"A practical and thorough guide to the fundamentals of IP Service Routing, the Alcatel-Lucent NRS I Certification has proven to be an invaluable tool for our Operations team. It is a key component of our IP knowledge curriculum. We are encouraging our employees to obtain this certification from Alcatel-Lucent."

—GLENN GARBELMAN
Director Video Operations Center (IP Operations)
AT&T

"We are pleased with the leadership Alcatel-Lucent is showing in IP training and network knowledge transfer. The SR Certification program courses are of high quality and supported with excellent practical labs. TELUS uses this training as part of our comprehensive strategy to introduce and manage our innovative suite of IP services in order to meet and exceed customer expectations."

—FRASER RAJAK

Vice-president, Service Management Data Centre and C.O. Operations
TELUS

Alcatel-Lucent Scalable IP Networks Self-Study Guide

Preparing for the Network Routing Specialist I (NRS 1) Certification Exam (4A0-100)

Kent Hundley
Alcatel-Lucent NRS I No. 1558

Wiley Publishing, Inc.

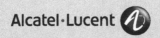

Alcatel-Lucent Scalable IP Networks Self-Study Guide: Preparing for the Network Routing Specialist I (NRS 1) Certification Exam (4A0-100)

Published by
Wiley Publishing, Inc.
10475 Crosspoint Boulevard
Indianapolis, IN 46256
www.wiley.com

Published by Wiley Publishing, Inc., Indianapolis, Indiana

Published simultaneously in Canada

ISBN: 978-0-470-42906-8

10 9 8 7 6 5 4 3 2 1

For general information on our other products and services please contact our Customer Care Department within the United States at (877) 762-2974, outside the United States at (317) 572-3993 or fax (317) 572-4002.

Wiley publishes in a variety of print and electronic formats and by print-on-demand. Some material included with standard print versions of this book may not be included in e-books or in print-on-demand. If this book refers to media such as a CD or DVD that is not included in the version you purchased, you may download this material at http://booksupport.wiley.com. For more information about Wiley products, visit www.wiley.com.

Library of Congress Control Number: 2009927345

About the Author

Kent Hundley (Alcatel-Lucent NRS I No. 1558) is a professional services IT consultant with more than 17 years of experience in the networking field. Kent has been a consultant for more than 12 years and has worked with numerous Fortune 100 enterprise clients and service provider customers in the areas of network architecture design, network operations, network management solutions, application analysis, and the design of security solutions. He is the author of several books on security and IP-related technologies and currently works as a consultant for a leading provider of solutions for managing networks and applications.

Credits

Executive Editor
CAROL LONG

Development Editor
SARA SHLAER

Technical Editors
GLENN WARNOCK, ANAND RAJ

Production Editor
CHRISTINE O'CONNOR

Copy Editor
CATE CAFFREY

Editorial Director
ROBYN B. SIESKY

Editorial Manager
MARY BETH WAKEFIELD

Production Manager
TIM TATE

Vice President and Executive
Group Publisher
RICHARD SWADLEY

Vice President and Executive Publisher
BARRY PRUETT

Associate Publisher
JIM MINATEL

Project Coordinator, Cover
LYNSEY STANFORD

Compositor
MAUREEN FORYS,
HAPPENSTANCE TYPE-O-RAMA

Proofreader
NANCY CARRASCO

Indexer
TED LAUX

Acknowledgments

I would like to express my thanks to Alcatel-Lucent for the opportunity to write this book and their support throughout this project. Without the access to their labs and continual assistance on technical matters, this work would not have been possible. I especially single out Glenn Warnock (Alcatel-Lucent SRA No. 2) for his tremendous help with reviewing the content and his assistance with numerous technical questions throughout the process, along with Anand Raj (Alcatel-Lucent SRA No. 14) for his technical support. I also extend my gratitude to Michael Anderson (Alcatel-Lucent SRA No. 24) for writing all the lab exercises. His input will certainly make this a valuable learning tool for those seeking the NRS I certification. And to Stephanie Chasse and Karyn Lennon, thank you for all of your ideas on the concept of this book, its design, and driving this team to get this book done.

I also extend a great thanks to Chris Butler for his efforts and contributions to the contents of the OSPF and BGP chapters. Of course, any flaws with the present work are entirely my own and not those of others.

Special thanks to the staff at Wiley Publishing for their untiring support and unwavering dedication to getting this project completed on time. In particular, Sara Shlaer played a key role in ensuring a successful outcome.

Most importantly, I thank my wife, Lori, and my children, Sophia and Patrick, for their love, support, and understanding during the nights and weekends I had to spend time away from our family to work. Although Sophia and Patrick are still too young to completely understand the particulars, they knew that I was not always available during our normal playtime and they had to "let daddy work on his book."

About the Contributing Author

Chris Butler, a Senior Network Architect currently working for the US Government, has 15+ years of experience designing and implementing networking and security solutions in the US Government, insurance, financial, and other commercial industries. He was the lead author for the book entitled, *IT Security Interviews Exposed: Secrets to Landing Your Next Information Security Job*. Chris lives and works in the DC Area with his wife and five children.

Contents at a Glance

Contents

Chapter 3: Data Link Overview   83

Chapter 4: Switched Networks, Spanning Tree, and VLANs   131

Chapter 7: Transport Layer Services—TCP and UDP   279

Chapter 8: Introduction to IP Routing   313

Chapter 9: OSPF   355

Chapter 10: BGP   393

Chapter 11: MPLS and VPN Services   427

Appendix A: Chapter Assessment Questions and Answers   469

Glossary   649

Foreword

The Internet continues to change the way the world communicates. New applications steadily emerge, facilitating meaningful links between information, content, and people. Video is increasingly a part of the web experience, and social networks have formed around all conceivable communities of interest. We have every reason to believe that highly collaborative multimedia applications will continue to flourish and that the Web 2.0 user experience will draw on innovative content distribution mechanisms.

Service providers need to build, operate, and maintain their IP networks to meet the demands of these new applications, and do so in a profitable manner. Your investment in this introductory certification from the SRC program will be critical to understanding how to balance the growth in transport costs associated with massive amounts of Internet traffic with the need to extract greater value from more sophisticated services.

Scaling routing performance while also scaling service sophistication requires meaningful changes to basic router and network design: an evolution from Internet routing to Service Routing. Five years after we introduced the world's first Service Router, the Alcatel-Lucent 7750 SR, this new approach has been widely embraced. From a standing start the 7750 SR family of routers has grown quickly to over 260 deployments around the world.

The need for Service Routing arises as providers attempt to implement more than basic Internet service on an IP/MPLS network. Any application that requires more than best-effort handling including VPNs, voice, and video requires a host of important new features to operate effectively. In addition to scaling in multiple dimensions, operational and resiliency considerations are central to making IP/MPLS platforms the common bearer of multi-service traffic.

In summary, a new era in building networks is upon us. With this certification you will be well positioned to help your employer or customer in this all-important transition, maximizing their opportunity and the value of their capital investments.

Basil Alwan
President, IP Division
Alcatel-Lucent

Introduction

This book is based on the Alcatel-Lucent's Scalable IP Networks course. It is designed to teach you the same material that is in the course and prepare you for the Alcatel-Lucent Network Routing Specialist I Certification exam (4A0-100). Like the course, this book teaches IP professionals the fundamentals of IP Service Routing, and so it is designed for network professionals with a limited knowledge of IP and Ethernet networking technologies.

While the primary focus of the book is to prepare you for the Alcatel-Lucent NRS I exam, bear in mind that the technologies discussed are also relevant to everyday networking activities and so the book can be useful as a reference even for those not intending to take the exam. However, the primary goal of this work is to prepare the reader to take the 4A0-100 exam, and thus not all topics are covered at the same level of detail that they might be for a general-purpose work on networking. Every effort has been made to cover the topics at a sufficient level of detail to prepare someone to take and pass the exam without giving too much information to overwhelm a network newcomer. The level of information for each topic has been carefully chosen to match the level of the exam.

Like the Alcatel-Lucent Scalable IP Networks course, the book has many objectives. Upon completing study of the topics contained in this work, the reader should be able to perform the following tasks:

- Describe the use of the Alcatel-Lucent 7750 Service Router (SR) and the Alcatel-Lucent 7450 Ethernet Service Switch (ESS) in the Internet.

- Execute basic commands with the Alcatel-Lucent SR command-line interface (CLI).

- Describe the purpose and operations of common Layer 2 technologies.

- Describe the IP forwarding process.

- Analyze an IP address with subnet mask and calculate subnet boundaries.

- Develop an IP address plan using IP subnetting and address summarization.

- Explain the differences between static routes and dynamic routing protocols.

- Configure static routes and dynamic routing in a single area OSPF network.

- Explain the purpose and basic features of BGP.

- Explain the purpose of MPLS and how it can be used to create tunnels across an IP network.

- Describe the MPLS-based VPN services supported on the Alcatel-Lucent 7750 SR: VPWS, VPLS, and VPRN.

Your success at understanding these objectives will determine your success on the exam. Each of these topics is covered in sufficient detail in this book to enable you to succeed when you take the Alcatel-Lucent NRS I exam if you apply yourself diligently to studying the materials. Some of the materials covered, such as IP subnetting, may be challenging and daunting to a network newcomer. However, we have strived to clearly explain the more difficult information and to provide guidance and examples that will help you understand the explanations. The Lab Exercises attached to the chapters will give you the opportunity to practice your new knowledge.

How This Book Is Organized

This book follows the outline of the Alcatel-Lucent Scalable IP Networks course. In the first chapter, we will give an introduction to the Internet and its history and a brief overview of the TCP/IP protocol suite. Chapter 2 examines the Alcatel-Lucent 7750 Services Router and the Alcatel-Lucent 7450 Ethernet Services Switch and provides an overview of the command-line interface used on both systems. Chapter 3 covers data link technologies, paying particular emphasis to the Ethernet protocol. Chapter 4 continues the discussion of Ethernet by looking at Ethernet switching and virtual LAN technology.

Chapter 5 looks at the IP protocol, including its addressing structure, and covers the concept of subnetting, complete with some sample exercises for creating subnets. Chapter 6 looks at the IP packet forwarding process and also some value-added services such as IP packet filtering. Chapter 7 concentrates on examining the upper transport layers of the IP stack and discusses both Transmission Control Protocol (TCP) and User Datagram Protocol (UDP). Chapter 8 begins a discussion of IP routing protocols and how they function in an IP network. Chapter 9 continues the discussion of IP routing by examining the Open Shortest Path First (OSPF) protocol. Chapter 10 concludes the discussion of IP routing with a discussion of the Border Gateway Protocol (BGP). We conclude in Chapter 11 with a discussion of Multi Protocol Label Switching (MPLS) and Virtual Private Networks (VPNs).

Each chapter begins with a few pre-assessment questions to give you a flavor of the chapter content, and a post-assessment quiz to test your understanding of the material. You can find all the assessment questions and their answers in Appendix A. Most chapters include a Lab Exercises section to give you practical experience to reinforce what you are learning. The Lab Exercises from all chapters are collected in Appendix B, along with the exercise solutions.

In topics related to networking, it is not possible to avoid TLAs (Three-Letter Acronyms) or acronyms in general. The acronyms are so heavily used in the networking industry that some of the terms are more readily recognized by their acronyms, rather than through the expanded term. For easy reference, most of the commonly used terms and acronyms in the book are listed along with their definitions in the Glossary at the end of the book.

Conventions Used in the Book

Alcatel-Lucent provides a modular approach for configuring the Alcatel-Lucent 7750 SR and Alcatel-Lucent 7450 ESS products. In this approach, most of the IP addressing and IP protocol features are configured in a modular fashion. The modular approach makes IP network designs simple and elegant. This makes node configurations easier to understand and maintain.

CLI commands are entered at the command-line prompt. Entering a command makes navigation possible from one command context (or level) to another. When you initially enter a CLI session, you are in the root context. At the root context, the prompt indicates the active Central Processor Module (CPM) slot and the name of the node. (For more information on CPM, see Chapter 2.) Navigate to another level by entering the name of successively lower contexts. As you change through the levels, the prompt also changes to indicate the context you are in. Listing 1 shows an example CLI navigation and prompt change according to the context.

Listing 1: Navigation and prompt change

```
A:AIRP_R01#
A:AIRP_R01# show
A:AIRP_R01>show#
```

The root prompt of Listing 1 indicates that the active CPM slot of the node is A and the name of the node is configured as AIRP_R01. In the listing, upon entering the command show, the prompt changes to indicate the show context. As you can see in this paragraph, when CLI codes are used inline along with the main text, they are indicated by the use of monofont text.

A standard set of icons are used throughout this book. A representation of these icons and their meanings are listed under the section, "Standard Icons."

Audience

This book is targeted for network professionals who have some experience with IP and Ethernet networks and who need to prepare for the Alcatel-Lucent NRS I exam (4A0-100). While the topics covered are of general use and information for any networking professional, the level of detail and the particular aspects of the technologies covered match explicitly what is needed to prepare for the exam.

This book assumes that the reader has a basic knowledge of networking, the Internet or IP protocol, and experience with binary numbers. Familiarity with configuring the Alcatel-Lucent 7750 Service Router or Alcatel-Lucent 7450 Ethernet Service Switch platforms will be helpful, but it is not required. In order to perform the labs in the book, you will need access to Alcatel-Lucent 7750 SR platforms. However, even if you do not have this access, you can still glean valuable information by reading through the labs to see the types of configuration tasks that are relevant to the topics under discussion.

Visit www.alcatel-lucent.com/src for additional information on the Alcatel-Lucent SRC Program.

Feedback Is Welcome

It would be our pleasure to hear back from you. Please forward your comments and suggestions for improvements to the following email address:

sr.publications@alcatel-lucent.com

Welcome to your preparation guide for the Alcatel-Lucent NRS I exam, and good luck with your studies and your career.

Kent Hundley
Alcatel-Lucent NRS I No.1558

The Alcatel-Lucent Service Routing Certification Program Overview

First in its class, the Alcatel-Lucent Service Routing Certification (SRC) Program offers extensive training to arm students with the skills, confidence, and credibility necessary to work in complex network environments. Through its rich focus on solutions and services, the SRC program meets the critical requirements for the third wave of IP innovation to meet service provider expectations. The Alcatel-Lucent SRC program is specifically designed to equip networking engineers, as well as operations and strategic planning staff, with the skills necessary to meet new operational challenges and to align network changes with their companies' business goals. Adding video and VoIP to the service mix creates an entirely new set of networking architectural challenges. The SRC program is unique in its ability to prepare service provider support staff to address these challenges, both now and in the future.

The SRC program offers four certifications:

- Alcatel-Lucent Network Routing Specialist I
- Alcatel-Lucent Network Routing Specialist II
- Alcatel-Lucent Triple Play Routing Professional
- Alcatel-Lucent Service Routing Architect

Based on their experience, expertise, and goals, students can choose which certification to follow. Certifications are awarded based on the successful completion of the relevant mandatory exams.

Courses from the SRC Program are delivered at Alcatel-Lucent sites globally. Visit www.alcatel-lucent.com/src for the latest class schedules.

Alcatel-Lucent provides credit for some Cisco and Juniper IP certifications. Visit www.alcatel-lucent.com/src/exemptions for a detailed overview of certification exemptions.

The *Scalable IP Networks Self-Study Guide* is published by the Alcatel-Lucent Service Routing Certification (SRC) Program (www.alcatel-lucent.com/src).

Alcatel-Lucent Scalable IP Networks Exam (4A0-100)

The Alcatel-Lucent Scalable IP Networks Exam is delivered by Prometric, a leading global provider of testing and assessment services. Prometric offers exam registration online, by telephone, or by walk-in (in selected locations). The exam is delivered in English in a secure and supervised environment at Prometric's global test sites. Participants have 75 minutes to answer 60 randomly generated questions. There are no exam prerequisites. Once Alcatel-Lucent has received the result for your exam (typically within 5 business days), an acknowledgment of your result will be sent to you.

Upon successful completion of the exam (4A0-100), participants will receive the Alcatel-Lucent Network Routing Specialist I Certification. The Alcatel-Lucent NRS I Certification is the introductory certification in the Alcatel- Lucent Service Routing Certification Program.

Standard Icons

Provider router

Enterprise router

Home

Office

Web server

File server

Enterprise server

Database server

Provider switch

ISP A POP

ISP B POP

IXP

Modem

Hub

Introduction To Networking

1

- The significance of the ARPANET
- The problems with having different protocols, and the solutions
- How the Internet evolved from a military-based network to a research-based network and then into a commercial network
- An overview of the modern Internet
- Differences between an Internet provider and a content provider
- Differences between traditional and modern ISP services
- The advantages of protocol layering
- The characteristics of the TCP/IP protocol layers, and how the layers work together
- The definition and development of the OSI Reference Model
- The similarities between the TCI/IP and OSI models of protocol

This chapter provides an introduction to the history and principles that underlie the Internet, the biggest network in the world. It is important that you have a foundational understanding of the hardware and software components that constitue the Internet in order to fully appreciate the remaining topics in the chapters that follow. The Internet has gone through large evolutionary changes in its lifetime, and these changes provide key insights into modern networking principles and design philosophies. We also discuss the development of the TCP/IP protocol, protocol layering, and the relationship of the OSI model to modern networking.

Pre-Assessment

The following assessment questions will help you understand what areas of the chapter you should review in more detail to prepare for the exam.

1. The original network that ultimately became the Internet was called
   A. NSFNET
   B. ARPANET
   C. DoDnet
   D. DARPA

2. The primary organization behind the development of the original Internet was
   A. IBM
   B. Digital Equipment Corporation (DEC)
   C. Stanford University
   D. the U.S. Department of Defense

3. Which of the following was *not* a primary design concern during the development of the original Internet?
   A. Reliability
   B. Bandwidth
   C. Interoperability
   D. Support for diverse network mediums

4. Which of the following was *not* a reason TCP was a superior transport protocol to NCP?

   A. Support for global addressing

   B. Support for end-to-end checksums

   C. Support for applications such as email

   D. Support for fragmentation and reassembly

5. Which of the following OSI layers is *not* paired with the correct implementation?

   A. Layer 7—Email

   B. Layer 3—TCP

   C. Layer 4—UDP

   D. Layer 2—PPP

You will find the answers to each of these questions in Appendix A. You can also download all of the CD materials for this book at `http://booksupport.wiley.com` to take all the assessment tests and review the answers.

1.1: Before the Internet

In the earliest days of computing circa the late 1960s, the majority of companies purchased only a single large system to handle all of their data processing needs. The systems were proprietary and closed, using hardware and software architectures that were compatible only with the same manufacturers's equipment. The basic components were large central mainframes that connected to intelligent communications "controllers," into which were plugged "dumb" terminals and printers. Network communication consisted entirely of the data sent between a terminal or printer and the mainframe. The terminals were incapable of local storage or configuration, and all intelligence in the entire system resided on the mainframe.

If companies wanted to expand their operations, they were locked into single vendors such as IBM or Digital Equipment Corporation. This led to serious compatibility issues when different organizations within a company or different companies needed to communicate with each other because cross-platform communication did not exist. There was no easy solution to this problem, and the dominant vendors had no incentive to ensure that their systems were compatible with those of other manufacturers.

The U.S. military found itself in an untenable situation when it realized that its different computer systems around the country could not communicate with each other because of proprietary systems and protocols. This meant that different sites could not share data or resources, and in the event of a disaster or systems failure, large amounts of information would be unavailable. *It was this realization of the need for systems that could share information and back each other up that drove the creation of the original "Internet."* In those early days, it was known as the *ARPANET*.

ARPANET: Genesis of the Internet

The ARPANET was conceived by the Advanced Research Projects Agency (ARPA) of the U.S. Department of Defense (DoD) to be the first cross-organizational communications network. It became the world's first packet-switched network, eventually leading to today's modern Internet. Its beginnings were humble, consisting of only four sites at Stanford, UC Santa Barbara, UCLA, and the University of Utah.

Owing to its military origins, in addition to information-sharing capabilities, the ARPANET was also designed with redundancy in mind. This was the Cold War era, and any communications system had to be able to survive a Soviet nuclear strike on any single or even multiple locations without complete failure. With this in mind, the system was designed with redundant packet switches, links, and a protocol to move data that could dynamically route around failed links and locations. Figure 1.1 shows an early drawing of the proposed network.

Connecting physical components and physical links was merely the first step in the development of the ARPANET, however. In order to make the system truly useful, it would have to support the ability for disparate devices to communicate with each other in a reliable fashion. These systems might be from a variety of manufacturers, and they might be connected to networks in various ways such as by radio or satellite.

As an example, in 1969 the Advanced Research Projects Agency (ARPA) had funded an experimental packet radio network under the direction of Professor Norman Abramson at the University of Hawaii called, appropriately enough, *ALOHANET*. The network connected sites spread around the Hawaiian Islands to a central time-sharing computer on the University of Hawaii campus. ALOHANET users could connect to the ARPANET, but the ALOHANET was not part of the ARPANET core, so from ARPANET's perspective, it was just a terminal connection.

Figure 1.1 The original ARPA network had only four nodes.

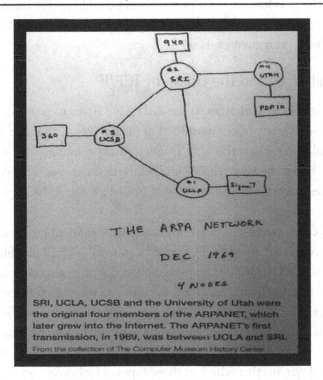

Other developments began to transpire to drive the ARPANET's need for heterogeneous communications. Robert Kahn, a Bolt, Baranek, and Newman researcher who had been instrumental in designing the ARPANET and improving its reliability, had been organizing an event to demonstrate the ARPANET. During this event in the spring of 1973, a new working group called the International Network Working Group (INWG) was organized.

One of the tasks that the INWG decided to undertake was to connect ARPANET and ALOHANET to some of the new packet-switching European networks to create a giant global network. Robert Kahn began a lengthy series of discussions with Vint Cerf, the INWG chairman, to find a solution to their mutual challenges.

Their model was an internetworking of ARPANET with ALOHANET and a satellite network (SATNET)—each of which used different communication protocols and different physical interfaces, optimized for that particular network's needs. Although the model was still in its infancy, the ARPANET designers were beginning to encounter various types of networks that needed to connect to their systems, and they faced a variety of challenges. The challenges faced by Kahn and Cerf would sow the intellectual seeds for the development of a protocol that could provide intercommunication across a wide variety of systems and physical infrastructures. These seeds would later bear fruit with the development of TCP/IP.

ARPANET Challenges and the Origin of TCP/IP

One of the biggest initial challenges to the ARPANET was to guarantee a high degree of reliability across a variety of communication media. Recall that the ARPANET was designed principally to support the U.S. DoD's military requirements, which meant that the network had to be very reliable under failure situations. The ARPANET had originally been designed to use the Network Control Protocol (NCP) for communication between end systems.

NCP provided connections and flow control between different processes running on different computers on the ARPANET. Applications such as email and file transfer were built to use NCP to send the required information and receive responses from other systems. While NCP provided many necessary features and was a good first step, it was not resilient enough to handle unreliable links such as packet radio and satellite links. (Think of the static that is sometimes encountered when listening to your favorite radio station, and imagine data packets encountering similar interference.) This posed a serious problem for interconnecting systems that relied on those types of technologies to the ARPANET.

NCP addressing proved to be problematic as well, since it only addressed next-hop nodes. This would be equivalent to being able to telephone only people in your own area code, or only address letters to people who lived in your same city. While still useful, such limitations would obviously prevent you from communicating outside of your immediate part of the world, and thus NCP addressing was hardly sufficient for the sort of global interconnections that ARPANET designers were contemplating.

If this weren't enough, each network that connected to the ARPANET had its own maximum packet size. In order to facilitate network communication, information is sent over the physical medium in discrete units called *packets*. A *packet* is equivalent to an envelope that holds a certain amount of information and no more. If you need to send more information than will fit in one envelope, you use multiple envelopes. On the ARPANET, various networks supported various maximum-sized packets (*envelopes*), so when a system needed to transfer information from one system to another, it often required unpacking one large envelope to fit into many smaller envelopes.

In order to alleviate these problems, Kahn undertook the development of a new host-to-host protocol. The new protocol would support global addressing, the ability to recover from lost packets, fragmentation and reassembly (the big-envelope-to-small-envelope problem), end-to-end checksums to verify that packet contents have not been altered in transit, and host-to-host flow control. He asked Cerf, who was by this time a professor at Stanford University, to help with the protocol development because he had experience with the design of NCP. To solicit the widest possible input for the project, Cerf ran a series of seminars at Stanford for students and visitors to discuss and challenge ideas as they were formed.

The outcome of this effort was a protocol whose success exceeded anything that its designers could possibly have envisioned. Cerf and Kahn presented their first version of the new protocol at a meeting of the INWG at Sussex University in the United Kingdom in September 1973. They called it the *Transmission Control Protocol* (TCP). And the rest, as the saying goes, is history.

A point on terminology is worth mentioning here. The original TCP included the addressing and other functions of the IP protocol; hence, the original protocol was known simply as *TCP* (the IP protocol is an important part of the TCP/IP protocol stack and will be discussed in detail in Chapter 5). After more work and discussions on the protocol, Kahn and Cerf decided in 1978 to split TCP into two discrete protocols, one called *TCP* and one called the *Internet Protocol* (IP). Each protocol would have separate functions. This new family of protocols became known as *TCP/IP*, and this is how we refer to it for the remainder of this chapter.

From War Room to Boardroom: The Internet Comes of Age

In 1980, the U.S. military adopted TCP/IP as a networking standard, and a "flag day" transition from NCP to TCP/IP was scheduled for ARPANET on January 1, 1983. The transition went reasonably smoothly, and this event marked the beginning of the *Internet* and the beginning of the end for the ARPANET.

Over the years, the ARPANET had become heavily utilized and burdened with congestion, and by 1985, it was reaching the end of its usefulness. In response, the National Science Foundation (NSF) initiated phase 1 development of the NSFNET. The NSFNET was created from a series of regional networks and peer networks. For example, the NASA Science Network was part of the original NSFNET. All of these networks were connected to a major backbone network to form the core NSFNET.

The NSFNET in its inception created a hierarchical network architecture and was more distributed than the ARPANET. The bottom tier consisted of university campuses and research institutions. These were connected to the middle tier (the regional networks). The regional networks were then connected to the main backbone network (the highest tier), consisting of six nationally funded supercomputers.

For many years, the NSFNET was reserved for research and educational purposes. Government agency networks were reserved for government-oriented missions exclusively. In fact, this policy continued into the early 1990s. However, as more peer networks began to be connected and new and different types of communications evolved, additional pressures mounted on the NSFNET administrators to provide additional connectivity and features.

As the NSFNET grew, there began to be a lot of commercial and general purpose interest in obtaining network access and interconnectivity. This, in turn, gave rise to an entire industry of network service providers (also known as *Internet service providers*, or ISPs) willing to fulfill this need for network connectivity. This growth in network connections began to occur on an international scale as networks outside the United States developed their own internetwork connections. These new and existing entities began to interconnect their networks in various ways, increasing the complexity of the infrastructure. Although the NSFNET clearly did not have the size and scope of the modern Internet, even at the early stages, the foundation was being laid for the evolution to the Internet as we know it today.

This growth was, in fact, anticipated by the founders of the INWG. The INWG actively encouraged the development of Internet and TCP/IP-related protocols with an eye toward the growth of internetworking. From the very beginning, anyone was allowed to participate in the development process merely by generating ideas for protocols to use on these emerging networks. These original documents were and still are known as *Requests For Comments* (RFCs). While today's RFCs are more formal and build on a rich and storied tradition of previous RFCs, they are still one of the major driving forces for innovation of new protocols and features.

The INWG evolved over the years into the Internet Engineering Task Force (IETF), which is now the standards body for TCP/IP and related protocols. Despite its importance, the IETF has never had an official charter. It still operates as an open organization where anyone representing research/commercial interests can contribute and improve the existing Internet protocols. IETF working groups enable individual contributors to meet and present and review their work with everyone else via the RFC process.

1.2: Service Providers and Content Providers

Anyone who can offer Internet connectivity could claim to be a service or Internet provider. The term *service provider* covers everything from a provider with a multi-million-dollar backbone and infrastructure providing Internet access to Fortune 100 companies, to a provider with a single router and access server in his garage providing dial-up Internet service to family and friends. The primary function of a service provider is to provide a simple connection to the Internet and possibly some very basic services such as email. Traditionally, a service provider did not go beyond this to give the customer additional application content.

In contrast, a *content provider* provides only information that is requested by the home user or small corporation. This information is typically resident on data servers. The access to these data servers occurs via application protocols (which will be discussed later). The most common example of an application protocol is the HTTP (hypertext transfer) protocol. (The group of servers that provide data via the HTTP protocol is often referred to collectively as the *World Wide Web*, or WWW). By using the HTTP protocol, users can access information from any server that "hosts" the particular information (the *website*) that is being sought by the user. For instance, using the HTTP protocol, the user can simply type **www.google.com** into a web browser such as Internet Explorer and obtain information from the website/data server that hosts www.google.com.

If the user happens to be in Ottawa, Canada and obtains services from ISP A, and the data server hosting the Google website happens to be in California, USA and is locally accessed by ISP B, then ISP A and ISP B will *peer* ("connect") with each other. *Peering* refers to a mutual agreement between two Internet service providers (ISPs) or, more generally, autonomous systems, to enable the exchange of information between each other's customers by direct or indirect interconnections. The indirect interconnection is via the *Internet Exchange Point* (IXP). Apart from Web access, which is the predominant Internet service, ISPs can also provide email access with multiple email accounts, data storage and, very recently, broadcast TV services.

Service providers can be broadly classified into three types or tiers, based on their size and functions:

- **Tier 1**—Tier 1 service providers serve mostly as transit providers. Because of their superior capital and resources, they are able to connect directly to any other major network and do not need to connect to a transit network to obtain service. By definition, a Tier 1 network does not purchase information transit from any other network to reach any other portion of the Internet. Therefore, in order to be a Tier 1 provider, a network must peer with every other Tier 1 network. A new network cannot become a Tier 1 without the implicit approval of every other Tier 1 network, since any one network's refusal to peer with it will prevent the new network from being considered a Tier 1 network. Examples of Tier 1 providers include AT&T, Global Crossing, and NTT Communications.

- **Tier 2**—Tier 2 service providers provide transit for some networks and also request transit service from Tier 1 providers to connect to other parts of the Internet. Examples of these types of providers are Bell Canada and British Telecom.

- **Tier 3**—Tier 3 service providers are smaller still than Tier 2 providers and require Tier 2 or Tier 1 providers for transiting to parts of the Internet. The Tier 3 service providers can provide reselling services for various Tier 2 providers to their customers. Examples of these types of providers would be most small providers that service only a single city or small regional network.

IXPs allow various Tier 1, 2, and 3 providers to exchange Internet data. The IXPs enable information exchange at local points, which avoids having to traverse or backhaul traffic through major points in order to reach the Internet. You can think of an IXP as serving the same purpose as a centralized train station or airline hub. Packets arrive from various providers and through the magic of Internet routing protocols are shunted off to the next provider's network for delivery to their ultimate destination. For example, in Figure 1.2, Tier 2 ISP A and Tier 2 ISP B must connect to each other through an IXP or through a Tier 1 ISP that has agreed to forward their traffic. An IXP would also connect multiple Tier 1 providers to each other in a similar fashion.

Figure 1.2 ISPs exchange data through an IXP.

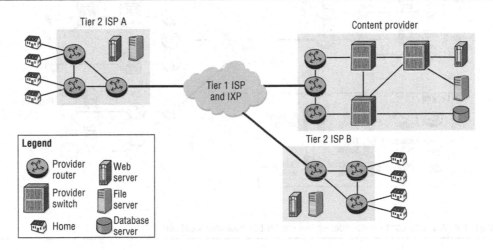

Enterprises can connect among their regional offices via Tier 2 or Tier 1 ISPs. An office in one region can connect to a Tier 2 ISP, while an office in another region may connect to a different Tier 2 ISP, but they will require a Tier 1 provider to link the two, as shown in Figure 1.3. If possible, connecting to a single service provider will usually provide increased service levels because all of the network transit points are under the control of a single provider. Some providers will even offer service guarantees for customer traffic as long as it does not leave their network, which can be very important for customers deploying services that are sensitive to delay, such as Voice over IP (VoIP).

For example, Figure 1.4 shows how a company may have its offices split into multiple regions around a country. It might be the case that Region 1 and Region 2 have a lot of interoffice application sharing, and thus connecting them to the same Tier 2 would provide adequate performance for less cost than connecting them to a Tier 1 provider. Similarly, Region 3 and Region 4 might have the same type of interoffice application-sharing requirement. In the event that Regions 1 and 2 and Regions 3 and 4 all need to communicate with each other, their respective providers could fulfill this need by using a Tier 1 provider network or IXP as a transit network.

In the next section, we take a closer look at service providers and their functions.

Figure 1.3 An IXP and a variety of tier providers connect regional offices.

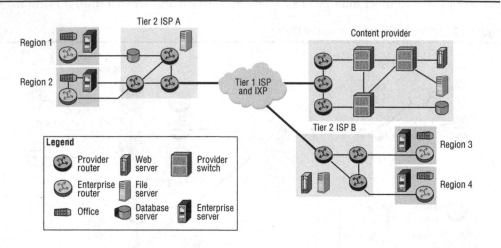

Figure 1.4 A single content provider serves content to multiple locations.

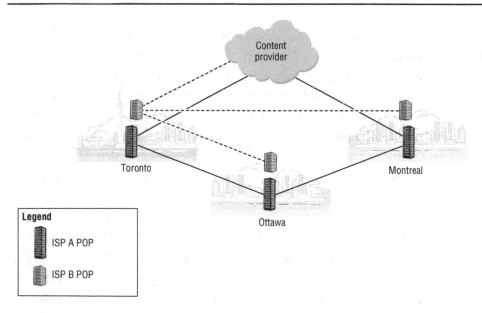

1.3: Modern Internet Service Providers

When the Internet was in its early commercial days, traditional ISPs provided access to basic services such as email and Web surfing via a modem dial-up. The connections were low speed with a theoretical limit of 56 Kbps at the peak of modem technology. Achieving the peak rate was rare, with actual speeds in the 28-Kbps to 36-Kbps range. The nature of the low-speed connections severely limited the range of services that ISPs could offer. Typical services consisted entirely of simple text-based web pages, email, and chatrooms. Additionally, the modem line often had to be shared with the home voice phone, so connectivity was limited to only those times when a connection was required. This paradigm changed dramatically as consumers began to have access to high-speed services such as DSL, and ISPs evolved to provide many additional services to customers.

Modern ISPs can be content providers or peer with several other content providers to provide their users with a myriad of services mainly categorized by voice, video, and data applications. The newer ISPs now compete with the traditional cable, satellite, and telecom providers. The bundling of these three major services that were offered as individual services in the past is referred to as *Triple Play*. In contrast, some of the cable and satellite providers are offering Internet services such as voice and data and also are able to peer with other ISPs and content providers and, in turn, compete with the telecom providers and other ISPs. Deregulation has also allowed companies who traditionally were able to offer only single services such as voice or cable, to offer new services in a wide-open, competitive services marketplace.

A major motivation behind the bundling of traditionally offered individual services is cost reduction. Another motivation is to offer customized services with varying price points. For example, ISP A may offer its end-users three packages: a basic service, a premium service, and an elite service. Each package is incrementally priced and consists of higher service utilization. The basic package could offer a 10 Megabits per second (Mbps) combined voice, Internet, and basic video service, whereas the premium and elite packages could be a 20 or 40 Mbps voice, very-high-speed Internet, and high-definition video services.

Apart from residential customer traffic, ISPs typically provide the business traffic needs for an enterprise whose traffic requirements with respect to bandwidth and timely delivery of an enterprise are well beyond that of the typical home user. A medium to large company may require the ISP's geographical presence to connect to its offices or other enterprise organizations. Additionally, the enterprises may require various types of services from an ISP such as web hosting or Layer 2/Layer 3 VPN (L2/L3 VPN) services for intersite connectivity.

This enterprise traffic via the ISP network is critical to the daily operations of the enterprise, and the delivery of this type of traffic is usually guaranteed by the ISP networks using *service level agreements* (SLAs). *Service level agreements* are contractual agreements between an ISP and its customers that define traffic guarantees and penalties resulting in payouts to the customers if the stated service level cannot be met for any reason. In order to provide these stated levels of service, the providers will limit the scope of the devices they will support. Normally, the provider will guarantee service levels up to a demarcation point.

Demarcation points serve as a means for the ISP to support the customer or other ISPs at a particular point characterized by equipment managed by the customer or the ISP. *Demarcation points* are essentially points at which delivery of packets becomes the responsibility of the customer or the provider, depending on the direction of packet delivery. A typical demarcation point for a home user would be the customer's DSL modem. The provider will test their signal up to the DSL modem and ensure that their signal has good quality up to that point. Beyond the DSL modem, it is the home user's responsibility to ensure that they have the correct connections from their computer to the modem.

All of these additions in terms of services and competing providers have led to exceptionally large growth of the Internet. Today, the Internet backbone has grown staggeringly complex compared to its humble beginning as the ARPANET. It is a collection of service providers that have connection points called *Points of Presence* (POPs) over multiple regions. The collection of POPs and the interconnections between them form the *provider networks.* Customers who require Internet service from a service provider are connected via access or hosting facilities in that provider's POP. The service providers have direct or indirect access to the data servers. The customers can be the "end-hosts" who receive the Internet service from their respective service providers.

One of the factors that make the backbone complex is that the customer of a service provider may also be a service provider for its own customers, and may connect to other service providers for certain data servers. What this means in practical terms is that a provider may or may not house the content that its customers use. The content can just as easily be stored on a different provider's network or on multiple provider networks as it can be on the customer's provider network. The peering and network connections of the providers make the actual location and delivery of the requested information transparent and seamless. Figure 1.4 illustrates how a single content provider can serve its content to multiple ISP POP locations.

As previously discussed, interconnections between providers are facilitated through exchange points known as IXPs. Because IXPs serve as the switching points for a large amount of traffic, it is critical that they switch packets from one provider network to another as quickly and reliably as possible. Having an IXP at the city level helps all the traffic between various ISPs and content providers to travel within the same city. In Figure 1.5, for instance, the ISP A POP and ISP B POP in Toronto can communicate via the Toronto IXP. If a content provider wants to peer with the IXP in a city, all the traffic between the ISP POPs in that city and the content provider is now localized. Without the presence of an IXP, the intracity inter-ISP traffic might have to be carried to an IXP in another city. This means that a user could be sitting at her apartment in Toronto and accessing a server at her office in downtown Montreal, but her traffic might be routed via Ottawa because of an out-of-town IXP.

Figure 1.5 Content goes through an IXP and is forwarded to various ISP POPs.

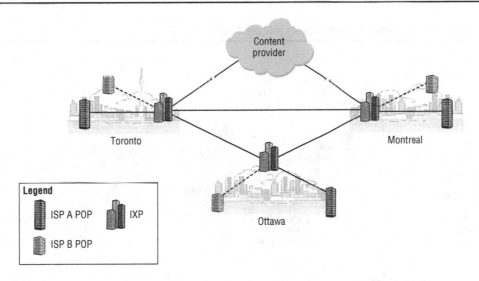

1.4: Overview of TCP/IP

For the Internet to work properly, the underlying components need a common way of communicating. This is achieved by providing common addressing to all the physical components. You can think of a physical device address the same way you think of a home address. Each address uniquely identifies a particular house somewhere in the world, and no two addresses are exactly alike. Similarly, the addressing is hierarchical, having a street address, a city, and a country (and a state, if you are in the United States). However, since these addresses are meant to be used solely by machines, they use only numeric addresses. In order to get data from one addressed host to another, you need a protocol that understands the addressing and knows how to get from point A to point B. On the Internet, this protocol is known appropriately enough as the *Internet Protocol* (IP), and the addresses are known as *IP addresses*.

An example of an IP address is *138.120.105.45*, and this address must be unique to a single computer. Delivering packets to a given IP address is again very similar to the methods that one would use to deliver mail to a person's home. The distribution of IP addresses is supervised by a centralized authority known as the *Internet Assigned Numbers Authority* (IANA), the way home addresses are issued by local government agencies. Indeed, the actual issuance of IP addresses is handled by different delegated Regional Internet Registry (RIR) agencies in different parts of the world, as shown in Figure 1.6.

Figure 1.6 Regional Internet Registry agents allocate IP addresses.

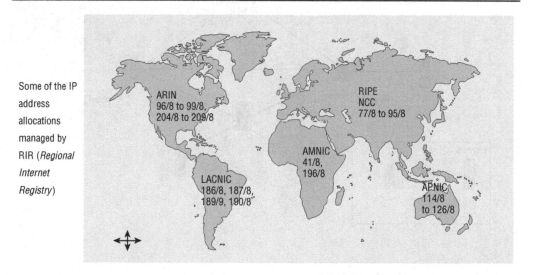

Some of the IP address allocations managed by RIR (*Regional Internet Registry*)

Just as with the postal system, the Internet provides a method for sending information from one place to another. On the Internet, information is sent in discrete units called *packets*. These *packets* actually consist of multiple pieces of information that are layered one on top of the other. Each piece of information is relevant to a particular process used by end-user computers or intermediate network devices. To continue the analogy, the layering of information can be compared to regular postal service, where there are several distinct functions:

- Creating the letter
- Enclosing the letter in an envelope, writing the sender's and recipient's addresses
- Choosing the type of delivery for the envelope (same day service, same week, etc.)
- Placing the appropriate stamp on the letter reflecting the service
- Physically sending the letter via carriers through air, water, or land

All these functions are relevant with transporting the letter to the proper destination. At the destination, the letter is received, and depending on the transport service, an acknowledgment of receipt may be sent back to the sender. The letter is simply then removed from the envelope, and its contents are then read.

Layering of TCP/IP information is treated in a similar fashion. The central difference is that TCP/IP is intended to transfer information to individual listening processes at a given IP address. A computer with a single IP address might provide numerous services such as email, web hosting, and data storage. TCP/IP allows for all of the IP packets to be delivered to the same computer system, and then unpacked and delivered to the individual process that requires that particular piece of information. TCP/IP also provides a reliable service, meaning it will re-send packets if it does not receive an acknowledgment of receipt. This layering approach, wherein service functions are distributed, is common of network protocols in general and TCP/IP in particular.

Each layer of the protocol layering stack adds the pertinent information (destination, error checks, etc.) at the beginning of the data, thereby adding more information to the data. The data en route to the receiver passes through several other systems that look only at the relevant header information for the layers that they are interested in and pass the data to another device. This would be similar in function to having envelopes inside other envelopes, with each envelope having different information.

For example, there might be an envelope that has just address information for an office building. Once the envelope is delivered to the building, the mail room would open the outer envelope, and inside there would be another envelope with a specific office location. None of the intermediate mail delivery systems would need to know about the exact office, so that information would be shielded from them.

The purpose of a network protocol suite is to define the protocols and technologies that support the interconnection of a diverse array of hardware and systems for deployment of a wide range of applications over the network. Anyone who has used an Internet application such as a web browser or email can appreciate the complexity of the systems required to support these applications. It is only due to our familiarity with these tools that we do not marvel that a user in Toronto, Canada can send an email quickly and effortlessly to a colleague in Pune, India whom he has never met face-to-face.

The layering of protocols provides a way to simplify this complex problem by segregating it into a number of smaller functions. Each layer performs a specific function that contributes to the overall functioning of the network. Systems participating in the protocols may not need to participate at every level, making it easier to move data from one point on the Internet to another with minimal effort. For example, network devices on the Internet may know only the destination address of information and need not know that the information in the packets is email or Web traffic, just as the intermediate mail sites need not know the exact office destination of the inside letter in our earlier example.

Understanding the TCP/IP Layers

The *TCP/IP protocol suite* (or "Internet protocol suite") is constructed around four layers of technology, as illustrated in Figure 1.7. The *application layer* provides all the services (e.g., web browsing and email) available to users of the Internet. The *network interfaces layer* includes all the hardware that comprises the physical infrastructure of the Internet. The two intermediate layers, the *transport layer* and *Internet Protocol layer*, provide a common set of services that are available to all Internet applications and that operate on all the hardware infrastructure of the Internet.

The Application Services Layer

The *application services layer* is the layer for the user. This layer only describes network applications. (Applications such as word processors and database programs are not considered network applications as they do not require network connectivity and are therefore not part of this layer.) Figure 1.8 lists some examples of network applications in the "Application services" box. Without network connectivity, these applications would be essentially useless.

Figure 1.7 The Internet Protocol suite is constructed around four layers.

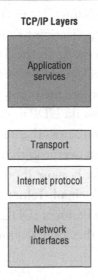

TCP/IP Layers

Application services

Transport

Internet protocol

Network interfaces

Figure 1.8 Example applications for the TCP/IP layers.

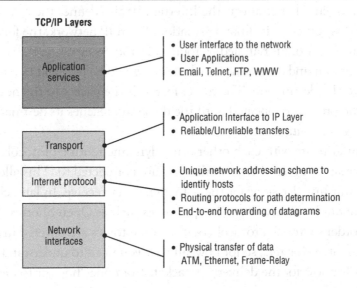

TCP/IP Layers

Application services
- User interface to the network
- User Applications
- Email, Telnet, FTP, WWW

Transport
- Application Interface to IP Layer
- Reliable/Unreliable transfers

Internet protocol
- Unique network addressing scheme to identify hosts
- Routing protocols for path determination
- End-to-end forwarding of datagrams

Network interfaces
- Physical transfer of data ATM, Ethernet, Frame-Relay

The Transport Layer

The *transport layer* is the application's interface to the network. The transport protocol provides a mechanism for an application to communicate with an application residing on another device in the network. In the TCP/IP protocol suite, there are two transport protocols: the *Transmission Control Protocol* (TCP), and the *User Datagram Protocol* (UDP). *TCP* is a connection-oriented protocol that provides an ordered and reliable transfer of data over the network. *UDP* is a connectionless protocol that supports the transfer of a single datagram across the network with no delivery guarantee. UDP is simpler and operates with less overhead than TCP. However, most Internet applications use TCP for data transfer because it provides a reliable transfer service. This includes HTTP (web browsing), email, Telnet, and FTP. Some applications, such as the Dynamic Host Configuration Protocol (DHCP) and the Trivial File Transfer Protocol (TFTP), use UDP because they only require a simple datagram transfer.

The Internet Protocol Layer

The *Internet Protocol layer* provides a common addressing plan for all hosts on the Internet as well as a simple, unreliable datagram transfer service between these hosts. IP is the common glue that connects the Internet. IP also defines the way a datagram (or packet) is routed to its final destination. In an IP network, the forwarding of packets across the network is handled by routers. IP routers examine the destination address of a datagram and determine which router would be the next hop to provide the best route to the destination. The router forwards the packet to the next hop router, where the process is repeated until the datagram reaches its destination. This is known as *hop-by-hop routing.*

Routers communicate with each other using dynamic routing protocols to exchange information about the networks they are connected to. This allows routers to make forwarding decisions for the datagrams they receive. In later chapters, you will learn about some key IP routing protocols such as Open Shortest Path First (OSPF) and Border Gateway Protocol (BGP). These topics are covered in much greater detail in later chapters, so for now, all that you need to understand is that routing protocols allow for the delivery of packets from one "hop" or router to the next in a predictable manner.

The Network Interfaces Layer

The *network interfaces layer* comprises the hardware that supports the physical interconnection of all network devices. The technologies of this layer are often designed in multiple layers themselves. The common attribute of all technologies of this layer is that they are able to forward IP datagrams or packets. There are many different technologies that operate at this layer, some of which are very complex. Some of the protocols commonly used at this layer include Asynchronous Transfer Mode (ATM), Frame-Relay, Point to Point Protocol (PPP), and Ethernet. However, there are many other protocols used; some are open standards, and some are proprietary.

The diversity of the network interfaces layer demonstrates one of the benefits of protocol layering. As new transmission technologies are developed, it is not necessary to make changes to the upper layers to incorporate these technologies into the network. The only requirement is that the new technology be able to support the forwarding of IP datagrams. For example, the original Ethernet standard only supported speeds up to 10 Mbps. Later came FastEthernet, which supported speeds up to 100 Mbps, and later still came GigabitEthernet, with speeds up to 1 Gbps. It is now not uncommon to encounter 10 Gbps Ethernet. Owing to the layering nature of TCP/IP, none of these changes at the lower layers required any changes to the upper protocols.

Forwarding Data

When a network application wants to communicate with another application across the network, it must first prepare the data in the specific format defined by the protocol to be used by the receiving application. A specific protocol is used so that the receiving application will know how to interpret the data it receives.

For example, in the case of a world wide web (WWW) request, the message consists of two parts, the message header and the body, as shown in Figure 1.9. The message header contains the sender's and receiver's addresses, as well as other information such as the urgency of the message and the nature of the message body. The format of the header and the nature of the addressing are defined by the application protocol. In the case of a WWW request the protocol is the hypertext transfer protocol (HTTP).

In addition to defining the format of the message, the protocol also specifies how the applications are expected to interact with each other, including the exchange of commands and the expected responses.

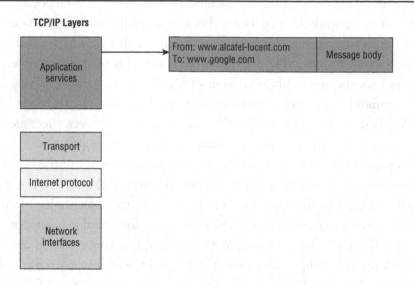

TCP treats all application data as a simple byte stream, including both the message header and the message body. TCP accepts the application's data and breaks it into segments for transmission across the network as required. To accomplish this reliable transfer, TCP packages the application data with a TCP header. On the receiving end of the connection, the TCP protocol removes the TCP header and reconstructs the application data stream exactly as it was received from the application on the sender's side of the network. In other words, TCP simply takes the data given to it by the upper layer application, and passes it to the upper layer application at the other end without trying to interpret the contents. Any protocol-specific formatting of the data is up to the upper layers.

As shown in Figure 1.10, the TCP and UDP headers carry source and destination addresses that identify the sending and recipient applications because a single host system may support multiple applications, as mentioned previously. These addresses are known as *port numbers*. Some port numbers are considered "well known" and should become familiar to you, such as port 80 for HTTP, port 21 for FTP, port 25 for Simple Mail Transfer Protocol (SMTP) and port 23 for Telnet. To transmit its segments of data across the network, TCP uses the services of the IP layer.

Figure 1.10 The transport layer specifies the TCP source and destination port numbers that will be used by the upper layer application.

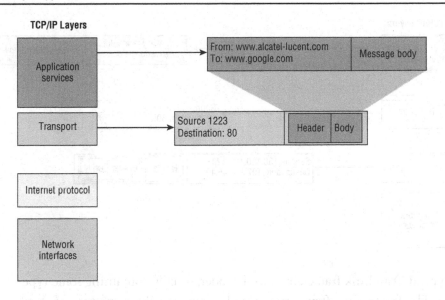

The IP layer provides a common addressing scheme across the network as well as a simple, unreliable datagram forwarding service between nodes in the network. Data from the transport layer is packaged in IP datagrams for transfer over the network. Each datagram travels independently across the network. The intermediate routers forward the datagram on a hop-by-hop basis based on the destination address. This allows for the network to dynamically route around any problems or failures in the network and deliver the packets as efficiently as possible. The packets may arrive out of order, so it is up to the upper layer TCP protocol to reassemble the message correctly.

As indicated in Figure 1.11, each datagram contains source and destination addresses that identify the end nodes in the network, and as you have seen, every node in an IP network is expected to have a unique IP address. IP uses the services of the underlying network interfaces such as Ethernet or ATM to accomplish the physical transfer of data.

The *data link layer* is the term used to describe the network interfaces used by IP for physically transmitting the data across the network. The units of data transmitted at the data link layer are usually known as *frames*. IP datagrams must always be encapsulated in some type of Data Link frame for transmission.

Figure 1.11 The network layer adds source and destination IP addresses so that the packet can be forwarded through the network.

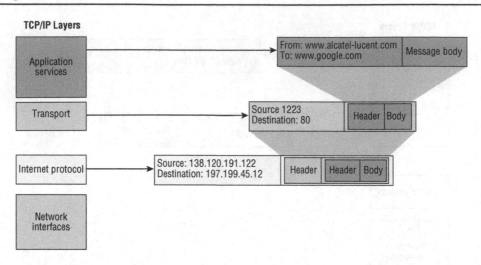

A typical Data Link frame contains a header, usually containing some type of address. The frame also often carries a trailer that contains some type of checksum to verify the integrity of the transmitted data. There are many types of technology used as network interfaces by IP, and they each have their own specific format and rules of operation. As noted earlier, the common characteristic is that the technologies are all capable of carrying IP datagrams.

The addressing at this layer identifies the two endpoints of a data exchange to the data link protocol. For example, Figure 1.12 shows the addressing of an Ethernet frame. Some Point-to-Point Protocols such as PPP may not use addresses if there is only one possible destination for the data. After all, you don't need addressing when two network devices can only send information to each other.

If it was not obvious from the preceding discussion, routers provide the critical traffic control of the IP datagrams across the Internet. Once the end-user's computer creates the packet and places it on the wire, its job is done until it receives a response. From the user's perspective, the information simply goes into a *black box* and gets sent to its destination, and a response is received. Behind the scenes, numerous, sometimes dozens, of routers reliably perform their duties accepting packets, examining the destination, looking up the next hop router for delivery, and forwarding the packet on its merry way. Along the way, the packet may cross Ethernet, ATM, Frame-Relay, PPP, and carrier pigeon to reach its intended destination (OK, maybe not really carrier pigeon, but you get the idea). Figure 1.13 illustrates this concept.

Figure 1.12 The data link layer adds source and destination MAC addresses for forwarding on the local network segments.

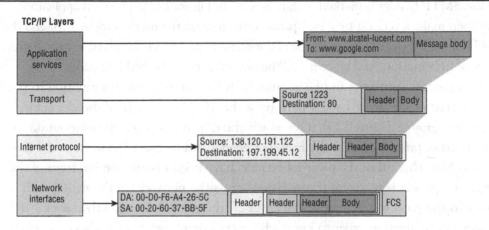

Figure 1.13 Data from applications is sent to the TCP/IP protocol stack where all the appropriate headers are added and the packet is sent on to the network for forwarding to its destination. As the packet travels through the network, the Layer 2 information is changed at each router, but the network, transport, and application information remain unchanged.

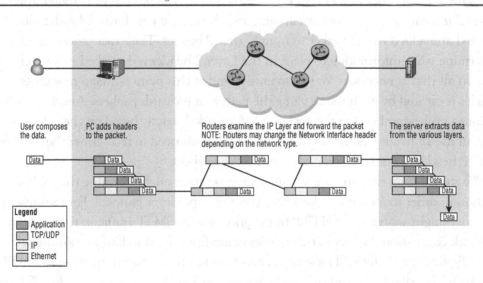

The process begins when the user composes data and hands it to a process on his or her computer for network processing. Assume that the user has composed an email and pressed the Send key in her email application. Behind the scenes, the email application will take the data the user has written and place an SMTP protocol header in front of it (the SMTP header is marked in darkest gray in Figure 1.13). The mail application will then make a request to a TCP process running on the user's computer to send the SMTP data. TCP will accept the SMTP information, possibly breaking it into discrete units of information, and place a TCP header in front of the SMTP header.

This process continues in like manner with TCP handing its information to the IP process that places an IP header in front of the TCP header (the IP header is marked in lightest gray in Figure 1.13), after which the IP process passes its information to the Ethernet process so that the Ethernet header can be placed in front of the IP header. Now that all of the protocol headers have been inserted one in front of the other, the packet is ready for transmission across the network. In the figure, each router in the path would remove the Layer 2/Ethernet header, read the Layer 3/IP header information in order to know what next hop to forward the packet to, place a new Layer 2 header onto the packet, and forward the packet out of the appropriate interface.

The reason for this is that Layer 2 headers are only used on local network connections such as Ethernet or a PPP link. Once the packet reaches the next router, the Layer 2 information is no longer relevant, and therefore a new Layer 2 header must be created and added to the packet in front of the IP header. The exact process used to determine what information to place in the Layer 2 header is described in later chapters, so all that is necessary for you to understand at this point is that a new Layer 2 header is created by each router along the path as it forwards packets. Another critical point to understand is that the packets are forwarded strictly based on the information in the IP header. None of the routers in the path need to read either the TCP or SMTP headers in order to properly forward the packets.

We should note that in some circumstances a router might examine the TCP information in order to forward packets based on the upper layer protocol. For example, a provider might wish to give HTTP traffic priority over SMTP traffic in the event of network congestion. However, this is a deviation from the standard forwarding process. Typically, a router will forward packets based only on the information in the IP header as described. It is only when the packet reaches the end-host that the TCP and SMTP headers are examined and removed.

At the destination host, the process previously described to create the packet is performed in the reverse direction, with each process removing the appropriate header and forwarding the remaining information, complete with upper layer headers, on to the next process. In our example, an Ethernet process would remove the Ethernet header, and then it would be processed by the IP, TCP, and SMTP processes, respectively.

 This is a simplified example for mail. In reality, the mail would be delivered to a mail server, and then the destination user would retrieve his or her email using a different protocol. However, the process performed at the mail server to receive the packets is as described.

That this process works so well and so reliably is a testament to the layered design of TCP/IP that provides for the segregation of responsibility required to allow for such diverse networks to intercommunicate seamlessly.

The OSI Reference Model

Up to this point, we have been discussing the TCP/IP layering model exclusively. However, the TCP/IP model is not the only game in town. The *Open Systems Interconnection* or *OSI Reference Model* represents a logical way of organizing how networks talk to each other so that all hardware and software vendors have an agreed-upon framework to develop networking technologies—similar to TCP/IP. The OSI model was created by the International Organization for Standardization (ISO) with the following goals:

- Simplify complex procedures into an easy-to-understand structure.
- Allow vendors to interoperate.
- Provide the ability to isolate problems from one layer that may be passed to other areas.
- Allow a modular plug-and-play functionality.
- Provide an independent layer design.

 The ISO is a network of national standards institutes based in Geneva, Switzerland. Its goal is to help promulgate standards that have been developed by consensus in particular fields of industry. The OSI model is simply one of many computer industry standards developed by the ISO, which, in turn, is simply one field of the many that have ISO-developed standards.

The OSI model is represented by the seven layers depicted in Figure 1.14. These layers may be grouped into two main areas, defined simply as the upper and lower layers.

Although a single device (e.g., a UNIX workstation) can execute all seven layers, this is not practical in real networks. The amount of traffic that needs to be moved through modern networks requires purpose-built devices that handle various layer functions. Two such examples are bridges, which are purpose-built for Layer 2 operation; and routers, which are purpose-built for Layer 3 operations.

Figure 1.14 The OSI reference model defines seven distinct layers.

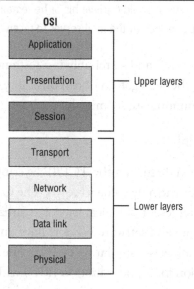

It is important to understand at the outset that the OSI model is simply that—a model. There are various protocols that implement services at each of the described layers of the model, but the model itself is simply a reference point for protocol designers. The OSI reference model was developed at the end of the 1970s, but the development of actual protocols to support the reference model was slow. (Recall that TCP had been developed in 1973 and thus predates the OSI model.) By the early 1990s, several OSI protocols (TP0-4, CLNS, CONS, X.400, and X.500) had been specified and commercial implementations attempted, but the success of TCP/IP and the weaknesses of OSI led to the complete adoption of TCP/IP for internetworking. OSI protocols were never in wide use, and today they are more of interest for historical ideas that didn't really catch on, like the Edsel or New Coke.

However, despite the failure of the actual OSI protocols, the OSI Reference Model terminology lives on and is widely used to describe the layering of network protocols. Indeed, much networking terminology derives from the OSI protocol suite. A very few remnants of OSI are still in use; for example, Lightweight Directory Access Protocol (LDAP), which is a derivation and simplification of X.500, and Intermediate System to Intermediate System (IS-IS), which was designed as an OSI routing protocol. IS-IS was later adapted to TCP/IP networks and is still a key routing protocol in many provider networks, while LDAP is used in some networks to provide user authentication services.

The following list maps the TCP/IP suite layers to the OSI model to see how they fit and where they differ. The TCP/IP suite differs from the OSI model in that the TCP/IP suite uses four protocol layers and the OSI model uses seven layers. Figure 1.15 shows the rough protocol layer relationship between the two models. It is "rough" because some of the functions of the TCP/IP layers bleed into the functions of the other OSI layers. This is not the fault of the TCP designers as after all, they were first to the party and their primary concerns were to design a practical protocol and not a protocol that fits neatly into the OSI model.

- **Network Interfaces**—The network interfaces layer defines the interface between hosts and network devices and contains the functionality of both the physical and data link layers of the OSI model. Protocols such as Ethernet describe both the framing of data (Layer 2) and the physical transmission of the frame over the media (Layer 1). This layer is often referred to as *Layer 2* or *L2* because it provides OSI Layer 2–type services to the IP layer.

- **Internet Protocol**—The IP layer provides a universal and consistent forwarding service across a TCP/IP network. IP provides services comparable to the OSI network layer and is sometimes referred to as a *Layer 3* (or *L3*) protocol. The OSI protocol CLNP corresponds most closely to IP.

- **Transport**—The transport layer comprises two main protocols, TCP and UDP. These transport protocols provide similar services to the OSI transport protocols. TCP is very similar to the OSI transport protocol, TP4. TCP and UDP may be referred to as *Layer 4 protocols*.

Figure 1.15 The TCP/IP layers do not map exactly to the OSI layers; multiple OSI layers are performed by a single TCP/IP layer.

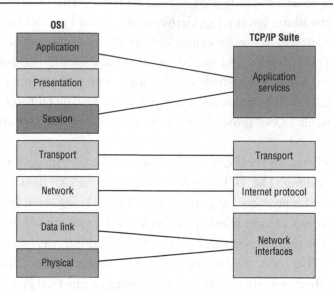

- **Application Services**—The application services provide end-user access to the Internet. Any of the services of the upper three OSI protocols that are required are incorporated into the application protocols. There are several Internet protocols that provide services similar to these OSI layers, although they do not follow the layering or service definitions of OSI. For example, MultIprotocol Mail Extensions (MIME) provides presentation-like services similar to SMTP. Application layer protocols are sometimes referred to as *Layer 7 protocols*.

The most important aspect of the OSI model is the terminology itself and not the particular implementation of protocols, which are, as previously stated, for the most part dead. You will often encounter vendor technologies that perform certain new functions such as "content switching" that purport to perform forwarding operations on Layer 4 or Layer 7. It is a key part of evaluating these claims and technologies that you understand what these layers entail and why having devices that understand these upper layers might be important for particular services.

Chapter Review

Now that you have completed this chapter, you should have a good understanding of the following topics. If you are not familiar with these topics, please go back and review the appropriate sections.

- The development of the ARPANET and its evolution to the modern Internet
- The function of the IETF and its relationship to the Internet
- The problems that the creation of TCP/IP was designed to solve
- The distinction between an Internet provider and a content provider
- The basic components of the Internet needed for it to function
- Protocol layering and why it is used
- The layers of the TCP/IP protocol
- The similarities and differences between the TCP/IP protocol and the OSI model

Post-Assessment

The following questions will test your knowledge and prepare you for the Alcatel-Lucent NRS I Certification Exam. Please review each question carefully and choose the most correct answer. You can compare your response with the answers listed in Appendix A. You can also download all of the CD content at http://booksupport .wiley.com to take all the assessment tests and review the answers. Good luck!

1. The original network that ultimately became the Internet was called
   A. NSFNET.
   B. ARPANET.
   C. DoDnet.
   D. DARPA.

2. The primary organization behind the development of the original Internet was
   A. IBM
   B. Digital Equipment Corporation (DEC)
   C. Stanford University
   D. the U.S. Department of Defense

3. Which of the following was *not* a primary design concern during the development of the original Internet?
   A. Reliability
   B. Bandwidth
   C. Interoperability
   D. Support for diverse network media

4. Which of the following was *not* a reason TCP was a superior transport protocol to NCP?
   A. Support for global addressing
   B. Support for end-to-end checksums
   C. Support for applications such as email
   D. Support for fragmentation and reassembly

5. Which of the following OSI layers is *not* paired with the correct implementation?

   A. Layer 7—Email

   B. Layer 3—TCP

   C. Layer 4—UDP

   D. Layer 2—PPP

6. Part of the growth of the ARPANET was driven by the ability of anyone to create and disseminate information about potential protocols and applications in a particular kind of document. These documents are known as

   A. Requests For Information.

   B. Protocol Revisions.

   C. Requests For Comments.

   D. Requests For Configurations.

7. ISPs connect to each other at well-defined network locations to exchange information. These connection points are known as

   A. ISPs.

   B. IXPs.

   C. BGPs.

   D. POPs.

8. A company that has locations throughout the country can obtain service at each location from a Tier 1, Tier 2, or Tier 3 provider. What is one reason a company might choose to connect all locations to a Tier 1 provider despite the higher costs involved?

   A. Sites at different tiers cannot communicate.

   B. Tier 3 providers don't use TCP/IP.

   C. Only Tier 1 providers provide content.

   D. A single provider could offer SLAs to each location.

9. Which of the following services would likely be offered by a content provider but *not* a service provider?

   A. Standard dial-up service

   B. Live video streaming from sports events

   C. Email service

   D. Basic Web Services

10. Which of the following accurately describes the TCP protocol?

    A. Connectionless with no guarantee of delivery

    B. Connectionless with guarantee of delivery

    C. Connection-oriented with guarantee of delivery

    D. None of the above

11. Originally, the IP protocol functions were performed by

    A. Ethernet.

    B. TCP.

    C. NCP.

    D. ALOHANET.

12. When an HTTP packet needs to be forwarded over the Internet, which of the following accurately describes the order of the headers as they would be placed in front of each other in the packet (assume the orginating device is on an Ethernet network)?

    A. HTTP, IP, TCP, Ethernet

    B. HTTP, TCP, IP, Ethernet

    C. HTTP, UDP, IP, Ethernet

    D. HTTP, IP, Ethernet

13. A router processing the packet described in Question 12 would need to examine and/or manipulate the headers for

    A. Ethernet only.

    B. IP only.

    C. TCP and IP only.

    D. IP and Ethernet only.

14. What would a router processing the packet described in Question 12 do with the Layer 2 header of the incoming packet?

   A. Remove the source Layer 2 address, add its own, and forward the packet.

   B. Remove the Layer 2 addresses and replace them with new addresses.

   C. Remove the entire Layer 2 header and create a new one based on the next hop interface.

   D. Leave the original Layer 2 header but forward the packet based on the destination address.

15. Most of the OSI-created protocols are no longer in use, although a few still provide some critically important functions. Which of the following describes an OSI protocol that is still in use?

   A. OSPF

   B. LDP

   C. TP0

   D. IS-IS

The Alcatel-Lucent 7750 SR and 7450 ESS Components and the Command-Line Interface

- The hierarchical structure of the Alcatel-Lucent 7750 SR and 7450 ESS CLI
- Basic CLI commands
- Configuring the hardware of the Alcatel-Lucent 7750 SR and 7450 ESS product lines
- The physical access options of the Alcatel-Lucent 7750 SR and 7450 ESS product lines
- Basic system configuration
- The Boot Options File

This chapter provides an introduction to the hardware and software architecture of the Alcatel-Lucent 7450 SR and 7750 ESS series devices. It also introduces you to the command-line interface (CLI) for configuration and management of SR/ESS products.

Pre-Assessment

The following assessment questions will help you understand what areas of the chapter you should review in more detail to prepare for the exam.

1. Which of the following is *not* a product in the Alcatel-Lucent 7750 SR/7450 ESS family?
   A. SR-12
   B. ESS-7
   C. SR-6
   D. ESS-1

2. Which of the following statements is false regarding the Alcatel-Lucent 7450 ESS series?
   A. It supports multiple chassis types.
   B. It supports OSFP, IS-IS, RIP, and BGP.
   C. It is used primarily for Ethernet aggregation.
   D. It can be managed via a console port or a dedicated Ethernet port on the SF/CPM.

3. Which of the following descriptions is correct?
   A. bof.cfg—7750/7450 configuration file
   B. cpm.tim—IOM image file
   C. config.cfg—Back-up configuration file
   D. boot.ldr—Bootstrap image file

4. Which of the following commands is *not* correctly described?
   A. `shutdown`—This command is used to disable an interface or protocol
   B. `exit all`—Logs out of the Alcatel-Lucent 7750 SR/7450 ESS device.

C. ?—Lists all commands in the current context.

D. [TAB]—This command is used for assistance with command completion

5. Which of the following is *not* a log stream type?

   A. Audit

   B. Change

   C. Main

   D. Security

You will find the answers to each of these questions in Appendix A. You can also download all of the CD materials for this book at http://booksupport.wiley.com to take all the assessment tests and review the answers.

2.1 The Alcatel-Lucent 7750 Service Router Family

There are three chassis types in the Alcatel-Lucent 7750 Service Router (SR) family, allowing for flexible deployments from the smallest POP (Point of Presence) to the largest ISP core. The Alcatel-Lucent 7750 SR-12 (shown in Figure 2.1) is the largest 7750 SR router and has a total of 12 front access card slots. Two card slots are dedicated for redundant common equipment; they cannot be used for any other purpose. Each of these slots can hold one Switch Fabric/Control Processor Module (SF/CPM), although only one SF/CPM is required for operation. A second SF/CPM provides complete redundancy of the fabric and the control processors. The purpose of the SF/CPM is to control access to the backplane of the 7750 for other cards in the chassis.

Figure 2.1 The Alcatel-Lucent 7750 SR-12. Two slots are dedicated for SF/CPM control cards; the other 10 slots are available for I/O Modules that provide network interfaces.

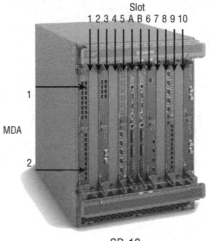

SR-12

There are two SF/CPM card options: 200 Gbps and 400 Gbps. The 200-Gbps cards provide 200-Gbps full-duplex switching and the 400-Gbps cards provide 400-Gbps half-duplex switching. When two Alcatel-Lucent 7750 SR SF/CPMs are installed, the traffic is load-shared across both of the switch fabrics. When two load-sharing SF/CPMs are installed, then two 200-Gbps cards provide a total of 400 Gbps full-duplex throughput, while two 400-Gbps cards provide 800 Gbps of full-duplex throughput. The backplane of the 7750 SR-12 supports 40-Gbps (full-duplex) through-put to each IOM slot.

Because two slots are reserved for SF/CPM modules, there are 10 remaining slots that can be used for Input/Output Module (IOM) base boards. The IOM cards provide physical network interfaces such as Gigabit Ethernet, Asynchronous Transfer Mode (ATM), Synchronous Optical NETwork, (SONET), and so on. An Alcatel-Lucent 7750 SR fully loaded with 10 IOM cards at full bandwidth can therefore produce 400 Gbps of full-duplex throughput.

The Alcatel-Lucent 7750 SR-7 chassis (shown in Figure 2.2) is a fully redundant system and has a total of seven front access slots. As with the SR-12, two card slots are dedicated for redundant SF/CPMs. The remaining five slots are used for IOM base boards.

Figure 2.2 The Alcatel-Lucent 7750 SR-7. Two slots are dedicated for SF/CPM control cards; the other five slots are available for I/O Modules that provide network interfaces.

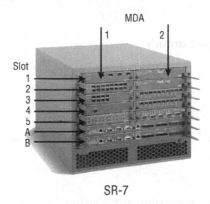

The Alcatel-Lucent 7750 SR-1 (shown in Figure 2.3) has the management, switch fabric, and one IOM base board integrated into the chassis. It is important to note that the SR-1 is a fixed form chassis and cannot accept new cards. The IOM base board, however, can accommodate two Media Dependent Adapters (MDAs) for physical interfaces. The 7750 SR-1 has an integrated switching system with 20 Gbps (full-duplex) of throughput. The 7750 SR-1 is a small form factor switch intended for installations where the rich 7750 SR service capabilities are required but with more modest interface and protocol scaling requirements such as a small POP.

Figure 2.3 The Alcatel-Lucent 7750 SR-1. The SF/CPM and one IOM base board are integrated into a fixed form chassis. The IOM base board can accommodate two Media Dependent Adapters (MDAs) for physical interfaces.

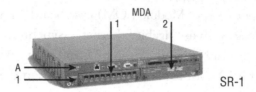

In addition to the physical components, the Alcatel-Lucent 7750 Service Router family supports a comprehensive set of service provider features. The list of features includes:

- Support for all industry standard routing protocols: Open Shortest Path First (OSPF), Intermediate System-Intermediate System (IS-IS), Border Gateway Protocol (BGP), and Routing Information Protocol (RIP)

- Multicast support

- BGP support with address families

- IPv6 support

- Supports Multi Protocol Label Switching (MPLS) and Label Distribution Protocol (LDP) with services capability

- Supports Virtual Private Networks (VPNs) including: Virtual Private Wire Service (VPWS), Virtual Private LAN Service (VPLS), and Virtual Private Routed Network (VPRN)

- Supports high availability with non-stop routing

- Supports Graceful Restart (GR) Helper Mode

The Alcatel-Lucent 7450 Ethernet Service Switch Group

Both the Alcatel-Lucent 7750 SR and 7450 Ethernet Service Switch (ESS) share the same robust service management, troubleshooting, and billing features. The 7450 ESS is based on the same technology foundation as the 7750 SR, but there are key differences between the two products. For example, the MDAs, IOMs, and fabric modules are not interchangeable between the two systems. The two product families have completely different chassis and modules, separate part numbers and list prices, distinct product feature roadmaps, and separate software loads.

The Alcatel-Lucent 7450 ESS capabilities are focused on enabling the delivery of metro Ethernet services only and do not support Layer 3 services such as MPLS/BGP VPNs and multicast. The 7450 ESS is also missing key functionality and scalability attributes such as BGP4 that are required in an edge router. Because of the differences in hardware architecture, there is no upgrade path to the Alcatel-Lucent 7750 SR or to a Provider Edge (PE) router.

Like the Alcatel-Lucent 7750 SR series, the Alcatel-Lucent 7450 ESS series has a variety of form factors that allows for deployment in diverse scenarios depending on the exact port density and aggregation technologies that are required. There are four different form factors in the Alcatel-Lucent ESS family. The 7450 ESS-12 (shown in Figure 2.4) is the largest and has a total of 12 front access card slots. Two card slots are dedicated for SF/CPM cards, and the remaining 10 slots can be used for any combination of IOM cards, just as with the 7750 SR-12.

Figure 2.4 The Alcatel-Lucent 7450 ESS-12. Two slots are dedicated for SF/CPM control cards; the other 10 slots are available for I/O Modules that provide network interfaces.

ESS 12

The Alcatel-Lucent 7450 ESS-7 and ESS-6 (shown in Figure 2.5) similarly provide two dedicated slots for the SF/CPM cards and five and four remaining slots for IOM cards, respectively. The ESS-7 and ESS-6 also have an integrated switching system with 100 Gbps and 80 Gbps (full-duplex) of throughput, respectively.

There is also an Alcatel-Lucent 7450 ESS-1 that is similar to the Alcatel-Lucent 7750 SR-1: it has the management, switch fabric, and one IOM base board integrated into the chassis. As with the 7750 SR-1, the IOM base board can accommodate two MDAs for physical interfaces and has an integrated switching system with 20 Gbps (full-duplex) of throughput.

Figure 2.5 The Alcatel-Lucent 7450 ESS-7 and ESS-6. Two slots are dedicated for SF/CPM control cards for both models. The other slots are available for I/O Modules that provide network interfaces.

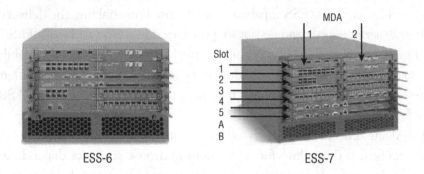

ESS-6   ESS-7

The differences between the Alcatel-Lucent 7750 SR series and the Alcatel-Lucent 7450 ESS series are summarized in Table 2.1.

Table 2.1 Differences between the Alcatel-Lucent 7750 SR Series and 7450 ESS Series

Type	7450 Ethernet Service Switch	7750 Service Router
Purpose	Primarily designed to support Ethernet aggregation services	Supports Ethernet, ATM, Frame-Relay, and VPRN services.
Platforms	ESS-1, ESS-6, ESS-7, and ESS-12	SR-1, SR-7, and SR-12
Redundancy Pwr/Control	ESS-6, ESS-7, and ESS-12	SR-7 and SR-12
MDA	Ethernet, POS	All Ethernet, ATM, POS, DS3/OC3 channelized

Control Plane versus Data Plane

One important architectural feature of the Alcatel-Lucent 7750 SR and 7450 ESS is the separation of control functions and data functions. Data functions involve the reception, processing, and forwarding of user application traffic. Data coming in from the remote network/customer site ingresses through the Media Dependent Adapters (MDAs), where the data is formatted (internal format). The data is then processed in the I/O Module, where the decision to switch happens (L2/L3 Forwarding information lookup) and the data packets are sent to the switch fabric (SF/CPM card). The switch fabric then forwards the data to the appropriate IOM, where it is sent to the appropriate egress MDA. Data plane operations happen only after the control plane has built the forwarding information and stored it in the IOM.

Control plane functions involve operations that build the L2 and L3 forwarding table information. These operations include receiving and maintaining L3 routing table information. (Building routing tables is covered in Chapter 5.) Building routing tables is a critical control function for any core service provider network, so it is very important that routers have the ability to maintain forwarding tables even when they have to process large amounts of data. Besides routing functions, the control plane also handles the router configuration and management functions. By separating the control and data functions, the Alcatel-Lucent 7750 SR and 7450 ESS can continue to perform their control plane functions even under the heaviest traffic loads. The separation of the control and data plane functions is shown in Figure 2.6.

In the next section, we will take a closer look at the physical components that comprise the Alcatel-Lucent 7750 SR and 7450 ESS.

Figure 2.6 The control plane and data plane functions use the same MDAs, but control packets are processed by the SF/CPM modules. Data packets are switched from the ingress IOM to the egress IOM without any handling by the control processor module (CPM).

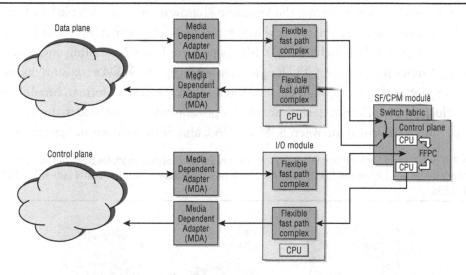

Physical Components of the Alcatel-Lucent 7750 SR and 7450 ESS Series

It is important to understand all of the different physical components that comprise an Alcatel-Lucent 7750 SR or 7450 ESS system. The systems themselves consist of a physical chassis with slots that house the cards that integrate into the card slots. The cards provide either the intelligence of the system if the card is a SF/CPM (shown in Figure 2.7) or physical interfaces if the card is an IOM.

Figure 2.7 SF/CPM cards plug into the chassis to provide intelligent data processing and forwarding.

Redundant SF/CPMs
supported on
SR7 and SR12

The IOMs are hot-swappable modules responsible for queuing, processing, and forwarding of data. An IOM contains two 10-Gbps traffic-processing programmable fast-path complexes. Each complex supports a pluggable MDA that allows a common programmable fast path to support all of the possible interface types. The IOM also contains a CPU section for managing the forwarding hardware in each Flexible Fast Path.

MDAs provide one or more physical interfaces, such as Ethernet, ATM, or SONET/Synchronous Digital Hierarchy (SDH). MDAs perform Layer 2 handling and pass incoming frames to the IOM CPU for processing. On egress, MDAs transmit outgoing frames out of the appropriate physical interface in the correct format. Small Form Factor Pluggable (SFP) transceivers are small optical modules available in a variety of formats. The relationship between IOMs, MDAs, and SFPs is shown in Figure 2.8.

Figure 2.8 Small Form Factor Pluggable (SFP) transceivers are small optical modules that plug into MDAs. MDAs themselves are add-on modules to IOM cards that provide interfaces for the Alcatel-Lucent 7750 SR and 7450 ESS.

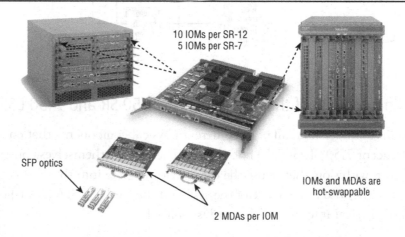

10 IOMs per SR-12
5 IOMs per SR-7

SFP optics

IOMs and MDAs are
hot-swappable

2 MDAs per IOM

How Packets Are Processed by the IOM

The primary function of the Alcatel-Lucent 7750 SR and 7450 ESS is to receive packets and make intelligent forwarding decisions. The IOM components previously discussed work in conjunction to accomplish this task. Data coming into the 7750/7450 (ingressing) go through the MDA, which provides the physical interface to the network. The MDA converts the physical format of the received data into an internal format and provides some minimal buffering. This step is necessary because the outgoing format of the data may differ from the incoming format; for example, an Ethernet frame does not have the same format as an ATM cell. Once the frame is converted to an internal format, it is then sent to the Flexible Fast Path complex (one for each MDA, maximum of two per IOM) for intelligent processing.

The Flexible Fast Path complex provides an array of intelligent service process features. Quality of service (QoS) is applied to classify and handle packets appropriately. This is an especially important step if there is latency-sensitive traffic in your network, such as Voice Over IP (VOIP). Any Access Control Lists (ACLs) are applied in real time to discard unwanted packets based on the configured security policy. Finally, the forwarding destination is determined (the destination IOM/MDA/port) in order to send the frame to the appropriate IOM card across the backplane fabric.

 QoS is a method of providing different levels of service to different users or applications by classifying and handling their data differently. QoS may involve forwarding data over different paths through a network or providing expedited forwarding. QoS is an advanced topic and is beyond the scope of this book. You can learn more about QoS and how it is implemented in an Alcatel-Lucent network in *Advanced QoS for Multi-Service IP/MPLS Networks* by Ramji Balakrishnan (Wiley, 2008).

If the data received is a user data packet, it is forwarded to the switch fabric. If it's a protocol control packet, then the control data is forwarded to the control plane. A user data packet, where the packet is intended for a user application such as email or file transfer, is the most typical scenario. A *control data packet* is a packet containing routing or management information and intended for the router CPM. This separation of the user data packet processing from the protocol control data packet processing ensures that the Alcatel-Lucent 7750 SR/7450 ESS system can be managed even when there are extremely high volumes of user traffic.

Figure 2.9 shows this processing of a packet upon ingress to an Alcatel-Lucent 7750 SR/7450 ESS system.

Figure 2.9 A packet ingresses the Alcatel-Lucent 7750 SR/7450 ESS through the MDA from an attached network. It is forwarded through the Flexible Fast Path complex to the switch fabric or the control plane.

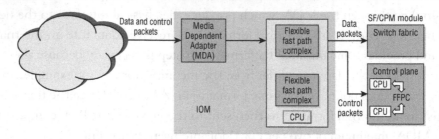

When data leaves the system (egressing), the process is very similar except that it is in the reverse direction. Data comes back to the IOM from the switch fabric if it is a user data packet, or from the control card in case of a CPM-generated packet. The packet is sent to the Flexible Fast Path complex responsible for the respective egress MDA for processing. Similar to the ingress, the Fast Path complex will provide QoS classification and buffer management, ACLs will be applied if configured, and then the data is framed and sent out of the correct port of the MDA. This process is shown in Figure 2.10.

Figure 2.10 A packet egressing the Alcatel-Lucent 7750 SR/7450 ESS is sent from the switch fabric to the Flexible Fast Path complex for processing. The data is then framed by the MDA and sent out to the network.

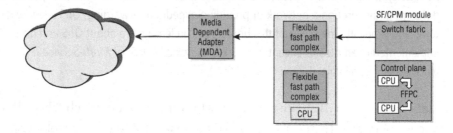

Basic Bootup Components

As with all computer systems, the Alcatel-Lucent 7750 SR and 7450 ESS series systems require a configuration or *boot* file that contains key information that is necessary for the system to function correctly. The 7750 SR and 7450 ESS systems use a Boot Options File (BOF) to configure the system for operations during the power-on process.

Each new system is shipped with a Compact Flash (CF) card that contains the files required to start the system. Each processor on an Alcatel-Lucent 7750 SR or 7450 ESS product can have three compact flashes: cf1, cf2, and cf3. The flash sizes can be 256M, 512M, 1G, and 2G. Flash cf3 is typically where the system files are stored, and that is where the system looks for the files when initializing. The cf1 and cf2 cards can be used to store debug and accounting logs.

The cf3 card contains the following directories and files located off of the root directory:

- **boot.ldr**—This file contains the system bootstrap image.
- **bof.cfg**—The bof.cfg file is user-configurable and contains information such as:
  - Management port IP address
  - Location of the image files (primary, secondary, and tertiary)
  - Location of the configuration files (primary, secondary, and tertiary)
- **TiMOS-m.n.Y.z**—This directory is named according to the major and minor software release, type of release, and version. For example, if the software release is Version 1.2 software release zero, the name would be *TiMOS-1.2.R.0*.

  On modular systems such as the Alcatel-Lucent 7750 SR-12 or the 7450 ESS-12, this directory contains two files, cpm.tim and iom.tim, for the SF/CPM and IOM cards, respectively. On fixed form chassis such as the 7750 SR-1 that have an integrated fabric/control and I/O, there is only one file, named *both.tim*.

  The cpm.tim image file is the software that is used to run on the Service Router or the Ethernet Services Switch. It is this software that is created and is tagged with a release number. This software contains all the features required to configure and run protocols on the Service Router/Ethernet Services Switch.

- **config.cfg**—This file contains the default configuration file. The default configuration file is very basic and provides just enough information to make the system operational. You can create other configuration files and point the system to them using the bof.cfg file.

The layout of the file system on the cf3 card is shown in Figure 2.11.

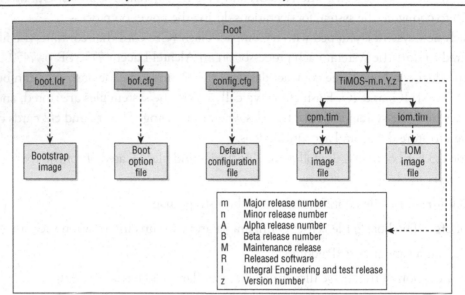

System Initialization Process

The Alcatel-Lucent 7750 SR and 7450 ESS series products go through a detailed step-by-step procedure to load all of their required software and configuration information in order to prepare the system for data processing. The entire initialization process is shown in Figure 2.12.

Most of the steps in the figure are self-explanatory. The system begins by running the boot.ldr file, which reads the bof.cfg files, waits briefly for any user intervention to halt the boot process, and then begins to load the system image file. If the system image file cannot be loaded, the initialization process fails. Once the system image is loaded, the system loads the configuration options found in the configuration file that is named in the bof.cfg file. The default name for the configuration file is *config.cfg*. The configuration file includes chassis, IOM, MDA, and port configurations, as well as system, routing, and service configurations. If the config file does not exist, the router will continue to boot, and a blank configuration will be used.

Figure 2.12 The initialization process for the Alcatel-Lucent 7750 SR and 7450 ESS series.

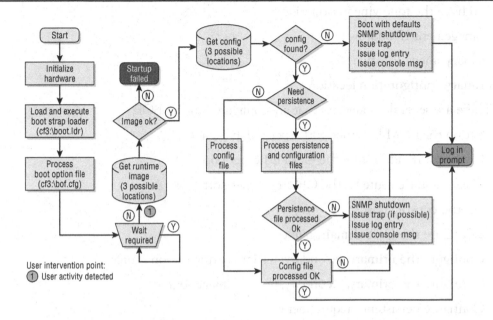

In addition to parsing the configuration information in the configuration file, the initialization process determines if persistence is configured on or off (the default is off). Persistence is required if the Alcatel-Lucent 7750 SR or 7450 ESS is managed by the 5620 Service Aware Manage (SAM) network manager. When persistence is turned on, the devices create an index file with the same file prefix name as the current configuration file. The index file contains a variety of index information (interface indexes, LSP ids, path IDs, etc.). The index file is built dynamically by the device operating system and does not contain configuration information entered by users. The index file is saved whenever the system configuration file is saved.

The index file ensures that the 5620 SAM has the same index data as the Alcatel-Lucent 7750 SR or 7450 ESS node after a system reboot. If a device reboots and the indexes stored on the SAM do not match the node indexes, a complete re-synchronization between the node and the SAM takes place automatically. This can be a very time-consuming and processor-intensive operation.

The Boot Options

The Boot Options File (BOF) stores parameters that specify the location of the image filename that the router will try to boot from and the configuration file that the router uses to configure the applications and interfaces. The most basic BOF configuration should have the following information:

- Management IP address
- Primary image location
- Primary configuration location

There are several parameters that are configured in the BOF:

1. Set up the CPM Ethernet port (speed, duplex, auto).
2. Create an IP address for the CPM Ethernet port.
3. Create a static route for the CPM Ethernet port.
4. Set the console port speed.
5. Configure the DNS domain name.
6. Configure the primary, secondary, tertiary configuration source.
7. Configure the primary, secondary, tertiary image source.
8. Configure persistence requirements.

The BOF configuration is done through the BOF command-line interface (CLI) context. Listing 2.1 shows some sample `bof` commands. Notice that the command-line prompt adds the `>bof` string when you are in the BOF context.

```
Listing 2.1  Example bof commands

SR-1# bof                                  # Change or create a bof file
SR-1>bof# address 10.10.10.2/24 primary    #Change/create CPM Port IP
                                           address
                                                   (must enter from
                                                   console)
SR-1>bof# speed 100                        # Set the CPM Ethernet Port
                                           speed to
                                                   100 Mbps.
SR-1>bof# primary-image cf3:/TIMOS.1.0.R0  # Set the primary image
                                           directory
SR-1>bof# primary-config cf3:/test.cfg     # Set the primary
                                           configuration file
                                                   to be test.cfg
SR-1>bof# save                             # Saves the bof
```

You see the information that is contained in the BOF by issuing the `show bof` command as shown in Listing 2.2:

```
Listing 2.2 The show bof command
A:sr1a# show bof
=====================================================================
BOF (Memory)
=====================================================================
    primary-image      cf3:\4.0.R9
    primary-config     cf3:\test\test_sr1a.cfg
    address            138.120.199.60/24 active
    autonegotiate
    duplex             full
    speed              100
    wait               3
    persist            on
    console-speed      115200
=====================================================================
```

The primary image location is one of the most important items in the BOF. If the router cannot find an image, it will remain in the boot cycle forever. This is obviously not conducive to a properly functioning network!

Besides the image location, the BOF also contains the name and location of the configuration file. In Listing 2.2, the primary configuration is located in cf3, the default location. When the router reboots, it performs two different operations. First, the boot loader executes the image file to boot the operating system. Then, it goes to card cf3, gets the configuration that is specified in the BOF, and loads the router with that configuration. In addition, after the primary configuration location has been defined, every time the operator inputs the command `admin save`, the current configuration is saved to the primary configuration file on the cf3 card.

The address that is referred to in the `show bof` output in Listing 2.2 is the address of the management port on the Control Processor Module (CPM). Notice the console speed—this is the default speed of the RS-232 port on the CPM. This speed can be changed here in the BOF, but this is rarely necessary. It is best practice to leave this setting at its default since anyone who needs access to the system from the console will try the default setting first. In an emergency an operator does not need to waste time trying to guess what the console speed setting is if it has been altered from the default.

2.2 Command-Line Interface

The Alcatel-Lucent 7750SR and 7450 ESS series product *command-line interface* (CLI) is a command-driven interface accessible through the console, Telnet, and Secure Shell (SSH). The CLI can be used for the configuration and management of SR/ESS products.

The *CLI command tree* is a hierarchical inverted tree similar to a DOS/UNIX directory structure. At the highest level is root. Below root are other levels with the major command groups; for example, configuration commands and show commands are levels immediately below root. Navigate down the tree by typing the name of the successively lower contexts. For example, typing **configure** or **show** at the root level navigates down to the configure or show context, respectively. Global commands, such as back, exit, info, and tree, can be entered at any level in the CLI hierarchy.

Sometimes the context you wish to navigate to can be specified in a specific context with a single keyword, such as:

```
SR>config# router
SR>config>router#
```

Sometimes a keyword and a user-supplied identifier are required:

```
SR>config>router# interface system
SR>config>router>if#
```

- You can view the hierarchical CLI command structure below your current position with the tree and tree detail commands.

- Use the info and info detail commands to display information about the current context level: info displays non-default information.

- info detail displays all configuration information, including defaults.

Whenever you are configuring from the CLI, the prompt provides key information depending on the symbols and text that are included as part of the prompt, as illustrated in Figure 2.13.

Figure 2.13 The CLI prompt provides key information such as the host name and current context.

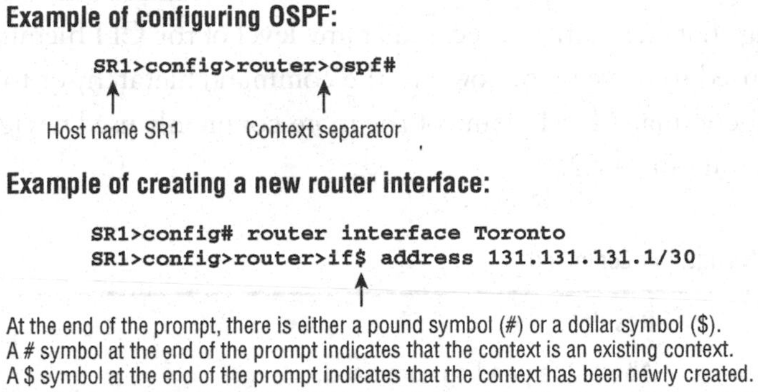

Example of configuring OSPF:

```
SR1>config>router>ospf#
```

Host name SR1   Context separator

Example of creating a new router interface:

```
SR1>config# router interface Toronto
SR1>config>router>if$ address 131.131.131.1/30
```

At the end of the prompt, there is either a pound symbol (#) or a dollar symbol ($).
A # symbol at the end of the prompt indicates that the context is an existing context.
A $ symbol at the end of the prompt indicates that the context has been newly created.

There are two very powerful tricks that you should be familiar with when typing commands at the CLI. The first is the use of context-sensitive help. If you know the beginning of the command but do not remember all of the extra parameters, you can enter <command> ?, where <command> is the beginning of the command such as ospf, interface, router, and the like. Using the ? provides the syntax and keywords associated with that command. Additionally, you can use the command completion option by pressing the [Tab] key after entering part or all of a command. If you enter part of the command and the text is unambiguous, the command will be completed automatically. If you enter part of a keyword that can have multiple endings and press the [Tab] key, possible options for completing the command will appear.

To summarize, command completion can be achieved by:

1. Abbreviation, if the keystrokes entered are unique:

```
SR1>config>router>os [ENTER]
SR1>config>router>ospf#
```

2. Using the [Tab] key or Spacebar to automatically complete the command:

```
SR1>config>router>os [TAB]
SR1>config>router>ospf

SR1>config>router>os [SPACEBAR]
SR1>config>router>ospf
```

If a match is not unique, the CLI displays all possible matches:

```
SR1>config# ro [TAB]
      router                router-ipv6
SR1>config# router
```

Console control commands are used for navigating in a CLI session and for displaying information about a console session. Many of these commands are global commands, meaning that they can be executed at any level of the CLI hierarchy. These commands are used to move up or down in the command hierarchy or to exit from a particular CLI command level. Some of the more commonly used navigation commands are shown in Table 2.2.

Table 2.2 Basic Navigation Commands

Command	Result
<Ctrl-c>	Aborts the pending command.
<Ctrl-z>	Terminates the pending command line and returns to the root context.
echo	Echoes the text that is typed (primary use is to display messages in an exec file).
back	Brings you back one context.
exit all	Brings you back to the root level.
up/down arrow	Lists previous command(s) to be repeated.
tree	Shows available commands from context.

There are two other special commands that deserve particular attention. The shutdown command is used to disable protocols and interfaces. This command is necessary to disable objects before they can be deleted. It is saved in the configuration file once the command is applied to an object.

The other special command is the use of the no form of any command. This form of the command can be used to remove commands that have been previously applied, such as no ospf or no bgp. To return to the shutdown command, for example, all ports on the Alcatel-Lucent 7750 SR and 7450 ESS systems are shut down by default when the system is first powered on and must be enabled with the no shutdown command.

To restore the settings after issuing a no command, you must reconfigure the router by re-entering the command you removed, rebooting from a configuration file that has the correct configuration, or doing an exec command on a configuration file that contains the correct settings. You can use an exec command to process a configuration file and restore the configuration stored in the file.

Table 2.3 shows a list of other useful global commands.

Table 2.3 Common Global Commands

Command	Result
info	Provides info on the configuration.
logout	Terminates the CLI session.
oam	Operations, Administration, and Maintenance (OAM) test suite (see the "Service OAM" section of the *7750 SR OS Services Guide*)
password	Changes the user CLI login password.
	Note: Not a global command; must be entered at the root level.
ping	Verifies the reachability of a remote host.
pwc	Displays the Present Working Context of the CLI session.
sleep	Causes the console session to pause operation (sleep) for 1 second or for the specified number of seconds (the primary use is to introduce a pause during the execution of an exec file).
ssh	Opens a secure shell connection to a host.
telnet	Telnets to a host.
traceroute	Determines the route to a destination address.
tree	Displays a list of all commands at the current level and all sublevels.
write	Sends a console message to a specific user or to all users with active console sessions.

There are also some useful commands to control the environment of the Alcatel-Lucent 7750 SR and 7450 ESS, such as the appearance of the prompt and the number of lines on the terminal screen. Some of these commands are displayed in Table 2.4.

Table 2.4 Sample CLI Environment Commands

Command	Result
alias	Enables the substitution of a command line by an alias.
create	Enables the create parameter check.
more	Configures whether CLI output should be displayed one screen at a time, awaiting user input to continue.
reduced-prompt	Configures the number of higher-level CLI context levels to display in the CLI prompt.
terminal	Configures the terminal screen length for the current CLI session.
time-display	Specifies whether time should be displayed in local or UTC format.

As previously mentioned, context-sensitive help for any command can be obtained through use of the ?.

Provisioning the Alcatel-Lucent SR/ESS Systems

The Alcatel-Lucent SR/ESS series products can be accessed in three ways: in-band ports such as on MDAs, a console port, and a CPM Ethernet management port. The *console port* is a DB-9 serial port on the SF/CPM card for a modular chassis or on the chassis itself for the SR-1 or ESS-1. The location of these ports is shown in Figure 2.14.

Figure 2.14 This figure shows the CPM serial console port and the CPM out-of-band Ethernet management port.

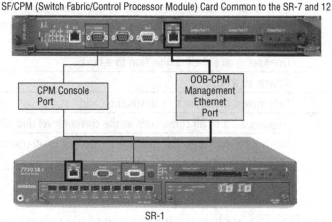

There are a few key points to keep in mind when provisioning the Alcatel-Lucent 7750 SR and 7450 ESS series. First, you have the ability to provision slots, IOMs, MDAs, and ports before or after they are physically installed. Second, you can also optionally specify which line cards are permitted to be installed in a particular slot and which MDAs are permitted to be installed in a particular IOM. A line card or MDA will not initialize unless the installed type matches the permitted type. This feature should be used with caution since it can prevent an IOM or MDA from functioning properly if it is installed in a card that is configured for a different type of hardware.

There is a certain order that should be followed when configuring the Alcatel-Lucent SR/ESS products. You should perform the following steps in the order listed:

1. Select a chassis slot and provision the IOM type for the slot.

2. Select an MDA slot and specify the MDA type for the slot.

3. Select a port and configure it.

Remember that IOMs, MDAs, and ports must be enabled with a `no shutdown` command. All ports are initially shut down when the products are initialized. Sample configuration steps for an IOM, MDA, and port are shown in Listings 2.3, 2.4, and 2.5 respectively.

Listing 2.3 IOM configuration example

```
SR1# configure card 1
SR1>config>card# card-type iom-20g
SR1>config>card# no shutdown
```

Listing 2.4 MDA configuration example

```
SR1>config>card# mda 1
SR1>config>card>mda# mda-type m60-10/100eth-tx
SR1>config>card>mda# no shutdown
```

Listing 2.5 Port configuration example

```
SR1# configure port 1/1/1
SR1>config>port# no shutdown .
```

There are many steps that are typically used to configure a system from startup. Not all of these steps will necessarily be followed for every system, but you can use this series of steps as a template for what is *typical* for initial setups.

1. Log in to the Alcatel-Lucent SR/ESS using console input.

2. Configure the system name and change the admin user password.

3. Configure the CPM Ethernet management IP address.

4. Configure additional BOF parameters.

5. Configure IOM cards.

6. Configure MDA cards.

7. View alarms.

8. Configure the system address.

9. Configure logs if required.

10. View the entire running config.

A few of the items in the typical configuration list deserve special attention. Although some of the items are optional, you must configure a system name, and you should always change the admin password.

- **System Name**—The system name can be any ASCII-printable string of up to 32 characters. The system name is configured in the `config` CLI context. If the name contains spaces, it must be enclosed in double quotes to delimit the start and end of the name. The system name becomes part of the CLI prompt. It is best practice not to use spaces in the system name. If you want to separate words or characters in the system name, use either an underscore or a dash.

- **Passwords**—The default login and password is `admin`. This password should be changed before your Alcatel-Lucent SR/ESS system is put into service. The system automatically creates at least one admin user (the default) and must retain at least one admin user unless you are using an external protocol such as RADIUS or TACACS+ to provide authentication. You can configure the following password parameters:

  - **Aging**—The maximum number of days (1 to 500) that a password remains valid before the user must change it. The default is no aging enforced.

  - **Attempts**—The number of unsuccessful login attempts allowed in a specified time period. If the configured threshold is exceeded, the user is locked out for a specified time.

    In the following example, a user is locked out for 10 minutes if four unsuccessful login attempts occur in a 10-minute period:

    ```
    Count: 4
    Time (minutes): 10
    Lockout (minutes): 10
    ```

  - **Authentication Order**—You can configure the order in which password authentication is attempted among RADIUS, TACACS +, and local methods.

- **Complexity**—You can use this parameter to specify if passwords must contain uppercase and lowercase characters, numeric characters, and special characters.

- **Minimum Length**—You can specify the minimum number of characters (1 to 8) required for a password.

There are various show commands that can be useful when configuring IOMs, MDAs, and ports. The show card command shows what IOM types a particular slot is configured to support and gives the status of the card (up or down). Similarly, the show mda command shows what MDA types a particular MDA is configured to support and the status of the MDA (up or down).

In addition to displaying the status of IOMs and MDAs, it is often useful to know the current version of the operating system running on an Alcatel-Lucent SR/ESS system and its current configuration. You can use the admin display-config command to display this information. Sample output from this command is shown in Listing 2.6.

Listing 2.6 A sample listing of the OS version and configuraion for an Alcatel-Lucent 7750 SR

```
A:acie_sr1a# admin display-config
# TiMOS-B-4.0.R9 both/hops ALCATEL SR 7750 Copyright (c) 2000-2007 Alcatel-
Lucent.
# All rights reserved. All use subject to applicable license agreements.
# Built on Tue Dec 19 15:56:05 PST 2006 by builder in /rel4.0/b1/R9/panos/
main
# Generated FRI DEC 22 16:00:41 2006 UTC
exit all
configure
#--------------------------------------------------------
echo "System Configuration"
#--------------------------------------------------------
    system
        name "acie_sr1a"
        snmp
            shutdown
        exit
        login-control
Press any key to continue (Q o quit)
```

Using Logs and Alarms

The Alcatel-Lucent 7750 SR and 7450 ESS products keep very extensive logs of events, alarms, traps, and debug/trace messages. The logs are used to monitor events and troubleshoot faults in the 7750 SR and 7450 ESS products. You can configure what type of logging information is captured and where you want to send the captured logging information. In some cases, you may want to save the logs to a secondary storage location for historical auditing purposes.

Applications and processes within the Alcatel-Lucent 7750 SR and 7450 ESS products generate event logs. The logs are divided into four types or *streams* of logs:

1. **Main**—Most normal logs not specifically directed to any other event stream

2. **Security**—Anything related to system security, such as failed login attempts

3. **Change**—Any events that affect the configuration or operation of the node

4. **Debug/Trace**—All output generated as a result of turning on debug/trace

These four streams of information are the source of all log entries. Events from any of these four streams are sent to an event log identified by a unique log identification (log ID) number from 1 to 100 (log IDs 99 and 100 are reserved for system use). Each log ID may contain events from more than one event stream. The configuration of each log ID includes determining which streams will create events in that log ID and the destination where the information for that log ID will be sent. You can think of a log ID as having inputs at one end from one or more of the four event streams and an output at the other end, with the log ID in the middle. Additionally, you can create a filter for each log ID to control the specific events that are sent to the log ID from each input stream. Refer to Figure 2.15 for a visual depiction of this process.

The log destination is configurable based on the contents of a log ID. A log ID can be directed to one of the following six destinations:

1. **Console**—The physical 9-pin console port of the Alcatel-Lucent 7750 SR/7450 ESS

2. **Session**—A console or Telnet session. *Sessions* are temporary log destinations that are valid only as long as the session lasts.

3. **Memory**—A circular buffer where the oldest entry is overwritten when the buffer is full

4. **File**—Event logs and accounting policy information can be directed to a file.

Figure 2.15 The relationship between log event sources, the log ID filter, the log IDs, and the log ID destinations. Note that the log ID filter policy is optional but recommended. Note also that the log ID destination options for the console and syslog are not shown.

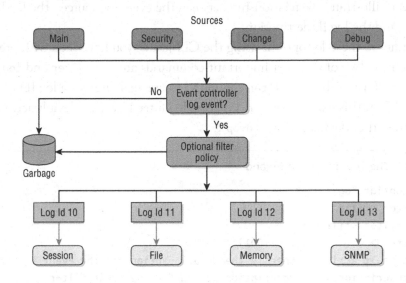

5. **Syslog**—Event log information can be sent to a syslog server.

6. **SNMP Trap Group**—Event log information can be sent to an SNMP trap group.

All events and traps are time-stamped and numbered per destination. Traps are sequence-numbered per destination and stored in memory. If the Alcatel-Lucent 5620 SAM should go offline for some reason, it may not receive some trap notifications. When the SAM comes back online, it will automatically recognize that it has missed some trap notifications because the last sequence number it has will be different from the sequence number in the Alcatel-Lucent SR/ESS system. The SAM will then update its records with the missing traps. If the in-memory notification log becomes full and some records are overwritten, the SAM will resynchronize itself with the Alcatel-Lucent SR/ESS system.

There are several steps that must be performed to configure logs:

1. Configure a log ID with a number from 1 to 98 (log IDs 99 and 100 are reserved for the system).

2. Identify the source(s) of the log ID.

3. Specify an optional filter to filter out certain log events.

4. Identify the destination of the log ID.

5. Examine the logs to view the events for that log ID.

Figure 2.15 illustrates the relationship between the event log sources, the log ID filter, the log ID, and the log ID destination.

You configure these log options using the CLI just as you have seen with previous commands. Two of the most important commands are `log filter` and `log id`. An example of using the `log filter` command to create a filter for a log ID is shown in Listing 2.7. In this example, we are creating log filter 14 with a default action of `forward` (the other default action is `drop`).

```
Listing 2.7 The log filter command
A:PE1>config# log filter
  - filter <filter-id>
  - no filter <filter-id>
 <filter-id>          : [1..1001]
 [no] default-action  - Specify the default action for the event filter
 [no] description     - Description string for the event filter
 [no] entry           + Configure an event filter entry
A:PE1>config# log filter 14
A:PE1>config>log>filter$ description "default filter"
A:PE1>config>log>filter$ default-action forward
A:PE1>config>log>filter$ back
A:PE1>config>log>filter# info detail
----------------------------------------------
            default-action forward
            description "default filter"
----------------------------------------------
```

Once the log filter is created, it is necessary to use the `log id` command to specify the source of the logs and the destination. Recall that there are four streams of logs: main, security, change, and debug/trace; and six possible destinations: console, session, memory, file, syslog, and SNMP trap. In Listing 2.8, we are configuring log ID 14 to forward the debug/trace input stream to the session destination.

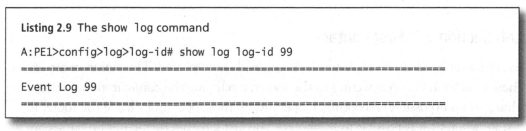

Listing 2.8 The `log id` command

```
A:PE1>config>log# log-id 14
A:PE1>config>log>log-id# from debug-trace
A:PE1>config>log>log-id# to session
A:PE1>config>log>log-id# filter 14
A:PE1>config>log>log-id# info detail
---------------------------------------------
            no description
            filter 14
            time-format utc
            from debug-trace
            to session
            no shutdown
---------------------------------------------
A:PE1>config>log>log-id#
```

It is important to note that there are two default logs: log 99, which is used for all severity levels of alarms; and log 100, which is used for serious errors. As you have seen previously, you can use a show command to view information about these and other logs. The show log log-id *xx*, where *xx* is the log ID you are interested in, is very useful for viewing the information in a particular log. Since the logs can store a large amount of information, additional options are available to show only specific information in a log. For example, the command show log-id 99 subject 1/1/1 would display information in the log only about port 1/1/1. There are other options as well, and as always liberal use of context-sensitive help via the ? can provide assistance on available command options. Sample output from a show log command for log ID 99 is shown in Listing 2.9.

Listing 2.9 The show log command

```
A:PE1>config>log>log-id# show log log-id 99
===================================================================
Event Log 99
===================================================================
```

(continued)

```
Description : Default System Log
Memory Log contents  [size=500    next event=25  (not wrapped)]
24 2006/08/17 15:30:55.29 UTC WARNING: SYSTEM #2006 - CHASSIS
"tmnxMDATable: Slot 1, MDA 2 configuration modified"
23 2006/08/17 15:30:55.29 UTC WARNING: SYSTEM #2007 - PORT
"Pool on Port 1/2/b.net-sap Modified managed object created"
........................
5 2006/08/17 15:30:55.29 UTC MINOR: CHASSIS #2004 - Mda 1/2
"Class MDA Module : wrong type inserted"
```

Now you should complete the lab exercises to assist you in reinforcing this chapter's features. These lab exercises are carefully designed to give you hands-on experience configuring many of the technology standards that have been discussed and should greatly aid you in your exam preparation.

Practice Lab: Alcatel-Lucent 7750/7450 Hardware and the CLI

The following lab is designed to reinforce your knowledge of the content in this chapter. Please review the instructions carefully and perform the steps in the order in which they are presented. The practice labs require that you have access to three or more Alcatel-Lucent 7750 SRs or Alcatel-Lucent 7450 ESSs in a non-production environment.

 These labs are designed to be used in a controlled lab environment. Please **DO NOT** attempt to perform these labs in a production environment.

Lab Section 2.1: First Contact

Every router needs to be configured, maintained, and updated. The common aspects of these operations are connecting to the router, modifying the configuration, saving the changes, and (possibly) rebooting. Hopefully, all these operations leave the router in a state whereby it is possible to *reconnect!* The first lab exercise focuses on basic connectivity for communicating with the router itself; the remaining exercises illustrate how to explore, modify, and save the router configuration. If you are familiar with the command line in DOS, UNIX, or Linux, you will see many similarities with the CLI in Alcatel-Lucent 7750/7450 routers.

Objective In this exercise, you will connect to the router's command-line interface (CLI), enter commands, then disconnect or reboot the router. You will need either physical access to the equipment or the IP address of the management port.

Validation You will know that you have succeeded if you get an interactive command prompt and are able to change the text of that prompt.

Throughout all the lab exercises, interaction with the router is exclusively through a text-based CLI. As previously mentioned, establishing the connection to the CLI is achieved via any (or all!) of three ways: a serial RS-232 port on the SF/CPM card; the dedicated Ethernet management (out-of-band) port on the SF/CPM card; or any regular Ethernet network (in-band) port. Each option is covered briefly below.

1. Connect to the router's CLI to get a login prompt:

   - **Via the Serial Port**—You will need physical access to the router to connect a laptop (or other suitable device) to the serial port with a serial cable. The default serial port settings are: 115000, N, 8, 1 with no flow control. For software, you will need a "terminal emulator" program; common options for MS Windows are Hyperterm, Kermit, PuTTY, and for Linux, minicom or seyon.

   - **Via the Management or Network Port**—You will need to know the configured address for the router. If there's no one to ask, or the equipment has never previously been set up, your only option is to connect via the serial port. For software, you should use an SSH program; common options for MS Windows are PuTTY; SecureCRT; OpenSSH; and for Linux, the built-in command ssh.

   In either case, if you don't immediately see the prompt login as:, pressing the [Enter] key should make it appear.

2. **Log In**—Routers are shipped with a default account admin and password admin. Try using these at the login prompt. If they don't work, you'll need to ask for a login account and password from the regular system administrator. If everything worked properly, you should see something like the following:

The code in bold text indicates user input.

```
login as: admin
TiMOS-B-6.1.R5 both/hops ALCATEL SR 7750 Copyright (c) 2000-2008
Alcatel-Lucent.
All rights reserved. All use subject to applicable license agreements.
Built Sun Dec 14 15:01:11 PST 2008 by builder /rel6.1/b1/R5/panos/main
admin@192.168.0.1's password:

*A:NS074661144#
```

3. **Executing Commands**—Executing a command is simple: Just type any valid command at the prompt. For this step, simply confirm the time setting and the OS version using the following commands:

```
*A:NS074661144# show time
Sat Jan  1 05:44:03 UTC 2000
*A:NS074661144# show version
TiMOS-B-6.1.R5 both/hops ALCATEL SR 7750 Copyright (c) 2000-2008
Alcatel-Lucent.
All rights reserved. All use subject to applicable license agreements.
Built Sun Dec 14 15:01:11 PST 2008 by builder /rel6.1/b1/R5/panos/main
*A:NS074661144#
```

3a. Does it matter if a command is typed in uppercase or lowercase?

3b. If a router is completely uninitialized, what time does it show?

3c. What is the OS version? Where else does the OS version appear?

Note the leading asterisk (*) in the CLI prompt. This is (normally) a reminder that the router has configuration changes that have not yet been saved. The next lab exercise covers this topic.

4. The router name appears after the first letter (A:), for example, NS074661144. Unless a proper name has been configured, the router generates this name from its serial number. According to best practices, every router should have a meaningful name that helps administrators identify it quickly. Configure a better name.

```
*A:NS074661144# configure system name Router1
*A:Router1#
```

4a. Does the router name *always* appear in the CLI prompt?

5. Disconnect from the router.

```
*A:Router1# log
```

Whatever software you're using to connect should either terminate or somehow show a disconnected state.

6. Reconnect to the router.

6a. Is the router name still the same as before disconnecting?

7. Reboot the router. Wait a minute or two and then reconnect.

```
*A:Router1# admin reboot now
```

7a. Is the router name still the same as before rebooting?

7b. Why or why not?

8. Reconfigure the router name to something meaningful to you.

Lab Section 2.2: What Is the Router Doing? Getting Help and Information

Most computer systems have some method of recording and reporting of significant events. MS Windows has the *Event Viewer*, UNIX and Linux have the command dmesg and the log files /var/log/messages. These are essential tools for diagnosing problems or anomalies with the system's behavior, or simply confirming that everything is working as it should. This lab looks at some of the facilities available on Alcatel-Lucent 7750/7450 equipment for getting help and information.

Objective In this exercise, you will become familiar with the boot traces and logging features available on Alcatel-Lucent 7750/7450 equipment. This exercise also demonstrates the help and auto-completion features of the CLI.

Validation You will know that you have succeeded if you feel at least a little more confident and competent with the CLI; if you can easily generate, edit, and correct typos; and if you can get help from the CLI.

1. Make sure you are logged in.

2. Using the command shown below, display and examine the complete log of bootup messages. These messages are an excellent source of information about how the router started up and what configuration files were used.

```
*A:Router1# show boot-messages
============================================================
cf3:/bootlog.txt
============================================================
Boot log started on CPU#0
   Build: X-6.1.R5 on Sun Dec 14 14:22:12 PST 2008 by builder
   CPUCTL FPGA version: 2C
Boot rom version is v29
>>>Testing mainboard FPGA chain...
>>>Validating SDRAM from 0x4D696368 to 0x61656C20
>>>Testing SDRAM from 0x416E6465 to 0x72736F6E
>>>Testing Compact Flash 1... Slot Empty
>>>Testing Compact Flash 2... Slot Empty
>>>Testing Compact Flash 3... OK (SILICONSYSTEMS INC 256MB)
Wales peripheral FPGA version is 0x14
MDA #1: Serial Number 'NS083662989'
Board Serial Number is 'NS074561259'
Chassis Serial Number is 'NS074661144'
Searching for boot.ldr on local drives:
Searching cf3 for boot.ldr...

[... Some lines omitted ...]

TiMOS BOOT LOADER
Time from clock is SAT JAN 01 00:00:00 2000 UTC
Switching serial output to sync mode...   done

Looking for cf3:/bof.cfg ... OK, reading

Contents of Boot Options File on cf3:
    primary-image     cf3:\6.1.R5
    address           192.168.183.108/27 active
    static-route      128.0.0.0/1 next-hop 192.168.183.97
    autonegotiate
    duplex            full
    speed             100
```

```
wait            3
persist         off
no li-local-save
no li-separate
console-speed   115200
[... Additional output omitted ...]
```

2a. Upon (re-)booting, what time does a router show?

2b. What are the settings for connecting to the router: Via the serial port? Via the management Ethernet port?

2c. In which file are the connection settings stored?

2d. Which piece of hardware provides the serial number that is used for the default router name?

3. On an uninitialized router, the time will always be incorrect. The next few steps are intended to show some of the excellent help features available through the CLI, so don't be afraid to experiment. Start typing the **admin set-time** command to set the time, but do not press the [Enter] key; type a question mark (?) instead to get a complete list of available options.

```
*A:Router1# admin set-time
 - set-time <date> <time>

<date>          : YYYY/MM/DD
<time>          : hh:mm[:ss]



*A:Router1# admin set-time
```

Notice that after displaying some help (the list of available options), the CLI re-typed your original command to leave you exactly where you were before typing the ?.

4. We all make mistakes from time to time. It's easy to interrupt or cancel at any time whatever has been typed: type **[Ctrl]+C** to kill everything that has been typed on the line.

```
*A:Router1# admin set-time ^C
*A:Router1#
```

5. It's easy to forget the exact spelling of a command. The CLI has help for this situation also: Type the word **admin** and only a part of **set-time**, and then press the [Space] or [Tab] key to have the system auto-complete the command.

```
*A:Router1# admin set[TAB]
*A:Router1# admin set-time
```

6. There are enough commands that it's sometimes possible to remember the first part of a command, but not the last. ["I know the word *time* is somewhere in the command, but I don't remember if it's at the start or the end."] The CLI provides help by listing all possible options. Type the first part of the command, press [Enter], and then use tree or tree detail to get a complete list of all options for that context.

```
*A:Router1# admin
*A:Router1>admin# tree
admin
|
+---application-assurance
|   |
|   +---upgrade
|
+---debug-save
|
+---disconnect
|
+---display-config
|
+---enable-tech
|
+---radius-discovery
|   |
|   +---force-discover
|
+---reboot
|
+---redundancy
|   |
|   +---force-switchover
|   |
|   +---synchronize
|
+---save
|
+---set-time
|
+---tech-support
*A:Router1>admin#
```

6a. What are the options for the reboot command used in the previous exercise? Which gives more information: using the "?" feature or the tree detail command?

7. There are two commands for getting out of a command subcontext: back or exit. If you enter a loooooong command and want to return to the original context, use exit. If you just want to go up a single level in the context, use back. Try either one to get out of the current context.

```
*A:Router1>admin# exit
*A:Router1#
```

8. Now that you're fully equipped to get help with commands, have a look to see what log files are recording on-going events in the router.

```
*A:Router1# show log log-collector
```

```
===============================================================================
Log Collectors
===============================================================================
Main                Logged   : 30                 Dropped  : 0
   Dest Log Id: 99    Filter Id: 0      Status: enabled    Dest Type: memory
   Dest Log Id: 100   Filter Id: 1001   Status: enabled    Dest Type: memory
Security            Logged   : 5                  Dropped  : 0
Change              Logged   : 8                  Dropped  : 0
Debug               Logged   : 0                  Dropped  : 0
LI                  Logged   : 25                 Dropped  : 0
===============================================================================
```

```
*A:Router1#
```

8a. How many main categories of events are there?

8b. From the above display, how many logs are actually actively recording events? (These are default logs that always exist.)

9. Have a look at a specific log.

```
*A:Router1# show log log-id 99


===============================================================================
Event Log 99
===============================================================================
Description : Default System Log
Memory Log contents  [size=500   next event=31  (not wrapped)]

30 2000/01/01 06:02:39.09 UTC WARNING: SYSTEM #2006 Base CHASSIS
"tmnxChassisTable: Chassis 1 configuration modified"

29 2000/01/01 00:00:17.24 UTC MINOR: CHASSIS #2002 Base Card 1
"Class IO Module : inserted"

28 2000/01/01 00:00:03.72 UTC WARNING: SNMP #2005 Base A/1
"Interface A/1 is operational"

27 2000/01/01 00:00:02.94 UTC MAJOR: SYSTEM #2005 Base SNMP daemon
"SNMP daemon initialization complete.
System configured with persistent SNMP indexes: false.
SNMP daemon admimistrative status: outOfService.
SNMP daemon operational status: outOfService."

26 2000/01/01 00:00:02.94 UTC MAJOR: SYSTEM #2023 Base SNMP
   administratively down
"The SNMP agent has changed state.  Administrative state is
  outOfService and operational state is outOfService."

25 2000/01/01 00:00:02.84 UTC MAJOR: SYSTEM #2004 Base System configured
"Bootup configuration complete. Configuration status: defaultBooted.
SNMP Persistent Indexes status: persistDisabled.
System configured with persistent indexes: false."*A:Router1#
[... Additional output omitted ...]
```

9a. How are log entries listed: from oldest to newest, or vice versa?

9b. Each log entry is numbered. Where does that number appear?

9c. Does the number of log entries identified by the log-collector correspond to what is printed out?

9d. Are there more options we could have used in this command? How can you find out?

Lab Section 2.3: Saving Configuration Changes

Alcatel-Lucent 7750/7450 routers provide two major configuration files required for initial access and maintaining configurations across resets. The following exercises show how these files are used.

Objective In this exercise, you will gain an understanding of the role, filename, and content of the Boot Options File (BOF), and become familiar with how to specify and save the configuration file.

Validation You will know you have succeeded if a directory listing of cf3: shows the two configuration files with recent time stamps.

1. Display and examine the content of the BOF.

```
*A:Router1# file type cf3:\bof.cfg
# TiMOS-B-6.1.R5 both/hops ALCATEL SR 7750 Copyright (c) 2000-2008
Alcatel-Lucent.
# All rights reserved. All use subject to applicable license agreements.
# Built on Sun Dec 14 15:01:11 PST 2008 by builder in
/rel6.1/b1/R5/panos/main

# Generated TUE JAN 01 16:33:15 2000 UTC

primary-image     cf3:\6.1.R5
address           192.168.0.1/27 active
static-route      128.0.0.0/1 next-hop 192.168.183.97
autonegotiate
duplex            full
speed             100
wait              3
persist           off
no li-local-save
no li-separate
console-speed     115200
```

   1a. For filenames, does it matter whether they are typed in uppercase or lowercase?

   1b. Can you identify where/how to specify the location for the desired OS version? (*Hint:* Find a match between the software version listed on the first line and one of the configuration lines.)

   1c. Can you use any of the CLI Help features to find out what storage devices exist, other than cf3?

2. The BOF collects together three main items: the connectivity details (multiple lines), where to find the desired OS version (one line), and where to find all remaining details of the configuration (one line, not shown in the previous step). Changing either the OS version or the configuration is so quick and easy because all it takes is editing either (or both) of these single lines and doing a reboot. Since an uninitialized router doesn't specify any configuration file, you will add this third item now.

```
*A:Router1# bof
*A:Router1>bof# primary-config cf3:\MAA-TestConfig.cfg
WARNING: CLI A valid config file does not exist at cf3:\MAA-TestConfig.cfg.
*A:Router1>bof#
```

3. The filename for the *primary* config is now set. In order to ensure that a router "always works and never stops," the Alcatel-Lucent 7750/7450 routers were designed to have other chances to find a valid config if the primary config is somehow unavailable. Use a CLI Help feature to find out how many additional chances are available.

   3a. If there are additional chances to find the config, are there also additional chances for finding the OS? If yes, how many?

4. The Alcatel-Lucent CLI has the same rules as any other editing task on a computer system: You may make as many changes as you wish before saving to a file, and you *must* save your changes or they will be lost when the system reboots. There is exactly one name that can be used for storing the BOF itself: `cf3:\bof .cfg`. Since there is only one name, there can only be one version or copy of the BOF. It isn't necessary to specify a filename when saving, only the `save` command.

```
*A:Router1>bof# save
Writing BOF to cf3:/bof.cfg
Saving BOF .... Completed.
*A:Router1>bof#
```

   4a. What exactly has been saved by the preceding command: just the BOF's three main items? or all other configuration details?

5. An Alcatel-Lucent 7750/7450 router has many, many configuration details, including a few that must at least have default values. The BOF now includes

a setting for *where* to save the configuration; it is now possible to save the configuration.

```
*A:Router1>bof# exit
*A:Router1# admin save
Writing file to cf3:\MAA-TestConfig.cfg
Saving configuration .... Completed.
A:Router1#
```

5a. What exactly has been saved by the above command: just the BOF's three main items? or all other configuration details?

5b. The admin save command didn't include a filename. What filename did the router use, and how did it choose it?

5c. What character has disappeared from the beginning of the prompt, as soon as the configuration was saved? What is the meaning of this character?

6. Verify that you have successfully created the expected configuration files. Confirm that the configuration files were, indeed, created by you: Print the current time, and check that the config files are time-stamped just a few minutes earlier.

```
A:Router1# file dir

Volume in drive cf3 on slot A has no label.

Volume in drive cf3 on slot A is formatted as FAT32.

Directory of cf3:\

01/01/2000  12:42a    <DIR>          6.1.R5
01/01/2000  08:54a             573 bof.cfg
01/01/2000  08:55a            5838 MAA-TestConfig.cfg

  [... Additional output omitted ...]

A:Router1#  show time
Sat Jan  1 08:57:03 UTC 2000
A:Router1#
```

6a. Compare the sample output above with your actual listing. Do you have *at least* the files bof.cfg and your main config file? (Depending on who has used the router before you, there could be many additional files.) If you don't have these two files, check and repeat the preceding steps carefully until you succeed.

6b. Is the time stamp on the config files a few minutes earlier than the current time (e.g., from the example above: 8:54 a.m. and 8:55 a.m. with the current time being a few minutes later at 8:57 a.m.)?

7. Repeat the steps above for each of the other routers.

8. Now that you know how to save the two main configuration files, make sure that you *save your work regularly* (even every few minutes)! The command prompt has a reminder symbol to make sure you know when you have unsaved changes.

For readers who don't like the anticipation of waiting, there's a practical application for saved configurations right within this book. We configure the OSPF protocol in Chapter 9 and ensure that it is saved(!). In Chapter 10, we use a different protocol, so the OSPF configuration is wiped clean. When we need OSPF again in Chapter 11, we rerun the saved configuration file to get a fully restored OSPF configuration.

Chapter Review

Now that you have completed this chapter, you should have a good understanding of the following topics. If you are not familiar with these topics, please go back and review the appropriate sections.

- Alcatel-Lucent 7750 SR and 7450 ESS product lines, including the various chassis types and card types
- CLI commands and navigation
- Useful commands in the CLI, including help options
- System start-up and boot files
- The Boot Options File (BOF) and default configuration files
- Basic system and hardware configuration
- Logs and alarms

Post-Assessment

The following questions will test your knowledge and prepare you for the Alcatel-Lucent NRS I Certification Exam. Please review each question carefully and choose the most correct answer. You can compare your response with the answers listed in Appendix A. You can also download all of the CD content at http://booksupport .wiley.com to take all the assessment tests and review the answers. Good luck!

1. Which of the following is *not* a product in the Alcatel-Lucent 7750 SR/7450 ESS family?

   A. SR-12

   B. ESS-7

   C. SR-6

   D. ESS-1

2. Which of the following statements is false regarding the Alcatel-Lucent 7450 ESS series?

   A. It supports multiple chassis types.

   B. It supports OSFP, IS-IS, RIP, and BGP.

   C. It is used primarily for Ethernet aggregation.

   D. It can be managed via a console port or a dedicated Ethernet port on the SF/CPM.

3. Which of the following descriptions is correct?

   A. bof.cfg—7750/7450 configuration file

   B. cpm.tim—IOM image file

   C. config.cfg—Back-up configuration file

   D. boot.ldr—Bootstrap image file

4. Which of the following commands is not correctly described?

   A. shutdown—This command is used to disable an interface or protocol.

   B. exit all—Logs out of the Alcatel-Lucent 7750 SR/7450 ESS device.

   C. ?—Lists all commands in the current context.

   D. [TAB]—This command is used for assistance with command completion.

5. Which of the following is not a log stream type?

A. Audit

B. Change

C. Main

D. Security

6. Which of the following descriptions of hardware for the Alcatel-Lucent 7750 SR/7450 ESS is correct?

A. IOMs plug into MDAs.

B. MDAs plug into SFPs.

C. SF/CPMs plug into IOMs.

D. IOMs plug into the chassis.

7. What file contains the system bootstrap image?

A. boot.cfg

B. image.ldr

C. boot.ldr

D. bof.cfg

8. The SF/CPM card has its own Ethernet interface for out-of-band management. This interface has its own IP address and default route. Where is this information stored?

A. boot.ldf

B. bof.cfg

C. config.cfg

D. cpm.tim

9. Which of the following correctly lists the order in which files are read by the Alcatel-Lucent 7750 SR/7450 ESS upon bootup?

A. boot.ldr, bof.cfg, system image, config.cfg

B. system image, boot.ldr, config.cfg, bof.cfg

C. boot.ldr, system image, bof.cfg, config.cfg

D. boot.ldr, bof.cfg, config.cfg, system image

10. During the boot process, an Alcatel-Lucent 7750 SR/7450 ESS checks to see if persistence is enabled. What is the purpose of persistence?

A. To ensure that the system saves routing table information when it reboots

B. To ensure that changes to the bof.cfg are saved

C. To ensure synchronization with the 5620 SAM

D. To ensure that config changes are stored in the config.cfg

11. What command would you use to enable an interface the first time you initialized an Alcatel-Lucent 7750 SR/7450 ESS?

A. `enable`

B. `no shutdown`

C. `interface enable`

D. `interface on`

12. Which of the following is the correct provisioning order you should follow when configuring an Alcatel-Lucent 7750 SR/7450 ESS for the first time?

A. IOM, port, MDA

B. Port, MDA, IOM

C. IOM, MDA, port

D. MDA, port, IOM

13. Which of the following is false regarding the logging mechanisms in the Alcatel-Lucent 7750 SR/7450 ESS?

A. Log IDs 99 and 100 are reserved for system usage.

B. You must configure at least one input stream for a log ID.

C. You must configure a filter for each log ID.

D. You must configure the destination for the events from the log ID.

14. What command would you use to display the configuration of your Alcatel-Lucent 7750 SR/7450 ESS?

A. `show config`

B. `admin display-config`

C. `display config`

D. `show admin config`

15. Which of the following values is *not* stored in the bof.cfg?

    A. The location of the primary boot image

    B. The list of IOM cards in the chassis

    C. The persist value

    D. The location of the primary config file

Data Link
Overview

- Layer 2 OSI
- Layer 2 protocols: PPP, ATM, and Time Division Multiplexing
- Ethernet overview
- Ethernet addressing and operation
- Ethernet physical cabling

This chapter provides an overview of several data link layer technologies, with particular attention and emphasis on Ethernet and its various standards. Ethernet is to the data link layer what IP and TCP are to the upper layers. There was a time in the history of networking when other standards such as Token-Ring were nearly as important as Ethernet, but that time has long since passed. It is safe to say that you cannot understand modern networking without understanding Ethernet, including its addressing schemes and physical standards. As such, the majority of this chapter will focus on providing you with an all-important understanding of this ubiquitous protocol. Additionally, we will cover two other very important protocols that you will encounter in Wide Area Networks: Point-to-Point Protocol (PPP) and Asynchronous Transfer Mode (ATM).

Pre-Assessment

The following assessment questions will help you understand what areas of the chapter you should review in more detail to prepare for the exam. You can also download all of the CD materials for this book at http://booksupport.wiley.com to take all the assessment tests and review the answers.

1. Which of the following is *not* a data link layer (OSI Layer 2) protocol?
   A. Ethernet
   B. ATM
   C. Cell-Relay
   D. PPP

2. Which of the following is *not* a function of PPP?
   A. Provides support for multiple upper-layer protocols
   B. Supports the connection of multiple devices on a single link
   C. Supports authentication
   D. Supports data integrity via a CRC on frame contents

3. Which of the following ATM AAL types is associated with an incorrect description?
   A. AAL3/4—Connection-oriented service
   B. AAL5—Connectionless service
   C. AAL2—Variable bit rate traffic
   D. AAL1—High bit rate traffic

4. Which of the following technologies ensures that a unicast packet is visible only to the device with the specific destination address?

   A. Ethernet

   B. Switched Ethernet

   C. Satellite

   D. Wireless LAN

5. The advantage of using multicast packets instead of broadcast packets is _____.

   A. Broadcasts are received by every host.

   B. Multicast is newer technology.

   C. Broadcasts are processed by every host.

   D. Multicast provides multiple addresses for flexibility.

   You will find the answers to each of these questions in Appendix A.

3.1 OSI Layer 2 Overview

In Chapter 1, we introduced the OSI model and discussed the various layers of the model. We discussed how the model is not itself a set of protocols, but merely an abstraction of the functions that must be performed by protocols in a hierarchical manner in order to facilitate network communications. We also briefly discussed the IP and TCP protocols and how they perform the functions of Layer 3 and Layer 4 in the OSI model, respectively. In this chapter, we examine the data link layer, Layer 2 of the OSI model, in more detail.

The first point to address is why the data link layer is needed at all. After all, we have addressing in Layer 3, so why is this not sufficient to move a packet from one system to another? The answer to this lies in the separation of duties performed by each layer, which provides for a wide variety of disparate technologies. It could be the case that a Layer 3 protocol such as IP could talk directly to the hardware layer and therefore bypass a need for a Layer 2 protocol. However, imagine how many different physical connections there might be, and then imagine how many different IP protocol stacks would have to be written.

IP would have to understand both Local Area Network (LAN) and Wide Area Network (WAN) technologies, phones and other mobile devices, PlayStations, and so on. There would have to be a large number of IP stacks, or the IP stack code would be enormously large to account for all the separate devices it would need to interact with. Any changes to the IP protocol would necessitate massive code changes for every conceivable type of hardware, and this seems very inefficient.

Enter the data link layer. By having the data link layer interact with the hardware and provide its own local addressing, the IP stack can be written with minimal understanding of the physical hardware. Indeed, Layer 3 protocols usually have no knowledge of the underlying physical infrastructure, nor do they need it, provided that the data link layer protocol is compatible with the Layer 3 protocol. The data link layer hides the details of the interaction with the physical medium entirely from upper protocols such as IP. In theory, this would allow IP to run over any possible physical medium, provided there was an appropriate data link layer protocol that understood how to communicate with both the upper-layer protocol and the lower layer physical connection. This has led to the mantra, "IP Over Everything."

Of course, the astute reader may immediately recognize that in some ways, this explanation simply moves the problem down a layer. If the data link layer must understand a wide variety of Layer 1 physical media, how is this necessarily better than simply having the Layer 3 protocol understand it? The truth is that in the real world, most data link layer protocols support only a very limited number of physical media. As you will see later, Ethernet can be run on only a few carefully specified physical media, and these specifications are part of the protocol itself. (Ethernet is therefore actually both a data link and a physical link layer protocol.) And, while other data link layer protocols such as PPP don't necessarily define the physical media they can use, by convention and common usage, there are only a few physical protocols that PPP stacks need to understand. The same holds true for other data link layer protocols. It is nevertheless true that separating interaction of the physical layer from Layer 3 has allowed for the IP protocol to exist relatively unchanged for more than 30 years. This is a remarkable achievement given the extraordinary evolution of hardware in that time period.

Types of Data Link Layer Protocols

There are many different data link layer protocols that have been used in the history of networking; however, many of them are of historical interest only. The most common protocols in use today are Ethernet, PPP, ATM, and Frame-Relay. In this chapter, we discuss Ethernet, PPP, and ATM, but with particular attention paid to Ethernet. PPP and ATM are primarily wide area protocols, whereas Ethernet is by far the dominant protocol in the local and campus network. Note that although the specifications of the various data link layer protocols can be quite diverse, all of these protocols perform many of the same functions. Once you understand how a particular Data Link protocol performs its functions, you can use this information to assist you in understanding other Data Link protocols as well.

Layer 2/Data Link networks can be classified broadly into three types:

- **Point-to-Point Networks**—Point-to-point network protocols do not usually require source and destination addresses since they are established between two networking devices only.

- **Circuit-Based Networks**—Circuit-based networks create virtual circuits between different devices over a shared infrastructure. Usually this involves manually mapping a path through network switches from one location to another.

- **Shared Networks**—Shared networks provide each device with a share of the underlying network medium such as a physical cable or a switch. All devices can send and receive traffic to each other directly through the shared medium.

The three protocols we will discuss each represents an example of these diverse network types. The PPP protocol is used on point-to-point links between two sites, ATM uses virtual circuits, and Ethernet is used over a shared medium. Despite the diversity of these and other Data Link protocols, they all share common characteristics. In particular, they will all have a Layer 2 frame that identifies particular fields that are required for Layer 2 operations.

These Layer 2 frames usually consist of:

- A circuit identifier in the case of circuit-based networks
- An address that directs the packet to the required destination in the case of shared media
- A fixed-length maximum size or maximum transmission unit (MTU) established between the source and receiving component. Data from higher layers is broken into fixed-length frames (covered later).
- An error check that is inserted by the source component and verified by the receiving component to verify data integrity on each data link segment

The next section discusses how a data link layer performs the function of transferring a packet across a network and how this function integrates into the complex process of interconnecting networks of varying types.

Scope of the Data Link Layer

The scope of a Data Link frame is the network itself. For example, in a typical scenario of IP/Ethernet, each IP subnet is considered to be one network. The Data Link frame remains intact while it traverses the Layer 2 devices in a particular IP subnet. If the IP packet needs to be routed to another subnet via an IP router, the original Data Link frame will be removed after it ingresses the IP router. When forwarding the IP packet out from the appropriate port, the IP router constructs a new Data Link frame with correct headers and Data Link addresses. This new Data Link header is used as the frame traverses the next subnet. This process continues until the destination host is reached. The application data sent between two host stations can traverse several physically different networks. Each network has a different Data Link header and may even use different Data Link protocols that depend on the physical wire itself, for example, Ethernet, PPP, ATM, or Frame-Relay.

In Figure 3.1, the end-hosts on the Layer 2 network communicate with each other using the specific Layer 2 (L2) protocol. The PCs on the left side of the Ethernet network do not require anything other than Ethernet L2 framing to talk to each other. The PCs on the right side of the network similarly require only ATM L2 framing to talk to each other. The L2 networks are separated by routers, which are Layer 3 OSI devices. The PCs on the Ethernet network can only communicate with the PCs on the ATM network through Layer 3 addresses. Note that the devices in the ATM cloud represent ATM switches and the devices in the Ethernet cloud represent Ethernet switches. The device connecting the two clouds is a router. We will discuss all of these concepts in this and later chapters.

Figure 3.1 Hosts on the Ethernet network communicate with each other using the Ethernet protocol, and hosts on the ATM network communicate using the ATM protocol. A router is required for hosts using different Layer 2 protocols to communicate with each other.

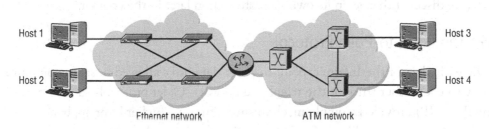

This separation of the differing networks by a router (Layer 3 device) provides many key features that might not be immediately obvious. First, any message from an Ethernet station to another Ethernet station is insulated from the ATM network. This means that no ATM station will ever have to concern itself with understanding an Ethernet frame. More than this, it means that the router will drop any packets that arrive at its Ethernet interface that are not intended for a device on the ATM network and vice versa. This means that a device can have assurance that it will not receive packets from an unrecognized Data Link protocol and it will not have to waste valuable processing time on extraneous data.

Another benefit is that each device needs to have a protocol stack only for its respective network. ATM devices need only an ATM protocol stack, and Ethernet devices need only an Ethernet stack. They may all have identical IP protocol stacks, and, indeed, this is probably the case if they are all running the same operating system (most OSs embed the TCP/IP protocol stack as part of the system itself). Finally, the separation provides protection in the event of a serious network malfunction on either network. The router will prevent errors relating to the Ethernet protocol from infecting the ATM network and vice versa. All hosts on the Ethernet network could be encountering serious problems, and the ATM hosts could still continue communicating with each other without any problems. This sort of network separation is a key part of good network design, and you will encounter it frequently.

3.2 Layer 2 Protocols: PPP, ATM, and Time Division Multiplexing

In the following sections, we examine some of the most important Layer 2 protocols. The protocols in this section comprise all of the most important Data Link protocols in use in modern networks with the exception of Ethernet. Because of its particular importance, we discuss Ethernet in its own separate section later in the chapter.

PPP: The Point-to-Point Protocol

In the early days of the Internet, point-to-point data links allowed hosts to communicate with each other through the telephone network. Older protocols such as Serial Line IP (SLIP) provided a simple mechanism for framing higher-layer applications for transmission along serial lines. Serial lines allow for data to be sent in a single-byte stream one after another in "serial," as opposed to allowing multiple byte streams in "parallel," hence the designation. By far the most typical serial lines continue to be dial-up modem connections to an ISP. SLIP, in accordance with RFC 1055, sent the datagram across the serial line as a series of bytes, and it used special characters to mark when a series of bytes should be grouped together as a datagram. SLIP was simple enough but could not control the characteristics of the connection. Because of its limitation and lack of features such as error detection, SLIP has largely been replaced by other protocols.

Today, the protocol of choice for this purpose is the Point-to-Point Protocol (PPP), which provides advantages such as link control to negotiate the link characteristics, network control to transfer multiple Layer 3 protocols, and authentication used by remote computers to dial into their Internet service. Figure 3.2 shows a typical configuration for which the SLIP protocol would have been used in the past, but today would be served by the PPP protocol stack installed on your home computer and on the ISP's router.

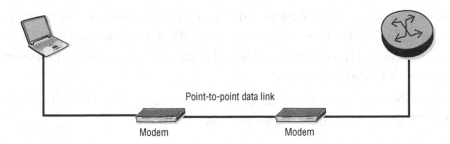

PPP is by far the dominant point-to-point protocol in use in modern networks. The frame itself is fairly simple and, in fact, has several fields that are not actually used. The reason for this is that the frame is derived from the frame for the High Level data link layer Control (HDLC) protocol designed by IBM. HDLC is still in use, but primarily only for connections to IBM mainframes. Some of the fields in the PPP header are relevant for HDLC but not for PPP and are retained mainly as historical artifacts. The PPP frame is shown in Figure 3.3, and the relevant fields are described in the following list.

Figure 3.3 The PPP frame header. The address and control fields are not used by PPP and are always set to default values.

Flag 0x7E	Address 0xFF	Control 0x03	Protocol First byte
Protocol Second byte	Data		
			Padding
Packing	Frame Check Sequence		Flag 0x7E

The relevant fields in the PPP frame are:

- **Flag**—The first flag field indicates the start of a PPP frame. It always has the value 01111110 binary (0x7E hexadecimal or 126 decimal). The last flag field indicates the end of a PPP frame. It always has the value 01111110 binary (0x7E hexadecimal or 126 decimal).

- **Address**—In HDLC this is the address of the destination of the frame but has no meaning in PPP. Therefore, it is always set to 11111111 (0xFF or 255 decimal), which is equivalent to a broadcast (it means "all stations").

- **Control**—This field is used in HDLC for various control purposes, but in PPP it is set to 00000011 (3 decimal).

- **Data**—Zero or more bytes of payload that contains either data or control information, depending on the frame type. For regular PPP data frames, the network-layer datagram, such as IP, is encapsulated here. For control frames, the control information fields are placed here instead.

- **Padding**—In some cases, additional dummy bytes may be added to pad out the size of the PPP frame to ensure a certain minimum size frame.

- **Frame Check Sequence (FCS)**—A checksum computed over the frame to provide basic protection against errors in transmission. This is a Cyclic Redundancy Check (CRC) code similar to the one used for other Layer 2 protocol error protection schemes such as the one used in Ethernet. It can be either 16 bits or 32 bits in size (the default is 16 bits). The FCS is calculated over the Address, Control, Protocol, Data, and Padding fields. Since the Address and Control fields are always the same, and the Protocol fields are always the same for IP, this essentially means that the Data field and the Padding field are the only fields that affect the CRC.

- **Protocol**—Identifies the protocol of the datagram encapsulated in the Information field of the frame. While there are several possible protocol fields, in the vast majority of cases, the IP protocol is the only one that is of concern. The hex number 0021 identifies IP version 4 as the upper-layer protocol.

A few more points are worth noting about the PPP protocol. First, unlike Ethernet, it does not specify any particular physical layer requirements. Indeed, PPP can operate across any Data Terminal Equipment (DTE)/Data Communications Equipment (DCE) interface. DTE/DCE is generic terminology for a physical interface between a "terminal" interface such as a PC and a "communication" interface such as a modem that provides the data communication. There are many standards for DTE/DEC such as Electronics Industry Alliance (EIA) RS-232 (the standard serial port on your PC provides this type of connection), Integrated Services Digital Network (ISDN), International Telecommunication Union—Telecommunication Standardization Sector (ITU-T) V.35, and so on. It is not important that you understand all the possible DTE/DEC standards, only that you understand that PPP supports all of them.

Another important point is that PPP provides several control protocols to build and control the connections between the end systems. Because PPP is more sophisticated than SLIP, it doesn't just start transmitting packets at will. Typically, a set-up function is performed by the Link Control Protocol (LCP) to determine factors such as encryption, compression, and authentication between the communicating systems. In addition to the LCP, the Network Control Protocol (NCP) provides control messages that allow for multiple upper-layer protocols to be used over the same physical point-to-point link in the event that protocols other than IP are needed.

Circuit-Switching and ATM

Circuit-switched protocols allow the transfer of user information as a unique set of packets identified by Virtual Circuits (VC). A VC can be thought of as a virtual connection through a network that may exist only for the duration of a particular network conversation. In some cases, the connection can exist for much longer than this. The reason the circuit is virtual is that a VC can be configured over an infrastructure that can support multiple connections. This is beneficial because if a given path fails, it is very easy to reconfigure the VC to take another path through the network. It also allows for multiple VCs to share the same physical infrastructure, resulting in economies of scale that cannot be achieved when each site requires its own dedicated physical point-to-point circuit.

In Figure 3.4, the switch on the left accepts traffic from each host PC into a virtual circuit and switches to another virtual circuit when going to the router. The virtual circuit number is the same between the host PC and the switch, and between the switch and the router. Traffic from each PC is uniquely identified by a virtual circuit number at every hop. This allows for many logical connections to be configured over a single physical connection and is the predominant way that WAN connections are handled in modern networks. The two most predominant circuit-switching technologies are Frame-Relay and Asynchronous Transfer Mode (ATM). In this chapter, we discuss ATM only because ATM is the more current and more widely used protocol. Most of the switching and virtual connection concepts associated with ATM are applicable to Frame-Relay as well.

ATM is a protocol that was the product of a long and arduous journey through various standards bodies and committees. Its original conception was to be a protocol that could support any type of traffic from voice and video to packet data and everything in between. Different types of traffic have different requirements, so it is difficult to find a "one size fits all" protocol. For example, voice traffic is extremely sensitive to excessive delays and thus usually needs small, fixed-length packets. Large file transfers, conversely, are not sensitive to delays and benefit from large packets that can transfer as much data in a single packet as possible.

Figure 3.4 ATM is an example of a circuit-switching protocol. Multiple logical circuits can exist on the same physical link.

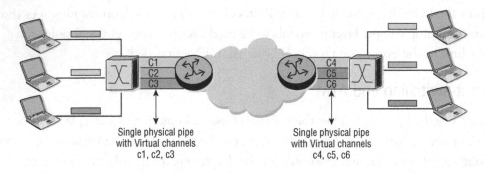

Single physical pipe
with Virtual channels
c1, c2, c3

Single physical pipe
with Virtual channels
c4, c5, c6

For many years, network engineers dreamed of a protocol that would support any application they needed and do it well. Out of this desire, ATM was born. Unfortunately, because ATM was designed with so many requirements in mind, it is a very complex protocol with a dizzying array of options and variations. We do not discuss all the possible options here, but we do cover the most essential characteristics of this important protocol.

ATM frames consist of fixed-length 53-byte *cells* that include a 5-byte header. As you will see later, this is much smaller than the largest Ethernet packets and is the result of a desire for a protocol that can support latency-sensitive applications such as voice traffic. ATM virtual circuits are identified by a Virtual Path Identification (VPI) and Virtual Channel Identification (VCI) pair. Quality of service (QoS) features are built into the ATM protocol, and five service classes are defined, as would be expected of a protocol designed from the ground up to support a large variety of applications. These and other features make ATM well-suited for carrying multiple kinds of services across the same physical infrastructure. The format of the ATM cell is shown in Figure 3.5, and the relevant fields are described below.

The relevant fields in the ATM frame are:

- **GFC**—4 bits of Generic Flow Control that is used to provide local functions, such as identifying multiple stations that share a single ATM interface. The GFC field is typically not used and is set to a default value.

- **VPI**—8 bits of Virtual Path Identifier that is used, in conjunction with the VCI, to identify the next destination of a cell as it passes through a series of switch routers on its way to its destination

Figure 3.5 The ATM cell format. Note the use of the Virtual Path (VPI) and Virtual Channel (VCI) identifiers to support virtual circuits over a single physical link.

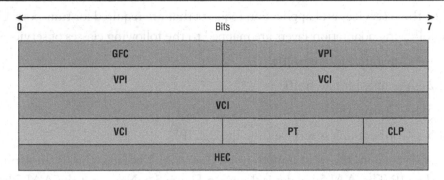

- **VCI**—16 bits of Virtual Channel Identifier that is used, in conjunction with the VPI, to identify the next destination of a cell as it passes through a series of switch routers on its way to its destination

- **PT**—3 bits of Payload Type. The first bit indicates whether the cell contains user data or control data. If the cell contains user data, the second bit indicates congestion, and the third bit indicates whether the cell is the last in a series of cells that represent a single ATM Adaptation Layer (AAL) 5 frame. AAL is a part of the protocol that takes upper-layer class of service information, such as from IP, and translates it into the correct ATM class of service (you'll learn more about this shortly).

- **CLP**—1 bit of Cell Loss Priority that indicates whether the cell should be discarded if it encounters extreme congestion as it moves through the network

- **HEC**—8 bits of Header Error Control that are a checksum calculated only on the header itself.

ATM cells are further encapsulated by ATM Adaptation Layers (AAL), which are responsible for the segmentation of higher-layer data into ATM cells and the reassembly of ATM cells received at the other end into higher-layer data. The segmentation/reassembly process is referred to as *Segmentation and Reassembly* (SAR), and it is a critical aspect of adapting ATM cells to upper-layer protocols like IP, which typically send data in much larger chunks than a 53-byte cell can accept. Another critical process is mapping upper-layer classes of service from the IP layer to connectionless ATM cells.

It is important to understand that, owing to the layering approach championed by the OSI model, upper-layer applications are not supposed to be aware of the intricacies of the underlying ATM protocol specifications. This means that a generic application may request a certain generic class of service such as *low latency*, and this request must then be *mapped* into an ATM class of service. Therefore, the AAL classification is related to these services and application requests that are required for transport. Usually the following adaptation layers are mapped to the following classes of service:

- AAL1—Constant bit rate traffic
- AAL2—Variable bit rate traffic
- AAL3/4—Connection-oriented service (usually)
- AAL5—Connectionless service (usually; e.g., IP)

For our discussion, the most important AAL is AAL5 because that is the service type used by IP. The AAL5 header is shown in Figure 3.6. Note that the AAL5 header could actually be called a *footer* since it follows the payload. The various descriptions for each class of service are described below.

Figure 3.6 The AAL5 header. AAL5 is the adaptation layer that is used by IP services.

Variable length	0-47	1	1	2	4 Bytes
PDU payload	PAD	UU	CPI	LI	CRC-32

PDU - Variable length user information field (broken into 48 byte segments)
PAD - Padding used to cell align the trailer between 0 and 47 bytes long
UU - CPCS user-to-user indication to transfer one byte of user information
CPI - Common Part Indication
LI - Length indicator

Classes of Service Types

- **Constant Bit Rate (CBR) Service**—AAL1 encapsulation supports a connection-oriented service wherein minimal data loss is required. Examples of this service include 64 Kbps voice, fixed-rate uncompressed video, and leased lines for private data networks.

- **Variable Bit Rate (VBR) Service**—AAL2 encapsulation supports a connection-oriented service in which the bit rate is variable but requires a bounded delay for delivery. Examples of this service include compressed packetized voice or video. The requirement on bounded delay for delivery is necessary for the receiver to reconstruct the original uncompressed voice or video.

- **Connection-Oriented Data Service**—For connection-oriented file transfer and data network applications in which a connection is set-up before data is transferred, this type of service has Variable Bit Rate and does not require bounded delay for delivery. Two AAL protocols were defined to support this service class and have been merged into a single type called *AAL3/4.*

- **Connectionless Data Service**—AAL5 encapsulation includes datagram traffic and data network applications in which no connection is set-up before data is transferred. This is used to transport IP/Ethernet/Frame-Relay applications.

 The most important points to remember about ATM are its use of small, fixed-length cells; its support for a variety of different applications; and its use of an adaptation layer to map service requests to the upper layers. You should also remember that AAL5 is used for IP data frames.

Time Division Multiplexing

Another technology for transferring data, usually over a WAN, is Time Division Multiplexing (TDM). In TDM, each host station sends information to a switch. The switch then transmits a frame to a router/switch at a constant data rate (e.g., 1.5 Mbps). This frame is then divided into many fixed timeslots (24), each slot being 64 Kbps. Each host can occupy one or more timeslots per frame. The key point is that each host PC is given a fixed data rate. If the host uses one timeslot, then its transmitting rate is 64K. If the pipe rate is 1.5 Mbps, the host will have to supply their next 64K in the next big frame. The TDM designation is used because each host gets a fixed amount of time, and those times are multitasked or *multiplexed* onto the same physical channel.

In Figure 3.7, each host PC transmits its characteristic frame (different slots appear as different shades of gray). The frames that are transmitted from the switch contain several timeslots. Within each of these frames, three of the timeslots are used by the respective PC hosts.

TDM is a digital technology in which individual signals are interleaved into a composite multiplexed signal. Recurring, fixed-length timeslots are created such that each individual signal is represented by a single channel. The total transmission bandwidth is split among the timeslots. The total composite signal includes the payload bits for the composing channels and overhead bits that create a frame structure that repeats at regular intervals.

Figure 3.7 Using a TDM circuit, each PC gets a fixed timeslot for its traffic.

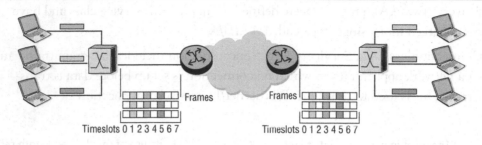

The frame structures of the DS-1 [ANSI95b] and the European E1 [ITU-T98a] signals are shown in Figure 3.8.

Figure 3.8 The frame structure for a DS-1 and a European E1 signal.

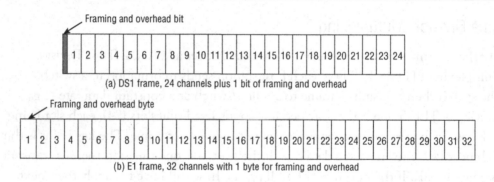

The DS-1 signal consists of 24 payload channels plus overhead. The basic frame of each of these signals repeats every 125 μs (microseconds), that is, 8,000 times per second. With 8 bits carried in each channel, this gives rise to a basic data rate of 64 Kbps for each channel. The requirement for this data rate stems from the need to sample the analog telephony signal 8,000 times per second and encode each sample in 8 bits. A DS-1 frame contains 24 channels, each consisting of 8 bits, plus 1 framing/overhead bit, leading to a total of 193 bits. Since the frame repeats every 125 μs (or 8,000 times a second), the total bit rate of the DS-1 signal is 1.544 Mbps. Similarly, the total bit rate of the E1 signal is 2.048 Mbps (32 channels of 8 bits, repeating every 125 μs).

Broadcast and Shared Access Data Links

Unlike point-to-point and circuit-switching networks, broadcast networks typically use a shared media to communicate to all the devices that are attached to that shared media simultaneously. For data to be reliably delivered from the source to the destination, each of the devices on the shared media is identified by a unique address. The frame that is sourced from the sending device is sent to all the devices sharing the media (broadcasting). All devices will receive the frame, but only the device whose address appears in the frame as the destination address will process the data. The rest of the devices will simply ignore the data. This may seem very inefficient, but it makes the protocol design very simple and supports services that require simultaneous transfer to all nodes on a segment.

 In later chapters, we will discuss technologies that mitigate this inefficiency.

To transmit data reliably, the device on the shared media must compose the frame, obtain control of the media, and then transmit the information. Since the media is shared, it is possible for multiple stations to transmit their information simultaneously, resulting in a collision. This collision causes data corruption. Depending on the protocol used, an algorithm needs to be followed to ensure a minimum number of collisions and also to ensure proper recovery from collisions. An example of a shared media protocol that is very commonly used today is Ethernet, but other shared media such as wireless LANs and satellites are also common, as shown in Figure 3.9.

Figure 3.9 Some examples of shared media technologies where every station receives the same information simultaneously.

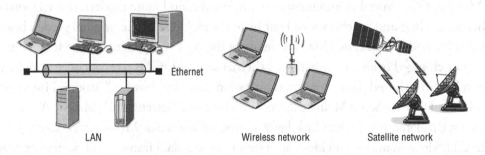

LAN   Wireless network   Satellite network

The remainder of this chapter will focus on the Ethernet protocol including its frame type, varieties, and protocol specifications.

As previously mentioned, it is critical that you have a very solid understanding of the Ethernet protocol because it is by far the dominant Data Link protocol in use in LANs today.

3.3 Ethernet Overview

Ethernet was originally designed by the Xerox Corporation, but the company was unsuccessful at launching the technology commercially. Later, Xerox joined with the Digital Equipment Corporation (DEC) to commercially standardize a suite of network products that would use the Ethernet technology. The Intel Corporation later joined the group, which then became known as *DEC-Intel-Xerox* (DIX). DIX developed and published the standard that was used for the original 10-Mbps version of Ethernet.

At its inception, the only medium capable of handling these speeds was a multidrop thick coaxial cable. This *thicknet* cable was very difficult to manage, and it is difficult to overstate how cumbersome it made network cabling. It had a very dense outer shell, and the network connections had to be inserted into the cable via a spike that literally punched through this outer shell to make a connection. (These cable connections were called, appropriately enough, *vampire taps* and were often unreliable.) There were very restrictive rules for how long the cables could be, how far apart stations had to be on the cable, and so on; and, in general, the original Ethernet standard was not user-friendly. It was, however, the start of something great.

Many of these initial requirements no longer exist, and more modern incarnations of Ethernet cabling and specifications bear little resemblance to the original garden hose thick cable and spiked taps. However, many of the core components of the technology have not changed from the early days. Ethernet was and still is a broadcast technology that relies on a shared media for communication. It uses a "passive," wait-and-listen protocol called *Carrier Sense Multiple Access with Collision Detection* (CSMA/CD)—much more on this later. It uses data link layer addressing known as *Media Access Control* (MAC) addresses, and it provides the ability to send a data frame to all devices on the network simultaneously (broadcasting). So while many things have changes from the early days at Xerox, some key concepts have remained the same.

In fact, even in the early days, Ethernet technology began to take hold of the industry. The Institute of Electrical and Electronics Engineers (IEEE) started project 802, which was to provide the industry with a framework for standardization of LAN technology. Because the technology was so diverse, the IEEE formed working groups in support of the different LAN technologies. The 802.3 working group was tasked with standardizing LANs based on the Ethernet technology.

Unfortunately, as previously mentioned in the discussion about ATM, a protocol designed by committee can be unnecessarily complex. In the case of Ethernet, two very similar but different standards were developed. Both of the standards are still in use, but the Ethernet II standard is by far the more widely accepted. The frame of each type is shown in Figure 3.10, with a description of each below.

Figure 3.10 The two Ethernet frame standards: 802.3 and Ethernet II.

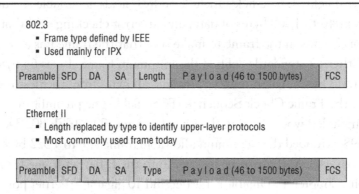

Figure 3.10 introduces a few new terms. IPX is Internet Packet eXchange, a protocol used exclusively by Novell. The SFD is the Start of Frame Delimiter, which is a 1-byte pattern, 10101011. The SFD is used to help Ethernet stations distinguish between noise on the link and the start of actual data. Finally, the DA is the destination address and the SA is the source address; these are Layer 2 address fields that we will discuss later in the chapter.

Ethernet supports two frame types, but they have been standardized so that all types can be transmitted on a common Ethernet network. The 16-bit field that follows the source address (SA) indicates whether the frame is Ethernet II or 802.3. If the value is 1,500 or less, the frame is treated as 802.3. If the value is greater than 1,500, the frame is treated as Ethernet II. The Ethernet II frame is normally used for transmission of IP datagrams.

Ethernet 802.3 was developed by the IEEE from the original Ethernet standard in 1983. IEEE Ethernet defines two layers—the lower MAC layer in 802.3 and an upper

LLC (Logical Link Control) layer in 802.2. These are sublayers of the OSI data link layer (Layer 2). The two layers were defined separately to provide additional link control features and so that common LLC frames could be used for different media types, such as Ethernet, Token-Ring, and Fiber Distributed Data Interface (FDDI). This allows bridging at Layer 2 between the different media types. There are three different 802.3 formats that were used for older protocols such as Novel Netware's IPX and Apple Computer's Appletalk protocols and OSI protocols. Today, these formats are rarely used. The Alcatel-Lucent 7750 SR uses the 802.3 format for the transmission of IS–IS routing updates; however, it uses Ethernet II for other traffic such as IP and MPLS.

A typical Ethernet frame is shown in Figure 3.11 and consists of a set of bits organized into several fields. These fields include address fields, a variable size data field that carries from 46 to 1,500 bytes of data, and an error-checking field that checks the integrity of the bits in the frame to make sure that the frame has arrived intact. The original Ethernet standards defined the minimum frame size as 64 bytes and the maximum as 1,518 bytes. These numbers include all bytes from the destination MAC address field to the Frame Check Sequence (FCS) field. The preamble and the SFD fields are not included when quoting the size of a frame. The IEEE 802.3ac standard released in 1998 extended the maximum allowable frame size to 1,522 bytes to allow for a virtual LAN (VLAN) tag to be inserted into the Ethernet frame format (VLANs are discussed in Chapter 4). Gigabit Ethernet and 10 gigabit Ethernet ports may support jumbo frames that can be 9,000 bytes.

Figure 3.11 A general Ethernet frame and its relevant fields.

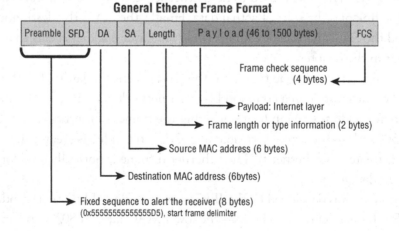

Ethernet Frames—Relevant Fields

- **Preamble**—This is a stream of bits used to allow the transmitter and receiver to synchronize their communication. The preamble is an alternating pattern of binary 56 ones and zeros. The preamble is immediately followed by the Start of Frame Delimiter.

- **Start of Frame Delimiter**—This is always 10101011 and is used to indicate the beginning of the frame information.

- **Destination Address (DA)**—This is the MAC address of the machine receiving data.

- **Source Address (SA)**—This is the MAC address of the machine transmitting data.

- **Length/Type**—The payload length or type field, also known as Ethertype. If the Ethernet frame is in the 802.3 format, this field is interpreted as length. If the Ethernet frame is in the Ethernet II or original DIX format, this field is interpreted as type, or Ethertype. The numeric value in this field determines whether the frame is an 802.3 frame or Ethernet II frame. If the value is less than 1,536 (hex value 0x600), it is an 802.3 frame. If the value is equal to or greater than 1,536, it is an Ethernet II frame.

- **Data/Padding (a.k.a. Payload)**—The data is inserted here. This is where the IP header and data are placed if you are running IP over Ethernet.

- **Frame Check Sequence (FCS)**—This is a part of the frame put in place to verify that the information each frame contains is not damaged during transmission. If a frame is corrupted during transmission, the FCS carried in the frame will not match with the recipient's calculated FCS. Any frames that do not match the calculated FCS will be discarded.

Figure 3.12 shows a real-world example of these standards with an Ethernet II frame captured by a packet capturing tool (commonly referred to as a *sniffer*). A description of the relevant fields follows.

The details of the captured frame information are shown below. Note that there are several different fields illustrated in the figure. The destination address, source address, and Ethertype information are for the L2 Ethernet header. The L3/IP information is for the IP header, and the TCP information is for the TCP header. Recall our discussion from Chapter 1 regarding how the different headers are placed one in front of the other for transmission, and you can see how the concept is actually put into practice. The bytes of each header follow along in a chain just as previously discussed.

Figure 3.12 An Ethernet frame captured using a packet sniffer. Relevant fields are highlighted.

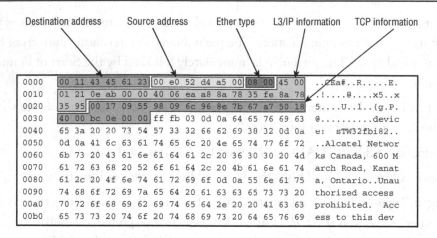

- **Ethernet II, Src**—FoundryN_d4:a5:00 (00:e0:52:d4:a5:00), Dst: Dell_45:61:23
  (00:11:43:45:61:23)

  - Destination: Dell_45:61:23 (00:11:43:45:61:23)

  - Source: FoundryN_d4:a5:00 (00:e0:52:d4:a5:00)

  - Type: IP (0x0800)

- **Internet Protocol, Src**—138.120.53.254 (138.120.53.254), Dst: 138.120.53.149
  (138.120.53.149)

  - Version: 4

  - Header length: 20 bytes

  - Differentiated Services Field: 0x00 (DSCP 0x00: Default; ECN: 0x00)

  - Total Length: 289

  - Identification: 0x0eab (3755)

  - Flags: 0x00

  - Fragment offset: 0

  - Time to live: 64

  - Protocol: TCP (0x06)

  - Header checksum: 0xeaa8 [correct]

- Source: 138.120.53.254 (138.120.53.254)

- Destination: 138.120.53.149 (138.120.53.149)

- **Transmission Control Protocol**—Src Port: 23 (23), Dst Port: 2389 (2389), Seq: 4, Ack: 1, Len: 249

  - Source port: 23 (23). This indicates the telnet protocol.

  - Destination port: 2389 (2389)

  - Sequence number: 4 (relative sequence number)

  - Next sequence number: 253 (relative sequence number)

  - Acknowledgement number: 1 (relative ack number)

  - Header length: 20 bytes

  - Flags: 0x0018 (PSH, ACK)

  - Window size: 16,384

  - Checksum: 0xbc0e [correct]

Many of these IP and TCP fields may be unfamiliar to you. All of the relevant IP and TCP fields will be covered in detail in later chapters, so it is not overly important that you try to understand them at this point. What is crucial is to see how the fields of the upper IP and TCP layers are *wrapped* or encapsulated in the data of the lower layers. Here, the IP and TCP headers are, from the perspective of the Ethernet protocol, simply bytes in its data payload. Similarly, from an IP packet's perspective, TCP fields are simply bytes in its data payload. This layering of headers mimics the layering of the OSI model that we have already discussed and helps you visualize what it means for a protocol stack to be *layered*.

Before we move on to Ethernet addressing, it is important to re-emphasize how Ethernet fits into the picture of the OSI model. Ethernet resides at the data link layer, and this layer can be subdivided further into two sublayers already mentioned, the Logical Link Control (LLC) and the Media Access Control (MAC). These sublayers are shown in Figure 3.13.

The LLC interfaces between the network interface layer and the higher L3 protocol and may provide additional functions such as flow control or retransmission. The MAC layer is responsible for determining the physical source and destination addresses for a particular frame and for the synchronization of data transmission and error checking. Additionally, at the physical layer, Ethernet transceivers use a link integrity test to continually monitor the data path for activity. The Ethernet II type of frame used for IP does not contain an LLC header and therefore does not provide any LLC functions. IP uses Ethernet II simply for the transmission of frames on a shared media. You can see in Figure 3.12 and the description that follows it that the upper-layer protocol is IP and the Ethernet frame header is using the *type* field, indicating the format is Ethernet II.

Figure 3.13 The LLC and MAC information are sub-layers of the data link layer of the OSI model.

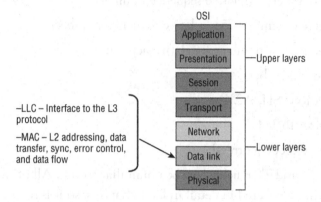

Ethernet Addressing and Operations

As previously mentioned, Ethernet has its own addressing scheme. The requirements for an Ethernet address are far less than that used by IP, and as such, the addressing scheme is much simpler. An Ethernet MAC address is a 48-bit (6 bytes) hexadecimal number consisting of only two (2) parts, the Organization Unit Identifier (OUI), which identifies the card's manufacturer, and a vendor assigned number. Each portion of the MAC address is 3 bytes. A MAC address is usually displayed in dashed hexadecimal notation as shown in Figure 3.14.

Figure 3.14 The format of an Ethernet MAC address.

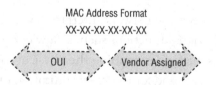

The OUI number is assigned by the IEEE to vendors such as Alcatel-Lucent. A few examples are Alcatel-Lucent Canada 00-80-21 and 00-DO-F6, Alcatel-Lucent USA 00-17-CC, and Alcatel-Lucent Italia 00-20-60. A list of various vendors' OUIs can be found at the IEEE website: `http://standards.ieee.org/regauth/oui/index.shtml`.

MAC addresses are used for delivering a frame from one device to another on an Ethernet network. The MAC address of each device on the network must be unique, and it is this uniqueness that allows an Ethernet frame to be delivered only to the station for which it is intended. In Figure 3.15, a station with the source address 00:e0:b1:88:0d:c0 is delivering a frame to station 00:14:22:c5:79:87.

Figure 3.15 Ethernet stations use unique MAC addresses to communicate with each other.

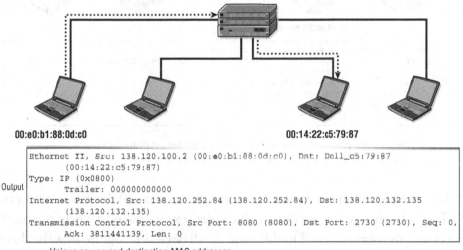

```
Ethernet II, Src: 138.120.100.2 (00:e0:b1:88:0d:c0), Dst: Dell_c5:79:87
        (00:14:22:c5:79:87)
Type: IP (0x0800)
        Trailer: 000000000000
Internet Protocol, Src: 138.120.252.84 (138.120.252.84), Dst: 138.120.132.135
        (138.120.132.135)
Transmission Control Protocol, Src Port: 8080 (8080), Dst Port: 2730 (2730), Seq: 0,
        Ack: 3811441139, Len: 0
```

– Unique source and destination MAC addresses
– Frame is meant for one particular destination or host.

The frame is sent to a hub that connects all devices on a four-node LAN. The hub, being a simple replicator, sends the frame out on all its ports except the port where the frame was received (the port attached to the source). Although all devices receive the frame, only the device whose MAC address matches the destination device processes the frame. This mode of addressing is called *unicast* because only a single device (*uni*) is the intended destination.

In contrast to unicast addressing, sometimes a device wants to send a message to all devices on the Ethernet segment. In such a case, there is a unique address that allows a station to send a *broadcast* or "all nodes" message that will be forwarded to and accepted by every device on the segment. In Figure 3.16, a device with a source address 00:13:ce:2b:6b:28 is sending a broadcast message to the special MAC address ff:ff:ff:ff:ff:ff, which means "all nodes."

Figure 3.16 The Ethernet destination MAC address ff:ff:ff:ff:ff:ff is the broadcast address which means "all hosts".

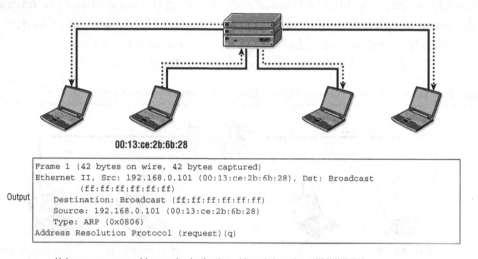

00:13:ce:2b:6b:28

```
Frame 1 (42 bytes on wire, 42 bytes captured)
Ethernet II, Src: 192.168.0.101 (00:13:ce:2b:6b:28), Dst: Broadcast
    (ff:ff:ff:ff:ff:ff)
  Destination: Broadcast (ff:ff:ff:ff:ff:ff)
  Source: 192.168.0.101 (00:13:ce:2b:6b:28)
  Type: ARP (0x0806)
Address Resolution Protocol (request)(q)
```

Output

– Unique source mac address only, destination address is broadcast (ff:ff:ff:ff:ff:ff).
– Frame is meant for all devices on the LAN in a broadcast domain.

In this example, the frame is sent to a hub that connects all devices on a four-node LAN. The hub sends the frame out on all its ports except the port where the frame was received (the port attached to the source). All devices recognize that the destination address (ff:ff:ff:ff:ff:ff) is a special address and will process the frame.

A broadcast message is actually a special case of the use of a *multicast* address, an address that is used by a group of nodes to receive messages intended just for that group. In this sense, the broadcast address is simply the special multicast group *all nodes*. There are special MAC address ranges that are reserved for multicast usage, and usage of these addresses typically requires additional configuration on a device via special software that makes use of the multicast functions. Figure 3.17 shows a device with source address 00:13:ce:2b:6b:28 sending to the multicast address 01:00:5e:01:01:01.

Figure 3.17 An Ethernet multicast MAC address is used to send a single Ethernet frame to multiple, but not all, hosts.

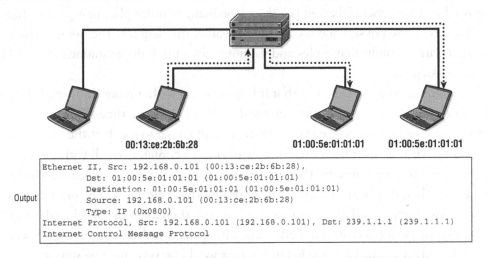

00:13:ce:2b:6b:28   01:00:5e:01:01:01   01:00:5e:01:01:01

```
Output
         Ethernet II, Src: 192.168.0.101 (00:13:ce:2b:6b:28),
             Dst: 01:00:5e:01:01:01 (01:00:5e:01:01:01)
             Destination: 01:00:5e:01:01:01 (01:00:5e:01:01:01)
             Source: 192.168.0.101 (00:13:ce:2b:6b:28)
             Type: IP (0x0800)
         Internet Protocol, Src: 192.168.0.101 (192.168.0.101), Dst: 239.1.1.1 (239.1.1.1)
         Internet Control Message Protocol
```

- Unique source mac address only, destination address is multicast group (01-00-5e-01-01-01).
- Frame is meant for only devices who are members of that group.

The frame is sent to a hub that connects all devices on a four-node LAN. The hub sends the frame out on all its ports except the port where the frame was received (the port attached to the source). All devices that are members of the particular group (239.1.1.1) IP addressing will process that message.

 There are special types of intelligent Ethernet switching devices that can understand when certain ports are configured for multicast and forward those messages to multicast-enabled devices only.

Ethernet Transmission—CSMA/CD

Since the origin of Ethernet, one of its defining characteristics has been the method by which an Ethernet host gains access to the shared medium. In simple terms, how does an Ethernet host actually start transmitting its information on the physical wire? The answer to this may seem obvious: Start transmitting when you are ready. And, in point of fact, this is exactly the way other data link layer technologies such as PPP and ATM work. When the host has data to send, the data link layer simply wraps a header around the upper-layer IP packet and starts sending it. However, it is important to remember the physical differences between the data link technologies previously discussed and Ethernet. Ethernet is a *shared* medium, meaning that many hosts share access to the same physical media. Recall the earlier discussion of the original thick Ethernet with its multidrop cables and vampire taps with multiple stations attached to the same physical wire.

What this means in practice is that it is quite possible that more than one host can attempt to send information on the physical media at the same time. This is equivalent to two—or more—people on a conference call trying to speak at the same time. For anyone who has ever been on a heavily populated conference call with lots of people trying to communicate, the problem is now obvious: Various speakers contend with each other, drowning out and garbling each other's messages. The original Ethernet designers were well aware of this problem, and therefore they developed a set of procedures or protocol that would allow each Ethernet attached station to gain access to the shared media when it needed it, but that would prevent any one station from monopolizing the conversation.

By limiting the size of the Ethernet packets, this ensured that a sending station could only send a single packet at a time once it had access to the physical media. Gaining access to the media in the first place was accomplished through a protocol called *Carrier Sense Multiple Access with Collision Detection* (CSMA/CD). Despite the complex acronym, CSMA/CD is very straightforward once you understand the purpose it is trying to accomplish: Make sure that only one host can access the shared media at a time, and provide for a corrective mechanism in the event that two or more hosts try to talk simultaneously.

Perhaps the easiest introduction to CSMA/CD comes by stepping through each term individually and summarizing how the terms translate into practice:

- **Carrier Sense (CS)**—Each Ethernet LAN-attached host continuously listens for traffic on the medium to determine when gaps between frame transmissions occur. In other words, "sense" (listen to) the "carrier" (the physical media).

- **Multiple Access (MA)**—LAN-attached hosts can begin transmitting any time that they detect that the network is quiet, meaning that no traffic is traveling across the wire. When the host senses that the carrier has no other host accessing the physical media, then it can begin transmitting.

- **Collision Detect (CD)**—If two or more LAN-attached hosts in the same CSMA/CD network or collision domain begin transmitting at approximately the same time, the bit streams from the transmitting hosts will interfere (collide) with each other, and both transmissions will be unreadable. In our conference call analogy, two speakers have stepped on each other's conversation. If that happens, each transmitting host must be capable of detecting that a collision has occurred before it has finished sending its respective frame. Each host must stop transmitting as soon as it has detected the collision and then must wait a random length of time as determined by a back-off algorithm before attempting to retransmit the frame. In this event, each transmitting host will transmit a 32-bit jam signal alerting all LAN-attached hosts of a collision before running the back-off algorithm. The purpose of the jam signal is to ensure that all hosts have received notice of the collision.

This process is depicted in Figure 3.18. All hosts constantly listen to the physical media ("carrier sense multiple access"). Host A determines that the line is not in use and begins transmitting. Hosts B, C, and D listen to Host A and do not transmit so that they can receive Host A's message.

Figure 3.18 All hosts listen to the Ethernet media to detect a transmission. Once Host A starts transmitting, then other stations will detect it and will not attempt to transmit.

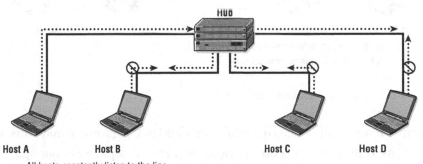

Host A Host B Host C Host D

- All hosts constantly listen to the line.
- Host A transmits.
- Host B, C, and D listen to Host A and do not transmit.
- All hosts receive Host A's message.

To return to our conference call analogy, this would translate into the following protocol: "Listen until no one else is speaking; start speaking when you have something to say; if anyone else starts speaking when you do, then roll a dice and wait that number of seconds to start speaking again."

The CSMA/CD protocol works reasonably well to reduce the chance of collisions and handle those that occur, but it does not and cannot prevent them. In Figure 3.19, both Hosts A and B could decide to transmit at once because no other hosts are transmitting a message on the line (idle line).

When Host A and Host B transmit frames at the same time, they will both detect collision or corruption of the data. Both Host A and Host B will generate a jam signal, which will be received by other hosts so that they discard the data that was just corrupted by a collision. A random back-off timer is then started on the transmitting hosts (this is an attempt to ensure that the hosts don't try to retransmit at the same time). Afterward, either Host A or Host B will initiate a transmission after they detect no other transmission on the line.

Figure 3.19 Host A and Host B may start to transmit simultaneously, resulting in a collision.

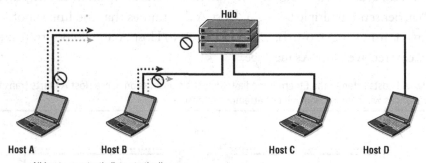

- All hosts constantly listen to the line.
- Host A and Host B transmit simultaneously.
- Messages collide.
- Both hosts back-off for a random time interval.

The astute reader will notice that while the CSMA/CD protocol may work well when you have only a few hosts on a network segment as depicted in our figures, it may not work so well when you have hundreds of hosts all busily attempting to transmit away. This is, in fact, correct, and large numbers of collisions were the bane of Ethernet network design for many years. Ethernet protocol designers searched for a way to reduce or eliminate collisions for Ethernet, and in the end they decided on an old solution that we have run into with ATM: Develop a switch that provides intelligence beyond that available with an Ethernet hub or long cable. One of the central capabilities that Ethernet switches provide is the ability for Ethernet hosts to communicate in *Full-Duplex* mode. Full-duplex operation is an optional MAC layer capability that allows simultaneous two-way transmission over point-to-point links. Full-duplex transmission involves no media contention, no collisions, and no need to schedule retransmissions. In effect, the shared Ethernet medium becomes a point-to-point link. There are exactly two hosts connected on a full-duplex point-to-point link, as shown in Figure 3.20.

Figure 3.20 Ethernet switches provide a dedicated, full-duplex link to each station and eliminate collisions.

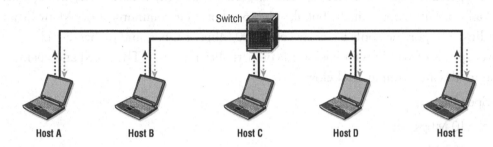

The link bandwidth is effectively doubled because each link can now support full-rate, simultaneous, two-way transmission.

Note that up to this point, the Ethernet operations we have been discussing have been implicitly *half-duplex*, because a host can either send or listen, but cannot do both at the same time. The original Ethernet standards provided for only half-duplex operations owing to the limitations of the physical hardware. With the development of Ethernet switches, conversations were no longer restricted to half-duplex "I talk then you talk" conversations. By connecting each Ethernet station directly to a centralized switch and using cabling that supports Full-Duplex mode, Ethernet designers eliminated collisions and also greatly increased the effective transmission rate of the protocol.

For example, 10Base-T working on half-duplex is efficient 30 percent to 40 percent of the time because of collisions, and as such, the effective throughput is only 3 to 4 Mb. This was a disadvantage of Ethernet over other competing standards at the time such as Token-Ring. In contrast, full-duplex ensures that data can be transmitted bi-directionally, so the effective rate of a 10-Mb full-duplex transmission is 20 Mb (i.e., 10 Mb each way). Hence, full-duplex transmissions are far more efficient than half-duplex. Switches and routers usually support full-duplex transmissions.

Even though there are clear advantages to Full-Duplex mode, most Ethernet devices still support Half-Duplex mode for backward-compatibility reasons. (You never know when someone might have 15-year-old devices that don't support Full-Duplex mode.) Therefore, when devices such as switches and hubs are interconnected, care must be taken to ensure that the proper transmission parameters are set on the ports. For switch-to-hub connections, the switch port must be set to half-duplex because the hub only supports half-duplex. For switch-to-switch, switch-to-host, or switch-to-router connections, full-duplex can and should be used.

It is possible to allow devices to "auto-negotiate" not only whether they will operate in Half- or Full-Duplex mode, but also the speed of their communication. Many Ethernet hosts support not only faster speeds of 100 Mbps, 1 Gbps, and higher, but also lower speeds of 10 Mbps for backward compatibility purposes. The speed and operation modes are summarized below:

- Speed
  - 10 Mbps
  - 100 Mbps
  - 1,000 Mbps
  - 10,000 Mbps
- Operation mode
  - Half-Duplex (CSMA/CD)?
  - Full-Duplex

If auto-negotiation is enabled, Ethernet nodes directly connected negotiate their speed as well as duplex mode prior to establishing a link. In theory, you could allow all Ethernet devices to auto-negotiate their speed and duplex mode. In practice, however, it is much better to manually set the speeds and modes of your devices to ensure that all of your Ethernet devices are operating at the speeds and modes you expect. Many network problems have been traced to a simple mismatch between speed or duplex mode on neighboring devices, so it is best practice to make certain that this situation does not arise in your network.

Ethernet Physical Standards

The original Ethernet standards are no longer used, and modern Ethernet takes advantage of enhanced data rates and distances through the use of twisted-pair and fiber optical cabling. There are four standards currently defined:

- **10 Mbps**—10Base-T Ethernet: twisted-pair or optical

- **100 Mbps**—100Base-T or Fast Ethernet: twisted-pair or optical
- **1,000 Mbps**—1000Base-T or Gigabit Ethernet: twisted-pair or optical
- **10,000 Mbps**—10 Gigabit Ethernet: twisted-pair or optical

10BaseT was the original IEEE 802.3i and is today's standard 802.3x. The transmission rate is 10 Mbps half-duplex or with 802.3x 10 Mbps full-duplex.

100BaseT is the IEEE 802.3u standard. It supports either Half-Duplex or Full-Duplex modes at 100-Mbps rates. There are several cabling options:

- **100Base-TX**—Two pairs of twisted-pair cable
- **100Base-T4**—Four pairs of twisted-pair cable
- **100Base-FX**—Optical cable

1000BaseT is also known as Gigabit Ethernet or simply GigE. It is IEEE standard 802.3ab and supports Full-Duplex mode only at 1,000 Mbps. If twisted-pair Cat 5e cabling is used, distances of up to 100 m are supported.

10,000BaseT is also known as TenGigabit Ethernet or TenGigE. It is IEEE standard 802.3ae and supports Full-Duplex mode only at 10 Gbps. The physical media is optical only, no twisted-pair.

These standards are summarized in Figure 3.21.

Figure 3.21 Physical specifications for all Ethernet standards.

Ethernet	Designation	Type	Wavelength	Distance	Fiber Type
10/100Base	TX	Copper	—	100 m	—
100Base	FX	Optical SFP	1310 nm	2 km	Multimode
	FX-SM	Optical SFP	1310 nm	25 km	Single-mode
Gigabit Ethernet	TX	Copper	—	100 m	—
	SX	Optical SFP	850 nm	550 m	Multimode
	LX	Optical SFP	1310 nm	10 km	Single-mode
	ZX	Optical SFP	1550 nm	70 km	Single-mode
	CWDM	Optical SFP	1470 nm to 1610 nm	70 km	Single-mode
10 gigabit Ethernet	LW/LR	Optical SFP	1310 nm	10 km	Single-mode
	EW/ER	Optical SFP	1550 nm	40 km	Single-mode
	SR	Optical SFP	850 nm	300 m	Multimode
	LR	Optical SFP	850 nm	10 km	Single-mode
	ZR	Optical SFP	1550 nm	80 km	Single-mode
	T	Copper	—	30-100 m	—
	CX4			15 m	

Now you should complete the lab exercises to assist you in reinforcing this chapter's features. These lab exercises are carefully designed to give you hands-on experience configuring many of the technology standards that have been discussed and should greatly aid you in your exam preparation.

Practice Lab: Configuring IOMs, MDAs, and Ports

The following lab is designed to reinforce your knowledge of the content in this chapter. Please review the instructions carefully and perform the steps in the order in which they are presented. The practice labs require that you have access to three or more Alcatel-Lucent 7750 SRs or Alcatel-Lucent 7450 ESSs in a non-production environment.

 These labs are designed to be used in a controlled lab environment. Please **DO NOT** attempt to perform these labs in a production environment.

Alcatel-Lucent 7750/7450 products are modular for flexibility, upgradability, and maintainability. A router is actually built from *many* modular components. The list of these components can be made to sound like a nursery rhyme: An SFP fits into an MDA, an MDA fits into an IOM, and an IOM fits into a chassis. None of the lab exercises in this book requires any configuration of the chassis, so exercises for this chapter deal with configuring everything from the IOM upward to the L2 Ethernet ports.

Except for the smallest members of the family, all routers start with the chassis. It contains power supply connections, mounts for cooling fans, the backplane with its associated circuitry, and, most importantly, space for adding large circuit boards (also known as *cards*). The largest router in the family accepts up to 12 cards. Except for the chassis, all components are hot-swappable.

As covered in Chapter 2, there are two main types of the large cards: Switch Fabric/Control Plane Modules (SF/CPMs) and I/O Modules (IOMs). All routers must have at least one and at most two SF/CPMs. Configuring SF/CPMs is a topic for a more advanced book, so these labs assume that the SF/CPM default mode is correct for all exercises. The exercises are structured so that each one deals with configuring a single component in the hierarchy: IOM cards, MDA cards, and ports.

The exercises in this lab are designed to integrate what you learned in Chapter 2 with the content of Chapter 3. The section "Basic Overview of Ethernet" covered some of the maximum frame sizes [maximum transmission units (MTUs) of normal and jumbo frames] and associated speeds (10 Mbps, 100 Mbps, 1 Gbps); see if you can spot some of these items in the final exercises where the Ethernet ports are configured.

Lab Section 3.1: A Full Deck of Cards

A fully loaded Alcatel-Lucent 7750 SRs or Alcatel-Lucent 7450 ESS can have up to 12 cards installed. Configuring these cards is a critical first step towards a fully operational device, so this is where we start for the first exercise.

Objective In this exercise, you will become familiar with the different cards that fit into the chassis and be able to recognize and identify them from the CLI. This exercise also covers the steps required to configure an IOM card.

Validation You will know you have succeeded if you can display the state of IOMs and if the IOMs show an operational state of Up.

1. Display and examine the current card configuration with the show card command.

   A:Router1# **show card**

```
===================================================================
Card Summary
===================================================================
Slot   Provisioned      Equipped         Admin     Operational
       Card-type        Card-type        State     State
-------------------------------------------------------------------
1                       iom2-20g         up        unprovisioned
A      sfm-400g         sfm-400g         up        up/active
B      sfm-400g                          up        down/standby
===================================================================
A:Router1#
```

   1a. In total, how many cards are physically present in the chassis? How many SF/CPMs? How many IOMs?

   1b. Referring to Chapter 2, what kind of labeling is used for the "two (2) card slots [...] dedicated for redundant SF/CPMs"?

1c. Referring to Chapter 2, how many different kinds of SF/CPM cards exist?

1d. Referring to Chapter 2, what kind of labeling is used for an IOM card(s)?

1e. (*Optional*) Is there any relationship between the first character of the prompt and any of the cards?

2. Configure the IOM card to the same type as Equipped. (Note: The specific card type may be different on your router.) Be ready to quickly type the show card command in order to catch the IOM in the process doing its own (local) bootup. Wait a few moments, and repeat the show card command to see the IOM in its final state.

```
A:Router1# configure card 1 card-type iom2-20g
*A:Router1# show card


===============================================================
Card Summary
===============================================================
Slot  Provisioned    Equipped       Admin    Operational
      Card-type      Card-type      State    State
---------------------------------------------------------------
1     iom2-20g       iom2-20g       up       booting
A     sfm-400g       sfm-400g       up       up/active
B     sfm-400g                      up       down/standby
===============================================================

*A:Router1# show card


===============================================================
Card Summary
===============================================================
Slot  Provisioned    Equipped       Admin    Operational
      Card-type      Card-type      State    State
---------------------------------------------------------------
1     iom2-20g       iom2-20g       up       up
A     sfm-400g       sfm-400g       up       up/active
B     sfm-400g                      up       down/standby
===============================================================

*A:Router1#
```

2a. Did the configuration command change the number of *physical* cards or the number of *available* cards?

2b. Why did the asterisk (*) reappear in the command prompt? What will make it disappear again?

3. Have a look at the main log to see if anything has been recorded as a result of these last few configuration changes. Remember: The log files are an *excellent* source of debugging and troubleshooting information!

```
*A:Router1# show log log-id 99


===================================================================
Event Log 99
===================================================================
Description : Default System Log
Memory Log contents  [size=500   next event=237  (not wrapped)]

236 2000/01/01 09:13:23.24 UTC MINOR: CHASSIS #2002 Base Mda 1/1
"Class MDA Module : inserted"

235 2000/01/01  09:13:23.24 UTC WARNING: SYSTEM #2009 Base CHASSIS
"Status of Card 1 changed administrative state: inService,
 operational state: inService"

234 2000/01/01  09:13:10.56 UTC WARNING: SYSTEM #2006 Base CHASSIS
"tmnxCardTable: Slot 1 configuration modified"

233 2000/01/01 09:13:10.55 UTC WARNING: SYSTEM #2007 Base PORT
"Pool on MDA 1/2 Modified managed object created"
[... Additional output omitted ...]
*A:Router1#
```

4. If it's ever necessary to remove an IOM, a two-step process ensures a clean shutdown.

```
*A:Router1# configure card 1 shutdown
*A:Router1# configure no card 1
*A:Router1# show card
```

```
===============================================================
Card Summary
===============================================================
Slot    Provisioned      Equipped        Admin    Operational
        Card-type        Card-type       State    State
---------------------------------------------------------------
1                        iom2-20g        up       unprovisioned
A       sfm-400g         sfm-400g        up       up/active
B       sfm-400g                         up       down/standby
===============================================================
```

*A:Router1#

Compare the output of the "show card" command with the output from the same command in Step 1. The IOM has successfully been removed from the configuration.

5. Reconfigure the IOM so that it is available for subsequent lab exercises. (Refer to Step 2.)

6. Have a look at the main log to see if anything has been recorded as a result of these last few configuration changes. Remember: The log files are an *excellent* source of debugging and troubleshooting information!

    *A:Router1# **show log log-id 99**

7. If your router has additional IOM cards and you want or need to use them for the exercises, you will need to repeat the configuration step for all additional IOM cards.

8. Repeat the preceding steps for each of the other routers.

Lab Section 3.2: An MDA for Every Need

There are many MDAs available for the Alcatel-Lucent 7750/7450 products: A recent version of the OS reports support for 42 different MDAs. The purpose of an MDA is to incorporate *all* circuitry that is specific to a particular type of Layer 2 connection, for example, Ethernet (both copper and fiber), Sonet/SDH (includes ATM), and OCx. Within these three broad categories, there are many different variations of MDAs to provide support for different speeds and numbers of connections. Having MDAs as a separate, modular component allows a customer to purchase and configure the right combination of connections that might be required for any particular network node.

Fortunately, the configuration process is very simple despite the large number of available MDAs.

Objective In this exercise, you will become familiar with recognizing, identifying, and configuring MDAs from the CLI.

Validation You will know you have succeeded if you can display the state of MDAs and if the MDAs show an operational state of Up.

1. Display and examine the current MDA configuration using the show mda command. Note that the exact output will depend entirely on your physical hardware.

   ```
   *A:Router1# show mda

   ===================================================================
   MDA Summary
   ===================================================================
   Slot  Mda  Provisioned       Equipped          Admin  Operational
                Mda-type          Mda-type          State  State
   -------------------------------------------------------------------
   1     1                       m10-1gb-sfp-b      up     unprovisioned
   ===================================================================
   ```

   1a. *Important!* Can you see any MDAs for IOMs that are *not* configured? Repeat the steps from the previous exercise to remove the IOM configuration and repeat the command to see the available MDAs.

   1b. In total, how many MDAs are physically plugged into an IOM(s)?

   1c. Which chassis slot/IOM is the m10-1gb-sfp-b MDA plugged into? Within that IOM, is the MDA plugged into the first or second MDA slot?

2. Generally, an MDA will always be configured to be the same as shown in the Equipped Mda-type column. Configure the available MDA(s). Note that the exact command will depend entirely on your physical hardware; follow the rule of configuring the type the same as shown in the previous command.

   ```
   *A:Router1# configure card 1 mda 1 mda-type m10-1gb-sfp-b
   *A:Router1#
   ```

   2a. What is the correspondence between the physical *location* of the MDA and the values specified in the above command?

   2b. Whether or not there was an asterisk in the prompt *before* issuing the configure command, will there be one *after* the command?

3. Display and examine all MDAs that are now visible.

```
*A:Router1# show mda

===============================================================
MDA Summary
===============================================================
Slot  Mda  Provisioned    Equipped       Admin   Operational
           Mda-type       Mda-type       State   State
---------------------------------------------------------------
1     1    m10-1gb-sfp-b  m10-1gb-sfp-b  up      up
===============================================================
*A:Router1#
```

3a. Did the configuration command change the number of *physical* MDAs or the number of *available* MDAs?

4. Have a look at the main log to see what has been recorded as a result of this configuration change. Here's one last reminder: The log files are an *excellent* source of debugging and troubleshooting information!

```
*A:Router1# show log log-id 99
```

5. As with IOMs, if it's ever necessary to remove an MDA, a two-step process ensures a clean shutdown.

```
*A:Router1# configure card 1 mda 1 shutdown
*A:Router1# configure card 1 no mda 1
*A:Router1# show mda

===============================================================
MDA Summary
===============================================================
Slot  Mda  Provisioned    Equipped       Admin   Operational
           Mda-type       Mda-type       State   State
---------------------------------------------------------------
1     1                   m10-1gb-sfp-b  up      unprovisioned
===============================================================
*A:Router1#
```

5a. Whether or not there was an asterisk in the prompt before issuing the configure command, will there be one *after* the command?

6. Reconfigure the MDA so that it is available for subsequent lab exercises.

7. If your router has additional MDAs and you want or need to use them for the exercises, you will need to repeat the configuration step for all additional MDAs. Don't forget to *save your configuration*.

8. Repeat the preceding steps for each of the other routers.

Lab Section 3.3: All Ports Up...To L2 Ethernet

The configuration process for the base hardware has a very definite hierarchy. First, the SF/CPM must be up-and-running in order to connect via the serial port or Ethernet management port. Next, the IOM(s) must be configured, followed by the MDA(s). An MDA will be neither visible nor configurable until its supporting IOM is fully configured; it is not possible to skip any preceding step. The same is true for individual ports: Everything in the hardware chain must be configured before ports become visible and configurable. Once they are configured, the raw hardware configuration is complete.

Objective In this exercise, you will become familiar with recognizing, identifying, and configuring ports from the CLI.

Validation You will know you have succeeded if you can display the state of ports and if the (required) ports show an operational state of Up.

1. Display and examine the current port configuration (show port command). Note that the exact output will depend entirely on your physical hardware. There's a lot of output; we'll just focus on a few of the most important items.

```
*A:Router1# show port

===============================================================
Ports on Slot 1
===============================================================
Port   Admin Link Port    Cfg  Oper LAG/ Port Port Port  SFP/XFP/
Id     State      State   MTU  MTU  Bndl Mode Encp Type  MDIMDX
---------------------------------------------------------------
1/1/1  Down  No   Down    9212 9212   -  netw null xcme  GIGE-T
1/1/2  Down  No   Down    9212 9212   -  netw null xcme  GIGE-T
1/1/3  Down  No   Down    9212 9212   -  netw null xcme  GIGE-T
1/1/4  Down  No   Down    9212 9212   -  netw null xcme  GIGE-T
1/1/5  Down  No   Down    9212 9212   -  netw null xcme
[... Additional output omitted ...]
1/1/10 Down  No   Down    9212 9212   -  netw null xcme
```

```
================================================================
Ports on Slot A
================================================================
Port  Admin Link Port    Cfg  Oper LAG/ Port Port Port   SFP/XFP/
Id    State      State   MTU  MTU  Bndl Mode Encp Type   MDIMDX
----------------------------------------------------------------
A/1   Up    Yes  Up      1514 1514   - netw null faste   MDI


================================================================
Ports on Slot B
================================================================
Port  Admin Link Port    Cfg  Oper LAG/ Port Port Port   SFP/XFP/
Id    State      State   MTU  MTU  Bndl Mode Encp Type   MDIMDX
----------------------------------------------------------------
B/1   Up    No   Ghost   1514 1514   - netw null faste
================================================================
*A:Router1#
```

1a. The output above is split into three main sections. The first section is all the output for which (single) piece of hardware?

1b. There are a total of 12 ports shown. How does the naming/labeling of the ports correspond with the SF/CPM, IOM, and MDA card numbering/labeling?

1c. The MDA is configured as m**10-1gb-sfp**-b, meaning 10 GigE ports using optical SFP connectors. How many ports have the SFP installed?

1d. The last port is listed with a port state of Ghost. Which card is it on? Does the card physically exist? What is the meaning of Ghost?

1e. With default settings, are ports in an Up or Down state? Is this consistent with other hardware (i.e., IOMs and MDAs)?

1f. What is the default MTU for a 10/100 FastE port? For a GigE port?

2. Configure a single port to a functional state.

```
*A:Router1# configure port 1/1/1 no shutdown
*A:Router1# show port
```

```
================================================================
Ports on Slot 1
================================================================
Port   Admin Link Port    Cfg  Oper LAG/ Port Port Port  SFP/XFP/
Id     State      State   MTU  MTU  Bndl Mode Encp Type  MDIMDX
----------------------------------------------------------------
1/1/1  Up    Yes  Up      9212 9212  -   netw null xcme  MDI GIGE-T
1/1/2  Down  No   Down    9212 9212  -   netw null xcme  GIGE-T
[... Additional output omitted ...]
*A:Router1#
```

2a. With the port operationally Up, what new information is available?

3. Multiple ports can be configured to a functional state, if done with a single command on one line.

```
*A:Router1# configure port 1/1/[2..10] no shutdown
*A:Router1# show port
[... Additional output omitted ...]
*A:Router1#
```

4. Single or multiple ports may be turned down with a single command.

```
*A:Router1# configure port 1/1/1 shutdown
*A:Router1# show port
[... Additional output omitted ...]
*A:Router1# configure port 1/1/[2..10] shutdown
*A:Router1# show port
[... Additional output omitted ...]
*A:Router1#
```

5. Don't forget to check the log files to see the corresponding entries for these operations.

6. Configure all ports Up that you need or want to use for the exercises. Remember to *save your configuration*.

7. Repeat the preceding steps for each of the other routers.

8. (*Optional*) Is it possible to shut down/remove an MDA while ports are still active? Do the ports retain their previous state when the MDA is reconfigured? Try it! (Don't worry, there's no risk of damaging the hardware.)

9. (*Optional*) If you have access to the physical hardware, try inserting and removing cables from a port and using a show port at each step to see the difference in the output.

Chapter Review

Now that you have completed this chapter, you should have a good understanding of the following topics. If you are not familiar with these topics, please go back and review the appropriate sections.

- The different types of Layer 2 protocols
- The basic functions of PPP, ATM, and TDM
- The different Ethernet frame types and how to differentiate them
- Ethernet addressing and operations, particularly CSMA/CD
- Understanding why full-duplex operations are important to Ethernet
- The different Ethernet physical cabling and speeds that are available

Post-Assessment

The following questions will test your knowledge and prepare you for the Alcatel-Lucent NRS I Certification Exam. Please review each question carefully and choose the most correct answer. You can compare your response with the answers listed in Appendix A. You can also download all of the CD content at http://booksupport.wiley.com to take all the assessment tests and review the answers. Good luck!

1. Which of the following is *not* a data link layer (OSI Layer 2) protocol?
   A. Ethernet
   B. ATM
   C. Cell-Relay
   D. PPP

2. Which of the following is *not* a function of PPP?
   A. Provide support for multiple upper-layer protocols.
   B. Support the connection of multiple devices on a single link.
   C. Support authentication.
   D. Support data integrity via a CRC on frame contents.

3. Which of the following ATM AAL types is associated with an incorrect description?
   A. AAL3/4—Connection-oriented service
   B. AAL5—Connectionless service
   C. AAL2—Variable bit rate traffic
   D. AAL1—High bit rate traffic

4. Which of the following technologies ensures that a unicast packet is visible only to the device with the specific destination address?
   A. Ethernet
   B. Switched Ethernet
   C. Satellite
   D. Wireless LAN

5. The advantage of using multicast packets instead of broadcast packets is _____.

A. Broadcasts are received by every host.

B. Multicast is newer technology.

C. Broadcasts are processed by every host.

D. Multicast provides multiple addresses for flexibility.

6. A PPP frame has several fields that are not used, like addressing. Why do these fields exist in the frame?

A. They are reserved for future use.

B. They are legacy fields from older versions of PPP headers.

C. PPP is based on the HDLC frame format.

D. PPP can be adapted for use on multi-point networks and might need the fields.

7. ATM uses 53-byte cells, which is quite a bit smaller than the maximum Ethernet frame. What is the purpose of having such a small cell size?

A. To support latency-sensitive applications like voice traffic

B. To provide less overhead on ATM switches

C. To support the use of multiple classes of service

D. To provide the ability to do switching in hardware

8. What is the purpose of the ATM Adaptation Layer?

A. It determines the amount of data in the cell.

B. It maps data from upper-layer service classes to ATM cells.

C. It adapts Ethernet frames to ATM cells.

D. It wraps a header around the ATM cell.

9. What are the two main types of Ethernet frames?

A. Thinnet and Thicknet

B. 10baseT and 100baseT

C. DIX Ethernet and Ethernet II

D. 802.3 and Ethernet II

10. Which of the following values for the Ethertype/length fields indicates an 802.3 frame (numbers are in decimal)?

    A. 64

    B. 1540

    C. 2048

    D. 9000

11. The original Thicknet standard had a maximum cable length as well as a minimum distance for stations to tap into the cable. Based on the description of CSMA/CD, what is the most likely reason for these distance requirements?

    A. A signal might be too weak to travel farther than the maximum distance.

    B. Every station on the wire had to be able to "detect" a collision in order to function properly.

    C. Too many taps in the cable would weaken the wire.

    D. Thicknet cable came in fixed lengths.

12. An Ethernet MAC address consists of _____.

    A. A 4-byte number in four parts

    B. A 4-byte number in two parts

    C. A 6-byte number in two parts

    D. A 6-byte number in four parts

13. When an Ethernet station wants to transmit information, the process it follows is _____.

    A. Just start transmitting.

    B. Listen for other stations transmitting; if none, then begin transmitting.

    C. Transmit whenever it receives the token.

    D. Issue a transmit request, and transmit when given authorization to do so.

14. What happens when two or more Ethernet stations attempt to transmit at the same time?

   A. This is impossible on half-duplex.

   B. The signal results in a collision, the stations stop, and the stations all wait the same amount of time to retransmit.

   C. The signal results in a collision, and the stations retransmit based on a configured priority.

   D. The signal results in a collision, and the stations stop and retransmit after waiting a random amount of time.

15. Which of the following Ethernet standards is not matched correctly?

   A. 10 Mb Ethernet—Fiber or copper cable

   B. 100 Mb Ethernet—Fiber or copper cable

   C. 1 Gig Ethernet—Fiber cable only

   D. All of the above are correct.

4

Switched Networks, Spanning Tree, and VLANs

- Ethernet devices and switching
- Ethernet link redundancy
- Ethernet path redundancy
- Virtual LANs

This chapter builds on the discussion of Ethernet technology in the previous chapter by examining how Ethernet is deployed in the network. We begin by focusing on Ethernet switch technology and how switches provide Ethernet services to devices across the network. We also examine how Ethernet networks can be built with redundancy, paying particular attention to the spanning tree protocol. Virtual LAN technology is also covered, and we show how this feature can be used to create multiple logical LANs over the same physical infrastructure. We also examine how a provider can use VLAN stacking to allow multiple customers to have overlapping VLANs and yet use the provider network as a common backbone.

Pre-Assessment

The following assessment questions will help you understand what areas of the chapter you should review in more detail to prepare for the exam. You can also download all of the CD materials for this book at `http://booksupport.wiley.com` to take all the assessment tests and review the answers.

1. When a frame with an unknown destination MAC address enters a switch, the switch will forward it out which ports?

    A. None

    B. All

    C. All unicast ports

    D. All except the port that received the frame

2. The primary difference in the way Ethernet hubs and Ethernet switches handle traffic is _____.

    A. Hubs forward broadcast traffic out every port, switches do not.

    B. Switches eliminate the need for thicknet cabling.

    C. Switches support multiple physical connections to hosts.

    D. Switches forward unicast traffic only to a specific destination port.

3. Which of the following is not true about Link Aggregation Groups?

    A. They protect against single or multiple link failures.

    B. They can contain up to eight physical links.

C. They can protect against a switch failure by calculating multiple paths to the root.

D. They can be configured to enter a down state if a certain number of links in the bundle fail.

4. Which of the following is not true of the STP protocol?

A. It calculates a root bridge.

B. It uses a cost value on each port to determine the path to the root bridge.

C. It ensures a loop-free topology.

D. It provides load-sharing capability.

5. The advantage of using VLANs is _____.

A. They can increase the security of your network.

B. They can interconnect multiple broadcast domains.

C. They can limit the amount of broadcast traffic between groups of devices.

D. Answers A and C, but not B.

You will find the answers to each of these questions in Appendix A.

4.1 Ethernet Devices: Hubs and Switches

In the previous chapter, we briefly mentioned devices that provide the physical Ethernet connections and forwarding of Ethernet frames. In this chapter, we describe these devices in much more detail and pay particularly close attention to how these devices function to transport Ethernet frames across the network.

The simplest Ethernet device is simply used to repeat an Ethernet signal along a wire and is called, appropriately enough, a *repeater*. Repeaters were needed in the days of thicknet cables because there were strict limits on the length of a single thicknet cable run. In modern networks these devices are rarely used or needed and are mentioned here only for historical purposes.

Ethernet Hubs

The next device to consider is the simplest multi-connection equipment: an Ethernet *hub*. Physically, a *hub* is a usually a small device that connects from four to eight Ethernet devices so that they can communicate with each other. The hub does this by providing a non-intelligent circuit board called a *backplane* that transmits electrical signals from any port to any other port. This transmission is done indiscriminately.

Any Ethernet frame that arrives on any port is automatically forwarded to every other port. In this way, a hub precisely mirrors the electrical function of the original Ethernet thicknet cable. Any device on a hub can talk to any other device on a hub and, indeed, there is no way to prevent this from happening. A hub provides no intelligent filtering or forwarding capabilities at all, and can be thought of as simply a "wire in a box." It should be noted that because a hub mimics the functions of an Ethernet wire, it is half-duplex only, so collisions can and often do occur. Figure 4.1 summarizes these points.

Ethernet Switches

While hubs provide some advantages to the days of long thicknet cable runs and vampire taps, they can obviously be improved on. For example, it would be better to have a hub forward an Ethernet frame only to that port or ports that actually need it. Also, it would be better if the hub provided full-duplex capabilities and avoided collisions. These features are, in fact, provided by an Ethernet *switch*. An *Ethernet switch* processes the Ethernet header information in the frame and determines what the destination MAC address is. It will then make an intelligent forwarding decision and send the frame only to the port that needs to receive that destination MAC address. Also,

Ethernet switches provide more intelligence in the backplane to buffer frames and prevent collisions on the backplane, enabling full-duplex conversations. These points are summarized in Figure 4.2.

Figure 4.1 Hubs and repeaters simply replicate and amplify the frames sent from each device; they do not inspect L2 headers and do not perform an intelligent forwarding. They provide only half-duplex operation.

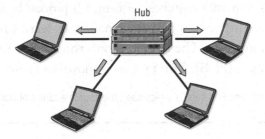

Hubs/Repeaters
- Signal amplification and replication
- Layer 1 devices that receive Ethernet frames and replicate across all other ports
- Do not inspect L2 frame headers
- Half duplex operation

Figure 4.2 (switch drawing only) Switches inspect L2 headers and will forward frames only to the specific port that has the destination address in the frame. They provide full-duplex operation.

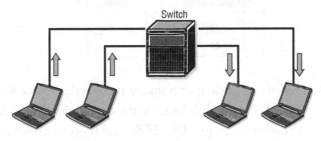

Switches
- Layer 2 device that inspects Ethernet frame headers
- Switches received Ethernet frames based on destination MAC address
- Full duplex operation

4.2 Ethernet Switching Operations

As mentioned in the previous section, Ethernet switches perform an intelligent forwarding operation. The Ethernet switch will forward a frame only to the port that needs to receive it. It performs this function by building a dynamic MAC address table that matches MAC addresses to ports so that it "knows" which ports correspond to which MAC addresses. Ethernet switches perform this process by using the source MAC address of packets arriving on ports to dynamically learn which MAC addresses are associated with an interface. The switch records this address information into a MAC forwarding database (FDB). This process is shown in Figure 4.3.

Figure 4.3 Switches build up their FDB table by recording the source address of frames as they enter each port on the switch.

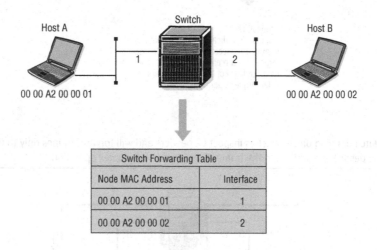

When the switch receives an Ethernet frame, it records the source MAC address and the interface on which it arrived. It looks at the destination MAC address of the frame, compares it to the entries in its MAC FDB, and then transmits the frame out of the appropriate interface. If no entry is found, the switch floods the frame out of all its interfaces except the interface on which the frame arrived. If the destination device exists, when it replies, the switch will learn the MAC address on the receiving port, and future flooding for that destination will be unnecessary. Through this flooding and learning process, an Ethernet switch will quickly build up its MAC FDB and will maintain it until the switch is rebooted, at which point the entire learning process begins again. The learning and flooding process is illustrated in Figure 4.4.

Figure 4.4 When a switch receives a frame with a destination address that is not in its FDB, it will flood the frame out each port. When the destination host responds, the switch records the reply frame's source MAC address in its FDB for future use.

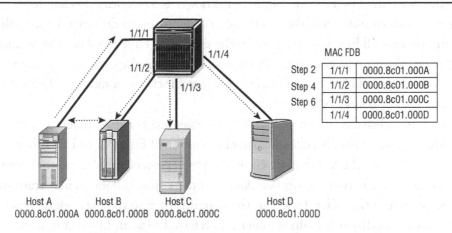

MAC FDB		
Step 2	1/1/1	0000.8c01.000A
Step 4	1/1/2	0000.8c01.000B
Step 6	1/1/3	0000.8c01.000C
	1/1/4	0000.8c01.000D

Host A
0000.8c01.000A

Host B
0000.8c01.000B

Host C
0000.8c01.000C

Host D
0000.8c01.000D

Step 1: Host A sends a frame to Host B
Step 2: The switch receives the frame on 1/1/1 and places the source in MAC FDB
Step 3: The destination is not in the MAC table so the switch floods the frame to all ports except the source
Step 4: Host B responds to Host A. The switch adds the source address of Host B to the MAC FDB
Step 5: The switch can now forward frames between Host A and Host B directly i.e. without flooding
Step 6 : Host C and Host D also send frames

There is an important caveat to the process as it has been described to this point. As discussed in the previous chapter, in addition to unicast Ethernet frames intended for a single destination, there are also broadcast frames intended for all stations and multicast frames intended for groups of devices. Normally, both types of frames are treated the same; they are flooded out of every port except the port it was received on. In other words, they are treated the same way as a unicast frame with a destination MAC that is not in the FDB. There are some switches that will also build special multicast FDB tables based on the multicast group destination address and therefore will only flood multicast frames to the required ports.

From this discussion it is clear that a switch will always flood a broadcast frame out of all its ports. A switch will never be able to use its FDB table to intelligently forward a broadcast frame. In the event that multiple switches are connected, every switch that receives the flooded broadcast frame will, in turn, flood the broadcast frame, and so on and so on. This process continues until a frame reaches all ports or encounters a device with a higher layer interface such as a router.

Routers operate at Layer 3 of the OSI model, and so an Ethernet frame would not be forwarded across a router. This boundary or domain that includes all of the Ethernet switches contained by a router boundary is known as a *broadcast domain*. It is important to understand that within a broadcast domain, every Ethernet device will receive and process all broadcast packets. In the event of a large number of broadcast packets, or *broadcast storm*, the processing at each station in the broadcast domain can be severely disrupted. This is one of many important functions of routers: They serve as broadcast packet boundaries.

In contrast to a broadcast domain, a *collision domain* exists between devices only within a single wire or hub. A *collision domain* is a group of Ethernet or Fast Ethernet devices in a CSMA/CD LAN that are connected by repeaters or hubs and that compete for access in the network. Only one device in the collision domain may transmit at any one time, and the other devices in the domain listen to the network to avoid data collisions. A collision domain is sometimes referred to as an *Ethernet segment*. Devices on a hub are in a single collision domain, whereas each device on a switch has its own collision domain between the device and its individual port. Figure 4.5 illustrates these different domains.

Figure 4.5 Hubs provide no separation for collision or broadcast domains, switches provide collision domain separation, and routers provide both collision and broadcast domain separation.

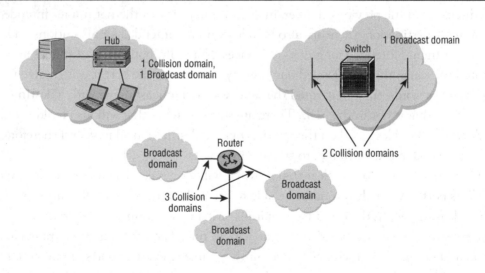

Figure 4.6 further illustrates the concepts of collision and broadcast domains. See if you can determine how many of each domain type exist in the figure (you can find the answer in the "Chapter Review" section).

Figure 4.6 Can you identify the collision and broadcast domains?

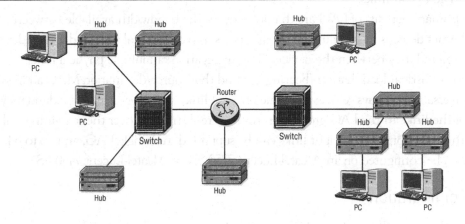

4.3 Ethernet Link Redundancy: LAG

With all networks, it is good design practice to provide for redundancy in the event of a failure. There are two basic types of redundancy available with Ethernet networks: link redundancy and path redundancy. Link redundancy is provided via the Link Aggregation Group (LAG) protocol. Path redundancy is provided by the Spanning Tree Protocol (STP). The primary difference between link redundancy and path redundancy is that the former does not provide redundancy in the event of a switch failure. For example, a failure of a single or multiple links between LAG-connected switches would be survivable. However, there are sometimes failures of an entire switch or blade in a switch, in which case, all available links on a particular path are lost. In such a case, full path redundancy would be required. These differences will become more apparent as we discuss each type of redundancy in more detail.

A LAG is based on the IEEE 802.3ad standard. LAG allows you to aggregate multiple physical links between Ethernet devices so that they are functionally equivalent to a single logical link. The 802.3ad standard specifies several important requirements for vendor implementations. First, all links in a LAG group must be full-duplex and must have the same speed. Second, the LAG implementation must not reorder frames as they are transmitted across the LAG group. This means that all frames transmitted between the same source/destination MAC address pair (referred to as a *conversation*) will be transmitted across the same physical link in the bundle. The result is that some links in the bundle may have more traffic than others, so traffic may not be perfectly load-balanced across all links.

The primary benefits of LAG are that it increases the bandwidth available between two Ethernet devices by grouping up to eight ports into one logical link, and it provides for link redundancy between the devices. The aggregation of multiple physical links allows for statistical load sharing (bearing in mind that source/destination MAC address pair conversations always go over the same physical link) and offers seamless redundancy. If one of the links in the LAG group fails, traffic is re-distributed over the remaining links in less than 1 second. Up to eight links can be supported in a single LAG, and up to 64 LAGs can be configured on an Alcatel-Lucent 7750 SR or Alcatel-Lucent 7450 ESS.

LAG Configuration

LAG can be statically configured between devices, or it can be forced dynamically through the use of the Link Aggregation Control Protocol (LACP). LACP is defined in IEEE standard 802.3ad (Aggregation of Multiple Link Segments). LACP provides a standardized method of implementing link aggregation among different manufacturers. It is important when planning a LAG implementation to consider whether you will configure the LAG groups statically or use LACP to create your groups dynamically. The advantage to static configuration is that you provide for more control in your network, but at the expense of increased management overhead. By using LACP, you reduce the need for configuration management, but you may end up with LAG groups that you did not expect.

When configuring LAG, there are several points to keep in mind. First, a maximum of eight ports can be included in a single LAG. Second, all ports in the LAG must have the same characteristics such as speed, duplex, and hold-timers. Finally, auto-negotiation of speed or duplex must *not* be configured for ports in the LAG. LAG ports should be configured for `no autonegotiate`. In general, the most important thing to keep in mind is that you are configuring ports that are supposed to function identically as part of a bundle. Therefore, you don't want to leave any of the settings of an individual port to chance, so configure your speed and duplex manually.

There are a few other LAG settings that should be noted. The LAG `port-threshold` determines the behavior of a LAG when the number of available links falls below the configured threshold value. In other words, how should the LAG behave when a certain number of physical links in the bundle fail? Two actions can be specified:

Option 1: down

```
configure lag <lag-id> port-threshold  <threshold value> action down
```

If the number of available links is less than or equal to the threshold value, the LAG is declared operationally down until the number of available links is greater than the threshold value.

Option 2: dynamic-cost

```
configure lag <lag-id>  port-threshold <threshold value> action dynamic-cost
```

When the number of available links is less than or equal to the threshold value, dynamic costing is used to determine the advertised LAG cost.

 The costing of the LAG only affects the link cost for a dynamic routing protocol.

Listing 4.1 illustrates an example of configuring a LAG group with the port-threshold option of down.

Listing 4.1: LAG group configuration example

```
Config> lag 1
Config>lag# description "LAG from PE1 to PE2"
Config>lag# port 2/1/1 2/2/1 3/1/1
Config>lag# port-threshold 2 action down
Config>lag# dynamic-cost
Config>lag# no shutdown
```

As illustrated in Listing 4.1, dynamic cost can actually be configured as a general command and not just as a port-threshold option. If dynamic cost is enabled, then it affects the OSPF routing protocol cost (we discuss the OSPF routing protocol and its cost metric in Chapter 9), even when the number of active links is greater than the port threshold. When dynamic cost is enabled and the number of active links is greater than the port-threshold value (0–7), the path cost is dynamically calculated whenever there is a change in the number of active links regardless of the specified port-threshold action.

For example, if the port-threshold value is 4 and there are eight links in the bundle, three links in the bundle could fail and no action would be taken because five links would still be active (the port-threshold would still not have been reached). In such a situation, if dynamic cost were enabled, then the OSPF cost of the link would be altered with each link failure even while the port threshold had not been reached, up to the point of reaching the port-threshold value. However, once the port-threshold value is reached, whatever action is set takes precedence. If the action is set to declare the LAG down, this action will be taken even if dynamic cost is enabled.

Another example should serve to drive this point home. In Figure 4.7, each physical link is configured with a cost of 100. Therefore, the cost of the logical link LAG 1 is 100/4 = 25 and LAG 2 is 100/3 = 33.

Figure 4.7 If dynamic cost is configured on the entire bundle, then the group will change its OSPF cost when a link fails, regardless of the port-threshold value as in LAG 1. Dynamic cost can also be configured to modify the cost only when the port threshold is reached as in LAG 2.

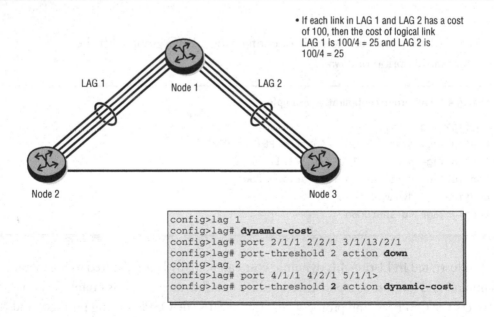

• If each link in LAG 1 and LAG 2 has a cost of 100, then the cost of logical link LAG 1 is 100/4 = 25 and LAG 2 is 100/4 = 25

LAG 1   Node 1   LAG 2

Node 2   Node 3

```
config>lag 1
config>lag# dynamic-cost
config>lag# port 2/1/1 2/2/1 3/1/13/2/1
config>lag# port-threshold 2 action down
config>lag 2
config>lag# port 4/1/1 4/2/1 5/1/1>
config>lag# port-threshold 2 action dynamic-cost
```

The LAG groups LAG1 and LAG2 are configured as follows:

- LAG1 has the `dynamic-cost` parameter configured. If a single link in LAG 1 fails, there are three active links and the port threshold is 2, so the `port-threshold` action is not executed. However since the `dynamic-cost` parameter is enabled on the LAG, the cost of LAG1 is dynamically computed to be 100/3 = 33. If another link in LAG1 fails, the number of active links matches the `port-threshold` and the `port-threshold` action is executed; therefore, LAG1 is declared operationally down.

- LAG2 does *not* have the `dynamic-cost` parameter configured. If a single link in LAG 2 fails, there are three active links and the port threshold is 2, so the port-threshold action is not executed. Since the `dynamic-cost` parameter is not enabled on the lag, the cost of LAG2 remains as 100/4 = 25. If another link in LAG2 fails, the number of active links matches the `port-threshold` and the `port-threshold` action is executed; therefore, the cost of LAG2 is dynamically calculated as 100/2 = 50.

Overall, LAG is a good solution for providing link redundancy between neighboring Ethernet devices. However, if you require end-to-end path redundancy, LAG cannot provide this functionality. In the next section, we examine how Ethernet path redundancy can be achieved.

4.4 Ethernet Path Redundancy: STP

In this section, we discuss the second type of redundancy: path redundancy provided via the Spanning Tree Protocol (STP). As previously mentioned, path redundancy provides an advantage over link redundancy by protecting you when an entire switch fails, and not just when individual links fail. However, there are some potential problems associated with providing path redundancy because of the nature of Ethernet switches. As you will see shortly, providing redundant Ethernet switch paths can result in broadcast storms due to constant "looping" of Ethernet frames. They may also lead to FDB table instability as switches might see source addresses coming in on different interfaces (recall the FDB learning process discussed previously).

 In the discussion that follows, the term *bridge* may be used as a substitute for *switch*. While a bridge typically only has two ports and switches typically have many more, for discussion purposes in this chapter, they are considered synonymous terms. In addition, STP behaves the same on both types of devices.

In order to understand the need for STP, you must first appreciate the nature of a loop in an Ethernet network. A loop exists in a network when a frame or packet exits one interface on a device and then re-enters the device on a second interface. Because switches and routers are computers and because computers are designed to perform the same function over and over under the same conditions, typically what will occur is that the switch or router will simply re-send the frame or packet back out the original exit interface.

If the frame or packet returns again on the same second interface, the router or switch will again re-send the data back out of the original interface, and so forth and so on indefinitely. As you will see in Chapter 5, IP packets have a "time to live" (TTL) field that gets decremented when each router processes the packet; this prevents an IP packet from existing forever on a network. No such field exists in an Ethernet frame, so other mechanisms must be employed.

The looping problem is exacerbated by Ethernet switches (as opposed to IP routers) because Ethernet switches are designed to flood frames out every port when a destination is unknown. In looping scenarios, it is often the case that the FDB table is unstable, resulting in excessive flooding. Without STP, broadcast traffic may increase exponentially because, as the switch receives multiple copies of a frame, it further replicates each frame and transmits them out one or more ports on the switch. Because of the L2 loop, the transmitted frames are received back and replicated again. This results in an exponential increase in Layer 2 traffic in the looped network. Since there is no TTL in Layer 2, this frame is copied and transmitted repeatedly until the switch gets overwhelmed with activity and possibly re-sets or locks up. This scenario is illustrated in Figure 4.8.

To see how a bridging loop can occur, consider the case in which no traffic has been transmitted on the network in Figure 4.8. Because no frames have been transmitted by any host, both Switch 1 and Switch 2 have an empty MAC FDB (they have not yet learned any MAC addresses). Let's examine the steps that occur when Host A sends a frame to Host B:

1. Host A sends a frame with the destination MAC address of Host B. One copy of the frame is received by Host B and processed.

2. The original frame from Host A is also received by Switch 1. Switch 1 records the source MAC of Host A to be on Segment 1. Since Switch 1 does not know where Host B is, it replicates the frame and sends it out the port connected to Segment 2.

Figure 4.8 Frames sent from Host A to Host B are forwarded from Segment 1 to Segment 2 by Switch 2, which is then forwarded from Segment 2 to Segment 1 by Switch 1 and then re-forwarded by Switch 2. This process continues ad infinitum.

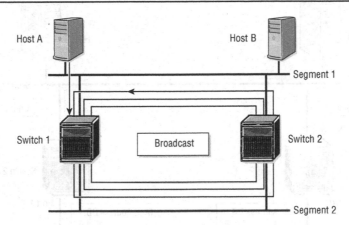

3. The original frame is also received by Switch 2 on Segment 1. Switch 2 also records the source MAC of Host A to be on Segment 1. Since Switch 2 does not know where Host B is, like Switch 1 it replicates the frame and sends it out the port connected to Segment 2.

4. Switch 2 receives the replicated frame from Switch 1 in Step 2 above via Segment 2. Switch 2 removes the existing entry for Host A in the MAC FDB and records that Host A belongs to the port attached to Segment 2. Switch 2 then replicates the frame and transmits it out the port attached to Segment 1, where it will be received by Switch 1 on Segment 1.

5. This process continues indefinitely as both Switch 1 and Switch 2 replicate the original frame from Host A onto Segments 1 and 2, causing excessive flooding and MAC FDB instability.

Figure 4.9 further illustrates this process at the port level. Switch 1 and Switch 2 will map the MAC address of Host A to Port 0 when it receives the original frame from Host A to Host B. Later, when the replicated frame from Switch 1 arrives at Port 1 of Switch 2, Switch 2 must remove its original entry for Host A and replace it with the new entry for Host A, mapping it to Port 1. This activity causes an unstable database as Switch 2 tries to keep up with the perceived location of Host A.

Figure 4.9 A further illustration of a loop created in a switched network when there are multiple active paths. The frame from Host A to Host B will continually circulate around the network.

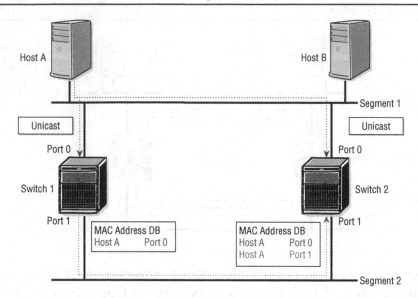

The problem should now be clear: When there are active redundant paths in an Ethernet switch network, frames can be forwarded indefinitely owing to the nature of the way switches learn MAC addresses and flood frames with an unknown destination. What is needed is a way to preserve redundant paths while avoiding this problem. In the next section, we will examine such a solution.

Using STP to Prevent Loops

The Spanning Tree Protocol (STP) was developed to solve these instability and broadcast-storm issues. It was invented in 1985 by Radia Perlman and was first published as a standard by the IEEE as *802.1D*. Revisions to STP were published in 1998 and 2004, and the Rapid Spanning Tree Protocol (RSTP) was introduced in 1998 as *IEEE 802.1w*. In 2004, the IEEE incorporated the changes of RSTP into the Spanning Tree Protocol and obsoleted previous versions. This version was published as *IEEE 802.1D-2004*. Because the current version of STP incorporates all the advances of RSTP, for the remainder of this chapter, we will just use the term *STP*. You should keep in mind that our use of the acronym from this point forward refers to the current version of STP published in 2004 and not previous, obsolete versions.

A few points about STP should be noted at the outset. First, STP is intended to prevent loops in an Ethernet switched network. It does this by selectively blocking ports to achieve a loop-free topology. That is, it determines what ports it can put into a non-functioning state to prevent loops from occurring, while still allowing frames to reach every destination in the Ethernet network. Second, STP uses a root/branch/leaf model, which determines a single path to each leaf spanning the entire switched network.

Finally, because end stations such as workstations or servers rarely act as Ethernet switches, they are usually not part of the STP protocol and do not participate in it. The first version of STP was slow at converging because of various issues with the protocol design. Many enhancements were introduced to improve convergence time with STP version IEEE 802.1d-2004, and the following discussion covers only the procedures in the current version. The exact mechanisms that STP uses to achieve a loop-free topology are the subject to which we now turn.

You should keep in mind throughout this discussion that the sole purpose of STP is to build an active loop-free topology (*active* in the sense that the ports that are blocked can change in response to changed network conditions). In Figure 4.10, STP would create a loop-free topology out of the physically looped network by blocking the ports that connect Switches C and E. All of the processes that make up STP are used to accomplish this seemingly trivial goal.

Spanning Tree topology can be thought of as a tree that includes the following components:

- A root (a root bridge/switch)
- Branches (LANs and designated bridges/switches)
- Leaves (end nodes)

Figure 4.10 STP will block the ports between Switches C and E, ensuring a loop-free topology in the switched network.

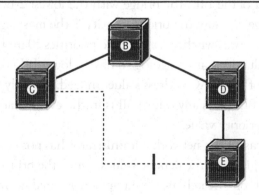

There are no disconnected components that are considered part of the tree. That is, the tree encompasses all of its leaves (end nodes), and there is usually only one tree for any Ethernet network (you will see later that each virtual LAN can have its own STP). There are no loops in the tree. If you trace a path from one leaf (end node) to any other leaf (end node), you'll find there is only one possible path. STP organizes and connects switches into a loop-free topology while leaving no segments isolated.

Selecting a Root Bridge

One of the key concepts to understand is how a root bridge is selected. The root bridge in a STP is critically important because it is the root bridge that serves as the starting point for building the STP *tree*. Think of the STP tree like a regular tree, except inverted with a single root at the top, leading to multiple branches with multiple leaves on each branch. The goal of the protocol is to have one and only one path from the bridge to each of the leaves. To facilitate this process, it is necessary to select one and only one root bridge. The way a root bridge is selected in based on a numeric value called the *bridge ID*.

Each bridge has a bridge ID (BID) that determines its priority for root bridge selection. The BID consists of 8 bytes built from (1) a 2-byte bridge priority and (2) the 6-byte MAC address of the bridge port with the lowest port ID on that switch. For example, if Port 0 (bridge/switch ports are usually numbered beginning with 0) on a given switch has a MAC address of 0060.1d20.5128 and a bridge priority of 10, the BID would be 10.0060.1d20.5128. The bridge with the lowest BID becomes the root bridge. Note that in practice, this means that if one bridge has a lower bridge priority than all other bridges, then it will always become the root bridge, regardless of the MAC addresses on each bridge.

Based on the format of the BID, the bridge with the lowest 2-byte bridge priority becomes the root bridge, because the bridge priority is the most significant part of the BID. For example, given two switches with bridge priorities 10 and 20, respectively, the bridge with priority value 10 is always going to have a lower BID than the bridge with priority 20, regardless of the MAC address value. Indeed, the only time that the MAC address portion of the BID plays any role at all is in the event that multiple switches have the same bridge priority value.

This might be the case if the network administrator has not configured the bridge priority manually and just took the default values. Since the bridge priority default value (32,768 by default on Alcatel-Lucent equipment) would normally be the same for switches from a common vendor, this would mean that all switches would have an equally low bridge priority (but not the same BID owing to differences in the MAC address portion of the BID).

In such a case where there is a tie for the lowest bridge priority, the switch with the lowest MAC address *among switches that share the same lowest bridge priority value* would become the root bridge. Note again that if you do not manually set the bridge priority, the device that becomes the root will be determined based on the MAC address of the bridge. Because it is difficult to determine where the lowest MAC address in a given Ethernet network will appear, it is considered best practice to manually set the priority of the switch that you want to serve as the root bridge for STP. This way a network administrator can determine in advance which switch will be the root bridge and not have to rely on the vagaries of the appearance of the lowest MAC address on a switch. Selection of the bridge with the lowest priority as the root is illustrated in Figure 4.11.

Figure 4.11 The root bridge is selected based on the bridge priority of 16, which is lower than the priority of the other bridges.

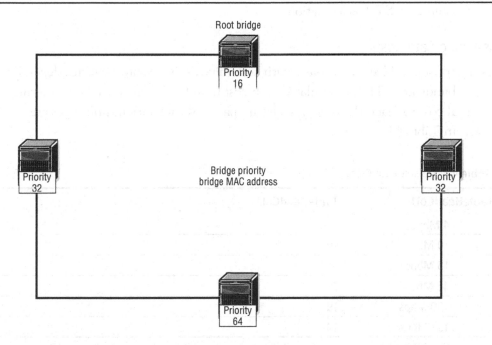

Note that in the figure there is one bridge of priority 16, two of priority 32, and one of priority 64. As shown, the bridge with priority 16 will become the root bridge because of its low priority. The election calculation for the root bridge by STP in Figure 4.11 is described in the following list:

1. After bridges/switches have initialized, root bridge election begins.

2. The bridge priority can be manually assigned. Since the priority field is 2 bytes or 16 bits, valid values range from 0 to 2^{16} = 65,535 (the default value for Alcatel-Lucent switches is 32,768).

3. Each bridge/switch sends its BID to every other bridge/switch. As described, the BID is 8 bytes: 2 bytes for bridge priority and 6 bytes that contain the MAC address of the lowest-numbered port on the bridge/switch.

4. Election of the root bridge is determined using the BID, which is made up of the priority and MAC address. The switch with the lowest BID value is selected as the root. In practice, this means that the bridge with the lowest configured bridge priority will become the root bridge.

5. Any subsequent physical change in the network after election of the root bridge will cause an STP recalculation.

Assigning Path Costs

Each port on a bridge/switch has a path cost value assigned automatically, depending on the bandwidth. The accumulated path cost from the bridge to the root determines the total cost to reach the root. The default path costs for various link types are shown in Table 4.1.

Table 4.1 Default Path Costs

TableHeadCol1	TableHeadCol2
4 Mbps	250
10 Mbps	100
16 Mbps	62
45 Mbps	39
100 Mbps	19
155 Mbps	14
622 Mbps	6
1 Gbps	4
10 Gbps	2

In the STP calculations, each switch must establish a single path to the root. By doing this, all loops are eliminated.

Three values are used in the STP port calculations:

- Port priority (has a default value but is configurable)
- Per port cost (the default value is dependent on bandwidth but is configurable)
- Port MAC address

After bridges/switches have initialized, and root and leaf bridges have been selected based on the bridge with the lowest bridge ID, each bridge port participating in the Spanning Tree is assigned either a root, designated, alternate, or back-up role. The designated port is the only port on a given LAN segment that can forward frames to/from that segment in order to avoid loops. The process that ports undergo to determine if they are a root port, designated port, or should go into a discard state is described below:

1. All ports on the root bridge automatically become designated ports.

2. A switch/bridge that is not a root bridge and has ports participating in STP is referred to as a *designated bridge/designated switch*.

3. The port on a designated bridge that is closest (least path cost) to the root bridge is elected as the root port. To determine the least path cost of each port, Bridge Protocol Data Units (BPDUs) are received from the root.

4. Non-root ports on each designated bridge providing the least cost path from a particular LAN segment (that the port is connected to) to the root bridge are elected as designated ports.

5. Non-root ports on the designated bridge that do not provide the least path cost from the LAN segment (that the port is connected to) to the root bridge are elected as alternate ports and go into the discard state.

This description can seem a little overwhelming, and STP can be confusing with all of its terminology. You should study Figure 4.12 and the explanation that follows it carefully as it illustrates all of the concepts mentioned in the previous steps.

Figure 4.12 The port is blocked because the path through that link to the root bridge is higher than the other path to the root bridge.

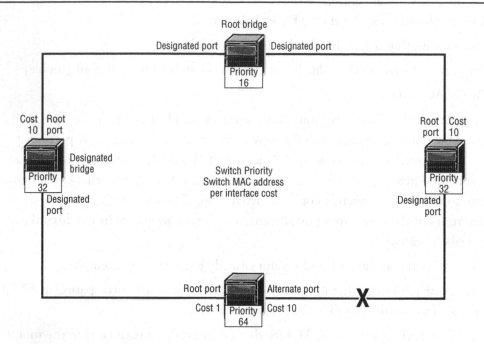

First notice that the switch with the lowest priority, 16, has been chosen as the root bridge. This means that all other bridges are designated bridges and will try to build a path to this bridge based on the lowest path cost. Next, notice that one path has a link that has been blocked because that path has a higher cost to the root bridge than the alternate path (*hint:* look at the cost on each link and add them up to determine the total path cost to the root bridge). If you study this diagram and understand why the root bridge was chosen and why a certain path was blocked while the alternative path was left open, you will have gone a long way toward understanding STP.

A few points about BPDUs are worth mentioning here. We have so far briefly described BDPUs as frames that are used to send STP messages, which is accurate, but there is more to it. First, as is probably obvious from the discussion so far, BPDUs are flooded throughout the switched network. This is what allows for the election of the root bridge; the BPDUs from every switch are transmitted to every other switch, so every switch knows which bridge has the lowest priority (or lowest BID if there are multiple bridges with the same lowest bridge priority).

Second, BPDUs are sent in an Ethernet frame with the port address as source and the STP multicast address 01:80:C2:00:00:00 as destination. This ensures that only bridges that are participating in STP will receive and process the BPDU frames. Finally, BPDUs are still transmitted and received on ports in the discard state. This ensures that the STP protocol can react quickly to changes in the network topology that might result in a new spanning tree. For example, if the originally chosen path to the root fails and a new root path must be chosen through a previously blocked port, it would be necessary to perform an STP recalculation.

More Details on STP

A few final words about STP port states merit some discussion before leaving this topic. When an STP port or switch is enabled on the network, the ports will transition between three states as the topology of the network is determined:

- **Discard State**—Initially, in the discard state, all data packets received on a port are dropped and no packets are transmitted, except Bridge Protocol Data Units (BPDUs). *BPDUs* are STP-specific packets originated by Ethernet switches as described previously.

- **Learning State**—In the learning state, MAC addresses are learned through packets received on the port, but no data packets are transmitted. Ports transition from learning to forwarding in a few seconds.

- **Forwarding State**—In the forwarding state, the port is fully functional and will receive and transmit packets normally.

We have now examined root bridge selection, how STP uses the cost of individual links to determine the path cost from each designated or non-root bridge to the root bridge, and how other higher cost paths are put into the discard state. There are actually two additional types of ports that you should be aware of that allow for fast reconvergence of STP in the event of a network failure: an *alternate port* and a *back-up port* (note that these ports are part of the RSTP enhancements and appear in the latest version of STP but not in prior versions). An *alternate port* is a port on the same network segment, but on a different switch that has a higher path cost to the root than the designated bridge for that segment. A *back-up port* is a port on the same network segment and on the same switch as the designated port that has a higher cost path to the root bridge. These types of ports are illustrated in Figure 4.13.

Figure 4.13 The current version of STP provides for very fast convergence in response to a switch/link failure by keeping track of ports that provide alternative paths to the root bridge. The back-up port is an alternative port on the same bridge, while the alternate port provides an alternative path on a different switch.

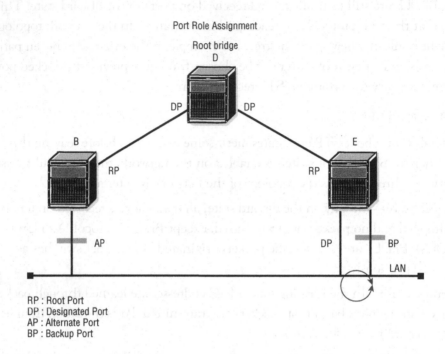

RP : Root Port
DP : Designated Port
AP : Alternate Port
BP : Backup Port

Both alternate and back-up ports remain in a discarding state unless there is a topology change that causes them to become the designated port. By keeping track of these additional ports, STP can allow a designated bridge to quickly transition its original root port to an alternative port in the event of a link or switch failure in the path to the root bridge. These enhancements are part of the RSTP changes made to STP in the 2004 release.

In the next section, we leave the topics of STP and redundancy and wrap up this chapter with a discussion of virtual LANs.

4.5 Virtual LANs

A *virtual LAN* (VLAN) is a mechanism that allows you to segregate devices, and their associated traffic from other devices and traffic, even when all of the devices are physically part of the same switched infrastructure. The astute reader may immediately wonder why you couldn't simply use a router to achieve this sort of separation. There is some merit to this question, as routers are the mechanisms that are typically used to segregate groups of Ethernet devices from one another. However, there are physical limitations on the deployment of routers, and those limitations may not match the physical locations for the deployment of devices in the same VLAN.

For example, you might have devices in multiple buildings that are part of the same segregated group, and there might be a multiple of these types of groups in each building. Your goal would be to allow the devices in the segregated group to communicate with each other, but not with any other Ethernet devices. This would be difficult to accomplish using traditional network segregation with routers, but it is trivially easy with VLAN technology.

There are two main reasons to use VLANs:

- To decrease the amount of broadcast traffic
- To increase the security of your network

Let's first examine the reasons for decreasing the amount of broadcast traffic in your network. Broadcast traffic is increased in direct proportion to the number of stations in the LAN, as illustrated in Figure 4.14. Note that *flat network* means a network without routers or without VLANs or both.

Figure 4.14 As broadcasts increase on a flat network, they quickly consume all available network resources.

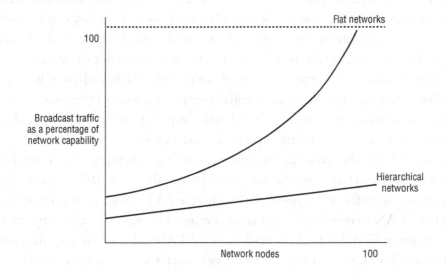

The use of VLANs allows for the isolation of groups of users so that one group is not interrupted by the broadcast traffic of another. By segregating a group of devices to a particular VLAN, a switch will block broadcasts from devices in that VLAN to devices that are not in that VLAN instead of flooding it out every port.

VLANs also have the benefit of added security by separating the network into distinct logical networks. Traffic in one VLAN is separated from another VLAN as if they were physically separate networks. If traffic is to pass from one VLAN to another, it must be routed. This logical separation regardless of physical location is a very powerful concept. For example, you could have a low security device and a high security device physically attached to the same Ethernet switch (indeed, they could be attached on adjacent physical ports). By configuring each device into a separate VLAN, neither device could communicate directly with the other without going through a router.

Creating and Using VLANS

While in theory there are many ways to create VLANs—such as by MAC address, IP address, workstation names, and so on—in practice, these methods are very cumbersome and ultimately unsupportable. The primary way that VLANs are created in modern networks is by physical port, and that is the method that we will address for the remainder of this chapter.

Each VLAN is identified by a VLAN ID (VID), which is usually a number such as 100, 101, and the like. They can reside on only a single switch, or they can be distributed throughout the entire network on each switch. You can think of a VLAN as a broadcast domain, and, in fact, that is exactly what it is (recall our earlier discussion of broadcast domains in Chapter 3). Each device in a VLAN, regardless of its physical location, can communicate directly with every other device in the same VLAN and cannot communicate outside of the VLAN except through a router. So with this background, let's examine how this process actually works.

In Figure 4.15, VLANs subdivide the Ethernet switch into multiple virtual switches. Note that there are no logical interconnections between these internal switches. Therefore, the broadcast traffic that is generated by a host in a VLAN stays within that VLAN, making the VLAN its own broadcast domain. Because broadcast traffic for a particular VLAN remains within that VLAN's borders, inter-VLAN or broadcast domain communication must occur through a Layer 3 device such as a router, as previously noted.

Figure 4.15 VLANs provide for logical separation of devices on the same physical switch.

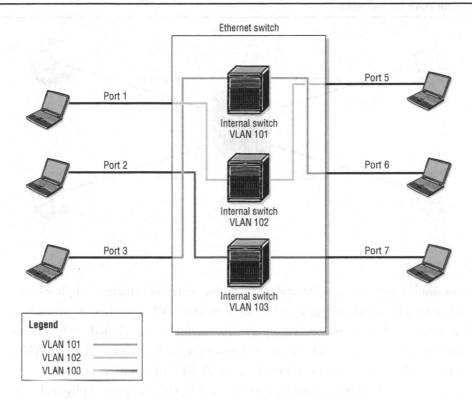

Hosts are typically not VLAN-aware (although Ethernet network card technology does exist to make hosts VLAN aware), and therefore no configuration is usually required on the hosts. The VLAN configuration is done when the switch and ports are assigned on a VLAN-by-VLAN basis.

Another example may be useful to illustrate intra-VLAN communication. In Figure 4.16, Host 1 sends out a broadcast. Because Host 4 is the only other member of the VLAN, it is the only host to receive the broadcast (both hosts are in VLAN 101).

The FDB entries behave much the same way in the VLAN model as they do in the standard switch model. The entries are updated based on the source address received on a given port. In Figure 4.16, the source address of the broadcast frame is only learned by VLAN 101 on the ingress port. The FDB for VLAN 102 will not know the source address of Host 1 after Host 1 transmits its broadcast packet. Therefore, in a VLAN environment, a separate FDB is kept for each VLAN. In this case, this means that the FDB for VLAN 101 will never learn about Host 3 or Host 2 and the FDB for VLAN 102 will never learn about Host 1 or Host 4.

Figure 4.16 Only hosts in common VLANs can communicate with each other. Switch 1 will keep a separate FDB for both VLAN 101 and VLAN 102.

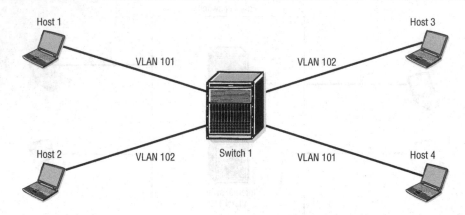

VLAN Trunking

These examples are very straightforward, but how do these principles apply when there are multiple switches? Figure 4.17 illustrates three VLANs that are shared across multiple switches. Frames ingressing a port in a particular VLAN will only be allowed to egress a port on the same VLAN, regardless of the switch it exits. The VLANs can span across multiple switches because common VLAN information is configured on both Switch 1 and Switch 2. Note that in Figure 4.17, there are three physical links between Switch 1 and Switch 2, one for each VLAN.

Of course, the problem with the design in Figure 4.17 is that it requires a separate physical link between the switches for each VLAN. That might be acceptable for two or three VLANs, but it is not a very scalable or practical solution. This is where VLAN "trunking" comes into play. VLAN trunking provides efficient interswitch forwarding of VLAN frames; it allows a single Ethernet port to carry frames from multiple VLANs instead of the "one link per VLAN" approach shown in Figure 4.17. This allows the use of a single high-bandwidth port, such as a gigabit Ethernet port or a LAG bundle, to carry the VLAN traffic between switches instead of one port per VLAN.

The sharing of VLANs between switches is achieved by the insertion of a header or "tag" with a 12-bit VID, which allows for $2^{12} = 4,094$ possible VLAN destinations for each Ethernet frame. A VID must be assigned for each VLAN. Assigning the same VID to VLANs on different connected switches can extend the VLAN (broadcast domain) across a network.

Figure 4.17 VLANs can be created across multiple switches. In this case, there is a separate physical interswitch link for each VLAN.

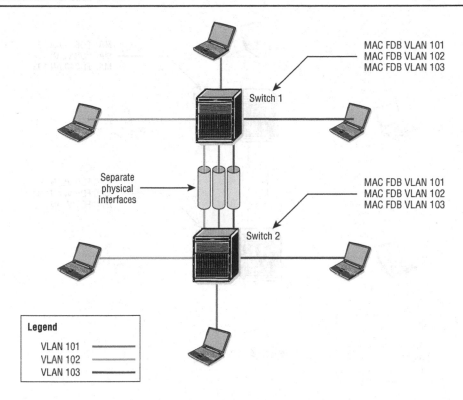

When a frame is leaving a switch with another switch as its destination, the egress switch will tag the frames with a VID so that the ingress switch knows which VLAN the frame belongs to. The IEEE 802.1q standard governs the format of the assigned tag. The procedure works by inserting a 32-bit VLAN header into the Ethernet frame of all network traffic for a VLAN as it exits the egress switch. The VID uses 12 bits of the 32-bit VLAN header. The ingress switch then uses the VID to determine which FDB it will use to find the destination.

After a frame reaches the destination switch port and before the frame is forwarded to the end destination, the VLAN header is removed. The use of a VLAN trunk is illustrated in Figure 4.18.

Figure 4.18 In this case, there is a single VLAN trunk port between the switches that carries traffic for all VLANs by tagging the frames with the correct VID on egress to the other switch.

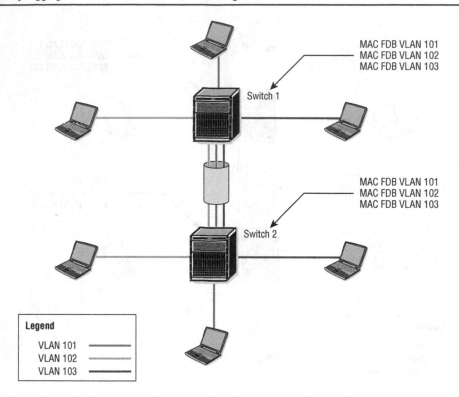

VLANs are separated within the trunk based on their VLAN IDs (802.1Q tags). The FDB at the destination switch designates the destination VLAN for the traffic on the VLAN trunk. Figure 4.19 illustrates the VLAN tag and how it is incorporated into the Ethernet frame that was discussed in Chapter 3.

The VLAN header can be broken down into two parts—the VLAN tag type and the tag control information. The *VLAN tag type* is a fixed value that is an indicator of a VLAN tag. It indicates that the Length/Type field can be found a further 4 bytes into the frame. Because the frame is a Q-tag frame and is longer, it needs to indicate that the Length/Type field is offset from the traditional location by 4 bytes.

Figure 4.19 VLAN tags are incorporated into the standard Ethernet frame through the addition of a VLAN tag field.

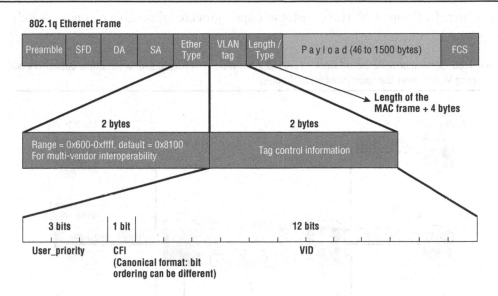

The tag control information has three parts:

1. **Priority Value (User Priority)**—A 3-bit value that specifies a frame's priority

2. **CFI**—A single bit. A setting of 0 means that the MAC address information is in its simplest form.

3. **VID**—A 12-bit value that identifies the VLAN that the frame belongs to. If the VID is 0, the tag header contains only priority information.

VLAN Use by Service Providers

There are some additional factors to consider for VLANs when they are examined from the perspective of a service provider. A restriction of Ethernet VLANs is the limited number of VIDs. With 12 bits used to define the VID, there are only $2^{12} = 4,096$ possibilities. Because VLANs 0 and 4095 are reserved, a Provider Edge (PE) router (connection to the customer) is really only capable of supporting 4,094 VLANs—not a significant number if it is compared with the expanding rates of networks. While 4,094 might seem sufficient, a single PE router might support hundreds or even thousands of customers, and the number of available VIDs can quickly evaporate.

One of the solutions to this restriction is *VLAN stacking*, also known as *Q-in-Q*. VLAN stacking allows the service provider to use Layer 2 protocols to connect customer sites. In Figure 4.20, three customers are connected through a common switch using VLAN stacking.

Figure 4.20 Service providers can "stack" VLAN ID information in order to support multiple customers with overlapping VLANs over the same provider backbone.

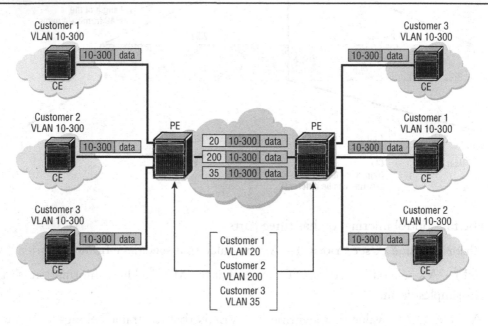

At the PE, the administrator has assigned a VLAN to represent the customer on that port. When the customer traffic arrives at the PE device, the PE switch simply inserts another VLAN tag in the frame in front of the first VLAN tag. It is this second or stacked VLAN tag that takes the customer traffic through the provider network. At the egress port of the PE equipment, the second or stack VLAN tag is removed, and the traffic is forwarded out the port.

This VLAN stacking allows Customers 1, 2, and 3 to use the same VLAN tags in their network. In theory, the service provider can support 4,094 customers, with each customer supporting 4,094 VLANs within their own network. Let's examine how this magic is accomplished by taking a look at the frames that support it.

In Figure 4.21, Customer 1 has sent a frame to the PE switch with a VLAN tag of 100. The PE switch inserts a second VLAN tag of 20. This tag number represents Customer

1 traffic. The second tag keeps Customer 1 traffic separate from Customer 2 and Customer 3 traffic and gives Customer 1 the ability to add 4,095 more associated VLANs.

Figure 4.21 Ethernet frames can support VLAN stacking by adding an additional VLAN tag to the standard frame.

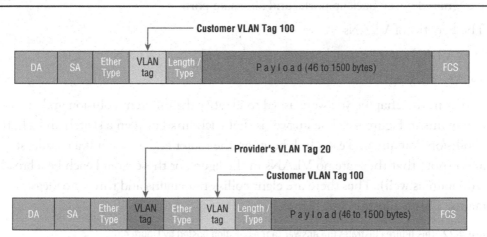

The VLAN tag that is inserted by the provider is the VLAN tag that is used in the provider network. When the frame has reached the appropriate egress port, the provider's VLAN tag is removed, and the frame with the customer's VLAN tag is forwarded out the egress port. Like we said: Magic!

Chapter Review

Now that you have completed this chapter, you should have a good understanding of the following topics. If you are not familiar with these topics, please go back and review the appropriate sections.

- The difference between a collision domain and a broadcast domain
- The difference between Ethernet hubs and Ethernet switches
- How bridges and switches operate
- The purpose of a switch FDB and how it is populated
- How switches forward unicast, multicast, and broadcast frames
- The different types of redundancy in an Ethernet-switched network
- How LAG load balances across multiple links

- Why STP is needed in an Ethernet switched network
- How the root bridge is selected
- BPDUs
- Designated ports, back-up ports, and alternate ports
- The benefits of VLANs
- How VLANs can be used between switches and what a VLAN trunk is
- VLAN stacking

Earlier in the chapter, you were asked to identify the different collision and broadcast domains in Figure 4.6. The answer is that each link between a switch and a hub is a collision domain, and each link between the router and a switch is a broadcast domain (note that there are no VLANs in the figure, or those would each be a broadcast domain as well). Thus there are eight collision domains and three broadcast domains. This is illustrated in Figure 4.22.

Figure 4.22 This figure illustrates the answer to the question posted by Figure 4.6.

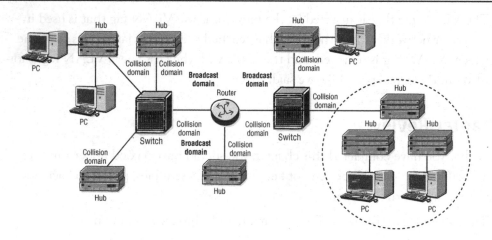

Post-Assessment

The following questions will test your knowledge and prepare you for the Alcatel-Lucent NRS I Certification Exam. Please review each question carefully and choose the most correct answer. You can compare your response with the answers listed in Appendix A. You can also download all of the CD content at `http://booksupport` `.wiley.com`. to take all the assessment tests and review the answers. Good luck!

1. When a frame with an unknown destination MAC address enters a switch, the switch will forward it out which ports?

    A. None

    B. All

    C. All unicast ports

    D. All except the port that received the frame

2. The primary difference in the way Ethernet hubs and Ethernet switches handle traffic is _____.

    A. Hubs forward broadcast traffic out every port, switches do not.

    B. Switches eliminate the need for thicknet cabling.

    C. Switches support multiple physical connections to hosts.

    D. Switches forward unicast traffic only to a specific destination port.

3. Which of the following is *not* true about Link Aggregation Groups?

    A. They protect against single or multiple link failures.

    B. They can contain up to eight physical links.

    C. They can protect against a switch failure by calculating multiple paths to the root.

    D. They can be configured to enter a down state if a certain number of links in the bundle fail.

4. Which of the following is *not* true of the STP protocol?

    A. It calculates a root bridge.

    B. It uses a cost value on each port to determine the path to the root bridge.

    C. It ensures a loop-free topology.

    D. It provides load-sharing capability.

5. The advantage of using VLANs is _____.

    A. They can increase the security of your network.

    B. They can interconnect multiple broadcast domains.

    C. They can limit the amount of broadcast traffic between groups of devices.

    D. A and C but not B

6. Which of the following statements is false?

    A. Routers provide broadcast domain separation.

    B. Hubs provide collision domain separation.

    C. VLANs provide broadcast domain separation.

    D. Switches provide collision domain separation.

7. The method that LAGs use to provide load balancing is best described as:

    A. Aggregates all source/destination conversations into a single conversation equally across all links

    B. Uses the same physical link for each source/destination conversation

    C. Statistically balances conversations based on the source MAC address

    D. Distributes egress frames equally across all links in the bundle

8. Given the following code:

```
Config> lag 1
Config>lag# description "LAG from PE1 to PE2"
Config>lag# port 1/1/1 1/1/2 1/1/3 1/1/4 1/1/5 1/1/6
Config>lag# port-threshold 2 action down
Config>lag# dynamic-cost
Config>lag# no shutdown
```

Which answer correctly describes what happens when Ports 1/1/5 and 1/1/6 fail?

    A. Nothing because the port threshold of 2 active links has not been reached

    B. The LAG begins using equal costing across all links because of the dynamic-cost parameter.

    C. The LAG updates its BPDUs and recalculates STP.

    D. The LAG changes its OSPF cost for the bundle but takes no other action.

9. What is the primary reason that Ethernet switched networks require STP?

   A. STP provides for link backup between switches.

   B. A loop-free topology is more efficient.

   C. Redundant paths can lead to broadcast storms and FDB instability.

   D. STP updates the OSPF routing protocol cost upon link failure.

10. The mechanism that STP uses to prevent loops in an Ethernet switched network is _____.

    A. STP elects a root and selectively blocks higher cost paths to the root from each bridge.

    B. STP blocks ports on all bridges that are not the root bridge.

    C. STP proactively changes all paths to the root bridge so that they are equal cost.

    D. STP uses BPDUs to set up a virtual path between each source and destination pair.

11. What determines how the root bridge is elected?

    A. The bridge priority

    B. The MAC address of the lowest switch port

    C. The bridge priority unless there is a tie, and then the lowest MAC address

    D. The BID unless there are multiple bridge priorities that are equal

12. What distinguishes an alternate port from a back-up port in STP?

    A. The alternate port has a higher path to the root.

    B. The back-up port has a lower priority.

    C. The back-up port is used only when the alternate port fails.

    D. The back-up port is on the same switch as the designated switch.

13. Which of the following is false regarding VLANs?

    A. They provide for broadcast domain separation.

    B. A single VLAN can exist on multiple switches.

    C. They require a separate physical connection per VLAN for interswitch links.

    D. They use a 12-bit VLAN ID to identify each VLAN.

14. Which STP port state is characterized by the port accepting and recording MAC address information, but not forwarding any frames out the port?

  A. Blocking

  B. Forwarding

  C. Listening

  D. Learning

15. The technology that allows multiple customers with the same VLANs to use the same provider backbone for their Ethernet traffic is known as _____.

  A. VLAN trunking

  B. VLAN tunneling

  C. VLAN stacking

  D. IEEE 802.1p

IP Addressing

- Internet Protocol
- IP addressing
- IP subnetting
- IP subnet address planning
- Practice creating IP subnets
- CIDR and route aggregation

We now turn to a discussion of the upper-layer protocols that provide network devices with the capability of delivering information anywhere in the world. In this chapter, we begin with an examination of the IP protocol. We examine the IP packet itself and its fields and discuss how these fields are used for forwarding information. We take a look at how IP addresses are constructed and manipulated to create a hierarchical addressing structure for your organization and how a properly created addressing scheme facilitates hierarchical routing. This discussion will lay the groundwork for you to tackle IP services and IP routing protocols in later chapters.

Pre-Assessment

The following assessment questions will help you understand what areas of the chapter you should review in more detail to prepare for the exam.

1. Which of the following is *not* a reason networks built on Ethernet alone cannot scale to a global network?

   A. Excessive broadcasts would make the network unusable.

   B. Ethernet lacks hierarchical addressing.

   C. Ethernet switches cannot build forwarding tables.

   D. Ethernet cables can only be of a limited length.

2. Which of the following is true about Layer 3 addressing?

   A. It is embedded in the device's firmware.

   B. It provides for a logical hierarchy.

   C. It allows for duplicate addresses on the Internet.

   D. Addresses are not required to be registered if they are used on the Internet.

3. Which of the following is false about the IP packet?

   A. The TTL field ensures that IP packets have a limited lifetime.

   B. The maximum size is 65,535 octets.

   C. The total length field includes the IP header.

   D. The current version is IPv5.

4. Which of the following is a valid host IP address?
    A. 192.168.300.4
    B. 255.70.1.1
    C. 224.0.0.1
    D. 10.254.1.1

5. An IP address has a first octet represented in binary as 11000001. What is the decimal equivalent?
    A. 190
    B. 193
    C. 192
    D. 11,000,001

You will find the answers to each of these questions in Appendix A. You can also download all of the CD materials for this book at http://booksupport.wiley.com to take all the assessment tests and review the answers.

5.1 Interconnecting Networks

In the previous chapter, we focused on Ethernet switches and their features as a way to build Ethernet networks. We described how Ethernet frames are sent from one Ethernet station to another and how Ethernet frames are processed by switches to achieve this communication. We also discussed how the use of VLANs allows for the separation of an Ethernet network into separate virtual networks for security purposes and also to provide protection from excessive broadcasts. A topic that we briefly touched on was communication between different VLANs or across routers, without fully defining exactly what routers are.

In this chapter, we discuss routing functions in some detail. But first, it is important to understand why a routing function is needed in the first place. The key to this topic is to understand why a Layer 3 protocol is necessary to interconnect Layer 2 networks such as Ethernet. The primary reason for this is that Layer 2 protocols such as Ethernet work on a local network only. In order to connect multiple Ethernet networks, you need a protocol that works at a higher layer: Layer 3.

The Need for Layer 3

In our discussion of Ethernet switches in Chapter 4, we mentioned that Ethernet-switched networks can provide for site- or campus-wide connectivity, and that VLANs enhance Ethernet network scalability. However, there are scalability limitations to an Ethernet network. There are several reasons for this. The first reason is that Ethernet addressing does not provide a structured hierarchy. Imagine an Ethernet switch with not just hundreds of MAC address entries in its FDB, but hundreds of thousands, and perhaps millions. Building such a list of entries and searching through it every time a switch needs to forward a packet could take an excessive amount of time and severely overload the CPU of the switch when it needs to forward hundreds of thousands of Ethernet frames every second.

If this problem were not enough, it is exacerbated by the fact that many protocols use Ethernet broadcasts at least part of the time to deliver information. Recall that a broadcast frame is sent out every port on an Ethernet switch except the one it was received on, and these broadcasts are received and processed by every device in a VLAN. In the case of a VLAN that might have hundreds of thousands of devices, every single one of them would receive and process each broadcast packet. Imagine a scenario in which every Ethernet-connected device was sending broadcast frames at the same time, resulting in millions of broadcast frames that need to be examined by every host.

Now include in the scenario mobile hosts such as laptops moving from one place to another and increasing the number of frames that need to be flooded (for Ethernet switches to "find" the hosts' new locations), and you have a completely unusable network. On top of all of this, there may be other Layer 2 protocols such as PPP or Frame-Relay involved in transferring the application messages from one device to another across a large network like the Internet (you can only run an Ethernet cable so far). How does an Ethernet frame get translated into a PPP or Frame-Relay frame? Ethernet and PPP have their own headers, their own frame size, and so on; thus, there would have to be a process to translate these completely different types of frames, just as you need a translator to translate English to Spanish or Russian to Japanese.

An additional problem to consider is how would an Ethernet station address a packet to a station that is non-Ethernet, or even determine what the non-Ethernet address was in the first place? All of these issues point to the need for a higher-layer protocol that can encapsulate the underlying Layer 2 frame, whether it's Ethernet, Frame-Relay, or something else. This protocol also needs a way to separate different Ethernet networks and create a boundary for Ethernet broadcasts. It needs a way to create hierarchical addressing and distribute addressing information across networks of an arbitrarily large size such as the Internet. This is exactly where Layer 3, the OSI network layer, enters the picture.

How Layer 3 Functions

One of the main functions of the network layer is to get the data compiled by the source to its destination or set of destinations, regardless of where this destination physically exists, via logical, hierarchical addressing. The network layer can be considered as the lowest layer in the TCP/OSI stack that is concerned with the end-to-end delivery of the application data. In this context, *end-to-end* means that IP is the first layer that can deliver information from any IP-capable device to any other IP-capable device, regardless of the underlying Layer 2 technologies. As mentioned earlier, it would be very difficult for an Ethernet device to deliver information to a non-Ethernet capable device, but not so for IP.

IP achieves this with the help of unique, logical addressing and with a standard set of protocols to aid in the dissemination of these addresses throughout the network and the forwarding of the data based on the addressing scheme. As previously mentioned, the network layer also functions to separate out various broadcast domains to prevent broadcasts from overwhelming your network. It does this by ensuring that a broadcast on one Ethernet network or VLAN is not forwarded to another unrelated network or VLAN. Put simply, Ethernet broadcasts are contained within an Ethernet segment and are not propagated "up" the protocol stack to the network or higher layers.

Devices that prevent these broadcasts from propagating from one Ethernet segment to another and use Layer 3 (L3) logical addressing to move data across a network are called *routers*. Routers inspect the L3 information, consult an L3 address forwarding table, and then forward data out through the right interface based on the forwarding table. The L3 addressing is a logical address that can be changed depending on the addressing plan. It is unlike a physical address (Ethernet MAC address) that is permanently programmed in the firmware.

An L3 address is unique and is used to identify all devices on the Internet. The addressing is based on a centralized plan, and the address distribution is controlled by a global authority known as the *Internet Assigned Numbers Authority* (IANA). The reason for this control of addresses is to ensure that every Internet device has a unique address. This unique addressing ensures that data is delivered properly from a source to its correct destination no matter where in the world the devices are located.

 Note that there are exceptions to the concept of unique addressing, which will be discussed in later chapters.

In order to properly forward packets based on L3 addressing, routers need a way to build a forwarding table of these addresses, just as Ethernet switches had to build a FDB table of L2 addresses. With routers this is accomplished through the use of a "routing protocol" that allows a router to automatically build up entries in the forwarding table for L3 addressing. Routers consult this table when receiving an L3 packet to decide which physical interface to send this data out of.

In addition to unique addressing and data forwarding, the network layer can get involved in *marking* the datagram specific to the application. This is to ensure differential treatment on the outbound packet by intermediate routers. This marking is what allows for different types of network traffic to be prioritized and forwarded differentially by intermediate routers and is a key component of quality of service (QoS) offerings by providers.

Layer 3 and Internet Protocol

By far the most widely used L3 protocol is the Internet Protocol (IP). The Internet Protocol (RFC 791) provides services that are roughly equivalent to the OSI network layer. IP provides a datagram (connectionless) transport service across a network. This service is sometimes referred to as *unreliable* because the protocol does not guarantee delivery or notify the end-host system about packets that are lost because of errors or network congestion. Note that this does not mean that IP is *unreliable* in the traditional sense of the term; it does not mean that IP drops large numbers of packets. It simply means that the IP layer does not itself worry about packet loss, but instead it relies on upper-layer protocols such as the Transmission Control Protocol (TCP) to handle re-transmissions in the event of dropped packets.

As an example of a situation that requires IP, examine the networks in Figure 5.1. The IP protocol is required in the figure because the physical networks connected to the user PCs are different between locations. One of the networks is ATM, one is Packet Over Sonet (POS), and one is Ethernet. It would be very difficult, if not impossible, for a simple L2 switch to handle transmission of a frame from one end-host to another in this scenario. With IP, the task becomes almost trivial.

Figure 5.1 There are end-hosts on ATM that need to communicate with hosts on Ethernet over a POS backbone. This situation requires IP routers to transfer the information from one L2 network to another.

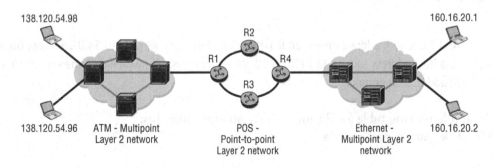

The IP layer is required to direct the data from the source PC to the destination PC in any direction. The routers play an important role in forwarding information based on the IP layer. The physical switches, which are TDM/ATM/POS or Ethernet-based, are only concerned with directing the user data to their nearest router. The routers inspect the IP information and direct the data out of the appropriate interface based on its IP address.

An example of how IP packets are forwarded may be useful at this point. The data composed on one of the PCs on the left in Figure 5.1 will have a source IP of 138.120.54.98 (we will explain the IP address later in this chapter) and a destination IP address of 160.16.20.1, the address of a host on the right in Figure 5.1. Since the destination IP address is not part of the local IP network, when data is sent out of the PC, it is sent to the router attached directly to the Layer 2 (ATM) switch by means of standard Layer 2 (ATM) forwarding, which we have previously discussed. The router R1 then has to make a choice and send the data out of one of its directly connected interfaces to either router R2 or R3. R2 and R3, in turn, will have to forward the packet out of their respective interfaces to R4 and then on to the Ethernet network.

For R1 to send the data out of the correct interface, it must have the knowledge to do so. This knowledge is created using routing protocols that run on all the routers involved to create the L3 forwarding table, also known as a *routing table*. In Figure 5.1, Routers R1–R4 will run the same routing protocol. Routing tables are constructed on every router using the routing protocols, and it is these tables that are referenced when the incoming data has to be forwarded out of the right interface.

Routing tables typically contain at a minimum the L3 network and the physical interface on the current router that is associated to the Layer 3 network. It is also common to have a "next-hop" entry for the network that lists the next router that will receive the packet.

 An L3 network address means an IP network address such as 138.120.54.0/24 as opposed to a host address such as 138.120.54.98. We will discuss this much more when we discuss IP address subnetting.

A sample routing table for R1 might have an entry like this:
```
R1# show router route-table
```

```
===============================================================================
Route Table (Router: Base)
===============================================================================
Dest Prefix                                 Type    Proto   Age        Pref
    Next Hop[Interface Name]                                 Metric
-------------------------------------------------------------------------------
160.16.20.0/24                              Local   Local   01d10h28m  0
    POStoR4                                                  0
```

```
----------------------------------------------------------------------
No. of Routes: 1
======================================================================

R1#
```

A sample entry for R4 might look like this:

```
R4# show router route-table


======================================================================
Route Table (Router: Base)
======================================================================
Dest Prefix                             Type    Proto    Age         Pref
      Next Hop[Interface Name]                           Metric
----------------------------------------------------------------------
160.16.20.0/24                          Local   Local    01d10h28m   0
      Ethernet                                               0
----------------------------------------------------------------------
No. of Routes: 1
======================================================================

R4#
```

The routers use these entries to keep forwarding packets based on the L3 addressing until the packet gets to a router that is *local* to the destination, meaning that it is on the same local network segment as the end station (e.g., the same Ethernet segment). Once the packet reaches the local router, the packet is then forwarded to the end-station using Ethernet framing and forwarding methods discussed in earlier chapters.

In the next section, we discuss the structure of an IP packet, its unique fields, and how they are used to assist with the addressing and forwarding functions.

5.2 The IP Header

Just as with Ethernet frames, there is a header for IP packets that contains very specific and important fields. Unlike the simplicity of the Ethernet header, however, there are numerous fields in an IP header. These fields provide important functionality to the IP layer that is not available to Ethernet. The IP header is shown in Figure 5.2, and the description of these fields follows.

Figure 5.2 An IP packet header. This header is for version 4 of IP; IP version 6 has a different header, but it is not yet in widespread use.

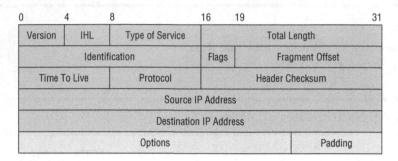

IP Header Fields

- **Version**—Always set this to the value 4, which is the current version of IP. (Note that there is a current version 6, but it is not yet in wide deployment. Version 6 IP has a different header.)

- **IHL (IP Header Length)**—A 4-bit field that contains the number of binary words (a *word* is 32 bits or 4 bytes) forming the header, usually five. This field is required because an IP packet can have options that increase the size of the header from 20 octets (bytes) up to a maximum of 60 octets (bytes). 60 bytes is the maximum because with a 4-bit field, the maximum value is $2^3 + 2^2 + 2^1 + 2^0 = 8 + 4 + 2 + 1 = 15$, and 15×4 bytes (*word*) = 60 bytes. The record route option can take up all 60 bytes when the recording router hops in a large network.

- **ToS (Type of Service)**—Also now known as *DSCP* (Differential Services Code Point). The ToS is an 8-bit field, usually set to 0, but that may indicate particular QoS needs from the network. The DSCP defines the way routers should queue packets while they are waiting to be forwarded and in some cases provides for packets to be forwarded along different paths based on priority.

- **Total Length**—A 16-bit field specifying the total length of the packet, including the header, in octets (bytes). The combined length of the header and the data can be at most 65,535 octets because this is the largest possible decimal number that can be described by 16 bits in binary.

- **Identification**—A 16-bit number that, together with the source address, uniquely identifies this packet; used during the reassembly of fragmented datagrams. IP allows an intermediate router to break apart an IP packet into smaller pieces in case a large packet needs to be forwarded over a network that supports only smaller packets. For example, a packet originating from an Ethernet network that might be 1,500 bytes may need to get forwarded over a PPP network that only supports frames 500 bytes in size. The ID field allows for packets to be broken up and then reassembled at the destination.

- **Flags**—Sequence of two flags (one of the 3 bits is unused) that controls whether routers are allowed to fragment a packet (i.e., the *Don't Fragment*, or DF, flag), and to indicate the parts of a packet to the receiver via the More Fragment (MF) flag.

- **Fragmentation Offset**—Offset from the start of the original sent packet, set by any router that performs IP fragmentation. Unused if fragmentation is not performed.

- **Time to Live (TTL)**—Number of hops/links that the packet may be routed over, decremented by most routers (used to prevent accidental routing loops). Recall our earlier discussion of Ethernet broadcast storms and how Ethernet frames can circulate forever because there is no mechanism to indicate to Ethernet switches that a frame should be discarded. The TTL field ensures that all IP packets have a limited lifetime.

- **Protocol**—An 8-bit field that indicates the type of transport data being carried (e.g., 6 = TCP, 17 = UDP).

- **Header Checksum**—This is a field for detecting errors in the IP header. The checksum is calculated by the transmitting router based on the contents of the IP header. It is calculated again by the receiver and compared with the value in the header. If they are different, the packet is discarded. The checksum is updated whenever the packet header is modified by a router (e.g., to decrement the TTL).

- **Source Address**—32-bit IP address of the original sender of the packet.

- **Destination Address**—32-bit IP address of the final destination of the packet.

- **Options**—Not normally used, but when used, the IP header length is greater than five 32-bit words to indicate the size of the options field. There are many options, but in modern networks most of them are no longer used. Originally one of the most common was the *strict source route* or *loose source route*. These options allowed for the sending station to specify to intermediate stations how the packet was to be routed. Modern routing protocols alleviate most of the need for these and other options. The padding field is used to make sure that the header ends on a 32-bit boundary in the event that options are used.

You should make sure that you become familiar with the fields of the IP header—especially the TTL, protocol, and addressing fields—and understand why they are needed. In the next section, we will begin an important discussion of IP addressing.

5.3 IP Addressing

An IPv4 (IP version 4) address is 32 bits long in binary format. It is normally expressed as four decimal numbers as a simpler representation for humans. Each decimal number is separated by a dot. This format is called *dotted-decimal notation*. The dotted-decimal format divides the 32-bit IP address into four octets of 8 bits each. These octets specify the value of each field as a decimal number, as shown in Figure 5.3. The range of each octet (byte) is from 0 to 255.

Figure 5.3 Routers represent IP addresses internally in binary format, while humans find it more convenient to use the decimal equivalent. Using the decimal version is fine, but there are operations that are performed on IP addresses that are best understood using binary.

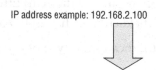

IP address example: 192.168.2.100

Binary equivalent: 11000000.10101000.00000010.01100100

Binary Addressing

When a novice is first introduced to the idea of binary addressing with IP, it is sometimes difficult to understand why the addresses are shown in binary when they can be just as easily represented in decimal, and decimal is what we humans are used to reading. The reason will make more sense once we get to IP address masking, but essentially the reason for discussing addressing in binary format is that it is much easier to determine what address a router is going to use when you examine the address the way the router sees it, and not as you might wish to see it. This allows you to perform the operation on the IP numbers the way the router performs the operations.

Routers are simply specialized computers, and computers work in and convert everything to binary. If you really want to understand IP addressing and how you can create subnets and use masks (topics to be discussed shortly), then it is essential that you take the time to understand the addressing in binary. It may seem like a lot of unnecessary work now, but the benefits of working the addressing in binary first and then converting to decimal will become apparent later in this chapter.

Examine Figure 5.3 in detail to see how the binary number shown equates to its decimal equivalent. The first important point is that both the binary and the decimal version of the address are not just a single number but, in fact, four separate numbers separated by a dot (.). Each part of the binary number is 8 bits, giving a total of a 32-bit address. Each bit in the binary number can be only a zero (0) or a one (1), equivalent to the "off" or "on" position of a circuit (this is why computers work in binary numbers). To convert a binary number to decimal, you raise the value 2 to the power of its position in the string 0 to 7, multiply it by 0 or 1 (whichever bit is in that position), and then add the resulting numbers.

 This is just like a decimal number, where 532 can be represented as 5 hundreds, 3 tens, and 2 ones as shown below:

Lowest position is furthest to the right = $2 \times 10^0 = 2 \times 1 = 2$

Next position (reading right to left) = $3 \times 10^1 = 3 \times 10 = 30$

Next position (reading right to left) = $5 \times 10^2 = 5 \times 100 = 500$

Adding these numbers gives you $2 + 30 + 500 = 532$.

Let's demonstrate using the example from Figure 5.3. The leftmost binary number is 11000000. The numbers are read from right to left, with the rightmost bit being the lowest value and the leftmost being the highest. This example can serve as a template for how you can calculate any number from any base. All numbers, regardless of the *base*—be it 10 (decimal) or 8 (hexadecimal) or 2 (binary)—can be calculated using this method.

In the examples that follow, we number the bits from left to right because that is how the number is naturally read, but remember that the lowest number is furthest on the right and the numbers increase in value going from right to left, just as in the decimal number 532, the 2 is the "ones" position, the 3 is in the "tens" position, and the 5 is in the "hundreds" position. When we say "n^{th} bit from left to right," this indicates that you read over n number of positions from left to right to find that bit position:

8th bit from left to right = 0 (value of the bit) $\times 2^0 = 0 \times 1 = 0$

7th bit from left to right = $0 \times 2^1 = 0 \times 2 = 0$

6th bit from left to right = $0 \times 2^2 = 0 \times 4 = 0$

5th bit from left to right = $0 \times 2^3 = 0 \times 8 = 0$

4th bit from left to right = $0 \times 2^4 = 0 \times 16 = 0$

3rd bit from left to right = $0 \times 2^5 = 0 \times 32 = 0$

2nd bit from left to right = $1 \times 2^6 = 1 \times 64 = 64$

1st bit from left to right = $1 \times 2^7 = 1 \times 128 = 128$

Adding all these numbers together (from right to left), you get $0 + 0 + 0 + 0 + 0 + 0 + 64 + 128 = 192$, which is, as indicated in Figure 5.3, the decimal equivalent for the first of the four dotted decimal numbers in the address. You can do the same thing for the other three octets to derive the decimal numbers from the binary. For the decimal number 168, the binary in Figure 5.3 is 10101000, calculated as:

8th bit from left to right = $0 \times 2^0 = 0 \times 1 = 0$

7th bit from left to right = $0 \times 2^1 = 0 \times 2 = 0$

6th bit from left to right = $0 \times 2^2 = 0 \times 4 = 0$

5th bit from left to right = $1 \times 2^3 = 1 \times 8 = 8$

4th bit from left to right = $0 \times 2^4 = 0 \times 16 = 0$

3rd bit from left to right = $1 \times 2^5 = 1 \times 32 = 32$

2nd bit from left to right = $0 \times 2^6 = 0 \times 64 = 0$

1st bit from left to right = $1 \times 2^7 = 1 \times 128 = 128$

Adding these numbers gives you $0 + 0 + 0 + 8 + 0 + 32 + 0 + 128 = 168$.

For the next dotted decimal position, the number is 2; this is derived from the binary 00000010:

8th bit from left to right = $0 \times 2^0 = 0 \times 1 = 0$

7th bit from left to right = $1 \times 2^1 = 1 \times 2 = 2$

6th bit from left to right = $0 \times 2^2 = 0 \times 4 = 0$

5th bit from left to right = $0 \times 2^3 = 0 \times 8 = 0$

4th bit from left to right = $0 \times 2^4 = 0 \times 16 = 0$

3rd bit from left to right = $0 \times 2^5 = 0 \times 32 = 0$

2nd bit from left to right = $0 \times 2^6 = 0 \times 64 = 0$

1st bit from left to right = $0 \times 2^7 = 0 \times 128 = 0$

Adding these numbers gives you $0 + 2 + 0 + 0 + 0 + 0 + 0 + 0 = 2$.

The final octet in the dotted decimal address is 100, derived from the binary 01100100:

8th bit from left to right = $0 \times 2^0 = 0 \times 1 = 0$

7th bit from left to right = $0 \times 2^1 = 0 \times 2 = 0$

6th bit from left to right = $1 \times 2^2 = 1 \times 4 = 4$

5th bit from left to right = $0 \times 2^3 = 0 \times 8 = 0$

4th bit from left to right = $0 \times 2^4 = 0 \times 16 = 0$

3rd bit from left to right = $1 \times 2^5 = 1 \times 32 = 32$

2nd bit from left to right = $1 \times 2^6 = 1 \times 64 = 64$

1st bit from left to right = $0 \times 2^7 = 0 \times 128 = 0$

Adding these numbers gives you $0 + 0 + 4 + 0 + 0 + 32 + 64 + 0 = 100$.

We now have all the decimal equivalents for the binary. Looking back, we now have 192 and then 168 and then 2 and then 100. Putting them together in dotted decimal, we get 192.168.2.100, which, as you can see, is the dotted decimal number from Figure 5.3.

This example should give you a feeling for how to calculate the decimal equivalent of a binary number, and it will serve you well to remember that the router is going to perform all its calculations based on the binary number and not its decimal equivalent. Later in this chapter, you will see why it is important to think in terms of binary and not decimal for certain operations.

A few more words on binary are important before moving on. First, you should become familiar with the most common 8-bit addressing numbers. If there is a 1 in every bit position for an 8-bit number (11111111), this would lead to a decimal value of $1 + 2 + 4 + 8 + 16 + 32 + 64 + 128 = 255$. You will see this number 255 or the *all ones* number again and again in this chapter. Another point is that once you know the decimal equivalents of each bit position, it is fairly easy to calculate from decimal to binary.

For example, if the decimal number is 128, it should be clear that this is a 1 in the highest bit position, and 0s in all the other positions like this: 10000000. Similarly, if the decimal number is 64, then this is a 1 in the second highest bit position, and 0s in all the other positions like this: 010000000, and so forth. You can also combine numbers to easily come up with the binary number; for example, the decimal 96 is easily calculated as 64 + 32 or 01100000.

One other important point is that routers often perform Boolean operations on the binary numbers. A Boolean operation is simply a logical operation such as an AND or an OR. In Boolean operations, you can think of a 0 as "false" and a 1 as "true," so that, for example, 0 (false) AND 1 (true) = 0 (false) (an AND operation requires everything to be 1 (true) in order for the operation to be true). Similarly, 1 (true) and 1 (true) = 1 (true).

You don't have to become a Boolean expert to work with IP addresses, just remember that 0 AND 1 = 0 and 1 AND 1 = 1, and you should be able to perform all the necessary operations. Now let's continue with a discussion of the parts of an IP address. When IP addressing was first envisioned, addresses were divided up into different types or *classes* of addresses. We will first examine how this approach worked and then discuss the more modern "classless" addressing approach.

Class-Based IP Addressing

The first part of an IP address identifies the network that a host will reside in. This is sometimes called a network *prefix*, much as an area or country code for a phone number might be called a prefix. The second part of an IP address identifies an individual host inside that network.

This creates a two-level hierarchy, as shown in Figure 5.4. All hosts in a given network share the same network prefix. However, the host numbers must be unique to each host. Conversely, hosts with different network prefixes may share the same host number. This is exactly like a phone number. Two people in the same area code cannot have the same phone number, but two people in different area codes can. The size of the network/host portions can be adjusted, as will be shown later in the chapter.

Figure 5.4 With class-based addressing, IP addresses have two parts: a network number or prefix and a host number.

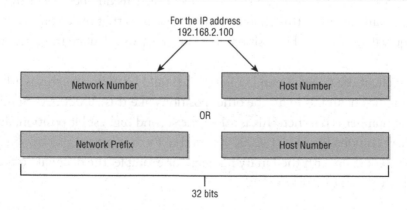

Recall that IP addressing follows a global plan and that IP addresses have to be registered with a central authority—the IANA. When addresses were first being assigned by the IANA, it was decided that to provide some form of flexibility to support the various sizes of networks that were being implemented, the IP address space should be divided into classes. The classes were defined as Class A, Class B, and Class C. This is referred to as *classful addressing* because the address space is split into predefined sizes. As shown in Figure 5.5, each class defines the boundary between the network and host at a different octet within the 32-bit address.

Figure 5.5 With class-based addressing, the first 3 bits of the first octet of the address determine how many bits were allocated for the network and how many for the host.

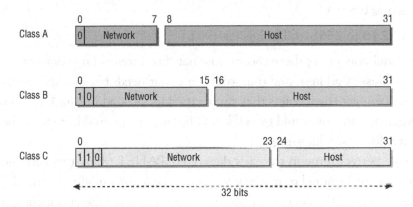

- **Class A (1 to 126)**—A Class A network has an 8-bit network prefix and, as shown in Figure 5.5, the highest-order bit is always set to 0, so the first octet always looks like 0*xxxxxxx*, where *x* can be either 0 or 1. This allows for a maximum of 128 networks that can be defined; however, two of the 128 networks are reserved. The 0.0.0.0 network is reserved for default routes, and the 127.0.0.0 network is reserved for loopback functions.

- **Class B (128 to 191)**—A Class B network has a 16-bit network prefix, and, as shown in Figure 5.5, the two highest-order bits are always set to 10 like 10*xxxxxx*, where *x* can be either 0 or 1. A maximum of 16,384 networks can be defined; the first 2 bits of the first octet MUST be 10, leaving 6 bits in the first octet that can be either 0 or 1. The next octet is also part of the network address (remember that it is a 16-bit prefix), which gives you another 8 bits that can be whatever value you want. Adding the 6 bits not reserved from the first octet with the 8 bits not reserved from the second octet gives you 14 bits that can be any value. Since each of the 14 bits can be either 0 or 1, that gives us $2^{14} = 16,384$ different possible networks.

- **Class C (192 to 223)**—A Class C network has a 24-bit network prefix, and, as shown in Figure 5.5, the three highest-order bits are always set to 110 like 110*xxxxx*. A maximum of 2,097,152 networks can be defined. The 2,097,152 number is similarly derived from the fact that you have 21 bits that can be any value (a 24-bit network prefix minus the first 3 bits that are required to be 110), which gives you $2^{21} = 2,097,152$.

- **Class D (224 to 239)**—Class D is used for multicast addresses (used in applications such as OSPF).

- **Class E (240 to 255)**—Class E is reserved.

The original concept of these classes was that if you were a large organization, you would get a Class A address, and that would suit your needs because you would have lots of hosts (you get three octets that can be used for host addressing). If you were a smaller organization, you would get a Class C because you would have fewer hosts (you get one octet for host addressing).

This made perfect sense in the early days of ARPANET when it was envisioned that perhaps a few hundred or maybe a thousand companies might ever need IP addressing. However, the concept of classes never envisioned the enormous growth of the Internet into the millions of hosts it has today. Many of the addressing problems of the modern Internet can be traced back to this early classification of the IP address space.

For example, an organization might only need a few Class Bs worth of IP addressing if they design their network properly, but they might have an entire Class A address space, and no other company can use those addresses because they were assigned to a specific company. Additionally, many modern networks are situated behind firewalls or other devices that hide the company's real addresses anyway, so even the largest global companies might need only a dozen or so addresses out of a possible 16M+ IP addresses that they could use (24 bits of host addressing for a Class A yields $2^{24} = 16,777,216$ possible host addresses).

The use of IP addressing in a haphazard way led to a crisis in the 1990s as ISPs began to run out of IP addresses to give to their customers, and it appeared that IPv4 had reached the end of its useful life. However, re-addressing measures and the abolition of the class-based addressing approach gave IPv4 new life but made the addressing schemes a bit more complicated, as we shall see. But first, let's take a look at some IP addressing examples to see how this works under the traditional classful approach.

In Figure 5.6, each router is connected to two or three networks via two or three interfaces. Every interface is identified by an IP address. The interfaces in the same network belong to the same network prefix or network class.

Figure 5.6 An example of five networks using different classes of addressing. Under classful IP addressing, the network portion and the host portion of the address are known based on the first octet of each address, that is, 192, 10, 172.

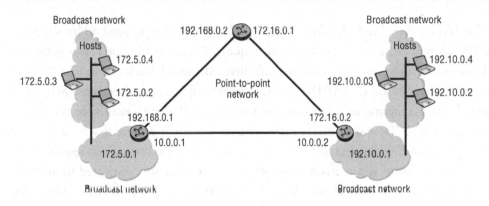

There are five classful networks in Figure 5.6:

In Class C: 192.168.0.0
            192.10.0.0

In Class B: 172.5.0.0
            172.16.0.0

In Class A: 10.0.0.0

This classful addressing made it simple to determine what portion of the address was for hosts, but it was very restrictive. It was also very wasteful, and it led to a depletion of available addressing. As the use of firewalls and Internet proxies became more prevalent, the need for each host in an organization to have an IP address that was routable on the Internet diminished. As a result of these developments, the IANA set aside certain ranges of IP addressing as *private*. These addresses are ranges that can be used by any organization, but they are not routable on the public Internet.

The creation of private addressing created an address space that is divided into two types: public address space and private address space. Understanding the difference is important and useful for a network administrator, especially if your organization is connected to the Internet. All of the *public address space* IP addresses are routable via the Internet and are managed by one of the three Regional Internet Registries (RIRs). Each RIR is responsible for a geographic region.

 Don't confuse RIRs with the Internet's Network Information Center, InterNIC, at www.internic.net and its designated registrars, such as Network Solutions, Inc. They handle *domain name* registration, not *address* registration.

The IANA distributes IP addresses to the RIRs. You must request address space, and IANA will either grant or deny your request. Alternatively, you can request the address space from your ISP [who then, in turn, allocates from its American Registry of Internet Numbers (ARIN)–allotted address space or makes the request on your behalf]. Receiving an address space from your ISP is the much more common approach as it obviates the need to try to obtain your own address space. In practice, if an organization is connected to a single provider, there is little if any reason for it to have its own address space. Even those organizations that are connected to multiple providers can usually get adequate functionality by using each provider's address space and load-balancing across each provider's network.

This system preserves address space and provides a central authority to prevent address-space collisions. When you are using a public address, you can send to and receive from all (unbroken) parts of the Internet. This means that all routers on the Internet know how to route data to your IP address. Because of this, not all address space is *portable*. If you own your address space, you can authorize an ISP to route it for you, but there is a chance that when you change providers or locations, it will no longer be possible to route your IP addresses to the new location. (You might, therefore, want to check before you travel with your address space.)

This is so because providers typically like to advertise and receive only large blocks of address space to prevent Internet routing tables from being overwhelmed. If every device on the Internet could move to any provider at will, then the Internet routing tables would become extremely large and inefficient, resulting in an unstable environment for every user. For customers who might want to change providers, the use of private addresses assists this process while still maintaining Internet routing stability.

Private IP Addressing

The IANA has reserved the following three blocks of IP address space for private intranets (local networks):

- 10.0.0.0 to 10.255.255.255
- 172.16.0.0 to 172.31.255.255
- 192.168.0.0 to 192.168.255.255

Any organization can use these private addresses in whatever way they want; they just cannot advertise them on the Internet or expect to send or receive traffic from other organizations using these addresses. These addresses are *private* and are expected to remain within a particular organization. It is quite common to find most customers using one or multiple of these address ranges in their internal network, performing an address translation function to map these private addresses to public addresses for communicating to other devices on the Internet.

In addition, IP addresses in the range of 169.254.0.0 to 169.254.255.255 are reserved for automatic private IP addressing. These IP addresses should not be used on the Internet. If you see an inbound packet to your network with a source address in the private range, it is either a configuration error on the sending device or an attempt by an attacker to obfuscate the origin of the sending device. A packet with a destination address in this range cannot be forwarded, so any incoming packets from this source are essentially a dead end, and the message cannot be returned. (Your provider would drop the packet because there would not be a destination for a private address range in its routing table.)

Types of IP Addresses

As with Ethernet addressing, there are three unique types of IP addressing: unicast, broadcast, and multicast. *Unicast address* refers to a specific IP address. A packet sent from a source to a specific destination address is referred to as a *unicast packet*. This packet is delivered to a single host or a single interface on the router; for example,

139.120.200.25 is a single host. Figure 5.7 illustrates a unicast packet being delivered to a single host across the network.

Figure 5.7 Unicast packets are delivered to a single host, usually along a single path through the network.

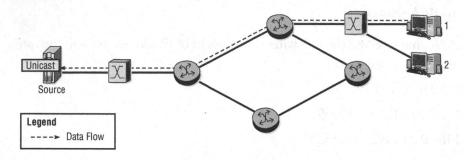

Broadcast address refers to all IP addresses in the broadcast domain. A packet sent from a source to all hosts in a broadcast domain (such as Ethernet) is referred to as a *broadcast packet*. The destination IP address in the update contains the network number and all 1s for the host address. For example, 138.120.255.255 specified in the destination IP header of a packet ensures that the packet will be delivered to all hosts in the 138.120.0.0 network. (The 255.255 part means *all hosts*.) Figure 5.8 illustrates a broadcast packet being flooded out to every host on the network.

Figure 5.8 A broadcast packet sent on a network segment will be sent to every host.

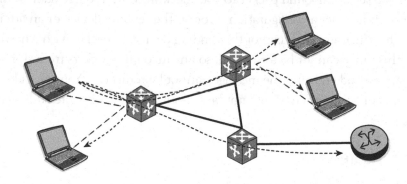

The multicast range of addresses is reserved for group membership applications. Multicast technology is an efficient way to deliver traffic to a group of destinations that want to receive that particular traffic. The group of destinations is characterized by an IP address in the multicast range of 239.0.0.0–239.255.255.255 that defines membership in that particular group. An example is broadcast TV service. When a host wants to receive traffic for a certain channel, it uses a group membership protocol for that channel identified by a multicast range address—239.1.1.1, for instance. Multicast routing protocols route traffic from its source to the various hosts that require the traffic. Figure 5.9 illustrates how multicast packets can be forwarded to various hosts throughout the network that are members of a particular multicast group.

Figure 5.9 Routers and switches can listen for multicast updates and build forwarding tables based on this information. In this way, multicasts can be forwarded to only those network segments and hosts that are members of a multicast group. In the figure, only Hosts 1, 6, and 3 will receive the multicast packets from the source.

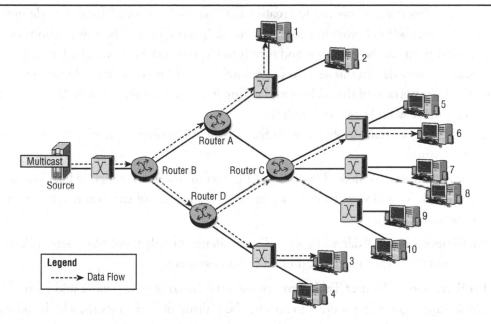

A final type of IP address is an anycast. An *anycast address* is created simply: You assign the same unicast address to two or more hosts. In theory, such hosts are functionally equivalent, and you would want to route packets to the "nearest" host. This works well in applications such as distributed websites. With the aid of dynamic routing protocols, the packets can find the nearest host, and in case that host is not available, traffic will be routed to the next nearest host.

5.4 IP Subnetting

Now that we have covered the basics of IP addressing, it's time to examine how a given IP address can be broken down into smaller networks. From the discussion so far, you have seen that the original classful addressing specified which part of the IP address was the network and which part was the host. For example, using classful addressing, the address 172.16.20.1 means network 172.16 and host 20.1 (172 is between 128 and 191).

This means that you could have up to 65,536 hosts (2^{16}) on this network. However, what if you needed more networks, and fewer hosts per network? After all, it is not typical to need 65K hosts on one network. This is where the concept of *subnetting* comes in. Subnetting allows you to create additional "subnetworks" from a single network, with each subnet providing for fewer hosts. Essentially, you borrow portions of the address from the host portion and give it to the network portion. The formula for this magic is revealed in this section (*hint*: it relies on using some of the binary bits from the host portion of the address and giving it to the network portion. See, we told you that binary would come in handy!)

There are three main problems with the classful addressing approach that we have been discussing:

- **Lack of Internal Address Flexibility**—Big organizations are assigned large, monolithic blocks of addresses that do not match the structure of their underlying internal networks well.

- **Inefficient Use of Address Space**—The existence of only three block sizes (Classes A, B, and C) leads to waste of limited IP address space.

- **Proliferation of Router Table Entries**—As the Internet grows, more and more entries are required for routers to handle the routing of IP datagrams, which causes performance problems for routers. Attempting to reduce inefficient address space allocation can lead to even more router table entries.

As shown in Figure 5.10, these problems were resolved by adding another layer of hierarchy to the addressing structure. Instead of being a simple two-level hierarchy that defines the network prefix and host number, a third level was introduced that defines a subnet number.

Figure 5.10 The use of subnetting allows you to "borrow" bits from the host portion of the classful address and use the data to create subnets of the primary network. Each of the subnets can contain a smaller number of hosts since there are fewer host bits available.

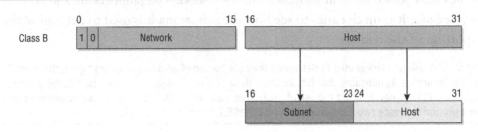

Adding a third level allowed network administrators the flexibility to manage their current network address in a manner that best suited their needs by assigning a distinct subnet number for each of their internal networks.

Identifying an IP Subnet

This immediately raises the question: How does one identify the subnet portion of a network? The answer is, through subnet masking. A *subnet mask* is a 32-bit binary number that accompanies an IP address. The mask "shadows" the IP address, and each bit in the mask corresponds to a complementary bit in the IP address. The mask is created so that it has 1 bit for each corresponding bit of the IP address that is part of its network ID or subnet ID, and a 0 for each bit of the IP address's host ID. Essentially, a binary *1* in the mask says "network or subnet ID" and a binary *0* says "host ID."

The actual operation is a logical AND of the bits in the host IP and the bits in the mask. The AND function is a Boolean logic operation that we previously mentioned. Recall that a Boolean AND amounts to just this: 1 AND 1 = 1, 1 AND 0 = 0. A mask always consists then of 1s for the network portion and 0s for the host portion. The mask thus tells TCP/IP devices which bits in the IP address belong to the network ID and subnet ID, and which are part of the host ID.

Here's an example to illustrate this concept. The subnet mask of 255.255.255.128 (or 11111111.11111111.11111111.10000000 in binary) has been chosen arbitrarily in Figure 5.11 and is applied to the IP address of 192.168.2.132, which is traditionally a Class C address. This subnet mask splits the Class C network of 192.168.2.0 into two subnetworks, each with 127 hosts. Note that 255 means "all 1s" in binary (recall this from our previous binary discussion). Also note that all addresses and masks are shown in binary. From our earlier example, you should be able to convert each of the binary addresses into dotted decimal addresses and vice versa. The numbers are shown in binary because it is much easier to see how the subnet mask is used to determine the host portion of the address.

Figure 5.11 A subnet mask is used to determine the host portion of an address. In this figure, there are 25 bits in the subnet mask, indicating that bits 26 through 32 (7 bits) are available for hosts. 192.168.2.0 would normally be a Class C network, but the use of the subnet mask indicates 1 bit (the 25th bit) is borrowed from the host portion to create two additional subnets: 192.168.2.0 and 192.168.2.128.

IP address	11000000.10101000.00000010.10000100
	LOGICAL AND
Subnet mask	11111111.11111111.11111111.10000000
	equals
Subnetwork	11000000.10101000.00000010.10000000
	192.168.2.128
Network Class C	192.168.2.0
Subnetwork	192.168.2.128
Host range	192.168.2.129 to 192.168.2.254

Note that without the mask, we would assume that 192.168.2.128 means "network 192.168.2.0" and that hosts 192.168.2.1 through 192.168.2.254 are all on the same network. With the mask 255.255.255.128, we know that there are two subnets because the leftmost bit in the fourth octet of the mask ($2^7 = 128$) has been "borrowed" from being a possible host bit to create two additional subnetworks—192.168.2.0 (giving hosts 0–127) and 192.168.2.128 (giving hosts 129–254). Figure 5.12 illustrates how these different subnets are created.

Notice in Figure 5.12 that the last octet now has 7 bits available for hosts because the leftmost bit has been used to create two subnets (the bit can be either 1 or 0, so two possible conditions means two subnets). Since there are 7 bits left and each bit has two possible values, the number of hosts available is then $2^7 = 128$. Note that to calculate the number of hosts or networks available, you just use the formula 2^n, where n is the number of bits available.

If the subnet is 192.168.2.0 (the leftmost bit in the last octet is 0), then the host address range is 1 (binary 00000001) up to 127 (binary 01111110). Binary 01111111 would be the "all 1s" or broadcast address for that subnet and therefore cannot be used for a host. Similarly, if the subnet is 192.168.2.128 (the leftmost bit in the last octet is

$1 = 2^7 = 128$), then the host address range is 129 (binary 10000001) up to 254 (binary 11111110). Again, binary 11111111 would be the "all 1s" or the broadcast address for that subnet and cannot be used for a host.

Figure 5.12 Using the subnet mask of 25 bits allows you to split the 192.168.2.0 network into two subnets that support 7 bits of host addressing instead of one network that supports 8 bits of host addressing. This is the essence of subnetting: It allows you to use portions of the address that would normally be used for host addresses to create additional subnetworks.

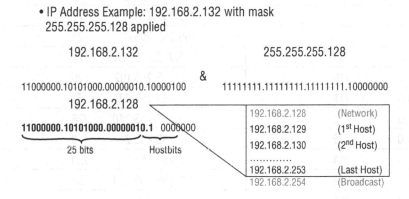

An IP address is always associated with a subnet mask. For example:

- IP:192.168.2.132 with a subnet mask of 255.255.255.128
- IP:192.168.2.132 with a subnet mask of 255.255.255.0

Another notation for subnet masking is using /x, where x represents the number of 1s in the subnet mask:

- 255.255.255.0 can be referred to as /24, as in 24 1s.
- 255.255.255.128 can be referred to as /25, as in 25 1s.
- IP:192.168.2.132/24 implies a subnet mask of 255.255.255.0.

This use of a number to indicate the mask is much less cumbersome than writing out the address and is a very common representation of an IP address and its associated mask. People will often refer to these as "24-bit mask" or "16-bit mask" and the like, so you should definitely be familiar with this representation and terminology.

The following table shows all possible subnet masks. You should be able to determine the binary equivalent from any of these based on our previous discussion.

Subnet Mask	/x Notation	Subnet mask	/x Notation
128.0.0.0	/1	255.255.128.0	/17
192.0.0.0	/2	255.255.192.0	/18
224.0.0.0	/3	255.255.224.0	/19
240.0.0.0	/4	255.255.240.0	/20
248.0.0.0	/5	255.255.248.0	/21
252.0.0.0	/6	255.255.252.0	/22
254.0.0.0	/7	255.255.254.0	/23
255.0.0.0	/8	255.255.255.0	/24
255.128.0.0	/9	255.255.255.128	/25
255.192.0.0	/10	255.255.255.192	/26
255.224.0.0	/11	255.255.255.224	/27
255.240.0.0	/12	255.255.255.240	/28
255.248.0.0	/13	255.255.255.248	/29
255.252.0.0	/14	255.255.255.252	/30
255.254.0.0	/15	255.255.255.254	/31
255.255.0.0	/16		

The assigned host address field of a subnet cannot contain all 0s or all 1s. The host number of all 0s is reserved for the network address, while the host number of all 1s is reserved for the broadcast address for that network or subnet. In Figure 5.13, 5 bits are used for the host address field. Using the formula of $32 - 2 = 30$, there are 30 assignable host addresses in this subnet. This means that each of the subnets that were created can support a maximum of 30 hosts. Using this decimal shortcut is fine, provided you understand how this number was derived from the binary. Using 5 bits yields $2^5 = 32$ possible host addresses. You then subtract the 0 host (00000) and the "all 1s" subnet broadcast (11111), giving you $32 - 2 = 30$ possible hosts for each subnet.

As illustrated in Figure 5.13, defining the host address for the tenth host in the subnet is relatively simple: You simply take the host bits and place them in the bit pattern that represents decimal 10 or binary 01010. This gives the host address of 192.168.1.10/27. If one of the other subnets is used (e.g., 192.168.1.96/27), defining the host address is a little more difficult; however, the concept remains the same.

Figure 5.13 Using a /27 means 27 bits are used for the subnet mask. This leaves 5 bits for the hosts on each subnet. Notice that it is easy to see what the hosts are when using binary, but it can be confusing trying to determine it in decimal.

Host address 0 192.168.1.0/27   11000000.10101000.00000001.00000000 **All 0 host**
Host address 1 192.168.1.1/27   11000000.10101000.00000001.00000001
Host address 2 192.168.1.2/27   11000000.10101000.00000001.00000010

....

Host address 29 192.168.1.29/27   11000000.10101000.00000001.00011101
Host address 30 192.168.1.30/27   11000000.10101000.00000001.00011110
Host address 31 192.168.1.31/27   11000000.10101000.00000001.00011111 **All 1 host**

Example:
Find all hosts in subnet address	192.168.1.96/27	
Total number of hosts	30	
First host	192.168.1.96 + 1/27	192.168.1.97/27
Tenth host	192.168.1.96 + 10/27	192.168.1.106/27
Last host	192.168.1.96 + 30/27	192.168.1.126/27
Broadcast address	192.168.1.96 + 31/27	192.168.1.127/27

Given a subnet address of 192.168.1.96/27 to define the tenth host address, the host bits are once again arranged in the bit pattern that represents decimal 10 or binary 01010. This is then added to the network prefix of 192.168.1.96/27 to give the host address of 192.168.1.106/27. To define the broadcast address for this network, the host bits would be all set to 1 or 11111. This is the binary representation of 31, so 31 would be added to the network address of 192.168.1.96, giving a broadcast address of 192.168.1.127/27 for this particular subnet.

As always, we recommend that you try to use the binary numbers when doing these exercises; it is easier to differentiate between the host and the network at the bit level.

IP Subnet Address Planning

As previously mentioned, class-based addressing is now obsolete and is very seldom used. Subnetting is very common for IPv4 addresses, and all modern routing protocols include the subnet mask as part of the route update. Because any subnet mask can be applied to any IP address, a network address can be referred to by a prefix with a subnet mask. For example, Class A IP address 10.0.0.0 can be referred to as *10.0.0.0/8*, where 8 is a subnet mask of 255.0.0.0, or network *10.0.0.0/16*, where 16 implies a subnet mask of 255.255.0.0. Similarly, an IP address of 138.120.24.253/25 has an extended network prefix of 138.120.24.128 (the first bit of the last octet is borrowed from the host portion to create two subnets, 138.120.24.0 and 138.120.24.128).

Routers use the network prefix of the destination IP address to route the traffic to a subnetted environment. Routers in the subnetted environment use the extended network prefix to route traffic between the individual subnets. The extended network prefix is a combination of the network prefix and the subnet number. The extended network prefix was originally defined by the subnet mask as described previously. When the bits in the subnet mask are set to 1, the router examining the address treats the corresponding bits in the destination IP address as part of the network address. The bits in the subnet mask that are set to 0 define the host portion of the address.

In the configuration of most modern routers, the extended network prefix can be represented by a decimal number that indicates the length of the subnet mask, as shown previously. This number represents the number of contiguous 1s in the subnet mask. It should be understood that this concept of representing the prefix length with a decimal number is strictly for the convenience of the user. The protocol still carries the four-octet subnet mask in its actual routing updates (and it is still converted to binary before being processed).

The purpose of all of this discussion of subnetting is not just to give you a background of what subnetting is, but ultimately to allow you to create your own IP addressing plan based on a given set of requirements. Like most endeavors, success in distributing IP addresses requires a plan. An addressing plan requires especially careful planning and consideration for future requirements. The network administrator cannot just look at the existing infrastructure in the assignment of addresses, but must also take into account future growth of hosts of all the subnets as well as future growth in the number of subnets that will be required.

The first planning step is to define the number of subnets that are required. In Figure 5.14, there is a requirement for nine subnets; therefore, using 3 host bits to create $2^3 = 8$ subnets would not meet the requirement. To meet this requirement, the administrator must use 4 host bits to create $2^4 = 16$ subnets. This now leaves room for future expansion.

The next step is to ensure that there is enough host space available to meet the requirements of the largest subnet. If the largest subnet requires 35 hosts, a $2^6 = 64$ host space must be used (6 bits must be reserved for hosts). Recall from our earlier discussion of "shortcuts" that you could have known this just by remembering that $2^5 = 32$, so 5 bits would not be enough. This size would also leave room for expansion because you can have up to $64 - 2 = 62$ hosts on each subnet, which is more than the required 35.

Figure 5.14 When planning a subnet design, you need to know how many subnets are required now and plan for a little future growth. The requirement here is for nine subnets, which means that at least 4 bits are needed because using 3 host bits would only yield eight subnets. You also need to know how many hosts will be needed on each subnet.

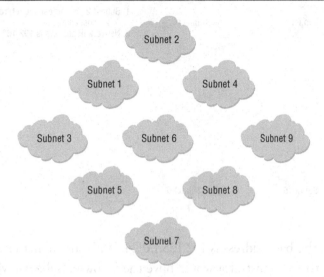

After the design is completed, the administrator must ensure that the organization's allocated IP address space is sufficient to meet current as well as future needs. First, the administrator must identify the bits required to provide the six needed subnets. Because the address is a binary address, the boundaries for the subnets are based on the power of 2.

In Figure 5.15, the administrator would require 3 bits of the existing host address to provide the necessary subnets: $2^3 = 8$ available subnets. This would give the subnets an extended prefix of 27 bits. The four-octet subnet mask would appear as 255.255.255.224 (the binary equivalent would be 11111111.11111111.11111111.11100000). Notice how the last octet in binary clearly shows the 3 bits borrowed from hosts to create the needed subnets.

Borrowing 3 out of 8 bits to create subnets would leave 5 bits of the last octet for host addresses. The calculation for usable or assignable host addresses as we have seen is $2^n - 2$, or in this case, $2^5 - 2$. Again, the reason why two host addresses must be subtracted from the total is because the host address 00000 (all 0s) is reserved for the network address and the host address of 11111 (all 1s) is reserved for the broadcast address of the subnet.

Figure 5.15 The goal is to subnet IP network 192.168.1.0/24 into at least 6 subnets, and ensure that each subnet has at least 20 host IP addresses.

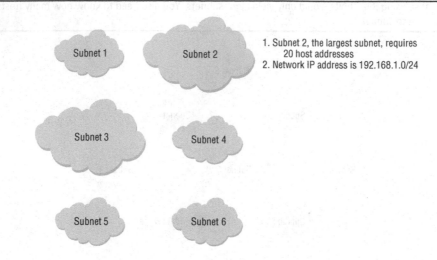

1. Subnet 2, the largest subnet, requires 20 host addresses
2. Network IP address is 192.168.1.0/24

In Figure 5.15, the base address is 192.168.1.0/24. With the subnet extended prefix we have defined, the administrator would have the following subnets, with each subnet supporting 30 hosts:

192.168.1.0/27	192.168.1.32/27	192.168.1.64/27
192.168.1.96/27	192.168.1.128/27	192.168.1.160/27
192.168.1.192/27	192.168.1.224/27	

The "/31" subnet mask is a special subnet mask where there are no network/broadcast addresses. In this case, using the example of 192.168.10.18/31 in the classical sense decodes to a subnet mask of 255.255.255.254 with a network address of 192.168.10.18 and a broadcast address of 192.168.10.19. Since there are no addresses reserved for host spaces, the devices need to be able to handle these addresses as two host addresses.

The "/32" subnet mask is another special subnet mask where there are no network/broadcast addresses and host addresses. There is only a single address that is reserved for loopback and the system address. The system address is a special loopback address that also serves as a router ID for routing protocols such as OSPF and BGP. *Loopback addresses* are internal logical addresses that are not associated with physical interfaces. It is important to note that only the *system* address is a "/32" address, and the loopback addresses can be associated to any subnet mask range. Loopback addresses are virtual and are not assigned to any interface on the router. Standard IP addresses are assigned to other interfaces on routers.

A *router interface* is a logical entity created in order to assign broadcast networks to physical Layer 2 networks connected to the router. It is also commonly referred to as a *Layer 3 interface* or *L3 interface*. It is almost always assigned an IP address. The IP address is applied along with the subnet mask associated with the broadcast domain. An interface is a logical entity, but it is almost always associated with a physical port. This is typically done to physically connect the router to a router, switch, hub, or a host. The other device attached to the router must also be configured with an IP address in the same broadcast network as the IP address assigned to the router interface.

An interface not associated with a physical port is associated with a loopback interface. These interfaces are considered internal to the router and represent broadcast domains within the router. These concepts are illustrated in Figure 5.16.

Figure 5.16 Most IP addresses are associated to a physical interface on a router. However, there is also an internal "system" address that is not associated with any single physical interface.

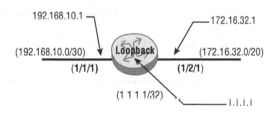

Figure 5.17 illustrates how you would add IP addresses to interfaces on an Alcatel-Lucent 7750 series router. Router A has two physical interfaces, one connected to the LAN network and one connected to Router B. Router A also has two logical interfaces, the system address and the loopback address, both of which are internal to Router A.

Figure 5.17 Router A has IP addresses on two physical interfaces and two logical interfaces.

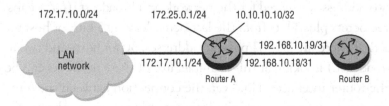

You can verify your configuration with the `show router interface` command. Your output should resemble Listing 5.1. Notice that some interfaces are loopback or system and others are associated with actual physical ports (i.e., 1/1/2, 1/1/1).

```
Listing 5.1 show router interface output

A:ASIN# show router interface
===============================================================================
Interface Table (Router: Base)
===============================================================================
Interface-Name                 Adm        Opr(v4/v6)  Mode     Port/SapId
   IP-Address                                                   PfxState
-------------------------------------------------------------------------------
loopback1                       Up         Up/--       Network  loopback
   172.25.0.1/24                                                n/a
system                          Up         Up/--       Network  system
   10.10.10.20/32                                               n/a
toLAN                           Up         Up/--       Network  1/1/2
   172.17.10.1/24                                               n/a
toRouterB                       Up         Up/--       Network  1/1/1
   192.168.10.18/31                                             n/a
-------------------------------------------------------------------------------
Interfaces : 4
===============================================================================
```

In the next section, we will illustrate more examples of IP subnetting and provide some practice exercises to hone your subnetting skills.

IP Subnets and VLSM Examples

All the networks in Figure 5.18 have a /27 network mask. This means that there are 30 hosts and two addresses reserved for the network and broadcast. (/27 means 24 bits for the first three octets plus 3 bits from the last octet, leaving 5 bits for host addressing. This means that there are $2^5 = 32$ possible addresses, 30 for hosts and two for the network and broadcast.) Looking at this example, five of these networks can be assigned to each of the router interfaces. However, the connection between the routers and that between one of the routers and the Internet only require two host addresses for their respective interfaces.

Figure 5.18 There are five networks that need IP address assignments. We need to create subnets from a common IP network address for all these networks.

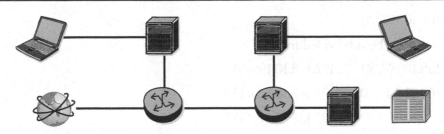

Subnets have been assigned to the network randomly, as shown in Figure 5.19. Each of the subnets supports 30 hosts. However, the link between the routers is a point-to-point link and only requires two host addresses. The broadcast networks attached to a switch could require 60 hosts each but are limited to 30 hosts. How do we rectify this situation?

Figure 5.19 Using 27 bits for the subnet mask, we could create eight subnets that can each support 30 hosts. However, 30 hosts may be too few for some subnets, and too many for others.

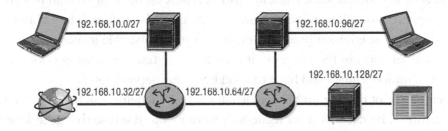

The solution is to assign different subnet masks to the network (this is very typical in real networks). Use a different mask (e.g., use /26 for 192.168.10.0/24) to generate subnetworks such as:

- 192.168.10.0/26
- 192.168.10.64/26
- 192.168.10.128/26
- 192.168.10.192/26

(all with 62 hosts each).

This is not enough to represent five networks, but take subnetwork 192.168.10.192/26 and apply a /30 to it:

- 192.168.10.192/26

which can then be subdivided into:

- 192.168.10.192/30   192.168.10.196/30
- 192.168.10.200/30   192.168.10.204/30
- 192.168.10.208/30   192.168.10.212/30

and so on.

Any one of the above addresses can be used to represent point-to-point links between the routers. You will have some subnets left over, but it is almost impossible to create a subnet plan that makes perfect use of all possible subnets.

This example illustrates a critical fact. When developing a subnet design, the network administrator must take into consideration the same questions that were asked when doing the traditional network design. At each level, the administrator must ensure that there are enough bits available for expansion. If the networks are spread out over several different sites, the administrator must ensure that enough bits are used to support those sites and any future sites that may be deployed. In addition, the administrator must envision how each site may further subdivide its network to support the subnetworks in the site itself. It is far better to have extra subnets for future use than to underestimate and have to re-address your network later.

Development of this hierarchical addressing scheme requires careful consideration and planning. The network must recursively work its way down so that each level has enough space in the host address range to support each requirement. This hierarchical addressing scheme is sometimes referred to as *variable-length subnet masking* (VLSM). If this hierarchical scheme is planned correctly before deployment, the multiple networks can then be aggregated into a single address that will help to reduce the number of routing entries in the backbone routers. This is an example of a VLSM solution to the problem in Figure 5.19.

Using different length subnet masks brings about a new set of challenges: how the different subnets and their various extended prefixes get advertised throughout the network. This requires the use of more modern routing protocols. The routing protocol used must be able to satisfy the following:

- The routing protocol must be able to carry the extended prefixes with each subnet advertised.

- The routers themselves must make forwarding decisions based on the longest match.
- The routing protocol must be able to perform summarization to support route aggregation.

Routing protocols such as OSPF and IS-IS support the use of VLSM. RIPv1 *does not* support the use or deployment of VLSM; however, RIPv2 *does* support the use of VLSM. Let's take a look at another example where VLSM is useful.

In the example in Figure 5.20, the organization is assigned the network IP address of 172.16.0.0/16, and it plans to design and deploy a VLSM network. Five subnets are required, each with a requirement of 2,000 hosts.

Figure 5.20 There are five networks that each require 2,000 hosts.

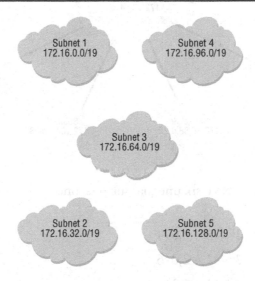

In typical Class B fashion, there is only one network with 65,534 hosts represented by the last 16 bits. We need five networks. Using some of the default Class B host bits should give us the required networks:

- **Option 1**—Using 2 bits out of 16 gives us $2^2 = 4$ networks and $2^{14} = 16,384$ hosts.
- **Option 2**—Using 3 bits out of 16 gives us $2^3 = 8$ networks and $2^{13} = 8,192$ hosts.
- **Option 3**—Using 4 bits out of 16 gives us $2^4 = 16$ networks and $2^{12} = 4,096$ hosts.

Option 2 or 3 can be used, but because only five networks are required. Option 2 is probably the best choice here because eight networks are more than required. However, if the network is bound to grow with no more than 4,000 hosts ever in any given subnet, Option 3 might be better because the network has been designed for 16 subnets and gives substantial room for growth.

In Figure 5.21, subnet 172.16.64.0/19 has been isolated and is now going to be further subdivided to support the six subnets that are located in the local campus. The total number of hosts supported in the /19 network is 8,194. This can be further subdivided into more subnetworks with a smaller number of hosts.

Figure 5.21 Subnet 3 has been further divided into six smaller subnets by using additional host bits. Notice that the smaller subnets do not need to have the same subnet mask.

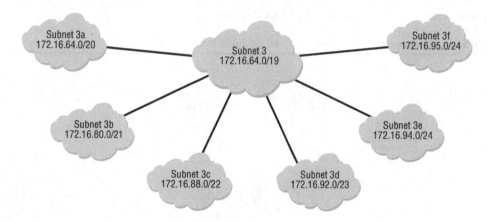

If the requirement is to have six unequal subnets, one option is to divide them as follows:

172.16.64.0/20:	$2^{12} - 2 = 4,094$
172.16.80.0/21:	$2^{11} - 2 = 2,046$
172.16.88.0/22:	$2^{10} - 2 = 1,022$
172.16.92.0/23:	$2^9 - 2 = 510$
172.16.94.0/24:	$2^8 - 2 = 254$
172.16.95.0/24:	$2^8 - 2 = 254$

Note that the sum of all valid hosts is 8,180. This is because by dividing further, two addresses are reserved for the subnetwork number and broadcast number for each subnet as we have previously discussed. Notice that the use of VLSM allows flexibility in the design of networks. Not all subnetworks or networks require the same number of hosts, so VLSM allows an administrator to create subnets with the required number of hosts while reserving enough bits for the creation of additional subnets.

Subnet Creation Exercises

Now that we have examined subnet creation, it is time to take a look at some practice exercises. In Figure 5.22, the administrator is tasked with taking the base address and subnetting it to support three subnets. Then the second subnet must be further subdivided to support four subnets. The administrator must then define the first, last, and broadcast addresses for the second sub-subnet. As an exercise, perform your own subnetting and check your answers at the end of this subsection.

Figure 5.22 The requirement is to subnet 138.120.0.0/16 into three subnets and then to further subnet one of those three into three additional subnets.

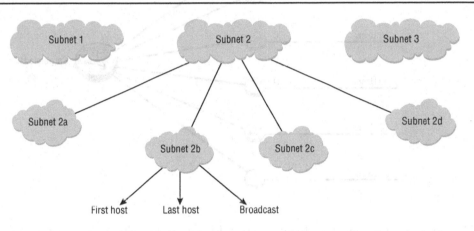

Subnet 1 network address: _____

Subnet 2 network address: _____

Subnet 3 network address: _____

Subnet 2a network address: _____

Subnet 2b network address: _____

Subnet 2c network address: _____

Subnet 2d network address: _____

Subnet 2b

First host address: _____

Last host address: _____

Broadcast address: _____

In Figure 5.23, the administrator is tasked with taking the base address 10.10.10.0/24 and subnetting it to support six subnets, ensuring that each subnet will support its host requirements.

Figure 5.23 The requirement is to create six subnets from 10.10.10.0/24. Each subnet must support the indicated number of hosts.

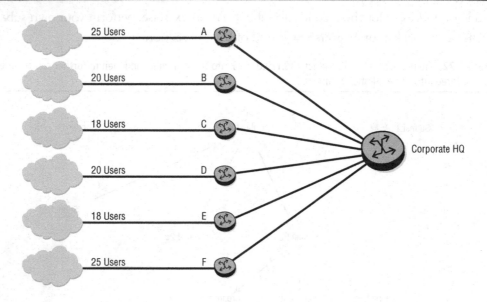

The next task for the administrator is to take one of the subnets and further subdivide it to support the point-to-point links that join the subnet routers to the main router. Given the IP address, use VLSMs to extend the use of the address. Provide a possible address for the following and check your answers at the end of this subsection:

HQA: _____

HQB: _____

HQC: _____

HQD: _____

HQE: _____

HQF: _____

Router A LAN: _____

Router B LAN: _____

Router C LAN: _____

Router D LAN: _____

Router E LAN: _____

Router F LAN: _____

These exercises and examples have now given you a solid understanding of IP address subnetting and the creation of an IP address plan. In the final section, we examine how proper subnet allocation and planning allow for hierarchical addressing that leads to more route stability and a better network.

Answers to Subnet Questions

The first exercise was based on Figure 5.22. A sample answer is shown below.

 Your answer may vary since there are multiple solutions that satisfy the requirement.

The starting address is 138.120.0.0/16. Since you need at least three major subnets (1, 2, and 3), you need to borrow 2 bits from the host portion of the address ($2^2 = 4$ possible subnets). This gives you a mask of /18 and four networks: 138.120.0.0/18, 138.120.64.0/18, 138.120.128.0/18, and 138.120.192.0/18. This example uses the first three subnets.

Subnet 1 network address: 138.120.0.0/18

Subnet 2 network address: 138.120.64.0/18

Subnet 3 network address: 138.120.128.0/18

Now, you need to further subdivide the 138.120.64.0/18 network into at least four subnets. Again, this means you need 2 more bits borrowed from the hosts ($2^2 = 4$ possible subnets), so your mask is now /20 and your subnets are: 138.120.64.0/20, 138.120.80.0/20, 138.120.96.0/20, and 138.120.112.0/20.

Subnet 2a network address: 138.120.64.0/20

Subnet 2b network address: 138.120.80.0/20

Subnet 2c network address: 138.120.96.0/20

Subnet 2d network address: 138.120.112.0/20

Subnet 2b

First host address: 138.120.80.1

Last host address: 138.120.95.254

Broadcast address: 138.120.95.255

The second exercise was based on Figure 5.23. You were tasked with taking the base address and subnetting it to support six subnets, ensuring that each subnet will support its host requirements.

 Your answer may vary since there are multiple solutions that satisfy the requirement.

You had to take one of the subnets and further subdivide it to support the point-to-point links that join the subnet routers to the main router. Given the IP address, you had to use VLSMs to extend the use of the address.

The starting address was 10.10.10.0/24. Since you need six addresses, you need to borrow 3 bits to give you eight total subnets (borrowing 2 bits yields only $2^2 = 4$ subnets, borrowing 3 bits gives $2^3 = 8$ subnets). This gives you the following subnets: 10.10.10.0/27, 10.10.10.32/27, 10.10.10.64/27, 10.10.10.96/127, 10.10.10.128/27, 10.10.10.160/27, 10.10.10.192/27, and 10.10.10.224/27.

This example uses the first six subnets for the LANs and the seventh subnet for the serial links. Note that since you have borrowed 3 bits from the 8-bit host address, which leaves 5 bits for hosts yielding $2^5 = 32$ addresses per subnet, subtracting two addresses for the subnet IP and the broadcast gives 30 hosts per subnet. Since none of the subnets requires more than 30 hosts, it doesn't matter how they are allocated, so just allocate them in order.

Router A LAN: 10.10.10.0/27

Router B LAN: 10.10.10.32/27

Router C LAN: 10.10.10.64/27

Router D LAN: 10.10.10.96/27

Router E LAN: 10.10.10.128/27

Router F LAN: 10.10.10.160/27

Now choose the next subnet, 10.10.10.192/27, to use for the serial links. Since the serial links only require two addresses per link, one for each end, you only need 2 bits for hosts (remember that we lose two addresses per subnet for the network and broadcast). Recall that you have 5 bits for hosts per subnet, which means that you can borrow 3 additional bits (5 – 2 needed for each serial link = 3 subnet bits). This yields the following subnets: 10.10.10.192/30, 10.10.10.196/30, 10.10.10.200/30, 10.10.10.204/30, 10.10.10.208/30, 10.10.10.212/30, 10.10.10.216/30, and 10.10.10.220/30.

HQA: 10.10.10.192/30

HQB: 10.10.10.196/30

HQC: 10.10.10.200/30

HQD: 10.10.10.204/30

HQE: 10.10.10.208/30

HQF: 10.10.10.212/30

This leaves two serial link subnets to spare.

5.5 CIDR and Route Aggregation—The End of Classful IP Addressing

With the rapid expansion of the Internet, IPv4 addresses were quickly becoming exhausted by the 1990s, and the sizes of routing tables were expanding exponentially. The response to these problems was the development and adaptation of Classless Inter Domain Routing (CIDR). CIDR eliminated the concept of address classes and replaced it with the concept of network prefixes. Rather than the first 3 bits defining the network mask, the network prefix alone now defines the network mask. This prefix mask is a method of defining the leftmost contiguous bits in the network portion of the routing table entry.

By eliminating the concept of address classes, CIDR allowed for a more efficient allocation of the IP address space. In addition, CIDR supports the concept of route aggregation, thus allowing a single route entry to represent multiple networks. As discussed previously, address planning is extremely important when subnets are first deployed. The subnets should be deployed so that they support the concept of aggregation, and when aggregation or summarization is applied, all subnets can be represented by as few entries as possible in the routing table. If you plan your network addressing from the central core outward to the edges of the network, your addressing scheme should naturally support this sort of hierarchy.

In Figure 5.24, Router A supports 256 different subnets with a /24 prefix. Rather than advertising all 256 subnets to Router B, the administrator can implement route aggregation and advertise them all as 10.10.0.0/16.

Figure 5.24 There are 256 routes in the routing table on Router A. Instead of advertising all 256 to Router B, it is better to summarize the subnets as a single aggregate route of 10.10.0.0/16 to reduce the routing table size and increase routing advertisement stability.

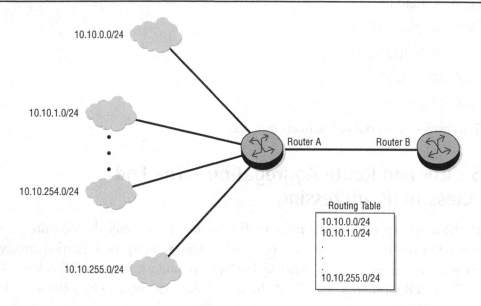

The example in Figure 5.24 is a simple example of route summarization, and it is easy to see that Router B only needs one entry of 10.10.0.0/16 to represent all 256 networks on Router A. However, route summarization is not always this simple, and it is important to understand the procedure for calculating a route summarization. In Figure 5.25, we'd like to summarize the eight networks on Router A. First, define the octet that will be manipulated by the aggregation. In this case, it is the third octet because the first two octets are always 10.15. Next, identify the original network prefix (/24), and then look to the left of the prefix line and identify the area where all the addresses have the same bit pattern. Draw a line down that portion. Look in between these two lines and ensure that all possible bit patterns are contained between the two lines. If this is the case, you can then summarize those bit patterns into (in this example) a /21 mask, as shown in Figure 5.25.

Figure 5.25 Draw a network line on the original network bit boundary (/24 in this case). This becomes the right bit boundary. Then draw a line where all the bits are common between the subnets (/21 in this case); this is the left bit boundary. Examine the subnets created by using the bits in between the lines. If all the subnets created by those bits are part of the range you want to summarize, then you can use the left bit boundary (/21 in this case) as a summary route.

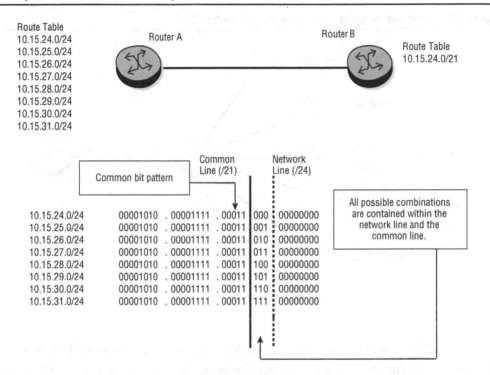

In Figure 5.26, the administrator is going to be using route aggregation on Router 1. What route or routes will be advertised to Router 2?

The solution starts by knowing what the lowest numbered subnet is and the prefix it uses. In this case, it is 10.15.1.32.0/28, so we know that at least this subnet will be advertised. The original prefix sets the right bit boundary at 28 bits, so now we have to find the left bit boundary. The easiest way to do this is to examine all of the subnets in binary. Since the first three octets are all the same, we will show only the fourth octet. We will list the subnets in numerical order and not in the order shown in the figure:

Subnet 32 = 2^5 = 1 in the 5th bit position = 00100000

Subnet 48 = $2^5 + 2^4$ = 1 in the 5th and 4th bit positions = 00110000

Subnet 64 = 26 = 1 in the 6th bit position = 01000000

Subnet 80 = 26 + 24 = 1 in the 6th and 4th bit positions = 01010000

Subnet 96 = 26 + 25 = 1 in the 6th and 5th bit positions = 011000000

Subnet 112 = 26 + 25 + 24 = 1 in the 6th, 5th, and 4th bit positions = 011100000

Figure 5.26 What route or routes will be advertised to Router 2?

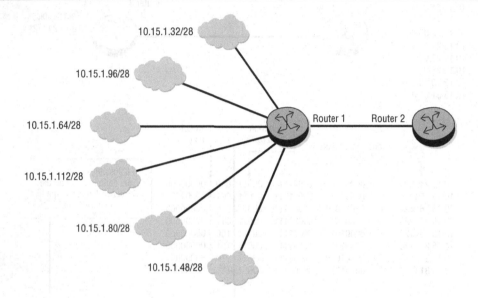

Figure 5.27 demonstrates the same procedure as Figure 5.25, but now there is a problem: Not all of the bit sequences between the network line and the common line are used! If you compare the "expected common line" to the "real common line," you will see that there are two bit patterns that are not part of the original six subnets.

The two bit patterns that fall outside of the range are 00000000 and 00010000, which translate into 0 and 16 in the fourth octet. The full subnet would be 10.15.1.0/28 and 10.15.1.16/28, which, as you can see from Figure 5.26, are not subnets that need to be summarized. The end result is that we can summarize the highest four subnets as a single aggregate CIDR route, and the lowest two subnets can be sent as a single aggregate of their own.

Looking again at Figure 5.27, you can see that the real common line for the highest numbered four subnets is /26, so we can summarize those subnets as 10.15.1.64/26 (the lowest subnet of the four is 64; /26 is the common line). The lowest two subnets, 10.15.1.32/28 and 10.15.1.48/28, can be sent as 10.15.1.32/27 because the common line for those two subnets falls at the 27th bit marker. The figure does not show this second split, but you can do this exercise yourself by moving the common line to the right 1 bit and seeing that both 10.15.1.32/28 and 10.15.1.48/28 can be summarized as a single aggregate, 10.15.1.32/27.

Figure 5.27 We would like to use common line /25, but there are bit patterns for subnets that are not part of the original six subnets. This means that we cannot aggregate all of these subnets into a single CIDR advertisement.

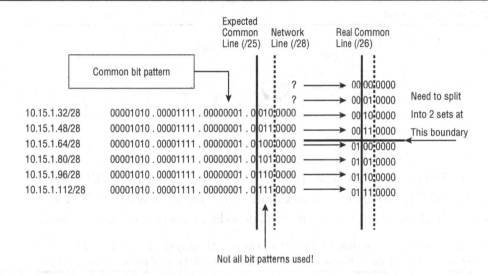

If any of the above examples are not clear, please review the procedures described again. It is very important that you understand how the aggregate routes were created and the procedure to follow. The most important thing to remember is to break down the subnets into binary because all of the operations described become much easier when you can see the actual bit patterns.

The next section concludes the chapter with a discussion of CIDR and VLSM.

CIDR versus VLSM

When you first look at CIDR and VLSM, they seem to both provide the same function, and they are, indeed, very similar. Both CIDR and VLSM imply the following:

- The routing protocol must carry network-prefix information with each advertised route.

- All routers must support the longest-match forwarding algorithm.

- Addresses must be allocated to support route aggregation.

The difference between the two is how the manipulation of the address space appears to the Internet. VLSM address manipulation is done on the address assigned to an organization and is invisible to the Internet because all the subnetting is internal to an organization. CIDR, on the other hand, manipulates addresses that are advertised to the Internet. This distinction is illustrated in Figure 5.28 and the figures that follow.

Figure 5.28 VLSM is used within an organization, whereas CIDR is used for aggregate routes that are advertised on the Internet.

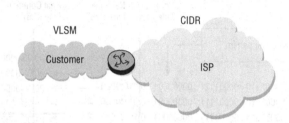

Figure 5.29 shows that an enterprise in its main location leases its IP addressing from the ISP. The ISP grants the enterprise ownership to its 100.1.1.0/24 block of addresses, and the enterprise divides its address block into many "/27" sub-blocks.

Figure 5.29 The enterprise is given the 100.1.0.0/23 address block by its ISP and then splits the block into multiple subnets. The ISP does not know or need to know how VLSM is used inside the enterprise.

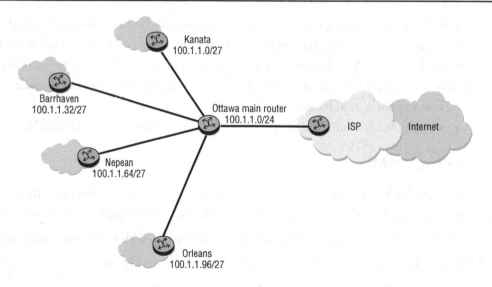

In Figure 5.30, the same enterprise customer exists in three different locations connected via the same ISP, who provides all the three locations with Internet access. The ISP dedicates the 100.1.0.0/20 block to this particular enterprise, and the ISP then divides the block into "/24" address blocks. If the same-size "/24" blocks are used, the enterprise can only add 13 more locations. This is an example where CIDR would be used to advertise an aggregate route from ISP 1 to ISP 2.

Figure 5.30 Here the ISP is providing multiple IP address blocks to the customer directly. In this case, ISP 1 would advertise a CIDR block to ISP 2.

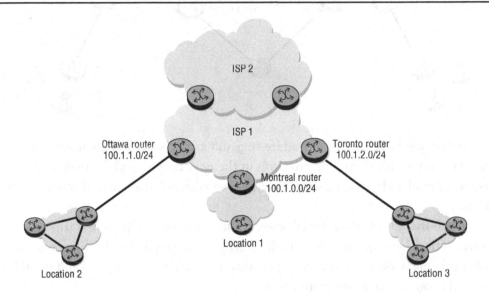

In Figure 5.31, the enterprise customer is dual-homed with ISP 1 and ISP 2. It needs ISP 1 mainly for Internet access. The Toronto office uses an IP address block of 101.1.0.0/24 to talk to ISP 2 and uses 100.1.0.2/24 to talk to ISP 1. In this scenario, ISP 1 would advertise a CIDR block for the 100.1 address ranges, and ISP 2 would advertise a CIDR block for the 101.1 address ranges. Typically, neither ISP 1 nor ISP 2 would advertise address ranges for the other ISP. This means that all inbound traffic from other ISPs with a destination address in the 100.1 range will go through ISP 1, and all inbound traffic from other ISPs with a destination address in the 101.1 range will go through ISP 2.

Figure 5.31 ISP 1 will advertise a CIDR route for the 100.1 blocks and ISP 2 will advertise a CIDR route for the 101.1 blocks.

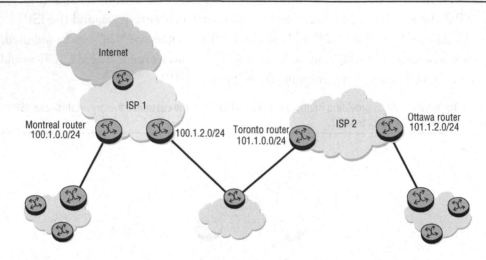

Now that you have reviewed IP addressing and its purposes, you are ready to hit the ground running with IP routing protocols in the next chapter and discover how all of these wonderful addressing schemes that are created get disseminated throughout the Internet.

Now you should complete the lab exercises to assist you in reinforcing this chapter's features. These lab exercises are carefully designed to give you hands-on experience configuring many of the technology standards that have been discussed and should greatly aid you in your exam preparation.

Practice Lab: IP Addressing and Routing

The following lab is designed to reinforce your knowledge of the content in this chapter. Please review the instructions carefully and perform the steps in the order in which they are presented. The practice labs require that you have access to three or more Alcatel-Lucent 7750 SRs or Alcatel-Lucent 7450 ESSs in a non-production environment.

 These labs are designed to be used in a controlled lab environment. Please **DO NOT** attempt to perform these labs in a production environment.

Lab Section 5.1: IP Addressing with Enterprise Customers

An ISP typically has one or more blocks of IP addresses that have been assigned to it by one of IANA's regional registries. The ISP might use one block of addresses for its residential broadband customers, another block for a college campus, and another block for a larger enterprise customer. The difficult part of the ISP's task is to split up and assign *just enough* of these addresses to each customer—enough to anticipate and allow future growth, but not so many that the ISP runs out of addresses. The ISP can allocate one block right after another so that the address numbering is consecutive without gaps, or intentionally leave gaps between the blocks for future growth. By sizing the blocks appropriately, multiple smaller blocks can later be grouped together as one single larger block. Maximizing block size helps minimize the number of unusable addresses and thus improves the efficiency of the ISP's overall address space. This exercise looks at one example with just a few of the typical constraints on utilization of the address space.

Objective In this exercise, you will design and implement an IP network addressing scheme that satisfies multiple addressing constraints and supports communications between multiple routers. Figure 5.32 provides the example network topology. This is a paper exercise.

Validation You will know you have succeeded by verifying your answers with the solutions provided in Appendix B.

Figure 5.32 A simplified diagram shows how an ISP connects to multiple sites of two different enterprises.

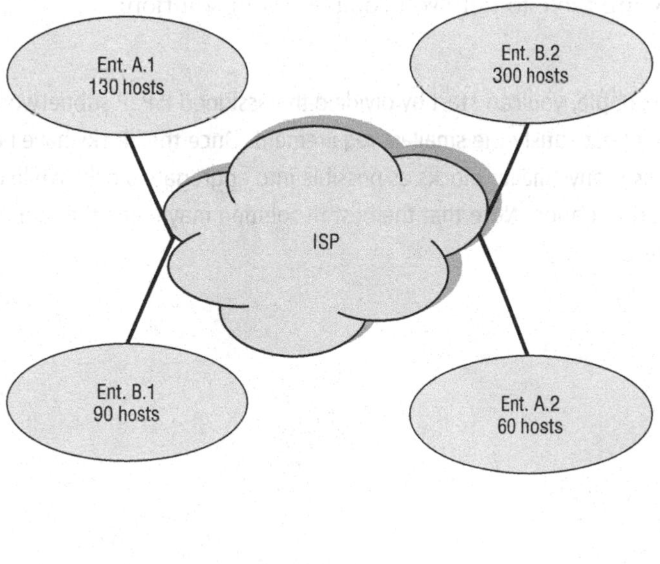

Requirements

Two enterprises, A and B, are connected to a central Tier 2 ISP. A.1 and A.2 are two of Enterprise A's locations connected to the Tier 2 ISP, and B.1 and B.2 are two of Enterprise B's locations connected to the same Tier 2.

The ISP has a public IP addressing space of 138.120.16.0/20. Enterprises A and B lease their IP addressing from their ISP. Enterprise A requires an IP addressing scheme that can scale to at most 30 nodes in location A.1 and 60 nodes in location A.2. Enterprise B requires an IP addressing scheme with at most 90 nodes in location B.1 and less than 300 nodes in location B.2. The ISP can only lease 500 IP addresses, distributed between the two enterprises, and will utilize the last part of its assigned subnetwork to connect to both the enterprises.

Your tasks are to:

1. Extract a 500 host subnetwork from the last part of the ISP IP network address of 138.120.16.0/20.

2. Divide the resulting subnetwork into unequal subnetworks satisfying all the site requirements for each of the enterprise locations.

 The subnetworks assigned to each location do not have to be a single aggregate block so long as they satisfy the number of addresses required.

3. Wherever possible, optimize address spaces among enterprise locations.

Use the following table to help you complete your solution:

 For this example, you can start by dividing the assigned ISP IP subnetwork into equal blocks that best satisfy the smallest requirement. Once the blocks have been assigned, combine as many smaller blocks as possible into aggregate blocks while obeying the rules for aggregation. Note that the best fit solution may mean that not all blocks can be aggregated.

Entity	Number of Host Addresses	IP Network
ISP Network	4094	138.120.16.0/20
Subnetwork assigned to Enterprises A and B	510	
Enterprise A		
Location A.1		
Location A.2		
Enterprise B		
Location B.1		
Location B.2		

Lab Section 5.2: IP Addressing with P, PE, and CE Routers

Real-world experience is certainly the best way to both learn and retain knowledge. It is, however, equally true that carrier grade routers are typically *very* expensive, so getting access for learning and experimenting may be difficult or even impossible. All remaining lab exercises have been designed to fully illustrate all configuration details, but with a minimum number of nodes. Reducing the amount of equipment to a minimum provides three important benefits: It is possible to complete all the configuration in a reasonable amount of time; it increases the probability of getting access to enough equipment; and (possibly most importantly) it minimizes the expense! Expect that you will need to adjust the exercises to match the particular hardware and cabling of your equipment. As a minimum, you will likely need to adjust port numbers. Specific details of the command output may differ, but the essential aspects should remain the same.

Objective In this exercise, you will design and implement an IP network addressing scheme to support the communications between the labeled routers shown in Figure 5.33. The IP addressing scheme will be used in the subsequent lab exercises throughout the book.

Validation You will know you have succeeded by verifying your answers with the solutions provided in Appendix B.

Figure 5.33 The Lab exercise uses this topology to demonstrate a simple IP addressing scheme.

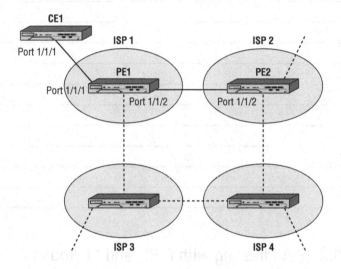

Note that in Figure 5.33, only the labeled routers joined by solid lines will actually be configured (i.e., PE1, PE2, CE1). The other routers, joined by dashed lines, represent the multitude of additional connections that might exist in a real-world scenario with many ISPs.

The focus of Figure 5.33 is the two ISPs: ISP 1 and ISP 2. A more typical network diagram would show routers that are entirely contained within the ISP's core network, having no connections to any customers. Such routers are referred to as *Provider* (P) routers and serve as transit points to other provider routers. *Provider Edge* (PE) routers have at least one connection to the ISP's customers and provide Internet and other network access for these customers. For the purposes of these lab exercises, all the ISP routers are considered PE routers.

CE1 is a *Customer Edge* (CE) router that represents customers of ISP 1. Such routers provide traffic from the ISP to the various customer entities.

Each ISP is assigned the following public address space by IANA:

- ISP 1 140.10.0.0/24
- ISP 2 150.10.0.0/24

Your task is to design an IP subnetwork based on the address space provided and assign the subnetworks to the various routers based on the following requirements, which are the same for both ISPs.

Requirements

1. The first 32 addresses in the assigned IP space for both ISPs are reserved for system and other internal loopback addresses on the PE router. Each of the routers in the ISP will require a system address from this block.

2. The next 64 addresses in the assigned IP space for both ISPs are reserved for future use.

3. All customer routers on both ISPs are connected to at most 60 hosts. So each ISP needs to assign two 60-host addressing schemes to represent all the customers.

4. All inter-router links including CE-PE router links within each ISP are point-to-point links; however, for the sake of convenience, they should be assigned /30-based addresses.

5. The ISP 1 and ISP 2 PE routers peer with each other. Consider that they are also physically connected to routers in ISP 3 and ISP 4, but do not peer.

When you are planning the addressing scheme, don't forget to consider future expansion and additional connections. You may find similarities with the exercise. From Lab 5.1, use the following table to help you complete your solution:

ISP Number 1			
Router	**Port**	**Interface Name**	**IP Address**
		Reserved for local loopbacks.	
		Reserved for future use.	
		Reserved for inter-router links.	
PE1		System	
		loopbackTest	
		toPE2	
		toCE1	
CE1		System	
		loopbackTest	
		toPE1	
		Aggregate	

ISP Number 2			
Router	**Port**	**Interface Name**	**IP Address**
		Reserved for local loop-backs.	
		Reserved for future use.	
		Reserved for inter-router links.	
PE2		System	
		loopbackTest	
		toP1	

Lab Section 5.3: Layer 3 Interfaces

In previous lab exercises, the equipment configuration finished at the L2 Ethernet level. Now that the L3 IP addressing scheme is complete, it is time to configure L3 interfaces on the router. This is not difficult, but there are some differences between physical interfaces and virtual or loopback interfaces. Look for the differences in the following exercises.

Objective In this exercise, you will configure the Layer 3 interfaces according to the IP addressing scheme listed in the tables in the previous exercise (Lab 5.2). This exercise assumes that all routers have been given suitable system names and configured up to the L2 Ethernet level.

Validation You will know you have succeeded if you can ping the L3 network interface of the adjacent router.

1. Using the following command, take a look at any existing interfaces on the router. Notice that the system interface is already created. This interface exists by default and cannot be removed. The only requirement is to assign the system interface with an IP address. By default, the system interface is automatically used by the various routing protocols as the router-id.

   ```
   *B:PE1# show router interface


   ===============================================================
   Interface Table (Router: Base)
   ===============================================================
   Interface-Name          Adm   Opr(v4/v6)  Mode    Port/SapId
     IP-Address                                       PfxState
   ---------------------------------------------------------------
   system                  Up    Down/--     Network system
     -                                               -
   ---------------------------------------------------------------
   Interfaces : 1
   ===============================================================
   *B:PE1#
   ```

   1a. Carefully examine the prompt for PE1. Which SF/CPM is currently active?

2. Assign a /32 IP address to the system interface in accordance with the addressing scheme from the previous section.

   ```
   *B:PE1# configure router
   *B:PE1>config>router# interface system
   *B:PE1>config>router>if# address 140.10.0.1/32
   *B:PE1>config>router>if# exit
   *B:PE1>config>router# show router interface
   ```

```
================================================================
Interface Table (Router: Base)
================================================================
Interface-Name          Adm   Opr(v4/v6)  Mode    Port/SapId
    IP-Address                                     PfxState
----------------------------------------------------------------
system                  Up    Up/--       Network system
    140.10.0.1/32                                  n/a
----------------------------------------------------------------
Interfaces : 1
================================================================
*B:PE1>config>router#
```

2a. Carefully examine the output for the router's system interface before and after the configuration command. What has changed?

2b. Knowing that the system interface exists by default, how many additional items need to be configured for it to be operational?

3. Assign IP addresses to the rest of the system interfaces on the CE and PE routers.

4. Create a loopback interface (for testing purposes). Note that a loopback interface needs two items in addition to the name: a /32 IP address and the special designation loopback.

```
*B:PE1>config>router# interface loopbackTest
*B:PE1>config>router>if$ address 140.10.0.11/32
*B:PE1>config>router>if$ loopback
*B:PE1>config>router>if$ exit
*B:PE1>config>router# show router interface


================================================================
Interface Table (Router: Base)
================================================================
Interface-Name          Adm   Opr(v4/v6)  Mode    Port/SapId
    IP-Address                                     PfxState
----------------------------------------------------------------
loopbackTest            Up    Up/--       Network loopback
    140.10.0.11/32                                 n/a
system                  Up    Up/--       Network system
    140.10.0.1/32                                  n/a
----------------------------------------------------------------
Interfaces : 2
================================================================
*B:PE1>config>router#
```

4a. Experiment with creating a loopback and leaving out either the IP address or the `loopback` designation. Other than the name, how many additional items need to be configured for the loopback to be operational?

5. Removing an interface is a simple two-step process. Remove the loopback interface now.

```
*B:PE1>config>router# interface loopbackTest shutdown
*B:PE1>config>router# no interface loopbackTest
*B:PE1>config>router#
```

5a. Experiment to see if it is possible to remove an interface that is operationally Up.

6. Re-create the loopback on PE1 and create loopbacks for the other CE and PE routers.

6a. Is there any conflict or problem with reusing the same name for an interface in more than one router? Are interface names local or global?

7. Create the *physical* inter-router interfaces. Note that a loopback interface needs two items in addition to the name: a /32 IP address and a physical port.

```
*B:PE1>config>router# interface toPE2
*B:PE1>config>router>if$ address 140.10.0.97/30
*B:PE1>config>router>if$ port 1/1/2
*B:PE1>config>router>if$ exit
*B:PE1>config>router# interface toCE1
*B:PE1>config>router>if$ address 140.10.0.101/30
*B:PE1>config>router>if$ port 1/1/1
*B:PE1>config>router>if$ exit
*B:PE1>config>router# show router interface
```

```
===============================================================
Interface Table (Router: Base)
===============================================================
Interface-Name      Adm   Opr(v4/v6)  Mode     Port/SapId
   IP-Address                                  PfxState
---------------------------------------------------------------
loopbackTest        Up    Up/--       Network  loopback
   140.10.0.11/32                              n/a
system              Up    Up/--       Network  system
   140.10.0.1/32                               n/a
toCE1               Up    Down/--     Network  1/1/1
   140.10.0.101/30                             n/a
```

```
toPE2                    Up      Down/--      Network 1/1/2
    140.10.0.97/30                            n/a
------------------------------------------------------------
Interfaces : 4
============================================================
*B:PE1>config>router#
```

7a. Note the operational state of the new interfaces. The command output shows evidence of another requirement for physical links to be operationally Up. What is that extra requirement? (One router's configuration was changed to demonstrate this requirement.)

8. Create the remaining inter-router interfaces for the CE and PE routers.

9. Now that L3 connectivity between all routers is configured, recheck the state of the interfaces to verify that they are all operationally Up. You can verify the configuration you entered with the info command: It shows everything that has been newly configured or changed from the default settings.

```
*B:PE1>config>router# info
--------------------------------------
#--------------------------------------
echo "IP Configuration"
#--------------------------------------
        interface "loopbackTest"
            address 140.10.0.11/32
            loopback
        exit
        interface "system"
            address 140.10.0.1/32
        exit
        interface "toCE1"
            address 140.10.0.101/30
            port 1/1/1
        exit
        interface "toPE2"
            address 140.10.0.97/30
            port 1/1/2
        exit
--------------------------------------
*B:PE1>config>router#
```

9a. What is the difference between the output from a `show` command versus an `info` command?

9b. Experiment with creating a physical interface and leaving out either the IP address or the port. Other than the name, how many additional items need to be configured for the interface to be operational?

9c. Experiment to find out if an interface can be both admin and operationally `Up/Up` on one side and not the other. What are the requirements for an interface to be admin and operationally `Up/Up`?

9d. Notice that all names in the output above are surrounded by quotation (" ") marks. The rule is that quotation marks are only necessary if the name contains a space. Experiment to see what happens if you try to configure an interface named `loopback Test` without using surrounding quotes.

The following table provides a convenient reference of the requirements for configuring L3 interfaces:

Interface Type	Name	Loopback	Subnet Mask	Port Config
System	system	Implicit	/32	None
Loopback	"Any String"	Explicit	/32	loopback
Normal	"Any String"	No	/1 - /31	Required

10. Check the route tables of the CE and PE routers. Notice the routes that now appear in the route table, and take note of their protocol type. There should be exactly one route for each interface that is operationally `Up`: four for PE1 and three for CE1 and PE2.

```
*B:PE1>config>router# show router route-table
```

```
===============================================================
Route Table (Router: Base)
===============================================================
Dest Prefix                    Type    Proto    Age        Pref
    Next Hop[Interface Name]                    Metric
---------------------------------------------------------------
140.10.0.1/32                  Local   Local    01h11m25s  0
    system                                      0
```

```
140.10.0.11/32                  Local    Local    00h00m45s   0
   loopbackTest                                               0
140.10.0.96/30                  Local    Local    00h44m49s   0
   toPE2                                                      0
140.10.0.100/30                 Local    Local    00h28m42s   0
   toCE1                                                      0
---------------------------------------------------------------
No. of Routes: 4
===============================================================
```

`*B:PE1>config>router#`

10a. Is there a difference between the outputs of the `show router interface` command and the `show router route-table` command? What is the difference?

11. Do the ultimate test to verify that interfaces are functioning properly: Use the `ping` command to check for connectivity from a router to the far end of each of the inter-router links, for example, between the two PE routers and between PE1 and CE1. You will need to think carefully to ensure that you use the correct IP address. (ICMP ping and ARP are covered more thoroughly in Chapter 6.)

```
*B:PE1>config>router# ping 140.10.0.97
PING 140.10.0.97 56 data bytes
64 bytes from 140.10.0.97: icmp_seq=1 ttl=64 time<10ms.
64 bytes from 140.10.0.97: icmp_seq=2 ttl=64 time<10ms.
64 bytes from 140.10.0.97: icmp_seq=3 ttl=64 time<10ms.
64 bytes from 140.10.0.97: icmp_seq=4 ttl=64 time<10ms.
64 bytes from 140.10.0.97: icmp_seq=5 ttl=64 time<10ms.

---- 140.10.0.97 PING Statistics ----
5 packets transmitted, 5 packets received, 0.00% packet loss
round-trip min < 10ms, avg < 10ms, max < 10ms, stddev < 10ms
*B:PE1>config>router#
```

Chapter Review

Now that you have completed this chapter, you should have a good understanding of the following topics. If you are not familiar with these topics, please go back and review the appropriate sections.

- The need for Layer 3 to interconnect Layer 2 networks
- The basic functions of IP
- The TTL, addressing, and protocol fields in the IP header
- The components of a dotted decimal IP address
- The difference between classful and classless IP addressing
- The difference between private and public IP addresses and identify the private IP address blocks
- How IP addresses are allocated
- Why subnetting is necessary and how subnet masks are used
- Understanding network addresses and broadcast addresses
- The importance of an IP address plan and how to create a plan based on customer requirements
- How to use VLSM to make efficient use of a given address space
- Route summarization and how to summarize a range of subnets into the least number of advertised routes
- The difference between VLSM and CIDR
- Configuring IP addressing on the various interfaces of a Alcatel-Lucent 7750

Post-Assessment

The following questions will test your knowledge and prepare you for the Alcatel-Lucent NRS I Certification Exam. Please review each question carefully and choose the most correct answer. You can compare your response with the answers listed in Appendix A. You can also download all of the CD content at `http://booksupport` `.wiley.com` to take all the assessment tests and review the answers. Good luck!

1. Which of the following is *not* a reason networks built on Ethernet alone cannot scale to a global?

    A. Excessive broadcasts would make the network unusable.

    B. Ethernet lacks hierarchical addressing.

    C. Ethernet switches cannot build forwarding tables.

    D. Ethernet cables can only be of a limited length.

2. Which of the following is true about Layer 3 addressing?

    A. It is embedded in the device's firmware.

    B. It provides for a logical hierarchy.

    C. It allows for duplicate addresses on the Internet.

    D. Addresses are not required to be registered if they are used on the Internet.

3. Which of the following is *not* true about an IP packet?

    A. The TTL field ensures that IP packets have a limited lifetime.

    B. The maximum size is 65,535 octets.

    C. The total length field includes the IP header.

    D. The current version is IPv5.

4. Which of the following is a valid host IP address?

    A. 192.168.300.4

    B. 255.70.1.1

    C. 224.0.0.1

    D. 10.254.1.1

5. An IP address has a first octet represented in binary as 11000001; the equivalent in decimal is _____.

   A. 190
   B. 193
   C. 192
   D. 11,000,001

6. The address 224.100.1.1 under traditional *classful* addressing would be _____.

   A. Class A
   B. Class B
   C. Class C
   D. None of the above

7. Which of the following is *not* a private address?

   A. 172.18.20.4
   B. 10.0.1.1
   C. 200.1.1.254
   D. 192.168.0.1

8. Which of the following is *not* a reason that subnetting is superior to class-based addressing?

   A. It reduces the Internet routing table size.
   B. You can identify the host portion of the address without the need for a mask.
   C. It creates greater internal address flexibility.
   D. It allows for more efficient use of address space.

9. Given a network address of 192.168.100.0/24, what is the maximum number of subnets you can create if each subnet must support at least seven hosts?

   A. 16
   B. 32
   C. 4
   D. 8

10. If your network address is 10.1.0.0/16 and you have subnetworks that all support at least 300 hosts, how many subnets do you have?

    A. 255

    B. 64

    C. 100

    D. 128

11. Which of the following is the correct representation of mask 255.192.0.0?

    A. /8

    B. /11

    C. /10

    D. /16

12. A network with a /30 mask allows you to have how many usable host addresses?

    A. 4

    B. 2

    C. 6

    D. 0

13. Given the address 10.1.1.0/24, the most correct description of 10.1.1.0 is _____.

    A. host 0 on the 10.1.1.0 subnet

    B. network 10.1.1.0

    C. illegal because 10.0.0.0 is a Class A

    D. subnet 10.1.1.0

14. The concept of allowing a single route entry to represent many network addresses is known as _____.

    A. CIDR

    B. Route aggregation

    C. VLSM

    D. classless addressing

15. How many subnets can be created from network 10.0.0.0/8 if each subnet must support at least 31 hosts?

   A. 2^{16}

   B. 2^{18}

   C. 2^{19}

   D. $2^{2}4$

16. Given network 175.100.0.0/16, if you create four subnets, how many addresses are available on each subnet?

   A. 16,384

   B. 4,096

   C. 16,382

   D. 4,094

17. What is the correct "all hosts" broadcast address for subnet 10.15.0.0/17?

   A. 10.15.255.255

   B. 10.15.0.255

   C. 10.15.127.255

   D. 10.15.128.255

18. Which of the following is *not* allowed?

   A. subnet 10.0.0.0/16

   B. subnet 10.255.0.0/16

   C. subnet 10.10.10.0/16

   D. host 10.10.10.0/32

19. Given network 135.100.0.0/16, you need nine subnets, and of these nine, one subnet needs to be split into 13 additional subnets. Choose the most likely masks you would create for this.

   A. /20 for the first eight subnets, /23 for the remaining 13

   B. /20 for the first eight subnets, /24 for the remaining 13

   C. /24 for all subnets

   D. /19 for the first eight subnets, /24 for the remaining 13

20. Given network 176.200.0.0/16 and a subnet that supports 4,387 hosts, what is the most likely mask for the subnet?

   A. /20

   B. /17

   C. /21

   D. /19

IP Forwarding and Services

- IP forwarding process
- Typical IP configurations
- Additional IP-related services
- IP filtering

$\mathbf{I}$n this chapter, we continue our discussion of the IP protocol by examining how IP packets are actually forwarded by a router. After examining this process, we look at some typical network configurations for a home network and how packets are sent from a home network to a service provider. We also examine some additional services that are needed in an IP network such as error messages and show how to discover a MAC address based on an IP address. Finally, we turn to the important topic of filtering to see how routers can selectively block certain IP packets based on particular security policies.

Pre-Assessment

The following assessment questions will help you understand what areas of the chapter you should review in more detail to prepare for the exam.

1. Which of the following is a function not performed by a router when forwarding an IP packet?

    A. Verify the IP header checksum.

    B. Decrement the TTL and ensure it is not zero.

    C. Send a "received" message to the originating router.

    D. Remove the existing L2 header and create a new L2 header before forwarding the IP packet to its next destination.

2. Which of the following highlights the differences between a traditional home user network and the modern user home network?

    A. Traditional home networks did not use routers.

    B. Modern home networks can use wireless access points.

    C. Modern home networks make use of a variety of new services such as Video on Demand and IP telephony.

    D. Traditional home networks did not rely on the IP protocol.

3. In a typical home network, when a PC needs to send an IP packet to a destination on the Internet it first sends the packet to _____.

    A. The designated router

    B. The cable modem

C. The router indicated in its BGP table

D. The default gateway

4. Which of the following statements regarding NAT is false?

   A. NAT is used for "many-to-one" translations.

   B. NAT alleviates the need for every home user device to have a public IP address.

   C. NAT typically makes use of private IP addressing.

   D. A NAT router maintains a translation database to perform the address conversions.

5. The process by which a home user's router requests and receives a public IP address from its service provider is known as _____.

   A. ARP

   B. DHCP

   C. ICMP

   D. OSPF

You will find the answers to each of these questions in Appendix A. You can also download all of the CD materials for this book at http://booksupport.wiley.com to take all the assessment tests and review the answers.

6.1 The IP Forwarding Process

We begin this chapter by discussing IP forwarding. *IP forwarding* refers to the process of moving transit packets from one router interface to another ("transit packets" in this context meaning packets whose destination is not the router itself). The forwarding process includes looking through the router forwarding table to find a match for the destination IP address and then sending the packet out the interface indicated in the forwarding table.

The process of forwarding IP packets is also often called *routing*. While the terms *forwarding* and *routing* are often used interchangeably, there is a subtle distinction between these processes. *Forwarding* means simply the process of examining the forwarding table and sending the packet out the correct destination interface. *Routing* is a more general term and includes not only the forwarding process just described, but the associated processes that a router uses to build the forwarding table as well.

Typically, there is a *routing protocol* that will be used to distribute information throughout a network from one router to another, thus allowing all routers to build up a routing table of destination addresses (routing protocols are discussed in Chapter 8). This routing table is then used to build the forwarding tables that are used to move packets to the actual router interfaces. On the Alcatel-Lucent 7750 SR, the routing table is maintained by the Control Processor Module (CPM). From the routing table, a forwarding table is constructed and downloaded to each line card (recall from Chapter 2 that a *line card* is a physical interface card that resides in an Alcatel-Lucent 7750 chassis).

To give you an idea of what a typical forwarding table looks like, Listing 6.1 shows actual output of the forwarding table on line card 1 of an Alcatel-Lucent 7750 SR-7.

```
Listing 6.1 Forwarding table output

A:P1# show router fib 1
===========================================================================
FIB Display
===========================================================================
Prefix                                                       Protocol
    NextHop
---------------------------------------------------------------------------
10.10.10.1/32                                                LOCAL
    10.10.10.1 (system)
10.10.10.2/32                                                OSPF
```

(continued)

```
      10.12.0.2 (toP2)
10.10.10.3/32                                                    OSPF
      10.13.0.2 (toP3)
10.12.0.0/24                                                     LOCAL
      10.12.0.0 (toP2)
10.13.0.0/24                                                     LOCAL
      10.13.0.0 (toP3)
10.23.0.0/24                                                     OSPF
      10.13.0.2 (toP3)
10.34.0.0/24                                                     OSPF
      10.13.0.2 (toP3)
192.168.1.0/24                                                  LOCAL
      192.168.1.0 (toPE1)
-------------------------------------------------------------------------

Total Entries : 8
-------------------------------------------------------------------------
```

The forwarding table is the information that a router uses to move packets from the ingress interface to the egress interface. When a packet comes in the router via a line card, the packet's destination IP address is compared with the contents of the forwarding table. If there is a match (longest/most specific match wins) with a prefix in the forwarding table, the packet is switched to the interface in Listing 6.1 as the next hop. For example, if the ingress packet has a destination IP address of 10.12.0.12, the destination IP addresses' longest match in the forwarding table is prefix 10.12.0.0/24. Since the next-hop interface for that prefix entry is (toP2), the packet will be switched to that interface and forwarded on the attached network.

This description of the forwarding process glosses over some of the key details that are involved in actually moving a packet from one interface to another. The astute reader may recall from earlier chapters our discussion of the IP frame check sequence and TTL fields and wonder how those are handled by routers. In actuality, there are many key actions that must be performed by routers to check for errors and make necessary changes to packets before simply forwarding them on to another destination. These key actions performed by a router are:

1. **Data Link Layer Frame Validation: Basic Frame Length and Frame Check Sequence (FCS) Verification**—When a router receives a frame from a LAN, the first task is to read the destination MAC address to ensure that the router is the

intended recipient of that frame. The next step, assuming that the router is the intended recipient of the frame, is to examine the FCS to see if there are any errors with the frame. If there are errors, the router discards the frame at this point.

2. **Network-Layer Protocol De-Multiplexing: Determination of the Upper Protocol That Needs to Receive the Encapsulated Data**—This is done so that after the L2 information has been removed, the payload is handed to the correct upper layer. Usually the upper layer will be IP.

3. **IP Packet Validation: Basic IP Header Verification**—The version number is verified, and the header checksum is calculated and verified. If either is not valid, the packet is dropped. The TTL field must be greater than 1; if the TTL = 1 or 0, the packet is discarded since this packet's time to live is finished. The TOS fields are also examined to determine if the packet requires special service handling.

4. **Forwarding Decision: Forwarding Table Lookup**—Check the forwarding table; if there is a match between the destination IP address in the packet and one of the prefixes (every single entry is checked looking for the longest match), the egress interface is chosen from the matching entry.

5. **Data Link Frame Construction: Packet Encapsulation**—The IP packet is now encapsulated in the L2 frame corresponding to the egress interface. If this is Ethernet, new source and destination MAC addresses are added including the type field, a new FCS is generated, and the packet is sent to the physical layer for transport.

Figure 6.1 demonstrates visually some of these key features. Note that the figure is "layered," with separate functions performed at the physical, data link, and network layers, just as we have been discussing repeatedly throughout previous chapters.

There are a few additional nuances to the forwarding process. For example, IP packets could be marked by an individual router with a certain Type of Service (ToS) for differential forwarding through the network. There may also be filters on interfaces that prevent a packet from being forwarded out of a particular interface.

However, although the forwarding process can be a bit more complicated than what we have shown, the basic process is as simple as described. You should be very familiar with this process as it is one of the central functions that routers perform in a network. Additional features of the forwarding process are important, but you need to make sure you completely understand the basic process that we have just explained.

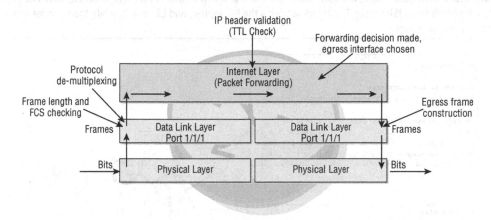

6.2 Typical IP Configurations

IP is the protocol of choice for routing in the Internet. Indeed, it is almost always the only choice because most providers only offer an IP transport service for their customers. It is used extensively in most service provider and carrier core networks. IP has evolved from being used simply to move data onto and around the Internet into providing a large variety of critical services to the home and business/enterprise. For example, IP is now used for delivering voice (phone), television, video, and other multimedia services to end consumers. As a result of this infusion of IP-based services, IP networks are now being created in the end-users' homes as well.

Figure 6.2 shows a very simple home network. There are two home PCs connected to a Layer 2 switch. The switch is then connected to a router that is in the service provider boundary. The demarcation point is the router interface toward the switch. The router interface is the demarcation point because the switch is owned by the home user, while the router is owned by the service provider.

Shown to the left in Figure 6.2 are the IP address outputs on both home computers. In order to communicate to the Internet, each of the computers must have a unique routable IP address. For traffic leaving the computers to the general Internet, a default gateway address is provided. The default gateway address is a network prefix that represents all possible destinations. It means "If you do not have a more specific prefix for the destination address, use this one."

Figure 6.2 A traditional home network setup. A PC and a laptop connect to a Layer 2 switch, which is, in turn, connected to an ISP router. The customer owns the PC, laptop, and L2 switch, while the provider owns and provides the router.

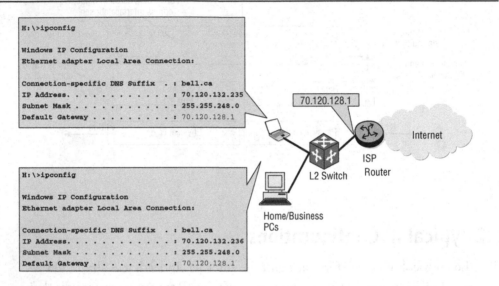

In this example, the default gateway address is the address of the interface on the ISP router facing the home network. Note that the default gateway is not the L2 switch because the switch is not operating at the IP layer. From the perspective of the computers and the router, the L2 switch is simply a transport to get IP packets back and forth to one another.

The home computers can communicate directly with each other since they are on the same network; communication between them does not have to go through the router. However, for the home PCs to access an Internet address outside of their network, for example, the eBay site, they must forward their packets to a router. An IP packet destined for the site would contain the source address of the computer and a destination address of eBay (76.67.217.148). The PC has no information about how to route the packet destined for the eBay server, and therefore it simply directs the packet to the default gateway. The default gateway will have the knowledge necessary to forward the packet to its final destination. Until recently, this was a very typical configuration for a home network, and it provided home users with basic Internet-related services.

In contrast, more modern home networks such as the one shown in Figure 6.3 support multiple services, and these services can be delivered on a single technology by a single or multiple providers. Home networks have evolved from a simple PC connected to a modem or a switch to multiple PCs, home televisions, and digital phones all connected via a single L2 technology to a home router that is managed at the home by the user and not by the provider. The router on one side of the network connection connects to the home network and on the other side connects to the service provider access device. The demarcation point in this case is the modem in Figure 6.3.

Figure 6.3 A modern home network that supports advanced user services such as IP telephony, Video on Demand (VoD), and interactive gaming over a high-speed Digital Subscriber Link (DSL) or cable Internet.

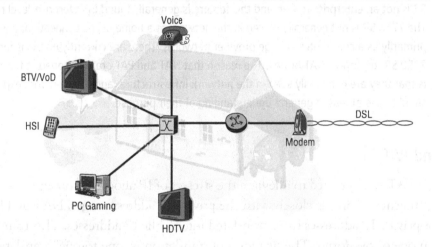

The data for all the services (in this single-provider, multiple-services scenario) is sent to the modem via DSL or cable technology. Every device in the home in this scenario requires an IP address to be able to connect to the Internet. There are several disadvantages to this configuration. First, it is not financially viable to have a unique public IP-routed address for every device in a home network. On top of this, it would not be a scalable solution. For the traffic to be received back to each device, the ISP would have to keep track of every home device for a single access point, and an ISP is typically not interested in maintaining multiple IP addresses for the average home user.

The best and most scalable solution is to have a home-managed router that assigns *private IP addresses* to each of the home devices and has a public IP address representing the home toward the ISP. Recall that private IP addresses are addresses that can be used by anyone for their own private networks, but that are not routable on the Internet. This makes them an ideal solution for large numbers of home networks that need to talk to each other on their local network, but that can all use a single (or sometimes multiple) public address to communicate with devices on the Internet. This magic is made possible by using Network Address Translation (NAT) or Port Address Translation (PAT). Let's examine how this process works.

 NAT and PAT are defined in Requests for Comments (RFC) 2663 and 3022. It is important to note that the Alcatel-Lucent 7750 SR does not currently support NAT or PAT. The 7750 SR is not an enterprise router, and this feature is generally found in enterprise-level routers. The 7750 SR is not generally placed in the network at a home user's connection; it is used primarily as a core router in large provider networks. There are currently no plans for the 7750 SR to support NAT or PAT. The reason that NAT and PAT are mentioned in this review is that they are commonly seen in the network infrastructure, and thus network experts should have at least a general understanding of their purpose.

NAT and PAT

NAT and PAT were created to alleviate the stresses of IP allocation on an ever-growing Internet. Working closely with the private IP address ranges, NAT and PAT allow for private IP addresses to be translated into public IP addresses. This translation can be in one of two forms. The first form of translation is "one-to-one" translation, or NAT. A single private IP address is translated to a single public IP address. In this form, the transport-layer port numbers (i.e., Transmission Control Protocol (TCP) or User Datagram Protocol (UDP)) are not monitored or modified. This allows for all applications to function normally without any change to the upper layers. The disadvantage of this form of translation is that there must be a pool of available addresses to support all the private IP-addressed clients. If all addresses in the pool are in use and a new device requests an address, it will fail because there is no available address within the pool of public addresses.

In Figure 6.4 the range of public IP addresses is from 192.1.1.2 to 192.1.1.254. Each client that sends traffic through the router will be mapped to a single IP address in the pool. If 253 clients are actively sending traffic through the router, the pool of available public IP addresses is completely consumed (because only 253 addresses are available). When the 254th client tries to send traffic out the router, the traffic cannot be sent because there are no available public IP addresses to use for NAT. Although this limits the number of clients that can simultaneously use this NAT router, it does not limit the types of applications that each client can be using because there are no changes to the upper-layer protocols.

Figure 6.4 NAT uses a pool of available public IP addresses that are mapped to private IP addresses when computers need to access the Internet. The IP address is one-to-one, and there are no changes to upper-layer protocols in the packets.

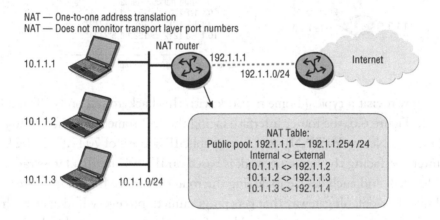

The second form of translation, PAT, is "many-to-one." A single public IP address supports multiple private IP addresses simultaneously. To accomplish this, the router must not only map the IP address of the client device, but it must also map the port number in use by the client. As translation occurs, the IP address is changed to a single public address. To keep track of the multiple streams of traffic from client devices, the upper-layer port numbers are mapped to unique port numbers in the database. This port change is transparent to the client.

Figure 6.5 illustrates a PAT router keeping track of source port numbers in its database.

Most modern applications do not have a problem with the change of upper-layer port. However, some applications (mostly legacy ones) require specific source and destination port numbers. If the router modifies the source port to one different from what the application expects, or requires, the application may not function properly. This is rarely a problem with more recently developed applications.

Figure 6.5 PAT uses a single public IP address that is mapped to many private IP addresses when computers need to access the Internet. PAT maintains a list of upper-layer ports and will alter the source port numbers if there is a duplication.

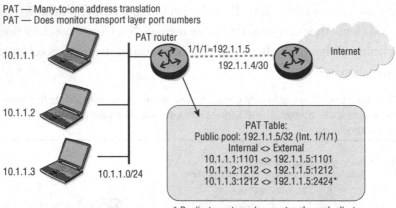

Let us now revisit a typical home network with this background on NAT and PAT services. In Figure 6.6, the router interface facing the ISP, sometimes referred to as the Wide Area Network (WAN) side, has a public IP address of 70.120.122.11/24. The router interface facing the home network is based on the private IP address range 192.168.10.0/24, and each device including the router interface has an IP address from that subnet. The default gateway that gets programmed into every IP device for Internet access will be the router interface address facing the home network, which in this case is 192.168.10.254/24. When any device attempts a TCP/UDP connection toward the Internet, the home router takes care of the address translation by using a port address translation table.

This configuration is probably familiar to anyone who has a small network at his or her own home. Most off-the-shelf home routers or wireless access points purchased at the store will be preconfigured with a private IP address range and are "plug and play." A user simply plugs the device into an outlet, runs a few wires or configures their PC with wireless network information, and can begin accessing the Internet within a matter of minutes. There is one key aspect missing from this picture, however. How does the single public IP address get assigned? Since new home users get connected each day and since there are many different ISPs that they might connect to, there must be a way to assign the public IP addresses dynamically. The protocol that supports this dynamic IP address assignment is known as Dynamic Host Control Protocol (DHCP).

Figure 6.6 All of the home network devices have their own private IP addresses in the 192.168.10.0/24 range. The router will use a PAT table to keep track of each address and port translation that occurs.

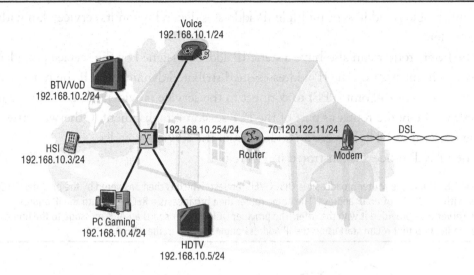

DHCP

How does the router in Figure 6.7 obtain the necessary public IP address that will be shared by the home network devices?

Figure 6.7 The router needs a way to determine what public IP address it needs to use. DHCP is the protocol that allows the router to get a dynamically assigned IP address.

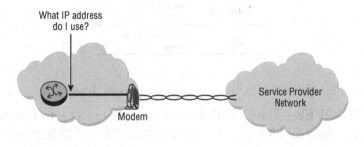

Every home router/PC that needs to connect to the Internet requires a public IP address. These IP addresses have to be requested from the Internet Assigned Numbers Authority (IANA) and its regional subsidiaries. A home user does not request an IP address from IANA, but from the service provider. The service providers are assigned IP address blocks depending on their size and business requirements, and supply their customers with addresses for their use. A home user is typically assigned a dynamic single IP address or multiple IP addresses depending on its service plan with its provider.

The home router can also have a static IP address assigned by the service provider. However, in most cases, the IP addresses are distributed dynamically. If the home router uses Point-to-Point (PPP) to connect to the service provider, the IP address can be sent to the home router as part of the PPP session establishment. Otherwise, the home router uses DHCP to get an address from the service provider.

The DHCP process is illustrated in Figure 6.8.

Figure 6.8 The home router broadcasts a DISCOVER request, which is then answered by the provider DHCP server with an OFFER of an IP address. The home router then broadcasts a REQUEST with the IP address of the server that provided it with the offer. The provider DCHP server sends an ACK message to the home router, indicating that it can start using the IP address originally sent in the OFFER.

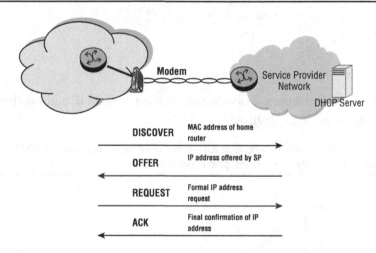

The following list describes each step in the process in detail:

1. **DHCPDISCOVER**—The DHCP client initiates the process by broadcasting a datagram destined for UDP port 68 (used by BOOTP and DHCP servers). This first datagram is known as a *DHCP discover message*, which is a request to any DHCP server that receives the message for configuration information. The DHCP discover message contains many fields, but the one that is most important contains the MAC address of the DHCP client.

2. **DHCPOFFER**—A DHCP server configured to lease addresses for the network on which the client computer resides constructs a response message known as a *DHCP offer* and sends it via broadcast to the computer that issued the DHCP discover. This broadcast is sent to UDP port 67 and contains the MAC address of the DHCP client. Also contained in the DHCP offer are the MAC and IP addresses of the DHCP server, as well as the values for the IP address and subnet mask that are being offered to the DHCP client.

   At this point, it is possible for the DHCP client to receive several DHCP offers, assuming that there are multiple DHCP servers with the capability to offer the DHCP client an IP address. In most cases, the DHCP client accepts the first DHCP offer that arrives.

3. **DHCPREQUEST**—The client selects an offer and constructs and broadcasts a DHCP request message. The *DHCP request message* contains the IP address of the server that issued the offer and the physical address of the DHCP client. The DHCP request performs two basic tasks. First, it tells the selected DHCP server that the client requests it to assign the DHCP client an IP address (and other configuration settings). Second, it notifies all other DHCP servers with outstanding offers that their offers were not accepted.

4. **DHCPACK**—When the DHCP server from which the offer was selected receives the DHCP request message, it constructs the final message of the lease process. This message is known as a *DHCP ack* (short for *acknowledgement*). The DHCP ack includes an IP address and subnet mask for the DHCP client. Optionally, the DHCP client is often also configured with IP addresses for the default gateway, several Domain Name Service (DNS) servers, and possibly one or two Windows Information Name Servers (WINS) servers.

   The DHCP servers maintain a list of assigned IP addresses and their lease times. Prior to the lease time expiry, the client that has sought an IP address via DHCP requests an IP address again. The server can choose to assign a different IP address or to renew the one previously assigned. In the case of a home gateway router that performs address translation, the home router performs the role of a client toward the service provider. It also performs the role of a DHCP server toward the home devices. IP-enabled devices at home request IP addresses from the home router, which assigns IP addresses in the private range. Both processes follow the procedures detailed above.

6.3 Additional IP-Related Services

In this section, we describe several services that IP uses to perform a variety of tasks related to the forwarding of packets. The two services discussed are a messaging service known as the *Internet Control Message Protocol* (ICMP) and the *Address Resolution Protocol* (ARP). ICMP, as the name implies, is a protocol that is used to construct and send messages in an IP network. These messages are normally sent in response to a network event such as congestion, dropped packets, and the like. ARP is used to translate an IP address into a MAC address so that a proper destination MAC address can be created in an Ethernet packet. Let's examine ICMP first.

ICMP

ICMP messages are constructed at the IP layer, often from a normal IP datagram that has generated an ICMP response. For example, each device (such as an intermediate router) that forwards an IP datagram must decrement the TTL field of the IP header by one. If the TTL reaches 0, an ICMP `time to live exceeded in transit` message is sent to the source of the datagram. IP creates the appropriate ICMP message with a new IP header (to get the ICMP message back to the original sending host) and transmits the resulting datagram in the usual manner. Each ICMP message is encapsulated directly in a single IP datagram, and thus, like UDP, ICMP does not guarantee delivery.

Figure 6.9 illustrates two very common ICMP messages: `echo request` and `echo reply`. These two ICMP messages are used by the well-known ping application. A host or router sends an ICMP echo request message to a specified destination. Any device that receives an echo request generates an echo reply and returns it to the original sender. The echo request contains an optional data area, and the echo reply contains a copy of the data sent in the echo request. The echo request and echo reply can thus be used to test whether a destination is reachable.

The use of the echo request and echo reply allows for a very simple test of network connectivity. In order for the echo request and echo reply to be received, the following network conditions must be true, which gives a quick and easy way to determine if a network is correctly forwarding IP packets:

- The IP software on the source computer must route the datagram.

Figure 6.9 Host A can determine if Host B is on the network and processing IP datagrams by sending an echo request command to Host B's IP address. The echo request is routed through the network to Host B, which then sends an echo reply message back to Host A's IP address. The ping application is the most common method of checking for host availability using echo request/echo reply.

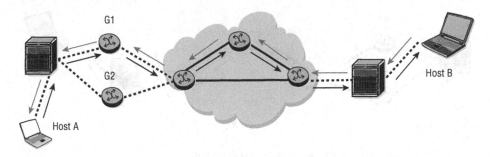

- The intermediate routers between the source and destination must be operating and must route the datagram correctly.
- The destination device must be running, and both ICMP and IP software must be working.
- All routers along the path must have the correct routes.

As mentioned, the ping application is the most common way to send an ICMP echo request and receive a reply. The command usually sends a series of echo request messages, captures the corresponding echo replies, and calculates the data return time and loss statistics. Nearly all modern operating systems including Linux, UNIX, and Windows include a ping program as a standard feature.

Another common ICMP message that is quite useful is the `destination unreachable` message. It is especially useful in determining when a particular IP device is no longer active. For example, a router could continue to send packets to a destination even after the destination is powered down without receiving an indication that the destination is down. The `destination unreachable` message can be sent from a router that is connected to the destination host network when it cannot reach the host, as illustrated in Figure 6.10.

There are many additional ICMP message types, but the ones we have discussed are the most common that you will encounter. Another very common and important IP service is the Address Resolution Protocol.

Figure 6.10 Host A is attempting to send packets to Host B, but Host B is no longer available. Without an ICMP message, it will be up to Host A's upper-layer protocols to time out the connection. As an alternative, if the network link to Host B is down, a router can send an ICMP `destination unreachable` message to Host A's IP process so that it can inform the upper-layer protocols.

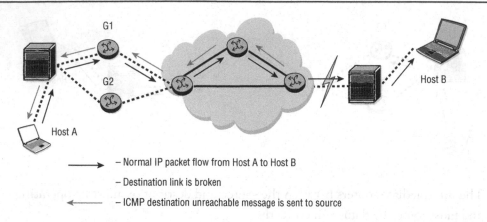

— Normal IP packet flow from Host A to Host B

— Destination link is broken

— ICMP destination unreachable message is sent to source

ARP

Recall from Chapter 3 that an Ethernet device has a hardware or MAC address associated with its Ethernet interface. In order for a device on an Ethernet (or other LAN) network to communicate with another device on the same Ethernet network, it must know the device's MAC address. However, in many cases, a device may just know another device's IP address, not its MAC address. In order to get the IP packet to its destination, a host must have some mechanism to match a destination IP address to a destination MAC address. This is the purpose of the Address Resolution Protocol.

ARP is defined in RFC 826. However, RFC 826 contained some ambiguities that were clarified in RFC 1122 (Host Network Requirements). As such, ARP implementations need to incorporate both RFC 826 and RFC 1122 in order to work reliably and consistently with other implementations. RFC 826 introduced the concept of an Address Resolution Protocol as a useful way for devices to locate the Ethernet hardware address of another IP host on the same local network. All Local Area Network (LAN) media—and many WAN media—now use ARP to locate the hardware addresses of other IP devices on the local network.

When a device needs to send an IP packet to another device on the local network, the IP software will first check to see if it knows the hardware address associated with the destination IP address (typically by consulting a cache of saved information from previous requests). If so, the sender just transmits the data to the destination system, using the protocols and addressing appropriate for whatever network medium is in use by the two devices. However, if the destination system's hardware address is not known, the IP software has to locate it before any data can be sent. At this point, IP will call on ARP to locate the hardware address of the destination system.

ARP performs this task by issuing an IP broadcast onto the network, requesting (ARP request) that the system that is using the specified IP address respond with its hardware address. If the destination system is powered up and on the network, it will see this broadcast (as will all of the other devices on the local network), and it will send an ARP response back to the original system. Note that the response is not broadcast back over the network, but is instead sent directly to the requesting system.

All the local devices should monitor the network for ARP broadcasts, and whenever they see a request for themselves (as indicated in the destination IP address field of the ARP request), they must generate a response packet and send it back to the requesting system. The response packet will consist of the local device's IP and hardware addresses. The response will also be marked as such, with the message-type field indicating that the current packet is an ARP response. The new ARP packet is then unicast directly to the original requester, where it is received and processed.

In Figure 6.11, Host 1 tries to ping Host 2. Host 1 looks in its cache of MAC addresses for the destination MAC address of Host 2. If it is not there, Host 1 queues the ICMP packet and sends an ARP request message. The ARP request is a broadcast message, and it is sent to all hosts in the broadcast domain. Each host opens the frame and checks the destination IP address. If it is not their address, the host ignores the packet. However, when Host 2 receives the request, it sees that it is the destination and sends an ARP reply. This ARP reply is transmitted in a frame that has the MAC address of Host 1 as its destination, and the MAC address of Host 2 as the source. Upon receiving the reply, Host 1 now learns the MAC address of Host 2 and is able to frame the ICMP message and send it to Host 2.

When the requesting system gets an ARP response, it stores the hardware and IP address pair of the requested device in a local cache, as illustrated in Figure 6.12. The next time that system needs to send data, it checks the local cache. If an entry is found, it uses that, eliminating the need to broadcast another request.

Figure 6.11 Host 1 issues a broadcast ARP request asking for Host 2's MAC address. Host 2 sees the request and sends a unicast ARP reply back to Host 1 with its MAC address.

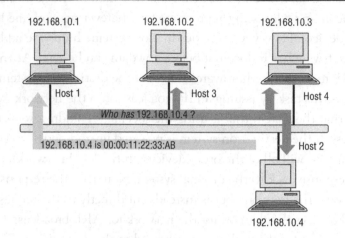

Figure 6.12 In order to reduce the number of ARP requests, IP hosts maintain an ARP cache that contains the answer to previous ARP requests. The entries in the ARP cache are saved for a limited amount of time and then discarded.

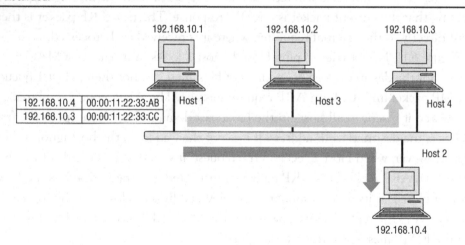

Likewise, the system that responded to the ARP broadcast stores the hardware and IP addresses of the system that sent the original broadcast. If it did not do so, it would have to issue its own ARP broadcast for Host 1's MAC address to find out where to send the ICMP echo response, which would create unnecessary network traffic. Note that IP addresses assigned to a host may not be static and can move around from host to host (recall our earlier discussion of DHC). Therefore, entries are removed from the ARP cache after a period of time. If the ARP cache does not time out, then the source may not be able to send its traffic to the right destination host. Several strategies exist that can alleviate the situation, but they are beyond the scope of this book.

The previous discussion addressed the use of ARP only within the confines of the same subnet. What happens if the destination host is not in the same subnet, as shown in Figure 6.13? Here, the process is different.

Figure 6.13 Host 1 wants to send an IP packet to Host 7, but Host 7 is not on its local network. Host 1 determines, based on its IP subnet mask, that Host 7 is on a distant network and issues an ARP request for its default gateway. The router responds with its MAC address, and then Host 1 sends the ICMP echo request to the router for forwarding.

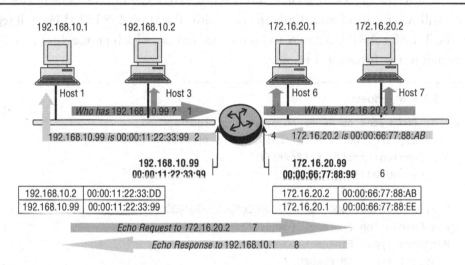

Host 1 wants to send traffic to Host 7, which is in a remote broadcast domain, and it wants to know if Host 7 can be reached. It tries to ping Host 7. However, in the absence of an ARP entry for 172.16.20.2, it needs to issue an ARP request. But, since 172.16.20.2 is not in the local broadcast domain, it issues an ARP request for its default gateway, which is the router interface in Figure 6.13.

Host 1 and Host 3 are programmed with a default gateway address in case they need to connect to hosts outside their local domain. For a local host to contact a remote host, it must send an ARP request to the default gateway. The router receives the broadcast on its interface in the 192.168.10.0 domain and issues an ARP response with its MAC address, and Host 1 can now form the IP packet for Host 7. Host 1 creates an IP packet that is then sent in an Ethernet frame to the router.

Using its forwarding table, the router decides to forward the packet out of the second interface. However, it does not have an ARP entry for the host 172.16.20.2. It therefore issues an ARP request in this broadcast domain. Upon receiving the ARP request, Host 7 responds with a unicast ARP response to the router. Note that ARP only works within the scope of a broadcast domain and therefore is never forwarded by a router. Just as with an IP host, the router maintains an ARP cache listing entries for the different broadcast domains it is connected to.

Listing 6.2 shows a packet capture of an ARP request. The capture shows a host with IP address 138.120.53.253 that is attempting to resolve the MAC address for a host with IP address 138.120.53.149. The destination MAC address of the Ethernet II frame is sent to the broadcast address ff:ff:ff:ff:ff:ff. All devices in the same broadcast domain will receive this frame. Only the host with IP address 138.120.53.149 will reply. The EtherType for ARP is 0x0806 and is used to indicate which protocol is being transported in the Ethernet II frame.

```
Listing 6.2 ARP request
Frame 31 (60 bytes on wire, 60 bytes captured)
Ethernet II, Src: 00:04:80:9f:78:00, Dst: ff:ff:ff:ff:ff:ff
    Destination: ff:ff:ff:ff:ff:ff
    Source: 00:04:80:9f:78:00
    Type: ARP (0x0806)
    Trailer: 000000000000000000000000000000000000
Address Resolution Protocol (request)
    Hardware type: Ethernet (0x0001)
    Protocol type: IP (0x0800)
    Hardware size: 6
    Protocol size: 4
    Opcode: request (0x0001)
    Sender MAC address: 00:04:80:9f:78:00
    Sender IP address: 138.120.53.253
    Target MAC address: 00:00:00_00:00:00
    Target IP address: 138.120.53.149
```

The fields in the packet include:

- **Hardware Type**—Each Layer 2 protocol is assigned a number used in this field. For example, Ethernet is 1.

- **Protocol Type**—Each protocol is assigned a number used in this field. For example, IP is 0x0800.

- **Hardware Size**—Size in bytes for hardware addressing. Ethernet addresses are 6 bytes in length.

- **Protocol Size**—Size in bytes for logical addressing. IPv4 addresses are 4 bytes in length.

- **Operation Code**—Specifies the operation the sender is performing. A value of 1 is for ARP request, and a value of 2 is for ARP reply.

- **Sender MAC Address**—The hardware MAC address of the sender

- **Sender IP Address**—The protocol address of the sender

- **Target MAC Address**—The hardware MAC address of the intended receiver. The MAC address is all 0s for a request.

- **Target IP Address**—The protocol address of the intended receiver

The packet capture in Listing 6.3 is the ARP reply in response to the ARP request in Listing 6.2. The Ethernet frame is a unicast frame and is sent only to the MAC address of the ARP request sender. All fields in the ARP reply packet have the same meaning as the ARP request packet. The main difference in the APR reply packet is the operation code (value of 2 for request) and the fully populated MAC addresses for the sender and the target. Note that the sender and target addresses have been swapped, but otherwise the fields are nearly identical to those previously described.

```
Listing 6.3 ARP reply

Frame 32 (42 bytes on wire, 42 bytes captured)
Ethernet II, Src: 00:11:43:45:61:23, Dst: 00:04:80:9f:78:00
    Destination: 00:04:80:9f:78:00
    Source: 00:11:43:45:61:23
    Type: ARP (0x0806)
Address Resolution Protocol (reply)
    Hardware type: Ethernet (0x0001)
    Protocol type: IP (0x0800)
    Hardware size: 6
    Protocol size: 4
    Opcode: reply (0x0002)
    Sender MAC address: 00:11:43:45:61:23
    Sender IP address: 138.120.53.149
    Target MAC address: 00:04:80:9f:78:00
    Target IP address: 138.120.53.253
```

Now that we have discussed some key services that use IP, it is time to conclude this chapter with a discussion of the important topic of IP filtering.

6.4 IP Filtering

One of the most important value-added services that can be provided by a router is the ability to filter IP packets based on a security policy. You can do this by creating a filter policy and applying it to an interface or interfaces on a router. *Filter policies*, also referred to as *access control lists*, are templates that are applied to services or network ports to control network traffic into (ingress) or out of (egress) a router interface. They can be created to filter based on IP and MAC addressing, protocol, or port matching criteria. Filters can be used on several interfaces, and the same filter can be applied to ingress traffic, egress traffic, or both. Ingress filters affect only inbound traffic destined for the routing complex, and egress filters affect only outbound traffic sent from the routing complex.

Configuring a service or network port with a filter policy is optional. If a service or network port is not configured with filter policies, all traffic is allowed on the ingress and egress interfaces (i.e., the default behavior on the port is "permit all"). By default, no filters are associated with services or interfaces; they must be explicitly created and associated. When you create a new filter, default values are provided although you must specify a unique filter ID for each new filter policy as well as each new filter entry and the associated actions. The filter entries specify the filter matching criteria. Only one ingress filter policy and one egress filter policy can be applied to a network interface at a time. All filter policies and entries are modifiable at the discretion of the network engineer.

Network filter policies control the forwarding and dropping of packets based on IP match criteria. Note that non-IP packets are not applied to IP match criteria, so the default action in the filter policy applies to these packets. If a default action is not explicitly configured, then the default action is to drop all non-matching packets. As an alternative action, the filter might simply allow the packet to be forwarded normally or forward it to a different next hop than would be indicated by the router's normal forwarding table.

A filter policy compares the match criteria specified in a filter entry to packets that are coming through the system, in the order the entries are numbered in the policy. When a packet matches all parameters in a particular filter entry, the system takes the specified action to drop or forward. If a packet does not match the entry parameters, the packet continues through the filter process. If the packet does not match any of the entries, the system executes the specified default action (i.e., "drop the packet unless a different default action is configured"). This process is illustrated in Figure 6.14. It is important to keep in mind that a single filter can have many entries, each with its own criteria to match. A packet will be examined against each entry, so the more entries that exist, the more processing that is required.

Figure 6.14 Incoming packets are compared against each filter entry in the filter policy. If there is a match, then the filter entry action is applied. If the entry is not a match, then each successive entry is checked until a match is found or the router reaches the end of the entries. If the end of the list is reached without a match, the default action is taken, or, if no default action is specified, the packet is dropped.

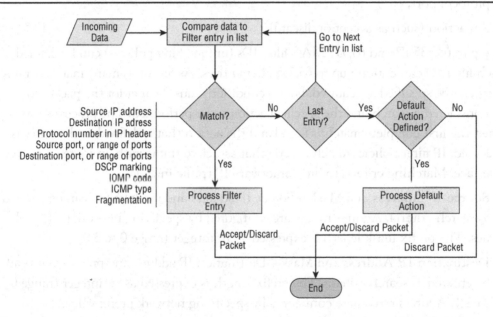

Each filter policy is assigned a unique filter ID and is defined with the following information:

- Scope
- Default action (such as accept or discard)
- Description (explain what the filter is for)
- At least one filter entry (the actual matching criteria)

The only parameter that is not straightforward is scope. The scope indicates whether the policy can be used only once or can be used many times. If the scope of the policy is exclusive, it can be applied to only a single entity (Service Access Point (SAP) or interface). If the scope is template, it can be applied to multiple entities (SAPs or interfaces).

For each filter policy, there can be numerous filter entries, but the policy must have at least one entry. This makes sense because it is the filter entries that determine the permit/deny actions of the policy. It would make little sense to have a policy with no matching criteria. For each filter entry, you must configure:

- Match criteria (IP address source or destination, upper-layer protocol, upper-layer protocol port, etc.)

- An action (such as accept or discard)

Up to 65,535 IP and 65,535 MAC filter IDs (unique filter policies) can be defined. Each filter ID can contain up to 65,535 filter entries. As few or as many match parameters can be specified as required, but all conditions must be met for the packet to be considered a match and the specified action to be performed. The process stops when the first complete match is found and the action that is defined in the entry is executed. IP filter policies match criteria that associate traffic with an ingress or egress interface. Matching criteria to drop or forward IP traffic include:

- **Source IP Address and Mask**—Source IP address and mask values can be entered as search criteria. Address ranges are configured by specifying network prefix values. The prefix mask length is expressed as an integer (range 0 to 32).

- **Destination IP Address and Mask**—Destination IP address and prefix values can be entered as search criteria. The prefix length is expressed as an integer (range 0 to 32). Address ranges are configured by specifying network prefix values.

- **Protocol**—Entering a protocol (e.g., TCP, UDP) allows the filter to search for the protocol specified in this field.

- **Source Port/Range**—Entering the source port number or port range allows the filter to search for matching TCP or UDP port and range values.

- **Destination Port/Range**—Entering the destination port number or port range allows the filter to search for matching TCP or UDP values.

- **DSCP Marking**—Entering a DSCP marking allows the filter to search for the DSCP marking specified in this field.

- **ICMP Code**—Entering an ICMP code allows the filter to search for the matching ICMP code in the ICMP header.

- **ICMP Type**—Entering an ICMP type allows the filter to search for the matching ICMP type in the ICMP header.

- **Fragmentation**—When fragmentation matching is enabled, a match occurs if packets have either the "More Fragments" bit set or have the fragment offset field of the IP header set to a non-zero value.

Several factors are important to keep in mind in the filter creation process:

- Creating a filter policy is always optional; they are not required.

- A specific filter must be explicitly associated with a specific service for packets to be matched.

- Each filter policy must consist of at least one filter entry.

- Each entry represents a collection of filter match criteria.

- When packets enter the ingress or egress ports, packets are compared to the criteria specified in the entry or entries.

- When you configure a large (complex) filter, it may take a few seconds to load the filter policy configuration and for it to be instantiated.

- The action keyword must be entered for the entry to be active. A filter entry without the action keyword is considered incomplete and is rendered inactive.

The process used to configure a filter is illustrated in Figure 6.15.

The major components of a filter policy are the filter ID and the entry ID. The *filter ID* is a numeric value between 1 and 65,535 that uniquely identifies the filter. Once the policy is created, you need to associate at least one filter entry with it and associate an ID with each entry. The *entry ID* determines the order in which entries are examined in ascending order.

Since each filter entry is examined until a match is found or the list of entries is exhausted, it is a best practice to place the most commonly used matches first so that processing of the other entries is reduced. You can include an optional description for each filter entry, but you must include a match criterion (IP addresses, upper-layer ports, etc.) and an action such as accept or discard.

Figure 6.15 The process used to create a filter policy. The filter must be created with its associated scope, description, and default action. Then, individual filter entries need to be created to specify what criteria the filter will examine in the IP packets. Finally, the policy must be applied to an interface or SAP.

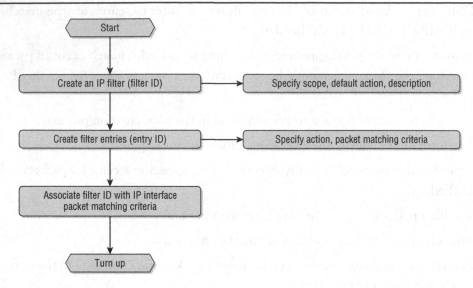

Creating filter policies and entries for the policies is very straightforward. There are, however, many options that can be used with individual filter entries. We will demonstrate some example filter policies to give you a better feel for how these filters are created and applied, but you should review the *Alcatel-Lucent 7750 SR OS Router Configuration Guide* to see all of the options that are available with filter policies and entries.

In Listing 6.4, IP Filter 1 is created. In the filter, the default action is to drop IP packets that do not meet the more explicit match settings. In the match settings, the filter is looking for all traffic sourced from IP subnet 1.2.3.0/24 that uses TCP at the transport layer and specifically uses TCP ports 666 to 999. If these criteria are met, the packet is forwarded.

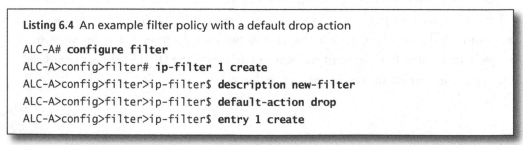

Listing 6.4 An example filter policy with a default drop action

```
ALC-A# configure filter
ALC-A>config>filter# ip-filter 1 create
ALC-A>config>filter>ip-filter$ description new-filter
ALC-A>config>filter>ip-filter$ default-action drop
ALC-A>config>filter>ip-filter$ entry 1 create
```

(continued)

```
ALC-A>config>filter>ip-filter>entry$ match src-ip 1.2.3.0/24
ALC-A>config>filter>ip-filter>entry$ match protocol tcp
ALC-A>config>filter>ip-filter>entry>match$ src-port range 666 999
ALC-A>config>filter>ip-filter>entry>match$ exit
ALC-A>config>filter>ip-filter>entry# action forward
ALC-A>config>filter>ip-filter>entry# ^z
ALC-A# configure router interface to-ALC-B
ALC-A>config>router>if# ingress
ALC-A>config>router>if>ingress# filter ip 1
ALC-A>config>router>if>ingress#
```

After the filter has been created, it must be associated with the ingress or egress of an interface. In Listing 6.4, the filter is applied to the ingress; note the use of the ingress command in the third line from the bottom.

In Listing 6.5, RTR-B (the name of the router) is configured to deny traffic from network 1.2.3.0/24 from entering the router on the interface toward RTR-C. This filter blocks all traffic received from that network from passing through to any other network in the topology. All other traffic received on the interface toRTR-C is allowed to enter because this is the default action.

Listing 6.5 An example filter policy with a default forward action

```
RTR-B# configure filter
RTR-B>config>filter# ip-filter 1 create
RTR-B>config>filter>ip-filter$ default-action forward
RTR-B>config>filter>ip-filter$ entry 1 create
RTR-B>config>filter>ip-filter>entry$ match src-ip 1.2.3.0/24
RTR-B>config>filter>ip-filter>entry# action drop
RTR-B# configure router interface toRTR-C
RTR-B>config>router>if# ingress
RTR-B>config>router>if>ingress# filter ip 1
```

In Listing 6.6, a filter has been created to permit only traffic from Host 1.2.3.4 to egress the interface toRTR-A. All other traffic egressing the interface toRTR-A will be dropped because this is the default action.

Listing 6.6 A filter policy with a single entry to permit packets with a source IP address of 1.2.3.4/34 and drop all other packets

```
RTR-B# configure filter
RTR-B>config>filter# ip-filter 1 create
RTR-B>config>filter>ip-filter$ default-action drop
RTR-B>config>filter>ip-filter$ entry 1 create
RTR-B>config>filter>ip-filter>entry$ match src-ip 1.2.3.4/32
RTR-B>config>filter>ip-filter>entry# action forward
RTR-B# configure router interface toRTR-A
RTR-B>config>router>if# egress
RTR-B>config>router>if>egress# filter ip 1
```

 You can examine an IP filter using the command show filter ip <filter number>.

Listing 6.7 shows the output for the sample configuration created in Listing 6.4. In the filter, the default action is to drop IP packets that do not meet the more explicit match settings. In the match settings, the filter is looking for all traffic sourced from IP subnet 1.2.3.0/24 that uses TCP at the transport layer and specifically uses application ports 666 to 999. If these criteria are met, the packet is forwarded.

Listing 6.7 Output of the show filter ip # command for the filter created in Listing 6.4

```
ALA-1# show filter ip 1
===============================================================
IP Filter
===============================================================
Filter Id    : 1                     Applied      : Yes
Scope        : Template              Def. Action  : Drop
Entries      : 1
Description : new-filter
---------------------------------------------------------------
Filter Match Criteria : IP
---------------------------------------------------------------
Entry        : 1
Log Id       : n/a
Src. IP      : 1.2.3.0/24      Src. Port      : 666..999
```

(continued)

```
Dest. IP        : 0.0.0.0/0         Dest. Port      : None
Protocol        : 6                 Dscp            : Undefined
ICMP Type       : Undefined         ICMP Code       : Undefined
Fragment        : Off               Option-present  : Off
Sampling        : Off               Int. Sampling   : On
IP-Option       : 0/0               Multiple Option : Off
TCP-syn         : Off               TCP-ack         : Off
Match action : Forwarded
Ing. Matches : 0       Egr. Matches   : 0
==================================================================================
```

You have now completed the examination of IP forwarding and services. In the next chapter, you will examine the upper-layer services, TCP and UDP.

Now you should complete the lab exercises to assist you in reinforcing this chapter's features. These lab exercises are carefully designed to give you hands-on experience configuring many of the technology standards that have been discussed and should greatly aid you in your exam preparation.

Practice Lab: ICMP and ARP

The following lab is designed to reinforce your knowledge of the content in this chapter. Please review the instructions carefully and perform the steps in the order in which they are presented. The practice labs require that you have access to three or more Alcatel-Lucent 7750 SRs or Alcatel-Lucent 7450 ESSs in a non-production environment.

 These labs are designed to be used in a controlled lab environment. Please **DO NOT** attempt to perform these labs in a production environment.

Internet Control Messaging Protocol (ICMP) is an IP protocol used to report on errors in the delivery of an IP datagram. When a destination address is unreachable, the router that cannot find the destination sends an ICMP "destination unreachable" message to the source of the IP datagram. ARP is a mechanism used to find out the MAC address corresponding to a specific IP address (if one doesn't already exist in the cache of Ethernet MAC addresses).

The lab exercises in this chapter have a dual purpose: to illustrate ARP and ICMP as well as show some basics of debugging on the Alcatel-Lucent 7750/7450 products.

Lab Section 6.1: Testing for ICMP and ARP

The last step in the previous chapter's lab exercises used the ping command. If a ping succeeds, it provides useful information in the form of reliability and latency statistics. If ping fails, however, it provides almost no diagnostic or troubleshooting information other than that "something" is broken. We have no indication whether the connectivity problem is with the source, the destination, or an intervening link between the two. By using debugging facilities, it is possible to narrow down and thus identify problems that may exist in any of these three areas.

Objective In this exercise, you will use show and debug commands to verify the functioning of the ARP table and the operation of ping commands.

Validation You will know you have succeeded if you are able to see debug output showing both ICMP request and reply packets on each router.

1. The first step to set up debugging is to define *what* information is desired and *where* it should go. Configure a log file that receives output from the debug/execution trace stream and delivers it to the terminal session. You may want to review the material on log files from Chapter 2 before continuing.

    ```
    *B:PE1# configure log log-id 33
    *B:PE1>config>log>log-id$ from debug-trace
    *B:PE1>config>log>log-id$ to session
    *B:PE1>config>log>log-id$ exit
    *B:PE1#
    ```

    1a. Can you use a CLI Help function to find out how many log files can be configured?

2. Configure which events will generate debug/execution trace information, for any listening log files.

    ```
    *B:PE1# debug router ip icmp
    ```

    2a. Use a CLI Help function to find out what other categories of events can be specified as a source of debug information. How many are there in the router ip context?

3. From CE1 and PE2, attempt to ping the IP address of PE1's interfaces. Observe the debug ICMP messages on the core routers.

```
*A:CE1>config>router# ping 140.10.0.101
PING 140.10.0.101 56 data bytes
64 bytes from 140.10.0.101: icmp_seq=1 ttl=64 time=10ms.
64 bytes from 140.10.0.101: icmp_seq=2 ttl=64 time<10ms.
[... Additional output omitted ...]


[ Output captured from PE1 terminal session ]
1 2000/01/01 13:53:45.62 UTC MINOR: DEBUG #2001 Base PIP
"PIP: ICMP
instance 1 (Base), interface index 4 (toCE1),
ICMP  ingressing on toCE1:
    140.10.0.102 -> 140.10.0.101
    type: Echo (8)  code: No Code (0)
"


2 2000/01/01 13:53:45.62 UTC MINOR: DEBUG #2001 Base PIP
"PIP: ICMP
instance 1 (Base), interface index 4 (toCE1),
ICMP  egressing on toCE1:
    140.10.0.101 -> 140.10.0.102
    type: Echo Reply (0)  code: No Code (0)
"
```

3a. Examine the output on PE1 carefully. Each ICMP packet is numbered in ascending order. Why are there 10 packets showing up on PE1 when CE1 only launched five ping requests?

3b. Can you find where the ingress/egress interface is identified?

4. Modify the ping command: The source IP address embedded in the ICMP Echo request packet should be the system interface address.

```
*A:CE1# ping 140.10.0.101 source 140.10.0.3
PING 140.10.0.101 56 data bytes
Request timed out. icmp_seq=1.
Request timed out. icmp_seq=2.
 [... Additional output omitted ...]
```

```
[ Output captured from PE1 terminal session ]
11 2000/01/01 14:04:50.33 UTC MINOR: DEBUG #2001 Base PIP
"PIP: ICMP
instance 1 (Base), interface index 4 (toCE1),
ICMP  ingressing on toCE1:
    140.10.0.3 -> 140.10.0.101
    type: Echo (8)  code: No Code (0)
"

12 2000/01/01 14:04:51.33 UTC MINOR: DEBUG #2001 Base PIP
"PIP: ICMP
instance 1 (Base), interface index 4 (toCE1),
ICMP  ingressing on toCE1:
    140.10.0.3 -> 140.10.0.101
    type: Echo (8)  code: No Code (0)
"
```

4a. How many ICMP requests appear on CE1? How many requests are successfully received by PE1? How many replies are sent?

4b. In which direction (ingress/egress) is all the traffic flowing under these circumstances? Why?

5. To verify ARP operation, turn on debug only for ARP on PE1. Start with an "empty" ARP cache by executing the following commands on each of the routers, and then start a ping to PE1 from either CE1 or PE2.

```
*A:CE1# clear router arp all

*B:PE1# clear router arp all
*B:PE1#
*B:PE1# show router arp

===============================================================
ARP Table (Router: Base)
===============================================================
IP Address      MAC Address      Expiry    Type    Interface
---------------------------------------------------------------
140.10.0.1      00:21:05:4d:41:41 00h00m00s Oth     system
140.10.0.11     00:21:05:4d:41:41 00h00m00s Oth     loopbackTest
140.10.0.97     00:1a:f0:57:72:6f 00h00m00s Oth[I]  toPE2
140.10.0.101    00:1a:f0:6c:6c:4c 00h00m00s Oth[I]  toCE1
```

```
------------------------------------------------------------------
No. of ARP Entries: 4
==================================================================

*B:PE1# debug router  ip no icmp
*B:PE1# debug router ip arp
*B:PE1# show debug
debug
    router "Base"
        ip
            arp
        exit
    exit
exit

*A:CE1# ping 140.10.0.101
[... Additional output omitted ...]

[ Output captured from PE1 terminal session ]
16 2000/01/01 14:17:06.19 UTC MINOR: DEBUG #2001 Base PIP
"PIP: ARP
instance 1 (Base), interface index 4 (toCE1),
ARP ingressing on toCE1
    Who has 140.10.0.101 ? Tell 140.10.0.102
"

17 2000/01/01 14:17:06.19 UTC MINOR: DEBUG #2001 Base PIP
"PIP: ARP
instance 1 (Base), interface index 4 (toCE1),
ARP egressing on toCE1
    140.10.0.101 is at 00:1a:f0:6c:6c:4c
"
```

5a. Why isn't the ARP table (cache) empty after issuing the
clear router arp all command? Which MAC/IP addresses remain?

5b. Why is there only a single ARP request/reply pair, instead of a pair for every
ping sent by CE1?

6. From PE1, ping the network interface address of both other routers. Observe whether ARP messages are generated. Verify that the ARP entry for the neighboring interfaces has been added.

```
*B:PE1# show router arp

===============================================================
ARP Table (Router: Base)
===============================================================
IP Address      MAC Address       Expiry    Type   Interface
---------------------------------------------------------------
140.10.0.1      00:21:05:4d:41:41 00h00m00s Oth    system
140.10.0.11     00:21:05:4d:41:41 00h00m00s Oth    loopbackTest
140.10.0.97     00:1a:f0:57:72:6f 00h00m00s Oth[I] toPE2
140.10.0.98     00:1a:f0:74:65:41 03h59m27s Dyn[I] toPE2
140.10.0.101    00:1a:f0:6c:6c:4c 00h00m00s Oth[I] toCE1
140.10.0.102    00:1a:f0:61:62:73 03h39m52s Dyn[I] toCE1
---------------------------------------------------------------
No. of ARP Entries: 6
===============================================================
*B:PE1#
```

6a. Were ARP messages generated? Why or why not?

6b. How many ARP entries are on each router at this point? Explain.

7. From PE1, attempt to ping the system interface address of both other routers. Observe whether ARP messages are generated.

7a. Were the pings successful? Why or why not?

7b. Were ARP messages generated? Why or why not?

7c. When a router is trying to reach a given IP, which comes first—checking the routing table or checking the ARP table?

Chapter Review

Now that you have completed this chapter, you should have a good understanding of the following topics. If you are not familiar with these topics, please go back and review the appropriate sections.

- How an incoming IP packet is processed and forwarded by a router
- The information contained in a router FIB table
- The purpose of a default gateway
- Understanding NAT and PAT and why they are used
- The purpose and operation of DHCP
- The purpose and operation of ARP
- The purpose of ICMP and how echo reply, echo request, and destination unreachable messages are used
- The concept of an IP filter and how they are created and applied on the Alcatel-Lucent 7750 SR

Post-Assessment

The following questions will test your knowledge and prepare you for the Alcatel-Lucent NRS I Certification Exam. Please review each question carefully and choose the most correct answer. You can compare your response with the answers listed in Appendix A. You can also download all of the CD content at `http://booksupport` `.wiley.com` to take all the assessment tests and review the answers. Good luck!

1. Which of the following is a function not performed by a router when forwarding an IP packet?

    A. Verify the IP header checksum.

    B. Decrement the TTL and ensure that it is not zero.

    C. Send a "received" message to the originating router.

    D. Remove the existing L2 header and create a new L2 header before forwarding the IP packet to its next destination.

2. Which of the following highlights the differences between a traditional home user network and the modern home user network?

    A. Traditional home networks did not use routers.

    B. Modern home networks can use wireless access points.

    C. Modern home networks make use of a variety of new services such as Video on Demand and IP telephony.

    D. Traditional home networks did not rely on the IP protocol.

3. In a typical home network, when a PC needs to send an IP packet to a destination on the Internet, it first sends the packet to _____.

    A. The designated router

    B. The cable modem

    C. The router indicated in its BGP table

    D. The default gateway

4. Which of the following statements regarding NAT is false?

   A. NAT is used for many-to-one translations.

   B. NAT is intended to alleviate the need for every home user device to have a public IP address.

   C. NAT typically makes use of private IP addressing.

   D. A NAT router maintains a translation database to perform the address conversions.

5. The process by which a home user's router requests and receives a public IP address from its service provider is known as _____.

   A. ARP

   B. DHCP

   C. ICMP

   D. OSPF

6. Which of the following is false about the DHCP process?

   A. The client broadcasts a discover message looking for DHCP servers.

   B. All DHCP servers will broadcast an offer message.

   C. A client will send a unicast accept message to the first DHCP server it receives a response from.

   D. All of the above statements are true.

7. The ping application relies on two common ICMP message types. Which answer is *not* one of these types?

   A. The echo receive ICMP type.

   B. The echo request ICMP type.

   C. The echo reply ICMP type.

   D. None of the above are ICMP message types used by ping.

8. Which of the following is true regarding ICMP `destination unreachable` messages?

   A. They are sent after failure to receive an Ethernet ACK.

   B. They are created by routers that cannot deliver an IP packet to its destination.

   C. They rely on the use of ICMP echo replies.

   D. They are originated by hosts that are about to reboot.

9. Which of the following is not usually involved in the ARP process when a host needs to send an IP packet to another host not on its own IP subnet?

A. The host needs to determine based on its mask that the destination host is not on its local subnet.

B. The host will issue an ARP request for the MAC address of its default gateway if it is not in its ARP cache.

C. The default gateway will determine if it needs to issue an ARP request for the destination host.

D. The default gateway will issue an ARP request for the MAC address of the originating host.

10. Which of the following is false regarding IP filters?

A. IP filters are not required on a router interface.

B. IP filters can filter on both IP addresses and upper-layer protocol port numbers.

C. IP filters will automatically permit IP packets by default unless otherwise configured.

D. Only one ingress and one egress filter can be applied per interface.

11. Which of the following is *not* a match criteria that can be used with IP filters?

A. Source or destination IP address

B. Source or destination port number

C. ICMP message type

D. Originating host name

12. Which of the following is *not* a valid IP filter command?

A. `ip-filter 10 create`

B. `default-action discard`

C. `entry 1 create`

D. `match dst-ip 10.5.1.0/24`

13. Which of the following IP filter entries would match packets from Network 11.1.1.0/24 to Host 5.1.1.1?

    A. `match src-ip 11.1.1.0/24`

    B. `match dst-ip 5.1.1.1/32`

    C. A and B together

    D. None of the above

14. You are creating a filter to permit packets to destination IP address 192.168.1.1/32. You want all other packets to be dropped. Which of the following commands is *not* required to support this policy?

    A. `ip-filter 1 create`

    B. `default-action drop`

    C. `entry 1 create`

    D. `match dst-ip 192.168.1.1/32`

15. Which of the following is *not* displayed with the use of the `show filter` command?

    A. The filter's default action

    B. The interfaces where the filter is applied

    C. The number of ingress and egress matches

    D. The entries in the filter

Transport Layer Services—TCP and UDP

- TCP connection-oriented services
- TCP guarantee of data delivery
- UDP connectionless services
- TCP and UDP use of port numbers for multiplexing

In this chapter we discuss the upper-layer transport protocols that are the application's interface to IP. We pay particular attention to the Transport Control Protocol (TCP) and how its features provide for the guaranteed delivery of data and management of congestion in the network. We also examine the User Datagram Protocol (UDP) and how it provides connectionless services for applications that do not require the overhead of TCP. Finally, we examine how port numbers are used by both TCP and UDP to provide *multiplexing*—the ability of a single TCP or UDP process to service multiple data streams based on discrete numbers that identify the upper-layer application.

Pre-Assessment

The following assessment questions will help you understand what areas of the chapter you should review in more detail to prepare for the exam. You can also download all of the CD materials for this book at http://booksupport.wiley.com to take all the assessment tests and review the answers.

1. Which of the following is *not* a transport layer protocol?

   A. TP4

   B. TCP

   C. RTP

   D. UDP

2. Which of the following statements about transport layer protocols is false?

   A. Most Internet applications use a transport layer protocol.

   B. Transport layer protocols can provide both reliable and unreliable services.

   C. Transport layer protocols provide end-to-end services for applications.

   D. Transport layer protocols require that additional software be added to your operating system.

3. Which of the following is *not* a characteristic of the TCP protocol?

   A. Reliable data transfer

   B. Connectionless operation

   C. Flow control supported

   D. Full-duplex operation

4. Which of the following is *not* a characteristic of the UDP protocol?

  A. Reliable data transfer

  B. Connectionless operation

  C. No flow control

  D. Appropriate for real-time traffic

5. Which of the following TCP flags is not matched with the correct definition?

  A. SYN—Indicates the start of a TCP connection.

  B. ACK—Acknowledges that a TCP segment has been received.

  C. FIN—Indicates the closing of a TCP session.

  D. RST—Re-sets the sequence numbers for a TCP session.

You will find the answers to each of these questions in Appendix A. You can also use the CD that accompanies this book to take all the assessment tests and review the answers.

7.1 Understanding the Transport Layer

As previously discussed, the transport layer is Layer 4 of the Open Systems Interconnection (OSI) model. The transport layer is designed to provide end-to-end control and information transfer of data sent from upper-layer applications. The goal of the transport layer is to relieve the upper layers from the need to provide reliable data transfer over an unreliable network protocol (such as Internet Protocol (IP)). The transport layer is the first layer of the OSI model that is concerned with ensuring the accurate delivery of data from one host to another. In the TCP/IP stack, the Transmission Control Protocol (TCP) and the User Datagram Protocol (UDP) provide services very similar to the OSI transport protocols and are therefore often referred to as *transport* or *Layer 4* protocols.

Internet applications such as Web browsing and email transfer use the services of the transport protocols. If the application needs a high level of service, such as reliable data transfer and flow control, the application typically uses TCP for data transfer as it provides these capabilities. If an application needs a simpler service with less overhead, the application may use UDP and perform any additional checking of data delivery itself.

 Although most higher-level protocols use TCP or UDP, there are a few higher-level protocols that do not use either of them. For example, the Open Shortest Path First (OSPF) routing protocol uses IP datagrams directly and does not use a transport layer protocol at all.

The transport layer protocols that are defined in the OSI model provide a wide range of services. TP0 (Transport Protocol 0) provides the lowest level of service, and TP4 (Transport Protocol 4) provides the highest level of service. The services provided by TP4 are very similar to those provided by TCP. Both TP4 and TCP are built to provide a reliable, connection-oriented, end-to-end transport service on top of an unreliable network service. The network service may lose packets, store packets, deliver packets in the wrong order, or even duplicate packets. Both protocols must be able to deal with the most severe problems (e.g., a subnetwork stores valid packets and sends them at a later date). Both TP4 and TCP have connect, transfer, and disconnect phases, and their principles of operation during these phases are also quite similar.

An application such as email that needs to transfer data across the Internet will use the services of an Internet transport protocol. Email uses TCP, because email needs a reliable data transfer service. The application data is first passed to the TCP services layer. The TCP layer then divides the application data into segments, if necessary (if, e.g., the amount of application data is larger than a single TCP segment can accommodate). Each TCP segment contains a TCP header. The size of the segments is based on the maximum transmission unit (MTU) size of the Layer 2 networks that are expected to be used for the transfer. The TCP segments are then passed to the IP services layer, where they are delivered across the network as IP datagrams. This encapsulation process is shown in Figure 7.1.

Figure 7.1 The application data is passed to the TCP layer, where it is divided into TCP segments and a TCP header is added to each segment. Each TCP segment is then passed to the IP layer, where an IP header is added before transmission onto the underlying data link layer.

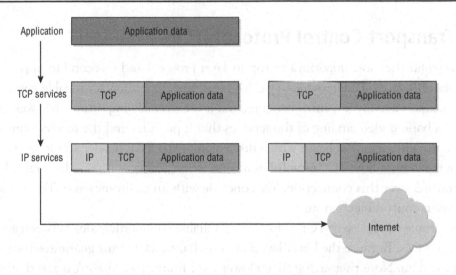

Each IP datagram contains the IP header and is routed across the network using the procedures described in Chapter 6. IP is an unreliable service, so if TCP determines that some of the IP datagrams were not received, TCP re-transmits the missing TCP segments. After the TCP segments are received by the receiving system, the TCP services layer supplies the application data to the receiving application exactly as the data was sent by the transmitting application. This is the reliable transfer service provided by TCP.

On a computer that is connected to the Internet, the TCP and IP services are usually provided as part of the operating system services. For example, all current versions of Windows, Linux, and Mac OS supply their own TCP/IP stack with the operating system. Most desktop and laptop systems purchased today come with a network card of some type that already has TCP/IP enabled, and thus there is usually very little configuration that needs to be done in order to access the Internet. Provided that the network you use provides the DHCP service as discussed in Chapter 6, it is normally a matter of simply plugging your computer into the network and starting your application.

In the next sections, we examine the TCP and UDP protocols and the services they provide in some detail. It should be noted that coverage of TCP will be much more comprehensive because TCP provides many more services than UDP and as such is a more complicated protocol.

7.2 Transport Control Protocol (TCP)

TCP is by far the most important transport layer protocol and is second in importance of topics only to IP. TCP provides a wealth of features that allow for reliable communication across virtually any infrastructure, and it is extremely important that you have at least a basic understanding of the services that it provides and the mechanisms it uses to provide them. We begin with a discussion of the TCP header and its options. We then examine how TCP establishes a connection and how it provides a reliable data transfer over this connection. We conclude with an examination of TCP's flow/congestion control mechanisms.

The primary purpose of TCP is to provide reliable communications between application services. Because the lower layers are unreliable, TCP must guarantee the delivery of the data. Note that saying that a lower layer is *unreliable* doesn't mean that the lower layers often fail. In fact, networks today are often very reliable. It simply means that the lower layers do not *guarantee* that a packet will be delivered. In all likelihood it will be delivered, but the lower layers do not have the onus of ensuring this occurs; TCP does.

The original TCP specification is provided in RFC 793. This RFC specifies the key functionality provided by TCP. Some of these functions are:

- **Data Transfer**—From the application-services viewpoint, TCP provides a contiguous stream of data through the network. TCP groups the bytes into segments and passes the segments to the IP for transmission to the destination. Note that this means that an application does not need to know or care how the data is transferred by TCP. It simply hands off a stream of data through an Application Programming Interface (API) call to the TCP service, and TCP handles the rest. This allows for an application developer to write very simple programming calls to TCP without having to specify how the data is to be transferred across the network.

- **Reliability**—TCP uses sequence numbers, which count each byte transmitted, and TCP waits for an acknowledgment from the receiving host. If the acknowledgment is not received within a specific interval, the data is re-transmitted. Note that this is a passive re-transmission system. The receiving host does not request missing data; it simply acknowledges only the data it has actually received. It is up to the sending TCP stack to recognize that it has not received acknowledgment for a particular segment and to re-send that segment.

- **Flow Control and Congestion Control**—*Flow control* refers to the capability of the receiver to control the rate at which data is sent by the sender by setting a "window size." *Congestion control* refers to the sender's ability to alter the rate at which it is sending based on network conditions such as packet drops.

- **Multiplexing**—Port numbers are used for multiplexing and de-multiplexing. This means that you can have many applications running simultaneously that all use TCP, with each having its own port number. TCP can seamlessly put all these streams of data into a TCP flow (*multiplex*) and then separate them out based on the port numbers each application is using (*de-multiplex*).

- **Logical Connections**—To support reliability and flow control, TCP must initialize and maintain status information for each connection. The status information contains sockets numbers, sequence numbers, and window size. These components combine to form a logical connection.

- **Full-Duplex**—A TCP connection is full-duplex: Either end may transmit data at any time. Note that this is not like a radio conversation, where only one party can talk at once. Here, each end of a TCP connection can send and receive at any time.

Figure 7.2 illustrates how TCP uses port numbers to differentiate conversations and how the protocol layers are "stacked" to provide the services layering we have been discussing throughout this book.

Figure 7.2 TCP uses port numbers to uniquely identify upper-layer applications and will pass the data it receives to the correct application on each end of a reliable connection. TCP makes use of the underlying unreliable IP layer to transfer data between Host A and Host B. If there are packet drops or packets arrive out of order, these issues will be handled by TCP. This will be transparent to the application layer above it and the network layer below it.

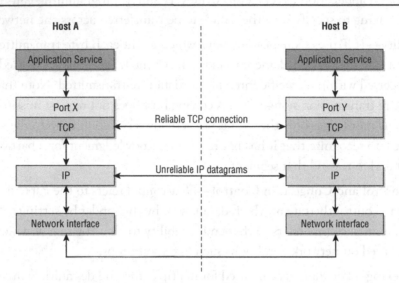

The TCP Header

Just as with IP, TCP has a header that contains the fields that TCP uses to provide the services previously mentioned. It is important that you become familiar with some of these key fields in order to fully understand how TCP uses these fields to enable the services it provides to the upper layers. The TCP header is illustrated in Figure 7.3.

The TCP header fields include:

- **Source and Destination Ports**—Port addresses identify the upper-layer applications that use the connection.

- **Sequence Number**—Each byte of data is assigned a sequence number. This 32-bit number ensures that data is correctly sequenced. The first byte of data that is sent by a station in a TCP header has its sequence number in this field (e.g., 58000). If this segment contains 700 bytes of data, the next segment sent by this station will have sequence number 58700 (i.e., 58000 + 700, so the formula to calculate the acknowledgment number is simply the last sequence number + the number of bytes in the last segment).

Figure 7.3 The fields in a TCP header. Note that there are many short fields with three-letter acronyms such as urg, ack, psh, and so on. These are known as *TCP flags*, and it is very important that you understand what these flags are for.

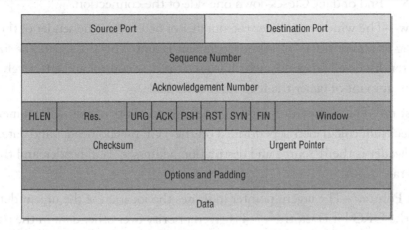

- **Acknowledgment Number**—This 32-bit number indicates the next sequence number that the sending device expects from the other station. Note that this is the *next* sequence number it is expecting, not the *current* sequence number. This is a key point to understand.

- **HLEN**—The header length provides the number of 32-bit words in the header. This is sometimes called the *Data Offset field*.

- **Reserved**—The value is always set to 0.

- **Code Bits**—The following flags indicate the type of header:

  - **URG**—Indicates that there is data in the segment that should be given priority and passed immediately to the application (e.g., [Ctrl]+C to abort an operation).

  - **ACK**—Acknowledgment, always present except in the initial packet of a TCP connection

  - **PSH**—Used by the application to indicate to TCP that the data should be transmitted immediately rather than buffered (e.g., to finish filling a segment). Also indicates to the receiver that data should be given immediately to the application. Intended to reduce overall latency that could be introduced by TCP.

  - **RST**—Re-sets the connection. This essentially tears down the connection.

- **SYN**—Synchronizes sequence numbers, only used during connection establishment.

- **FIN**—End of data. Closes down one side of the connection.

- **Window**—The window indicates the number of octets that the sender of the ACK is willing to accept before an acknowledgment is sent. This is the window size parameter discussed previously, which is used for flow control and effectively represents the amount of buffer the receiver has available.

- **Checksum**—The checksum is used to verify the integrity of the TCP segment. The checksum calculation is performed on the TCP pseudo-header and data. The *pseudo-header* is the IP source and destination addresses, TCP header, and the TCP data.

- **Urgent Pointer**—The urgent pointer indicates the location of the urgent data. When the URG bit is set, this data is given priority over other data in the data stream. It should be noted that this and the URG flag are rarely used in modern applications.

- **Options**—Several options are defined for TCP. The most common is the TCP Maximum Segment Size (MSS) (details below).

The MSS defines the largest segment that will be sent on the TCP connection. The value is an estimate by the TCP of the size of datagrams that can be accommodated on the connection without fragmentation. Usually each side sends the MTU value of its Layer 2 connection in the MSS field. The lower of the two values is then used by both sides as the MSS. For example, the MTU of Ethernet is 1,514, while the MTU of a PPP connection might be 500. If both ends sent their respective MTUs, then 500 would be chosen as the MSS since the lowest MSS is always chosen.

However, the problem with determining the MSS using only the two endpoints is that there may be a link in the middle of the connection that has a smaller MTU than either end. In this case, all full-size packets will have to be fragmented by IP to traverse this link. (Recall the discussion of IP fragmentation from Chapter 5.) Fragmentation is an inefficient operation and should be avoided if possible because it places unnecessary strain on the fragmenting router. To avoid this, TCP may perform Path MTU Discovery in which TCP attempts to find the MTU that is supported across the connection and use this MTU as the MSS. However, Path MTU Discovery is not always supported by a particular vendor's TCP implementation, and thus sometimes IP fragmentation is unavoidable.

Establishing a TCP Connection—The Three-Way Handshake

Before TCP can transmit any data, it must first establish a connection from the sender to the receiver, similar to someone picking up a phone to call another party. This process is called the *three-way handshake* and is illustrated in Figure 7.4.

Figure 7.4 The TCP three-way handshake. Host A sends a SYN request with a starting sequence number, an acknowledgement number set to zero, and the SYN bit set. Host B acknowledges this by sending a response with its own sequence number, an acknowledgement number equal to Host A's sequence number plus 1, and the SYN and ACK bits set. Host A then responds with a new sequence number equal to its initial sequence number plus 1, an acknowledgement number equal to Host B's sequence number plus 1, and the ACK bit set. Once these three packets are exchanged, the handshake is complete and communication can begin.

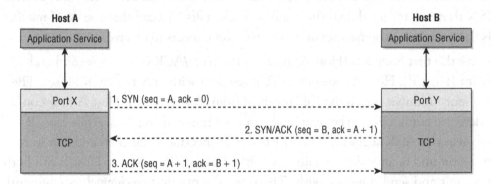

Figure 7.4 shows how a three-way handshake is performed. In a TCP session, data is not transmitted until the three-way handshake is successfully completed and the session is considered open. The opening TCP segments include the initial sequence numbers from both sides, and these sequence numbers increase throughout the TCP conversation. The MSS is also agreed on during the three-way handshake. After a session is established between the two hosts, data can be transferred until the session is interrupted or shut down. The data is sent in TCP segments, which are a combination of the data and a TCP header.

There are three steps to establish the TCP session, (hence the term *three-way handshake*). These steps are:

- One endpoint (Host A) sends a TCP segment with the SYN bit set in the header. This indicates that the host wishes to establish a TCP connection. Note this means that if the SYN bit is set, it is always the beginning of a conversation; it should never be set otherwise. TCP also selects a 32-bit sequence number to use for the session. This number is included in the TCP header and is known as the *Initial*

Sequence Number (ISN). The acknowledgement field is 0 since the sender does not yet have any idea what the ISN is for the receiving side of the conversation.

- The other endpoint (Host B) receives the SYN segment, and, if an application is ready to accept the connection, TCP sends a second segment with the SYN and the ACK bits set in the header. Note that the SYN bit is set because TCP conversations are full-duplex, so the receiving station is opening up its own "reverse" connection to the original sender so that it can send data independently of the data stream that it is receiving from the sender. TCP on Host B also selects its sequence number for the session and transmits the number as its ISN. TCP also sends a value in the acknowledgement field of the TCP header. This number is the value of the ISN that was received from the original sender plus 1 (recall that the *ACK number* is the number of the next segment the receiver expects to receive).

- After the first endpoint (Host A) receives the SYN/ACK from the second endpoint (Host B), Host A transmits a TCP segment with only the ACK bit set. The sequence number sent is the ISN received from Host B, plus 1. Host A now considers the connection to be open and can start transmitting data. After Host B receives the ACK segment, it considers the connection to be open and can start to transmit and receive data. Again, note that TCP is full-duplex, so Host B can both transmit and send simultaneously. There are, essentially, two *channels* of communication between Host A and Host B.

TCP Reliable Data Transfer

If an application requires reliable transfer of its data across the network, it will use TCP to obtain that service. TCP is responsible for ensuring that all data is received and sent to the receiving application in the order in which it was sent. This means that TCP will order the data for the application, even if the data arrives out of order. Since TCP ensures delivery even if some packets are dropped, it will wait to receive missing data before passing it to the upper-layer application. This technique is known as *positive acknowledgement with re-transmission* because TCP actively acknowledges only the data that was actually received; it does not request information that has not been received. It is up to the sender to notice out-of-order or duplicate acknowledgements and re-send missing data.

Each segment that is sent by TCP has an identifying sequence number transmitted in the TCP header. This sequence number indicates the number of the first byte of data in the overall data stream for this connection. The receiver acknowledges receipt of this data by transmitting an acknowledgement number that indicates the next byte of data in the stream that the receiver expects to receive. If some of the data is lost, the receiver will continue to send the same acknowledgement number that indicates the bytes that were received successfully. The sender maintains a re-transmission timer. If the sender does not receive an acknowledgement for some bytes of data that were sent, the data will be re-transmitted when the re-transmission timer expires.

Because the TCP segments are transmitted over an unreliable network service (IP network), the segments may arrive at the destination in a different order from that in which they were originally sent. The sequence numbers are used by the receiver to reconstruct the data stream and ensure that the data is provided to the application in the same order that the data was sent. Figure 7.5 illustrates an example of a TCP conversation when data is lost during the conversation.

Figure 7.5 TCP sends SEQ number 27000, which is acknowledged by the receiver, and the receiver indicates it expects to receive 27500 next. The sender then sends two segments with numbers 27500 and 28000, but 27500 is lost. The receiver does not acknowledge that it received 28000 because this would indicate to the sender that it received both 27500 and 28000. Instead, the receiver repeats the acknowledgement, indicating that it is still expecting 27500, which is how the sender recognizes that 27500 was lost and that it needs to re-send. Once 27500 is received, the receiver requests segment 29000 since it has already received 28000 and 28500.

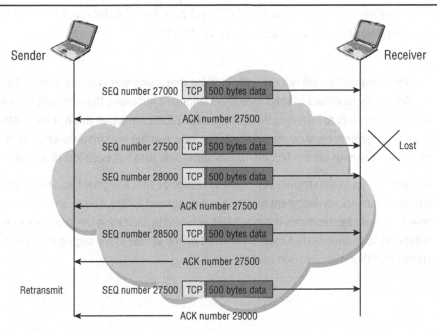

Figure 7.5 shows reliable data transfer between two hosts:

1. The sender sends a TCP segment with 500 bytes of data on an established connection. The sequence number is 27000.

2. The receiver acknowledges the receipt of this data with an acknowledgement number of 27500.

3. The sender sends another segment of 500 bytes with a sequence number of 27500. This segment is lost by the network (unreliable service).

4. The sender sends another segment of 500 bytes with a sequence number of 28000. This segment is successfully received by the receiver and is buffered.

5. The receiver sends an acknowledgement number of 27500 because the receiver still has not received the segment that contains the 500 bytes of data in the overall data stream.

6. The sender sends another segment of 500 bytes with a sequence number of 28500. This segment is received and buffered. Another acknowledgement of 27500 is sent.

7. The re-transmission timer expires for the sender, and the missing segment that contains 27500 is re-transmitted.

8. The receiver receives the segment 27500 and now has the data up to byte 29000. The receiver sends an acknowledgement of 29000.

The receiving station will not explicitly indicate that a segment was lost. Notice that the sender simply continues to send an acknowledgment indicating that the next sequence number it expects to receive is the lost segment 27500. Note that this is a *duplicate acknowledgement* because the acknowledgement number sent from the receiver is the same as a previous acknowledgment, indicating that data has been lost in transit.

It is entirely up to the sending TCP agent to recognize that a segment was lost based on this duplicate acknowledgment and to re-send segment 27500. The receiver will always only acknowledge segments it has actually received by indicating the sequence number it expects to receive next; it must be inferred by the sender that a segment was lost in transit and that it must re-send data.

TCP Flow Control

If a TCP sender waits to receive acknowledgement for each segment that it sends before sending another segment, the effective throughput of the connection can be greatly limited over the bandwidth that is supported by the transmission media. This is not significant on a high-speed LAN because the acknowledgements are received very quickly. However, if the network Round Trip Time (RTT) is long, the sender may spend a significant amount of time waiting for acknowledgements.

To increase the overall throughput on TCP connections, TCP allows the sender to send more than one segment without waiting for an acknowledgement. This provides a higher overall throughput because TCP spends less time waiting for acknowledgements. However, there is a danger of overwhelming the TCP receiver with too much data. To avoid overwhelming the receiver, the amount of data that can be sent to the receiver before receiving an acknowledgment must be controlled. To accomplish this, the received data is buffered in a preset amount of buffer space until it is requested by the application.

The amount of buffer space is specified in the TCP header window-size parameter. When the receiver sends an acknowledgement, the receiver's TCP header sets the value of the window-size parameter to specify the amount of buffer space (in bytes) that is available. This is the maximum amount of data that the sender can send before it receives the next acknowledgement. If the receiver's buffer becomes full, the receiver sends a window size of 0 and the sender cannot transmit any more data. When the receiving application requests the data and the TCP buffer space is available, the receiver sends an updated window size and the sender can start to transmit more data.

The window value is always set by the receiver, which provides a flow control mechanism for the receiver. Figure 7.6 illustrates an example of TCP flow control in which the receiver is receiving data faster than it can process it and therefore advertises a window size of 0 to halt the transfer of data from the sender.

The TCP flow control process works as follows:

1. The sender received an ACK from a previous transmission that indicates a window size of 5,000 bytes.

2. The sender has 3,000 bytes to send and transmits them in three 1,000-byte segments, one after the other.

3. The receiver buffers the received data and sends an ACK to acknowledge all the received data. The receiver sets the window size to 2,000.

Figure 7.6 The sender is transmitting data faster than the host can receive it. The first advertised window size is 5,000 in the first acknowledgment. After additional data is received, the receiver reduces its window size to 2,000 in the next acknowledgment. After still more data is received, the receiver reduces its window size to 0, effectively halting the sender from receiving any additional data until the receiver's buffer is cleared and it sends a non-zero window size to the sender. At this point, the sender can resume its transmission.

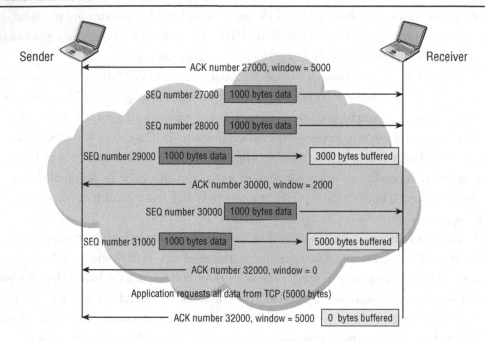

4. The sender has more data to send. Because the last window size was 2,000, the sender cannot send more than 2,000 bytes. This data is sent in two 1,000-byte segments.

5. The receiver buffers the 2,000 bytes as they are received. Because the application has not requested any data, the initial 3,000 bytes received are still being buffered.

6. The receiver's buffer is now full, and an ACK with a window value of 0 is sent.

7. Even if the sender has more data to send, the sender must not transmit any more data because the window size is currently 0.

8. The application requests data from TCP, and the 5,000 bytes are taken from the buffer. The buffer is now empty, and an ACK is transmitted to re-set the window size to 5,000.

9. When the sender receives the new window size, the sender can now transmit more data.

It is rare, given the CPU processing power of modern computers, for a TCP process to reduce its window size to zero in order to stop the data flow completely. What is more likely is for the window size to reduce slightly, as some segments are processed to slow down the sending host slightly, and then for the receiver to send an increased window size to allow the sender to begin transmitting more rapidly.

TCP Operation

A somewhat typical TCP conversation is shown in Figure 7.7. Here, an entire (albeit short) TCP conversation is shown from start to finish. Note that this is a simplified example in which Host 1 is sending data to Host 2, but Host 2 is simply acknowledging the data and is not sending any data of its own to Host 1. Host 2 *could* send data of its own to Host 1 because TCP is a full-duplex protocol; it is just not doing so in this example.

Figure 7.7 A short but complete TCP conversation from start to finish. The three-way handshake starts the TCP conversation, data is transferred with sequence and acknowledgement numbers, and the window size fluctuates slightly. The conversation is closed at the end with FIN and FIN + ACK bits set. Wnd=the advertised TCP Window and LEN=the length of the data in the TCP segment.

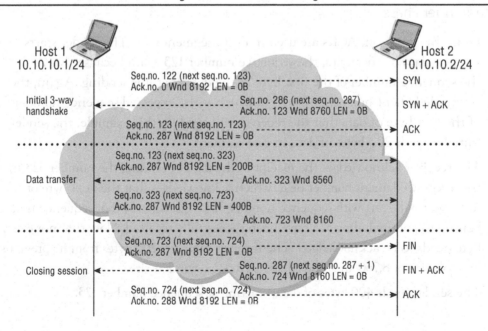

The process is outlined in the following lists:

Initial Three-Way Handshake Phase

1. The session begins with Host 10.10.10.1/24, which initiates a SYN that contains the sequence number 122, which is the ISN. There are only zeros in the acknowledgment field because this field is not used in the SYN segment. The window size of the sender starts as 8,192 octets.

2. The receiving host sends its ISN (286) in the sequence number field and acknowledges the sender's sequence number by incrementing the number by 1 (123); the receiver expects this value to be the starting sequence number of the data bytes that the sender will send next. This is called the *SYN-ACK segment*. The receiver's window size starts as 8,760.

3. When the SYN-ACK is received, the sender issues an ACK that acknowledges the receiver's ISN by incrementing the ISN by 1 and placing the value in the acknowledgment field (287). The sender also sends the same sequence number that it sent previously (123). These three segments that are exchanged to establish the connection never contain any data.

Data Transfer Phase

1. From this point on, ACKs are used in every segment sent. The sender starts sending data by specifying the sequence number 123 again because this is the sequence number of the first byte of the data that it is sending. Again, the acknowledgment number 287 is sent, which is the expected sequence number of the first byte of data that the receiver will send. In this example, the sender initially sends 200 bytes of data in one segment.

2. The receiver acknowledges the receipt of the data by sending the number 323 in the acknowledgment number field, which acknowledges that the next byte of data to be sent will start with sequence number 323. It is assumed that sequence numbers up to and including 323 have been successfully received. Note that not every byte needs to be acknowledged. The receiver subtracts 200 bytes from its previous window size of 8,760 and sends 8,560 as its new window size.

3. The sender sends 400 bytes of data, starting at sequence number 323.

Closing Session Phase

1. The receiver acknowledges receipt of the data with the number 723 (323 + 400). The receiver subtracts 400 bytes from the previous window size of 8,560 and sends the new window size of 8,160.

2. The sender transmits the expected sequence number 723 in a FIN because, at this point, the application needs to close the session. The receiver sends a FIN-ACK that acknowledges the FIN and increments the acknowledgment sequence number by 1 to 724, which is the number that the receiver will expect on the final ACK. Note that each side must send its own FIN that must be ACKed, just as each side had to send its own SYN that had to be ACKed.

3. The sender transmits the final ACK, which confirms the sequence number 724.

We have covered all of the steps in this process already, with the exception of the FIN bit. When either side of a TCP conversation wants to close the connection, it sends a segment with the FINished TCP flag set. This indicates to the other side that one side of the conversation is closing its connection. The other host will either send an ACK bit to acknowledge the FIN, or as in our example, it will respond with both the ACK bit and its own FIN bit set to close its end of the session. Two FINs are needed because TCP is full-duplex and each end can continue sending data even if the other host closes a portion of its connection. While additional data can still be sent by one end of the connection even after the initial FIN, in practice, it is typical to see the FIN, FIN + ACK, ACK sequence illustrated in Figure 7.7.

Congestion Control in TCP

In addition to these standard flow control abilities, TCP also has the ability to react to congestion in the underlying network infrastructure. Recall from our discussion of IP that there is no true congestion control at the IP layer. Although ICMP contains a *source quench* message type that is intended for congestion control, this message type is not used for end-to-end congestion control. The normal behavior of an IP router when there is congestion is to queue packets for a relatively short period. If the queuing space is depleted, additional packets are discarded. When packets are discarded, this means that they must be re-sent by the TCP layer, which is inefficient. It is far better to slow down the rate at which packets are sent and have them delivered than to re-send packets that have been dropped.

TCP implements a congestion control mechanism to help manage congestion on an end-to-end connection. A variety of different algorithms are used, but TCP congestion control typically has two phases: slow start and congestion avoidance. In *slow start* mode, after a TCP connection is established, data is not immediately transmitted in amounts up to the maximum value that is allowed by the TCP window size. Instead, transmission by the sender is limited by the *congestion window*. The *congestion window value* is initially set to one or two segments and is a value maintained by the *sender*, not a value advertised by the receiver like the window size. Each time a segment is acknowledged, the congestion window is increased, which allows the sender to slowly ramp up its sending rate. In other words, the sender starts slow and then ramps up the rate until it reaches the maximum allowed by the receiver's advertised window size—hence the term *slow start*.

Slow start is useful to ensure that a sender does not overwhelm the network at the beginning of a TCP conversation, but networks can often encounter congestion after a TCP conversation has already been established. Therefore, other mechanisms are needed to handle this situation. When congestion is detected (either through the receipt of duplicate ACKs or the expiry of a timer that measures the round trip time), TCP enters *congestion avoidance*. The congestion window is reduced to slow down the sender and then gradually increased until congestion is encountered again. This process continues through the life of the TCP connection.

An important point to remember is that even with the congestion window tracking on the sender, the maximum transmission rate is ultimately controlled by the TCP window size because this is the receiver's flow control mechanism. If the window size is less than the size allowed by the congestion window, the transmission rate will never exceed the size specified by the TCP window. In other words, the sender will always send segments at the rate specified by its own congestion window or the size of the receiver's advertised window, *whichever is less*. Figure 7.8 illustrates the concepts of TCP congestion control and how TCP adapts to network congestion.

The following steps lead you through Figure 7.8:

1. During the three-way handshake to establish the connection, the receiving side specified a window size of 8,000. An MSS of 1,000 bytes has also been established for the connection.

Figure 7.8 A typical TCP transfer of data, where the sender is using a congestion window (cwnd) to control the rate at which it is sending. The cwnd is increased until it exceeds the receiver's advertised window or congestion is detected. When congestion is detected, the receiver reduces its cwnd accordingly, and then the process starts over.

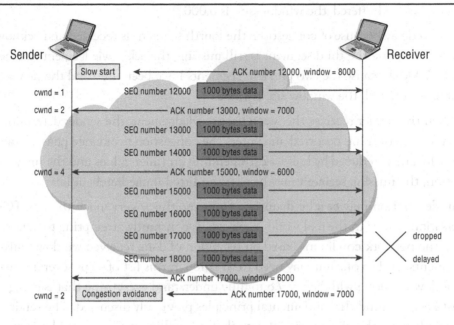

2. Because this is the start of the session, the sender is in the slow start phase and, therefore, sets its congestion window (cnwd) value to 1. The sender transmits one segment of 1,000 bytes even though there is more data to send, and a window size of 8,000 is specified by the receiver (i.e., it sends the lesser of the cwnd and the receiver's advertised window size).

3. The first segment is acknowledged by the receiver with a window size of 7,000, and the segment is buffered. The sender increases its cnwd value to 2. The sender can now transmit two segments of 1,000 bytes each. Note that the sender is ramping up the rate at which it is sending.

4. The receiving application has used the previous segment, but the two new segments are buffered and are acknowledged with a window size of 6,000.

5. Because the sender received an acknowledgement for two more segments, the sender increases the cnwd value by 2 to 4. The sender then transmits four segments of 1,000 bytes each.

6. The third segment is dropped because of congestion, and the fourth segment is delayed. When the first two segments are received, an acknowledgement (17000) is sent. Because the previously buffered segments have been used and the two new segments are buffered, the window size is 6,000.

7. After a delay because of congestion, the fourth segment is received and acknowledged. Because the third segment is still missing, the acknowledgement number is still 17000. Because the two previous segments have been used and the new segment is buffered, the window size is 7,000.

8. When the sender receives the second acknowledgement, the sender determines that congestion has occurred and enters the congestion avoidance phase. The cnwd value is reduced by half to 2. Depending on timer values and the implementation, the missing segment may be re-transmitted immediately or later.

This description may be a bit daunting. However, this is very much the way TCP conversations occur in the real world. Each side is constantly attempting to adjust itself to the network conditions based on reception of data, received windows, missing segments, and so on. You may need to go through this list of steps several times while following along with Figure 7.8 to fully understand everything that is going on. Just keep in mind the fundamental principles previously discussed. The sender is going to advertise the window size of data that it is willing to receive, and it is going to acknowledge the data that it has already received. It is up to the sender to send at the rate of its congestion window or TCP window, whichever is less, and to recognize that a segment it has sent has been dropped based on the ACK numbers received from the receiver. You should review these steps until you are confident the process is completely clear to you.

In the next section, we review UDP, which, as you will see, is a much simpler protocol with far fewer features.

7.3 User Datagram Protocol (UDP)

The original User Datagram Protocol specification is found in RFC 768, which describes the key aspects of the protocol. Unlike TCP, which has many features and can provide reliable communication across an unreliable infrastructure, UDP is far simpler and provides no guarantees of delivery. However, UDP is still a very useful transport-layer protocol. TCP provides its features and reliability at the cost of additional overhead and complexity. The rich feature set of TCP is not required by every application—one size does *not* fit all. For example, the Domain Name Service (DNS) protocol uses UDP for its name-to-IP address lookups because it is faster and the application can simply send another request if the first request is not answered in a reasonable amount of time.

Most of the time, the answer is received before a TCP connection would have even been established. Not only does this increase overall user response time for name resolution, but also it lowers the overall overhead on the DNS server because it does not have to manage thousands of TCP connections from clients. Instead, it can simply issue a UDP response without setting up and tearing down TCP connections. Other applications besides DNS use UDP, so it is important that you have a basic understanding of this protocol and how it works, even though it is far simpler than TCP.

Capabilities of UDP

UDP provides a simple, connectionless, unreliable datagram delivery service. The service is similar to the service that is provided by IP, although UDP has port addresses to support multiplexing between different applications. UDP is used when an application does not need a reliable transfer mechanism or if the application needs to avoid the additional overhead of TCP. The term *unreliable* refers simply to the fact that UDP does not provide flow control, acknowledgement, or re-transmission capabilities like those provided by TCP. These capabilities require additional overhead and slow down communication. Therefore, UDP may be used for applications in which real-time factor is more critical than packet loss, such as Voice over IP or DNS. We will examine a few of these services in detail to give you a taste for the types of applications that make use of UDP.

The Domain Name System (DNS) resolves domain names (e.g., www.alcatel-lucent .com) to an IP address. This is a simple query and response. As a result, the overhead of establishing a connection is not worthwhile. If the query or response is dropped, the host sends the query again. If DNS were to use TCP, the DNS server would have to accept and process a TCP request from every client that required a name lookup. Since DNS lookups are very common, the DNS server could potentially have to process hundreds or even thousands of TCP connection requests every few seconds. The DNS server would then have to tear down these connections once the request had been processed, causing more overhead. All of this is in order to send information that will likely fit in a single packet. This extra processing is not required for a simple service such as DNS, and it is far more efficient and practical to use UDP.

Another application that makes use of UDP is Remote Procedure Call (RPC). RPC supports interprocess communication across a network. Many implementations of RPC manage the reliability and sequencing of data and use UDP as a simple datagram delivery service to avoid the overhead of TCP. Like DNS, RPC often requires only a very simple query-response messaging service. While the response of these messages is very important, it is usually more important to alleviate potential overhead on the systems making and receiving the queries. Unless the network infrastructure is very unreliable, these queries are almost always answered in a timely fashion, while avoiding the connection setup and teardown overhead of TCP.

UDP is also widely used for real-time audio and video streaming. Because these applications often have real-time constraints, re-transmitting lost data is not a viable option, and the application uses other methods to handle missing data. Many of these applications use Real Time Protocol (RTP), which includes a mechanism for carrying sequence and timing information. Timing information is not provided in TCP, and this is important for many real-time applications. RTP data therefore uses UDP for its transport and again avoids the overhead and complexity of TCP.

The UDP Header

The UDP header is shown in Figure 7.9.

Figure 7.9 The UDP header contains only port, length, and checksum fields. It does not have many of the fields that the TCP header has because UDP is a much simpler transport protocol.

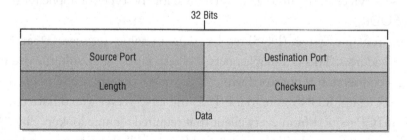

The UDP header is obviously very simple compared to the TCP header. There are no synchronization, sequence, or acknowledgment fields. The header only contains the source and destination application port number, a length field for the length of the data, and a checksum. Therefore, the UDP datagram has very little overhead and is useful for applications that are real-time data streams such as Voice Over IP, or applications that require only simple query-response services such as DNS or RPC. Other applications that use UDP include the Simple Network Management Protocol (SNMP) and DHCP (recall our previous discussion of DHCP in Chapter 6).

UDP Similarities with TCP

Despite the differences with TCP, UDP does show some similarities with its more sophisticated cousin owing to their common requirement to function as a transport protocol. For example, UDP is similar to TCP in its use of port numbers to identify the receiving and sending application processes. UDP uses the port numbers in the multiplexing and de-multiplexing operations. This function is necessary to allow UDP (and TCP) to provide services to many upper-layer applications at the same time. Figure 7.10 illustrates this multiplexing aspect of UDP and includes the port numbers for a few well-known UDP applications.

Figure 7.10 UDP uses port numbers to multiplex applications just as with TCP. Some of the more common UDP applications are DNS, DHCP, and TFTP.

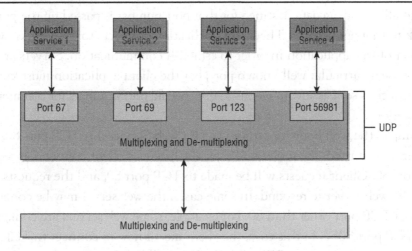

The following are some of the most common well-known UDP port numbers:

- Port 53—Domain Name Service (DNS)
- Port 67—Dynamic Host Configuration Protocol (DHCP)

- Port 69—Trivial File Transfer Protocol (TFTP)
- Port 123—Network Timing Protocol (NTP)
- Port 161—Simple Network Management Protocol (SNMP)
- Port 520—Routing Information Protocol (RIP)

In the next section, we discuss how TCP and UDP use port numbers to multiplex conversations to many upper-layer applications simultaneously.

7.4 Port Numbers and Sockets

Although they differ in numerous respects, both TCP and UDP contain a source and destination port number in their headers. These port numbers allow multiple applications to use the transport protocol simultaneously on the same physical connection. This capability is known as *transport-level multiplexing*. If several transport sessions are active for a system on the network, the data is de-multiplexed based on the source address and port number when the data arrives. This allows TCP or UDP to identify the unique application process that the incoming data is destined for.

Typically, a server application listens for connections on a well-known port. This means that all incoming data destined for that port number is passed up the protocol stack to that application. The client application connects to the well-known port number of the application in order to establish communication. Servers are not required to use a particular well-known port, but the client application must know the port to connect to so it is advantageous to use specific port numbers for commonly used applications.

For example, the well-known port for HTTP (Web Services) is TCP port 80. When the web server is started, the server will typically listen for client connection requests on TCP port 80. Client requests will be made to TCP port 80, and the requests will be passed to the web server to respond. In some cases, the web server may be configured to listen to a TCP port other than 80. For example, some web servers are configured to listen on TCP port 8080. In this case, the client must know to connect to TCP port 8080. If the request is made to TCP port 80, there will be no response since there is no process listening to TCP port 80. Figure 7.11 illustrates some of the most common TCP and UDP ports. You should become familiar with these ports.

Figure 7.11 Both TCP and UDP use port numbers to multiplex and de-multiplex multiple applications. Some of the more common applications for both transport protocols are listed in the figure.

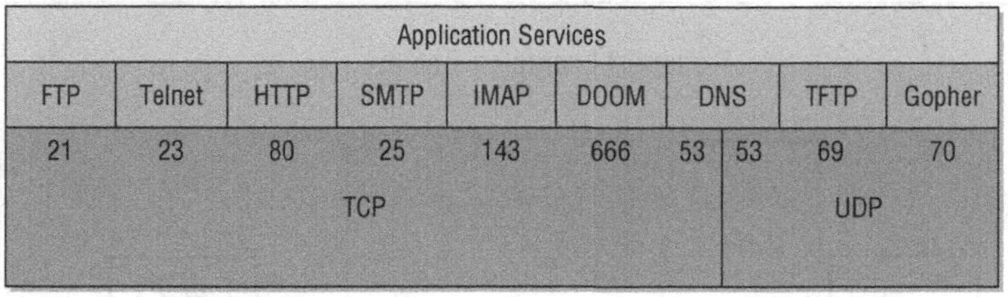

Application Services									
FTP	Telnet	HTTP	SMTP	IMAP	DOOM	DNS	DNS	TFTP	Gopher
21	23	80	25	143	666	53	53	69	70
TCP							UDP		

Ports identify an application service. This allows the transport layer to differentiate between application services. Each process that needs to communicate with another process identifies itself to the transport layer by using one or more port numbers. A port is a 16-bit number that is used by the host-to-host protocol to identify to which higher-level protocol or application service the port must deliver incoming messages. There are two types of port numbers:

- **Well-Known Ports**—Well-known port numbers belong to standard services. The port numbers range from 1 to 1023 and are assigned by the IANA.

- **Ephemeral Ports**—Client applications do not require well-known port numbers because they initiate communications with servers to well-known ports; they do not usually need to listen for connections. The host system allocates each client process a port number for only as long as the process needs the port number and then may reuse it later (hence the term *ephemeral*). The port numbers range from 1024 to 65535 and are not controlled by the IANA. Because the host dynamically assigns the port number to the client application, the port number may vary each time that the client application is started.

Sockets are very similar to ports, but a socket is actually a combination of IP address and port information. Sockets are used to identify the network connection between applications. Although applications on different hosts can be differentiated using IP addresses and destination addresses, it is impossible to differentiate between two sessions on the same hosts for the same application using IP addressing alone. The combination of a protocol (i.e., TCP or UDP), IP address, and port number uniquely identifies a socket on each end. Figure 7.12 illustrates an example of a server using sockets to uniquely identify client conversations.

Figure 7.12 Multiple instances of the same application can be initiated between the same hosts because TCP and UDP use both source and destination ports to uniquely identify each session. The destination port is the same for each application session, but the source ports for each session are unique.

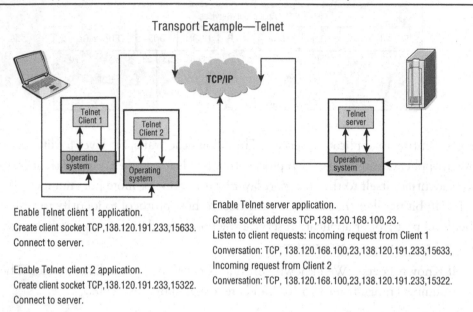

Transport Example—Telnet

Enable Telnet client 1 application.
Create client socket TCP,138.120.191.233,15633.
Connect to server.

Enable Telnet client 2 application.
Create client socket TCP,138.120.191.233,15322.
Connect to server.

Enable Telnet server application.
Create socket address TCP,138.120.168.100,23.
Listen to client requests: incoming request from Client 1
Conversation: TCP, 138.120.168.100,23,138.120.191.233,15633,
Incoming request from Client 2
Conversation: TCP, 138.120.168.100,23,138.120.191.233,15322.

In Figure 7.12, there are two Telnet sessions originating from client 138.120.191.233. The IP address and destination port numbers are not enough for the Telnet server to differentiate between the two Telnet sessions since both sessions have the same source IP address and destination port on the server. In this case, the source port numbers, which are unique for each client session, are required for the Telnet server to differentiate between the packets of each of the sessions. In the example, note that the Client 1 session has a source port of 15633 and the Client 2 session has a source port of 15322. This allows both the server and the workstation to uniquely identify the proper application to receive the data.

Chapter Review

Now that you have completed this chapter, you should have a good understanding of the following topics. If you are not familiar with these topics, please go back and review the appropriate sections..

- The purposes of a transport protocol
- Compare and contrast TCP and UDP.

- The TCP three-way handshake
- The fields in the TCP header and their functions
- How TCP provides reliable data transfer
- TCP's flow control mechanisms
- How TCP reacts to network congestion
- The fields in the UDP header and their functions
- Why UDP is used for real-time applications
- Application ports
- The difference between well-known ports and ephemeral ports
- How the same application can have multiple sessions between two hosts and how each session is uniquely identified

Post-Assessment

The following questions will test your knowledge and prepare you for the Alcatel-Lucent NRS I Certification Exam. Please review each question carefully and choose the most correct answer. You can compare your response with the answers listed in Appendix A in the back of this book. You can also download all of the CD content at `http://booksupport.wiley.com` to take all the assessment tests and review the answers. Good luck!

1. Which of the following is *not* a transport layer protocol?

    A. TP4

    B. TCP

    C. RTP

    D. UDP

2. Which of the following statements about transport layer protocols is false?

    A. Most Internet applications use a transport layer protocol.

    B. Transport layer protocols can provide both reliable and unreliable services.

    C. Transport layer protocols provide end-to-end services for applications.

    D. Transport layer protocols require additional software be added to your operating system.

3. Which of the following is *not* a characteristic of the TCP protocol?

    A. Reliable data transfer

    B. Connectionless operation

    C. Flow control supported

    D. Full-duplex operation

4. Which of the following is *not* a characteristic of the UDP protocol?

    A. Reliable data transfer

    B. Connectionless operation

    C. No flow control

    D. Appropriate for real-time traffic

5. Which of the following TCP flags is *not* matched with the correct definition?

    A. SYN—Indicates the start of a TCP connection.

    B. ACK—Acknowledges that a TCP segment has been received.

    C. FIN—Indicates the closing of a TCP session.

    D. RST—Re-sets the sequence numbers for a TCP session.

6. A TCP sequence or acknowledgment number consists of _____ bits.

    A. 30

    B. 64

    C. 24

    D. 32

7. After a client initiates a connection request to a server with the SYN bit set, the server usually responds with a packet that has the _____ bit set.

    A. SYN

    B. ACK

    C. SYN and ACK

    D. SYN, ACK, and URG

8. Which of the following TCP bits is set to indicate that an application wishes to close an open connection?

    A. RST

    B. FIN

    C. URG

    D. ACK

9. When operating in slow start mode, which of the following describes the mechanisms to throttle the amount of data sent?

    A. The receiver's advertised window size

    B. The sender's congestion window and the sender's advertised window size

    C. The sender's congestion window and the receiver's advertised window size

    D. The maximum segment size and the URG pointer

10. Which of the following are possible mechanisms by which a TCP sending process could recognize that packets it sent to a receiver had been dropped by the network?

    A. An RSND bit from the receiving TCP process

    B. Duplicate ACK numbers

    C. An advertised window size of 0

    D. An ICMP `source quench` message

11. Given the values `MSS=1000 bytes`, `cwnd value=6`, `window size=5000`, and sender's `SN=5000`, what will be the ACK number from the receiving station after the sender sends its next set of segments to the receiving station?

    A. 6000

    B. 11001

    C. 11000

    D. 10000

12. Which of the following types of applications would be least likely to use the UDP protocol?

    A. A "request-response" application

    B. An application that is sensitive to packet loss

    C. An application that is sensitive to delay

    D. A real-time application

13. TCP provides many advanced features missing from UDP. Which of the following is an advantage that UDP has over TCP?

    A. It provides reliable data transfer.

    B. It can recover gracefully from packet loss.

    C. It reacts to network congestion.

    D. It adds little overhead to the data transfer.

14. Which of the following is least likely to be used as an ephemeral port?

    A. 1025

    B. 53212

    C. 1487

    D. 65938

15. DNS is a unique protocol in terms of its transport selection because simple name lookups use UDP, while "zone transfers" that transfer a large amount of name resolution information from one DNS server to another use TCP. What is the least likely reason for using this approach?

    A. Name lookups are simple request-response.

    B. TCP is a reliable protocol.

    C. An unreliable zone transfer could result in serious name resolution discrepancies in a network.

    D. UDP cannot be used for bulk file transfers.

Introduction to IP Routing

- IP routing concepts
- The IP routing table
- Building the IP routing table and its components
- Static and default routes
- Distance vector and link state routing protocols

In this chapter, we begin the discussion of the very important topic of IP routing. In previous chapters, we have discussed how routers forward IP packets without describing how an IP router knows where to forward the IP packet. It is now time to discuss this process in some detail. In this chapter, we cover the basics of IP routing and the processes and methods that are used to build an IP routing table. We also discuss how to manually configure IP routes and examine how the specific types of IP routing protocols build dynamic routing tables. This information will lay the groundwork for the discussion of specific routing protocols in the next chapters.

Pre-Assessment

The following assessment questions will help you understand what areas of the chapter you should review in more detail to prepare for the exam.

1. An IP router normally uses which of the following pieces of information to forward an IP packet?

   A. The destination IP address only

   B. The source and destination IP address

   C. The destination IP address and the destination TCP port

   D. The destination IP address, the TTL, and the ToS

2. The two main categories of routing protocols are IGP and _____.

   A. OSPF

   B. Link state

   C. BGP

   D. EGP

3. Which of the following is *not* a characteristic of an IGP?

   A. It is intended for networks under a common administrative control.

   B. It is used between ASes.

   C. There are not as many policy enforcement features as an EGP.

   D. IGPs can be distance vector or link state protocols.

4. A router can run multiple routing protocols that each have their own table of routing information. A router selects the best route for each destination from all routing sources and puts them in the _____.

   A. Routing Link Database

   B. Routing Information Base

   C. Routing Table

   D. ARP Table

5. Which of the following pairings is *not* correct?

   A. EGP—BGP4

   B. Link state—OSPF

   C. IGP—RIP

   D. Distance vector—IS-IS

You will find the answers to each of these questions in Appendix A. You can also download all of the CD materials for this book at `http://booksupport.wiley.com` to take all the assessment tests and review the answers.

8.1 IP Routing Concepts and Purposes

From our discussion of the Internet Protocol (IP) protocol in previous chapters, you should realize by now that the creation and transmission of IP packets form the basis of all network communications on the Internet. Earlier chapters illustrated the IP packet format and features, and we demonstrated the basics of how IP packets are forwarded by routers. A key topic that we have not yet discussed is how information about IP address locations is actually used by routers in order to forward packets to their proper destination. Recall that IP addressing is global in scope, and all routers on the Internet need to understand how to forward a packet to its final destination, regardless of where that IP destination is physically located. This forwarding process is referred to as *routing*, and it is to this topic that we now turn.

IP routing can be defined as the set of tasks involved in sending an IP packet from the IP source device to the IP destination device across an IP network. The packet enters the IP network via a router and is sent to another router in the network, which then sends it to another router, and so on, until the packet reaches its destination. In theory, the number of routers an IP packet can cross is limited only by the TTL field, but in reality, an IP packet rarely needs to traverse more than 15 to 20 routers to reach its destination. Each of the routers in an IP network uses its routing table to determine how to forward packets. The routing table serves as a destination lookup for IP packets, allowing a router to find a matching next hop for the destination so that it knows what router to forward the packet to next.

The routing tables can be created manually by the network administrator, or they can be created automatically by protocols that run on every router. The routing table maintains a list of IP networks and the physical interfaces on the router to reach these networks. Using the routing table as a source for lookup information, the router forwards the IP packet to its destination. It would be possible for a network administrator to manually configure all the possible destinations into a routing table without the need for a protocol to handle this task. However, this is not a very practical solution. Even using Classless Internet Domain Routing (CIDR) notation, there could be thousands of addresses to configure on each router. Additionally, in the event of a change in the network or a network failure, the administrator would have to reconfigure a large number of routes in a short amount of time. Therefore, for all but a very few limited situations, use of a dynamic routing protocol is by far the preferred solution for creating routing tables.

IGPs and EGPs

Dynamic routing protocols can be divided into two main categories: Interior Gateway Protocols (IGPs) and Exterior Gateway Protocols (EGPs). Although there are some technical differences in the feature support of IGPs and EGPs, the principal difference is the administrative scope of the routing protocol. An IGP is intended for use in a network that is under the control of a single entity or administrative group, usually a single company, school, or organization. This single network entity is usually referred to as an *Autonomous System* (AS). IGPs such as Routing Information Protocol (RIP) and Open Shortest Path First (OSPF) are normally used for routing only within a single AS. The goal of an IGP is to find the lowest-cost route to every destination within the network, but it has limited information about destinations outside of the AS in which it functions.

IGPs can be further divided into distance vector and link state protocols. *Distance vector routing protocols* normally use a hop-count metric to determine the best route to a destination regardless of the bandwidth capability of the network links along the path. Each router that participates in a distance vector routing protocol does not have a complete topological view of the network; the router only knows the best next hop to the destination. For example, a typical distance vector routing protocol would have an entry for 10.0.0.0/8 to next-hop router 1.1.1.1 out of a specific interface. Other than the hop count, it does not have any additional information about the route and would not know the entire path to reach network 10.0.0.0/8. RIP is a classic example of a distance vector protocol.

On the other hand, *link state routing protocols* operate in a fundamentally different way than distance vector protocols. Link state protocols use a cost metric that is a representation of the link status and the physical bandwidth of the router interfaces along the entire path to each destination. Link state protocols select a path based on the route that has the least cost, which is usually representative of the path that has the most physical bandwidth. Each router that participates in a link state routing protocol has a complete topological view of the network. This is accomplished by a process known as *flooding*. Link state protocols propagate all of the information about their links and routes throughout the entire AS so that each router has a common view of the entire AS network (this procedure is covered in detail later in this chapter). Common link state protocols are OSPF and Intermediate System to Intermediate System (IS-IS).

In contrast to an IGP, the goal of an EGP is to provide routes *between* autonomous systems. EGPs normally have special features that allow them to handle larger numbers of routes than IGPs, and they also have features that allow them to implement policy enforcement that may exist between the ASes. For example, a service provider might prefer paths through a neighboring provider because of certain business agreements, even though a different provider might technically have a lower metric route to a particular destination. Because an EGP must work within these policy constraints, the protocol will not necessarily choose the lowest-cost route the way an IGP would.

BGPv4 is the current EGP used in the Internet. BGP is a path vector protocol that chooses a routing path based on the number of autonomous systems that must be traversed rather than on the number of routers that the path must traverse. BGP also performs policy-based routing because policies can be used in many different ways to influence the ways a preferred route is chosen in addition to a simple "shortest AS" decision. Figure 8.1 illustrates these basic divisions between IGP versus EGP and distance vector versus link state routing protocols.

IP Forwarding Using the Routing Table

The basic process of IP routing is best illustrated with an example. Examine Figure 8.2, paying particular attention to the routing tables for each router that is shown.

Figure 8.1 Routing protocols can be divided into IGPs and EGPs. IGPs can be further divided into distance vector and link state protocols.

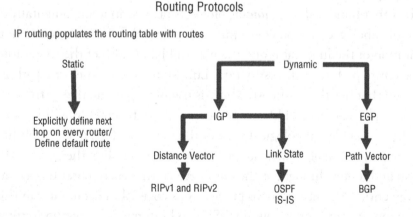

Figure 8.2 The basic process of IP forwarding. Each router examines an ingress packet's destination address and searches for a match in its routing table. If a matching route is found, the packet is forwarded out of the designated interface. Each router will reframe the L2 header but leave the IP and upper layers unchanged.

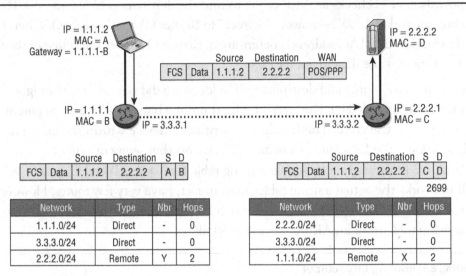

Assuming that the routing tables exist on the routers in this figure, the basic flow of a packet of data through a network can be described as follows:

1. Device A (1.1.1.2) needs to send data to Server D (2.2.2.2). Because Device A is not located on the same Local Area Network (LAN) segment as Device D, Device A must use the default gateway (1.1.1.1) for the LAN segment. Device A issues an Address Resolution Protocol (ARP) request for the 1.1.1.1 address to learn the Media Access Control (MAC) address of the gateway. The router responds with the MAC B address. Device A can now encapsulate the data, as shown in the top block diagram in the figure. Note that the source and destination IP addresses identify the overall source and destination devices; the frame source and destination addresses identify the path across one Ethernet segment.

2. When the frame arrives at Router B, the router removes the L2 header and trailer, examines the IP header, checks the routing table for an entry that matches the destination IP address in the IP packet, and determines that the data needs to be sent to Router C. Router B determines this by finding the entry for the 2.2.2.0/24 network in its routing table and getting the next hop (NH) value, which in this case is "IP-C," that is, Router C. To send the data, Router B encapsulates the data in a Packet Over Sonet (POS)/Point-to-Point Protocol (PPP) frame and forwards the data.

3. Router C removes the IP datagram from the PPP frame and checks its routing table. Because the destination IP network is directly connected to its Ethernet port, Router C checks its ARP cache to find the destination MAC address. (Note that network 2.2.2.0/24 shows as "Direct" in Router C's routing table.) When the destination L2 MAC address is determined, Router C creates the frame of data and forwards the data to Server D.

Note that the source and destination IP addressing did not change throughout the movement of the data. However, the L2 framing changed over each segment that the packet traversed. The IP address identifies a device within the entire network topology; the L2 address identifies a device on that segment only.

Figure 8.2 illustrated a very simple routing table for Routers B and C, and in very small networks the actual routing tables may, in fact, have very few routes. However, in most networks, the routing tables are much larger. Listing 8.1 illustrates the output of a routing table from an Alcatel-Lucent 7750 SR.

Listing 8.1 Routing table output

```
Listing 8.1 Routing table output
A:PE1# show router route-table
===============================================================
Route Table (Router: Base)
===============================================================
Dest Prefix                        Type    Proto   Age        Pref
      Next Hop[Interface Name]                                 Metric
---------------------------------------------------------------
10.1.2.0/24                        Local   Local   03d23h08m  0
      to-p2r1                                                  0
10.1.3.0/24                        Local   Local   03d23h08m  0
      to-p3r1                                                  0
10.1.4.0/24                        Local   Local   04d00h34m  0
      to-p4r1                                                  0
10.2.3.0/24                        Remote  OSPF    00h41m00s  10
      10.1.2.21                                                2000
10.2.4.0/24                        Remote  OSPF    00h41m00s  10
      10.1.2.21                                                2000
10.3.4.0/24                        Remote  OSPF    04d00h16m  10
      10.1.3.31                                                2000
```

(continued)

```
10.10.10.11/32              Local   Local   06d18h33m   0
    system                                              0
10.10.10.21/32             Remote   OSPF    00h41m04s   10
    10.1.2.21                                           1000
-------------------------------------------------------------------
No. of Routes: 8
===================================================================
```

The major components of the routing table are described below:

- **Dest Prefix**—The network that has been advertised to this router. The terms *prefix* and *network* are used interchangeably. Note that each prefix has an associated network mask in CIDR notation, that is, /24, /32, and so on.

- **Type**—The type of interface. This indicates whether the destination prefix belongs to a locally attached network or to a remote network. Locally attached networks indicate that the router is directly attached to the network and does not need to forward packets to another router for that network destination.

- **Protocol**—If the destination network is not directly attached to the router, the routing protocol that was used to advertise the destination prefix to this router is displayed. The protocols can be, for example, RIP, OSPF, BGP, and static.

- **Age**—How long this entry has been in the routing table. As we will see, when using distance vector routing protocols, this value will be very short because routes are constantly advertised. Conversely, link state protocols advertise updates only when a change occurs.

- **Preference**—A unit of measurement that indicates the preference of one routing protocol over another routing protocol. This value is necessary in the event that the same prefix is advertised to the router from multiple routing sources.

- **Next Hop**—Packets should be forwarded to this IP address to reach the destination prefix.

- **Metric**—The numerical value used by a routing protocol to calculate the best route to a destination. Depending on the routing protocol, the metric is usually a hop count or a cost that is assigned to a network link. Unlike a preference, which is used to determine the preference for a route among multiple routing sources, a metric is used to determine the preferred route within a single routing source such as OSPF.

Building a Routing Table

All routing protocols serve the same purpose: to find paths through a network and store the paths in a routing table. The paths are also called *routes*, or more specifically, *IP routes*. These routes are advertised to neighbors using mechanisms and procedures that are specific to each routing protocol. Each router in a network needs to populate its routing table so that it can forward IP data packets. Figure 8.3 describes a routing protocol operation that is based on a distance vector protocol. (Distance vector protocols are discussed in detail later in this chapter.)

Figure 8.3 Distance vector routing protocols operate by having each router send information about its directly connected networks to its neighbors. Routers R2 and R3 will send information about their directly connected networks to R1 so that it can build its routing table. R1 would then send its own independent updates of the information in its routing table to any router on Network A. A distance vector routing protocol would never send updates directly from R2 and R3 to routers on Network A.

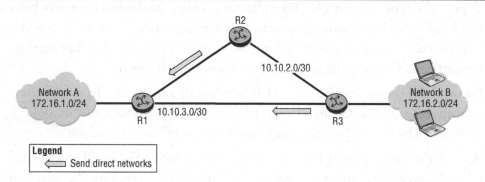

When Routers R2 and R3 are turned on, they both send information about their locally attached networks to their neighbors. As a result, R1 receives and processes these routing updates and places them in its routing table. In this way, R1 builds a routing table that contains both its locally attached networks and the networks that are directly attached to R2 and R3.

Routing updates are a type of network advertisement made by one router to another router. An update is part of the distance vector routing protocol that runs between the routers in order to exchange the updates. A typical routing update consists of the following components:

- A network address with a network mask (also known together as a network prefix)

- A metric associated with the prefix

- The IP address of the next hop to reach this network prefix

R1 uses this information, including its locally discovered networks, and builds a routing information base (RIB). The RIB is protocol-dependent and will normally contain routes from multiple sources such as direct, static, and some routing protocol such as RIP or OSPF.

In Figure 8.4, R1 builds a RIB, which collects and maintains all of the information from its neighbors. If routers R2 and R3 obtain new network information, the routers send this as an advertisement to router R1. Router R1 would then update the information in the RIB if necessary.

Figure 8.4 Routers R2 and R1 send routing updates to R1. R1 uses this information to build a protocol-independent RIB that contains all available routes from all sources. R1 then uses all of this information from different routing sources, including its local interfaces, to build its routing table.

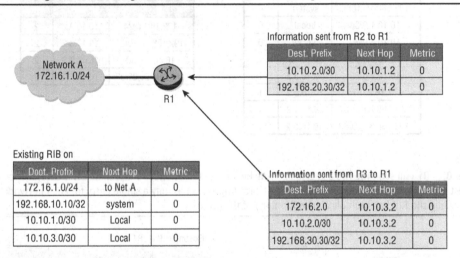

If new updates are received from their directly attached neighbors, Routers R2 and R3 build their respective RIBs and then propagate this information to other neighbors. Note that a router would not advertise the route back to the neighbor it received the update from. Figure 8.5 illustrates new updates sent from Routers R2 and R3 to Router R1 so that R1 will update its RIB.

In Figure 8.6, Router R1 takes the information from the RIB and generates a routing table. Using an algorithm, Router R1 will calculate the best path to a particular network. The parameter that is used in the algorithm to differentiate between two advertisements about the same network from two different neighbors is referred to as the *metric* or *cost*. In this example, the *metric* is the hop count or the number of hops that the destination network is from the source R1. Hop count is a very commonly used metric for distance vector routing protocols.

Figure 8.5 If there are changes to the routing information on R2 and R3, they will send new updates to R1. R1 will enter this new information into the RIB and then recalculate a new routing table.

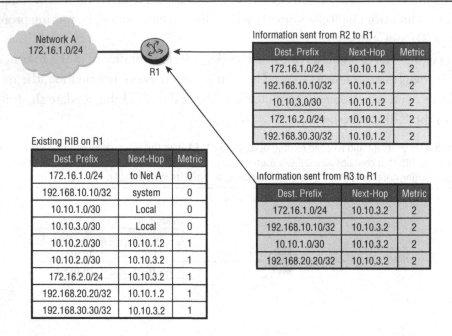

Information sent from R2 to R1

Dest. Prefix	Next-Hop	Metric
172.16.1.0/24	10.10.1.2	2
192.168.10.10/32	10.10.1.2	2
10.10.3.0/30	10.10.1.2	2
172.16.2.0/24	10.10.1.2	2
192.168.30.30/32	10.10.1.2	2

Existing RIB on R1

Dest. Prefix	Next-Hop	Metric
172.16.1.0/24	to Net A	0
192.168.10.10/32	system	0
10.10.1.0/30	Local	0
10.10.3.0/30	Local	0
10.10.2.0/30	10.10.1.2	1
10.10.2.0/30	10.10.3.2	1
172.16.2.0/24	10.10.3.2	1
192.168.20.20/32	10.10.1.2	1
192.168.30.30/32	10.10.3.2	1

Information sent from R3 to R1

Dest. Prefix	Next-Hop	Metric
172.16.1.0/24	10.10.3.2	2
192.168.10.10/32	10.10.3.2	2
10.10.1.0/30	10.10.3.2	2
192.168.20.20/32	10.10.3.2	2

Figure 8.6 R1 will scan the RIB and calculate the best route to each network prefix. In this case, it chooses the best route based on the metric. Note that R1's routing table has only a single entry for each network prefix, while the RIB has multiple entries for many of the prefixes.

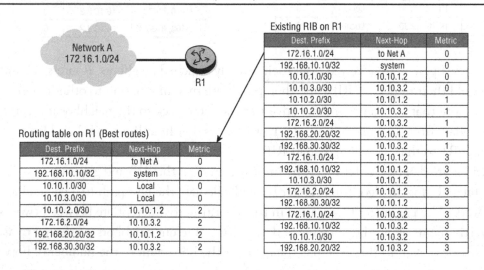

Existing RIB on R1

Dest. Prefix	Next-Hop	Metric
172.16.1.0/24	to Net A	0
192.168.10.10/32	system	0
10.10.1.0/30	10.10.1.2	0
10.10.3.0/30	10.10.3.2	0
10.10.2.0/30	10.10.1.2	1
10.10.2.0/30	10.10.3.2	1
172.16.2.0/24	10.10.3.2	1
192.168.20.20/32	10.10.1.2	1
192.168.30.30/32	10.10.3.2	1
172.16.1.0/24	10.10.1.2	3
192.168.10.10/32	10.10.1.2	3
10.10.3.0/30	10.10.1.2	3
172.16.2.0/24	10.10.1.2	3
192.168.30.30/32	10.10.1.2	3
172.16.1.0/24	10.10.3.2	3
192.168.10.10/32	10.10.3.2	3
10.10.1.0/30	10.10.3.2	3
192.168.20.20/32	10.10.3.2	3

Routing table on R1 (Best routes)

Dest. Prefix	Next-Hop	Metric
172.16.1.0/24	to Net A	0
192.168.10.10/32	system	0
10.10.1.0/30	Local	0
10.10.3.0/30	Local	0
10.10.2.0/30	10.10.1.2	2
172.16.2.0/24	10.10.3.2	2
192.168.20.20/32	10.10.1.2	2
192.168.30.30/32	10.10.3.2	2

For example, Routers R2 and R3 both advertise the destination network 172.16.2.0/24 to Router R1. R2 advertises 172.16.2.0/24 with a metric of 2. R3 previously advertised 172.16.2.0/24 with a metric of 0 because this network was directly attached to R3. Any local networks on a particular router are considered to be the lowest metric or 0. When R1 receives the update from R2 and R3, R1 installs both the updates in its RIB and adds the value 1 to the metric advertised by both R2 and R3. In this case, the 172.16.2.0/24 update from R2 will be installed in the R1 RIB with a metric of 3 (2 + 1); the update from R3 will be installed with a metric of 1 (0 + 1). Because R1 receives the update about 172.16.2.0/24 from R2 and R3, a metric of 1 will be added to their individual advertised metrics (R1 counts itself as 1 hop, and therefore will add 1 to the route).

The routing table on R1 is built from the existing RIB on R1. The best routes, depending on the algorithm used, are sent to the routing table, and this will be used to forward the IP packets. The best routes in our example are the routes with the lowest cost or hop count to the particular destination. Note also for advertisements about a prefix that contains equal metrics, that the route selection algorithm must use a differentiator to install one route in the routing table.

For example, in Figure 8.6, network 10.10.2.0/30 is the network that is directly attached to Routers 2 and 3. Therefore, when prefix 10.10.2.0/30 is advertised to R1 from R2 and R3, the advertisement contains the same metric (0 in this case since both R2 and R3 are directly connected to this prefix). R1 updates its RIB with both the updates: There are two entries for 10.10.2.0/30, one with next hop 10.10.1.2 (R2) and one with next hop 10.10.3.2 (R3). However, R1 chooses to install only the update from R2 (next hop 10.10.1.2 in the routing table). The criteria for selecting a prefix from several available equal cost routes are entirely routing protocol-dependent.

IP Forwarding Details

Let's examine the process of router IP forwarding in a little more detail. The process is shown step-by-step in Figure 8.7 and is described in the following list.

1. An IP packet enters Router R1.
2. The IP packet's destination address is compared to the entries in the R1 forwarding table.

Figure 8.7 An IP packet arrives at the ingress to Router R1. R1 looks at the destination IP address and searches for a matching entry in its routing table. R1 finds a match and forwards the packet out the appropriate interface to the next hop indicated in its routing table (R3, in this case). R3 follows the same process as R1, determines that the route is local, and forwards the packet to its local network.

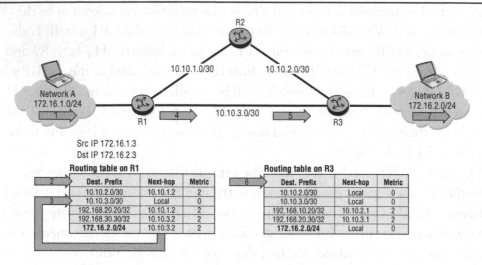

3. The longest entry matching the destination is found, and the next-hop IP address is examined. The local interface corresponding to the next-hop IP address is then determined by re-examining the R1 forwarding table.

4. The IP packet is then forwarded to the corresponding local interface and out of Router R1 to its next-hop R3.

5. The IP packet enters Router R3.

6. R3 examines its routing table to find a matching destination for the IP address. It determines that the network is local and that it does not need to forward the packet to any other routers.

7. R3 puts the correct L2 header on the IP packet and forwards it to the destination device.

These procedures are actually the result of two separate functions that routers perform. One function of routers is simply to forward packets as we have described. The other function is to use routing protocols to build routing tables so that the forwarding process has the information it needs to operate correctly. The terms *control plane* and *data plane* are often used when referring to these routing update and packet forwarding processes.

These terms simply refer to the two basic functions performed by routers. The *data plane* is simply the reception and forwarding of IP packets by a router. One of the primary functions of routers is to forward data (IP packets)—hence the term *data plane* to describe this function. The *control plane* is simply the sending and receiving of routing protocol updates to allow for the dissemination of routing protocol information. The routing updates provide information about how to *control* the flow of IP packets through a network—hence the designation *control plane*. Figure 8.8 illustrates this difference.

Figure 8.8 The control plane function consists of routing protocol updates that are exchanged only between routers to build the routing table. The data plane function consists of the procedures to forward IP packets using the information contained in routing tables.

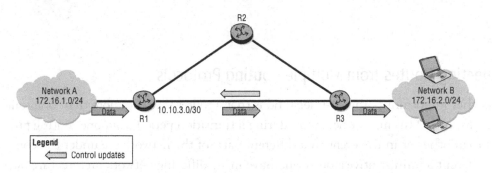

It is important to realize that despite the examples presented so far, a router's neighbor interface may not always be point-to-point. In Figure 8.9, Routers R1, R2, and R3 are connected to a common broadcast domain. In such cases, the process of building the IP forwarding table is the same except that R1 must use its Address Resolution Protocol (ARP) table to determine the L2 address of the next-hop router. (Recall our discussion of the ARP protocol from Chapter 6.)

Figure 8.9 illustrates these steps:

1. R1 has one interface that is configured toward the broadcast domain.

2. When R3 and R2 send updates about their local networks to R1, they include the IP address of their interface on the broadcast domain.

3. R1 installs network 172.16.9.0/24 with a next hop of 10.10.10.3 and network 172.16.2.0/24 with a next hop of 10.10.10.2.

4. When R1 needs to send an IP packet to R2 or R3, it will obtain the L2 address for these routers from its ARP table and forward the packets with the correct L2 header.

Figure 8.9 R1 needs to forward an IP packet to network 172.16.2.0/24. It examines its routing table and determines that R3 is the next hop. Since R3 and R1 share a common Ethernet segment, R1 will issue an ARP request for the MAC address of R3's IP address or retrieve the MAC address from its ARP table if an entry already exists for R3. Once R1 has the MAC address of R3, it will use this address to create the L2 header for the IP packet and forward the frame using the Ethernet protocol.

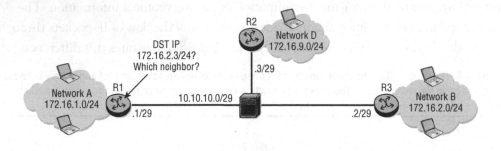

Selecting Routes from Multiple Routing Protocols

Another important point to understand is that a router may run more than one routing protocol. This may be necessary during a transition period from one routing protocol to another or in the event that different parts of the network are under the control of different administrative groups who have made differing network architecture decisions. In Figure 8.10, the R1–R2 and R2–R3 interfaces are running OSPF, and the R1–R5 and R5–R3 interfaces are running RIP.

Figure 8.10 Router R1 receives updates about Network B prefix 172.16.9.0/24 from both the OSPF and RIP routing protocols. Metrics from different routing protocols are not directly comparable, so R1 must use a priority mechanism to determine which routing update to enter in its routing table. The Alcatel-Lucent 7750 router prefers OSPF over RIP by default.

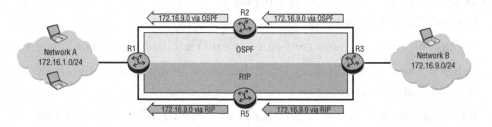

Network B can be advertised on both the interfaces of R3, each running a different protocol. Therefore, this network is advertised to R1 by both RIP and OSPF. R1

has to decide which entry to install in its routing table. In order to choose between the two updates, R1 uses the preference attribute presented in Listing 8.1. The preference parameter indicates the router's preference of one routing update source over another source. By default, on the Alcatel-Lucent 7750 SR, routes learned from OSPF are preferred over routes learned from RIP. Therefore, the route learned from OSPF is installed in the routing table on R1. (Note that the protocol with a lower preference value is preferred.)

When a routing protocol learns routes from its neighbors, the protocol populates its RIBs with the routes. Each protocol stores the routes it has learned from its neighbors in its RIB. Therefore, there is a RIB for each routing protocol. For each destination in the RIB, the routing protocol chooses the best route based on the lowest metric. The best routes are sent to the Routing Table Manager (RTM). This process is illustrated in Figure 8.11. Notice that RIP has its RIB, and OSPF has its own separate RIB.

Figure 8.11 A router maintains an RIB for each routing protocol. If there are identical network prefixes in multiple routing protocol RIB's, the Routing Table Manager uses a protocol hierarchy to determine which routes to place in the routing table.

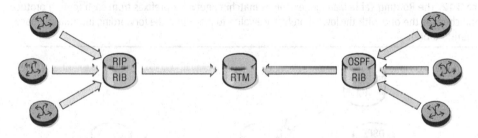

Because metrics from different protocols are not comparable, the RTM uses the preference value to choose from all of the best routes that it receives. The lower the protocol's preference, the more likely that the best or active route will be selected from that protocol. Because the router must have a method for determining the *best* route, different protocols should not be configured with the same preference. Table 8.1 lists the default preference values that are assigned to each routing protocol on the Alcatel-Lucent 7750 SR. All of the preference values, with the exception of the preference for directly attached networks, are configurable, keeping in mind that each routing protocol needs to have a distinct preference value.

Table 8.1 Default Preference Table

Route type	Preference	Configurable
Direct attached	0	No
Static	5	Yes
OSPF internal	10	Yes
IS-IS Level 1 internal	15	Yes
IS-IS Level 2 internal	18	Yes
RIP	100	Yes
OSPF external	150	Yes
IS-IS Level 1 external	160	Yes
IS-IS Level 2 external	165	Yes
BGP	170	Yes

The best routes from the RTM are placed in the forwarding information base (FIB), also commonly referred to as the *routing table*. This process is illustrated in Figure 8.12.

Figure 8.12 The Routing Table Manager examines matching network prefixes from each routing protocol RIB and chooses the one with the lowest preference value to place into the forwarding information base (FIB/routing table).

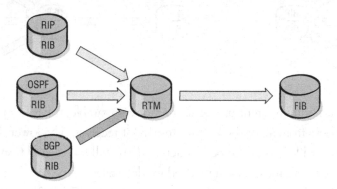

- The RTM may receive a best route from multiple protocols

- Selection is based on lowest preference value

- The RTM sends its best route to the FIB

- This route is the active route and is used for forwarding

The FIB is distributed to the various line cards on the Alcatel-Lucent 7750 SR and is used to forward incoming IP packets. Distributing the FIB to the line cards reduces overall CPU processing on the router and increases the packet forwarding rate of the router.

Now that we have examined the process of routing advertisement and building routing tables, we will turn to the differing procedures used by routing protocol types. In the next section, we examine the simplest "protocol" for building routing tables: static routing.

8.2 Static and Default Routes

Static routes are manually configured by a network administrator. They describe the remote destination network and the next hop that a packet must be forwarded to in order to reach the destination. The destination can be one network or a range of networks. Note that for two routers to forward data to each other bidirectionally, a static route needs to be configured on both routers; otherwise, one router could send packets, but the receiving router would not know how to forward return packets.

By default, a static route is created with a preference of 5 and a metric of 1. However, these parameters can be changed to accommodate different configuration needs. If the preference and metric parameters are left at the default values, a static route is always preferred over a route learned from a dynamic routing protocol. By adjusting the preference value, the user can define a secondary route that will be used if the dynamic protocol fails to provide a route. Alternatively, a second static route can be configured as a backup to the primary static route by assigning a higher metric to the secondary route.

Static routing saves bandwidth and processing because there are no routing advertisements or updates. Static routing also allows you to override any decision by a routing protocol. However, any changes to the routes must be made manually, so there is no real-time response if a destination becomes unreachable. For this reason, static routes are often only used in extremely simple network configurations, such as where there may be only a single path to a network, or as a backup to a route advertised by a routing protocol.

In Figure 8.13, the corporate headquarters network is connected to two remote sites. The corporate site provides the remote sites with resources and Internet access. Because the corporate network is connected through one link to each of the sites, all traffic from corporate to the remote sites will traverse these single links. A remote network like this, with only one connection to the backbone network, is often referred to as a *stub network*. When you have a stub network, it is rarely necessary to run a routing protocol over the link as there is only a single path to reach the stub network.

Figure 8.13 There is only one path to reach Remote site 1 and Remote site 2. A static route can be configured on R1 to send all traffic for 192.168.1.0/24 to CR1, and a static route can be configured on R5 to send all traffic for 172.16.0.0/24 to CR2.

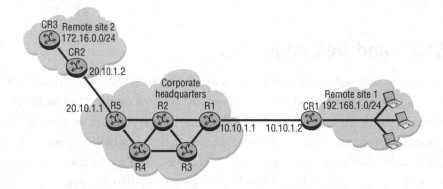

By configuring a static route on R1, traffic destined for network 192.168.1.0/24 will exit out of the interface on R1 to CR1. A static route configured on R5 will send traffic to CR2. If R2 or any of the other corporate routers wants to reach either remote site, they must also be configured with a static route in the correct direction. In order for traffic to flow in both directions, the remote networks must also be configured with static routes to reach the corporate network.

Notice that it would be cumbersome to configure a large number of static routes on CR1 and CR2 for each network that is reachable through each router's single link to corporate headquarters. It would also be unnecessary since all routes would point to the same next hop. It would be very useful in this case to have a way to simply specify that "all" routes are reachable through a static route to a certain next hop. This functionality is achieved through the use of a default route.

A *static default route* in the routing table is a wildcard entry that fits any destination. The route is used when the destination address of a packet does not match any other entry in the routing table—hence the term *default*. The default route is followed when no other routes match. A default route is often used on a stub network when there is only one path to reach the other remote networks. The default route is a static route with a network address and mask of 0.0.0.0.

In Figure 8.14, for Remote site 1 to access the resources of the corporate headquarters network, it does not need to list every entry in its routing table for every resource that it needs to send traffic to. Therefore, it uses the default route to match any possible route. The default route is the longest match in the routing table when nothing else matches.

Figure 8.14 Router CR1 can be configured with a default route to send all packets for all destinations to R1 since the only path to all networks from Remote site 1 is through R1. The command to configure the default route on CR1 is shown in Listing 8.2.

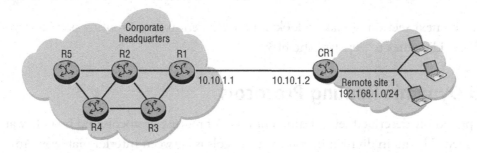

Static and default routes are very valuable for certain limited situations, so you should be familiar with their syntax. Listing 8.2 illustrates the syntax to configure static routes. Default route configuration is simply a special case of a static route in which both the route and the mask are 0.0.0.0.

Listing 8.2 Static route configuration

Context: config>router>
Syntax1:   [**no**] **static-route** {*ip-prefix/mask* | *ip-prefix netmask*}
[**preference** *preference*] [**metric** *metric*] [**tag** *tag*] [**enable** | **disable**]
[**next-hop** *ip-address* | *ip-int-name*]

Syntax2:   [**no**] **static-route** {*ip-prefix/mask* | *ip-prefix netmask*}
[**preference** *preference*] [**metric** *metric*] [**tag** *tag*] [**enable** | **disable**]
indirect *ip-address*

Syntax3:   [**no**] **static-route** {*ip-prefix/mask* | *ip-prefix netmask*}
[**preference** *preference*] [**metric** *metric*] [**tag** *tag*] [**enable** | **disable**]
black-hole

(continued)

```
Example for the default route on CR1 in figure 8.14:
config>router> static-route 0.0.0.0/0 next-hop 10.10.1.1
Example:    config>router> static-route 10.1.1.0/24 next-hop
10.2.2.2
Example     config>router> static-route 10.1.1.0/24 next-hop
10.2.1.2 preference 10
Example     config>router> static-route 10.1.1.0/24 next-hop
10.2.1.2 preference 10 metric 100
```

In the next section, we take a look at how different types of routing protocols work and provide routes to populate the FIB.

8.3 Dynamic Routing Protocols

We previously described several different types of routing protocols and how they are classified. The main division in routing protocols is between Interior Gateway Protocols (IGPs), which as explained earlier are used within the same AS, and Exterior Gateway Protocols (EGPs), which are used among different ASes. We will examine EGPs in Chapter 10, but here we concentrate on IGPs.

Within IGPs, there are two main types of protocols: distance vector and link state. We will examine both types of IGPs in this section, beginning with a discussion of distance vector protocols.

With a distance vector routing algorithm (sometimes referred to as *Bellman-Ford* after the original algorithm designers), a router passes a copy of its entire routing table periodically to all its neighbors. These regular updates between routers communicate topology changes because each router is continually receiving a current copy of the entire routing table from its neighbor. All that each router is aware of is a metric (distance) to a particular route and its next hop (vector). Note that the router does not have a picture of the topology; it simply knows the next router that it sends packets to for a given destination and the associated metric for that route.

Figure 8.15 illustrates the distance vector routing process.

The update process is outlined in the following list:

1. RTR-B receives a routing update from RTR-A.

2. RTR-B uses the information received from RTR-A to recalculate its routing table.

Figure 8.15 RTR-B receives a complete routing table from RTR-A. RTR-B uses this information to recalculate its routing table and then sends its complete routing table to RTR-D. Note that RTR-B sends its own routing table to RTR-D; it does not forward RTR-A's routing table to RTR-D.

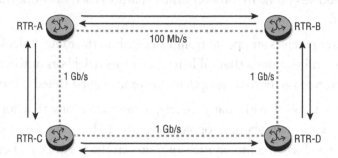

3. RTR-B then sends its routing table to RTR-D.

4. This same step-by-step process occurs in all directions between direct-neighbor routers.

It is critical to understand that when using a distance vector protocol, a routing table is not transmitted beyond the immediate neighbor. For example, RTR-D does not receive a routing update directly from RTR-A. RTR-D receives the routing updates only from its directly connected neighbors, so RTR-D is only aware of RTR-A's routes via RTR-B and RTR-C. For this reason, distance vector protocols are sometimes called *routing by rumor* because each router relies solely on the information provided to it by its neighbors and not from the original source of the route.

Figure 8.16 illustrates the distance vector step-by-step process for updating all routers in a network when a topology change occurs.

Figure 8.16 A router running a distance vector routing protocol receives updates from its neighbors, processes the update and recalculates its own routing table, and then sends updates about its routing table to its other neighbors.

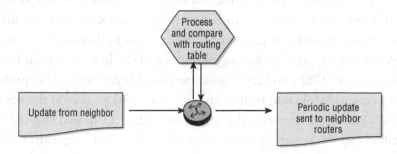

- Each router sends its entire routing table to each of its adjacent neighbors. This table includes reachable addresses, a value that represents the distance metric, and the IP address of the first router on the path to each network that the router knows about.

- As each router receives an update from its neighbor, the router calculates a new routing table and transmits that table to each of its neighbors at the next timed interval (distance vector routing updates occur at regular timed intervals).

- In a very large network with many routers, it can take a long time for all the routers in the network to know about a topology change. (This is referred to as *convergence*, when all routers have a common view of routes in the network.) Therefore, distance vector protocols have a high convergence time, which is very undesirable.

Distance vector routing protocols were the first routing protocols designed. As such, they have several limitations that you may have already observed. First, they use periodic updates to send the routing tables. This means that a route may have changed since the most recent update and packets may be forwarded to the wrong destination until the next update occurs. Additionally, periodic updates use unnecessary bandwidth and CPU processing resources when there are no changes to the network. Also, each router receives information only from its neighboring router. In certain situations in which a network link is going up and down rapidly (*flapping*), this can lead to routing loops. A *routing loop* occurs where router R1 thinks a route's next hop is R2, and R2 thinks its next hop is R1, and so packets get continually forwarded back and forth between R1 and R2 until the TTL is reached and they are discarded. Routing loops are very undesirable and need to be avoided at all costs.

Owing to these and other limitations, a new type of routing protocol was developed known as a *link state routing protocol*. In contrast to the limited information a router uses with distance vector protocols, link state routing protocols maintain a complete database of topology information. While distance vector protocols have nonspecific information about distant networks, link state routing protocols maintain full knowledge of distant routers and how they interconnect. That is, they have a view of the entire internetwork topology, including all routes and the links that must be traversed to reach those routes. OSPF and IS-IS are examples of link state routing protocols.

Link state protocols function by flooding link state packets (LSPs) throughout the network. LSPs are used to transmit the information that is required to build the topological database, which is used by the Shortest Path First (SPF) algorithm to build an

SPF tree. An *SPF tree* is simply a view of all the routes in the network and the shortest path needed to reach them. Using the SPF tree, link state protocols build a routing table of paths to each network destination. When a link state topology changes, all of the routers must become aware of the change so they can update their routing table accordingly. This involves the propagation of common routing information simultaneously to all routers in the network. Figure 8.17 summarizes this process.

Figure 8.17 RTR-A keeps a database of links and how those links form a path to each network. RTR-A will be able to determine from the updates it receives that it can reach network 2.2.2.0/24 via interface 1/1/1 through RTR-C and then on to RTR-B, but it will know that it can also reach the network through interface 1/1/2 to RTR-B directly, and this will likely be the lower cost and preferred path.

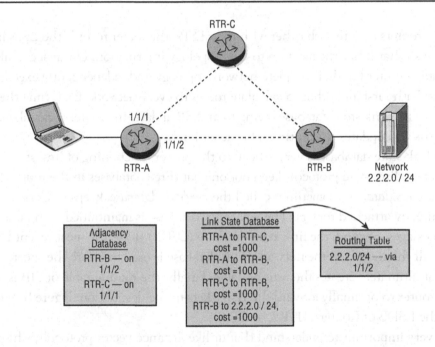

To achieve information convergence, each router performs a series of procedures to build its routing table. First, it keeps track of all of its neighboring routers. Second, it builds an LSP that lists neighbor router names and link metrics (cost). This includes new neighbors, changed metrics, and links to neighbors that are down. These steps are illustrated in Figure 8.18.

Figure 8.18 When link state protocols are used, each router keeps a database of each of its links and the associated cost for each link. The cost is usually based on a default value that is a function of the speed of the interface.

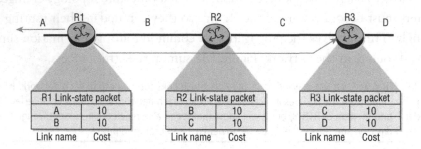

Once routers update each other with their LSPs, the router records the LSPs in its database so that it has the most up-to-date topology information. Using accumulated LSP data, a router builds a complete network topology and independently executes the Shortest Path First algorithm to calculate routes to every network. Each time there is a change to the link state database owing to an LSP update, the router recalculates the best paths and updates the routing table accordingly.

The link state database is very crucial to the proper functioning of link state protocols. In fact, link state protocols keep not one but three databases in the router. First, the *adjacency database*, sometimes called the *neighbor database*, keeps track of all of the other directly attached routers. The adjacency database is maintained with periodic *Hello* messages. Second, the link state database (LSDB) stores the most recent LSPs sent by all the routers in the network. This database is used to create the shortest path tree that ultimately creates the routing table. Finally, the routing table or FIB is used by the router to optimally forward the IP packets to the destination. Figure 8.19 illustrates the LSDB of Routers R1, R2, and R3.

It is very important to understand that unlike distance vector protocols, which periodically update their entire routing table, link state protocols are driven by topology changes. When a router recognizes a topology change (i.e., link down, neighbor down, new link, or new neighbor), the router must notify its neighbors of this change so that they can record the change and rerun the SPF algorithm. To accomplish this, the router that recognizes the changes sends new link state information about the change by flooding it throughout the network. When each router receives the new link state information, the router must update its topological database and send the information to its neighbors. Each router then independently runs the SPF algorithm against the new topological database to update its routing table. Figure 8.20 illustrates this process.

Figure 8.19 Each router using a link state protocol will maintain a link state database that contains all the information for all links in the network. Note that each router should share a common view of the links in the network because each LSP is flooded to every router. Each router independently runs the Shortest Path First algorithm based on the link state database to calculate its individual route to each destination.

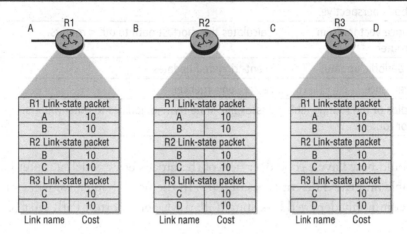

Figure 8.20 When a link state router detects a topology change, it floods the new LSP information to other link state routers. Each router records the new LSP in its link state database and then each independently runs the Shortest Path First algorithm to update its routing table.

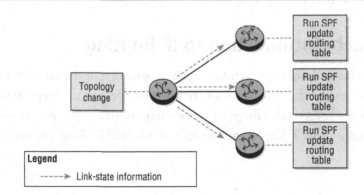

At the end of this process, every router possesses a common view of the entire network and has received information directly from other routers in order to independently build its topological view. This is in stark contrast to the view of a router running a distance vector protocol in which each router has only a limited amount of information about the network that it received from its neighboring routers. This and other differences between the different types of IGPs are summarized in Table 8.2.

Table 8.2 Distance Vector versus Link State

Distance Vector	Link State
Views the network topology from the neighbor's perspective.	Gets a common view of the entire network topology.
Adds distance vectors from router to router.	Calculates the shortest path to other routers.
Frequent, periodic updates	Event-triggered updates
Slow convergence	Faster convergence
Passes copies of the routing table to neighbor routers.	Passes link state routing updates to other routers.

You should now have a good overview of the processes by which a router builds its routing table and the different types of IGPs. In the next chapter, we will examine the most commonly deployed link state IGP: the Open Shortest Path First (OSPF) protocol.

Now you should complete the lab exercises to assist you in reinforcing this chapter's features. These lab exercises are carefully designed to give you hands-on experience configuring many of the technology standards that have been discussed and should greatly aid you in your exam preparation.

Practice Lab: Introduction to IP Routing

The following lab is designed to reinforce your knowledge of the content in this chapter. Please review the instructions carefully and perform the steps in the order in which they are presented. The practice labs require that you have access to three or more Alcatel-Lucent 7750 SRs or Alcatel-Lucent 7450 ESSs in a non-production environment.

 These labs are designed to be used in a controlled lab environment. Please **DO NOT** attempt to perform these labs in a production environment.

Up to this point in the labs, it is only possible to ping addresses on the interfaces that are directly connected to a router. Locally attached networks, that is, the subnets associated with interfaces, are the only networks known by the router. As seen in the last step of the lab exercises in Chapter 6, any attempt to ping the system interface of a remote router will fail, since the remote *system* interface is not directly attached to the local router, and thus no route exists to the destination.

This set of exercises looks at *static routes*, and a particular kind of static route called a *default route*. Static routes are one method of populating the routing table, thus enabling traffic to reach non-local networks. Note that all information for static routes is determined and manually entered by the administrator and thus is subject to the usual limitations of humans. Exercises in later chapters look at two other well-known protocols—OSPF and BGP—for automatically generating and propagating routing table information.

Lab Section 8.1: Static Routes

The Chinese philosopher Lao Tzu said, "A journey of a thousand miles starts with [just] one step." This idea is equally true for routing traffic to any final destination: Each router along the path only needs to be concerned with a single additional step, known as a *next hop*. If every router has the correct information, and sends traffic one additional step, the traffic should ultimately end up where it's supposed to go.

In routing terms, a *destination* is a range of addresses, or subnet addresses, connected to a particular router. A typical static route is a rule that combines these two parts: a destination subnet and the next-hop router. We'll see exactly how to write these rules on the Alcatel-Lucent 7750/7450 products.

Objective In this exercise, you will configure a pair of static routes between PE1 and PE2 so that each router can reach the other's system interface.

Validation You will know you have succeeded if both PE routers can ping the system interface of the adjacent PE router.

1. The first part of a static route is the subnet, so it always includes a subnet mask (even for a single address!). This example uses a /32 subnet (a single address) for the system interface of the adjacent PE router. Traffic must step (or hop) across to reach the IP interface at the far end of the link. The next hop address is always the IP address for the interface at the far end of the link, not the IP address of the near end of the link. Since the next hop is always a single address, it never has a subnet mask.

   On PE1, configure a static route using the following command syntax.

   ```
   *B:PE1# configure router static-route 150.10.0.1/32 next-hop 140.10.0.98
   *B:PE1#
   ```

1a. What is the destination subnet in the preceding command?

1b. What is the next-hop address in the above command?

1c. Is the new subnet range anywhere within the 140.10.0.0/24 range of ISP 1, or is it completely external?

2. Confirm that the route table has a new entry.

```
*B:PE1# show router route-table

===============================================================
Route Table (Router: Base)
===============================================================
Dest Prefix                      Type    Proto   Age        Pref
    Next Hop[Interface Name]                     Metric
---------------------------------------------------------------
140.10.0.1/32                    Local   Local   01h11m25s  0
    system                                        0
140.10.0.11/32                   Local   Local   00h00m45s  0
    loopbackTest                                  0
140.10.0.96/30                   Local   Local   00h44m49s  0
    toPE2                                         0
140.10.0.100/30                  Local   Local   00h28m42s  0
    toCE1                                         0
150.10.0.1/32                    Remote  Static  00h04m06s  5
    140.10.0.98                                   1
---------------------------------------------------------------
No. of Routes: 5
===============================================================
*B:PE1#
```

3. Confirm that a debug log is still configured using the show log log-collector command (from Lab 2.2 in Chapter 2). All logs except 99 and 100 disappear every time you log out. If necessary, re-create the log (see Lab 6.1 in Chapter 6). Do the same for router PE2.

4. Turn on debugging for ICMP only (see Lab 6.1 in Chapter 6). Do the same for router PE2.

5. Test the new static route by pinging the system interface of PE2 from PE1.

```
*B:PE1# ping 150.10.0.1
PING 150.10.0.1 56 data bytes
```

```
1 2000/01/01 13:49:07.77 UTC MINOR: DEBUG #2001 Base PIP
"PIP: ICMP
instance 1 (Base), interface index 3 (toPE2),
ICMP  egressing on toPE2:
   140.10.0.1 -> 150.10.0.1
   type: Echo (8)  code: No Code (0)
"
 [... Additional output omitted ...]
Request timed out. icmp_seq=1.
Request timed out. icmp_seq=2.
[... Additional output omitted ...]



[ Output captured from PE2 terminal session ]
*A:PE2#
1 2000/01/01 13:48:12.54 UTC MINOR: DEBUG #2001 Base PIP
"PIP: ICMP
instance 1 (Base), interface index 3 (toPE1),
ICMP  ingressing on toPE1:
   140.10.0.1 -> 150.10.0.1
   type: Echo (8)  code: No Code (0)
"
```

5a. Did PE1 successfully transmit a ping request? How do you know?

5b. Did PE2 successfully receive a ping request? How do you know?

5c. What are the exact source and destination addresses in the ping packets?

5d. Does PE1 have a correct, functioning route to the system address of PE2?

5e. Was the ping command successful? How do you know?

5f. Explain why or why not the ping was successful.

6. Compare the source address for this last ping command with the one from Lab Exercise 6.1 in Chapter 6. Compare also the "type" of route in the routing table for the ping destination in each case. (Refer to Step 2 above, and Step 10 in Lab Exercise 5.3 in Chapter 5.)

   6a. By default, what source address is used when a ping destination is a *Local* route? By default, what source address is used when a ping destination is a *Remote* route? (This is a good rule to remember!)

7. Repeat the necessary steps above to build a static route on PE2 that points to the system interface on PE1. Be sure to confirm that it appears correctly in the route table on PE2.

```
*A:PE2# configure router static-route 140.10.0.1/32 next-hop 140.10.0.97
*A:PE2#
```

8. Repeat the test of pinging the system interface of PE2 from PE1. (You may want to turn off debugging to make it easier to distinguish the output.)

8a. Did PE1 successfully transmit a ping request? How do you know?

8b. Did PE2 successfully receive a ping request? How do you know?

8c. What are the exact source and destination addresses in the ping packets?

8d. Does PE1 have a correct, functioning route to the system address of PE2? Does PE2 have a functioning route to the system interface of PE1?

8e. Was the ping command successful? How do you know?

8f. Explain why the ping was successful or not.

9. Test both PE routers to determine whether you can ping the loopback interfaces of the remote PE router.

9a. Which loopback interfaces are reachable, if any? Explain why or why not?

10. Removing a static route requires typing the *exact* route again, except with the option no in front of static-route. Remove the static route. (Try making some intentional typing mistakes in the addresses, to see what kind of error messages you get.)

```
*A:PE2# configure router no static-route 140.10.0.1/32 next-hop
140.10.0.97
*A:PE2#
```

10a. How can you confirm that a static route has been successfully removed?

11. As the last step, use the ping command to verify that both PE routers have a correct, functioning static route to the other router's system interface.

11a. What did you learn? For successful communication, how many routes are required between a source and destination? Do *not* forget this important rule!!!

Lab Section 8.2: Default Routes and Router Logic

In the previous exercise, the static routes were fairly simple: Traffic destined for a particular subnet was sent to a particular next-hop address. In this lab, we use three different kinds of static routes. These are shown in Figure 8.21 as *aggregate routes*, *default routes*, and *simple routes*. Together they provide enough flexibility to handle just about every situation.

Figure 8.21 Three different types of static routes are used from CE to PE and from PE to PE in this lab exercise.

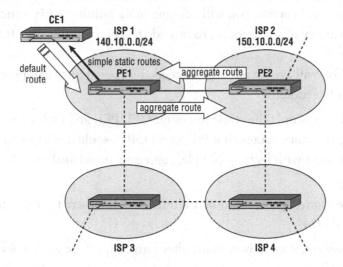

Consider for a moment the CE1 router. Since there is only one single connection to the rest of the (Inter)network, the next-hop address would *always* be the same for every single static route. It seems pointless to have many, many static routes all giving the same next hop. A *default route* provides a solution—a single routing entry that effectively says: "Any other destination uses [PE1] as the next hop." This route will be used for any destination subnet that isn't local to CE1.

Next, let's look at the network from PE2's perspective. All hosts in the subnet 140.10.0.0/24 exist *somewhere* within ISP 1. Exactly where a host resides within ISP 1 isn't a concern for PE2; that's PE1's job to sort out. All PE2 needs to know is that any address within 140.10.0.0/24 should be forwarded to PE1 as the next hop. PE2 uses an *aggregate route* for the /24 subnet without considering whether every single possible host within that range actually exists. (In fact, there may be many addresses and entire blocks for which *no* hosts exist!) The key point of the aggregate route is that there are *no hosts outside of ISP 1 for the 140.10.0.0/24 range*. Likewise for PE1: It should be configured so that traffic for all possible hosts in the 150.10.0.0/24 range is sent via PE2.

This set of lab exercises makes use of all three types of routes (simple, aggregate, and default) to get full connectivity between the routers with a minimum number of entries in each router's routing table. The CE device uses a default route toward PE1; PE1 will use simple static routes toward the subnets associated with CE1; and both PE routers will use aggregate routes for the neighbor's IP subnet.

Objective In this exercise, you will become more familiar with static routes by configuring a variety of static routes to provide full connectivity to all interfaces from all routers.

Validation You will know you have succeeded if every router can ping every interface on every other router.

1. Figure 8.21 shows only the static routes for CE1, PE1, and PE2. Complete the figure by drawing the static routes that ISP 3 and ISP 4 would use to reach 140.10.0.0/24. Label each route with its type (simple, aggregate, or default) and the `next-hop` interface.

    1a. For the *shortest* path, how many alternatives are there for ISP 3 to reach 140.10.0.0/24?

    1b. For the *shortest* path, how many alternatives are there for ISP 4 to reach 140.10.0.0/24?

    1c. If ISP 3 does not use the shortest path, can traffic still reach 140.10.0.0/24?

2. Remove all previously configured static routes (see the previous exercise). Confirm that all static routes have been removed (see the previous exercise; all routes should have a type of `Local`).

3. Configure aggregate static routes between PE1 and PE2. Confirm that you can ping every interface on PE2 from PE1 and vice versa.

   ```
   *B:PE1# configure router static-route 150.10.0.0/24 next-hop 140.10.0.98
   *B:PE1#
   *A:PE2# configure router static-route 140.10.0.0/24 next-hop 140.10.0.97
   *A:PE2#
   ```

4. Configure simple static routes on PE1 for all interfaces on CE1.

```
*B:PE1# configure router static-route 140.10.0.3/32 next-hop 140.10.0.102
*B:PE1# configure router static-route 140.10.0.12/32 next-hop 140.10.0.102
*B:PE1#
```

4a. Why is a pair of routes to CE1 necessary, instead of just a single route?

5. Configure a default route on CE1 that points to PE1.

```
*A:CE1# configure router static-route 0.0.0.0/0 next-hop 140.10.0.101
*A:CE1#
```

6. Use a show command to verify the static routes on all three routers.

```
*B:PE1# show router route-table
===============================================================
Route Table (Router: Base)
===============================================================
Dest Prefix              Type    Proto   Age       Pref
    Next Hop[Interface Name]                Metric
---------------------------------------------------------------
140.10.0.1/32            Local   Local   02d22h03m  0
    system                                  0
140.10.0.3/32            Remote  Static  00h06m41s  5
    140.10.0.102                            1
140.10.0.11/32           Local   Local   02d20h45m  0
    loopbackTest                            0
140.10.0.12/32           Remote  Static  00h06m27s  5
    140.10.0.102                            1
140.10.0.96/30           Local   Local   02d21h37m  0
    toPE2                                   0
140.10.0.100/30          Local   Local   02d21h21m  0
    toCE1                                   0
150.10.0.0/24            Remote  Static  00h57m02s  5
    140.10.0.98                             1
---------------------------------------------------------------
No. of Routes: 7
===============================================================
*B:PE1>config>router#
```

```
*A:PE2# show router route-table
===============================================================
Route Table (Router: Base)
===============================================================
Dest Prefix                     Type    Proto   Age          Pref
    Next Hop[Interface Name]                     Metric
---------------------------------------------------------------
140.10.0.0/24                   Remote  Static  00h58m13s    5
    140.10.0.97                                  1
140.10.0.96/30                  Local   Local   02d20h51m    0
    toPE1                                        0
150.10.0.1/32                   Local   Local   02d21h20m    0
    system                                       0
150.10.0.11/32                  Local   Local   02d21h19m    0
    loopbackTest                                 0
---------------------------------------------------------------
No. of Routes: 4
===============================================================
*A:PE2#


*A:CE1# show router route-table
===============================================================
Route Table (Router: Base)
===============================================================
Dest Prefix                     Type    Proto   Age          Pref
    Next Hop[Interface Name]                     Metric
---------------------------------------------------------------
0.0.0.0/0                       Remote  Static  00h01m48s    5
    140.10.0.101                                 1
140.10.0.3/32                   Local   Local   02d21h20m    0
    system                                       0
140.10.0.12/32                  Local   Local   02d21h21m    0
    loopbackTest                                 0
140.10.0.100/30                 Local   Local   02d21h19m    0
    toPE1                                        0
---------------------------------------------------------------
No. of Routes: 4
===============================================================
*A:CE1#
```

6a. Can you account for each of the routes in each router's routing table?

7. Verify the proper operation of the routes by pinging between each pair of adjacent routers. If any ping fails, confirm that there are no mistakes in any route type, subnet/mask, or next-hop values.

8. Use `ping` and `traceroute` between CE1 and PE2. Confirm that each router can reach the other's `system` and `loopback` interfaces.

8a. How is it possible for CE1 to reach PE2 when there is no route for the 150.10.0.0/24 subnet in CE1's routing table?

8b. How is it possible for PE2 to reach CE1 when there is no specific route to CE1 interfaces in PE2's routing table?

9. Using `ping` (and, optionally, `traceroute`), confirm that every router can reach every configured interface on every other router.

10. (*Optional*) Use `traceroute` to verify that PE2 can reach CE1. Use `traceroute` again to attempt connectivity with one of the aggregate customer IPs on CE1 and notice the difference in the output.

```
*A:PE2# traceroute 140.10.0.3
traceroute to 140.10.0.3, 30 hops max, 40 byte packets
  1  140.10.0.97 (140.10.0.97)    <10 ms  <10 ms  <10 ms
  2  140.10.0.3 (140.10.0.3)     <10 ms  <10 ms  <10 ms
*A:PE2#
*A:PE2# traceroute 140.10.0.193
traceroute to 140.10.0.193, 30 hops max, 40 byte packets
  1  140.10.0.97 (140.10.0.97)    <10 ms !N  <10 ms !N  <10 ms !N
*A:PE2#
```

10a. The marker `!N` means the router at the far end of the link has *no* route to the destination, so it will drop all such packets. Is there any way to improve the handling of these packets? Try out your solution!

Chapter Review

Now that you have completed this chapter, you should have a good understanding of the following topics. If you are not familiar with these topics, please go back and review the appropriate sections.

- The purpose of IP routing
- The components of a IP routing table and their functions
- The Routing Table Manager
- Static routing and default routing
- The steps to configure a default route
- The purpose of a dynamic routing protocol
- The benefits of a dynamic routing protocol over static routes
- The concepts of convergence and routing loops
- Comparing distance vector routing protocols with link state routing protocols
- The differences between an IGP and an EGP

Post-Assessment

The following questions will test your knowledge and prepare you for the Alcatel-Lucent NRS I Certification Exam. Please review each question carefully and choose the most correct answer. You can compare your response with the answers listed in Appendix A in the back of this book. You can also download all of the CD content at http://booksupport.wiley.com to take all the assessment tests and review the answers. Good luck!

1. An IP router normally uses which of the following pieces of information to forward an IP packet?

    A. The destination IP address only

    B. The source and destination IP address

    C. The destination IP address and the destination TCP port

    D. The destination IP address, the TTL, and the ToS

2. The two main categories of routing protocols are IGP and _____.

    A. OSPF

    B. Link state

    C. BGP

    D. EGP

3. Which of the following is *not* a characteristic of an IGP?

    A. It is intended for networks under a common administrative control.

    B. It is used between ASes.

    C. There are not as many policy enforcement features as an EGP.

    D. It includes distance vector and link state protocols.

4. A router can run multiple routing protocols that each have their own table of routing information. A router selects the best route for each destination from all routing sources and puts them in the _____.

    A. Routing Link Database

    B. Routing Information Base

    C. Routing Table

    D. ARP Table

5. Which of the following pairings is *not* correct?

  A. EGP—BGP4

  B. Link state—OSPF

  C. IGP—RIP

  D. Distance vector—IS-IS

6. In which situation would you be most likely to use a static default route?

  A. In small networks

  B. On links with only a single path to other routers

  C. When you have older routers

  D. On a low-bandwith link

7. It is said that distance vector protocols have a longer convergence time than link state protocols. What is the most likely reason for this?

  A. Link state protocols send less information.

  B. Link state protocols keep track of neighbors via Hello updates.

  C. The shortest path algorithm is much faster to calculate than the calculation performed by a distance vector protocol.

  D. Distance vector protocols rely on updates only from neighbors.

8. There are many advantages of link state protocols over distance vector protocols. Which of the following is a potential advantage of distance vector?

  A. Distance vector sends its entire routing table in updates.

  B. Distance vector does not require extensive processing to build the routing table.

  C. Distance vector sends updates at timed intervals.

  D. Distance vector relies on neighbors to report routing updates.

9. When a link state router receives an LSP update, it uses what algorithm to calculate its routing table?

  A. OSPF

  B. Spanning tree

  C. SPF

  D. Least cost

10. Which of the following is most likely to be used for forwarding IP packets from a stub network?

A. A static route

B. A default route

C. A floating static route

D. OSPF with the "stub area" feature

11. The forwarding of packets on a router is a function of the data plane. The use of a routing protocol to build routing tables is a function of _____.

A. The routing plane

B. The control plane

C. The OSPF plane

D. The protocol plane

12. Link state protocols flood LSP information throughout the network to each router. These LSPs are stored in _____.

A. The routing table

B. The FIB

C. The routing database

D. The link state database

13. If there are multiple identical network prefixes advertised by different routing protocols, the Routing Table Manager chooses the route to place in the routing table based on _____.

A. It enters a route based on the lowest metric value.

B. It enters a route based on the highest preference value.

C. It enters a route based on the lowest preference value.

D. It enters a route for each protocol in the routing table.

14. Using a link state protocol, which of the following best describes the view each router has of all the links in the network after all LSPs have been flooded?

   A. Each router has a common view of the network.

   B. Each router has a unique view of the network based on its location.

   C. Each router knows about only those LSPs originated from its neighbors.

   D. Each router knows about all LSPs but uses only LSPs from its neighbors to construct its view.

15. Which of the following is the most accurate explanation of the information a distance vector routing protocol sends to neighboring routers?

   A. It sends Hello updates.

   B. It sends its entire routing table.

   C. It floods LSPs.

   D. It sends its entire routing table and its neighbors' routing tables.

OSPF

- Overview of OSPF
- The OSPF router ID
- OSPF point-to-point neighbor adjacencies
- OSPF link state flooding
- OSPF sequence numbers
- OSPF metrics

In this chapter, we build on our discussion of IP routing protocols by examining the specific link state protocol OSPF, or Open Shortest Path First. OSPF is an important routing protocol widely used in enterprise and service provider networks today. Having a foundational understanding of its mechanics is extremely important. OSPF has many complex features, and a detailed discussion of all of them has filled entire books. In this chapter, we introduce you to only the most important aspects of the protocol to give you a foundation for understanding the basics. Primarily, we focus on how OSPF discovers neighbor routers and exchanges link state information with other routers. We examine how link state information is flooded throughout a network so that each router has an identical view of the topology and look at how OSPF determines the shortest path to each network destination using this information.

Pre-Assessment

The following assessment questions will help you understand what areas of OSPF you should review in more detail to prepare for the exam.

1. OSPF discovers neighbors _____.
   A. Only by manually configuring the router
   B. By flooding updates
   C. Using Hello advertisements
   D. Using a host table

2. Which of the following is *not* a feature of the OSPF protocol?
   A. Supports authentication.
   B. Provides a loop-free topology.
   C. Uses the Shortest Path First algorithm.
   D. Uses a hop count–based metric.

3. Which logical interface is recommended for defining a router ID?
   A. Ethernet interface
   B. Chassis interface
   C. MAC address
   D. System interface

4. What is the primary purpose of the OSPF router ID?

   A. To elect a designated router

   B. To uniquely identify an OSPF router

   C. To trace sequence numbers

   D. To support LSA flooding

5. LSA updates are sent in response to network changes and _____.

   A. Every 30 minutes

   B. After the Hello timer expires

   C. When the DR detects the BDR has failed

   D. Every 30 minutes provided new information needs to be transmitted

You will find the answers to each of these questions in Appendix A. You can also download all of the CD materials for this book at `http://booksupport.wiley.com` to take all the assessment tests and review the answers.

9.1 Introduction to OSPF

In the previous chapter, we discussed IP routing protocols and examined the distance vector and link state types of Interior Gateway Protocols. As mentioned in our prior chapter, link state protocols are the more modern routing protocols and are the ones typically found in today's large networks. A very popular link state protocol is Open Shortest Path First (OSPF). OSPF has undergone several Request For Comments (RFC) revisions, and the most current specification is found in RFC 2328. In this chapter, we will provide an overview of OSPF and its basic functions. While we will not cover all of the advanced features of OSPF, this chapter will give you a foundational understanding of the most important OSPF concepts.

The IS-IS Link State Routing Protocol

IS-IS (Intermediate System to Intermediate System) is another popular link state routing protocol. Although it has some significant differences from OSPF, IS-IS uses the same databases and the same SPF algorithm and has a similar approach to flooding updates through the network.

OSPF is a typical link state protocol and uses several techniques to ensure each router has a loop-free topological view of the network and to achieve fast convergence time. OSPF begins the process of building a topological view of the network by sending *Hello* packets out on each of its connected networks. These Hello packets are sent to a specific multicast address and are picked up by any OSPF routers on a common network. In order to ensure two-way communication, the Hello packets include a list of all the other OSPF routers that a given router has received Hello packets from.

Therefore, a router knows it is on a common network segment with other OSPF routers when it sees Hellos with its own information in the update. Once OSPF routers detect the Hello updates from each other, they begin an exchange of network database information with the ultimate purpose of building a common view of the network. When the routers have completed this exchange of information, they are said to have formed an *adjacency*.

Note how similar the process of forming an adjacency seems to the process distance vector protocols use to exchange routing tables, covered in Chapter 8. And, indeed, in some ways the process is very similar. However, there are some very specific differences. Primarily, adjacent routers are exchanging *topology information*, not routing tables. The information in the link state database allows each router to build an independent routing table based on a common view of the network.

This point needs to be understood at the outset of any OSPF discussion. Each OSPF router uses the Shortest Path First (SPF) algorithm to determine a loop-free view of each destination in the network from its link state database. This database is built up from information about its own connected networks, information from adjacent routers, and information originated from other OSPF routers in the network via a flooding process.

OSPF propagates information not only to its neighboring, adjacent routers, but to all OSPF routers throughout the network. It does this by flooding updates to all OSPF routers. These updates are known as Link State Advertisements (LSAs). There are several different types of LSAs, but the one of primary interest is the router LSA (type 1).

A router LSA describes a router and its connected links. This is the information that is flooded by the routers throughout the OSPF network. When there is a change to any link in the network, the affected routers will update all their adjacent neighbors, and the neighbors will, in turn, flood this information to other adjacent routers in a reliable manner. OSPF runs directly on top of the IP protocol and implements its own reliable transmission methods to ensure that updates are not lost even over an unreliable network transport.

The Shortest Path First Algorithm

Once a router receives an LSA, it updates the information in its link state database and then calculates a shortest path tree to all network destinations with itself as the root. The exact SPF algorithm is complex, but the basic principle is that a router will create a tree view of the network with itself as the root and paths to all other routers and links as branches on a tree. The algorithm ensures that there is only a single path to any given network and that it is the lowest cost to that network. This ensures that the view each router creates is loop-free and the "shortest path" to each destination—hence the *Shortest Path First* algorithm.

Additional OSPF Features

There a few additional features that may be found in OSPF networks. In some situations, it may be advisable to ensure that only OSPF routers that have a specific password can communicate with each other. This would prevent any unauthorized OSPF-speaking devices from injecting LSAs into the network. OSPF supports the use of authentication to support this feature.

Additionally, in large networks, it might be useful to have a hierarchy so that a router does not need a complete view of the entire network. OSPF supports this need through the use of areas. An *area* can be thought of as a small subset of the entire network where each router in the area has a common view of the networks inside the area, but only certain routers (area border routers or ABRs) have information about networks and routers outside of the area. This allows all of the non-ABR routers to have a much smaller link state database while still allowing every router to reach networks outside the area by way of an ABR. A more thorough discussion of areas is beyond the scope of this work.

In addition to these features, OSPF differentiates between interface types. Some interfaces such as Ethernet are referred to as *broadcast interfaces* because they support sending information to all other devices on the network simultaneously. Other interfaces such as serial links are referred to as *point-to-point* because there are only two devices on the network.

OSPF handles broadcast networks differently than point-to-point networks and uses mechanisms to ensure that not all routers on a broadcast network need to form adjacencies with all other routers. However, this adds additional overhead, and it is considered best practice to configure broadcast interfaces, such as Ethernet, as point-to-point whenever possible. In this chapter, we concentrate on configuring OSPF in a point-to-point manner on an Ethernet network.

The following list summarizes these features along with several other features of the OSPF protocol that you should be aware of:

- Link state protocol with fast convergence and inherent loop prevention mechanisms.

- Highly scalable; can support the largest enterprise networks.

- Uses the SPF algorithm to calculate the routing table.

- Default cost metric takes into account the physical bandwidth of the port or the cost can be set manually.

- Supports hierarchy using areas.
- Authentication support using passwords or MD5 hash
- Traffic engineering extensions for Multi Protocol Label Switching (MPLS)
- OSPF version 2 (RFC 2328) is a widely deployed, well-known protocol for IPv4.
- OSPF version 3 (RFC 5340) is standardized and supports IPv6.

In the next section, we begin examining how some of these key features work in OSPF by looking at particular implementation characteristics. We start with a discussion of the OSPF router ID.

 The Alcatel-Lucent implementation of OSPF version 2 for routing IPv4 conforms to the specifications detailed in RFC 2328.

9.2 Router IDs and Their Function

The astute reader may have already noticed that OSPF has many features that require it to track information about all of the routers in the network (e.g., to determine how to build a loop-free tree to each destination). In order to do this, OSPF requires a unique method of identifying each router it exchanges information with. This allows an OSPF router to develop an accurate picture of all of the links and routers in the network. The element that OSPF uses to uniquely identify a router is the *router ID*. The router ID is used as an identifier in Link State Updates that are sent to other routers, and it is the mechanism used by each router to identify all other routers.

The *router ID* is a 32-bit number assigned to each router running OSPF. Routers running OSPF use the router ID of neighboring routers to establish adjacencies and to flood LSAs. A router ID can be configured explicitly, or if no router ID is configured, the system ID of the router is used. If no system ID is configured, the last 4 octets (32 bits) of the router's chassis MAC address are used. The chassis MAC address is found with the command show chassis.

In Figure 9.1, Router R1 has a router ID of 1.1.1.1 and Router R2 has a router ID of 2.2.2.2. This enables both routers and any other router in the OSPF network to uniquely identify them.

In the next section, we examine how the router ID is used during the adjacency process to exchange link state database information.

Figure 9.1 Each OSPF router must have a router ID to uniquely identify it. Router R1 has a router ID of 1.1.1.1, and Router R2 has a router ID of 2.2.2.2.

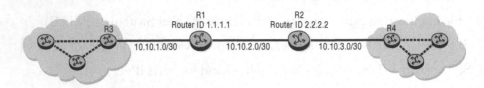

 Changing an OSPF router ID is not preemptive; therefore, configuring a new router ID will not take effect until the OSPF process is restarted.

The router ID used for OSPF can be configured explicitly via the command:

```
configure router router-id <router-id>
```

The router ID is specified in dotted decimal notation, much like an IP address. If the router ID is specified in this manner, the router ID would also be used for other routing protocols such as Border Gateway Protocol (BGP). If you would like to use a different router ID for other routing protocols, you can override this high-level router ID and create an OSPF-specific router ID with the command:

```
configure router ospf router-id <router-id>
```

 Overriding the high-level router ID with an OSPF-specific router ID is supported in Alcatel-Lucent 7750 Release 6.0 and later.

If a `router-id` is not configured in the `config->router` context, the router's system interface IP address is used. To configure a system interface, use the command:

```
configure router interface system address <ip-address>/32
```

OSPF Point-to-Point Adjacencies

As already discussed, OSPF is based on routers exchanging link state information with each other. Two OSPF routers must create an OSPF neighbor adjacency before they can exchange routing information. On point-to-point OSPF networks, neighboring routers automatically become fully adjacent with each other once they detect each other via OSPF Hello updates. For example, in Figure 9.2, R2 becomes fully adjacent with both R1 and R3. All neighbor adjacencies in the point-to-point network are indicated with the arrows in the figure.

Figure 9.2 In order to exchange link state information with each other, neighboring OSPF routers must build an adjacency. OSPF routers that are connected to each other on point-to-point links always form adjacencies. The adjacency process begins once each router sees its own router ID in the Hello packets from the other router. Once routers become adjacent, they exchange full link state tables with each other.

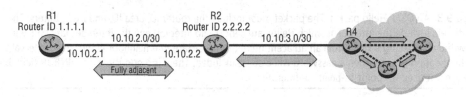

Because OSPF routers on point-to-point networks automatically become adjacent, the only configuration necessary is to enable OSPF on the interfaces and ensure that they are configured with the same area and Hello timers. Hello timers control the frequency with which OSPF Hello packets are sent and how often they are timed out. Hello timers have default values, so if they are not changed, OSPF routers configured with the same area on a point-to-point link should automatically become adjacent without any additional configuration.

However, routers can be connected on a shared broadcast segment, such as Ethernet, rather than a point-to-point segment. On a broadcast segment, additional steps are performed by the protocol to reduce the amount of OSPF control traffic that flows between routers on the segment. This involves electing designated routers (DRs) and back-up designated routers (BDRs) to handle adjacency formation.

On an OSPF broadcast network, DRs and BDRs are the only OSPF routers that form adjacencies with other OSPF routers on the segment. This significantly reduces the number of adjacencies that each router must create and maintain.

A detailed discussion of DRs and BDRs is beyond the scope of this book; we examine only the point-to-point scenario for ease of discussion and because configuring Ethernet connected routers as OSPF point-to-point is considered a best practice. Note that the default OSPF interface type is broadcast for router Ethernet interfaces and you must explicitly configure them as point-to-point. The steps necessary to configure an Ethernet interface as OSPF point-to-point will be presented later in this chapter.

DRs and BDRs are covered in the "Alcatel-Lucent Interior Routing Protocols" course. See the Alcatel-Lucent website at www.alcatel-lucent.com/src for more information.

To begin the process of forming an adjacency, routers send Hello messages out of each OSPF-enabled interface. The Hello packets are the basic process by which OSPF routers discover neighboring routers. A router will include the address of other routers it has received Hello updates from, ensuring that neighbor routers will see each other's router ID in their respective Hello updates. The most important fields in a Hello packet are noted in Figure 9.3.

Figure 9.3 An OSPF Hello packet. The packet must include the router ID, area ID, and Hello timers. The Hello timers include the interval at which Hellos are sent (Hello interval) and the interval that OSPF will wait without receiving a Hello from an adjacent neighbor to declare that neighbor down (dead interval). If authentication is used, then a password will also be included. There is a priority and a DR/BDR field, but these are not used for point-to-point configurations.

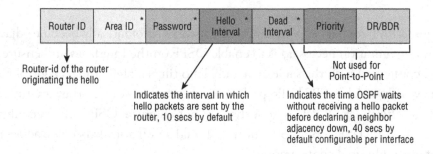

Parameters that are denoted with an asterisk in the figure must be set the same on both routers to form an adjacency or to keep an adjacency alive. These parameters are:

- **Area ID**—Used for OSPF hierarchy; it must be configured even if there is only a single area and it must be the same on all adjacent routers

- **Password**—Used only for OSPF authentication

- **Hello Interval**—The interval at which Hello updates are sent; defaults to 10 seconds.

- **Dead Interval**—The time OSPF waits without receiving a Hello update to mark a neighbor down; defaults to 40 seconds.

Forming an OSPF Adjacency

Hello packets are sent between routers to form an adjacency and to proceed to an exchange of link state tables. They are also used as a keep-alive after the adjacency is formed. On point-to-point links, OSPF traffic is always sent to the reserved multicast address 224.0.0.5.

Although Hello messages are important, they are only the beginning of the process of forming an adjacency. Let's examine the entire process of forming an adjacency from beginning to end. In Figure 9.4, Routers R1 and R2 have been rebooted and therefore need to form a new adjacency.

Figure 9.4 Routers R1 and R2 have been rebooted and need to form an adjacency. They are initially in the OSPF down state. The routers begin sending OSPF Hello packets and proceed to the OSPF init state. Once the routers see their own router ID in a neighbor's Hello updates, they move to the two-way state and are ready to begin an exchange of link state database information.

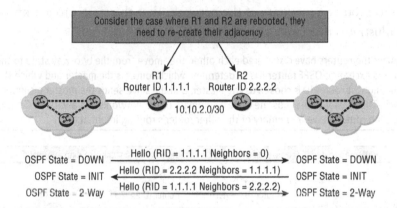

The process of forming an adjacency proceeds through several distinct stages:

1. When both routers are first powered up, they are in the OSPF down state.

2. Both OSPF routers send OSPF Hello packets to discover each other and proceed to the init state.

3. When the discovery process is complete, the routers are in a two-way state and are ready to exchange routing information.

Once routers have moved to the two-way state, this indicates that they are ready to begin the exchange of their link state database information. This process begins when the routers move from the two-way state to the ExStart state.

In the ExStart state, both routers send database description (DBD) packets to establish a master–slave relationship. The highest router ID becomes the master. Maximum transmission unit (MTU) checking is also performed in the `ExStart` state. The OSPF MTU from both neighbors must match to proceed beyond the `exchange start` state. The OSPF MTU can be configured explicitly on the OSPF interface. If the MTU is not configured, the physical port MTU becomes the OSPF MTU. Therefore, if an OSPF MTU is not configured, the physical port MTUs must match to create an adjacency. The OSPF MTU determines the maximum size of the OSPF control (CTL) packets, which is typically the size of the Link State Update and Link State Request packets.

Once the master–slave relationship is established during the `ExStart` state, the database description is first sent by the slave router to the master router to provide a summary of the networks that the slave router knows about. The master router then sends the slave router a summary of the networks that the master router knows about. Figure 9.5 illustrates this process.

Figure 9.5 After the routers have discovered each other, they move from the two-way state to the exchange state. The routers exchange OSPF router IDs to determine which router is the master and which the slave. The router with the highest router ID is chosen as the master, and the slave sends the master a summary of the networks it has. The master then sends the slave a summary of the networks it is aware of. Once this process is completed, both routers have a summary of the other router's routing information.

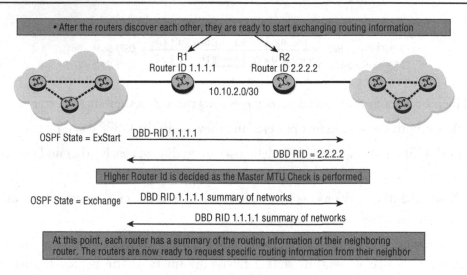

Once the master and slave routers exchange their summary information, the `exchange` state is now complete. The routers now proceed to the `loading` state. In the loading state, routers use a specific OSPF packet type, called a *Link State Advertisement* (LSA), to describe their routing information. In this state, both routers go through a Request, Reply, and Acknowledge sequence until each router has a full view of its neighbor's link state information. At this point, both routers have an identical link state database and are considered fully adjacent. Once the link state database is fully up to date, the routers run the SPF algorithm to calculate the best path to each destination in the network and use this information to build their routing table. The steps in the loading stage are shown in Figure 9.6.

Figure 9.6 After OSPF routers complete the exchange state, they move to the loading state. In the loading state, the routers go through a series of request–reply–acknowledge steps to request information on specific LSAs. Once this process is complete the OSPF is in a full state—both routers have an identical link state database.

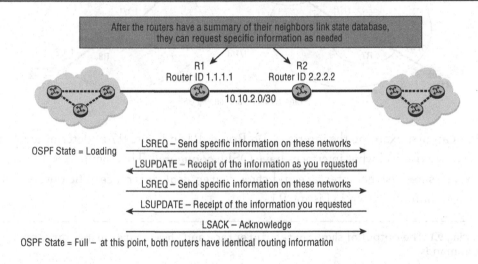

Now that we have finished examining the steps in the OSPF database exchange process, it will be useful to take a look at some common OSPF commands.

OSPF Commands

There are several OSPF commands that are useful for examining the state of OSPF on a router. For the following command output, the network shown in Figure 9.7 will be used.

Figure 9.7 A sample network topology. For the examples that follow, only routers R1, R2, R3, R5, and R7 have been enabled for OSPF.

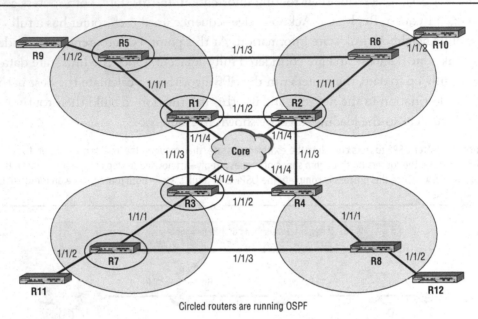

Circled routers are running OSPF

We can first examine the interfaces on Router R1 in Figure 9.7 to determine what interfaces exist and what interfaces have OSPF configured. The commands, respectively, are show router interface and show router ospf interface. The output from each command is shown in Listing 9.1.

Listing 9.1 The output of show router interface and show router ospf interface commands

```
*A:AIRP_R01>show>router# interface

===============================================================================
Interface Table (Router: Base)
===============================================================================
Interface-Name                   Adm        Opr(v4/v6)  Mode     Port/SapId
   IP-Address                                                    PfxState
-------------------------------------------------------------------------------
L1                               Up         Up/--       Network  loopback
   172.16.2.1/24                                                 n/a
```

(continued)

```
L2                              Up        Up/--      Network loopback
    172.16.3.1/24                                              n/a
-
system                          Up        Up/--      Network system
    172.16.1.1/32                                             n/a
toR2                            Up        Up/--      Network 1/1/2
    172.31.12.1/24                                            n/a
toR3                            Up        Up/--      Network 1/1/3
    172.31.13.1/24                                            n/a
toR4                            Up        Up/--      Network 1/1/4
    172.31.14.1/24                                            n/a
toR5                            Up        Up/--      Network 1/1/1
    172.16.15.1/24                                            n/a
-------------------------------------------------------------------
Interfaces : 7
===================================================================
*A:AIRP_R01>show>router#
*A:AIRP_R01>show>router>ospf# interface
===================================================================
OSPF Interfaces
===================================================================
If Name          Area Id      Designated Rtr  Bkup Desig Rtr  Adm  Oper
-------------------------------------------------------------------
toR5             0.0.0.0      0.0.0.0         0.0.0.0         Up   PToP
toR2             0.0.0.0      0.0.0.0         0.0.0.0         Up   PToP
toR3             0.0.0.0      0.0.0.0         0.0.0.0         Up   PToP
toR4             0.0.0.0      0.0.0.0         0.0.0.0         Up   PToP
-------------------------------------------------------------------
No. of OSPF Interfaces: 4
===================================================================
*A:AIRP_R01>show>router>ospf#
```

There are several points of interest in the output of these commands. First, note that the number of interfaces on R1 is seven and the number of interfaces for OSPF is four. Not all active interfaces on R1 are configured for OSPF. The Oper flag for the toR2, toR3, toR4, and toR5 interfaces indicate that the interfaces are point-to-point (PToP). Because the interfaces are Ethernet, this means that the interfaces have been explicitly configured as OSPF point-to-point. (You will see how to do this later in the chapter.) How do you know that the interfaces are Ethernet? The easiest way is to use the show port command and examine the output for ports 1/1/1, 1/1/2, 1/1/3, and 1/1/4 (the ports that correspond to the OSPF enabled interfaces). The output of this command is shown in Listing 9.2. You can see that the port type is faste, that is, fastethernet.

Listing 9.2 Listing of the show port command

```
*A:AIRP_R01# show port


===============================================================================
=
Ports on Slot 1
===============================================================================
=
Port    Admin Link Port  Cfg  Oper LAG/ Port Port Port  SFP/XFP/
Id      State      State MTU  MTU  Bndl Mode Encp Type  MDIMDX
-------------------------------------------------------------------------------
--
1/1/1   Up    Yes  Up    1514 1514   -  netw null faste MDI
1/1/2   Up    Yes  Up    1514 1514   -  netw null faste MDI
1/1/3   Up    Yes  Up    1514 1514   -  netw null faste MDI
1/1/4   Up    Yes  Up    1514 1514   -  netw null faste MDI
1/1/5   Down  No   Down  1514 1514   -  netw null faste
1/1/6   Down  No   Down  1514 1514   -  netw null faste
1/1/7   Down  No   Down  1514 1514   -  netw null faste
1/1/8   Down  No   Down  1514 1514   -  netw null faste
1/1/9   Down  No   Down  1514 1514   -  netw null faste
1/1/10  Down  No   Down  1514 1514   -  netw null faste
1/1/11  Down  No   Down  1514 1514   -  netw null faste
1/1/12  Down  No   Down  1514 1514   -  netw null faste
1/1/13  Down  No   Down  1514 1514   -  netw null faste
1/1/14  Down  No   Down  1514 1514   -  netw null faste
1/1/15  Down  No   Down  1514 1514   -  netw null faste
1/1/16  Down  No   Down  1514 1514   -  netw null faste
1/1/17  Down  No   Down  1514 1514   -  netw null faste
1/1/18  Down  No   Down  1514 1514   -  netw null faste
1/1/19  Down  No   Down  1514 1514   -  netw null faste
1/1/20  Down  No   Down  1514 1514   -  netw null faste
1/1/21  Down  No   Down  1514 1514   -  netw null faste
1/1/22  Down  No   Down  1514 1514   -  netw null faste
```

(continued)

```
1/1/23      Down   No   Down     1514 1514     - netw null faste
1/1/24      Down   No   Down     1514 1514     - netw null faste
1/1/25      Down   No   Down     1514 1514     - netw null faste
1/1/26      Down   No   Down     1514 1514     - netw null faste
1/1/27      Down   No   Down     1514 1514     - netw null faste
1/1/28      Down   No   Down     1514 1514     - netw null faste
1/1/29      Down   No   Down     1514 1514     - netw null faste
1/1/30      Down   No   Down     1514 1514     - netw null faste
*A:AIRP_R01#
```

Another point to note is that one of the interfaces is a system interface. The IP address of the system interface will be used as the OSPF router ID unless a different OSPF router ID is explicitly configured. You determine the OSPF router ID using the `show router ospf status` command as shown in Listing 9.3. Notice that the router ID is the same as the system interface, indicating that a specific OSPF router ID has not been configured.

```
Listing 9.3 The output of the show router ospf status command

*A:AIRP_R01# show router ospf status


===================================================================
OSPF Status
===================================================================
OSPF Cfg Router Id            : 0.0.0.0
OSPF Oper Router Id           : 172.16.1.1
OSPF Version                  : 2
OSPF Admin Status             : Enabled
OSPF Oper Status              : Enabled
Graceful Restart              : Disabled
GR Helper Mode                : Disabled
Preference                    : 10
External Preference           : 150
Backbone Router               : True
Area Border Router            : False
AS Border Router              : False
Opaque LSA Support            : True
Traffic Engineering Support   : False
```

(continued)

```
RFC 1583 Compatible         : True
Demand Exts Support         : False
In Overload State           : False
In External Overflow State  : False
Exit Overflow Interval      : 0
Last Overflow Entered       : Never
Last Overflow Exit          : Never
External LSA Limit          : -1
Reference Bandwidth         : 100,000,000 Kbps
Init SPF Delay              : 1000 msec
Sec SPF Delay               : 1000 msec
Max SPF Delay               : 10000 msec
Min LS Arrival Interval     : 1000 msec
Init LSA Gen Delay          : 5000 msec
Sec LSA Gen Delay           : 5000 msec
Max LSA Gen Delay           : 5000 msec
Last Ext SPF Run            : Never
Ext LSA Cksum Sum           : 0x0
OSPF Last Enabled           : 03/13/2009 23:10:03
*A:AIRP_R01#
```

The configuration for the interfaces and OSPF information for Router R1 are shown in Listings 9.4 and 9.5. First, you must create the interfaces that will participate in the OSPF routing protocol. On Router R1 we have created the system interface and two other interfaces, toR2 and toR5. You must assign them to a particular port and give them an IP address. Note that the system interface does not require a port. Next, you have to configure the interfaces for OSPF. You do this by creating an OSPF area ID, 0.0.0.0 in this case, and assigning interfaces to this area. As mentioned previously, the interfaces need to be configured as type point-to-point since they are Ethernet and will default to OSPF interface type broadcast by default.

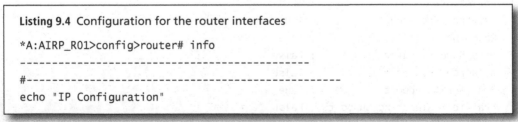

Listing 9.4 Configuration for the router interfaces

```
*A:AIRP_R01>config>router# info
-----------------------------------------------
#-----------------------------------------------------
echo "IP Configuration"
```

(continued)

```
#-------------------------------------------------
        interface "L1"
            address 172.16.2.1/24
            loopback
        exit
        interface "L2"
            address 172.16.3.1/24
            loopback
        exit
        interface "system"
            address 172.16.1.1/32
        exit
        interface "toR2"
            address 172.31.12.1/24
            port 1/1/2
        exit
        interface "toR3"
            address 172.31.13.1/24
            port 1/1/3
        exit
        interface "toR4"
            address 172.31.14.1/24
            port 1/1/4
        exit
        interface "toR5"
            address 172.16.15.1/24
            port 1/1/1
        exit
```

Listing 9.5 Configuration for the OSPF commands on the interfaces

```
*A:R1>config>router>ospf# info
    area 0.0.0.0
        interface "toR5"
            interface-type point-to-point
        exit
```

(continued)

```
        interface "toR2"
            interface-type point-to-point
        exit
        interface "toR3"
            interface-type point-to-point
        exit
        interface "toR4"
            interface-type point-to-point
        exit
    exit
```

Once OSPF is configured on an interface, it will begin to issue OSPF Hello messages on each interface. Other routers will see the Hello messages and will eventually form an adjacency with R1 and exchange link state database information. You can easily see a router's OSPF neighbors using the show router ospf neighbor command as shown in Listing 9.6. Note that R1 has two neighbors in a Full state, indicating that they have formed an adjacency and exchanged full link state database information.

Listing 9.6 The output of the show router ospf neighbor command

```
*A:AIRP_R01# show router ospf neighbor

===============================================================================
OSPF Neighbors
===============================================================================
Interface-Name            Rtr Id          State     Pri  RetxQ   TTL
-------------------------------------------------------------------------------
toR5                      172.16.254.1    Full      1    0       38
toR2                      255.0.0.0       Full      1    0       31
toR3                      255.0.0.0       Full      1    1       38
-------------------------------------------------------------------------------
No. of Neighbors: 3
===============================================================================
```

In a single area point-to-point network, only the router LSAs (Type 1 LSAs) will be used to create the link state database. In more complex topologies, there are other types of LSAs exchanged. In the next section, we examine the process by which LSAs are flooded throughout a network in response to a change in the network.

9.3 Link State Updates and Flooding

Link State Advertisements (LSAs) describe the network topology, including router interfaces and destination networks. Each LSA is flooded throughout an area. The collection of link information from all routers and networks forms the protocol's topological database. The distribution of topology database updates takes place between adjacent routers. A router sends LSAs to advertise its state according to the configured interval and when the router's state changes.

When a router discovers a routing table change or detects a change in the network link state information, it is advertised to other routers to maintain identical topological databases. Link State Advertisements flood the area, with each router forwarding the received LSA to its adjacent routers in a reliable manner. The flooding mechanism ensures that all routers in an area have the same topological database. There are some key points to keep in mind when considering OSFP LSAs:

- OSPF LSAs are flooded in OSPF Link State Update packets. Each Link State Update may contain several LSAs.

- Each OSPF Link State Update is acknowledged by the adjacent routers that receive the update.

- Each OSPF LSA has a maximum age of 60 minutes; after this time a router will delete the LSA from its database.

- OSPF LSAs are refreshed by the originating router every 30 minutes, ensuring that they do not get flushed by adjacent routers.

- Every OSPF router generates a Type 1 Router LSA to flood their local topology information within the OSPF area.

- On point-to-point single area OSPF networks, only Type 1 Router LSAs are required to convey topology information to each other.

Router LSAs on point-to-point networks are always flooded to multicast IP address 224.0.0.5. This is the same multicast address used for OSPF Hello packets while forming and maintaining an OSPF neighbor adjacency. Figure 9.8 illustrates the flooding process. Note that R2 sends its LSAs out on network 10.10.2.0/30 in a Link State Update packet, and it is received by Router R1. R1 will acknowledge its receipt of the Link State Update and will then send the information in the Link State Update on to network 10.10.1.0/24, where it will be received and acknowledge by Router R3 and so on until all OSPF routers have received the Link State Update and all routers have acknowledged its receipt.

Figure 9.8 R2 will flood information on its LSAs whenever there is a topology change or every 30 minutes. R2 begins the flooding process by sending its LSAs to the multicast address 224.0.0.5 on each OSPF interface. In this case, R2 floods its LSAs out its interface on the 10.10.2.0/30 network, where it will be received and processed by Router R1. Router R1 will acknowledge receipt of the LSA update and then forward the LSA information on to network 10.10.1.0/30, where it will be received and processed by Router R3. R3 will perform the same acknowledgement and forwarding process as R1, and this process continues until every OSPF router has received and acknowledged the LSA update information.

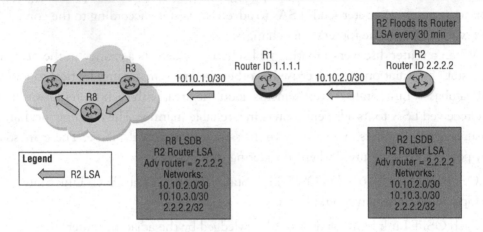

You can examine the Link State Advertisements from other OSPF routers using the `show router ospf database` command as shown in Listing 9.7. Note that each LSA is displayed including the type of LSA (typically a Type 1 router LSA), the advertising router ID, and the age. It is important to point out again that a router will have LSAs from non-adjacent routers owing to the flooding mechanism. This is normal in an OSPF network. Each router must have exactly the same link state information in its database in order for them to have a common view of the network.

Listing 9.7 The output of `show router ospf database` is used to display LSA advertisements from other OSPF routers.

```
*A:AIRP_R01# show router ospf database

===============================================================================
OSPF Link State Database (Type : All)
===============================================================================
Type    Area Id      Link State Id    Adv Rtr Id     Age  Sequence   Cksum
-------------------------------------------------------------------------------
Router  0.0.0.0      172.16.1.1       172.16.1.1     72   0x8000000d 0xec7c
```

(continued)

```
Router  0.0.0.0      172.16.254.1    172.16.254.1    365  0x80000004 0x78e
Router  0.0.0.0      172.18.1.1      172.18.1.1       78  0x80000004 0x84e4
Router  0.0.0.0      255.0.0.0       255.0.0.0         8  0x800001a7 0x2154
---------------------------------------------------------------------------
No. of LSAs: 4
===========================================================================
```

You can get even more information on a particular LSA using the show router ospf database <router id> detail command. In Listing 9.8, we used LSA for Router 172.16.254.1. Note the sequence number information.

Listing 9.8 The output for information on a particular LSA using show router ospf database <routerid> detail

```
*A:AIRP_R01>show>router>ospf# database 172.16.254.1 detail

===========================================================================
OSPF Link State Database (Type : All) (Detailed)
===========================================================================
---------------------------------------------------------------------------
Router LSA for Area 0.0.0.0
---------------------------------------------------------------------------
Area Id         : 0.0.0.0              Adv Router Id    : 172.16.254.1
Link State Id   : 172.16.254.1 (2886794753)
LSA Type        : Router
Sequence No     : 0x80000004           Checksum         : 0x78e
Age             : 475                  Length           : 48
Options         : E
Flags           : None                 Link Count       : 2
Link Type (1)   : Point To Point
Nbr Rtr Id (1)  : 172.16.1.1           I/F Address (1)  : 172.16.15.5
No of TOS (1)   : 0                    Metric-0 (1)     : 1000
Link Type (2)   : Stub Network
Network (2)     : 172.16.15.0          Mask (2)         : 255.255.255.0
No of TOS (2)   : 0                    Metric-0 (2)     : 1000
===========================================================================
```

OSPF uses a sequence number to ensure that LSAs are not transmitted around the OSPF area indefinitely. It also uses an acknowledgement process to guarantee reliability of LSA transmission to neighboring routers. The algorithm used by the OSPF router to process received LSAs is as follows:

1. If the sequence number in the LSA is lower than the one in the database, the incoming link state information is discarded, and the receiving router will update the sending router with the corresponding information in its own database. Note that this is because a higher sequence number means that the receiving router already has more current information than it is receiving from the transmitting router.

2. If the sequence number is the same, an acknowledgement is sent. The incoming link state information is then discarded because the receiving router already has this information in its database.

3. If the sequence number is higher, the new link state information is populated in the topological database, an acknowledgement is sent, and the link state information is forwarded to its neighbors using the flooding process previously described.

Note that in all cases the receiving router will either send an acknowledgement or, in the case of reception of a lower sequence number, will update the sending router with the more current LSA. OSPF ensures that the LSA flooding process is reliable through the use of this acknowledgement process. Figure 9.9 illustrates the flooding process for an LSA with sequence number 123.

Figure 9.9 The LSA with sequence number 123 is flooded from router R2 throughout the OSPF network. Every router will receive the LSA update and acknowledge its receipt. If a router has a sequence number for the LSA that is higher than the one it receives, it will discard the LSA with sequence number 123 and update its adjacent router with the more current LSA.

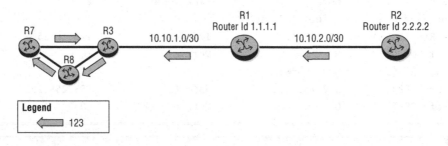

We have now discussed the fundamentals of the OSPF routing protocol. The most important points to remember are that OSPF uses LSAs to send updates about the router interfaces to all other routers through the flooding process described previously. OSPF ensures that this process is reliable through the use of acknowledgements. The distribution of LSAs ensures that all routers in the network have a common view of the entire topology. The final step in the process is for each router to calculate the shortest path to each destination based on the metrics for each link. We will conclude the chapter examining OSPF metrics and how they are used in the SPF calculation.

OSPF Metrics and SPF Calculation

In OSPF, all interfaces have a cost value or routing metric used in the OSPF link state calculation. As explained in Chapter 8, the metric value is configured based on hop count, bandwidth, or other parameters, to compare different paths through an AS. OSPF uses cost values to determine the best path to a particular destination: the lower the cost value, the more likely the interface will be used to forward data traffic.

The OSPF metric advertised in the router LSA for an interface is automatically calculated by dividing a *reference bandwidth* by the interface bandwidth. On the Alcatel-Lucent 7750 Service Router, the default reference bandwidth is 100 Gbps. So, for example, the default cost for a 1-Gbps interface would be (100 Gbps)/(1 Gbps) = 100. The default cost for a 100-Mbps interface would be (100 Gbps)/(0.1 Gbps) = 1,000. Lower metrics are better, so a 100 metric is preferred over a 1,000 metric, and the 1-Gbps interface would thus be preferred over the 100-Mbps interface. Listing 9.9 illustrates the output of the `show router ospf interface <interfacename> detail` command. You can see that the metric is 1,000 for the `Oper Metric`, indicating that the speed of the interface is 100 Mbps (this is the fastethernet interface we looked at earlier). Note that this command also displays a lot of OSPF-related statistics such as the number of Link State Updates received and transmitted.

> **Listing 9.9** Listing of the output to see the metric for an OSPF interface using the `show router ospf interface <interfacename> detail` command
>
> ```
> *A:AIRP_R01>show>router>ospf# interface toR5 detail
>
>
> ===============================================================================
> OSPF Interface (Detailed) :  toR5
> ===============================================================================
> ```

(continued)

```
------------------------------------------------------------------------
Configuration
------------------------------------------------------------------------
IP Address      : 172.16.15.1
Area Id         : 0.0.0.0            Priority        : 1
Hello Intrvl    : 10 sec            Rtr Dead Intrvl : 40 sec
Retrans Intrvl  : 5 sec             Poll Intrvl     : 120 sec
Cfg Metric      : 0                 Advert Subnet   : True
Transit Delay   : 1                 Auth Type       : None
Passive         : False             Cfg MTU         : 0
------------------------------------------------------------------------
State
------------------------------------------------------------------------
Admin Status    : Enabled           Oper State      : Point To Point
Designated Rtr  : 0.0.0.0           Backup Desig Rtr : 0.0.0.0
IF Type         : Point To Point    Network Type    : Transit
Oper MTU        : 1500              Last Enabled    : 03/13/2009 23:29:14
Oper Metric     : 1000              Bfd Enabled     : No
Te Metric       : 1000              Te State        : Down
Admin Groups    : None
Ldp Sync        : outOfService      Ldp Sync Wait   : Disabled
Ldp Timer State : Disabled          Ldp Tm Left     : 0
------------------------------------------------------------------------
Statistics
------------------------------------------------------------------------
Nbr Count       : 1                 If Events       : 3
Tot Rx Packets  : 599               Tot Tx Packets  : 595
Rx Hellos       : 228               Tx Hellos       : 226
Rx DBDs         : 4                 Tx DBDs         : 3
Rx LSRs         : 1                 Tx LSRs         : 1
Rx LSUs         : 4                 Tx LSUs         : 362
Rx LS Acks      : 362               Tx LS Acks      : 3
Retransmits     : 0                 Discards        : 0
Bad Networks    : 0                 Bad Virt Links  : 0
Press any key to continue (Q to quit)
```

As an alternative to accepting the cost based on the interface speed, the OSPF metric of an interface can be configured in the OSPF interface context. Figure 9.10 illustrates an example of an OSPF interface metric that has been manually configured. Note that the default metric of system and loopback interfaces on a router is zero.

Figure 9.10 Router R1 has a configured OSPF metric of 674 on its interface to network 10.10.2.0/30. It is using the default metric on its interface to network 10.10.1.0/30 (metric 100 indicates a 1-Gbps interface). The default metric for the system interface is 0.

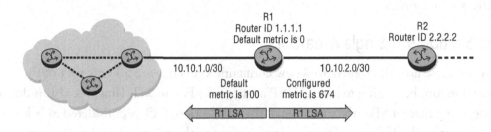

We have now examined the key aspects of the OSPF routing protocol. Your understanding of the topics that have been covered will be reinforced through the use of the exercises and questions that follow. In the next chapter, we will turn to the most popular EGP protocol: the Border Gateway Protocol (BGP).

Now you should complete the lab exercises to assist you in reinforcing this chapter's features. These lab exercises are carefully designed to give you hands-on experience, configuring many of the technology standards that have been discussed and should greatly aid you in your exam preparation.

Practice Lab: Open Shortest Path First (OSPF)

The following lab is designed to reinforce your knowledge of the content in this chapter. Please review the instructions carefully and perform the steps in the order in which they are provided. The practice labs require that you have access to three or more Alcatel-Lucent 7750 SRs or Alcatel-Lucent 7450 ESSs in a non-production environment.

 These labs are designed to be used in a controlled lab environment. Please **DO NOT** attempt to perform these labs in a production environment.

In the previous chapter, the static routes were configured entirely manually. There were many possible sources of mistakes: determining the correct IP address of the next-hop interface; typing mistakes of either subnet, mask, or next-hop values; or forgotten routes. Any single mistake could potentially severely disrupt the flow of traffic.

Routing protocols were designed to automate the preceding tasks and thereby eliminate as many sources of error as possible. In this lab, we use OSPF to duplicate the connectivity of the previous lab, but without requiring any manual configuration of addresses or subnets.

Lab Section 9.1: Single Area OSPF

This exercise uses the routers in a new configuration. They are all now part of the same domain, belonging to a single ISP as shown in Figure 9.11. (Imagine this is due to a corporate merger.) For the purposes of this lab section, CE1 is considered as belonging to part of the ISP core. There are no changes to the addressing scheme.

Objective In this exercise, you will configure a single area OSPF network. This lab will demonstrate the different databases that are created by the OSPF routing protocol.

Validation You will know you have succeeded if every router can ping *every interface* on *every* other router.

Figure 9.11 This configuration of three routers allows us to explore the key aspects of OSPF routing.

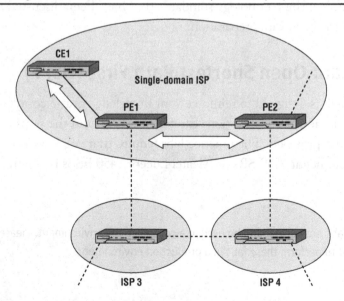

Please remove all static routes configured on CE1 and the PE devices in the previous labs. Refer to Lab Section 8.1 in Chapter 8. Confirm that all routes have been removed by ensuring that each router's routing table contains only routes of type Local.

1. The first step is to enable the OSPF routing process on the router:

```
*B:PE1# configure router ospf
*B:PE1>config>router>ospf$
```

2. Next define the area that the interfaces will be placed in. Remember that the area must match on the interfaces on both ends of a link for OSPF to establish an adjacency. The objective of this exercise is to configure a single area OSPF network; therefore, you should use the same area number.

```
*B:PE1>config>router>ospf$ area 0
*B:PE1>config>router>ospf>area$
```

3. Within this area, enter all the interfaces on which OSPF should be running and sending out its advertisements. The system interface is a special case and should *always* be included in OSPF. In this case, place all the local interfaces into the OSPF process area 0. Do *not* include the loopback interfaces; they are used to demonstrate another feature of OSPF in a later step.

```
*B:PE1>config>router>ospf>area$ interface system
*B:PE1>config>router>ospf>area>if$ exit
*B:PE1>config>router>ospf>area# interface toPE2
*B:PE1>config>router>ospf>area>if$ exit
*B:PE1>config>router>ospf>area# interface toCE1
*B:PE1>config>router>ospf>area>if$ exit
*B:PE1>config>router>ospf>area# exit
*B:PE1>config>router>ospf#
```

4. Continue with configuring OSPF on all other routers in the domain. Don't forget to include the system interfaces!

4a. How many routes are in each route table?

4b. What is the preference and metric value of each OSPF route?

5. Use a show command to look at the OSPF neighbors of each router.

```
*B:PE1>config>router>ospf# show router ospf neighbor

===============================================================
OSPF Neighbors
===============================================================
Interface-Name      Rtr Id        State  Pri  RetxQ   TTL
---------------------------------------------------------------
toPE2               150.10.0.1    Full   1    0       35
toCE1               140.10.0.3    Full   1    0       34
---------------------------------------------------------------
No. of Neighbors: 2
===============================================================
*B:PE1>config>router>ospf#
```

5a. How many neighbors do you see on PE1? PE2? CE1?

5b. What is the state of the adjacencies? What should they be? Why?

6. Use a show command to display the OSPF Link State database. This database is a listing of all LSAs that have been received by the router. It is these LSAs that the SPF algorithm uses to create the forwarding table.

```
*B:PE1>config>router>ospf# show router ospf database

===============================================================
OSPF Link State Database (Type : All)
===============================================================
Type     Area Id   Link State Id   Adv Rtr Id   Age   Sequence    Cksum
---------------------------------------------------------------
Router   0.0.0.0   140.10.0.1      140.10.0.1   522   0x80000008  0x1b9b
Router   0.0.0.0   140.10.0.3      140.10.0.3   515   0x80000005  0xd83d
Router   0.0.0.0   150.10.0.1      150.10.0.1   502   0x80000005  0xae57
Network  0.0.0.0   140.10.0.97     140.10.0.1   522   0x80000001  0xefa4
Network  0.0.0.0   140.10.0.101    140.10.0.1   537   0x80000001  0x7523
---------------------------------------------------------------
No. of LSAs: 5
===============================================================
*B:PE1>config>router>ospf#
```

6a. What type of LSAs are in the database?

6b. Is the database consistent on all routers? Is the database *identical* on all routers?

7. The previous command only showed a *summary* of each LSA. Use the `detail` option at the end of the command to see the full LSA information.

```
*B:PE1# show router ospf database detail
[... OR ...]
*B:PE1 # show router ospf database 140.10.0.1 detail
```

8. Confirm using `ping`, and optionally `traceroute`, that each router can reach every interface configured in OSPF on every other router. Note that the loopbacks have *not* been configured in OSPF and therefore should *not* be reachable from remote routers. If any interface isn't reachable, double-check that you have correctly configured that interface into OSPF.

9. We will use loopback interfaces to demonstrate how to distribute external or static routes into OSPF. To enable a router to distribute external routes, it must be identified as an *Autonomous System Border Router* (ASBR). Each router will distribute its loopback interface, so make each router an ASBR.

```
*B:PE1>config>router>ospf# asbr
*B:PE1>config>router>ospf#
```

9a. Can the ASBR designation be limited to a particular area? Try issuing the `asbr` command within the context config ➤ router ➤ ospf ➤ area 0.

10. A routing policy defines which external routes are distributed into OSPF. It is impossible to distribute external routes without a policy. A lengthy discussion of policy implementation on the Alcatel-Lucent 7750/7450 products is a topic for an advanced course. For this exercise, please follow the commands below, which create and *apply* an export policy to OSPF. Repeat this process on all routers.

```
*B:PE1# configure router policy-options
[For layout considerations, the prompt is shorted below.]
>policy-options# begin
>policy-options# policy-statement DistributeLB
>policy-options>policy-statement$ entry 10
>policy-options>policy-statement>entry$ from protocol direct
>policy-options>policy-statement>entry# action accept
>policy-options>policy-statement>entry>action# exit
>policy-options>policy-statement>entry# exit
>policy-options>policy-statement# exit
>policy-options# commit
>policy-options# exit all
```

```
[...The full prompt is shown again below...]
*B:PE1#
*B:PE1# configure router ospf
*B:PE1>config>router>ospf# export DistributeLB
*B:PE1>config>router>ospf#
```

10a. Can the export policy be assigned only to a particular area? Try issuing the export command within the context config ➤ router ➤ ospf ➤ area 0.

11. Confirm using ping, and optionally traceroute, that each router can reach every interface configured in OSPF on every other router, including loopbacks. If any interface isn't reachable, double-check that you have correctly configured that interface into OSPF and that the router is designated as **asbr**.

12. Use a show command to display the routing table on each router. Compare the result with the routing tables you obtained in Exercise 8.2. Verify the Protocol column to ensure that none of the routes is static.

```
*B:PE1# show router route-table
===============================================================
Route Table (Router: Base)
===============================================================
Dest Prefix                     Type    Proto   Age        Pref
    Next Hop[Interface Name]                    Metric
---------------------------------------------------------------
140.10.0.1/32                   Local   Local   03d02h27m  0
    system                                      0
140.10.0.3/32                   Remote  OSPF    02h16m53s  10
    140.10.0.102                                100
140.10.0.11/32                  Local   Local   03d01h09m  0
    loopbackTest                                0
140.10.0.12/32                  Remote  OSPF    00h09m57s  150
    140.10.0.102                                1
140.10.0.96/30                  Local   Local   03d02h01m  0
    toPE2                                       0
140.10.0.100/30                 Local   Local   03d01h45m  0
    toCE1                                       0
150.10.0.1/32                   Remote  OSPF    02h16m39s  10
    140.10.0.98                                 100
150.10.0.11/32                  Remote  OSPF    00h09m45s  150
    140.10.0.98                                 1
```

```
----------------------------------------------------------------
No. of Routes: 8
================================================================
*B:PE1>config>router#
```

12a. What is the preference value for a route generated from an OSPF interface?
What is the preference value for routes distributed via an export policy?

The next set of lab exercises shows how to completely remove all configuration for a routing protocol in two quick steps. For the moment, however, don't forget to save the configuration on *all* your routers! Since the exercises in Chapter 11 require OSPF, it will save time if the fully functional configurations are saved *now* with a separate configuration name (refer to Lab Section 2.3 in Chapter 2, "Saving Configuration Changes").

```
*B:PE1# bof primary-config cf3:\OSPF-Full.cfg
WARNING: CLI A valid config file does not exist at cf3:\OSPF-Full.cfg.
*B:PE1# admin save
Writing file to cf3:\OSPF-Full.cfg
Saving configuration .... Completed.
*B:PE1# bof primary-config cf3:\MAA-TestConfig.cfg
*B:PE1#
```

Chapter Review

Now that you have completed this chapter, you should have a good understanding of the following topics. If you are not familiar with these topics, please go back and review the appropriate sections.

- The purpose of and importance of OSPF as an interior gateway routing protocol
- The features of OSPF
- The concept of route selection in OSPF
- Understand an OSPF router ID and explain why it is used.
- The steps for OSPF routers to form an adjacency
- How Link State Updates are flooded through an OSPF network in response to a network change
- Common commands used when configuring OSPF on an Alcatel-Lucent 7750 SR and why they are used

Post-Assessment

The following questions will test your knowledge and prepare you for the Alcatel-Lucent NRS I Certification Exam. Please review each question carefully and choose the most correct answer. You can compare your response with the answers listed in Appendix A in the back of this book. Good luck!

1. OSPF discovers neighbors _____.

    A. Only by manually configuring the router

    B. By flooding updates

    C. Using Hello advertisements

    D. Using a host table

2. Which of the following is *not* a feature of the OSPF protocol?

    A. It supports authentication.

    B. It provides a loop-free topology.

    C. It uses the Shortest Path First algorithm.

    D. It uses a hop count–based metric.

3. Which logical interface is recommended for defining a router ID?

    A. Ethernet interface

    B. Chassis interface

    C. MAC address

    D. System interface

4. What is the primary purpose of the OSPF router ID?

    A. To elect a designated router

    B. To uniquely identify an OSPF router

    C. To trace sequence numbers

    D. To support LSA flooding

5. LSA updates are sent in response to network changes and _____.

   A. Every 30 minutes

   B. After the Hello timer expires

   C. When the DR detects the BDR has failed

   D. Every 30 minutes provided new information needs to be transmitted

6. What does it mean to say that two OSPF routers are *adjacent*?

   A. The routers are physically connected on a point-to-point link.

   B. The routers are on a common network segment and have exchanged database information.

   C. The routers have exchanged Hello packets.

   D. The routers are in a single area.

7. What is required for OSPF routers on a point-to-point network to form an adjacency?

   A. The DR must form an adjacency first.

   B. The neighbor IP address must be configured.

   C. They will automatically become adjacent provided certain OSPF configuration values match.

   D. Nothing. OSPF routers on point-to-point links will always become adjacent.

8. Which of the following hello packet values is *not* involved in the adjacency process on point-to-point links?

   A. The area ID

   B. The priority

   C. The Hello timer

   D. The dead timer

9. In addition to having correct OSPF settings in the Hello packets, another value that can prevent routers from forming an adjacency in the event of a mismatch is _____.

   A. The AS number

   B. The OSPF MTU

   C. The OSPF metric

   D. The MPLS TE

10. The command to display the Link State Updates that a router has received is _____.

   A. `show router ospf status`

   B. `show router ospf links`

   C. `show router ospf summary`

   D. `show router ospf database`

11. There are many different types of LSAs in OSPF. The most common LSA type in point-to-point networks is _____.

   A. The area LSA

   B. The router LSA

   C. The network LSA

   D. The summary LSA

12. If an OSPF router receives an LSA with a sequence number that is *equal* to the sequence number it already has for that LSA, it will _____.

   A. Silently drop the LSA.

   B. Send a rejection notice to the sending router.

   C. Drop the LSA and send an acknowledgement.

   D. Drop the LSA and forward it to its adjacent routers.

13. Which of the following is false regarding the Shortest Path First algorithm that OSPF uses?

   A. It determines the optimal route to each network.

   B. It creates a loop-free path to each network.

   C. It is run only on the router that originates an LSA update.

   D. It runs every time a new LSA is received.

14. Which of the following correctly identifies the order of steps for two OSPF routers to become fully adjacent?

   A. Exchange, Loading, SPF, Adjacent

   B. Exchange, ExStart, Loading

   C. ExStart, Exchange, Loading, Full

   D. ExStart, Exchange, Loading, Adjacent

15. Which of the following default metrics is *not* correct for the given interface speed?

    A. 1 Gbps link = 100

    B. 16 Mbps link = 6,250

    C. 1.544 Mbps link = 64,766

    D. 622 Mbps link = 16

BGP

10

- Interior and exterior gateway protocols
- Autonomous systems
- BGP history and features
- BGP packet details and operations
- Case studies demonstrating BGP

In this chapter, we complete our discussion of IP routing protocols by examining the most widely used Exterior Gateway Protocol: Border Gateway Protocol, or BGP. BGP use is ubiquitous in the Internet between content providers, and BGP is used in many cases between a content provider and its customers. BGP is an extraordinarily scalable and flexible routing protocol, and it has many advanced features that make it well suited for implementing policy-based forwarding decisions between networks under different administrative control. The goal of this chapter is not to examine all of these features in detail, but to give you an introduction to the fundamental principles that underlie the operation of BGP and its basic functions.

In this chapter, we examine how BGP fits into the overall family of routing protocols that we discussed in Chapter 8 and review its history and features. We will also investigate how BGP establishes and maintains peering sessions between routers and take a look at some of the details of BGP packets. We end the chapter by reviewing some BGP case studies to give you a better appreciation for how BGP is implemented in typical situations.

Pre-Assessment

The following assessment questions will help you understand what areas of BGP you should review in more detail to prepare for the exam.

1. The primary purpose of an EGP is to _____.
    A. Handle large routing tables.
    B. Distribute routing information between ASes.
    C. Support routing inside a large enterprise network.
    D. Provide a default route to the Internet.

2. Which of the following is false regarding ASes?
    A. The assignment of public AS numbers is controlled by RIRs.
    B. 65,001 is a private AS number.
    C. An IGP is required for routing within the AS.
    D. They usually contain routers under the control of different administrative groups.

3. Which logical interface is preferred for creating internal BGP sessions?

    A. Ethernet interface

    B. Chassis interface

    C. MAC address

    D. System interface

4. Which of the following is true regarding BGP neighbors?

    A. They can be discovered automatically.

    B. They need to be directly connected.

    C. They can be in the same or different AS.

    D. Not all internal BGP speakers need to have the same information about routes outside the AS.

5. Two BGP routers configured as neighbors communicate using _____.

    A. TCP on a variable port

    B. UDP on a fixed port

    C. TCP on a fixed port

    D. IP using a fixed protocol

You will find the answers to each of these questions in Appendix A. You can also download all of the CD materials for this book at http://booksupport.wiley.com to take all the assessment tests and review the answers.

10.1 Interior and Exterior Gateway Protocols

In Chapter 8, we first introduced the topic of Interior Gateway Protocols (IGPs) and Exterior Gateway Protocols (EGPs). You will recall from that chapter that an IGP is designed to route between networks within an organization. The networks within the organization may use private or public addresses that are typically not advertised to other organizations, and the networks are all typically under the control of a single administrative group. This is an essential point in understanding the key difference between an IGP and an EGP. It is not just the scale of the network that determines that an EGP should be used, although that is certainly a factor.

What is more important is that EGPs are typically used when there are different parts of a network that are under different administrative control. When this occurs, there may be policy decisions that affect routing between these different networks that are more nuanced than merely finding the shortest path. This policy control and the ability to support very-large-scale routing are the primary factors that motivate the use of an EGP such as the Border Gateway Protocol.

 Version 4 is the current version of BGP, so BGP is often referred to as *BGPv4*. However, since older versions of BGP are rarely used, for the remainder of this chapter, any discussion of BGP features and operations refers to version 4.

BGP provides many features to control traffic flows between organizations connecting to the Internet. BGP is able to scale to very large networks, which is an important requirement in order to manage the 200,000+ routes of the Internet. BGP provides extensive policy control through the use of various route preference attributes that are more complicated and feature-rich than anything provided in an IGP, such as Open Shortest Path First (OSPF).

We discussed Autonomous Systems (ASes) in Chapter 8, and you will recall this term is synonymous with a network under a single administrative control. BGP uses the concept of an AS extensively, and as you will see, this and other features allow BGP to handle networks of enormous scale. It is key, however, to remember that an IGP such as OSPF is still required for routing within the AS. BGP is used to exchange routing information between ASes and for the routing of traffic that is in transit through the AS. The next AS will have its own IGP with its own routing. The details of the routing within each AS are hidden from other ASes; BGP handles routes that are exchanged between ASes.

As an example of the need for AS-based forwarding, consider Figure 10.1. In this figure, the enterprise offices need the address information of the content providers. However, the information from the content provider must traverse many Internet Service Provider (ISP)s, and each ISP runs its own choice of IGP. When the origin of the prefix is the content provider that runs OSPF as their IGP and the Tier 2 ISP runs IS-IS, the prefix would have to be relearned in the Tier 2 ISP as an Intermediate System to Intermediate System (IS-IS) prefix, and, therefore, the prefix could lose its original attributes. Every other ISP in the path of the prefix toward the enterprise would need to relearn the prefix in the protocol of its choice, meaning that a large number of routing protocol redistributions would have to take place.

Figure 10.1 Network traffic between the enterprise and the content provider must traverse many ISPs. Each ISP runs its own choice of IGP configured to its particular needs. BGP provides a common protocol to accommodate routing between all of the ISPs.

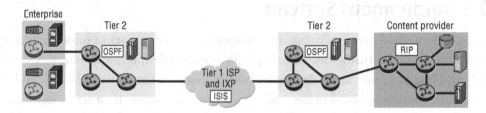

Although end-to-end routing can be achieved in this scenario by a process of continually re-distributing from one routing protocol into another, there are several disadvantages to such an approach. First, router re-distribution removes the metrics of the original protocol and uses the metrics of the new protocol. The result is a loss of the "best path" attribute of the route. Also, router re-distribution needs to be managed carefully with extensive policies. This is because route re-distribution must generally be bi-directional.

If routes from ISP 1 need to appear in ISP 2's routing tables, then routes from ISP 2 would also need to appear in ISP 1's routing tables. This mutual re-distribution can lead to routing loops because routes originating from ISP 1 might be re-distributed to ISP 2 and then re-redistributed back to ISP 1. This is a highly undesirable situation, and you should take great care to avoid it.

An additional issue is that distributing the Internet addresses into an IGP is not a scalable design because most routers are not designed to handle the large number of Internet prefixes. Many routers within an AS may be small office routers with limited

CPU and memory; they would not be capable of handling hundreds of thousands of routing entries. It would also be highly inefficient to distribute those routes to all routers within an AS since many enterprise ASes may have only one, or at most a handful of exit points out of the AS. There would be no reason to have entries for thousands of routes that all point to the same destination.

All of these issues lead to the conclusion that Internet route distribution requires a common protocol to run between all of the routers that are involved in the transfer of network prefixes from one AS to another. What is needed is an EGP that can accept routes from various internal IGPs within each AS, summarize their AS origin, and keep track of the hundreds of thousands of routes originating from thousands of ASes. These are the requirements that drive the need for an EGP such as BGP. In the next section, we examine the concept of ASes in a little more detail.

10.2 Autonomous Systems

We have mentioned previously that an *Autonomous System* is a set of routers under a single technical administration. ASes typically use a single Interior Gateway Protocol (IGP) and common metrics to determine how to route packets within the AS, and use an inter-AS routing protocol to determine how to route packets to other ASes. The use of the term *Autonomous* System stresses the fact that even when multiple IGPs and metrics are used, the administration of an AS appears to other ASes to have a single coherent interior routing plan. To networks outside the AS, it presents a consistent picture of the destinations that are reachable in and through it. None of the details of the routing inside the AS are known or need to be known to other ASes.

A key point that we have not yet discussed is how an AS is identified on the Internet. Just as with IP addresses, a globally unique identification number is used to distinguish individual ASes. An AS number is a 16-bit field, yielding $2^{16} = 65,535$ possible AS numbers. The assignment of these AS numbers is controlled by independent organizations called Regional Internet Registries (RIRs) with the charter to manage their growth across the Internet. Just as with IP addressing, there is a concept of public AS numbers and private AS numbers, as illustrated in Figure 10.2.

The difference between public AS numbers and private AS numbers is summarized as follows.

Figure 10.2 Public AS numbers range from 0 to 64,511. Private AS numbers range from 64,512 to 65,535. Public AS numbers are needed to peer with other ASes, while private AS numbers can be used within an AS. AS 200 and AS 400 are peering with AS 300, so all AS numbers are public. Inside AS 300, private AS numbers can be used such as 65,002 and 65,003.

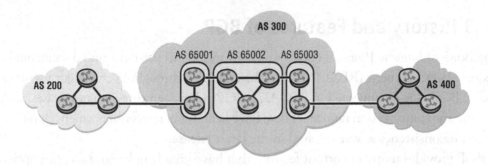

Public AS numbers:

- Are assigned by the IANA or a regional authority.
- Must be used when connecting to other autonomous systems on the Internet.
- Range from 0 to 64,511.

Private AS numbers:

- Are assigned by ISPs (for some clients) or local BGP administrators.
- Are not allowed to be advertised to other ISPs or on the Internet.
- Range from 64,512 to 65,535.

Regional Internet Registries (RIRs) are suborganizations beneath the IANA, and they are used to control the distribution and use of AS numbers. RIRs are nonprofit corporations established for the purpose of administration and registration of IP address space and AS numbers on behalf of the IANA. There are currently five RIRs:

- **AfriNIC**—Africa, portions of the Indian Ocean
- **APNIC**—Portions of Asia, portions of Oceania
- **ARIN**—Canada, the United States, and many Caribbean and North Atlantic islands
- **LACNIC**—Latin America, portions of the Caribbean
- **RIPE NCC**—Europe, the Middle East, Central Asia

The concept of AS numbers is important to keep in mind as you further examine the history and features of BGP. As you will see, the concept of a path to particular ASes is key to forwarding operations in BGP.

10.3 History and Features of BGP

The Border Gateway Protocol (BGP) was born in 1989 as version 1 and documented in Request For Comment (RFC) 1105. BGP has survived through several major revisions. Today, BGPv4 is documented in RFC 4271. BGPv4 has seen three major releases, while keeping the same version number. There have been numerous enhancements, and several inconsistencies were resolved in the latest release.

BGP provides many important features that have greatly reduced the consumption of the IPv4 address space. These critical features have essentially prolonged the life of IPv4. These features include but are not limited to the following:

- Configured neighbors can be any reachable devices, not just directly connected devices.

- Unicast exchange of information

- Reliable route exchange via TCP using well-known port 179

- Periodic keep-alive for session management

- Event-driven routing updates

- Robust metrics

A key strength of BGP is that it enables the implementation of administrative policies to manage traffic flow between autonomous systems based on virtually any policy. BGP is extraordinarily scalable and can handle not only large numbers of ASes and IP network routes, but also large numbers of neighbors and a high rate of network changes. It is the protocol of choice for service providers and runs on all Internet-connected routers.

BGP is the fundamental building block of the Internet and is used by every service provider in the world for service-provider interoperability, and is the most feature-rich and scalable routing protocol in use in the world. It supports the current requirements of the Internet and, with extended capabilities such as multiple protocol families and extended AS numbers, it is well-positioned for the future.

The Alcatel-Lucent implementation of BGP version 4 for routing IPv4 conforms to the specifications detailed in RFC 4271.

As alluded to in the features list, BGP is not a discovery protocol like OSPF, and as such, BGP neighbors must be manually configured to connect to each other. However, BGP neighbors need not be directly connected. The only requirement for BGP neighbors is that they can establish a TCP session with each other to exchange routes. If two or more BGP routers can establish TCP sessions and exchange routes, they will become *peers*. BGP peers can either be in the same AS or in different ASes.

Within an AS, an IGP is required to route traffic between BGP peers so that they can establish a TCP session. Using an IGP provides the ability to have BGP peers that are not directly connected to each other. Between ASes, BGP peers are normally directly connected, so no IGP is usually necessary to establish those types of sessions. In the rare case in which BGP peers in different ASes are not directly connected, static routes are normally used to provide the routing to establish a TCP session. BGP sessions between routers in different ASes are known as *external BGP* (eBGP) sessions, while sessions between routers in the same AS are *internal BGP* (iBGP) sessions. Figure 10.3 illustrates the distinction between iBGP and eBGP.

Figure 10.3 Peer connections between routers in different ASes are known as *external BGP* (eBGP) sessions, while peer connections within the same AS are known as *internal BGP (iBGP)* sessions. The routers in AS 65,004 and AS 65,001 have an eBGP session with routers in AS 65,002. Peering inside AS 65,002 are iBGP sessions.

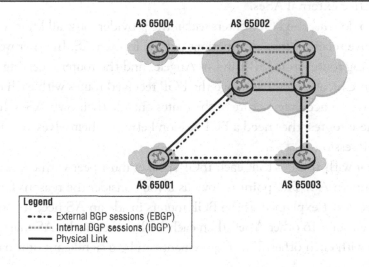

eBGP implementation can be very simple. External interfaces are typically used in order to learn more quickly when the physical interface goes down. The failure of an external-facing interface provides the advantage of immediately tearing down the TCP session on port 179 connection, which provides for a decreased convergence time throughout the network. In some cases, there may be multiple links between eBGP speakers for redundancy, in which case, a logical loopback interface can be used.

iBGP speakers almost always use the system interface to establish their TCP session. A system interface provides much greater stability than a physical interface. For example, today's highly resilient networks provide many paths out of a core router to a neighboring router, so there may be many paths that packets can traverse between iBGP speakers. Using the Alcatel-Lucent system interface to create the iBGP session allows for any alternative path to be used to create and maintain the session. It is considered a best practice to use the system interface especially with iBGP to ensure that BGP sessions continue to operate as long as there is at least a single usable path between BGP peers.

The question may arise as to why you would need BGP within an AS since the entire purpose of BGP is to propagate routing information between different ASes. The answer lies in the fact that all content providers, and even some enterprise networks, have multiple connections to other ASes. A provider might have a connection to ISP 1 in Los Angeles on one router and a connection to ISP 2 in Chicago on another router. The provider would receive routes about networks from both ISP 1 and ISP 2, and then it must make intelligent decisions about how best to forward packets to the respective external ASes.

In order to do this, the BGP routers *within* the provider must all know what routes the others have received from destinations outside its own AS. In other words, the router receiving routes from ISP 1 in Los Angeles and the router receiving routes from ISP 2 in Chicago must exchange the BGP received routes with each other so they both have an accurate picture of the routes outside their own ASes. In order to exchange these routes, they need a BGP session between themselves, and hence the need of iBGP sessions.

One caveat with iBGP is that each iBGP speaker must peer with every other iBGP speaker within an AS. This point is obvious if you consider the reasons for having iBGP that were just explained. If the BGP routers inside an AS need a consistent picture of the routes to other ASes, then each BGP router in the AS must exchange information with each other. This requirement can be a significant drawback to iBGP, and it directly affects configuration complexity. There are some options in BGP to mitigate this drawback; however, they are beyond the scope of this book. All that you really need to understand is that all iBGP routers must have a consistent view of the BGP routes reachable through external ASes.

Now that we have discussed the general principle of BGP peering, we will next examine how BGP builds its routing tables and makes forwarding decisions. One of the key factors in such a discussion is the BGP tracking metrics that administrators can manipulate to make routing policy decisions. In the next section, we briefly examine some of the most important metrics that BGP uses to make its routing decisions.

10.4 BGP Metrics

BGP is a path vector routing protocol that carries routing information between ASes. The designation *path vector* means that BGP updates carry a sequence of AS numbers that must be traversed to reach a given network destination; that is, the AS "path" to each network. In the simplest possible BGP configuration, BGP selects the best path to a given network based on the shortest AS path. So, the network that was advertised from an AS that is the fewest ASes away would be the "best" path to that destination. However, BGP provides many more metrics and attributes that allow for much greater routing policy control than simply using the shortest AS path. RFC 4271 outlines the many metric types (also known as *attributes*) to choose from, to implement BGP policies. There are, in general, two major classes of attributes:

- Well-known attributes (mandatory or discretionary)
- Optional attributes (transitive or non-transitive)

According to RFC 4271, well-known mandatory attributes must be supported by every BGP implementation. In addition, well-known discretionary attributes must also be supported in every BGP implementation, with the only difference being that the latter is not required to be present in every routing update.

Optional attributes can be either transitive or non-transitive. Optional attributes are not always supported in every BGP implementation, which is a key difference from the well-known attributes. If a router receives a route with a transitive optional attribute set, it will pass this information along intact to other BGP speakers regardless of whether the BGP speaker understands it or not. If a particular BGP implementation does not recognize an optional non-transitive attribute, then it is quietly dropped and no action is taken.

Well-known mandatory attributes are, as you might expect, the most important. There are only three well-known mandatory attributes:

- Origin—Indicates the original source of the route such as whether it originated in a BGP statement or was re-distributed from an IGP. This attribute is typically used to prefer routes from one origin over another given other metrics are the same, such as AS path.

- AS-Path—Indicates the series of ASes that must be traversed to reach a particular network destination. The shortest AS path to a destination is preferred and is usually the "best" route to a particular destination.

- Next-hop—Indicates the next BGP router to forward packets to for a particular network destination. The next hop must be reachable via a static route or IGP if it is not directly connected.

Although there are many other attributes, interesting policy decisions can be configured using only these three. For example, in Figure 10.4, there are two links between AS 65,200 and AS 65,250. Without considering other factors, those two links would normally be considered of equal *cost* since routes advertised over each link would be from the same AS.

Figure 10.4 In a simple BGP configuration, Router C would have two equal cost paths from its AS 65,250 to AS 65,200, one through its eBGP session to Router B and one through its eBGP session to Router A. Because both Router B and Router A are in the same AS, the path cost for each eBGP session is the same.

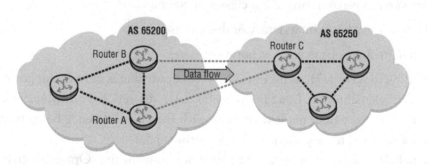

However, BGP can easily be configured to prefer routes advertised over one link by changing the origin of the routes advertised over one of the links. If the origin of routes advertised over one link is preferred over the origin of those advertised over a different link, for example, then that link will be used as the primary route. An ISP might want to do this because of certain policy arrangements with a neighboring ISP.

This is only a very simple example of the sorts of policy decisions that can be made using BGP attributes.

Further discussion of BGP policies is beyond the scope of this book, but you can understand the basic operation of BGP by keeping in mind just these three mandatory attributes. Of course, many more attributes are available that can be used to influence BGP routing policies. In fact, it is the use of these additional attributes that complicates the configuration and use of BGP.

BGP is an extraordinarily powerful routing protocol, and newcomers to network routing often want to see it used in their network. However, not every connection to the Internet requires BGP, and its power can also lead to unnecessary complexity. As with many things, often the simpler solution is the best solution. In the next section, we review when to use and when not to use BGP.

10.5 When to Use BGP

When should you use BGP? As mentioned above, BGP can accommodate virtually any number of policies. This flexibility can be somewhat of a double-edged sword. BGP is administratively much more complex than an IGP. BGP updates include path information that is used for routing policy enforcement and loop detection between ASes. Adding to the complexity of BGP is the fact that topology and routing table sizes become much larger than in an IGP environment. The increased size of the tables means that factors such as CPU loading, memory utilization, update generation, and route processing have greater implications in BGP.

Keeping these factors in mind, there are several considerations you need to account for when making a decision to use BGP. You *should* use BGP in the following cases:

- You are an ISP and need to pass client traffic from one AS to another AS.
- You need to multi-home to several ISPs because of company requirements.
- Traffic flow between your company and other companies must be carefully managed and controlled.

You *should not* use BGP in the following cases:

- You do not need to have more than one connection to the Internet, or, in the event of multiple connections, you do not care about optimizing the route to destinations in other ASes.
- The company network engineers do not understand how BGP works.
- The routers and physical links to the ISP cannot handle the load of BGP traffic.

As of Q2 2009, the routing table for the Internet core consists of over 280,000 routes.

Assuming that your requirements are such that you require BGP, it is important to understand how BGP actually operates to build routing tables. It is to this topic that we now turn.

10.6 Packet Details and Operation

Neighbor relationships in BGP are somewhat different from what is normal in the IGP world. Traditionally, neighbors are always directly connected routers. With BGP, this is not the case. Neighbors may be directly connected, but it is not required because BGP uses unicast TCP/IP for neighbor establishment. Neighbor relationships can be established with any IP-reachable device properly configured as a BGP speaker. At the application layer, BGP functions similarly to other TCP/IP applications, such as Telnet, FTP, and HTTP. BGP may be viewed as an application because it uses registered port number 179 in the TCP/IP model. Figure 10.5 illustrates establishment of a BGP session.

Figure 10.5 BGP peer establishment functions much like other protocols that use TCP. Both BGP peers initiate TCP connections to create the session. Once a session is established, OPEN messages are exchanged, and then one of the TCP sessions is removed. Once the peers have exchanged keep-alive messages, the session is established and they can exchange updates. Afterward, keep-alive messages are exchanged and update messages sent when there is a network change.

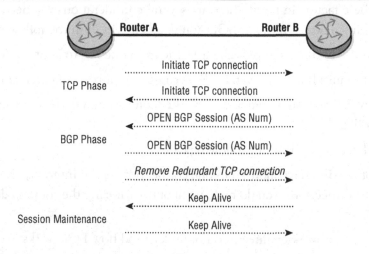

Once a BGP peer is established, the BGP speakers exchange UPDATE messages. The purpose of the UPDATE is to exchange Network Layer Reachability Information (NLRI) as it occurs in the network. The CIDR block or prefix is contained within this NLRI. Also included are the prefix length, full AS path to the destination, and the next hop (recall that the AS path and next hop are mandatory attributes). The origin, AS path, and next hop attributes we briefly touched on earlier in the chapter are also included in the NLRI. NLRI updates announce new reachability information to BGP speakers, and they also indicate when a destination should be withdrawn if it is no longer reachable.

BGP Update Processing

This exchange of NLRI between BGP speakers is a critical operation in BGP. This exchange can occur in both directions, meaning that a BGP speaker can both send and receive to the same peer. This NLRI exchange is stored in routing tables on the router based on the metrics associated with each NLRI.

Conceptually speaking, each BGP implementation maintains three different routing information bases (RIBs) within the running BGP process:

- **Loc-RIB**—The Loc-RIB (local routing information base) is the so-called *master* routing table in BGP. This Loc-RIB is separate from the main routing table for the router itself.

- **Adj-RIB-In**—For each neighbor, the BGP process maintains an Adj-RIB-In (adjacent routing information base incoming) containing the NLRI received from that particular neighbor.

- **Adj-RIB-Out**—For each neighbor, the BGP process maintains an Adj-RIB-Out (adjacent routing information base outgoing) containing the NLRI to be sent to a particular neighbor.

The BGP process uses all of the information contained within these three tables to make routing decisions. It is also possible to have visibility into each of these tables to confirm expected results of a particular BGP configuration. For example, you may have provisioned a BGP peer with a customer where you provide only a default route (0.0.0.0). If that route is not properly received on the customer peer, then the default route is withdrawn automatically, and traffic is sent via an optional path. To confirm that you are, in fact, sending the default route *to* your customer, you could check the

Adj-RIB-Out. The customer could also confirm what is *incoming* from the ISP by reviewing the Adj-RIB-In table.

The BGP process considers all of the NLRI in all of the RIBs and populates the main routing tables with feasible routes. While further details are beyond the scope of this book, the topics covered up to this point should give you a basic understanding of the purpose of BGP and the concepts associated with its use.

In the next section, we examine some sample case studies to further illustrate the principles we have covered.

10.7 BGP Case Studies

In this section, we review several use cases to help you better understand how BGP is implemented in various scenarios. The Alcatel-Lucent 7750 series family of routers is designed to work effectively in each of the scenarios below. These use cases represent real-world scenarios with best practice design principles.

Use Case I

Figure 10.6 illustrates two different customers that have different requirements for BGP peering with their providers. ISP 1 and ISP 2 will be running BGP because they are acting as transit providers for their customers to the Internet. As we have discussed, the Internet is made up of hundreds of thousands of routers and AS numbers. Some of the larger Internet providers are shown in the Internet cloud, and they interconnect and share routes between each other using eBGP. There are two enterprise customers shown in Figure 10.6: Enterprise Customer 1 and Enterprise Customer 2.

Customer 1 has a single connection to ISP 1 and is borrowing address space from that provider (subnet 209.217.64.64/26). This customer will use a default route to ISP 1. ISP 1 will have a route back to its customer's subnet using either static routes or a dynamic routing protocol. ISP 1, using BGP, will advertise its aggregate network of 209.217.64.0/18 to its upstream providers in the Internet cloud using eBGP. From the Internet it will appear as though 209.217.64.64/26 is not being advertised and only the aggregate will be seen (209.217.64.0/18) coming from AS 7788, which belongs to ISP 1. (It is considered a best practice to summarize and not leak specific subnets in most cases.)

Figure 10.6 Different customers with different BGP peering requirements. Customer 1 has only a single connection to the Internet, but Customer 2 has multiple connections to different providers.

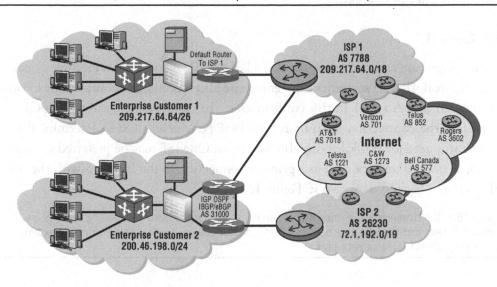

Customer 2 has two connections for redundancy: one to ISP 1 and one to ISP 2. Customer 2 has its own IP address block, which it received from ARIN. We mentioned earlier in this chapter that in most cases, there is no need to run a complex routing protocol like BGP unless you have multiple connections to the Internet, as is the case with Customer 2. Customer 2 might require redundant connectivity to the Internet because either it needs the extra bandwidth or it simply cannot afford to be offline from the Internet if a link fails. The server in the Customer 2 cloud could be offering important files and must be online for continuous operation. This is a situation in which Customer 2 needs to run BGP.

When Customer 2 advertises its network 200.46.198.0/24 via BGP, from the Internet it will appear as though the network is reachable from AS 31,000. (Customer 2 will have received this public AS from ARIN or an RIR.) In fact, other BGP routers on the Internet will see 200.46.198.0/24 with two *paths*. One path will be 200.46.198.0/24 from AS 31,000, 26,230 (through ISP 2), and another path for this same address space coming from AS 31,000, 7,788 (through ISP 1).

Since BGP is a path-vector protocol, in most cases the path used by the Internet (from AT&T, as an example) will make its route selection to reach Customer 2 based on the shortest AS-PATH (the fewest number of ASes in the path). There are several route metrics used in BGP for route selection, and they are covered in detail in Alcatel-Lucent's BGP course.

Use Case II

In the second use case, an enterprise has a large OSPF network with multiple Local Area Network (LAN) segments. The enterprise also has multiple connections to two ISPs (AS 47 and AS 395). In this configuration, the enterprise will often run BGP to manage the connections with their ISPs. BGP policies are used to determine the path that is used for traffic leaving the enterprise. One ISP may be preferred for some routes, or one ISP may be used as a primary connection to the Internet, with the other ISP used as a backup, as shown in Figure 10.7.

Figure 10.7 The customer has multiple BGP connections to different providers. Internally, the customer routers will determine the best route based on OSPF, and BGP will be used to determine the best external AS to forward packets to for Internet routes.

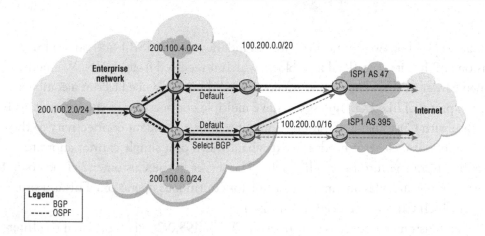

Within the enterprise network, internal routing information is exchanged with OSPF. The enterprise networks are summarized as 100.200.0.0/20 and advertised to the ISPs and onward to the Internet with BGP. In this scenario, the enterprise uses a private AS number, and its routes are advertised by the ISPs using their AS numbers.

The full set of Internet routes is not exported into OSPF. Instead, a default route is advertised by the Internet-connected routers. Some subsection of the BGP routes that are received may be advertised into the enterprise in order to influence the route for traffic that egresses the enterprise network.

Use Case III

In the third use case, an enterprise is connected to its two ISPs (AS 47 and AS 395). Routing information is exchanged between the enterprise and the two ISPs using BGP, as described in the previous use case. Both ISPs are Tier 2 ISPs, which means that they purchase transit capacity from one or more Tier 1 ISPs. Similar to the enterprise, the Tier 2 ISPs pay the Tier 1 providers to carry their traffic.

The Tier 1 providers carry *transit traffic*. This is traffic that originated outside their network and has a destination outside their network. A Tier 2 ISP may be connected to more than one Tier 1 ISP, or may have transit arrangements with other Tier 2 ISPs. Multiple connections are often used to provide the ISP with a redundant path to all Internet destinations, as shown in Figure 10.8.

Figure 10.8 ISP interconnections will use BGP to allow transit traffic destined for other ASes to flow through it to the next AS in the path.

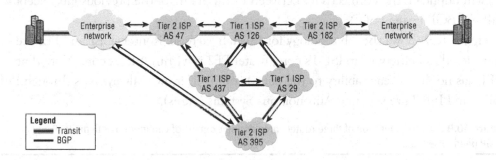

An ISP with multiple connections to the Internet usually needs to control the path used for its traffic. The reason may be to ensure the shortest path, but often is related to cost or other considerations.

This completes the discussion of BGP and its use cases. You can apply the information you have learned in this chapter by following along in the lab exercises.

Now you should complete the lab exercises to assist you in reinforcing this chapter's features. These lab exercises are carefully designed to give you hands-on experience configuring many of the technology standards that have been discussed and should greatly aid you in your exam preparation.

Practice Lab: BGP Routing

The following lab is designed to reinforce your knowledge of the content in this chapter. Please review the instructions carefully for each lab and perform the steps in the order in which they are provided. The practice labs require that you have access to three or more Alcatel-Lucent 7750 SRs in a non-production environment. Note that the Alcatel-Lucent 7450 ESSs do not have the BGP capabilities required for these lab exercises.

 These labs are designed to be used in a controlled lab environment. Please **DO NOT** attempt to perform these labs in a production environment.

Although there are quite a variety of routing protocols, BGP is the de facto standard for routers handling the global routing table (i.e., for the Internet). No course on routing protocols would be complete without some discussion of BGP. In this lab, we will duplicate the connectivity between PE1 and PE2 of the previous lab, except we will use BGP instead of OSPF.

Figure 10.9 shows the lab topology for this lab exercise. Routers CE1 and PE1 are considered as being within ISP 1's core; router PE2 is within ISP 2's core. Note that CE1 has no direct reachability to the outside of ISP 1; it must always pass through PE1. ISP 1 and ISP 2 are separate Autonomous Systems (ASes).

Figure 10.9 This configuration of three routers provides an example of configuring both an iBGP and an eBGP peering session.

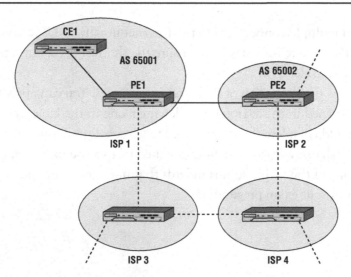

Lab Section 10.1: External BGP Routing

We use External BGP (eBGP), or BGP between routers in different ASs, to provide a tidy example of basic BGP configuration. After establishing EBGP in this section, we'll add additional connectivity in the next section.

Objective In this exercise, you will configure two BGP Autonomous Systems, using eBGP peering. You will configure the BGP routing protocol and required policies to connect the two different Autonomous Systems together and exchange routing information.

Validation You will know you have succeeded if each PE router can ping *every interface* on the other PE router.

Removing OSPF is the first step before configuring BGP, since this exercise uses BGP exclusively between PE1 and PE2. In most cases, removing a routing protocol is a simple two-step process: Shut down the protocol and specify no *xxx* (where *xxx* is a protocol name).

1. Remove OSPF from PE2 only. Remove just the interface to PE2 from PE1's OSPF configuration.

```
*A:PE2# configure router
*A:PE2>config>router# ospf shutdown
*A:PE2>config>router# no ospf
*A:PE2>config>router#

*B:PE1# configure router
*B:PE1>config>router# ospf area 0 no interface toPE2
*B:PE1>config>router# exit
*B:PE1#
```

2. Confirm whether OSPF has been successfully removed.

```
*A:PE2>config>router# show router status

===================================================
Router Status (Router: Base)
===================================================
                    Admin State      Oper State
---------------------------------------------------
Router              Up               Up
OSPFv2              Not configured   Not configured
```

```
RIP                 Not configured  Not configured
ISIS                Not configured  Not configured
[... Additional output omitted ...]
BGP                 Not configured  Not configured
[... Additional output omitted ...]

Max IPv4 Routes     No Limit
Max IPv6 Routes     No Limit
Total IPv4 Routes   3
Total IPv6 Routes   0
[... Additional output omitted ...]
ECMP Max Routes     1
Triggered Policies  No
=======================================================
*A:PE2>config>router#
```

2a. Has OSPF been removed from PE2? What other routing protocols are running on PE2?

2b. There is another method of confirming that OSPF is no longer running between PE1 and PE2. What is it?

2c. The output shows three IPv4 routes on PE2. Where do they come from? Explain the results. (*Hint:* Look at the routing table for details.)

3. Assign the AS number to each router as shown in Figure 10.9.

```
*B:PE1>config>router# autonomous-system 65001
*B:PE1>config>router#


*A:CE1>config>router# autonomous-system 65001
*A:CE1>config>router#


*A:PE2>config>router# autonomous-system 65002
*A:PE2>config>router#
```

4. The PE routers are external BGP (eBGP) peers since they have *different* AS numbers. eBGP peers typically use the IP address of the connecting network interface as the neighbor address. On *each* PE router, configure the far end router within a group called eBGP. The far end router should be listed with its IP address and AS number.

```
*B:PE1>config>router# bgp
*B:PE1>config>router>bgp$ group eBGP
*B:PE1>config>router>bgp>group$ neighbor 140.10.0.98
*B:PE1>config>router>bgp>group>neighbor$ peer-as 65002
*B:PE1>config>router>bgp>group>neighbor$ exit
*B:PE1>config>router>bgp>group# exit
*B:PE1>config>router>bgp#
```

5. Once both PE routers are configured, verify that they have successfully established a peer relationship.

```
*B:PE1>config>router>bgp# show router bgp summary
===============================================================
 BGP Router ID : 140.10.0.1   AS : 65001   Local AS : 65001
===============================================================
BGP Admin State       : Up        BGP Oper State    : Up
Total Peer Groups     : 1         Total Peers       : 1
[... Additional output omitted ...]


===============================================================
BGP Summary
===============================================================
Neighbor
               AS PktRcvd InQ Up/Down   State|Rcv/Act/Sent
                  PktSent OutQ          (Addr Family)
---------------------------------------------------------------
140.10.0.98
            65002      7    0 00h02m46s 0/0/0 (IPv4)
                       7    0
===============================================================
*B:PE1>config>router>bgp#
```

5a. Have the two PE routers exchanged any route information? How can you verify this?

5b. In the output above, what does the output column Rcv/Act/Sent mean?

6. Check directly with BGP to see the details of routes advertised to the PE neighbor.

```
*B:PE1# show router bgp neighbor 140.10.0.98 advertised-routes
===============================================================
 BGP Router ID : 140.10.0.1   AS : 65001   Local AS : 65001
===============================================================
 Legend -
 Status codes  : u - used, s - suppressed, h - history,
                 d - decayed, * - valid
 Origin codes  : i - IGP, e - EGP, ? - incomplete, > - best


===============================================================
 BGP IPv4 Routes
===============================================================
 Flag  Network                      LocalPref   MED
       Nexthop                                  VPN Label
       As-Path
===============================================================
 No Matching Entries Found
===============================================================
 *B:PE1#
```

7. BGP, like other distance vector protocols, requires an export policy to advertise routes to other BGP peers. Apply an export policy on both PE routers. For convenience, reuse the export policy (e.g., DistributeLB) created in Lab Section 9.1 in Chapter 9. It actually exports all local (i.e., *direct*) interfaces.

```
*B:PE1>config>router>bgp# export DistributeLB
*B:PE1>config>router>bgp#
```

7a. Have the two PE routers exchanged any route information? What three commands can be used to verify this? (You may need to wait a few moments before seeing the final results.)

7b. What is the preference value for BGP routes? How does that compare with OSPF? Which one is *better*, that is, has higher precedence?

7c. At this point in time, how many routes are in the routing table? Explain your answer.

8. Confirm that each PE router can ping every interface on the other PE router. If not, check that you have used the correct addresses and AS numbers in the configurations and have applied the policy correctly on both routers.

Lab Section 10.2: Internal BGP Routing

Shifting from eBGP to iBGP can cause a few extra configuration issues. This lab exercise looks at potential issues and solutions for next-hop values and route preference values.

Objective In this exercise you will add an iBGP peering configuration to the existing eBGP setup. You will configure the BGP routing protocol and required policies to ensure that routing information flows correctly between iBGP and eBGP peers.

Validation You will know you have succeeded if every router can ping *every* interface on *every* other router.

1. Confirm that OSPF is still up and running correctly between PE1 and CE1.

   1a. What commands can be used to verify OSPF operation? (*Hint:* There are at least three different alternatives.)

2. PE1 and CE1 are internal BGP (iBGP) peers since they have the same AS number. iBGP peers typically use the system IP address as the neighbor address (which is why an IGP like OSPF is necessary to resolve that address). On both PE1 and CE1, configure the far end router within a group called iBGP. Just like eBGP, the far end router should be listed with an IP address and AS number.

   ```
   *B:PE1>config>router>bgp# group iBGP
   *B:PE1>config>router>bgp>group$ neighbor 140.10.0.3
   *B:PE1>config>router>bgp>group>neighbor$ peer-as 65001
   *B:PE1>config>router>bgp>group>neighbor$ exit
   *B:PE1>config>router>bgp>group# exit
   *B:PE1>config>router>bgp#
   ```

3. Once both PE1 and CE1 routers are configured, verify that they have successfully established a peer relationship.

   ```
   *B:PE1>config>router>bgp# show router bgp summary
   ===============================================================
    BGP Router ID : 140.10.0.1   AS : 65001   Local AS : 65001
   ===============================================================
   BGP Admin State        : Up        BGP Oper State     : Up
   Total Peer Groups      : 2         Total Peers        : 2
   [... Additional output omitted ...]


   ===============================================================
   ```

```
BGP Summary
===============================================================
Neighbor
                AS PktRcvd InQ  Up/Down   State|Rcv/Act/Sent
                   PktSent OutQ           (Addr Family)
---------------------------------------------------------------
140.10.0.3
             65001        5    0 00h01m41s 0/0/6 (IPv4)
                          7    0
140.10.0.98
             65002      139    0 01h08m17s 3/2/4 (IPv4)
                        140    0
===============================================================
*B:PE1>config>router>bgp#
```

3a. Has PE1 exchanged any routes with CE1? How can you verify this?

3b. In the output above, what do the values in the column `Rcv/Act/Sent` tell you?

3c. At this point in time, how many routes are in PE1's routing table? Explain your answer.

3d. How does PE1 learn about CE1's interfaces: through OSPF, BGP, or both? What does the routing table say? Explain your answer.

4. Configure the export policy on CE1 so that its interfaces are exported by BGP.

4a. Have the two PE routers exchanged any route information? (You may need to wait a few moments before seeing the final results.)

4b. What is the preference value for BGP routes?

4c. At this point in time, how many routes are in the routing table? Explain your answer.

4d. How does PE1 learn about CE1's interfaces: through OSPF, BGP, or both? What does the routing table say? Explain your answer.

5. Check the routing tables on CE1 and PE2.

5a. Does either router have routes to the other's system and loopback interfaces?

6. Each router advertises its routes specifying a next hop of the local router's network interface. Since PE1 sits between CE1 and PE2, neither of those two routers knows

how to reach the far router's network interface. Confirm what route information is being sent to CE1.

```
*B:PE1# show router bgp neighbor 140.10.0.3 advertised-routes
===============================================================
 BGP Router ID : 140.10.0.1   AS : 65001   Local AS : 65001
===============================================================
 Legend -
 Status codes  : u - used, s - suppressed, h - history,
                 d - decayed, * - valid
 Origin codes  : i - IGP, e - EGP, ? - incomplete, > - best


===============================================================
BGP IPv4 Routes
===============================================================
Flag  Network                       LocalPref   MED
      Nexthop                                   VPN Label
      As-Path
---------------------------------------------------------------

[... Additional output omitted ...]

?     150.10.0.1/32                 100         None
      140.10.0.98                               -
      65002

?     150.10.0.11/32                100         None
      140.10.0.98                               -
      65002


---------------------------------------------------------------
Routes : 6
===============================================================
*B:PE1>config>router>bgp#
*B:PE1>config>router>bgp#
```

6a. What specific IP address does PE2 specify as the next-hop address to reach its interfaces?

6b. Is that address known to CE1? (In Step 1 of the previous exercise, did you remember to remove the toPE2 interface from PE1's OSPF configuration?)

7. A common technique to fix the issue of an unreachable `next-hop` interface is to have eBGP routers *change* that address to their local address. Configure PE1 to set the next-hop address on all routes advertised/passed along to its iBGP peers.

```
*B:PE1>config>router>bgp# group iBGP next-hop-self
*B:PE1>config>router>bgp#
```

7a. Confirm what route information is now being sent to CE1. (You may need to wait a few moments before seeing the final result.)

7b. What specific interface does PE1 choose for the next-hop address?

7c. Is that address known to CE1?

7d. Why is an IGP still needed among iBGP peers?

8. Confirm whether each router can ping all interfaces on every other router.

8a. Can every router reach every interface?

8b. Do the ping results for each router correlate with the routing table information for that router? Explain your answer.

9. BGP routers will only pass along, as a default, learned BGP routes that are the *best* routes. On PE1, confirm which protocol is selected for the routes learned from CE1. (*Hint:* Look at the routing table.)

9a. Why does the Routing Table Manager (RTM) always choose the one protocol as the source of routes from CE1?

9b. Does the chosen protocol fit the specifications in the export policy for BGP (i.e., the DistributeLB policy)?

10. Modify the policy on PE1 so that it will include all routes learned within the AS.

 In a real-world environment, it may not be required to distribute the CE1 routes into another Autonomous System. It is a design decision and done here for illustrative purposes.

```
*B:PE1>config>router>bgp# exit all
*B:PE1# configure router policy-options
[For layout considerations, the prompt is shorted below.]
>policy-options# begin
>policy-options# policy-statement DistributeLB
>policy-options>policy-statement# entry 20
```

```
>policy-options>policy-statement>entry$ from protocol ospf
>policy-options>policy-statement>entry# action accept
>policy-options>policy-statement>entry>action# exit
>policy-options>policy-statement>entry# exit
>policy-options>policy-statement# exit
[...The full prompt is shown again below...]
*B:PE1>config>router>policy-options# commit
*B:PE1>config>router>policy-options# exit
*B:PE1#
```

10a. Note the numbering of the new entry. Does this replace or add to the existing entry?

10b. Does the new entry add an extra condition (an AND function) or an alternative condition (an OR function)?

10c. What is the purpose of the begin and commit keywords?

11. Compare the routing tables on PE1 and PE2. Look carefully at the routes for the CE1 system and loopback interfaces. (You may need to wait a few moments before seeing the final results.)

11a. What is the next-hop address that appears on PE1 and PE2 for routes to CE1? Is it the same?

11b. What kind of BGP peering relationship exists between PE1 and PE2?

11c. Is the next-hop-self attribute required for eBGP peers?

If you have done everything correctly, every router should be able to ping *every* interface on *every* other router.

Chapter Review

Now that you have completed this chapter, you should have a good understanding of the following topics. If you are not familiar with these topics, please go back and review the appropriate sections.

- The purpose of and importance of BGP as an exterior routing protocol
- Autonomous systems in BGP
- The basic features of BGP

- The need to have an IGP within the AS to support communication between BGP peers
- The difference between iBGP and eBGP
- The three mandatory attributes used by BGP to determine the best route to network destinations
- The three tables used by the BGP routing process
- Example case studies that show the peering between ISPs and how BGP controls the distribution of routes and the flow of transit traffic

Post-Assessment

The following questions will test your knowledge and prepare you for the Alcatel-Lucent NRS I Certification Exam. Please review each question carefully and choose the most correct answer. You can compare your response with the answers listed in Appendix A in the back of this book. Good luck!

1. The primary purpose of an EGP is to _____.
   A. Handle large routing tables.
   B. Distribute routing information between ASes.
   C. Support routing inside a large enterprise network.
   D. Provide a default route to the Internet.

2. Which of the following is false regarding ASes?
   A. The assignment of public AS numbers is controlled by RIRs.
   B. 65,001 is a private AS number.
   C. An IGP is required for routing within the AS.
   D. They usually contain routers under the control of different administrative groups

3. Which logical interface is preferred for creating internal BGP sessions?
   A. Ethernet interface
   B. Chassis interface
   C. MAC address
   D. System interface

4. Which of the following is true regarding BGP neighbors?
   A. They can be discovered automatically.
   B. They need to be directly connected.
   C. They can be in the same or different AS.
   D. Not all internal BGP speakers need to have the same information about routes outside the AS.

5. Two BGP routers configured as neighbors communicate using _____.

   A. TCP on a variable port

   B. UDP on a fixed port

   C. TCP on a fixed port

   D. IP using a fixed protocol

6. The primary purpose of iBGP is _____.

   A. To ensure that routers inside an AS have a common view of networks outside the AS

   B. To ensure that the IGP has multiple exit points from an AS

   C. To serve as back-up routers to eBGP

   D. To exchange routes with external ASes

7. By default, BGP will choose the best path to a given network destination based on _____.

   A. The sum of the interface speeds to a destination

   B. The shortest AS path

   C. The AS that is configured with special non-discretionary attributes

   D. The AS that re-distributed the route from OSPF into BGP

8. Once BGP peers establish a connection, they send routing updates to each other using _____.

   A. A keep alive message

   B. A next-hop update

   C. An update message

   D. A networks message

9. By looking only at the BGP configuration statements on two routers, you can tell if they are iBGP peers or eBGP peers because _____.

   A. The statement says `iBGP` or `eBGP`.

   B. The statement contains the word *internal* or *external*.

   C. Internal peering statements are configured separately.

   D. The AS number is associated with each peer statement.

10. The command to display the status of your BGP process is _____.

A. `show router bgp process`

B. `show router bgp summary`

C. `show router bgp info`

D. `show router bgp status`

11. In the event that a previously advertised network becomes unreachable, BGP will _____.

A. Advertise the route with a null AS-path.

B. Tear down the peer connection.

C. Send a withdraw message.

D. Update its route table but take no other action.

12. In which of the following situations would you be least likely to use BGP?

A. A service provider with multiple connections to other providers

B. An enterprise with multiple connections to the same ISP

C. An enterprise with multiple connections to different ISPs

D. A service provider with a single connection to a higher-level ISP

13. The three well-known mandatory attributes in BGP are _____.

A. Origin, AS-path, and community

B. AS-path, community, and next-hop

C. AS-path, peer, and next-hop

D. AS-path, origin, and next-hop

14. A BGP router usually does not need to receive a full Internet routing table if _____.

A. It is the single exit point for an AS.

B. It is one of several exit points from an AS.

C. It is part of a transit AS.

D. It is providing updates to downstream providers.

15. All of the following are reasons that using BGP between ASes is preferable to using IGP route re-distribution except _____.

A. Route re-distribution loses the metrics of the original IGP.

B. Route re-distribution can lead to routing loops.

C. BGP provides a consistent interface for route exchange across various ASes.

D. Route re-distribution provides for greater policy control.

MPLS and VPN Services

11

- Service networks building blocks—CE, PE, and P devices
- MPLS fundamentals
- VPN services—VPWS, VPLS, and VPRN

In this final chapter, we round out our discussion of Alcatel-Lucent NRS I exam topics with a discussion of service networks. To this point, our discussion has focused on technologies such as Ethernet and IP and how they provide network connectivity. In this chapter, we focus on how providers can use their underlying network infrastructure to provide value-added services to customers above and beyond simple Internet connectivity. Primarily we focus on Multi Protocol Label Switching (MPLS) and its use in the provider network to implement customer Virtual Private Networks (VPNs). We also discuss the various types of VPN services that can be supplied by an MPLS network.

Pre-Assessment

The following assessment questions will help you understand what areas of the chapter you should review in more detail to prepare for the exam.

1. Which of the following accurately describes a P device?

   A. It is used exclusively by the customer.

   B. It is responsible for adding and removing labels.

   C. It swaps label information and forwards packets.

   D. It creates an LSP in the provider network.

2. Which of the following is false regarding an SDP?

   A. It provides transport tunnel encapsulation.

   B. It is specific to a single service.

   C. The SDP ID is locally unique.

   D. LDP can be used as the signaling protocol.

3. Which of the following is *not* an accurate description of a VPN?

   A. A series of point-to-point tunnels configured on client equipment

   B. A tunnel technology created in a provider network

   C. A function of MPLS networks to create private communities of users

   D. Any network that includes encryption

4. Which of the following is false regarding LDP?

   A. It is used to define unidirectional paths through the network.

   B. The LDP protocol is specifically intended for label distribution

   C. It is the only method for distributing labels in an MPLS network.

   D. It describes a path through the MPLS network based on the IGP.

5. Which of the following term–definition pairs is incorrect?

   A. push—add a label

   B. swap—replace a label

   C. label distribution protocol—series of labels and next hop interfaces

   D. pop—remove a label

You will find the answers to each of these questions in Appendix A. You can also download all of the CD materials for this book at http://booksupport.wiley.com to take all the assessment tests and review the answers.

11.1 Services Overview

In previous chapters, we focused our discussions on particular technologies such as Ethernet, IP, TCP, and IP routing. These technologies are the all-important building blocks for service providers to create scalable networks and provide connectivity to customers for access to the Internet. In the early days of Internet networking, deploying these technologies and providing simple Internet connections was sufficient to maintain a profitable business.

Those days are now long past. In the modern global economy, service providers often compete with many other providers on razor-thin margins for customers, and it is necessary to provide additional services to customers above and beyond simple undifferentiated access to the Internet. Additionally, providers need to make the most efficient use possible of their infrastructures, using whatever capacity is available while ensuring the least amount of congestion. It is these two primary concerns that drive the needs for a "services"-based model of network connectivity.

In a services model, additional technology is overlaid on top of the existing network infrastructure in order to provide for fine-tuned packet forwarding based on service-specific information. In addition to fine-tuned forwarding, a services-based network provides the ability to separate traffic based on customer origin or type of traffic. This allows providers to give customers value-added services such as virtual private networks or enhanced quality of service (QoS) levels for a price premium.

In a VPN service, the provider ensures that traffic from each customer is logically separated over a shared physical infrastructure. A VPN can be thought of as a series of *tunnels* connecting various customer sites, where all traffic to and from each site is internal to the customer. In this sense, all the traffic is *private* because none of Customer A's sites can send or receive traffic to Customer B's sites and vice versa. It is *virtual* because, in reality, traffic from each customer passes through the same physical links and router interfaces, and the separation is done completely through advanced service configuration in the providers' equipment.

Similarly, a services network allows a provider to differentiate traffic based on individual customer or traffic class. Different types of traffic can be routed differently over separate network paths. Some paths can be reserved for customers willing to pay a premium for service level guarantees, while other traffic can be routed over paths that do not provide the same guarantees. This model can allow a service provider to continue to provide standard service levels to the average customer, while recouping additional revenue from customers who require a higher level of service, all over the same physical infrastructure.

This type of model lowers the provider's overall costs and network management overhead, while simultaneously increasing network flexibility. New customers can be added to various service levels with little or no changes to the existing service provider network. It is these requirements that drive the need for a services-based network model, and the remainder of this chapter focuses on the technologies that allow service providers to implement these requirements.

The Building Blocks of MPLS and VPN Services

Several key features are required to build networks capable of providing the services just described. These functions are performed by the provider equipment already in place and are not new types of physical equipment. The same Alcatel-Lucent 7750 SR and Alcatel-Lucent 7450 ESS products that provide standard IP services provide these additional types of services. A standard architecture for a services-based provider network is shown in Figure 11.1.

Figure 11.1: These are the key components of a Services-Bases Network: Customer Edge, Provider Edge, and Provider Core.

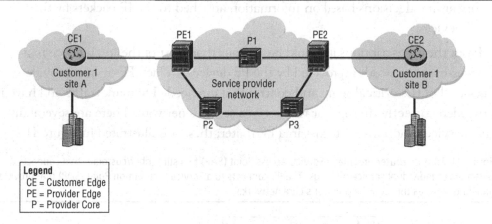

There are a few new terms in the figure that need to be introduced:

- **Customer Edge Devices**—A Customer Edge (CE) device resides on the customer premises. The CE device provides access to the service provider network over a link to one or more Provider Edge (PE) routers. The end-user typically owns and operates these devices. The CE devices are unaware of tunneling protocols or VPN services that are provided by the service provider. From the customer's perspective, whatever device they use to connect to their provider is a CE. Typical examples of a CE would be a home networking router or wireless access point.

- **Provider Edge Devices**—A Provider Edge (PE) device has at least one interface that is directly connected to a CE device. In addition, a PE device usually has at least one interface that connects to the service Provider Core devices, or provider routers. Because the PE device must be able to connect to different CE devices over different access media, the PE device is usually able to support many different interface types. The PE device is the customer's gateway to the VPN services offered by the service provider. It is the PE device that determines what, if any, special services need to be provided to the traffic arriving at the provider network from the CE devices.

- **Provider Router**—Provider (P) routers are located in the Provider Core network. The P router supports the service provider's bandwidth and switching requirements over a geographically dispersed area. The P router does not connect directly to the customer equipment. P routers typically do not know or care about the different services that are being provided to individual customers and instead simply make forwarding decisions based on information attached to the IP packets by the PE devices.

From these descriptions it should be obvious that most of the intelligence in a services-based network is provided by the PE devices. In fact, PE devices provide almost all of the critical setup and control that are needed to mark traffic and have it forwarded correctly throughout the rest of a services network. There are several distinct service functions that exist in a PE router; these are illustrated in Figure 11.2.

Figure 11.2: A PE router provides a Service Access Point (SAP) to a subscriber/customer that connects customers to individual service offerings. The PE connects to a Service Distribution Point (SDP) that provides tunneling services through the provider's core network.

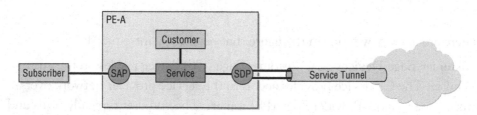

A *Service Access Point* (SAP) provides the logical entity that serves as the customer access to whatever services are provided by the PE. A *Service Distribution Point* (SDP) is the method that a service uses to connect to another router's services. SDPs have several important features:

- They provide the transport tunnel encapsulation that the service will be using (such as MPLS/RSVP-TE, MPLS/LDP, or IP/GRE).
- SDP IDs are locally unique; the same SDP ID can be used on another router.
- An SDP is not specific to one service; many services can use the same SDP.

When describing the services at a PE, there are several additional points to keep in mind. First, the terms *customer* and *subscriber* are used synonymously. Second, a customer ID is assigned when the customer account is created. This allows a provider to uniquely identify services configured for a particular customer throughout their network. In order to provision a service, a customer ID must be associated with the service at the time of the service creation. In other words, the services provided by a PE are entirely customer-driven; the service itself exists only as a service for particular customers.

At this point, you may be asking yourself what exactly we mean by a *service*, so it is time to firm up these concepts by examining one of the most important customer services: Virtual Private Networks.

Understanding VPN Services

The term *Virtual Private Network* (VPN) has a long and somewhat confusing history in networking. For much of its history, the term *VPN* referred to the use of encryption and tunneling to create private IP tunnels over a public network such as the Internet. Various technologies such as IPSec and SSL were, and still are, used to create these encrypted tunnels. In principle, there is nothing wrong with this approach, and many organizations still use it. However, it is not a very scalable solution. Each device that is participating in the VPN tunnels must be configured with the correct tunnel and encryption information.

Additionally, traditional VPN tunnels are point-to-point, so in order to provide any-to-any connectivity, a tunnel must be configured on each endpoint to every other endpoint. A further limitation is that the VPN controls are entirely at the Customer Edge. Not only is the provider typically not aware of the VPN services, but it is unable to provide any additional level of service to the customer owing to the use of encryption. These scalability and lack of service guarantee limitations led to the introduction of *provider-based VPN services.*

In order to provide a VPN service, the service provider encapsulates the customer data to traverse the service provider network. Depending on the nature of the VPN service, the encapsulation of the Layer 2 and Layer 3 headers may be included. The customer data must be transported without any changes across the service provider network from one customer site to another customer site. This way the provider can attach any additional information to the original packet needed for forwarding inside the provider network, and then strip off this information and forward the packet using standard Layer 2 and Layer 3 information at the destination CE.

In order to accomplish this, an additional header is added to the customer data for transport across the service provider network. Instead of routing or switching the data across the service provider's network using the customer's Layer 2 or Layer 3 headers, the data traverses the network using a header that is added at the edge of the service provider network. Therefore, the customer data in the packets is effectively tunneled across the service provider network unchanged. Figure 11.3 illustrates a packet arriving from a CE as it is switched across a provider network in provider-controlled tunnels.

Figure 11.3: Packets from the source CE arrive at the ingress PE and are encapsulated with a tag that allows them to be forwarded through the provider network along specific paths. The forwarding path is based on this provider-created tag. The tag is removed before the packet is forwarded to the destination CE so that the original packet arrives at the destination CE unchanged.

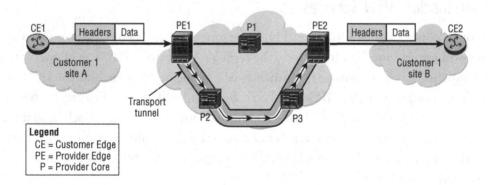

There are several important points to note about Figure 11.3. First, the existence of a tunnel is completely transparent to the CE device. The details of the tunnel, its characteristics, and how it is implemented are not known nor do they need to be known by the customer's equipment. This allows for substantially easier and more manageable customer device deployment. Also, all of the tunnel information in the provider network is enabled and controlled on the PE devices. The PE devices set up the tunnel, mark the packets inbound from CE devices, and then forward them on to the rest of the provider network. Provider P routers simply forward the packets based on the information marked on them by the PE devices.

One additional point is that the provider VPN service typically does not include encryption, although it can if the customer desires it. Encryption is not normally necessary because the customer packets are usually contained within a single provider and do not cross any physical components where multiple parties would have access to the data. It is possible that some customers may have requirements for encrypted traffic even though their packets never traverse more than a single provider. In such a case, the encryption would simply be another service provided at the PE device.

Now that we have discussed the VPN service in general terms, it is time to examine specifically how this service is commonly implemented. By far the most commonly used technology to implement customer VPNs is Multi Protocol Label Switching.

Understanding MPLS

In a *Multi Protocol Label Switching* (MPLS) network, routers are categorized as Label Edge Routers (LERs) or Label Switch Routers (LSRs). The LERs are the endpoints of the MPLS tunnels, known as *Label Switched Paths* (LSPs), and are normally at the edge of the network. The LSRs are at the core of the network and provide the connectivity between the LERs.

 Using our earlier terminology, the LERs are PE devices, and the LSRs are P devices. Do not be confused by this new terminology. LER and LSR are the MPLS-specific terms, whereas PE and P are more generic terms for a services-based network. When discussing MPLS, we will typically use the terms *LER* and *LSR*, but from a services network perspective, they are simply the PE and P devices already discussed.

Figure 11.4 illustrates conceptually how LERs and LSRs interoperate. Note that this picture is identical in concept to the manner in which PE and P devices interoperate.

Figure 11.4: Routers in an MPLS network are characterized as Label Edge Routers (LERs) and Label Switch Routers (LSRs). LERs control the addition and removal of provider labels, while LSRs simply forward the customer data based on the provider labels.

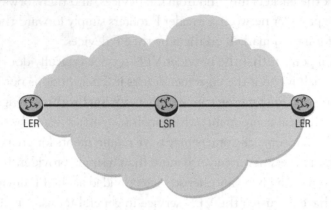

The purpose of MPLS is to provide a tunneling service to forward customer packets across the provider network based on information other than simply IP address destination. In order to provide this service, MPLS will mark packets inbound from the customer devices (CE) with a special header called a *label*. The *label* is simply an additional header that is added to packets inbound to the provider network.

These labels are used to make the forwarding decision for incoming traffic, rather than using the IP address. This basically turns the Layer 3, routed network into a switched network. This provides several advantages over traditional IP routing that we will discuss shortly. For now, the most important point to understand is that the LERs mark the packets with label information based on provider-configured policies. By marking the packets, the provider network can differentiate customer traffic based on the labels, for example, by forwarding differently labeled packets over a preferred path.

The MPLS-enabled routers (LERs and LSRs) use a signaling protocol to distribute labels across the network. The method for distributing labels through the network depends on the signaling protocol being used, either Label Distribution Protocol (LDP) or Resource Reservation Protocol (RSVP).

 In this chapter, we will discuss LDP at a high level. RSVP and LDP are covered in more detail in the Alcatel-Lucent MPLS course.

Understanding LDP

The *Label Distribution Protocol* (LDP) is a signaling protocol that is used in an MPLS network to distribute label information to LERs and LSRs. In this way, it is very similar to an IP routing protocol, except that instead of distributing IP network address information, it distributes label information. Before LDP can be enabled on a router, the network must be running a routing protocol. The routing protocol allows LDP to know which destinations it needs to generate labels for. Once a peering session is established, the routers check their routing tables and send out a label associated with networks that they see.

In Figure 11.5, an LDP session is established between Router 2 and Router 3. Router 3 checks its routing table for networks that are reachable through it and sends a label to Router 2 to represent those networks. For example, Router 3 sends a label with the value 20 to represent networks 10.1.1.0/24 and 10.1.2.0/24.

Figure 11.5: Router 3 uses LDP to send information to Router 2 associating label 20 with networks 10.1.1.0/24 and 10.1.20.0/24. Router 3 will place a 20 label on all packets it receives with a destination to Router 3 networks and forward it out Interface 1.

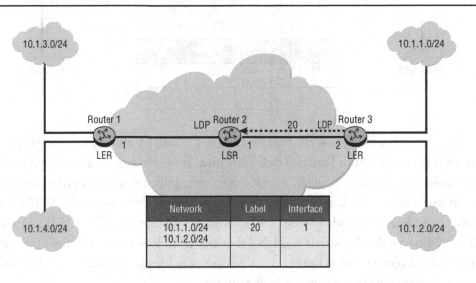

Each time Router 2 receives a packet destined for the 10.1.1.0/24 or 10.1.2.0/24 network, the router pushes the label (20) onto the packet and forwards the packet on the interface that takes the MPLS frame to Router 3. Because Router 3 originated the label (20), the router knows that any MPLS frame coming in with the label (20) is destined for a network that is terminated from it. Router 3 removes the label (20) from the frame, does a Layer 3 lookup, and routes the packet to its destination using standard IP forwarding mechanisms.

Figure 11.6 further illustrates the LDP set-up process, this time by examining the process as it relates to Router 1 and Router 2.

Figure 11.6: Router 2 uses LDP to update Router 1 with label information about the networks on Router 3. Router 2 sends label 10 to Router 1, so Router 1 will tag any packets with a destination address of the networks on Router 3 with a 10 tag and forward it to Router 2. Router 2 will swap the 10 tag with a 20 tag and forward the packets on to Router 3.

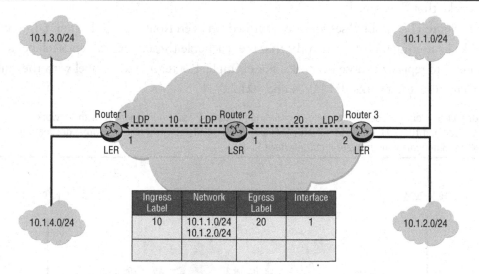

In Figure 11.6, LDP is now enabled on Router 1. Router 1 will set up a peering session with Router 2 just as Router 3 did. This time, however, Router 2 will send label information to Router 1. Router 2 checks its routing table for networks that are reachable through it and sends a label to Router 1 to represent those networks. In this case, Router 2 sends a label with a value of 10 to Router 1 to represent the 10.1.1.0/24 and 10.1.2.0/24 networks. Note that the label that is sent to Router 1 is not the same label that Router 2 received from Router 3. Labels are only locally significant, so they only need be unique within a particular MPLS router.

Now that Router 1 has label information, it can use MPLS to forward packets for networks 10.1.1.0/24 and 10.1.2.0/24. When Router 1 receives a packet destined for the 10.1.1.0/24 or 10.1.2.0/24 network, Router 1 pushes a label (10) onto the packet and sends it to Router 2. At this point, Router 2's function has changed. Now, when it receives an MPLS frame with the label 10, it *swaps* (switches) out the label 10, replaces it with the label 20, and sends it to Router 3. Router 3's function remains the same. Router 3 removes the label 20 and routes the packet to its destination.

Figure 11.7 shows the complete LSP setup from Router 1 to Router 3. Router 1's function is to perform a Layer 3 lookup, and if the packet is destined for one of the networks supported by Router 3, Router 1 pushes (encapsulates the packet in an MPLS frame) the appropriate label onto the packet. This is the function of the ingress LER, to apply the correct label to packets when they enter the provider network.

When Router 2 receives the MPLS frame, it examines the label, swaps the ingress label for the appropriate egress label, and sends the frame out of the appropriate interface to its destination. Router 2 now functions as an LSR and is basically performing a Layer 2 switch function, switching the packet from one interface to another and creating a new label header. When receiving the MPLS frame, Router 3 examines the label and *pops* (removes the packet from the MPLS frame) the label, performs a Layer 3 lookup, and routes the packet to the appropriate network.

Figure 11.7: A complete tunnel is set up between Router 1 and Router 3. Router 1 is the provider ingress and will apply a 10 label to packets with a destination of 10.1.1.0/24 or 10.1.2.0/24. The packet is forwarded to Router 2 with label 10, and Router 2 swaps label 20 for label 10 and forwards it to Router 3. Router 3 pops the label from the packet and forwards the original packet to its destination CE.

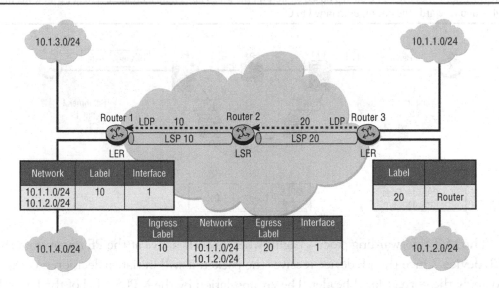

Note that LSPs are unidirectional. For bidirectional communications, an additional LSP must be set up in the opposite direction. For example, in Figure 11.7, devices on the network 10.1.3.0/24 attached to Router 1 can send packets to network 10.1.1.0/24 attached to Router 3 because the necessary label information has been distributed throughout the network. However, Router 1 has not disseminated label information about networks 10.1.3.0/24 and 10.1.4.0/24 to Router 2, so neither Router 2 nor Router 3 has any information on the labels necessary to reach those networks. The process of distributing label information described above would have to be performed for Router 1 networks in the same manner as it was for Router 3 networks in order to establish bidirectional LSPs.

In the next section, we dive deeper into the inner workings of the MPLS protocol.

11.2 MPLS in Detail

Now that we have examined some MPLS basics, let's take a more detailed look at the entire MPLS forwarding process. Figure 11.8 shows a typical example of a provider MPLS network. (Note that in Figure 11.8 the LER and LSP routers are labeled with the more generic PE and P terms, emphasizing the interchangeability of these terms.)

Figure 11.8: PE1 applies an MPLS label to the packet from CE1. The packet is then forwarded through the provider network devices P2 and P3 based entirely on the MPLS label until it arrives at PE2. PE2 removes the label and forwards the packet unchanged to CE2.

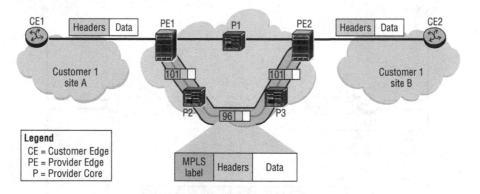

The MPLS forwarding process begins when packets arrive at the PE router from the CE device. Once the PE device receives the packet, it will initiate a decision process to apply the correct label header. The encapsulation by the MPLS label of the Layer 2 header that is received from the CE device depends on whether a Layer 2 or Layer 3

VPN service is offered by the carrier. (The different types of VPN services are discussed later in this chapter.)

As discussed previously, in an MPLS network the PE and P devices have some special terminology. The first PE router is called the *Ingress Label Edge Router* (iLER). The iLER encapsulates the customer packets with an MPLS label based on provider-configured policies. The intermediate routers (usually P routers) are called *Label Switching Routers* (LSRs). LSRs make switching decisions that are based on the MPLS label. The LSR reads the label in the incoming MPLS frame, makes a switching decision, swaps the label, and then transmits the MPLS frame out of the appropriate port or interface.

The last PE router on the LSP is the Egress Label Edge Router (eLER). The eLER is the termination point of the LSP, or the end of the tunnel. The egress LER removes the MPLS label and forwards the customer packets to the CE device. As previously mentioned, the CE devices neither know nor need to know about any of the MPLS-specific information. The MPLS labels are applied by the iLER as the packets enter the provider network and are removed by the eLER as the packets leave the provider network. The entire process is completely transparent to the customer.

Let's examine the entire process a packet undergoes from the time it leaves the origination CE to the time it arrives at the destination CE device. For the purposes of this discussion, we will assume that LDP has already distributed label information to all PE and P routers. In Figure 11.8, CE1 sends a data frame toward CE2. On an Ethernet interface, this is a normal IP datagram that is encapsulated in Ethernet. CE1 is not aware of the MPLS LSP that originates on PE1. The packet that is sent from CE1 to PE1 is unlabeled because the CE does not run MPLS and is unaware of any of the details of the MPLS provider network.

When the packet reaches PE1, an MPLS label is applied to the frame. This label corresponds to the LSP that ends on PE2. The MPLS label encapsulates the unlabeled packet that was received from CE1. The labeled MPLS packet is then sent along the LSP to P2. P2 processes the MPLS packet and checks its MPLS table to perform a label swapping operation. It reads the label value of 101, performs a table lookup, switches the packet out of the appropriate interface to P3, and applies the label value of 96.

P3 performs a similar label swap operation and switches the MPLS packet out from its interface to PE2 with the label value 101. Note that, by coincidence, this is the same label value that is used by PE1. Recall, however, that this is not a problem because labels are locally significant to the router. When PE2 receives the labeled packet, PE2 performs a lookup on the received label value of 101. Because P2 is an edge router that is directly connected to CE2, PE2 strips the MPLS label and then forwards the unlabeled packet to CE2. As with CE1, CE2 is totally unaware of any MPLS information in the Provider Core. CE2 receives the same packet as though CE1 and CE2 were directly connected.

Because MPLS tunnels are unidirectional, two LSPs are required for bidirectional communication. Therefore, traffic that is sent between two customer sites may follow different paths over the network. As you can see from Figure 11.9, the MPLS path is defined by the labels that are used to switch along the path. The egress router of the LSP signals the label that should be used for the LSP to the next upstream router. The upstream router will transmit data; data flows from upstream to downstream. LSPs can be manually configured, but either LDP or RSVP is usually used to distribute label information throughout an MPLS network.

Figure 11.9: CE routers have no knowledge of the MPLS labeling process inside the provider network. Labels are assigned at the ingress PE router and removed at the egress PE router. Within the provider cloud, packets are switched from one interface to another on P routers based entirely on the labels applied to packets by the PE routers. Two LSPs are required for bidirectional data transfer.

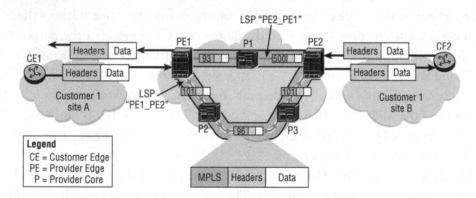

When LDP is the label signaling protocol, the LSP always follows the path chosen by the Interior Gateway Protocol (IGP). An LSR that has LSPs passing through or ending on the router distributes a label for each LSP to all its LDP neighbors. An upstream router may receive labels for a specific LSP from multiple neighbors, and it then chooses the downstream router to use based on the next hop that is determined by the IGP. This means that the next-hop LSR for the LSP is the same as the next-hop router that is chosen by the IGP; the label that is used is the one signaled by that neighbor.

When RSVP is the label signaling protocol, labels are specifically requested by the ingress router for the LSP. The request travels along the path to the egress LSR, which generates a label for the LSP. This path may follow the IGP, in which case, the path will be the same as the one used by LDP. A second option is that the path of the LSP may be explicitly specified, partially or completely. A third option is that a traffic engineering–enabled routing protocol will be used to choose a path that meets some specific constraints.

RSVP also allows additional, redundant paths to be created that can be used for fast failover if the original LSP fails. The services that are transported over an LSP are then protected so that a failover to the back-up LSP can be performed much more quickly than when only the IGP is relied on.

Now that we have examined the MPLS structure in some detail, it is time to turn our attention to the various sorts of VPN services that can be provisioned over the services network.

11.3 VPN Services in Detail

Recall from our earlier discussion that a VPN is a way to provide customers with connections that seem to them to be private over a physical network infrastructure that is shared by multiple customers. MPLS is the key technology that allows providers to implement VPN services for customers. Service routers use MPLS to provide a variety of VPN services over their core IP/MPLS network. The service provider can offer simple, transparent Layer 2 and Layer 3 VPN services to multiple customers over a single network. Three different types of services are supported: VPWS, VPLS, and VPRN. The remainder of this section will focus on the differences in these three types of VPN services.

- **Virtual Private Wire Service**—Virtual Private Wire Service (VPWS) is a simple Layer 2 service that emulates a single leased line or circuit between two locations. The customer has no knowledge of the service provider network; the service acts as a simple point-to-point connection between customer sites. The VPWS can emulate an Ethernet connection (epipe), a Frame-Relay connection (fpipe), an ATM connection (apipe), or a TDM connection such as a T1 or E1 circuit (cpipe). The Layer 2 frames of customer data are encapsulated in MPLS labels and tunneled across the service provider network.

- **Virtual Private LAN Service**—Virtual Private LAN Service (VPLS) is a Layer 2 multipoint service that can be used to interconnect more than two customer locations. From the customer's perspective, VPLS looks as though a simple Layer 2 LAN switch exists between the different customer locations. The Ethernet frames of customer data are encapsulated in MPLS labels and tunneled across the service provider network. In this way, the VPLS is very similar to the VPWS in that from the customer's perspective, it is a Layer 2 service. The difference is that the provider's MPLS network allows for more than a single connection between two sites.

- **Virtual Private Routed Network**—Virtual Private Routed Network (VPRN) is a Layer 3 service that makes the service provider network appear as a simple IP router that connects two or more customer locations. VPRN allows the CE devices to exchange route information with VPRN as if it were an IP router. The IP packets containing customer data are encapsulated in MPLS labels and tunneled across the service provider network.

VPWS

VPWS is the simplest of the VPN services that an MPLS network can provide. A sample VPWS configuration is shown in Figure 11.10.

Figure 11.10: VPWS provides a simple Layer 2 service that emulates a point-to-point line between two sites. From the CE perspective, the MPLS network is a single wire that connects them.

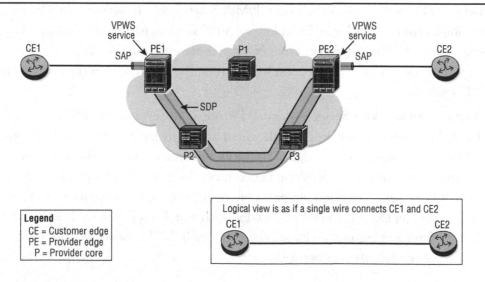

VPWS is a simple point-to-point service, emulating a simple Layer 2 connection between two customer locations. The customer frame is not checked, and Media Access Control (MAC) learning is not performed by VPWS. The customer Layer 2 frames are encapsulated in MPLS labels and switched across the service provider network transparently.

The ingress PE receives customer data on a Service Access Point (SAP) that is associated with a specific service. The SAP may be a port, a port with a specific Virtual Local Area Network (VLAN) tag in the case of an Ethernet port, or a port with a specific circuit ID in the case of ATM or Frame-Relay. The customer data is then encapsulated with a service label by the ingress PE. Because many services may be configured on the PE, the service label identifies the specific service that the data belongs to. The service label value is signaled to the ingress PE by the egress PE when the service is initialized by the provider.

After the data is encapsulated with the service label, the data must be forwarded over the correct Service Distribution Point (SDP) that is defined by the service. A second, outer label is added to the data. This label identifies the LSP that will be used to transport the MPLS packet to the far end of the tunnel—the egress PE device. The data is label switched along the LSP using this outer label.

The egress PE removes the MPLS-encapsulated data from the SDP. The inner, service label is used to identify the service that the data belongs to, and, after the labels are removed, the data is transmitted on the appropriate SAP for the service. In other words, the service label is used to de-multiplex the data from the SDP to the appropriate service.

CE devices are never aware of SDPs and SAPs. The CE devices transmit to the ingress PE device, possibly using a specific VLAN tag, and then receive an unlabeled packet from the egress PE device. This process is illustrated in Figure 11.11.

VPLS

VPLS is similar to VPWS, with SAPs to provide customer access and SDPs to provide the transport connection across the network to the remote PEs of the service. However, VPLS is a multipoint service that supports multiple access points (as opposed to a VPWS, which is only point-to-point with two access points). VPLS acts as a logical Layer 2 switch that connects all of the CE devices that are attached to the service. Figure 11.12 illustrates the physical and logical view of an example VPLS.

Figure 11.11: In a VPWS service, the MPLS network uses both an MPLS tag for transporting the data and an inner service label for de-multiplexing the service at the SDP. PE2 pops the MPLS tag and then determines which service the frame belongs to based on the service label before forwarding the packet to CE2.

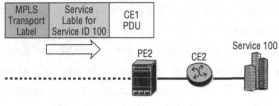

PE2 strips the MPLS label

PE2 then looks at the service label to determine which service the frame belongs to

PE2 then makes the appropriate forwarding decision for the destination customer site

Figure 11.12: VPLS emulates a private LAN service that can connect multiple customer sites. From the customer's perspective, the service is a simple Layer 2 switch service. Multiple services can be provided over a single CE by using different SAPs at the provider ingress.

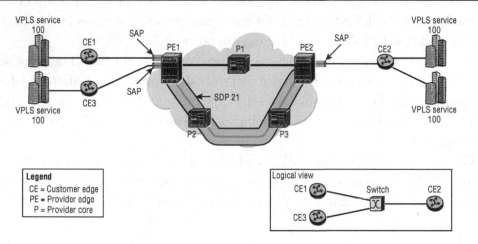

Because VPLS emulates a switched Ethernet service, a MAC address forwarding database (FDB) must be maintained for each VPLS. When a unicast frame with an unknown source address arrives on a SAP or an SDP, VPLS learns the address, in the same way that an Ethernet switch learns a MAC address on its ports. The VPLS FDB associates MAC addresses with SAPs and SDPs, but is otherwise similar to an Ethernet switch.

When an Ethernet frame arrives on a SAP or an SDP, a lookup is performed in the FDB for the destination address. If there is an entry for the address, the frame is forwarded to the appropriate SAP or SDP. If there is no entry for the address, the frame is flooded to all other SAPs and SDPs, which is similar to the flooding of an unknown frame on an Ethernet switch. Figure 11.13 illustrates the FDB table on PE routers that must maintain MAC address to service mapping information.

Figure 11.13: In a VPLS, the PE devices maintain an FDB to keep track of MAC addresses, service IDs, and SAPs. The PEs will tag the packets with the appropriate service ID and MPLS label for forwarding through the MPLS network.

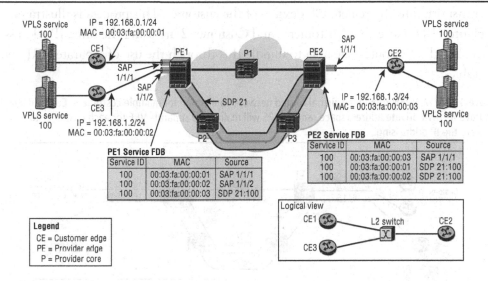

VPRN

A VPRN is a class of VPN that allows the connection of multiple sites in a routed domain over a service provider IP/MPLS network. VPRN is a Layer 3 service (as opposed to VPWS and VPLS, which are Layer 2 services). From the customer's perspective, all of the sites appear to be connected to a private routed network that is administered by the service provider for that customer only. Each PE router providing VPRN services maintains a separate IP forwarding table for each VPRN. Each customer of the service provider has its own private IP address space and, therefore, may have overlapping IP addresses.

The VPRN service uses VPN Routing and Forwarding Instances (VRFs) within the PE device to maintain forwarding information on a per-customer basis. A *VRF* is a logical private forwarding (routing) table that securely isolates the routing information of one customer from the next customer, and also from the routes of the Provider Core network. Each PE maintains multiple separate VRFs that are based on the number of distinct VPRN services that the PE supports.

Each CE router becomes a routing peer of the provider PE router that it is directly connected to. Routes are exchanged between the CE and the PE routers. The PE devices in a VPRN service exchange routes with each other so that the routes can be transmitted to the remote CE devices of the customer. This process is illustrated in Figure 11.14. Note that Customer 1 and Customer 2 are using the same IP address space, but the PE routers are able to handle this through the use of separate VRF routing tables.

Figure 11.14: A VPRN provides a virtual routed network connection for multiple customers. Each customer can have its own private address space, and the PE will maintain a separate VRF for each customer to separate the IP addressing.

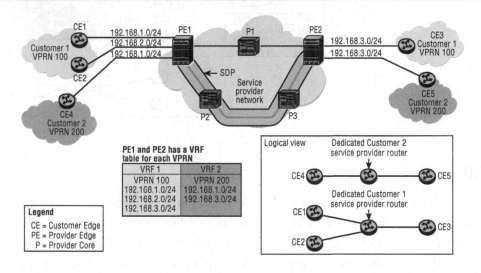

The transport of customer data is similar to a VPWS or VPLS, except that the Layer 2 headers are removed and the IP datagrams are encapsulated with the MPLS headers. Customer data arrives at a VPRN SAP, is encapsulated with an inner service label and an outer transport label, and is then carried across the network using MPLS. The main difference from a customer perspective is that the provider network appears as a routed IP network, and therefore either the customer devices must peer to the provider equipment using an IP routing protocol, or static routes must be configured.

The types of VPN services provided to a customer are driven by the particular requirements of the customer. All of the VPN services have their benefits and drawbacks, and the *right* VPN services can only be determined after carefully examining your customer's needs. Whatever service is required by your customer, the Alcatel-Lucent 7750 SR products can support their individual use case.

Now that we have examined MPLS and VPN concepts, you should complete the lab exercises to assist you in reinforcing these protocol features.

Practice Lab: Services

The following lab is designed to reinforce your knowledge of the content in this chapter. Please review the instructions carefully and perform the steps in the order in which they are provided.

Note that unlike previous labs, the labs in this chapter require a *fourth* piece of equipment that is capable of generating and responding to ping packets as a minimum. You will also need to have the capability of statically configuring its IP address. If your Alcatel-Lucent equipment has copper (i.e., wired) Ethernet ports, a simple desktop or laptop computer is more than sufficient. If not, you will need a fourth Alcatel-Lucent 7750/7450 router with suitable connections.

 These labs are designed to be used in a controlled lab environment. Please **DO NOT** attempt to perform these labs in a production environment.

The exercises for this chapter are split into two sections. The first section creates the supporting infrastructure for services. This infrastructure is not specific to any particular service but can support multiple services in just about any imaginable combination. The second section implements a VPLS service between the PE nodes.

As noted in Lab Section 5.2 in Chapter 5, all lab exercises have been designed to fully illustrate all configuration details but with a minimum number of nodes. While a VPLS across a single pair of routers may seem trivial (see Figure 11.15), please keep in mind that a real network could potentially have *dozens* of routers between PE1 and PE2 and that these additional routers could span a city, a continent, or even the entire globe.

Figure 11.15: The Service Provider Core network provides the infrastructure to connect geographically separate customer equipment in a seamless, invisible fashion.

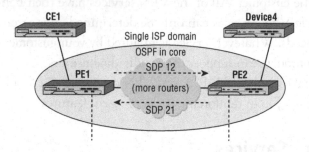

Lab Section 11.1: Services Framework

Figure 11.15 shows the topology for this section. The VPN framework resides within the domain of a single ISP. The edge routers (PE1 and PE2) are the only ones shown explicitly, although there could be many other Provider Core (P) routers. The network cloud is a reminder that the edge routers may have a direct link or may be joined by many intervening routers. An IGP is always a necessity; we'll reuse most of the configuration from Chapter 9. The task in this section is to build SDPs (shown as dotted arrows) between the PE routers.

Objective In this exercise, you will configure OSPF as the core IGP within a single domain, configure LDP, and create a full mesh of SDPs between PE routers. This creates the infrastructure to support the VPLS service in the next section.

Validation You will know you have succeeded if the SDPs between the PE routers are admin and operationally Up after completing all steps, and the two customer-facing (Ethernet) ports are in access mode.

The BGP configuration from the previous chapter's exercises is not needed for this chapter. Although BGP should not interfere with these exercises, you are advised to remove it completely for the sake of simplicity and ease of debugging. The command outputs for these exercises were obtained with BGP removed.

Part 1: IGP Configuration

1. (*Optional*) Completely remove the BGP configuration on *all* routers. (Refer to Lab Section 10.1 in Chapter 10.)

```
*B:PE1# configure router
*B:PE1>config>router# bgp shutdown
*B:PE1>config>router# no bgp
*B:PE1>config>router# exit
*B:PE1#
```

1a. What command(s) can you use to verify that BGP has been successfully removed? (Refer to Lab Section 10.1 in Chapter 10.)

2. Restore the full OSPF configuration that you saved at the end of Chapter 9. Do this on all routers. (If you don't have saved config files, you will need to complete all the configuration steps from Chapter 9 on all routers.)

```
*B:PE1# exec cf3:\OSPF-Full.cfg
System Configuration
System Security Configuration
Log Configuration
System Security Cpm Hw Filters Configuration
QoS Policy Configuration
Card Configuration
Port Configuration
[... Additional output omitted ...]
Router (Network Side) Configuration
OSPFv2 Configuration
[... Additional output omitted ...]
Executed 225 lines in 0.0 seconds from file cf3:\OSPF-Full.cfg
*B:PE1#
```

3. Unlike in Lab Section 9.1 in Chapter 9, CE1 is now exclusively part of the customer network and is no longer considered as part of the ISP core. Since the role of CE1 has changed for this lab, it no longer participates in the ISP's core routing. On PE1, remove the toCE1 interface from OSPF. (Don't change the OSPF configuration on CE1; it will be modified in a later step.) Verify that OSPF is no longer running between PE1 and CE1.

```
*B:PE1# configure router ospf
*B:PE1>config>router>ospf# area 0
```

```
*B:PE1>config>router>ospf>area# no interface toCE1
*B:PE1>config>router>ospf>area# exit all
*B:PE1# show router ospf neighbor

===============================================================
OSPF Neighbors
===============================================================
Interface-Name      Rtr Id        State   Pri  RetxQ   TTL
---------------------------------------------------------------
toPE2               150.10.0.1    Full    1    0       35
---------------------------------------------------------------
No. of Neighbors: 1
===============================================================
*B:PE1#
```

3a. What tells you that OSPF is no longer running between PE1 and CE1?

Part 2: LDP and SDP Configuration

Running an IP/MPLS-based service requires a protocol for exchanging labels between the ISP's routers; we'll use the Label Distribution Protocol (LDP) for ease of deployment. The LDP labels provide the required support to run Service Distribution Point (SDPs).

A VPLS service requires a full mesh of SDPs. The term *full mesh* means every PE router has an SDP to every other PE router participating in the service. In this exercise, since we only have two PE routers, we only need a pair of SDPs in order for PE1 and PE2 to be fully meshed.

1. LDP must be enabled on *all* router interfaces within the Provider Core. Unlike OSPF or BGP, the default state for LDP is disabled. You *must* remember to do no shutdown to enable LDP. Configure LDP on both PE routers.

   ```
   *B:PE1# configure router ldp
   *B:PE1>config>router>ldp$ interface-parameters
   *B:PE1>config>router>ldp>if-params$ interface toPE2
   *B:PE1>config>router>ldp>if-params>if$ exit
   *B:PE1>config>router>ldp>if-params# exit
   *B:PE1>config>router>ldp# no shutdown
   *B:PE1>config>router>ldp#
   ```

2. Once both routers have LDP configured, verify that LDP is correctly configured on both PE routers and that they have established an LDP session.

```
*B:PE1>config>router>ldp# show router ldp interface

===============================================================
LDP Interfaces
===============================================================
Interface      Adm Opr  Hello Hold  KA     KA      Transport
                        Factor Time Factor Timeout Address
---------------------------------------------------------------
toPE2          Up  Up   3     15    3      30      System
---------------------------------------------------------------
No. of Interfaces: 1
===============================================================
*B:PE1>config>router>ldp#
*B:PE1>config>router>ldp# show router ldp session

===============================================================
LDP Sessions
===============================================================
Peer LDP Id    Adj Type  State        Msg Sent  Msg Recv  Up Time
---------------------------------------------------------------
150.10.0.1:0   Link      Established  60        61        0d 00:02:36
---------------------------------------------------------------
No. of Sessions: 1
===============================================================
*B:PE1>config>router>ldp# exit
*B:PE1#
```

Every SDP is identified by a numeric label. It's a best practice to design or pick a convention for the numbering scheme, and *stick to it!* We'll use the convention of two digits: the first digit for the near end router and the second digit for the far end router. As an example, an SDP from PE1 to PE2 will be labeled **12.**

3. On PE1, configure an SDP to PE2; on PE2, configure an SDP to PE1. For the first attempt, do not use the parameter **create** when defining the SDP. For the second attempt, don't forget to use the attribute mpls! Like LDP, the default state for an SDP is disabled. Don't forget the no shutdown command.

```
*B:PE1# configure service
*B:PE1>config>service# sdp 12 mpls
MINOR: CLI 'create' is mandatory while creating SDP.
*B:PE1>config>service# sdp 12 mpls create
*B:PE1>config>service>sdp$ far-end 150.10.0.1
*B:PE1>config>service>sdp$ ldp
*B:PE1>config>service>sdp$ no shutdown

*B:PE1>config>service>sdp$
```

4. After both SDPs have been configured, verify that they are both admin and operationally Up. (In some circumstances, you may need to wait a few moments before the SDPs will be Up.) If not, confirm that you have entered all the parameters correctly.

```
*B:PE1>config>service# show service sdp


===============================================================
Services: Service Destination Points
===============================================================
SdpId  Adm MTU  Opr MTU  IP address    Adm  Opr  Deliver Signal
---------------------------------------------------------------
12     0        9190     150.10.0.1    Up   Up   LDP     TLDP
---------------------------------------------------------------
Number of SDPs : 1
---------------------------------------------------------------
===============================================================
*B:PE1>config>service#
```

5. Removing an SDP is the familiar two-step process: Shut down the SDP and delete it with no sdp. Remove one of the SDPs for practice.

```
*B:PE1>config>service# sdp 12 shutdown
*B:PE1>config>service# no sdp 12
*B:PE1>config>service#
```

6. On each PE router, verify the state of any SDPs (see Step 4).

   6a. Is it possible to get a single SDP in the Up state?

7. Re-create the missing SDP and again verify that they are both admin and operationally Up.

Part 3: Customer-Facing Configuration

This section provides all the steps for configuring the customer-facing Service Access Points (SAPs) on the PE routers. It may not be obvious at first glance why there are so many steps. There is a chain of logic that goes something like this:

A. Customer equipment connects to a VPLS via a SAP.

B. SAPs can only be created on Ethernet ports that are set to access mode.

C. A port with an existing interface *cannot* be changed to access mode.

D. So we first need to remove any interfaces on network ports.

If that doesn't make complete sense, don't worry because the steps below guide the way. Don't be afraid to experiment to see what kind of error messages you get if you miss a step or do it incorrectly.

1. Remove the existing network interface on PE1 that faces CE1. Use the familiar two-step process: Shut down first, then delete.

```
*B:PE1# configure router
*B:PE1>config>router# interface toCE1 shutdown
*B:PE1>config>router# no interface toCE1
*B:PE1>config>router# exit
*B:PE1#
```

1a. What error message do you get if you try to remove an interface that is *not* shut down?

2. Configure the port facing customer equipment as an access port.

```
*B:PE1# configure port 1/1/1
*B:PE1>config>port# shutdown
*B:PE1>config>port# ethernet mode access
*B:PE1>config>port# no shutdown
*B:PE1>config>port# exit
*B:PE1#
```

2a. There are only two states for a port: One is access mode. What is the name of the other mode? (Use the CLI Help!)

2b. What error message do you get if a port is *not* shut down when you try to change modes?

3. On PE2, configure the corresponding customer-facing port as an access port. This exercise assumes that Device 4 is connected to port 1/1/1. If you are using a different port, you will need to adapt the commands given below. (Also, if you have configured a network interface on that port, you will need to remove it first.)

```
*A:PE2# configure port 1/1/1
*A:PE2>config>port# shutdown
*A:PE2>config>port# ethernet mode access
*A:PE2>config>port# no shutdown
*A:PE2>config>port# exit
*A:PE2#
```

Part 4: Verification

A general first step for troubleshooting services is to check that nothing has been (accidentally) left in a (shut)down state. The next step is to check that nothing was skipped or missed while building the configuration.

1. **IGP Verification**—Confirm that OSPF is running throughout the provider network (i.e., just PE1 and PE2 in this case). Confirm that routes for every interface appear in the routing table. Confirm that all interfaces within the provider network respond to a ping. (Remember that customer-facing ports are now operating as SAPs, not network interfaces.)

2. **LDP Verification**—Confirm that LDP has successfully exchanged all labels that will be necessary for PE1 and PE2 to send data back and forth. Each router needs a pair of labels—one to reach the far router and one offered to the far router to send data back to the local router.

```
*B:PE1# show router ldp bindings active


===========================================================
Legend:  (S) - Static
===========================================================
LDP Prefix Bindings (Active)
===========================================================
Prefix         Op   IngLbl  EgrLbl  EgrIntf  EgrNextHop
-----------------------------------------------------------
140.10.0.1/32  Pop  131071   --      --        --
150.10.0.1/32  Push   --     131071  1/1/2    140.10.0.98
-----------------------------------------------------------
No. of Prefix Bindings: 2
===========================================================
*B:PE1#
```

2a. One label is to reach the far router. Is that the Push or the Pop label?

2b. One label is offered to the far router to send data back to the local router. Is that the Push or the Pop label?

3. SDP Verification—Confirm that the SDPs are both admin and operationally Up.

4. Customer-Facing SAP Verification—Confirm that the customer-facing ports are in access mode. Confirm that the port itself is admin and operationally Up.

```
*B:PE1# show port 1/1/1


===========================================================
Ethernet Interface
===========================================================
Description       : 10/100/Gig Ethernet SFP
Interface         : 1/1/1     Oper Speed      : 1 Gbps
Link-level        : Ethernet  Config Speed    : 1 Gbps
Admin State       : up        Oper Duplex     : full
Oper State        : up        Config Duplex   : full
Physical Link     : Yes       MTU             : 1514
[... 4 lines of output omitted ...]


Configured Mode   : access    Encap Type      : null
Dot1Q Ethertype   : 0x8100    QinQ Ethertype  : 0x8100
PBB Ethertype     : 0x88e7
[... Additional output omitted ...]
*B:PE1#
```

Lab Section 11.2: VPLS Example

A VPLS is a Layer 2 service that connects multiple sites in a single LAN. It's like creating a virtual switch from a network of Service Routers. In this lab, we will configure the actual VPLS across the PE nodes as shown in Figure 11.16. The PE devices will connect to each other in a full mesh topology using mesh-type SDPs. The CE devices will be configured to use the same subnet (i.e., addresses from a single LAN). The operation of the VPLS will be demonstrated using ping, traceroute, and (optionally) OSPF.

 Note that after the service reference topology has been configured, adding additional services from edge-to-edge does not require any further modification of the supporting infrastructure.

Figure 11.16: Customer equipment connects to the Provider Edge via a SAP. To the customer, the SAP in a VPLS behaves identically to a port on an Ethernet switch.

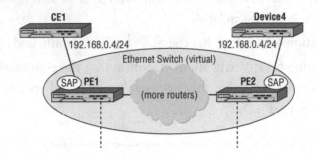

Objective In this exercise, you will configure a VPLS service between PE routers. You will also demonstrate the ability of customer equipment to communicate across this VPLS as if it were a simple Ethernet switch.

Validation You will know you have succeeded if the CE devices can ping each other and if traceroute shows the CE devices as being only a single (virtual!) hop away from each other.

Part 1: Provider Edge VPLS Configuration

1. Create a VPLS service. Every service is identified with a numeric name. The actual value isn't as important as the fact that it should be unique within the ISP's domain. Repeat the configuration on both PE1 and PE2, using an *identical* service number on both routers. Like SDPs, the default state for a service is disabled. Don't forget the no shutdown command!

    ```
    *B:PE1# configure service
    *B:PE1>config>service# vpls 22 customer 1 create
    *B:PE1>config>service>vpls$ no shutdown
    *B:PE1>config>service>vpls$
    ```

    1a. What happens if you forget to use the keyword create when first creating a VPLS?

2. SDPs are used to distribute services across multiple Service Routers. In terms of a VPLS, an SDP is needed to every other router that has an SAP participating in the VPLS. Add the required SDPs to the VPLS configuration on each PE router,

specifying that they operate in mesh mode. Be careful with your typing: PE1's SDP to PE2 was identified as *12* when created; PE2's SDP to PE1 was identified as *21*.

```
*B:PE1>config>service>vpls$ mesh-sdp 12 create
*B:PE1>config>service>vpls>mesh-sdp$ exit
*B:PE1>config>service>vpls#

*A:PE2>config>service>vpls$ mesh-sdp 21 create
*A:PE2>config>service>vpls>mesh-sdp$ exit
*A:PE2>config>service>vpls#
```

2a. What happens if you forget to use the keyword create when first creating a mesh SDP?

3. Add the SAPs to attach CE devices to the VPLS.

```
*B:PE1>config>service>vpls# sap 1/1/1 create
*B:PE1>config>service>vpls>sap$ exit
*B:PE1>config>service>vpls#

*A:PE2>config>service>vpls# sap 1/1/1 create
*A:PE2>config>service>vpls>sap$ exit
*A:PE2>config>service>vpls#
```

3a. What happens if you forget to use the keyword create when first creating a SAP?

4. Confirm that the VPLS is both admin and operationally Up on each router. Check the status summary of the service, as well as the detailed status for all the service components: SAPs and SDPs.

```
*B:PE1# show service service-using

===============================================================
Services
===============================================================
ServiceId  Type  Adm  Opr  CustomerId  Last Mgmt Change
---------------------------------------------------------------
22         VPLS  Up   Up   1           01/01/2000 16:53:17
---------------------------------------------------------------
Matching Services : 1
---------------------------------------------------------------
===============================================================
```

```
*B:PE1#
*B:PE1>config>service>vpls# show service id 22 base

===========================================================
Service Basic Information
===========================================================
Service Id          : 22          Vpn Id            : 0
Service Type        : VPLS
Customer Id         : 1
Last Status Change: 01/01/2000 16:56:01
Last Mgmt Change  : 01/01/2000 16:53:17
Admin State         : Up          Oper State        : Up
MTU                 : 1514        Def. Mesh VC Id : 22
SAP Count           : 1           SDP Bind Count  : 1
Snd Flush on Fail : Disabled      Host Conn Verify: Disabled
Propagate MacFlush: Disabled
Def. Gateway IP   : None
Def. Gateway MAC  : None


-----------------------------------------------------------
Service Access & Destination Points
-----------------------------------------------------------
Identifier              Type  AdmMTU  OprMTU  Adm  Opr
-----------------------------------------------------------
sap:1/1/1               null  1514    1514    Up   Up
sdp:12:22 M(150.10.0.1) n/a   0       9190    Up   Up
===========================================================
*B:PE1>config>service>vpls#
```

If the service isn't completely Up, start with the troubleshooting steps from Section 11.1: Check that nothing has been (accidentally) left in a (shut)down state. Then check that nothing was skipped or missed while building the configuration.

Note that just like an Ethernet switch, the state of a VPLS service doesn't depend on the CE equipment being properly configured. If the VPLS is down, looking at the customer equipment will *not* help you find or fix the problem.

Part 2: Customer Device Configuration

For this exercise, we will treat CE1 and Device4 as traditional routers. Their interfaces will use addresses from a common subnet, even though they are on opposite sides of a service (which may span a city, a continent, or the globe). The VPLS service will join these two devices in the same way an Ethernet switch would join them.

The minimum requirements for Device4 are that it be capable of sending and responding to pings. We will, however, walk through the full configuration in case Device4 is an Alcatel-Lucent 7750/7450 device.

Determine whether you have the ability to set the IP address of Device4. Set it to **192.168.0.4** if you can. If not, carefully note the address and subnet mask of the interface connected to PE2. You will need to adapt the examples below to give PE1 a compatible IP address and mask so that it is part of the same subnet as PE2.

1. Reconfigure the interface on CE1 that connects to PE1. It should now use an address of 192.168.0.1/24. (We will leave the name of the interface the same, even though a new name like toISP or toVPLS would be more appropriate to this exercise.)

   ```
   *A:CE1# configure router
   *A:CE1>config>router# interface toPE1
   *A:CE1>config>router>if# address 192.168.0.1/24
   *A:CE1>config>router>if# exit
   *A:CE1>config>router# exit
   *A:CE1#
   ```

2. Assuming that Device4 is an Alcatel-Lucent 7750/7450 device, configure the basic router settings and the interface to PE2. If Device4 is some other device and you are able to set the IP address and subnet mask, do so now.

   ```
   *A:NS074662074# configure system name Dev4-CE2
   *A:Dev4-CE2# configure card 1 card-type iom-20g-b
   *A:Dev4-CE2# configure card 1 mda 1 mda-type m10-1gb-sfp-b
   *A:Dev4-CE2# configure port 1/1/1 no shutdown
   *A:Dev4-CE2# configure router
   *A:Dev4-CE2>config>router# interface system
   *A:Dev4-CE2>config>router>if# address 150.10.0.2/32
   *A:Dev4-CE2>config>router>if# exit
   *A:Dev4-CE2>config>router# interface toVPLS
   *A:Dev4-CE2>config>router>if$ address 192.168.0.4/24
   *A:Dev4-CE2>config>router>if$ port 1/1/1
   *A:Dev4-CE2>config>router>if$ exit
   *A:Dev4-CE2>config>router#
   ```

3. (*Optional*) On Device4, create OSPF area 0. Add the system interface and interface connecting to the PE2.

```
*A:Dev4-CE2>config>router# ospf
*A:Dev4-CE2>config>router>ospf$ area 0
*A:Dev4-CE2>config>router>ospf>area$ interface system
*A:Dev4-CE2>config>router>ospf>area>if$ exit
*A:Dev4-CE2>config>router>ospf>area# interface toVPLS
*A:Dev4-CE2>config>router>ospf>area>if$ exit
*A:Dev4-CE2>config>router>ospf>area# exit
*A:Dev4-CE2>config>router>ospf# exit
*A:Dev4-CE2>config>router#
```

4. Confirm basic connectivity between the CE devices by pinging the interfaces on the 192.168.0.0/24 subnet. If there is no response, verify the previous configuration steps and correct as necessary. Pay particular attention to the configuration of addresses on CE1 and Device4.

```
*A:CE1# ping 192.168.0.4
PING 192.168.0.4 56 data bytes
64 bytes from 192.168.0.4: icmp_seq=1 ttl=64 time<10ms.
64 bytes from 192.168.0.4: icmp_seq=2 ttl=64 time<10ms.
64 bytes from 192.168.0.4: icmp_seq=3 ttl=64 time<10ms.
64 bytes from 192.168.0.4: icmp_seq=4 ttl=64 time<10ms.
64 bytes from 192.168.0.4: icmp_seq=5 ttl=64 time<10ms.

---- 192.168.0.4 PING Statistics ----
5 packets transmitted, 5 packets received, 0.00% packet loss
round-trip min < 10ms, avg < 10ms, max < 10ms, stddev < 10ms
*A:CE1#
```

Part 3: Verification

CE Network Connectivity

1. On CE1 or Device4, run a `traceroute` to the 192.168.0.x address on the other device.

```
*A:CE1# traceroute 192.168.0.4
traceroute to 192.168.0.4, 30 hops max, 40 byte packets
  1  192.168.0.4 (192.168.0.4)    <10 ms  <10 ms  <10 ms
*A:CE1#
```

1a. How many routers does CE1 see between itself and Device4?

1b. Does CE1 see the connection to Device4 as routed or switched (at Layer 2)? Explain your answer.

2. On CE1 or Device1, try to ping any of the interfaces on PE1 or PE2.

2a. Are any PE interfaces reachable?

3. (*Optional*) If Device4 has OSPF configured, check the adjacencies and LSA database on CE1 and Device4. (Refer to Lab Section 9.1 in Chapter 9.)

3a. How many OSPF adjacencies are there on each CE device?

3b. Are there any adjacencies with, or LSAs from, the PE routers?

3c. From CE1, which system interfaces can you ping? PE1? PE2? Device4?

3d. Explain the results.

3e. Are the OSPF sessions on the CE devices connected in any way to the OSPF sessions on the PE devices?

4. On one of the PE devices, shut down the SDP to the other PE device. Repeat Steps 1–3 above.

```
*B:PE1# configure service sdp 12 shutdown
*B:PE1#
```

4a. Explain the results. (*Hint:* Check the status of the VPLS service.)

5. Re-enable the SDP that you shut down in the previous step. You may need to wait a few moments for everything to return to its previous state.

```
*B:PE1# configure service sdp 12 no shutdown
*B:PE1#
```

VPLS Service Connectivity

6. There are now two CE devices connected to the VPLS. Check to see if this has affected the quantity or state of the services present on each PE device.

```
*B:PE1# show service service-using
*B:PE1#
```

6a. How many services are there on each PE device?

6b. What is the status of each service?

7. On each PE device, you can see the MAC database per service using the following command. Compare the exact contents of the two databases.

```
*B:PE1# show service id 22 fdb detail


===============================================================
Forwarding Database, Service 22
===============================================================
ServId  MAC                 Source-Id    Type  Last Change
                                         /Age

---------------------------------------------------------------
22      00:1a:f0:5c:6e:1b  sdp:12:22    L/0   01/01/2000 18:39:25
22      00:1a:f0:5c:73:c5  sap:1/1/1    L/0   01/01/2000 16:58:14

---------------------------------------------------------------
No. of MAC Entries: 2
===============================================================
*B:PE1#
```

7a. Are the databases identical or different? If different, what is different? Explain the results.

7b. How many local MAC addresses are in the CE1 table?

7c. How many remote MAC addresses are in the CE1 table?

Chapter Review

Now that you have completed this chapter, you should have a good understanding of the following topics. If you are not familiar with these topics, please go back and review the appropriate sections.

- The different types of routers and their function in a VPN services-based network
- The concept of tunneling and its role in providing VPN services
- How MPLS can be used as a method of tunneling and label switching
- The three major VPN services: VPWS, VPLS, and VPRN
- SAPs, SDPs, and their application to VPN services

Post-Assessment

The following questions will test your knowledge and prepare you for the Alcatel-Lucent NRS I Certification Exam. Please review each question carefully and choose the most correct answer. You can compare your response with the answers listed in Appendix A. You can also download all of the CD content at http://booksupport .wiley.com to take all the assessment tests and review the answers. Good luck!

1. Which of the following accurately describes a P device?

   A. It is used exclusively by the customer.

   B. It is responsible for adding and removing labels.

   C. It swaps label information and forwards packets.

   D. It creates an LSP in the provider network.

2. Which of the following is false regarding an SDP?

   A. It provides transport tunnel encapsulation.

   B. It is specific to a single service.

   C. The SDP ID is locally unique.

   D. LDP can be used as the signaling protocol.

3. Which of the following is *not* an accurate description of a VPN?

   A. A series of point-to-point tunnels configured on client equipment

   B. A tunnel technology created in a provider network

   C. A function of MPLS networks to create private communities of users

   D. Any network that includes encryption

4. Which of the following is false regarding LDP?

   A. It is used to define unidirectional paths through the network.

   B. It is a protocol specifically intended for label distribution.

   C. It is the only method for distributing labels in an MPLS network.

   D. It describes a path through the MPLS network based on the IGP path.

5. Which of the following term–definition pairs is incorrect?

    A. push--add a label

    B. swap--replace a label

    C. label distribution protocol--series of labels and next-hop interfaces

    D. pop--remove a label

6. The most commonly used label distribution protocol is _____.

    A. OSPF

    B. BGP

    C. LDP

    D. RIP

7. Which of the following is *not* a type of VPN?

    A. VPWS

    B. VPNM

    C. VPLS

    D. VPRN

8. A VPN that provides a simple point-to-point service between two destinations is a _____.

    A. VPNM

    B. VPLS

    C. VPWS

    D. None of the above

9. The VPN service that must maintain a table of MAC addresses is _____.

    A. VPWS

    B. VPLS

    C. VPRN

    D. Both A and B

10. The VPN service that requires encryption is _____.

   A. VPRN

   B. VPNM

   C. VPLS

   D. None of the above

11. The VPN service that appears to the customer as a private routed network is _____.

   A. VPNM

   B. VPRN

   C. VPLS

   D. VPWS

12. As a packet traverses an MPLS network, it passes through a router that removes one label and replaces it with another. The router it passed through was a _____ router.

   A. PE

   B. CE

   C. LER

   D. P

13. A packet arrives at a router with a label, and the router cannot perform any operations on it. The router is most likely a _____.

   A. LSR

   B. PE

   C. LER

   D. None of the above

14. In an MPLS network, the customer routers have no knowledge of how the MPLS features are implemented. The benefits of this include:

   A. Ease of CE configuration

   B. Allows for very scalable VPN solutions

   C. Lowers CE management overhead

   D. All of the above

15. The relationship between LDP and an IGP is best described as

   A. LDP paths are preferred over IGP routes.

   B. LDP uses IGP next-hop information.

   C. LDP re-distributes labels into IGP.

   D. IGP tags network destinations with LDP information.

A

Chapter Assessment Questions and Answers

Assessment Questions

Chapter 1

1. The original network that ultimately became the Internet was called _____.

   A. NSFNET

   B. ARPANET

   C. DoDnet

   D. DARPA

2. The primary organization behind the development of the original Internet was _____.

   A. IBM

   B. Digital Equipment Corporation (DEC)

   C. Stanford University

   D. U.S. Department of Defense

3. Which of the following was *not* a primary design concern during the development of the original Internet?

   A. Reliability

   B. Bandwidth

   C. Interoperability

   D. Support for diverse network mediums

4. Which of the following was *not* a reason TCP was a superior transport protocol to NCP?

   A. Support for global addressing

   B. Support for end-to-end checksums

   C. Support for applications such as email

   D. Support for fragmentation and reassembly

5. Which of the following OSI layers is *not* paired with the correct implementation?

    A. Layer 7—Email

    B. Layer 3—TCP

    C. Layer 4—UDP

    D. Layer 2—PPP

6. Part of the growth of the ARPANET was driven by the ability of anyone to create and disseminate information about potential protocols and applications in a particular kind of document. These documents are known as _____.

    A. Requests For Information

    B. Protocol Revisions

    C. Requests For Comments

    D. Requests For Configurations

7. ISPs connect to each other at well-defined network locations to exchange information. These connection points are known as _____.

    A. ISPs

    B. IXPs

    C. BGPs

    D. POPs

8. A company that has locations throughout the country can obtain service at each location from a Tier 1, Tier 2, or Tier 3 provider. What is one reason a company might choose to connect all locations to a Tier 1 provider despite the higher costs involved?

    A. Sites at different tiers cannot communicate.

    B. Tier 3 providers don't use TCP/IP.

    C. Only Tier 1 providers provide content.

    D. A single provider could offer SLAs to each location.

9. Which of the following services would likely be offered by a content provider but *not* a service provider?

   A. Standard dial-up service

   B. Live video streaming from sports events

   C. Email service

   D. Basic web services

10. Which of the following accurately describes the TCP protocol?

    A. Connectionless with no guarantee of delivery

    B. Connectionless with guarantee of delivery

    C. Connection-oriented with guarantee of delivery

    D. None of the above

11. Originally the IP protocol functions were performed by _____.

    A. Ethernet

    B. TCP

    C. NCP

    D. ALOHANET

12. When an HTTP packet needs to be forwarded over the Internet, which of the following accurately describes the order of the headers as they would be placed in front of each other in the packet (assume that the originating device is on an Ethernet network)?

    A. HTTP, IP, TCP, Ethernet

    B. HTTP, TCP, IP, Ethernet

    C. HTTP, UDP, IP, Ethernet

    D. HTTP, IP, Ethernet

13. A router processing the packet described in Question 12 would need to examine and/or manipulate which headers?

    A. Ethernet only

    B. IP only

    C. TCP and IP only

    D. IP and Ethernet only

14. What would a router processing the packet described in Question 12 do with the Layer 2 header of the incoming packet?

    A. Remove the source Layer 2 address, add its own, and forward the packet.

    B. Remove the Layer 2 addresses and replace them with new addresses.

    C. Remove the entire Layer 2 header and create a new one based on the next-hop interface.

    D. Leave the original Layer 2 header but forward the packet based on the destination address.

15. Most of the OSI-created protocols are no longer in use, although a few still provide some critically important functions. Which of the following describes an OSI protocol that is still in use?

    A. OSPF

    B. LDP

    C. TP0

    D. IS-IS

Chapter 2

1. Which of the following is *not* a product in the Alcatel-Lucent 7750 SR/7450 ESS family?

    A. SR-12

    B. ESS-7

    C. SR-6

    D. ESS-1

2. Which of the following statements is false regarding the Alcatel-Lucent 7450 ESS series?

    A. It supports multiple chassis types.

    B. It supports OSFP, IS-IS, RIP, and BGP.

    C. It is used primarily for Ethernet aggregation.

    D. It can be managed via a console port or a dedicated Ethernet port on the SF/CPM.

3. Which of the following descriptions is correct?

  A. bof.cfg—7750/7450 configuration file

  B. cpm.tim—IOM image file

  C. config.cfg—Back-up configuration file

  D. boot.ldr—Bootstrap image file

4. Which of the following commands is not correctly described?

  A. shutdown—This command is used to disable an interface or protocol.

  B. exit all—Logs out of the Alcatel-Lucent 7750 SR/7450 ESS device.

  C. ?—Lists all commands in the current context.

  D. [TAB]—This command is used for assistance with command completion.

5. Which of the following is not a log stream type?

  A. Audit

  B. Change

  C. Main

  D. Security

6. Which of the following descriptions of hardware for the Alcatel-Lucent 7750 SR/7450 ESS is correct?

  A. IOMs plug into MDAs.

  B. MDAs plug into SFPs.

  C. SF/CPMs plug into IOMs.

  D. IOMs plug into the chassis.

7. What file contains the system bootstrap image?

  A. boot.cfg

  B. image.ldr

  C. boot.ldr

  D. bof.cfg

8. The SF/CPM card has its own Ethernet interface for out-of-band management. This interface has its own IP address and default route. Where is this information stored?

   A. boot.ldf

   B. bof.cfg

   C. config.cfg

   D. cpm.tim

9. Which of the following correctly lists the order in which files are read by the Alcatel-Lucent 7750 SR/7450 ESS upon bootup?

   A. boot.ldr, bof.cfg, system image, config.cfg

   B. system image, boot.ldr, config.cfg, bof.cfg

   C. boot.ldr, system image, bof.cfg, config.cfg

   D. boot.ldr, bof.cfg, config.cfg, system image

10. During the boot process, an Alcatel-Lucent 7750 SR/7450 ESS checks to see if persistence is enabled. What is the purpose of persistence?

    A. To ensure that the system saves routing table information when it reboots

    B. To ensure that changes to the bof.cfg are saved

    C. To ensure synchronization with the 5620 SAM

    D. To ensure that config changes are stored in the config.cfg

11. What command would you use to enable an interface the first time you initialized an Alcatel-Lucent 7750 SR/7450 ESS?

    A. enable

    B. no shutdown

    C. interface enable

    D. interface on

12. Which of the following is the correct provisioning order you should follow when configuring an Alcatel-Lucent 7750 SR/7450 ESS for the first time?

    A. IOM, port, MDA

    B. Port, MDA, IOM

    C. IOM, MDA, port

    D. MDA, port, IOM

13. Which of the following is false regarding the logging mechanisms in the Alcatel-Lucent 7750 SR/7450 ESS?

   A. Log-ids 99 and 100 are reserved for system usage.

   B. You must configure at least one input stream for a log-id.

   C. You must configure a filter for each log-id.

   D. You must configure the destination for the events from the log-id.

14. What command would you use to display the configuration of your Alcatel-Lucent 7750 SR/7450 ESS?

   A. `show config`

   B. `admin display-config`

   C. `display config`

   D. `show admin config`

15. Which of the following values is *not* stored in the bof.cfg?

   A. The location of the primary boot image

   B. The list of IOM cards in the chassis

   C. The persist value

   D. The location of the primary config file

Chapter 3

1. Which of the following is *not* a data link layer (OSI Layer 2) protocol?

   A. Ethernet

   B. ATM

   C. Cell-Relay

   D. PPP

2. Which of the following is *not* a function of PPP?

   A. Provide support for multiple upper-layer protocols.

   B. Support the connection of multiple devices on a single link.

   C. Support authentication.

   D. Support data integrity via a CRC on frame contents.

3. Which of the following ATM AAL types is associated with an incorrect description?

   A. AAL3/4—Connection-oriented service

   B. AAL5—Connectionless service

   C. AAL2—Variable bit rate traffic

   D. AAL1—High bit rate traffic

4. Which of the following technologies ensures that a unicast packet is visible only to the device with the specific destination address?

   A. Ethernet

   B. Switched Ethernet

   C. Satellite

   D. Wireless LAN

5. The advantage of using multicast packets instead of broadcast packets is:

   A. Broadcasts are received by every host.

   B. Multicast is newer technology.

   C. Broadcasts are processed by every host.

   D. Multicast provides multiple addresses for flexibility.

6. A PPP frame has several fields that are not used, like addressing. Why do these fields exist in the frame?

   A. They are reserved for future use.

   B. They are legacy fields from older versions of PPP headers.

   C. PPP is based on the HDLC frame format.

   D. PPP can be adapted for use on multi-point networks and might need the fields.

7. ATM uses 53-byte cells, which is quite a bit smaller than the maximum Ethernet frame. What is the purpose of having such a small cell size?

   A. To support latency-sensitive applications like voice traffic

   B. To provide less overhead on ATM switches

   C. To support the use of multiple classes of service

   D. To provide the ability to do switching in hardware

8. What is the purpose of the ATM Adaptation Layer?

    A. It determines the amount of data in the cell.

    B. It maps data from upper-layer service classes to ATM cells.

    C. It adapts Ethernet frames to ATM cells.

    D. It wraps a header around the ATM cell.

9. What are the two main types of Ethernet frames?

    A. Thinnet and Thicknet

    B. 10baseT and 100baseT

    C. DIX Ethernet and Ethernet II

    D. 802.3 and Ethernet II

10. Which of the following values for the Ethertype/length fields indicates an 802.3 frame (numbers are in decimal)?

    A. 64

    B. 1540

    C. 2048

    D. 9000

11. The original Thicknet standard had a maximum cable length as well as a minimum distance for stations to tap into the cable. Based on the description of CSMA/CD, what is the most likely reason for these distance requirements?

    A. A signal might be too weak to travel farther than the maximum distance.

    B. Every station on the wire had to be able to "detect" a collision in order to function properly.

    C. Too many taps in the cable would weaken the wire.

    D. Thicknet cable came in fixed lengths.

12. An Ethernet MAC address consists of _____.

    A. A 4-byte number in four parts

    B. A 4-byte number in two parts

    C. A 6-byte number in two parts

    D. A 6-byte number in four parts

13. When an Ethernet station wants to transmit information, the process it follows is _____.

    A. Just start transmitting.

    B. Listen for other stations transmitting; if none, then begin transmitting.

    C. Transmit whenever it receives the token.

    D. Issue a transmit request, and transmit when given authorization to do so.

14. What happens when two or more Ethernet stations attempt to transmit at the same time?

    A. This is impossible on half-duplex.

    B. The signal results in a collision, the stations stop, and the stations all wait the same amount of time to retransmit.

    C. The signal results in a collision, and the stations retransmit based on a configured priority.

    D. The signal results in a collision, and the stations stop and retransmit after waiting a random amount of time.

15. Which of the following Ethernet standards is not matched correctly?

    A. 10 Mb Ethernet—Fiber or copper cable

    B. 100 Mb Ethernet—Fiber or copper cable

    C. 1 Gig Ethernet—Fiber cable only

    D. All of the above are correct.

Chapter 4

1. When a frame with an unknown destination MAC address enters a switch, the switch will forward it out which ports?

    A. None

    B. All

    C. All unicast ports

    D. All except the port that received the frame

2. The primary difference in the way Ethernet hubs and Ethernet switches handle traffic is _____.

   A. Hubs forward broadcast traffic out every port, switches do not.

   B. Switches eliminate the need for thicknet cabling.

   C. Switches support multiple physical connections to hosts.

   D. Switches forward unicast traffic only to a specific destination port.

3. Which of the following is *not* true about Link Aggregation Groups?

   A. They protect against single or multiple link failures.

   B. They can contain up to eight physical links.

   C. They can protect against a switch failure by calculating multiple paths to the root.

   D. They can be configured to enter a down state if a certain number of links in the bundle fail.

4. Which of the following is *not* true of the STP protocol?

   A. It calculates a root bridge.

   B. It uses a cost value on each port to determine the path to the root bridge.

   C. It ensures a loop-free topology.

   D. It provides load-sharing capability.

5. The advantage of using VLANs is _____.

   A. They can increase the security of your network.

   B. They can interconnect multiple broadcast domains.

   C. They can limit the amount of broadcast traffic between groups of devices.

   D. A and C but not B

6. Which of the following statements is false?

   A. Routers provide broadcast domain separation.

   B. Hubs provide collision domain separation.

   C. VLANs provide broadcast domain separation.

   D. Switches provide collision domain separation.

7. The method that LAGs use to provide load balancing is best described as:

    A. Aggregates all source/destination conversations into a single conversation equally across all links

    B. Uses the same physical link for each source/destination conversation

    C. Statistically balances conversations based on the source MAC address

    D. Distributes egress frames equally across all links in the bundle

8. Given the following code:

    ```
    Config> lag 1
    Config>lag# description "LAG from PE1 to PE2"
    Config>lag# port 1/1/1 1/1/2 1/1/3 1/1/4 1/1/5 1/1/6
    Config>lag# port threshold 2 action down
    Config>lag# dynamic-cost
    Config>lag# no shutdown
    ```

    Which answer correctly describes what happens when Ports 1/1/5 and 1/1/6 fail?

    A. Nothing because the port threshold of 2 active links has not been reached

    B. The LAG begins using equal costing across all links because of the dynamic-cost parameter.

    C. The LAG updates its BPDUs and recalculates STP.

    D. The LAG changes its OSPF cost for the bundle but takes no other action.

9. What is the primary reason that Ethernet switched networks require STP?

    A. STP provides for link backup between switches.

    B. A loop-free topology is more efficient.

    C. Redundant paths can lead to broadcast storms and FDB instability.

    D. STP updates the OSPF routing protocol cost upon link failure.

10. The mechanism that STP uses to prevent loops in an Ethernet switched network is _____.

    A. STP elects a root and selectively blocks higher cost paths to the root from each bridge.

    B. STP blocks ports on all bridges that are not the root bridge.

    C. STP proactively changes all paths to the root bridge so that they are equal cost.

    D. STP uses BPDUs to set up a virtual path between each source and destination pair.

11. What determines how the root bridge is elected?

   A. The bridge priority

   B. The MAC address of the lowest switch port

   C. The bridge priority unless there is a tie, and then the lowest MAC address

   D. The BID unless there are multiple bridge priorities that are equal

12. What distinguishes an alternate port from a back-up port in STP?

   A. The alternate port has a higher path to the root.

   B. The back-up port has a lower priority.

   C. The back-up port is used only when the alternate port fails.

   D. The back-up port is on the same switch as the designated switch.

13. Which of the following is false regarding VLANs?

   A. They provide for broadcast domain separation.

   B. A single VLAN can exist on multiple switches.

   C. They require a separate physical connection per VLAN for interswitch links.

   D. They use a 12-bit VLAN ID to identify each VLAN.

14. Which STP port state is characterized by the port accepting and recording MAC address information, but not forwarding any frames out the port?

   A. Blocking

   B. Forwarding

   C. Listening

   D. Learning

15. The technology that allows multiple customers with the same VLANs to use the same provider backbone for their Ethernet traffic is known as _____.

   A. VLAN trunking

   B. VLAN tunneling

   C. VLAN stacking

   D. IEEE 802.1p

Chapter 5

1. Which of the following is *not* a reason networks built on Ethernet alone cannot scale to a global?

   A. Excessive broadcasts would make the network unusable.

   B. Ethernet lacks hierarchical addressing.

   C. Ethernet switches cannot build forwarding tables.

   D. Ethernet cables can only be of a limited length.

2. Which of the following is true about Layer 3 addressing?

   A. It is embedded in the device's firmware.

   B. It provides for a logical hierarchy.

   C. It allows for duplicate addresses on the Internet.

   D. Addresses are not required to be registered if they are used on the Internet.

3. Which of the following is *not* true about an IP packet?

   A. The TTL field ensures that IP packets have a limited lifetime.

   B. The maximum size is 65,535 octets.

   C. The total length field includes the IP header.

   D. The current version is IPv5.

4. Which of the following is a valid host IP address?

   A. 192.168.300.4

   B. 255.70.1.1

   C. 224.0.0.1

   D. 10.254.1.1

5. An IP address has a first octet represented in binary as 11000001; the equivalent in decimal is _____.

   A. 190

   B. 193

   C. 192

   D. 11,000,001

6. The address 224.100.1.1 under traditional *classful* addressing would be _____.

   A. Class A

   B. Class B

   C. Class C

   D. None of the above

7. Which of the following is *not* a private address?

   A. 172.18.20.4

   B. 10.0.1.1

   C. 200.1.1.254

   D. 192.168.0.1

8. Which of the following is *not* a reason that subnetting is superior to class-based addressing?

   A. It reduces the Internet routing table size.

   B. You can identify the host portion of the address without the need for a mask.

   C. It creates greater internal address flexibility.

   D. It allows for more efficient use of address space.

9. Given a network address of 192.168.100.0/24, what is the maximum number of subnets you can create if each subnet must support at least seven hosts?

   A. 16

   B. 32

   C. 4

   D. 8

10. If your network address is 10.1.0.0/16 and you have subnetworks that all support at least 300 hosts, how many subnets do you have?

   A. 255

   B. 64

   C. 100

   D. 128

11. Which of the following is the correct representation of mask 255.192.0.0?

   A. /8

   B. /11

   C. /10

   D. /16

12. A network with a /30 mask allows you to have how many usable host addresses?

   A. 4

   B. 2

   C. 6

   D. 0

13. Given the address 10.1.1.0/24, the most correct description of 10.1.1.0 is _____.

   A. Host 0 on the 10.1.1.0 subnet

   B. Network 10.1.1.0

   C. Illegal because 10.0.0.0 is a Class A

   D. Subnet 10.1.1.0

14. The concept of allowing a single route entry to represent many network addresses is known as _____.

   A. CIDR

   B. Route aggregation

   C. VLSM

   D. Classless addressing

15. How many subnets can be created from network 10.0.0.0/8 if each subnet must support at least 31 hosts?

   A. 2^{16}

   B. 2^{18}

   C. 2^{19}

   D. 2^{24}

16. Given network 175.100.0.0/16, if you create four subnets, how many addresses are available on each subnet?

 A. 16,384

 B. 4,096

 C. 16,382

 D. 4,094

17. What is the correct "all hosts" broadcast address for subnet 10.15.0.0/17?

 A. 10.15.255.255

 B. 10.15.0.255

 C. 10.15.127.255

 D. 10.15.128.255

18. Which of the following is *not* allowed?

 A. subnet 10.0.0.0/16

 B. subnet 10.255.0.0/16

 C. subnet 10.10.10.0/16

 D. host 10.10.10.0/32

19. Given network 135.100.0.0/16, you need nine subnets, and of these nine, one subnet needs to be split into 13 additional subnets. Choose the most likely masks you would create for this.

 A. /20 for the first eight subnets, /23 for the remaining 13

 B. /20 for the first eight subnets, /24 for the remaining 13

 C. /24 for all subnets

 D. /19 for the first eight subnets, /24 for the remaining 13

20. Given network 176.200.0.0/16 and a subnet that supports 4,387 hosts, what is the most likely mask for the subnet?

 A. /20

 B. /17

 C. /21

 D. /19

Chapter 6

1. Which of the following is a function not performed by a router when forwarding an IP packet?

   A. Verify the IP header checksum.

   B. Decrement the TTL and ensure that it is not zero.

   C. Send a "received" message to the originating router.

   D. Remove the existing L2 header and creates a new L2 header before forwarding the IP packet to its next destination.

2. Which of the following highlights the differences between a traditional home user network and the modern home user network?

   A. Traditional home networks did not use routers.

   B. Modern home networks can use wireless access points.

   C. Modern home networks make use of a variety of new services such as Video on Demand and IP telephony.

   D. Traditional home networks did not rely on the IP protocol.

3. In a typical home network, when a PC needs to send an IP packet to a destination on the Internet, it first sends the packet to _____.

   A. The designated router

   B. The cable modem

   C. The router indicated in its BGP table

   D. The default gateway

4. Which of the following statements regarding NAT is false?

   A. NAT is used for many-to-one translations.

   B. NAT is intended to alleviate the need for every home user device to have a public IP address.

   C. NAT typically makes use of private IP addressing.

   D. A NAT router maintains a translation database to perform the address conversions.

5. The process by which a home user's router requests and receives a public IP address from its service provider is known as _____.

   A. ARP

   B. DHCP

   C. ICMP

   D. OSPF

6. Which of the following is false about the DHCP process?

   A. The client broadcasts a discover message looking for DHCP servers.

   B. All DHCP servers will broadcast an offer message.

   C. A client will send a unicast accept message to the first DHCP server it receives a response from.

   D. All of the above statements are true.

7. The ping application relies on two common ICMP message types. Which answer is *not* one of these types?

   A. The echo receive ICMP type.

   B. The echo request ICMP type.

   C. The echo reply ICMP type.

   D. None of the above are ICMP message types used by ping.

8. Which of the following is true regarding ICMP `destination unreachable` messages?

   A. They are sent after failure to receive an Ethernet ACK.

   B. They are created by routers that cannot deliver an IP packet to its destination.

   C. They rely on the use of ICMP echo replies.

   D. They are originated by hosts that are about to reboot.

9. Which of the following is not usually involved in the ARP process when a host needs to send an IP packet to another host not on its own IP subnet?

   A. The host needs to determine based on its mask that the destination host is not on its local subnet.

   B. The host will issue an ARP request for the MAC address of its default gateway if it is not in its ARP cache.

C. The default gateway will determine if it needs to issue an ARP request for the destination host .

D. The default gateway will issue an ARP request for the MAC address of the originating host .

10. Which of the following is false regarding IP filters?

  A. IP filters are not required on a router interface.

  B. IP filters can filter on both IP addresses and upper-layer protocol port numbers.

  C. IP filters will automatically permit IP packets by default unless otherwise configured.

  D. Only one ingress and one egress filter can be applied per interface.

11. Which of the following is *not* a match criteria that can be used with IP filters?

  A. Source or destination IP address

  B. Source or destination port number

  C. ICMP message type

  D. Originating host name

12. Which of the following is *not* a valid IP filter command?

  A. `ip-filter 10 create`

  B. `default-action discard`

  C. `entry 1 create`

  D. `match dst-ip 10.5.1.0/24`

13. Which of the following IP filter entries would match packets from network 11.1.1.0/24 to host 5.1.1.1?

  A. `match src-ip 11.1.1.0/24`

  B. `match dst-ip 5.1.1.1/32`

  C. A and B together

  D. None of the above

14. You are creating a filter to permit packets to destination IP address 192.168.1.1/32. You want all other packets to be dropped. Which of the following commands is *not* required to support this policy?

   A. `ip-filter 1 create`

   B. `default-action drop`

   C. `entry 1 create`

   D. `match dst-ip 192.168.1.1/32`

15. Which of the following is *not* displayed with the use of the `show filter` command?

   A. The filter's default action

   B. The interfaces where the filter is applied

   C. The number of ingress and egress matches

   D. The entries in the filter

Chapter 7

1. Which of the following is *not* a transport layer protocol?

   A. TP4

   B. TCP

   C. RTP

   D. UDP

2. Which of the following statements about transport layer protocols is false?

   A. Most Internet applications use a transport layer protocol.

   B. Transport layer protocols can provide both reliable and unreliable services.

   C. Transport layer protocols provide end-to-end services for applications.

   D. Transport layer protocols require additional software be added to your operating system.

3. Which of the following is *not* a characteristic of the TCP protocol?

   A. Reliable data transfer

   B. Connectionless operation

   C. Flow control supported

   D. Full-duplex operation

4. Which of the following is *not* a characteristic of the UDP protocol?

   A. Reliable data transfer

   B. Connectionless operation

   C. No flow control

   D. Appropriate for real-time traffic

5. Which of the following TCP flags is *not* matched with the correct definition?

   A. SYN—Indicates the start of a TCP connection.

   B. ACK—Acknowledges that a TCP segment has been received.

   C. FIN—Indicates the closing of a TCP session.

   D. RST—Re-sets the sequence numbers for a TCP session.

6. A TCP sequence or acknowledgment number consists of _____ bits.

   A. 30

   B. 64

   C. 24

   D. 32

7. After a client initiates a connection request to a server with the SYN bit set, the server usually responds with a packet that has the _____ bit set.

   A. SYN

   B. ACK

   C. SYN and ACK

   D. SYN, ACK, and URG

8. Which of the following TCP bits is set to indicate that an application wishes to close an open connection?

   A. RST

   B. FIN

   C. URG

   D. ACK

9. When operating in slow start mode, which of the following describes the mechanisms to throttle the amount of data sent?

   A. The receiver's advertised window size

   B. The sender's congestion window and the sender's advertised window size

   C. The sender's congestion window and the receiver's advertised window size

   D. The maximum segment size and the URG pointer

10. Which of the following are possible mechanisms by which a TCP sending process could recognize that packets it sent to a receiver had been dropped by the network?

    A. An RSND bit from the receiving TCP process

    B. Duplicate ACK numbers

    C. An advertised window size of 0

    D. An ICMP source quench message

11. Given the values MSS=1000 bytes, cwnd value=6, window size=5000, and sender's SN=5000, what will be the ACK number from the receiving station after the sender sends its next set of segments to the receiving station?

    A. 6000

    B. 11001

    C. 11000

    D. 10000

12. Which of the following types of applications would be least likely to use the UDP protocol?

    A. A "request-response" application

    B. An application that is sensitive to packet loss

    C. An application that is sensitive to delay

    D. A real-time application

13. TCP provides many advanced features missing from UDP. Which of the following is an advantage that UDP has over TCP?

    A. It provides reliable data transfer.

    B. It can recover gracefully from packet loss.

    C. It reacts to network congestion.

    D. It adds little overhead to the data transfer.

14. Which of the following is least likely to be used as an ephemeral port?

    A. 1025

    B. 53212

    C. 1487

    D. 65938

15. DNS is a unique protocol in terms of its transport selection because simple name lookups use UDP, while "zone transfers" that transfer a large amount of name resolution information from one DNS server to another use TCP. What is the least likely reason for using this approach?

    A. Name lookups are simple request-response.

    B. TCP is a reliable protocol.

    C. An unreliable zone transfer could result in serious name resolution discrepancies in a network.

    D. UDP cannot be used for bulk file transfers.

Chapter 8

1. An IP router normally uses which of the following pieces of information to forward an IP packet?

    A. The destination IP address only

    B. The source and destination IP address

    C. The destination IP address and the destination TCP port

    D. The destination IP address, the TTL, and the ToS

2. The two main categories of routing protocols are IGP and _____.

   A. OSPF

   B. Link state

   C. BGP

   D. EGP

3. Which of the following is *not* a characteristic of an IGP?

   A. It is intended for networks under a common administrative control.

   B. It is used between ASes.

   C. There are not as many policy enforcement features as an EGP.

   D. It includes distance vector and link state protocols.

4. A router can run multiple routing protocols that each have their own table of routing information. A router selects the best route for each destination from all routing sources and puts them in the _____.

   A. Routing Link Database

   B. Routing Information Base

   C. Routing Table

   D. ARP Table

5. Which of the following pairings is *not* correct?

   A. EGP—BGP4

   B. Link state—OSPF

   C. IGP—RIP

   D. Distance vector—IS-IS

6. In which situation would you be most likely to use a static default route?

   A. In small networks

   B. On links with only a single path to other routers

   C. When you have older routers

   D. On a low-bandwidth link

7. It is said that distance vector protocols have a longer convergence time than link state protocols. What is the most likely reason for this?

   A. Link state protocols send less information.

   B. Link state protocols keep track of neighbors via Hello updates.

   C. The shortest path algorithm is much faster to calculate than the calculation performed by a distance vector protocol.

   D. Distance vector protocols rely on updates only from neighbors.

8. There are many advantages of link state protocols over distance vector protocols. Which of the following is a potential advantage of distance vector?

   A. Distance vector sends its entire routing table in updates.

   B. Distance vector does not require extensive processing to build the routing table.

   C. Distance vector sends updates at timed intervals.

   D. Distance vector relies on neighbors to report routing updates.

9. When a link state router receives an LSP update, it uses what algorithm to calculate its routing table?

   A. OSPF

   B. Spanning tree

   C. SPF

   D. Least cost

10. Which of the following is most likely to be used for forwarding IP packets from a stub network?

   A. A static route

   B. A default route

   C. A floating static route

   D. OSPF with the "stub area" feature

11. The forwarding of packets on a router is a function of the data plane. The use of a routing protocol to build routing tables is a function of _____.

   A. The routing plane

   B. The control plane

   C. The OSPF plane

   D. The protocol plane

12. Link state protocols flood LSP information throughout the network to each router. These LSPs are stored in _____.

   A. The routing table

   B. The FIB

   C. The routing database

   D. The link state database

13. If there are multiple identical network prefixes advertised by different routing protocols, the Routing Table Manager chooses the route to place in the routing table based on _____.

   A. It enters a route based on the lowest metric value.

   B. It enters a route based on the highest preference value.

   C. It enters a route based on the lowest preference value.

   D. It enters a route for each protocol in the routing table.

14. Using a link state protocol, which of the following best describes the view each router has of all the links in the network after all LSPs have been flooded?

   A. Each router has a common view of the network.

   B. Each router has a unique view of the network based on its location.

   C. Each router knows about only those LSPs originated from its neighbors.

   D. Each router knows about all LSPs but uses only LSPs from its neighbors to construct its view.

15. Which of the following is the most accurate explanation of the information a distance vector routing protocol sends to neighboring routers?

    A. It sends Hello updates.

    B. It sends its entire routing table.

    C. It floods LSPs.

    D. It sends its entire routing table and its neighbors' routing tables.

Chapter 9

1. OSPF discovers neighbors _____.

    A. Only by manually configuring the router

    B. By flooding updates

    C. Using Hello advertisements

    D. Using a host table

2. Which of the following is *not* a feature of the OSPF protocol?

    A. It supports authentication.

    B. It provides a loop-free topology.

    C. It uses the Shortest Path First algorithm.

    D. It uses a hop count–based metric.

3. Which logical interface is recommended for defining a router ID?

    A. Ethernet interface

    B. Chassis interface

    C. MAC address

    D. System interface

4. What is the primary purpose of the OSPF router ID?

    A. To elect a designated router

    B. To uniquely identify an OSPF router

    C. To trace sequence numbers

    D. To support LSA flooding

5. LSA updates are sent in response to network changes and _____.

   A. Every 30 minutes

   B. After the Hello timer expires

   C. When the DR detects the BDR has failed

   D. Every 30 minutes provided new information needs to be transmitted

6. What does it mean to say that two OSPF routers are *adjacent?*

   A. The routers are physically connected on a point-to-point link.

   B. The routers are on a common network segment and have exchanged database information.

   C. The routers have exchanged Hello packets.

   D. The routers are in a single area.

7. What is required for OSPF routers on a point-to-point network to form an adjacency?

   A. The DR must form an adjacency first.

   B. The neighbor IP address must be configured.

   C. They will automatically become adjacent provided certain OSPF configuration values match.

   D. Nothing. OSPF routers on point-to-point links will always become adjacent.

8. Which of the following hello packet values is *not* involved in the adjacency process on point-to-point links?

   A. The area ID

   B. The priority

   C. The Hello timer

   D. The dead timer

9. In addition to having correct OSPF settings in the Hello packets, another value that can prevent routers from forming an adjacency in the event of a mismatch is _____.

   A. The AS number

   B. The OSPF MTU

   C. The OSPF metric

   D. The MPLS TE

10. The command to display the Link State Updates that a router has received is _____.

A. `show router ospf status`

B. `show router ospf links`

C. `show router ospf summary`

D. `show router ospf database`

11. There are many different types of LSAs in OSPF. The most common LSA type in point-to-point networks is _____.

A. The area LSA

B. The router LSA

C. The network LSA

D. The summary LSA

12. If an OSPF router receives an LSA with a sequence number that is *equal* to the sequence number it already has for that LSA, it will _____.

A. Silently drop the LSA.

B. Send a rejection notice to the sending router.

C. Drop the LSA and send an acknowledgement.

D. Drop the LSA and forward it to its adjacent routers.

13. Which of the following is false regarding the Shortest Path First algorithm that OSPF uses?

A. It determines the optimal route to each network.

B. It creates a loop-free path to each network.

C. It is run only on the router that originates an LSA update.

D. It runs every time a new LSA is received.

14. Which of the following correctly identifies the order of steps for two OSPF routers to become fully adjacent?

A. Exchange, Loading, SPF, Adjacent

B. Exchange, ExStart, Loading

C. ExStart, Exchange, Loading, Full

D. ExStart, Exchange, Loading, Adjacent

15. Which of the following default metrics is *not* correct for the given interface speed?

    A. 1 Gbps link = 100

    B. 16 Mbps link = 6,250

    C. 1.544 Mbps link = 64,766

    D. 622 Mbps link = 16

Chapter 10

1. The primary purpose of an EGP is to _____.

    A. Handle large routing tables.

    B. Distribute routing information between ASes.

    C. Support routing inside a large enterprise network.

    D. Provide a default route to the Internet.

2. Which of the following is false regarding ASes?

    A. The assignment of public AS numbers is controlled by RIRs.

    B. 65,001 is a private AS number.

    C. An IGP is required for routing within the AS.

    D. The AS usually contain routers under the control of different administrative groups.

3. Which logical interface is preferred for creating internal BGP sessions?

    A. Ethernet interface

    B. Chassis interface

    C. MAC address

    D. System interface

4. Which of the following is true regarding BGP neighbors?

    A. They can be discovered automatically.

    B. They need to be directly connected.

    C. They can be in the same or different AS.

    D. Not all internal BGP speakers need to have the same information about routes outside the AS.

5. Two BGP routers configured as neighbors communicate using _____.

   A. TCP on a variable port

   B. UDP on a fixed port

   C. TCP on a fixed port

   D. IP using a fixed protocol

6. The primary purpose of iBGP is _____.

   A. To ensure that routers inside an AS have a common view of networks outside the AS

   B. To ensure that the IGP has multiple exit points from an AS

   C. To serve as back-up routers to eBGP

   D. To exchange routes with external ASes

7. By default, BGP will choose the best path to a given network destination based on _____.

   A. The sum of the interface speeds to a destination

   B. The shortest AS path

   C. The AS that is configured with special non-discretionary attributes

   D. The AS that re-distributed the route from OSPF into BGP

8. Once BGP peers establish a connection, they send routing updates to each other using _____.

   A. A keep alive message

   B. A next-hop update

   C. An update message

   D. A networks message

9. By looking only at the BGP configuration statements on two routers, you can tell if they are iBGP peers or eBGP peers because _____.

   A. The statement says iBGP or eBGP.

   B. The statement contains the word *internal* or *external*.

   C. Internal peering statements are configured separately.

   D. The AS number is associated with each peer statement.

10. The command to display the status of your BGP process is _____.

  A. `show router bgp process`

  B. `show router bgp summary`

  C. `show router bgp info`

  D. `show router bgp status`

11. In the event that a previously advertised network becomes unreachable, BGP will _____.

  A. Advertise the route with a null AS-path.

  B. Tear down the peer connection.

  C. Send a withdraw message.

  D. Update its route table but take no other action.

12. In which of the following situations would you be least likely to use BGP?

  A. A service provider with multiple connections to other providers

  B. An enterprise with multiple connections to the same ISP

  C. An enterprise with multiple connections to different ISPs

  D. A service provider with a single connection to a higher-level ISP

13. The three well-known mandatory attributes in BGP are _____.

  A. Origin, AS-path, and community

  B. AS-path, community, and next-hop

  C. AS-path, peer, and next-hop

  D. AS-path, origin, and next-hop

14. A BGP router usually does not need to receive a full Internet routing table if _____.

  A. It is the single exit point for an AS.

  B. It is one of several exit points from an AS.

  C. It is part of a transit AS.

  D. It is providing updates to downstream providers.

15. All of the following are reasons that using BGP between ASes is preferable to using IGP route re-distribution except _____.

    A. Route re-distribution loses the metrics of the original IGP.

    B. Route re-distribution can lead to routing loops.

    C. BGP provides a consistent interface for route exchange across various ASes.

    D. Route re-distribution provides for greater policy control.

Chapter 11

1. Which of the following accurately describes a P device?

    A. It is used exclusively by the customer.

    B. It is responsible for adding and removing labels.

    C. It swaps label information and forwards packets.

    D. It creates an LSP in the provider network.

2. Which of the following is false regarding an SDP?

    A. It provides transport tunnel encapsulation.

    B. It is specific to a single service.

    C. The SDP ID is locally unique.

    D. LDP can be used as the signaling protocol.

3. Which of the following is *not* an accurate description of a VPN?

    A. A series of point-to-point tunnels configured on client equipment

    B. A tunnel technology created in a provider network

    C. A function of MPLS networks to create private communities of users

    D. Any network that includes encryption

4. Which of the following is false regarding LDP?

    A. It is used to define unidirectional paths through the network.

    B. It is a protocol specifically intended for label distribution.

    C. It is the only method for distributing labels in an MPLS network.

    D. It describes a path through the MPLS network based on the IGP path.

5. Which of the following term–definition pairs is incorrect?
   A. Push—Add a label
   B. Swap—Replace a label
   C. Label distribution protocol—Series of labels and next-hop interfaces
   D. Pop—Remove a label

6. The most commonly used label distribution protocol is _____.
   A. OSPF
   B. BGP
   C. LDP
   D. RIP

7. Which of the following is *not* a type of VPN?
   A. VPWS
   B. VPNM
   C. VPLS
   D. VPRN

8. A VPN that provides a simple point-to-point service between two destinations is a _____.
   A. VPNM
   B. VPLS
   C. VPWS
   D. None of the above

9. The VPN service that must maintain a table of MAC addresses is _____.
   A. VPWS
   B. VPLS
   C. VPRN
   D. Both A and B

10. The VPN service that requires encryption is _____.
   A. VPRN

B. VPNM

C. VPLS

D. None of the above

11. The VPN service that appears to the customer as a private routed network is _____.

   A. VPNM

   B. VPRN

   C. VPLS

   D. VPWS

12. As a packet traverses an MPLS network, it passes through a router that removes one label and replaces it with another. The router it passed through was a _____ router.

   A. PE

   B. CE

   C. LER

   D. P

13. A packet arrives at a router with a label, and the router cannot perform any operations on it. The router is most likely a _____.

   A. LSR

   B. PE

   C. LER

   D. None of the above

14. In an MPLS network, the customer routers have no knowledge of how the MPLS features are implemented. The benefits of this include _____.

   A. It makes CE configuration easier.

   B. It allows for very scalable VPN solutions.

   C. It lowers CE management overhead.

   D. All of the above

15. The relationship between LDP and an IGP is best described as

    A. LDP paths are preferred over IGP routes.

    B. LDP uses IGP next-hop information.

    C. LDP re-distributes labels into IGP.

    D. IGP tags network destinations with LDP information.

Answers to Assessment Questions

Chapter 1

1. B. ARPANET

   NSFNET was the follow-on network, DARPA is an organization, and DoDnet does not exist.

2. D. The U.S. Department of Defense

   All of the other answers are incorrect.

3. B. Bandwidth

   The network needed to support diverse systems in a reliable manner over diverse media. There was not a great need for large amounts of bandwidth.

4. C. Support for applications such as email

   NCP provided support for applications like email; it did not provide any of the features in the other answers.

5. B. Layer 3-TCP

   TCP is a Layer 4 protocol. The other answers are incorrect.

6. C. Requests For Comments

   The other answers are incorrect.

7. B. IXPs

   The other answers don't address the question.

8. D. A single provider could offer SLAs to each location.

   A single provider can offer SLAs because the traffic would be contained entirely within its own network; other providers can provide the services in the other answers.

9. B. Live video streaming from sports events

Live streaming video for sports events would clearly fall into the *content* scope of services. The other services are all commonly offered by all service providers.

10. C. Connection-oriented with guarantee of delivery

"Connection-oriented with guarantee of delivery" describes the basic functions of using TCP. The other answers are incorrect.

11. B. TCP

Originally the functions of both TCP and IP were in a single TCP protocol.

12. B. HTTP, TCP, IP, Ethernet

The headers are placed in front of each other in order of the protocol stack from the highest layer down, so the order would be application, Layer 4 (TCP), Layer 3 (IP), and then Layer 2 (Ethernet).

13. D. IP and Ethernet only

A router would remove the Ethernet (Layer 2) header, examine the IP (Layer 3) address to determine how to forward the packet, and then replace the Layer 2 header for the appropriate next-hop interface.

14. C. Remove the entire Layer 2 header and create a new one based on the next-hop interface.

Answer B is incorrect because the next-hop interface might be a different layer technology so the router cannot simply replace addresses; it must create a new Layer 2 header. The other answers don't describe the forwarding process correctly.

15. D. IS-IS

IS-IS is a routing protocol developed by the ISO that is still in use in many provider networks. The other answers are either not ISO protocols or are no longer in use.

Chapter 2

1. C. SR-6

This is not a product in the SR line; the SR line contains SR-12, SR-7, and SR-1.

2. B. It supports OSPF, IS-IS, RIP, and BGP.

The Alcatel-Lucent 7450 ESS is designed primarily as an Ethernet aggregation point and so it does not support provider protocols like BGP.

3. D. boot.ldr—Bootstrap image file

This is the only correct pairing.

4. B. `exit all`—Logs out of the Alcatel-Lucent 7750 SR/7450 ESS device.

The `exit all` command takes you to the root context but does not log you out.

5. A. Audit

This is not a valid log stream type.

6. D. IOMs plug into the chassis.

An IOM card supports two MDAs that provide the physical ports for a chassis.

7. C. boot.ldr

This is the file that contains the bootstrap image, and it is the first file that is read upon system startup.

8. B. bof.cfg

The bof.cfg stores the boot file configuration parameters such as the Ethernet management IP, the location of the config file, and the system image file.

9. A. boot.ldr, bof.cfg, system image, config.cfg

This is the correct order.

10. C. To ensure synchronization with the 5620 SAM

The persistence option is only needed if the 5620 SAM is used to manage your Alcatel-Lucent device.

11. B. `no shutdown`

By default, all the ports and cards on an Alcatel-Lucent 7750 SR/7450 ESS are down and need to have the `no shutdown` command used to enable them.

12. C. IOM, MDA, port

This is the correct provisioning order.

13. C. You must configure a filter for each log-id.

Configuration of a filter for a log-id is optional.

14. B. `admin display-config`

This is used to show the configuration of your Alcatel-Lucent device.

15. B. The list of IOM cards in the chassis

This value is not stored in the bof.cfg.

Chapter 3

1. C. Cell-Relay

   There is no protocol called *Cell-Relay*; the other answers are all Data Link protocols.

2. B. Support the connection of multiple devices on a single link.

   There is an address field, but it is not used as there is no need for addressing on a point-to-point link.

3. D. AAL1—High bit rate traffic

   AAL1 is constant bit rate traffic.

4. B. Switched Ethernet

   An Ethernet switch will forward the frame to the correct port based on a destination address in its FDB; all the other technologies broadcast all frames to all devices.

5. C. Broadcasts are processed by every host.

   Depending on the switch technology in use, multicast packets might also be received by every host, but every host would not *process* the multicast packets if they are not in the multicast group. Every device must strip the Ethernet header and examine the contents of the upper layers of a broadcast to determine if the packet is intended for it or not. This is a major disadvantage for broadcast traffic.

6. C. PPP is based on the HDLC frame format.

   The HDLC protocol used the fields that PPP does not, and the fields are a legacy of this.

7. A. To support latency-sensitive applications like voice traffic

   This is the primary factor behind the small size of the cells. The other answers don't address the core reason for the size of the cells.

8. B. It maps data from upper-layer service classes to ATM cells.

   ATM supports many classes of service, but data from upper-layer protocols must be mapped to the 53-byte ATM cells For example, IP datagrams are encapsulated in an AAL5 frame, which is then encapsulated in individual ATM cells.

9. D. 802.3 and Ethernet II

   These are the two main types of Ethernet frames. The other answers are incorrect.

10. A. 64

A value less than 1536 indicates an 802.3 frame.

11. B. Every station on the wire had to be able to "detect" a collision in order to function properly.

Based on our description of CSMA/CD, it is implied that each station needs to be able to determine when other stations are transmitting, which means that each station needs to be within a certain distance of other stations so that the electrical signals can reach it in no more than a fixed amount of time.

12. C. A 6-byte number in two parts

The two parts are the vendor OUI and the vendor-chosen hardware address.

13. B. Listen for other stations transmitting; if none, then begin transmitting.

This is a brief description of the "carrier sense multiple access" part of the CSMA/CD protocol.

14. D. The signal results in a collision, and the stations stop and retransmit after waiting a random amount of time.

This is a brief description of how Ethernet stations retransmit after collision. They wait a random amount of time to try to ensure that the same stations don't transmit at the same time again.

15. C. 1 Gig Ethernet—Fiber cable only

Gigabit Ethernet can run over copper cabling as well.

Chapter 4

1. D. All except the port that received the frame

This is how switches work until they build up their FDB.

2. D. Switches forward unicast traffic only to a specific destination port.

This is opposed to hubs that act like a "wire in a box" and forward frames out every port. Both hubs and switches forward broadcast traffic out all ports.

3. C. They can protect against a switch failure by calculating multiple paths to the root.

This is a description of STP, not LAG.

4. D. It provides load-sharing capability.

   STP cannot provide load-sharing because only a single path exists between each segment and the root bridge to avoid loops.

5. D. A and C but not B

   VLANs do not provide routing between broadcast domains although they do create separate broadcast domains.

6. B. Hubs provide collision domain separation.

   Hubs simply forward all frames out all ports and so do not provide collision domain separation.

7. B. Uses the same physical link for each source/destination conversation.

   This method is used to ensure that there is no frame reordering as required by the 802.3ad standard.

8. D. The LAG changes its OSPF cost for the bundle but takes no other action.

   This is because the "dynamic-cost" option is configured on the bundle so that each time a link fails, the OSPF cost is updated. No other action is taken because the threshold is 2 and there are still four out of six active links functioning.

9. C. Redundant paths can lead to broadcast storms and FDB instability.

   This describes the problem of loops in a switched network, which is the primary reason to use STP.

10. A. STP elects a root and selectively blocks higher cost paths to the root from each bridge.

    This is an accurate description of the way STP functions to prevent loops.

11. C. The bridge priority unless there is a tie, and then the lowest MAC address

    This is an accurate description of how a root bridge is selected. Answer D is wrong because the BID is always used to determine the root bridge (note the *unless* qualifier). In fact, answer C describes what the BID is: bridge priority plus MAC address.

12. D. The back-up port is on the same switch as the designated switch.

    The alternate port is on a non-designated switch on the same segment.

13. C. They require a separate physical connection per VLAN for interswitch links.

    This is not true if a VLAN trunk is used between the switches.

14. D. Learning

In this state, the bridge learns information about MAC addresses but does not yet forward frames.

15. C. VLAN stacking

VLAN stacking allows a provider to stack its own VLAN information in front of the customer's VLAN information to support customers with overlapping VLANs.

Chapter 5

1. C. Ethernet switches cannot build forwarding tables.

Ethernet switches, in fact, do build FDB tables of MAC addresses. The other answers are all factors that prevent Ethernet from creating global networks.

2. B. It provides for a logical hierarchy.

This is one of the main reasons that IP can support global networks—the use of hierarchical addressing.

3. D. The current version is IPv5.

The current version is IPv4, and the next version is IPv6.

4. D. 10.254.1.1

10.254.1.1 is the only valid host address. The other addresses are either out of supported IP address ranges, are in the broadcast range (255), or are multicast (224).

5. B. 193

Calculate this as $2^8 + 2^7 + 2^0 = 128 + 64 + 1 = 193$.

6. D. None of the above

This is a Class D or multicast address. You can tell this by examining the first octet in binary: 224 = 128 + 64 + 32 = 11100000. The first 3 bits are 1, so this indicates that it is a Class D address.

7. C. 200.1.1.254

The private address ranges are 10.0.0.0/8, 172.16.0.0/12, and 192.168.0.0/16.

8. B. You can identify the host portion of the address without the need for a mask.

This is true for classful addressing, but not for classless addressing. Using classless addressing, you need the subnet mask to determine how many bits are used for the subnet and how many for the host.

9. **A. 16**

If you need seven hosts per subnet, this means that you need to leave at least 4 bits for each subnet because $2^4 - 2 = 14$ available hosts. This leaves 4 bits ($8 - 4 = 4$) for the subnet, which means you can have $2^4 = 16$ subnets. 3 bits for each subnet is not sufficient because two addresses (all zeros and all ones) cannot be used.

10. **D. 128**

The trick here is recognizing that if you need 300 hosts per subnet, then you need to use more than 8 bits of the IP address for hosts because you can only have 255 max hosts for an 8-bit octet. If you borrow one of the bits from the third octet, this gives you a maximum of 510 hosts, and leaves 7 bits of the third octet for subnets. $2^7 = 128$, so you can have 128 subnets.

11. **C. /10**

The key here is to remember that 255 means "all 1s," so you know that the first octet has all the bits used and therefore the mask is at least /8. 192 translates into the highest 2 bits of the next octet: $2^7 + 2^6 = 128 + 64 = 192$, so this means that 10 bits are used so the subnet mask is /10.

12. **B. 2**

The key here is "usable" host addresses. A /30 leaves 2 bits for hosts, which would translate into $2^2 = 4$. However, the 0 host is the subnet address and the "all 1s" host is the broadcast, so those addresses cannot be used. This leaves only two usable host addresses.

13. **D. subnet 10.1.1.0**

B is not as correct because technically 10.1.1.0 is a subnet of network 10.0.0.0.

14. **B. Route aggregation**

CIDR is a technology that implements route aggregation, but the question asks what the "concept" is called, and the concept is route aggregation.

15. **B. 2^{18}**

The key is to determine how many bits are available for subnetting. We know we need 31 hosts, so we know we need at least 5 bits because $2^5 = 32$. However, we lose 2 bits for each subnet for the subnet and broadcast address, so we actually need 6 bits for the hosts because using 5 bits would only give us 30 hosts per subnet. Since there are 24 total available bits for subnets on network 10.0.0.0/8, $24 - 6$ host bits = 18 subnet bits, and $2^{18} = 262,144$ available subnets.

16. C. 16,382

If there are four subnets, that means we have used 2 of the available host bits because $2^2 = 4$. This leaves $16 - 2 = 14$ bits for subnets, and $2^{14} - 2 = 16,382$.

17. C. 10.15.127.255

Using a /17 means that we have used 1 bit for the subnet, leaving 7 bits in the third octet. The "all 1s" means to set all of those bits to 1 and all the bits in the last octet to 1. This means that the last octet is 255 (8 bits set to 1) and the 3rd octet is 127 (highest bit is $2^7 = 128$, so $255 - 128 = 127$).

18. C. subnet 10.10.10.0/16

This value cannot be used as a subnet address since the host portion is not all zeros. The other network addresses given all have the host portion all zeros. Any valid address can be used as a host address.

19. B. /20 for the first eight subnets, /24 for the remaining 13

Because nine subnets are needed, we need to use 4 bits of the host address in the third octet because $2^4 = 16$ possible subnets (3 bits would only yield eight subnets). Then we need 13 more subnets, which means we need to take another 4 bits to give us 16 more possible subnets ($2^4 = 16$). This means we need $16 + 4 = /20$ for the first eight subnets and $16 + 4 + 4 = /24$ for the remaining 13 subnets.

20. D. /19

We need to determine how many bits are needed to support 4,387 hosts. We know that using 8 bits gives us 255 hosts (all 1s for a single octet). If we double this by using an additional bit, that gives us 510 hosts; double again gives 1,020; double again gives us 2,040; double again gives us 4,080; and double again gives us 8,160. We had to double five times to get the desired number of hosts, which means we had to take 5 bits + original 8 bits = 13 total bits for hosts from the available 16 (/16 was the original network). This leaves 3 bits left for subnetting ($16 - 13 = 3$), so /16 + 3 bits = /19 subnet mask.

Chapter 6

1. C. Send a "received" message to the originating router.

IP does not guarantee delivery and does not attempt to inform the transmitting router that packets have been received. Acknowledgement and recovery from packet drops is performed by higher layer protocols.

2. C. Modern home networks make use of a variety of new services such as Video on Demand and IP telephony.

Traditional home networks used only basic services such as Web browsing and email.

3. D. The default gateway

A default gateway is the IP forwarding device that end-user IP devices send data to for routing on the Internet.

4. A. NAT is used for many-to-one translations.

PAT is used for many-to-one translations, while NAT is used for one-to-one translations.

5. B. DHCP

This is the protocol used to receive a dynamic IP address for a home router.

6. C. A client will send a unicast message to the first DHCP server it receives a response from.

The response is actually a broadcast message so that any other DHCP servers know they were not chosen by the requesting device.

7. A. The echo receive ICMP type.

This is not an ICMP message type.

8. B. They are created by routers that cannot deliver an IP packet to its destination.

The `destination unreachable` message is intended to inform the source host that the destination address is unavailable.

9. D. The default gateway will issue an ARP request for the MAC address of the originating host.

This is not necessary because the default gateway will cache this data based on the information in the original ARP request from the originating host.

10. C. IP filters will automatically permit IP packets by default unless otherwise configured.

The default action for an IP filter is to discard packets.

11. D. Originating host name

This is because the host name is not part of an IP packet.

12. B. `default-action discard`

The command should be `default-action drop`.

13. C. A and B together

Both A and B are required to match on the source IP address range and the destination IP address host.

14. B. `default-action drop`

`default-action drop` is not required because the default action, if no other action is configured, is to drop packets that do not match any entries in the filter policy.

15. B. The interfaces where the filter is applied

This is not shown; all the other answers are part of the `show filter` output.

Chapter 7

1. C. RTP

TCP, UDP, and TP4 are transport protocols.

2. D. Transport layer protocols require additional software be added to your operating system.

All modern OSes come with a TCP/IP stack that includes the TCP transport protocol.

3. B. Connectionless operation

TCP always requires the establishment of a connection.

4. A. Reliable data transfer

UDP does not provide reliable data transfer because it does not guarantee delivery.

5. D. RST—Re-sets the sequence numbers for a TCP session

RST indicates that a TCP connection is unavailable, if, for example, an attempt is made to connect to a port that is not available.

6. D. 32

There are 32 bits in a sequence number.

7. C. SYN and ACK

Both bit sets are included in the packet.

8. B. FIN

   FIN indicates that one side of an open connection wishes to initiate a close.

9. C. The sender's congestion window and the receiver's advertised window size

   The sender will send the lower of the two values.

10. B. Duplicate ACK numbers

    This indicates that the receiver has not received at least one segment and that segment must be re-sent.

11. D. 10000

    The sender can never send more than the advertised window size, which is 5000 (even if its congestion window is higher). If the initial sequence number is 5000, then the next sequence number expected by the receiver is always the sequence number (5000) + the number of bytes sent (5000) = 10000.

12. B. An application that is sensitive to packet loss

    This is because UDP does not guarantee delivery so it would be better to use TCP to avoid packet loss.

13. D. It adds little overhead to the data transfer.

    UDP does not require connection establishment and has a small header, so it adds very little overhead to an application.

14. D. 65938

    This is outside the acceptable range of ephemeral ports, 1024–65535.

15. D. UDP cannot be used for bulk file transfers.

    While it is usually better not to use UDP for bulk file transfers, it can be done (TFTP uses UDP for bulk file transfers). The other answers are all good reasons for DNS to use both TCP and UDP for different functions.

Chapter 8

1. A. The destination IP address only
   This is normally the only information that is used to determine how to forward an IP packet.

2. D. EGP

   IGP and EGP are the two main types of routing protocols.

3. B. It is used between ASes.

   IGPs are used exclusively inside a single AS.

4. C. Routing table

   Each routing protocol has its own RIB, and the RTM selects routes from each RIB to place in the routing table/FIB.

5. D. Distance vector—IS-IS

   IS-IS is a link state routing protocol.

6. B. On links with only a single path to other routers

   This is by far the most common situation to use a static route; you might use them in small networks, but even in small networks, routing protocols have an advantage over static routes.

7. D. Distance vector protocols rely on updates only from neighbors.

   Link state protocols flood LSPs throughout the network, and then each router calculates the routes independently so convergence can be very fast. Distance vector protocols have to wait for each router to recalculate its own routing table before sending an update leading to slower convergence.

8. B. Distance vector does not require extensive processing to build routing tables.

   Link state protocols rely on calculating paths using the Shortest Path First algorithm. If you have older routers with slower CPUs, this can take additional time to create the routing table. Distance vector protocols do not perform this sort of complex algorithm.

9. C. SPF

   The Shortest Path First algorithm is used by link state routing protocols.

10. B. A default route

    While technically this is a type of static route, it is more accurate to call it a default route. This is the type of route most likely to be found on stub networks.

11. B. The control plane

    This is the function that is used to build routing tables.

12. D. The link state database

This is where link state information is stored to build the routing table.

13. C. It enters the lowest preference value in the routing table.

The RTM prefers the routing protocol with the lowest preference value.

14. A. Each router has a common view of the network.

Each router receives the same LSPs and should have the same link state database. It then builds a path to each network using the SPF algorithm to create its routing table.

15. B. It sends its entire routing table.

This is how distance vector protocols update neighbor routers.

Chapter 9

1. C. Using Hello advertisements

OSPF sends Hello packets to the 224.0.0.5 multicast IP address to discover other OSPF routers.

2. D. It uses a hop count–based metric.

OSPF uses a cost value on each interface that is based on the bandwidth of the link; it does not use a hop count.

3. D. System interface

It is recommended that you use the system interface as the router ID.

4. B. To uniquely identify an OSPF router

Every OSPF router must have a router ID to uniquely identify it for purposes of building the SPF tree and identifying its LSA updates.

5. A. Every 30 minutes

LSA updates are sent every 30 minutes in order to refresh the LSA. They are sent regardless of whether changes have occurred.

6. B. The routers are on a common network segment and have exchanged database information.

Routers that have shared database information are referred to as *adjacent*. Not all neighbor OSPF routers become adjacent.

7. C. They will automatically become adjacent provided certain OSPF configuration values match.

The area ID and Hello and dead timers must match in the Hello packets.

8. B. The priority

The priority value is only applicable on OSPF broadcast networks.

9. B. The OSPF MTU

This is based on the interface MTU and must match on each router.

10. D. `show router ospf database`

This command displays the LSAs that have been received from other OSPF routers.

11. B. The router LSA

The router LSA carries the local topology information for each router in the network.

12. C. Drop the LSA and send an acknowledgment

The router already has the information so it will drop the LSA, but all LSAs must be acknowledged.

13. C. It is run only on the router that originates an LSA update.

Whenever an LSA update is flooded throughout the network, all routers must rerun the SPF algorithm.

14. C. ExStart, Exchange, Loading, Full

This is the correct order.

15. D. 622-Mbps link = 16

(100 Gbps)/(622 Mbps) = 160, not 16.

Chapter 10

1. B. Distribute routing information between ASes

BPG is an EGP protocol so it is used between different ASes.

2. D. The AS usually contains routers under the control of different administrative groups.

An AS is usually under the control of a single group.

3. D. System interface

This is the preferred interface for internal BGP sessions because iBGP peers are often not directly connected to each other.

4. C. They can be in the same or different AS.

You can have both internal BGP and external BGP sessions.

5. C. TCP on a fixed port

BGP uses TCP port 179.

6. A. To ensure that routers inside an AS have a common view of networks outside the AS

This is to ensure that routers inside the AS choose the correct exit point for routes in other ASes.

7. B. The shortest AS path

BGP uses AS path information to choose the best route to each destination.

8. C. An update message

The BGP update message contains the NLRI, or route information, exchanged by BGP peers.

9. D. The AS number is associated with each peer statement.

You must configure an AS number for each neighbor, and this allows you to determine if the peer is internal or external. Internal peers have the same AS number.

10. B. `show router bgp summary`

This command is used to see the state of your BGP information. There is no `show router bgp status` command as there is for other routing protocols.

11. C. Send a withdraw message

BGP will actively send withdraw messages to its peers to remove previously advertised routes that are no longer available.

12. B. An enterprise with multiple connections to the same ISP

In such a situation, the enterprise can use equal cost default routes to load balance across the multiple links; there is no need to complicate the routing with BGP.

13. D. AS-path, origin, and next-hop

These attributes are included with every BGP network update for each destination.

14. A. It is the single exit point for an AS.

If there is only one exit point from an AS, there is little reason for a BGP router to receive full Internet routing tables.

15. D. Route re-distribution provides for greater policy control.

BGP provides for much greater policy control than simple IGP route re-distribution.

Chapter 11

1. B. It is responsible for adding and removing labels.

Answer A is a CE, and answer C is a P. D is partially correct, but B is the more accurate answer.

2. B. It is specific to a single service.

SDPs are not specific to a single service and can support multiple services.

3. D. Any network that includes encryption

Encryption can be a part of a VPN, but the correct description of a VPN should include a way to privatize communications between user communities. The other answers speak to this, but answer D does not.

4. C. It is the only method for distributing labels in an MPLS network.

LDP is only one method of distributing labels; RSVP can be used as well as other protocols.

5. C. Label distribution protocol—Series of labels and next-hop interfaces

This description is the Label Switched Path.

6. C. LDP

LDP is the most common label distribution protocol.

7. B. VPNM

VPNM is not a type of VPN.

8. C. VPWS

VPWS is a VPN that emulates a point-to-point service between two destinations.

9. B. VPLS

VPLS is a VPN that must maintain a table of MAC addresses.

10. D. None of the above

None of the VPN services provided by an MPLS network require encryption.

11. B. VPRN

VPRN is a VPN that appears to a customer as a private routed network.

12. D. P

P routers swap labels and forward them to other P or PE routers.

13. D. None of the above

PE, LSR, and LER routers can all understand labels. The router is most likely a CE router, which is not one of the choices.

14. D. All of the above

Transparency of the MPLS features to a CE device has all of the benefits listed.

15. B. LDP uses IGP next-hop information.

LDP and IGPs do not re-distribute information directly or compete with each other for paths as they perform completely different functions, although LDP does use the information from IGP to populate the next-hop interfaces for labels.

B

Lab Exercises and Solutions

The lab exercises that appear throughout the book are gathered in this appendix. The solutions to the exercise questions appear at the end of the appendix.

Chapter 2: Alcatel-Lucent 7750/7450 Hardware and the Command Line Interface

The following lab is designed to reinforce your knowledge of the content in this chapter. Please review the instructions carefully and perform the steps in the order in which they are presented. The practice labs require that you have access to three or more Alcatel-Lucent 7750 SRs or Alcatel-Lucent 7450 ESSs in a non-production environment.

 These labs are designed to be used in a controlled lab environment. Please **DO NOT** attempt to perform these labs in a production environment.

Lab Section 2.1: First Contact

Every router needs to be configured, maintained, and updated. The common aspects of these operations are connecting to the router, modifying the configuration, saving the changes, and (possibly) rebooting. Hopefully, all these operations leave the router in a state whereby it is possible to *reconnect!* The first lab exercise focuses on basic connectivity for communicating with the router itself; the remaining exercises illustrate how to explore, modify, and save the router configuration. If you are familiar with the command line in DOS, UNIX, or Linux, you will see many similarities with the CLI in Alcatel-Lucent 7750/7450 routers.

Objective In this exercise, you will connect to the router's command-line interface (CLI), enter commands, then disconnect or reboot the router. You will need either physical access to the equipment or the IP address of the management port.

Validation You will know that you have succeeded if you get an interactive command prompt and are able to change the text of that prompt.

Throughout all the lab exercises, interaction with the router is exclusively through a text-based CLI. As previously mentioned, establishing the connection to the CLI is achieved via any (or all!) of three ways: a serial RS-232 port on the SF/CPM card;

the dedicated Ethernet management (out-of-band) port on the SF/CPM card; or any regular Ethernet network (in-band) port. Each option is covered briefly below.

1. Connect to the router's CLI to get a login prompt:

   - **Via the Serial Port**—You will need physical access to the router to connect a laptop (or other suitable device) to the serial port with a serial cable. The default serial port settings are: 115000, N, 8, 1 with no flow control. For software, you will need a "terminal emulator" program; common options for MS Windows are Hyperterm, Kermit, PuTTY, and for Linux, minicom or seyon.

   - **Via the Management or Network Port**—You will need to know the configured address for the router. If there's no one to ask, or the equipment has never previously been set up, your only option is to connect via the serial port. For software, you should use an SSH program; common options for MS Windows are PuTTY; SecureCRT; OpenSSH; and for Linux, the built-in command ssh.

   In either case, if you don't immediately see the prompt login as:, pressing the [Enter] key should make it appear.

2. **Log In**—Routers are shipped with a default account admin and password admin. Try using these at the login prompt. If they don't work, you'll need to ask for a login account and password from the regular system administrator. If everything worked properly, you should see something like the following:

   ```
   login as: admin
   TiMOS-B-6.1.R5 both/hops ALCATEL SR 7750 Copyright (c) 2000-2008
   Alcatel-Lucent.
   All rights reserved. All use subject to applicable license agreements.
   Built Sun Dec 14 15:01:11 PST 2008 by builder /rel6.1/b1/R5/panos/main
   admin@192.168.0.1's password:

   *A:NS074661144#
   ```

 The code in bold text indicates user input.

3. **Executing Commands**—Executing a command is simple: Just type any valid command at the prompt. For this step, simply confirm the time setting and the OS version using the following commands:

```
*A:NS074661144# show time
Sat Jan  1 05:44:03 UTC 2000
*A:NS074661144# show version
TiMOS-B-6.1.R5 both/hops ALCATEL SR 7750 Copyright (c) 2000-2008
Alcatel-Lucent.
All rights reserved. All use subject to applicable license agreements.
Built Sun Dec 14 15:01:11 PST 2008 by builder /rel6.1/b1/R5/panos/main
*A:NS074661144#
```

3a. Does it matter if a command is typed in uppercase or lowercase?

3b. If a router is completely uninitialized, what time does it show?

3c. What is the OS version? Where else does the OS version appear?

 Note the leading asterisk (*) in the CLI prompt. This is (normally) a reminder that the router has configuration changes that have not yet been saved. The next lab exercise covers this topic.

4. The router name appears after the first letter (A:), for example, NS074661144. Unless a proper name has been configured, the router generates this name from its serial number. According to best practices, every router should have a meaningful name that helps administrators identify it quickly. Configure a better name.

```
*A:NS074661144# configure system name Router1
*A:Router1#
```

4a. Does the router name *always* appear in the CLI prompt?

5. Disconnect from the router.

```
*A:Router1# log
```

Whatever software you're using to connect should either terminate or somehow show a disconnected state.

6. Reconnect to the router.

6a. Is the router name still the same as before disconnecting?

7. Reboot the router. Wait a minute or two and then reconnect.

   `*A:Router1# admin reboot now`

7a. Is the router name still the same as before rebooting?

7b. Why or why not?

8. Reconfigure the router name to something meaningful to you.

Lab Section 2.2: What Is the Router Doing? Getting Help and Information

Most computer systems have some method of recording and reporting of significant events. MS Windows has the *Event Viewer*, UNIX and Linux have the command `dmesg` and the log files /var/log/messages. These are essential tools for diagnosing problems or anomalies with the system's behavior, or simply confirming that everything is working as it should. This lab looks at some of the facilities available on Alcatel-Lucent 7750/7450 equipment for getting help and information.

Objective In this exercise, you will become familiar with the boot traces and logging features available on Alcatel-Lucent 7750/7450 equipment. This exercise also demonstrates the help and auto-completion features of the CLI.

Validation You will know that you have succeeded if you feel at least a little more confident and competent with the CLI; if you can easily generate, edit, and correct typos; and if you can get help from the CLI.

1. Make sure you are logged in.

2. Using the command shown below, display and examine the complete log of bootup messages. These messages are an excellent source of information about how the router started up and what configuration files were used.

```
*A:Router1# show boot-messages
===============================================================
cf3:/bootlog.txt
===============================================================
Boot log started on CPU#0
   Build: X-6.1.R5 on Sun Dec 14 14:22:12 PST 2008 by builder
   CPUCTL FPGA version: 2C
Boot rom version is v29
>>>Testing mainboard FPGA chain...
>>>Validating SDRAM from 0x4D696368 to 0x61656C20
```

```
>>>Testing SDRAM from 0x416E6465 to 0x72736F6E
>>>Testing Compact Flash 1... Slot Empty
>>>Testing Compact Flash 2... Slot Empty
>>>Testing Compact Flash 3... OK (SILICONSYSTEMS INC 256MB)
Wales peripheral FPGA version is 0x14
MDA #1: Serial Number 'NS083662989'
Board Serial Number is 'NS074561259'
Chassis Serial Number is 'NS074661144'
Searching for boot.ldr on local drives:
Searching cf3 for boot.ldr...

[... Some lines omitted ...]

TiMOS BOOT LOADER
Time from clock is SAT JAN 01 00:00:00 2000 UTC
Switching serial output to sync mode...    done

Looking for cf3:/bof.cfg ... OK, reading

Contents of Boot Options File on cf3:
     primary-image    cf3:\6.1.R5
     address          192.168.183.108/27 active
     static-route     128.0.0.0/1 next-hop 192.168.183.97
     autonegotiate
     duplex           full
     speed            100
     wait             3
     persist          off
     no li-local-save
     no li-separate
     console-speed    115200
[... Additional output omitted ...]
```

2a. Upon (re-)booting, what time does a router show?

2b. What are the settings for connecting to the router: Via the serial port? Via the management Ethernet port?

2c. In which file are the connection settings stored?

2d. Which piece of hardware provides the serial number that is used for the default router name?

3. On an uninitialized router, the time will always be incorrect. The next few steps are intended to show some of the excellent help features available through the CLI, so don't be afraid to experiment. Start typing the **admin set-time** command to set the time, but do not press the [Enter] key; type a question mark (?) instead to get a complete list of available options.

```
*A:Router1# admin set-time
  - set-time <date> <time>

 <date>                : YYYY/MM/DD
 <time>                : hh:mm[:ss]


 *A:Router1# admin set-time
```

Notice that after displaying some help (the list of available options), the CLI re-typed your original command to leave you exactly where you were before typing the ?.

4. We all make mistakes from time to time. It's easy to interrupt or cancel at any time whatever has been typed: type **[Ctrl]+C** to kill everything that has been typed on the line.

```
*A:Router1# admin set-time ^C
*A:Router1#
```

5. It's easy to forget the exact spelling of a command. The CLI has help for this situation also: Type the word **admin** and only a part of **set-time**, and then press the [Space] or [Tab] key to have the system auto-complete the command.

```
*A:Router1# admin set[TAB]
*A:Router1# admin set-time
```

6. There are enough commands that it's sometimes possible to remember the first part of a command, but not the last. ["I know the word *time* is somewhere in the command, but I don't remember if it's at the start or the end."] The CLI provides help by listing all possible options. Type the first part of the command, press [Enter], and then use tree or tree detail to get a complete list of all options for that context.

```
*A:Router1# admin
*A:Router1>admin# tree
admin
 |
```

```
+---application-assurance
|   |
|   +---upgrade
|
+---debug-save
|
+---disconnect
|
+---display-config
|
+---enable-tech
|
+---radius-discovery
|   |
|   +---force-discover
|
+---reboot
|
+---redundancy
|   |
|   +---force-switchover
|   |
|   +---synchronize
|
+---save
|
+---set-time
|
+---tech-support
*A:Router1>admin#
```

6a. What are the options for the `reboot` command used in the previous exercise? Which gives more information: using the "?" feature or the `tree detail` command?

7. There are two commands for getting out of a command subcontext: `back` or `exit`. If you enter a loooooong command and want to return to the original context, use `exit`. If you just want to go up a single level in the context, use `back`. Try either one to get out of the current context.

```
*A:Router1>admin# exit
*A:Router1#
```

8. Now that you're fully equipped to get help with commands, have a look to see what log files are recording on-going events in the router.

```
*A:Router1# show log log-collector


=====================================================================
Log Collectors
=====================================================================
Main                 Logged  : 30            Dropped  : 0
  Dest Log Id: 99    Filter Id: 0    Status: enabled   Dest Type: memory
  Dest Log Id: 100   Filter Id: 1001 Status: enabled   Dest Type: memory
Security             Logged  : 5             Dropped  : 0
Change               Logged  : 8             Dropped  : 0
Debug                Logged  : 0             Dropped  : 0
LI                   Logged  : 25            Dropped  : 0
=====================================================================

*A:Router1#
```

8a. How many main categories of events are there?

8b. From the above display, how many logs are actually actively recording events? (These are default logs that always exist.)

9. Have a look at a specific log.

```
*A:Router1# show log log-id 99


=====================================================================
Event Log 99
=====================================================================
Description : Default System Log
Memory Log contents  [size=500    next event=31  (not wrapped)]

30 2000/01/01 06:02:39.09 UTC WARNING: SYSTEM #2006 Base CHASSIS
"tmnxChassisTable: Chassis 1 configuration modified"

29 2000/01/01 00:00:17.24 UTC MINOR: CHASSIS #2002 Base Card 1
"Class IO Module : inserted"

28 2000/01/01 00:00:03.72 UTC WARNING: SNMP #2005 Base A/1
"Interface A/1 is operational"

27 2000/01/01 00:00:02.94 UTC MAJOR: SYSTEM #2005 Base SNMP daemon
```

```
"SNMP daemon initialization complete.
System configured with persistent SNMP indexes: false.
SNMP daemon admimistrative status: outOfService.
SNMP daemon operational status: outOfService."

26 2000/01/01 00:00:02.94 UTC MAJOR: SYSTEM #2023 Base SNMP
   administratively down
"The SNMP agent has changed state.  Administrative state is
   outOfService and operational state is outOfService."

25 2000/01/01 00:00:02.84 UTC MAJOR: SYSTEM #2004 Base System configured
"Bootup configuration complete. Configuration status: defaultBooted.
SNMP Persistent Indexes status: persistDisabled.
System configured with persistent indexes: false."*A:Router1#
[... Additional output omitted ...]
```

9a. How are log entries listed: from oldest to newest, or vice versa?

9b. Each log entry is numbered. Where does that number appear?

9c. Does the number of log entries identified by the log-collector correspond to what is printed out?

9d. Are there more options we could have used in this command? How can you find out?

Lab Section 2.3: Saving Configuration Changes

Alcatel-Lucent 7750/7450 routers provide two major configuration files required for initial access and maintaining configurations across resets. The following exercises show how these files are used.

Objective In this exercise, you will gain an understanding of the role, filename, and content of the Boot Options File (BOF), and become familiar with how to specify and save the configuration file.

Validation You will know you have succeeded if a directory listing of cf3: shows the two configuration files with recent time stamps.

1. Display and examine the content of the BOF.

```
*A:Router1# file type cf3:\bof.cfg
# TiMOS-B-6.1.R5 both/hops ALCATEL SR 7750 Copyright (c) 2000-2008
Alcatel-Lucent.
```

```
# All rights reserved. All use subject to applicable license agreements.
# Built on Sun Dec 14 15:01:11 PST 2008 by builder in
/rel6.1/b1/R5/panos/main

# Generated TUE JAN 01 16:33:15 2000 UTC

primary-image     cf3:\6.1.R5
address           192.168.0.1/27 active
static-route      128.0.0.0/1 next-hop 192.168.183.97
autonegotiate
duplex            full
speed             100
wait              3
persist           off
no li-local-save
no li-separate
console-speed     115200
```

1a. For filenames, does it matter whether they are typed in uppercase or lowercase?

1b. Can you identify where/how to specify the location for the desired OS version? (*Hint:* Find a match between the software version listed on the first line and one of the configuration lines.)

1c. Can you use any of the CLI Help features to find out what storage devices exist, other than cf3?

2. The BOF collects together three main items: the connectivity details (multiple lines), where to find the desired OS version (one line), and where to find all remaining details of the configuration (one line, not shown in the previous step). Changing either the OS version or the configuration is so quick and easy because all it takes is editing either (or both) of these single lines and doing a reboot. Since an uninitialized router doesn't specify any configuration file, you will add this third item now.

```
*A:Router1# bof
*A:Router1>bof# primary-config cf3:\MAA-TestConfig.cfg
WARNING: CLI A valid config file does not exist at cf3:\MAA-TestConfig.cfg.
*A:Router1>bof#
```

3. The filename for the *primary* config is now set. In order to ensure that a router "always works and never stops," the Alcatel-Lucent 7750/7450 routers were designed to have other chances to find a valid config if the primary config is somehow unavailable. Use a CLI Help feature to find out how many additional chances are available.

3a. If there are additional chances to find the config, are there also additional chances for finding the OS? If yes, how many?

4. The Alcatel-Lucent CLI has the same rules as any other editing task on a computer system: You may make as many changes as you wish before saving to a file, and you *must* save your changes or they will be lost when the system reboots. There is exactly one name that can be used for storing the BOF itself: `cf3:\bof.cfg`. Since there is only one name, there can only be one version or copy of the BOF. It isn't necessary to specify a filename when saving, only the **save** command.

```
*A:Router1>bof# save
Writing BOF to cf3:/bof.cfg
Saving BOF .... Completed.
*A:Router1>bof#
```

4a. What exactly has been saved by the preceding command: just the BOF's three main items? or all other configuration details?

5. An Alcatel-Lucent 7750/7450 router has many, many configuration details, including a few that must at least have default values. The BOF now includes a setting for *where* to save the configuration; it is now possible to save the configuration.

```
*A:Router1>bof# exit
*A:Router1# admin save
Writing file to cf3:\MAA-TestConfig.cfg
Saving configuration .... Completed.
A:Router1#
```

5a. What exactly has been saved by the above command: just the BOF's three main items? or all other configuration details?

5b. The `admin save` command didn't include a filename. What filename did the router use, and how did it choose it?

5c. What character has disappeared from the beginning of the prompt, as soon as the configuration was saved? What is the meaning of this character?

6. Verify that you have successfully created the expected configuration files. Confirm that the configuration files were, indeed, created by you: Print the current time, and check that the config files are time-stamped just a few minutes earlier.

```
A:Router1# file dir

 Volume in drive cf3 on slot A has no label.

 Volume in drive cf3 on slot A is formatted as FAT32.

Directory of cf3:\

01/01/2000  12:42a    <DIR>         6.1.R5
01/01/2000  08:54a               573 bof.cfg
01/01/2000  08:55a              5838 MAA-TestConfig.cfg

 [... Additional output omitted ...]

A:Router1#  show time
Sat Jan  1 08:57:03 UTC 2000
A:Router1#
```

6a. Compare the sample output above with your actual listing. Do you have *at least* the files bof.cfg and your main config file? (Depending on who has used the router before you, there could be many additional files.) If you don't have these two files, check and repeat the preceding steps carefully until you succeed.

6b. Is the time stamp on the config files a few minutes earlier than the current time (e.g., from the example above: 8:54 a.m. and 8:55 a.m. with the current time being a few minutes later at 8:57 a.m.)?

7. Repeat the steps above for each of the other routers.

8. Now that you know how to save the two main configuration files, make sure that you *save your work regularly* (even every few minutes)! The command prompt has a reminder symbol to make sure you know when you have unsaved changes.

For readers who don't like the anticipation of waiting, there's a practical application for saved configurations right within this book. We configure the OSPF protocol in

Chapter 9 and ensure that it is saved(!). In Chapter 10, we use a different protocol, so the OSPF configuration is wiped clean. When we need OSPF again in Chapter 11, we rerun the saved configuration file to get a fully restored OSPF configuration.

Chapter 3: Configuring IOMs, MDAs, and Ports

The following lab is designed to reinforce your knowledge of the content in this chapter. Please review the instructions carefully and perform the steps in the order in which they are presented. The practice labs require that you have access to three or more Alcatel-Lucent 7750 SRs or Alcatel-Lucent 7450 ESSs in a non-production environment.

 These labs are designed to be used in a controlled lab environment. Please **DO NOT** attempt to perform these labs in a production environment.

Alcatel-Lucent 7750/7450 products are modular for flexibility, upgradability, and maintainability. A router is actually built from *many* modular components. The list of these components can be made to sound like a nursery rhyme: An SFP fits into an MDA, an MDA fits into an IOM, an IOM fits into a chassis, and the chassis bolts into an equipment rack. None of the lab exercises in this book requires any configuration of the chassis, so exercises for this chapter deal with configuring everything from the IOM upward to the L2 Ethernet ports.

Except for the smallest members of the family, all routers start with the chassis. It contains power supply connections, mounts for cooling fans, the backplane with its associated circuitry, and, most importantly, space for adding large circuit boards (also known as *cards*). The largest router in the family accepts up to 12 cards. Except for the chassis, all components are hot-swappable.

As covered in Chapter 2, there are two main types of the large cards: Switch Fabric/Control Plane Modules (SF/CPMs) and I/O Modules (IOMs). All routers must have at least one and at most two SF/CPMs. Configuring SF/CPMs is a topic for a more advanced book, so these labs assume that the SF/CPM default mode is correct for all exercises. The exercises are structured so that each one deals with configuring a single component in the hierarchy: IOM cards, MDA cards, and ports.

The exercises in this lab are designed to integrate what you learned in Chapter 2 with the content of Chapter 3. The section "Basic Overview of Ethernet" covered some of the maximum frame sizes [maximum transmission units (MTUs) of normal and jumbo frames] and associated speeds (10 Mbps, 100 Mbps, 1 Gbps); see if you can spot some of these items in the final exercises where the Ethernet ports are configured.

Lab Section 3.1: A Full Deck of Cards

A fully loaded Alcatel-Lucent 7750 SRs or Alcatel-Lucent 7450 ESS can have up to 12 cards installed. Configuring these cards is a critical first step towards a fully operational device, so this is where we start for the first exercise.

Objective In this exercise, you will become familiar with the different cards that fit into the chassis and be able to recognize and identify them from the CLI. This exercise also covers the steps required to configure an IOM card.

Validation You will know you have succeeded if you can display the state of IOMs and if the IOMs show an operational state of Up.

1. Display and examine the current card configuration with the show card command.

```
A:Router1# show card


===============================================================
Card Summary
===============================================================
Slot   Provisioned     Equipped        Admin     Operational
       Card-type       Card-type       State     State
---------------------------------------------------------------
1                      iom2-20g        up        unprovisioned
A      sfm-400g        sfm-400g        up        up/active
B      sfm-400g                        up        down/standby
===============================================================
A:Router1#
```

1a. In total, how many cards are physically present in the chassis? How many SF/CPMs? How many IOMs?

1b. Referring to Chapter 2, what kind of labeling is used for the "two (2) card slots [...] dedicated for redundant SF/CPMs"?

1c. Referring to Chapter 2, how many different kinds of SF/CPM cards exist?

1d. Referring to Chapter 2, what kind of labeling is used for an IOM card(s)?

1e. (*Optional*) Is there any relationship between the first character of the prompt and any of the cards?

2. Configure the IOM card to the same type as `Equipped`. (Note: The specific card type may be different on your router.) Be ready to quickly type the `show card` command in order to catch the IOM in the process doing its own (local) bootup. Wait a few moments, and repeat the `show card` command to see the IOM in its final state.

```
A:Router1# configure card 1 card-type iom2-20g
*A:Router1# show card
```

```
===============================================================
Card Summary
===============================================================
Slot   Provisioned      Equipped        Admin     Operational
       Card-type        Card-type       State     State
---------------------------------------------------------------
1      iom2-20g         iom2-20g        up        booting
A      sfm-400g         sfm-400g        up        up/active
B      sfm-400g                         up        down/standby
===============================================================
*A:Router1# show card
```

```
===============================================================
Card Summary
===============================================================
Slot   Provisioned      Equipped        Admin     Operational
       Card-type        Card-type       State     State
---------------------------------------------------------------
1      iom2-20g         iom2-20g        up        up
A      sfm-400g         sfm-400g        up        up/active
B      sfm-400g                         up        down/standby
===============================================================
*A:Router1#
```

2a. Did the configuration command change the number of *physical* cards or the number of *available* cards?

2b. Why did the asterisk (*) reappear in the command prompt? What will make it disappear again?

3. Have a look at the main log to see if anything has been recorded as a result of these last few configuration changes. Remember: The log files are an *excellent* source of debugging and troubleshooting information!

```
*A:Router1# show log log-id 99


=====================================================================
Event Log 99
=====================================================================
Description : Default System Log
Memory Log contents  [size=500   next event=237  (not wrapped)]

236 2000/01/01 09:13:23.24 UTC MINOR: CHASSIS #2002 Base Mda 1/1
"Class MDA Module : inserted"

235 2000/01/01  09:13:23.24 UTC WARNING: SYSTEM #2009 Base CHASSIS
"Status of Card 1 changed administrative state: inService,
 operational state: inService"

234 2000/01/01  09:13:10.56 UTC WARNING: SYSTEM #2006 Base CHASSIS
"tmnxCardTable: Slot 1 configuration modified"

233 2000/01/01 09:13:10.55 UTC WARNING: SYSTEM #2007 Base PORT
"Pool on MDA 1/2 Modified managed object created"
[... Additional output omitted ...]
*A:Router1#
```

4. If it's ever necessary to remove an IOM, a two-step process ensures a clean shutdown.

```
*A:Router1# configure card 1 shutdown
*A:Router1# configure no card 1
*A:Router1# show card
```

```
===============================================================
Card Summary
===============================================================
Slot    Provisioned        Equipped        Admin    Operational
        Card-type          Card-type       State    State
---------------------------------------------------------------
1                          iom2-20g        up       unprovisioned
A       sfm-400g           sfm-400g        up       up/active
B       sfm-400g                           up       down/standby
===============================================================
*A:Router1#
```

Compare the output of the "show card" command with the output from the same command in Step 1. The IOM has successfully been removed from the configuration.

5. Reconfigure the IOM so that it is available for subsequent lab exercises. (Refer to Step 2.)

6. Have a look at the main log to see if anything has been recorded as a result of these last few configuration changes. Remember: The log files are an *excellent* source of debugging and troubleshooting information!

```
    *A:Router1# show log log-id 99
```

7. If your router has additional IOM cards and you want or need to use them for the exercises, you will need to repeat the configuration step for all additional IOM cards.

8. Repeat the preceding steps for each of the other routers.

Lab Section 3.2: An MDA for Every Need

There are many MDAs available for the Alcatel-Lucent 7750/7450 products: A recent version of the OS reports support for 42 different MDAs. The purpose of an MDA is to incorporate *all* circuitry that is specific to a particular type of Layer 2 connection, for example, Ethernet (both copper and fiber), Sonet/SDH (includes ATM), and OCx. Within these three broad categories, there are many different variations of MDAs to provide support for different speeds and numbers of connections. Having MDAs as a separate, modular component allows a customer to purchase and configure the right combination of connections that might be required for any particular network node. Fortunately, the configuration process is very simple despite the large number of available MDAs.

Objective In this exercise, you will become familiar with recognizing, identifying, and configuring MDAs from the CLI.

Validation You will know you have succeeded if you can display the state of MDAs and if the MDAs show an operational state of Up.

1. Display and examine the current MDA configuration using the show mda command. Note that the exact output will depend entirely on your physical hardware.

   ```
   *A:Router1# show mda


   ===============================================================
   MDA Summary
   ===============================================================
   Slot  Mda   Provisioned    Equipped          Admin   Operational
               Mda-type       Mda-type          State   State
   ---------------------------------------------------------------
   1     1                    m10-1gb-sfp-b     up      unprovisioned
   ===============================================================
   ```

   1a. *Important!* Can you see any MDAs for IOMs that are *not* configured? Repeat the steps from the previous exercise to remove the IOM configuration and repeat the command to see the available MDAs.

   1b. In total, how many MDAs are physically plugged into an IOM(s)?

   1c. Which chassis slot/IOM is the m10-1gb-sfp-b MDA plugged into? Within that IOM, is the MDA plugged into the first or second MDA slot?

2. Generally, an MDA will always be configured to be the same as shown in the Equipped Mda-type column. Configure the available MDA(s). Note that the exact command will depend entirely on your physical hardware; follow the rule of configuring the type the same as shown in the previous command.

   ```
   *A:Router1# configure card 1 mda 1 mda-type m10-1gb-sfp-b
   *A:Router1#
   ```

   2a. What is the correspondence between the physical *location* of the MDA and the values specified in the above command?

   2b. Whether or not there was an asterisk in the prompt *before* issuing the configure command, will there be one *after* the command?

3. Display and examine all MDAs that are now visible.

```
*A:Router1# show mda

===============================================================
MDA Summary
===============================================================
Slot  Mda   Provisioned    Equipped       Admin   Operational
            Mda-type       Mda-type       State   State
---------------------------------------------------------------
1     1     m10-1gb-sfp-b  m10-1gb-sfp-b  up      up
===============================================================

*A:Router1#
```

3a. Did the configuration command change the number of *physical* MDAs or the number of *available* MDAs?

4. Have a look at the main log to see what has been recorded as a result of this configuration change. Here's one last reminder: The log files are an *excellent* source of debugging and troubleshooting information!

```
*A:Router1# show log log-id 99
```

5. As with IOMs, if it's ever necessary to remove an MDA, a two-step process ensures a clean shutdown.

```
*A:Router1# configure card 1 mda 1 shutdown
*A:Router1# configure card 1 no mda 1
*A:Router1# show mda

===============================================================
MDA Summary
===============================================================
Slot  Mda   Provisioned    Equipped       Admin   Operational
            Mda-type       Mda-type       State   State
---------------------------------------------------------------
1     1                    m10-1gb-sfp-b  up      unprovisioned
===============================================================

*A:Router1#
```

5a. Whether or not there was an asterisk in the prompt before issuing the configure command, will there be one *after* the command?

6. Reconfigure the MDA so that it is available for subsequent lab exercises.

7. If your router has additional MDAs and you want or need to use them for the exercises, you will need to repeat the configuration step for all additional MDAs. Don't forget to *save your configuration*.

8. Repeat the preceding steps for each of the other routers.

Lab Section 3.3: All Ports Up...To L2 Ethernet

The configuration process for the base hardware has a very definite hierarchy. First, the SF/CPM must be up-and-running in order to connect via the serial port or Ethernet management port. Next, the IOM(s) must be configured, followed by the MDA(s). An MDA will be neither visible nor configurable until its supporting IOM is fully configured; it is not possible to skip any preceding step. The same is true for individual ports: Everything in the hardware chain must be configured before ports become visible and configurable. Once they are configured, the raw hardware configuration is complete.

Objective In this exercise, you will become familiar with recognizing, identifying, and configuring ports from the CLI.

Validation You will know you have succeeded if you can display the state of ports and if the (required) ports show an operational state of Up.

1. Display and examine the current port configuration (show port command). Note that the exact output will depend entirely on your physical hardware. There's a lot of output; we'll just focus on a few of the most important items.

```
*A:Router1# show port
```

```
===============================================================================
Ports on Slot 1
===============================================================================
Port   Admin Link Port   Cfg  Oper LAG/ Port Port Port  SFP/XFP/
Id     State      State  MTU  MTU  Bndl Mode Encp Type  MDIMDX
-------------------------------------------------------------------------------
1/1/1  Down  No   Down   9212 9212   -  netw null xcme  GIGE-T
1/1/2  Down  No   Down   9212 9212   -  netw null xcme  GIGE-T
1/1/3  Down  No   Down   9212 9212   -  netw null xcme  GIGE-T
1/1/4  Down  No   Down   9212 9212   -  netw null xcme  GIGE-T
1/1/5  Down  No   Down   9212 9212   -  netw null xcme
```

```
[... Additional output omitted ...]
1/1/10 Down  No   Down    9212 9212    - netw null xcme


===============================================================
Ports on Slot A
===============================================================
Port  Admin Link Port   Cfg Oper LAG/ Port Port Port  SFP/XFP/
Id    State      State  MTU MTU  Bndl Mode Encp Type  MDIMDX
---------------------------------------------------------------
A/1   Up    Yes  Up     1514 1514    - netw null faste MDI


===============================================================
Ports on Slot B
===============================================================
Port  Admin Link Port   Cfg Oper LAG/ Port Port Port  SFP/XFP/
Id    State      State  MTU MTU  Bndl Mode Encp Type  MDIMDX
---------------------------------------------------------------
B/1   Up    No   Ghost  1514 1514    - netw null faste
===============================================================
*A:Router1#
```

1a. The output above is split into three main sections. The first section is all the output for which (single) piece of hardware?

1b. There are a total of 12 ports shown. How does the naming/labeling of the ports correspond with the SF/CPM, IOM, and MDA card numbering/labeling?

1c. The MDA is configured as m10-1gb-sfp-b, meaning 10 GigE ports using optical SFP connectors. How many ports have the SFP installed?

1d. The last port is listed with a port state of Ghost. Which card is it on? Does the card physically exist? What is the meaning of Ghost?

1e. With default settings, are ports in an Up or Down state? Is this consistent with other hardware (i.e., IOMs and MDAs)?

1f. What is the default MTU for a 10/100 FastE port? For a GigE port?

2. Configure a single port to a functional state.

```
*A:Router1# configure port 1/1/1 no shutdown
*A:Router1# show port
```

```
=================================================================
Ports on Slot 1
=================================================================
Port   Admin Link Port   Cfg  Oper LAG/ Port Port Port   SFP/XFP/
Id     State      State  MTU  MTU  Bndl Mode Encp Type   MDIMDX
-----------------------------------------------------------------
1/1/1  Up    Yes  Up     9212 9212    - netw null xcme   MDI GIGE-T
1/1/2  Down  No   Down   9212 9212    - netw null xcme   GIGE-T
[... Additional output omitted ...]
*A:Router1#
```

2a. With the port operationally Up, what new information is available?

3. Multiple ports can be configured to a functional state, if done with a single command on one line.

```
*A:Router1# configure port 1/1/[2..10] no shutdown
*A:Router1# show port
[... Additional output omitted ...]
*A:Router1#
```

4. Single or multiple ports may be turned down with a single command.

```
*A:Router1# configure port 1/1/1 shutdown
*A:Router1# show port
[... Additional output omitted ...]
*A:Router1# configure port 1/1/[2..10] shutdown
*A:Router1# show port
[... Additional output omitted ...]
*A:Router1#
```

5. Don't forget to check the log files to see the corresponding entries for these operations.

6. Configure all ports Up that you need or want to use for the exercises. Remember to *save your configuration.*

7. Repeat the preceding steps for each of the other routers.

8. (*Optional*) Is it possible to shut down/remove an MDA while ports are still active? Do the ports retain their previous state when the MDA is reconfigured? Try it! (Don't worry, there's no risk of damaging the hardware.)

9. (*Optional*) If you have access to the physical hardware, try inserting and removing cables from a port and using a show port at each step to see the difference in the output.

Chapter 5: IP Addressing and Routing

The following lab is designed to reinforce your knowledge of the content in this chapter. Please review the instructions carefully and perform the steps in the order in which they are presented. The practice labs require that you have access to three or more Alcatel-Lucent 7750 SRs or Alcatel-Lucent 7450 ESSs in a non-production environment.

 These labs are designed to be used in a controlled lab environment. Please **DO NOT** attempt to perform these labs in a production environment.

Lab Section 5.1: IP Addressing with Enterprise Customers

An ISP typically has one or more blocks of IP addresses that have been assigned to it by one of IANA's regional registries. The ISP might use one block of addresses for its residential broadband customers, another block for a college campus, and another block for a larger enterprise customer. The difficult part of the ISP's task is to split up and assign *just enough* of these addresses to each customer—enough to anticipate and allow future growth, but not so many that the ISP runs out of addresses. The ISP can allocate one block right after another so that the address numbering is consecutive without gaps, or intentionally leave gaps between the blocks for future growth. By sizing the blocks appropriately, multiple smaller blocks can later be grouped together as one single larger block. Maximizing block size helps minimize the number of unusable addresses and thus improves the efficiency of the ISP's overall address space. This exercise looks at one example with just a few of the typical constraints on utilization of the address space.

Objective In this exercise, you will design and implement an IP network addressing scheme that satisfies multiple addressing constraints and supports communications between multiple routers. Figure 5.32 provides the example network topology. This is a paper exercise.

Validation You will know you have succeeded by verifying your answers with the solutions provided at the end of this appendix.

Figure 5.32 A simplified diagram shows how an ISP connects to multiple sites of two different enterprises.

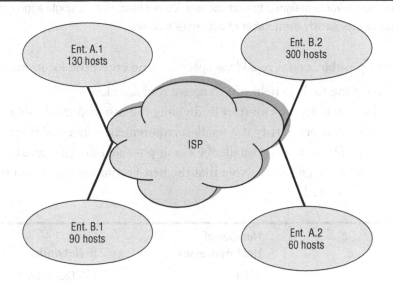

Requirements

Two enterprises, A and B, are connected to a central Tier 2 ISP. A.1 and A.2 are two of Enterprise A's locations connected to the Tier 2 ISP, and B.1 and B.2 are two of Enterprise B's locations connected to the same Tier 2.

The ISP has a public IP addressing space of 138.120.16.0/20. Enterprises A and B lease their IP addressing from their ISP. Enterprise A requires an IP addressing scheme that can scale to at most 30 nodes in location A.1 and 60 nodes in location A.2. Enterprise B requires an IP addressing scheme with at most 90 nodes in location B.1 and less than 300 nodes in location B.2. The ISP can only lease 500 IP addresses, distributed between the two enterprises, and will utilize the last part of its assigned subnetwork to connect to both the enterprises.

Your tasks are to:

1. Extract a 500 host subnetwork from the last part of the ISP IP network address of 138.120.16.0/20.

2. Divide the resulting subnetwork into unequal subnetworks satisfying all the site requirements for each of the enterprise locations.

The subnetworks assigned to each location do not have to be a single aggregate block so long as they satisfy the number of addresses required.

3. Wherever possible, optimize address spaces among enterprise locations.

Use the following table to help you complete your solution:

Hint: for this example, you can start by dividing the assigned ISP IP subnetwork into equal blocks that best satisfy the smallest requirement. Once the blocks have been assigned, combine as many smaller blocks as possible into aggregate blocks while obeying the rules for aggregation. Note that the best fit solution may mean that not all blocks can be aggregated.

Entity	Number of Host Addresses	IP Network
ISP Network	4094	138.120.16.0/20
Subnetwork assigned to Enterprises A and B	510	
Enterprise A		
Location A.1		
Location A.2		
Enterprise B		
Location B.1		
Location B.2		

Lab Section 5.2: IP Addressing with P, PE, and CE Routers

Real-world experience is certainly the best way to both learn and retain knowledge. It is, however, equally true that carrier grade routers are typically *very* expensive, so getting access for learning and experimenting may be difficult or even impossible. All remaining lab exercises have been designed to fully illustrate all configuration details, but with a minimum number of nodes. Reducing the amount of equipment to a minimum provides three important benefits: It is possible to complete all of the configuration in a reasonable amount of time; it increases the probability of getting access to enough equipment; and (possibly most importantly) it minimizes the expense! Expect that you will need to adjust the exercises to match the particular hardware and cabling of your equipment. As a minimum, you will likely need to adjust port numbers. Specific details of the command output may differ, but the essential aspects should remain the same.

Objective In this exercise, you will design and implement an IP network addressing scheme to support the communications between the labeled routers shown in Figure 5.33. The IP addressing scheme will be used in the subsequent lab exercises throughout the book.

Validation You will know you have succeeded by verifying your answers with the solutions provided at the end of this appendix.

Figure 5.33 The Lab exercise uses this topology to demonstrate a simple IP addressing scheme.

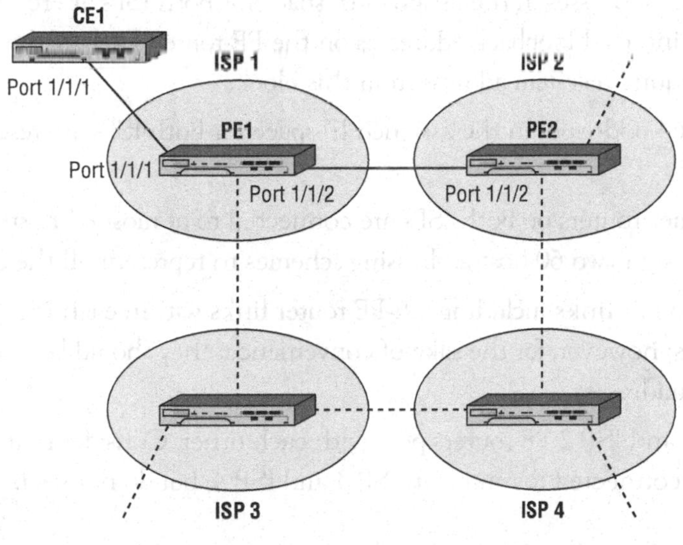

Note that in Figure 5.33, only the labeled routers joined by solid lines will actually be configured (i.e., PE1, PE2, CE1). The other routers, joined by dashed lines, represent the multitude of additional connections that might exist in a real-world scenario with many ISPs.

The focus of Figure 5.33 is the two ISPs: ISP 1 and ISP 2. A more typical network diagram would show routers that are entirely contained within the ISP's core network, having no connections to any customers. Such routers are referred to as *Provider* (P) routers and serve as transit points to other provider routers. *Provider Edge* (PE) routers have at least one connection to the ISP's customers and provide Internet and other network access for these customers. For the purposes of these lab exercises, all the ISP routers are considered PE routers.

CE1 is a *Customer Edge* (CE) router that represents customers of ISP 1. Such routers provide traffic from the ISP to the various customer entities.

Each ISP is assigned the following public address space by IANA:

- ISP 1 140.10.0.0/24
- ISP 2 150.10.0.0/24

Your task is to design an IP subnetwork based on the address space provided and assign the subnetworks to the various routers based on the following requirements, which are the same for both ISPs.

Requirements

1. The first 32 addresses in the assigned IP space for both ISPs are reserved for system and other internal loopback addresses on the PE router. Each of the routers in the ISP will require a system address from this block.

2. The next 64 addresses in the assigned IP space for both ISPs are reserved for future use.

3. All customer routers on both ISPs are connected to at most 60 hosts. So each ISP needs to assign two 60-host addressing schemes to represent all the customers.

4. All inter-router links including CE-PE router links within each ISP are point-to-point links; however, for the sake of convenience, they should be assigned /30-based addresses.

5. The ISP 1 and ISP 2 PE routers peer with each other. Consider that they are also physically connected to routers in ISP 3 and ISP 4, but do not peer.

When you are planning the addressing scheme, don't forget to consider future expansion and additional connections. You may find similarities with the exercise. From Lab 5.1, use the following table to help you complete your solution:

ISP Number 1			
Router	Port	Interface Name	IP Address
		Reserved for local loopbacks.	
		Reserved for future use.	
		Reserved for inter-router links.	
PE1		System	
		loopbackTest	
		toPE2	
		toCE1	
CE1		System	
		loopbackTest	
		toPE1	
		Aggregate	

ISP Number 2			
Router	Port	Interface Name	IP Address
		Reserved for local loopbacks.	
		Reserved for future use.	
		Reserved for inter-router links.	
PE2		System	
		loopbackTest	
		toP1	

Lab Section 5.3: Layer 3 Interfaces

In previous lab exercises, the equipment configuration finished at the L2 Ethernet level. Now that the L3 IP addressing scheme is complete, it is time to configure L3 interfaces on the router. This is not difficult, but there are some differences between physical interfaces and virtual or loopback interfaces. Look for the differences in the following exercises.

Objective In this exercise, you will configure the Layer 3 interfaces according to the IP addressing scheme listed in the tables in the previous exercise (Lab 5.2). This exercise assumes that all routers have been given suitable system names and configured up to the L2 Ethernet level.

Validation You will know you have succeeded if you can ping the L3 network interface of the adjacent router.

1. Using the following command, take a look at any existing interfaces on the router. Notice that the system interface is already created. This interface exists by default and cannot be removed. The only requirement is to assign the system interface with an IP address. By default, the system interface is automatically used by the various routing protocols as the router-id.

   ```
   *B:PE1# show router interface


   ===============================================================
   Interface Table (Router: Base)
   ===============================================================
   Interface-Name          Adm    Opr(v4/v6)  Mode      Port/SapId
      IP-Address                                         PfxState
   ---------------------------------------------------------------
   system                  Up     Down/--     Network system
      -                                                  -
   ---------------------------------------------------------------
   Interfaces : 1
   ===============================================================
   *B:PE1#
   ```

   1a. Carefully examine the prompt for PE1. Which SF/CPM is currently active?

2. Assign a /32 IP address to the system interface in accordance with the addressing scheme from the previous section.

```
*B:PE1# configure router
*B:PE1>config>router# interface system
*B:PE1>config>router>if# address 140.10.0.1/32
*B:PE1>config>router>if# exit
*B:PE1>config>router# show router interface


===============================================================
Interface Table (Router: Base)
===============================================================
Interface-Name       Adm    Opr(v4/v6)  Mode    Port/SapId
   IP-Address                                   PfxState
---------------------------------------------------------------
system               Up     Up/--       Network system
   140.10.0.1/32                                n/a
---------------------------------------------------------------
Interfaces : 1
===============================================================
*B:PE1>config>router#
```

2a. Carefully examine the output for the router's system interface before and after the configuration command. What has changed?

2b. Knowing that the system interface exists by default, how many additional items need to be configured for it to be operational?

3. Assign IP addresses to the rest of the system interfaces on the CE and PE routers.

4. Create a loopback interface (for testing purposes). Note that a loopback interface needs two items in addition to the name: a /32 IP address and the special designation loopback.

```
*B:PE1>config>router# interface loopbackTest
*B:PE1>config>router>if$ address 140.10.0.11/32
*B:PE1>config>router>if$ loopback
*B:PE1>config>router>if$ exit
*B:PE1>config>router# show router interface
```

```
=================================================================
Interface Table (Router: Base)
=================================================================
Interface-Name          Adm    Opr(v4/v6)  Mode    Port/SapId
    IP-Address                                      PfxState
-----------------------------------------------------------------
loopbackTest            Up     Up/--       Network loopback
    140.10.0.11/32                                  n/a
system                  Up     Up/--       Network system
    140.10.0.1/32                                   n/a
-----------------------------------------------------------------
Interfaces : 2
=================================================================

*B:PE1>config>router#
```

4a. Experiment with creating a loopback and leaving out either the IP address or the `loopback` designation. Other than the name, how many additional items need to be configured for the loopback to be operational?

5. Removing an interface is a simple two-step process. Remove the loopback interface now.

```
*B:PE1>config>router# interface loopbackTest shutdown
*B:PE1>config>router# no interface loopbackTest
*B:PE1>config>router#
```

5a. Experiment to see if it is possible to remove an interface that is operationally Up.

6. Re-create the loopback on PE1 and create loopbacks for the other CE and PE routers.

6a. Is there any conflict or problem with reusing the same name for an interface in more than one router? Are interface names local or global?

7. Create the *physical* inter-router interfaces. Note that a loopback interface needs two items in addition to the name: a /32 IP address and a physical port.

```
*B:PE1>config>router# interface toPE2
*B:PE1>config>router>if$ address 140.10.0.97/30
*B:PE1>config>router>if$ port 1/1/2
*B:PE1>config>router>if$ exit
*B:PE1>config>router# interface toCE1
*B:PE1>config>router>if$ address 140.10.0.101/30
*B:PE1>config>router>if$ port 1/1/1
```

```
*B:PE1>config>router>if$ exit
*B:PE1>config>router# show router interface

===============================================================
Interface Table (Router: Base)
===============================================================
Interface-Name          Adm    Opr(v4/v6)   Mode    Port/SapId
   IP-Address                                        PfxState
---------------------------------------------------------------
loopbackTest            Up     Up/--        Network loopback
   140.10.0.11/32                                   n/a
system                  Up     Up/--        Network system
   140.10.0.1/32                                    n/a
toCE1                   Up     Down/--      Network 1/1/1
   140.10.0.101/30                                  n/a
toPE2                   Up     Down/--      Network 1/1/2
   140.10.0.97/30                                   n/a
---------------------------------------------------------------
Interfaces : 4
===============================================================
*B:PE1>config>router#
```

7a. Note the operational state of the new interfaces. The command output shows evidence of another requirement for physical links to be operationally Up. What is that extra requirement? (One router's configuration was changed to demonstrate this requirement.)

8. Create the remaining inter-router interfaces for the CE and PE routers.

9. Now that L3 connectivity between all routers is configured, recheck the state of the interfaces to verify that they are all operationally Up. You can verify the configuration you entered with the info command: It shows everything that has been newly configured or changed from the default settings.

```
*B:PE1>config>router# info
-------------------------------------
#-------------------------------------
echo "IP Configuration"
#-------------------------------------
        interface "loopbackTest"
            address 140.10.0.11/32
            loopback
```

```
            exit
            interface "system"
                address 140.10.0.1/32
            exit
            interface "toCE1"
                address 140.10.0.101/30
                port 1/1/1
            exit
            interface "toPE2"
                address 140.10.0.97/30
                port 1/1/2
            exit
-----------------------------------------

    *B:PE1>config>router#
```

9a. What is the difference between the output from a show... command versus an info... command?

9b. Experiment with creating a physical interface and leaving out either the IP address or the port. Other than the name, how many additional items need to be configured for the interface to be operational?

9c. Experiment to find out if an interface can be both admin and operationally Up/Up on one side and not the other. What are the requirements for an interface to be admin and operationally Up/Up?

9d. Notice that all names in the output above are surrounded by quotation (" ") marks. The rule is that quotation marks are only necessary if the name contains a space. Experiment to see what happens if you try to configure an interface named loopback Test without using surrounding quotes.

The following table provides a convenient reference of the requirements for configuring L3 interfaces:

Interface Type	Name	Loopback	Subnet Mask	Port Config
System	system	Implicit	/32	None
Loopback	"Any String"	Explicit	/32	loopback
Normal	"Any String"	No	/1 – /31	Required

10. Check the route tables of the CE and PE routers. Notice the routes that now appear in the route table, and take note of their protocol type. There should be exactly one route for each interface that is operationally Up: four for PE1 and three for CE1 and PE2.

```
*B:PE1>config>router# show router route-table


===================================================================
Route Table (Router: Base)
===================================================================
Dest Prefix                     Type    Proto   Age         Pref
    Next Hop[Interface Name]                     Metric
-------------------------------------------------------------------
140.10.0.1/32                   Local   Local   01h11m25s   0
    system                                       0
140.10.0.11/32                  Local   Local   00h00m45s   0
    loopbackTest                                 0
140.10.0.96/30                  Local   Local   00h44m49s   0
    toPE2                                        0
140.10.0.100/30                 Local   Local   00h28m42s   0
    toCE1                                        0
-------------------------------------------------------------------
No. of Routes: 4
===================================================================
*B:PE1>config>router#
```

10a. Is there a difference between the outputs of the show router interface command and the show router route-table command? What is the difference?

11. Do the ultimate test to verify that interfaces are functioning properly: Use the ping command to check for connectivity from a router to the far end of each of the inter-router links, for example, between the two PE routers and between PE1 and CE1. You will need to think carefully to ensure that you use the correct IP address. (ICMP ping and ARP are covered more thoroughly in Chapter 6.)

```
*B:PE1>config>router# ping 140.10.0.97
PING 140.10.0.97 56 data bytes
64 bytes from 140.10.0.97: icmp_seq=1 ttl=64 time<10ms.
64 bytes from 140.10.0.97: icmp_seq=2 ttl=64 time<10ms.
64 bytes from 140.10.0.97: icmp_seq=3 ttl=64 time<10ms.
64 bytes from 140.10.0.97: icmp_seq=4 ttl=64 time<10ms.
64 bytes from 140.10.0.97: icmp_seq=5 ttl=64 time<10ms.
```

```
---- 140.10.0.97 PING Statistics ----
5 packets transmitted, 5 packets received, 0.00% packet loss
round-trip min < 10ms, avg < 10ms, max < 10ms, stddev < 10ms
*B:PE1>config>router#
```

Chapter 6: ICMP and ARP

The following lab is designed to reinforce your knowledge of the content in this chapter. Please review the instructions carefully and perform the steps in the order in which they are presented. The practice labs require that you have access to three or more Alcatel-Lucent 7750 SRs or Alcatel-Lucent 7450 ESSs in a non-production environment.

 These labs are designed to be used in a controlled lab environment. Please **DO NOT** attempt to perform these labs in a production environment.

Internet Control Messaging Protocol (ICMP) is an IP protocol used to report on errors in the delivery of an IP datagram. When a destination address is unreachable, the router that cannot find the destination sends an ICMP "destination unreachable" message to the source of the IP datagram. ARP is a mechanism used to find out the MAC address corresponding to a specific IP address (if one doesn't already exist in the cache of Ethernet MAC addresses).

The lab exercises in this chapter have a dual purpose: to illustrate ARP and ICMP as well as show some basics of debugging on the Alcatel-Lucent 7750/7450 products.

Lab Section 6.1: Testing for ICMP and ARP

The last step in the previous chapter's lab exercises used the ping command. If a ping succeeds, it provides useful information in the form of reliability and latency statistics. If ping fails, however, it provides almost no diagnostic or troubleshooting information other than that "something" is broken. We have no indication whether the connectivity problem is with the source, the destination, or an intervening link between the two. By using debugging facilities, it is possible to narrow down and thus identify problems that may exist in any of these three areas.

Objective In this exercise, you will use show and debug commands to verify the functioning of the ARP table and the operation of ping commands.

Validation You will know you have succeeded if you are able to see debug output showing both ICMP request and reply packets on each router.

1. The first step to set up debugging is to define *what* information is desired and *where* it should go. Configure a log file that receives output from the debug/execution trace stream and delivers it to the terminal session. You may want to review the material on log files from Chapter 2 before continuing.

```
*B:PE1# configure log log-id 33
*B:PE1>config>log>log-id$ from debug-trace
*B:PE1>config>log>log-id$ to session
*B:PE1>config>log>log-id$ exit
*B:PE1#
```

   1a. Can you use a CLI Help function to find out how many log files can be configured?

2. Configure which events will generate debug/execution trace information, for any listening log files.

```
*B:PE1# debug router ip icmp
```

   2a. Use a CLI Help function to find out what other categories of events can be specified as a source of debug information. How many are there in the router ip context?

3. From CE1 and PE2, attempt to ping the IP address of PE1's interfaces. Observe the debug ICMP messages on the core routers.

```
*A:CE1>config>router# ping 140.10.0.101
PING 140.10.0.101 56 data bytes
64 bytes from 140.10.0.101: icmp_seq=1 ttl=64 time=10ms.
64 bytes from 140.10.0.101: icmp_seq=2 ttl=64 time<10ms.
[... Additional output omitted ...]

[ Output captured from PE1 terminal session ]
1 2000/01/01 13:53:45.62 UTC MINOR: DEBUG #2001 Base PIP
"PIP: ICMP
instance 1 (Base), interface index 4 (toCE1),
ICMP  ingressing on toCE1:
   140.10.0.102 -> 140.10.0.101
   type: Echo (8)  code: No Code (0)
"
```

```
2 2000/01/01 13:53:45.62 UTC MINOR: DEBUG #2001 Base PIP
"PIP: ICMP
instance 1 (Base), interface index 4 (toCE1),
ICMP  egressing on toCE1:
   140.10.0.101 -> 140.10.0.102
   type: Echo Reply (0)  code: No Code (0)
"
```

3a. Examine the output on PE1 carefully. Each ICMP packet is numbered in ascending order. Why are there 10 packets showing up on PE1 when CE1 only launched five ping requests?

3b. Can you find where the ingress/egress interface is identified?

4. Modify the ping command: The source IP address embedded in the ICMP Echo request packet should be the system interface address.

```
*A:CE1# ping 140.10.0.101 source 140.10.0.3
PING 140.10.0.101 56 data bytes
Request timed out. icmp_seq=1.
Request timed out. icmp_seq=2.
 [... Additional output omitted ...]

[ Output captured from PE1 terminal session ]
11 2000/01/01 14:04:50.33 UTC MINOR: DEBUG #2001 Base PIP
"PIP: ICMP
instance 1 (Base), interface index 4 (toCE1),
ICMP  ingressing on toCE1:
   140.10.0.3 -> 140.10.0.101
   type: Echo (8)  code: No Code (0)
"


12 2000/01/01 14:04:51.33 UTC MINOR: DEBUG #2001 Base PIP
"PIP: ICMP
instance 1 (Base), interface index 4 (toCE1),
ICMP  ingressing on toCE1:
   140.10.0.3 -> 140.10.0.101
   type: Echo (8)  code: No Code (0)
"
```

4a. How many ICMP requests appear on CE1? How many requests are successfully received by PE1? How many replies are sent?

4b. In which direction (ingress/egress) is all the traffic flowing under these circumstances? Why?

5. To verify ARP operation, turn on debug only for ARP on PE1. Start with an "empty" ARP cache by executing the following commands on each of the routers, and then start a ping to PE1 from either CE1 or PE2.

```
*A:CE1# clear router arp all

*B:PE1# clear router arp all
*B:PE1#
*B:PE1# show router arp

===============================================================
ARP Table (Router: Base)
===============================================================
IP Address      MAC Address       Expiry      Type    Interface
---------------------------------------------------------------
140.10.0.1      00:21:05:4d:41:41 00h00m00s   Oth     system
140.10.0.11     00:21:05:4d:41:41 00h00m00s   Oth     loopbackTest
140.10.0.97     00:1a:f0:57:72:6f 00h00m00s   Oth[I]  toPE2
140.10.0.101    00:1a:f0:6c:6c:4c 00h00m00s   Oth[I]  toCE1
---------------------------------------------------------------
No. of ARP Entries: 4
===============================================================

*B:PE1# debug router ip no icmp
*B:PE1# debug router ip arp
*B:PE1# show debug
debug
    router "Base"
        ip
            arp
        exit
    exit
exit

*A:CE1# ping 140.10.0.101
[... Additional output omitted ...]

[ Output captured from PE1 terminal session ]
```

```
16 2000/01/01 14:17:06.19 UTC MINOR: DEBUG #2001 Base PIP
"PIP: ARP
instance 1 (Base), interface index 4 (toCE1),
ARP ingressing on toCE1
   Who has 140.10.0.101 ? Tell 140.10.0.102
"

17 2000/01/01 14:17:06.19 UTC MINOR: DEBUG #2001 Base PIP
"PIP: ARP
instance 1 (Base), interface index 4 (toCE1),
ARP egressing on toCE1
   140.10.0.101 is at 00:1a:f0:6c:6c:4c
"
```

5a. Why isn't the ARP table (cache) empty after issuing the `clear router arp all` command? Which MAC/IP addresses remain?

5b. Why is there only a single ARP request/reply pair, instead of a pair for every ping sent by CE1?

6. From PE1, ping the network interface address of both other routers. Observe whether ARP messages are generated. Verify that the ARP entry for the neighboring interfaces has been added.

```
*B:PE1# show router arp

===============================================================
ARP Table (Router: Base)
===============================================================
IP Address      MAC Address        Expiry    Type   Interface
---------------------------------------------------------------
140.10.0.1      00:21:05:4d:41:41  00h00m00s Oth    system
140.10.0.11     00:21:05:4d:41:41  00h00m00s Oth    loopbackTest
140.10.0.97     00:1a:f0:57:72:6f  00h00m00s Oth[I] toPE2
140.10.0.98     00:1a:f0:74:65:41  03h59m27s Dyn[I] toPE2
140.10.0.101    00:1a:f0:6c:6c:4c  00h00m00s Oth[I] toCE1
140.10.0.102    00:1a:f0:61:62:73  03h39m52s Dyn[I] toCE1
---------------------------------------------------------------
No. of ARP Entries: 6
===============================================================
*B:PE1#
```

6a. Were ARP messages generated? Why or why not?

6b. How many ARP entries are on each router at this point? Explain.

7. From PE1, attempt to ping the system interface address of both other routers. Observe whether ARP messages are generated.

7a. Were the pings successful? Why or why not?

7b. Were ARP messages generated? Why or why not?

7c. When a router is trying to reach a given IP, which comes first—checking the routing table or checking the ARP table?

Chapter 8: Introduction to IP Routing

The following lab is designed to reinforce your knowledge of the content in this chapter. Please review the instructions carefully and perform the steps in the order in which they are presented. The practice labs require that you have access to three or more Alcatel-Lucent 7750 SRs or Alcatel-Lucent 7450 ESSs in a non-production environment.

 These labs are designed to be used in a controlled lab environment. Please **DO NOT** attempt to perform these labs in a production environment.

Up to this point in the labs, it is only possible to ping addresses on the interfaces that are directly connected to a router. Locally attached networks, that is, the subnets associated with interfaces, are the only networks known by the router. As seen in the last step of the lab exercises in Chapter 6, any attempt to ping the system interface of a remote router will fail, since the remote *system* interface is not directly attached to the local router, and thus no route exists to the destination.

This set of exercises looks at *static routes*, and a particular kind of static route called a *default route*. Static routes are one method of populating the routing table, thus enabling traffic to reach non-local networks. Note that all information for static routes is determined and manually entered by the administrator and thus is subject to the usual limitations of humans. Exercises in later chapters look at two other well-known protocols—OSPF and BGP—for automatically generating and propagating routing table information.

Lab Section 8.1: Static Routes

The Chinese philosopher Lao Tzu said, "A journey of a thousand miles starts with [just] one step." This idea is equally true for routing traffic to any final destination: Each router along the path only needs to be concerned with a single additional step, known as a *next hop*. If every router has the correct information, and sends traffic one additional step, the traffic should ultimately end up where it's supposed to go.

In routing terms, a *destination* is a range of addresses, or subnet addresses, connected to a particular router. A typical static route is a rule that combines these two parts: a destination subnet and the next-hop router. We'll see exactly how to write these rules on the Alcatel-Lucent 7750/7450 products.

Objective In this exercise, you will configure a pair of static routes between PE1 and PE2 so that each router can reach the other's system interface.

Validation You will know you have succeeded if both PE routers can ping the system interface of the adjacent PE router.

1. The first part of a static route is the subnet, so it always includes a subnet mask (even for a single address!). This example uses a /32 subnet (a single address) for the system interface of the adjacent PE router. Traffic must step (or hop) across to reach the IP interface at the far end of the link. The next hop address is always the IP address for the interface at the far end of the link, not the IP address of the near end of the link. Since the next hop is always a single address, it never has a subnet mask.

   On PE1, configure a static route using the following command syntax.

   ```
   *B:PE1# configure router static-route 150.10.0.1/32 next-hop 140.10.0.98
   *B:PE1#
   ```

   1a. What is the destination subnet in the preceding command?

   1b. What is the next-hop address in the above command?

   1c. Is the new subnet range anywhere within the 140.10.0.0/24 range of ISP 1, or is it completely external?

2. Confirm that the route table has a new entry.

   ```
   *B:PE1# show router route-table
   ```

```
===================================================================
Route Table (Router: Base)
===================================================================
Dest Prefix                  Type    Proto   Age        Pref
    Next Hop[Interface Name]                  Metric
-------------------------------------------------------------------
140.10.0.1/32                Local   Local   01h11m25s  0
    system                                    0
140.10.0.11/32               Local   Local   00h00m45s  0
    loopbackTest                              0
140.10.0.96/30               Local   Local   00h44m49s  0
    toPE2                                     0
140.10.0.100/30              Local   Local   00h28m42s  0
    toCE1                                     0
150.10.0.1/32                Remote  Static  00h04m06s  5
    140.10.0.98                               1
-------------------------------------------------------------------
No. of Routes: 5
===================================================================
*B:PE1#
```

3. Confirm that a debug log is still configured using the show log log-collector command (from Lab 2.2 in Chapter 2). All logs except 99 and 100 disappear every time you log out. If necessary, re-create the log (see Lab 6.1 in Chapter 6). Do the same for router PE2.

4. Turn on debugging for ICMP only (see Lab 6.1 in Chapter 6). Do the same for router PE2.

5. Test the new static route by pinging the system interface of PE2 from PE1.

```
*B:PE1# ping 150.10.0.1
PING 150.10.0.1 56 data bytes

1 2000/01/01 13:49:07.77 UTC MINOR: DEBUG #2001 Base PIP
"PIP: ICMP
instance 1 (Base), interface index 3 (toPE2),
ICMP egressing on toPE2:
    140.10.0.1 -> 150.10.0.1
    type: Echo (8)  code: No Code (0)
"

[... Additional output omitted ...]
```

```
Request timed out. icmp_seq=1.
Request timed out. icmp_seq=2.
[... Additional output omitted ...]


[ Output captured from PE2 terminal session ]
*A:PE2#
1 2000/01/01 13:48:12.54 UTC MINOR: DEBUG #2001 Base PIP
"PIP: ICMP
instance 1 (Base); interface index 3 (toPE1),
ICMP  ingressing on toPE1:
    140.10.0.1 -> 150.10.0.1
    type: Echo (8)  code: No Code (0)
"
```

5a. Did PE1 successfully transmit a ping request? How do you know?

5b. Did PE2 successfully receive a ping request? How do you know?

5c. What are the exact source and destination addresses in the ping packets?

5d. Does PE1 have a correct, functioning route to the system address of PE2?

5e. Was the `ping` command successful? How do you know?

5f. Explain why or why not the ping was successful.

6. Compare the source address for this last `ping` command with the one from Lab Exercise 6.1 in Chapter 6. Compare also the "type" of route in the routing table for the ping destination in each case. (Refer to Step 2 above, and Step 10 in Lab Exercise 5.3 in Chapter 5.)

  6a. By default, what source address is used when a ping destination is a *Local* route? By default, what source address is used when a ping destination is a *Remote* route? (This is a good rule to remember!)

7. Repeat the necessary steps above to build a static route on PE2 that points to the system interface on PE1. Be sure to confirm that it appears correctly in the route table on PE2.

  ```
  *A:PE2# configure router static-route 140.10.0.1/32 next-hop 140.10.0.97
  *A:PE2#
  ```

8. Repeat the test of pinging the system interface of PE2 from PE1. (You may want to turn off debugging to make it easier to distinguish the output.)

8a. Did PE1 successfully transmit a ping request? How do you know?

8b. Did PE2 successfully receive a ping request? How do you know?

8c. What are the exact source and destination addresses in the ping packets?

8d. Does PE1 have a correct, functioning route to the system address of PE2? Does PE2 have a functioning route to the system interface of PE1?

8e. Was the ping command successful? How do you know?

8f. Explain why the ping was successful or not.

9. Test both PE routers to determine whether you can ping the loopback interfaces of the remote PE router.

9a. Which loopback interfaces are reachable, if any? Explain why or why not?

10. Removing a static route requires typing the *exact* route again, except with the option no in front of static-route. Remove the static route. (Try making some intentional typing mistakes in the addresses, to see what kind of error messages you get.)

```
*A:PE2# configure router no static-route 140.10.0.1/32 next-hop
140.10.0.97
*A:PE2#
```

10a. How can you confirm that a static route has been successfully removed?

11. As the last step, use the ping command to verify that both PE routers have a correct, functioning static route to the other router's system interface.

11a. What did you learn? For successful communication, how many routes are required between a source and destination? Do *not* forget this important rule!!!

Lab Section 8.2: Default Routes and Router Logic

In the previous exercise, the static routes were fairly simple: Traffic destined for a particular subnet was sent to a particular next-hop address. In this lab, we use three different kinds of static routes. These are shown in Figure 8.21 as *aggregate routes*, *default routes*, and *simple routes*. Together they provide enough flexibility to handle just about every situation.

Consider for a moment the CE1 router. Since there is only one single connection to the rest of the (Inter)network, the next-hop address would *always* be the same for every single static route. It seems pointless to have many, many static routes all giving the same next hop. A *default route* provides a solution—a single routing entry that effectively says: "*Any* other destination uses [PE1] as the next hop." This route will be used for any destination subnet that isn't local to CE1.

Figure 8.21 Three different types of static routes are used from CE to PE and from PE to PE in this lab exercise.

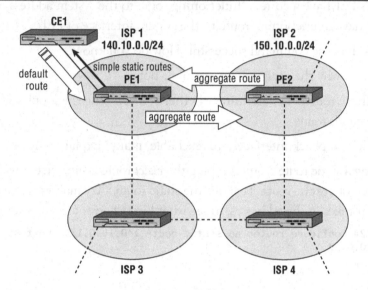

Next, let's look at the network from PE2's perspective. All hosts in the subnet 140.10.0.0/24 exist *somewhere* within ISP 1. Exactly where a host resides within ISP 1 isn't a concern for PE2; that's PE1's job to sort out. All PE2 needs to know is that any address within 140.10.0.0/24 should be forwarded to PE1 as the next hop. PE2 uses an *aggregate route* for the /24 subnet without considering whether every single possible host within that range actually exists. (In fact, there may be many addresses and entire blocks for which *no* hosts exist!) The key point of the aggregate route is that there are *no hosts outside of ISP 1 for the 140.10.0.0/24 range*. Likewise for PE1: It should be configured so that traffic for all possible hosts in the 150.10.0.0/24 range is sent via PE2.

This set of lab exercises makes use of all three types of routes (simple, aggregate, and default) to get full connectivity between the routers with a minimum number of entries in each router's routing table. The CE device uses a default route toward PE1; PE1 will use simple static routes toward the subnets associated with CE1; and both PE routers will use aggregate routes for the neighbor's IP subnet.

Objective In this exercise, you will become more familiar with static routes by configuring a variety of static routes to provide full connectivity to all interfaces from all routers.

Validation You will know you have succeeded if every router can ping every interface on every other router.

1. Figure 8.21 shows only the static routes for CE1, PE1, and PE2. Complete the figure by drawing the static routes that ISP 3 and ISP 4 would use to reach 140.10.0.0/24. Label each route with its type (simple, aggregate, or default) and the next-hop interface.

    1a. For the *shortest* path, how many alternatives are there for ISP 3 to reach 140.10.0.0/24?

    1b. For the *shortest* path, how many alternatives are there for ISP 4 to reach 140.10.0.0/24?

    1c. If ISP 3 does not use the shortest path, can traffic still reach 140.10.0.0/24?

2. Remove all previously configured static routes (see the previous exercise). Confirm that all static routes have been removed (see the previous exercise; all routes should have a type of Local).

3. Configure aggregate static routes between PE1 and PE2. Confirm that you can ping every interface on PE2 from PE1 and vice versa.

        *B:PE1# configure router static-route 150.10.0.0/24 next-hop 140.10.0.98
        *B:PE1#
        *A:PE2# configure router static-route 140.10.0.0/24 next-hop 140.10.0.97
        *A:PE2#

4. Configure simple static routes on PE1 for all interfaces on CE1.

        *B:PE1# configure router static-route 140.10.0.3/32 next-hop 140.10.0.102
        *B:PE1# configure router static-route 140.10.0.12/32 next-hop 140.10.0.102
        *B:PE1#

    4a. Why is a pair of routes to CE1 necessary, instead of just a single route?

5. Configure a default route on CE1 that points to PE1.

        *A:CE1# configure router static-route 0.0.0.0/0 next-hop 140.10.0.101
        *A:CE1#

6. Use a show command to verify the static routes on all three routers.

```
*B:PE1# show router route-table
===============================================================
Route Table (Router: Base)
===============================================================
Dest Prefix                      Type     Proto    Age        Pref
    Next Hop[Interface Name]                        Metric
---------------------------------------------------------------
140.10.0.1/32                    Local    Local    02d22h03m  0
    system                                          0
140.10.0.3/32                    Remote   Static   00h06m41s  5
    140.10.0.102                                    1
140.10.0.11/32                   Local    Local    02d20h45m  0
    loopbackTest                                    0
140.10.0.12/32                   Remote   Static   00h06m27s  5
    140.10.0.102                                    1
140.10.0.96/30                   Local    Local    02d21h37m  0
    toPE2                                           0
140.10.0.100/30                  Local    Local    02d21h21m  0
    toCE1                                           0
150.10.0.0/24                    Remote   Static   00h57m02s  5
    140.10.0.98                                     1
---------------------------------------------------------------
No. of Routes: 7
===============================================================
*B:PE1>config>router#

*A:PE2# show router route-table
===============================================================
Route Table (Router: Base)
===============================================================
Dest Prefix                      Type     Proto    Age        Pref
    Next Hop[Interface Name]                        Metric
---------------------------------------------------------------
140.10.0.0/24                    Remote   Static   00h58m13s  5
    140.10.0.97                                     1
140.10.0.96/30                   Local    Local    02d20h51m  0
    toPE1                                           0
150.10.0.1/32                    Local    Local    02d21h20m  0
    system                                          0
150.10.0.11/32                   Local    Local    02d21h19m  0
    loopbackTest                                    0
---------------------------------------------------------------
No. of Routes: 4
===============================================================
*A:PE2#

*A:CE1# show router route-table
```

```
========================================================
Route Table (Router: Base)
========================================================
Dest Prefix               Type    Proto   Age        Pref
    Next Hop[Interface Name]                Metric
--------------------------------------------------------
0.0.0.0/0                 Remote  Static  00h01m48s  5
        140.10.0.101                       1
140.10.0.3/32             Local   Local   02d21h20m  0
        system                             0
140.10.0.12/32            Local   Local   02d21h21m  0
        loopbackTest                       0
140.10.0.100/30           Local   Local   02d21h19m  0
        toPE1                              0
--------------------------------------------------------
No. of Routes: 4
========================================================
*A:CE1#
```

6a. Can you account for each of the routes in each router's routing table?

7. Verify the proper operation of the routes by pinging between each pair of adjacent routers. If any ping fails, confirm that there are no mistakes in any route type, subnet/mask, or next-hop values.

8. Use `ping` and `traceroute` between CE1 and PE2. Confirm that each router can reach the other's `system` and `loopback` interfaces.

8a. How is it possible for CE1 to reach PE2 when there is no route for the 150.10.0.0/24 subnet in CE1's routing table?

8b. How is it possible for PE2 to reach CE1 when there is no specific route to CE1 interfaces in PE2's routing table?

9. Using `ping` (and, optionally, `traceroute`), confirm that every router can reach every configured interface on every other router.

10. (*Optional*) Use `traceroute` to verify that PE2 can reach CE1. Use `traceroute` again to attempt connectivity with one of the aggregate customer IPs on CE1 and notice the difference in the output.

```
*A:PE2# traceroute 140.10.0.3
traceroute to 140.10.0.3, 30 hops max, 40 byte packets
  1  140.10.0.97 (140.10.0.97)    <10 ms  <10 ms  <10 ms
```

```
  2  140.10.0.3 (140.10.0.3)     <10 ms  <10 ms  <10 ms
*A:PE2#
*A:PE2# traceroute 140.10.0.193
traceroute to 140.10.0.193, 30 hops max, 40 byte packets
  1  140.10.0.97 (140.10.0.97)     <10 ms !N  <10 ms !N  <10 ms !N
*A:PE2#
```

10a. The marker !N means the router at the far end of the link has *no* route to the destination, so it will drop all such packets. Is there any way to improve the handling of these packets? Try out your solution!

Chapter 9: Open Shortest Path First (OSPF)

The following lab is designed to reinforce your knowledge of the content in this chapter. Please review the instructions carefully and perform the steps in the order in which they are provided. The practice labs require that you have access to three or more Alcatel-Lucent 7750 SRs or Alcatel-Lucent 7450 ESSs in a non-production environment.

 These labs are designed to be used in a controlled lab environment. Please **DO NOT** attempt to perform these labs in a production environment.

In the previous chapter, the static routes were configured entirely manually. There were many possible sources of mistakes: determining the correct IP address of the next-hop interface; typing mistakes of either subnet, mask, or next-hop values; or forgotten routes. Any single mistake could potentially severely disrupt the flow of traffic.

Routing protocols were designed to automate the preceding tasks and thereby eliminate as many sources of error as possible. In this lab, we use OSPF to duplicate the connectivity of the previous lab, but without requiring any manual configuration of addresses or subnets.

Lab Section 9.1: Single Area OSPF

This exercise uses the routers in a new configuration. They are all now part of the same domain, belonging to a single ISP as shown in Figure 9.11. (Imagine this is due to a corporate merger.) For the purposes of this lab section, CE1 is considered as belonging to part of the ISP core. There are no changes to the addressing scheme.

Objective In this exercise, you will configure a single area OSPF network. This lab will demonstrate the different databases that are created by the OSPF routing protocol.

Validation You will know you have succeeded if every router can ping *every interface* on *every* other router.

Figure 9.11 This configuration of three routers allows us to explore the key aspects of OSPF routing.

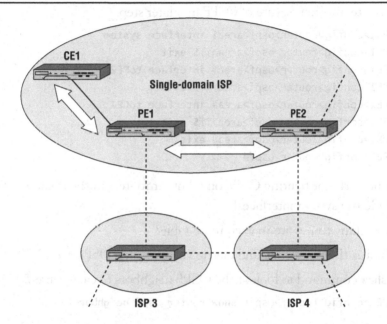

 Please remove all static routes configured on CE1 and the PE devices in the previous labs. Refer to Lab Section 8.1 in Chapter 8. Confirm that all routes have been removed by ensuring that each router's routing table contains only routes of type `Local`.

1. The first step is to enable the OSPF routing process on the router:

   ```
   *B:PE1# configure router ospf
   *B:PE1>config>router>ospf$
   ```

2. Next define the area that the interfaces will be placed in. Remember that the area must match on the interfaces on both ends of a link for OSPF to establish an

adjacency. The objective of this exercise is to configure a single area OSPF network; therefore, you should use the same area number.

```
*B:PE1>config>router>ospf$ area 0
*B:PE1>config>router>ospf>area$
```

3. Within this area, enter all the interfaces on which OSPF should be running and sending out its advertisements. The `system` interface is a special case and should *always* be included in OSPF. In this case, place all the local interfaces into the OSPF process area 0. Do *not* include the `loopback` interfaces; they are used to demonstrate another feature of OSPF in a later step.

```
*B:PE1>config>router>ospf>area$ interface system
*B:PE1>config>router>ospf>area>if$ exit
*B:PE1>config>router>ospf>area# interface toPE2
*B:PE1>config>router>ospf>area>if$ exit
*B:PE1>config>router>ospf>area# interface toCE1
*B:PE1>config>router>ospf>area>if$ exit
*B:PE1>config>router>ospf>area# exit
*B:PE1>config>router>ospf#
```

4. Continue with configuring OSPF on all other routers in the domain. Don't forget to include the system interfaces!

4a. How many routes are in each route table?

4b. What is the preference and metric value of each OSPF route?

5. Use a `show` command to look at the OSPF neighbors of each router.

```
*B:PE1>config>router>ospf# show router ospf neighbor
```

```
===========================================================
OSPF Neighbors
===========================================================
Interface-Name     Rtr Id       State   Pri  RetxQ   TTL
-----------------------------------------------------------
toPE2              150.10.0.1   Full    1    0       35
toCE1              140.10.0.3   Full    1    0       34
-----------------------------------------------------------
No. of Neighbors: 2
===========================================================
*B:PE1>config>router>ospf#
```

5a. How many neighbors do you see on PE1? PE2? CE1?

5b. What is the state of the adjacencies? What should they be? Why?

6. Use a show command to display the OSPF Link State database. This database is a listing of all LSAs that have been received by the router. It is these LSAs that the SPF algorithm uses to create the forwarding table.

```
*B:PE1>config>router>ospf# show router ospf database
```

```
===================================================================
OSPF Link State Database (Type : All)
===================================================================
Type    Area Id   Link State Id  Adv Rtr Id   Age  Sequence    Cksum
-------------------------------------------------------------------
Router  0.0.0.0   140.10.0.1     140.10.0.1   522  0x80000008  0x1b9b
Router  0.0.0.0   140.10.0.3     140.10.0.3   515  0x80000005  0xd83d
Router  0.0.0.0   150.10.0.1     150.10.0.1   502  0x80000005  0xae57
Network 0.0.0.0   140.10.0.97    140.10.0.1   522  0x80000001  0xefa4
Network 0.0.0.0   140.10.0.101   140.10.0.1   537  0x80000001  0x7523
-------------------------------------------------------------------
No. of LSAs: 5
===================================================================
```

```
*B:PE1>config>router>ospf#
```

6a. What type of LSAs are in the database?

6b. Is the database consistent on all routers? Is the database *identical* on all routers?

7. The previous command only showed a *summary* of each LSA. Use the detail option at the end of the command to see the full LSA information.

```
*B:PE1# show router ospf database detail
[... OR ...]
*B:PE1 # show router ospf database 140.10.0.1 detail
```

8. Confirm using ping, and optionally traceroute, that each router can reach every interface configured in OSPF on every other router. Note that the loopbacks have *not* been configured in OSPF and therefore should *not* be reachable from remote routers. If any interface isn't reachable, double-check that you have correctly configured that interface into OSPF.

9. We will use loopback interfaces to demonstrate how to distribute external or static routes into OSPF. To enable a router to distribute external routes, it must be identified as an *Autonomous System Border Router* (ASBR). Each router will distribute its loopback interface, so make each router an ASBR.

```
*B:PE1>config>router>ospf# asbr
*B:PE1>config>router>ospf#
```

   9a. Can the ASBR designation be limited to a particular area? Try issuing the asbr command within the context config ➤ router ➤ ospf ➤ area 0.

10. A routing policy defines which external routes are distributed into OSPF. It is impossible to distribute external routes without a policy. A lengthy discussion of policy implementation on the Alcatel-Lucent 7750/7450 products is a topic for an advanced course. For this exercise, please follow the commands below, which create and *apply* an export policy to OSPF. Repeat this process on all routers.

```
*B:PE1# configure router policy-options
[For layout considerations, the prompt is shorted below.]
>policy-options# begin
>policy-options# policy-statement DistributeLB
>policy-options>policy-statement$ entry 10
>policy-options>policy-statement>entry$ from protocol direct
>policy-options>policy-statement>entry# action accept
>policy-options>policy-statement>entry>action# exit
>policy-options>policy-statement>entry# exit
>policy-options>policy-statement# exit
>policy-options# commit
>policy-options# exit all
[...The full prompt is shown again below...]
*B:PE1#
*B:PE1# configure router ospf
*B:PE1>config>router>ospf# export DistributeLB
*B:PE1>config>router>ospf#
```

   10a. Can the export policy be assigned only to a particular area? Try issuing the export command within the context config ➤ router ➤ ospf ➤ area 0.

11. Confirm using ping, and optionally traceroute, that each router can reach every interface configured in OSPF on every other router, including loopbacks. If any

interface isn't reachable, double-check that you have correctly configured that interface into OSPF and that the router is designated as **asbr**.

12. Use a show command to display the routing table on each router. Compare the result with the routing tables you obtained in Exercise 8.2. Verify the Protocol column to ensure that none of the routes is static.

```
*B:PE1# show router route-table
===============================================================
Route Table (Router: Base)
===============================================================
Dest Prefix                    Type    Proto   Age        Pref
    Next Hop[Interface Name]                    Metric
---------------------------------------------------------------
140.10.0.1/32                  Local   Local   03d02h27m  0
    system                                      0
140.10.0.3/32                  Remote  OSPF    02h16m53s  10
    140.10.0.102                                100
140.10.0.11/32                 Local   Local   03d01h09m  0
    loopbackTest                                0
140.10.0.12/32                 Remote  OSPF    00h09m57s  150
    140.10.0.102                                1
140.10.0.96/30                 Local   Local   03d02h01m  0
    toPE2                                       0
140.10.0.100/30                Local   Local   03d01h45m  0
    toCE1                                       0
150.10.0.1/32                  Remote  OSPF    02h16m39s  10
    140.10.0.98                                 100
150.10.0.11/32                 Remote  OSPF    00h09m45s  150
    140.10.0.98                                 1
---------------------------------------------------------------
No. of Routes: 8
===============================================================
*B:PE1>config>router#
```

12a. What is the preference value for a route generated from an OSPF interface? What is the preference value for routes distributed via an export policy?

The next set of lab exercises shows how to completely remove all configuration for a routing protocol in two quick steps. For the moment, however, don't forget to save the configuration on *all* your routers! Since the exercises in Chapter 11 require OSPF, it will save time if the fully functional configurations are saved *now* with a separate configuration name (refer to Lab Section 2.3 in Chapter 2, "Saving Configuration Changes").

```
*B:PE1# bof primary-config cf3:\OSPF-Full.cfg
WARNING: CLI A valid config file does not exist at cf3:\OSPF-Full.cfg.
*B:PE1# admin save
Writing file to cf3:\OSPF-Full.cfg
Saving configuration .... Completed.
*B:PE1# bof primary-config cf3:\MAA-TestConfig.cfg
*B:PE1#
```

Chapter 10: BGP Routing

The following lab is designed to reinforce your knowledge of the content in this chapter. Please review the instructions carefully for each lab and perform the steps in the order in which they are provided. The practice labs require that you have access to three or more Alcatel-Lucent 7750 SRs in a non-production environment. Note that the Alcatel-Lucent 7450 ESSs do not have the BGP capabilities required for these lab exercises.

 These labs are designed to be used in a controlled lab environment. Please **DO NOT** attempt to perform these labs in a production environment.

Although there is quite a variety of routing protocols, BGP is the de facto standard for routers handling the global routing table (i.e., for the Internet). No course on routing protocols would be complete without some discussion of BGP. In this lab, we will duplicate the connectivity between PE1 and PE2 of the previous lab, except we will use BGP instead of OSPF.

Figure 10.9 shows the lab topology for this lab exercise. Routers CE1 and PE1 are considered as being within ISP 1's core; router PE2 is within ISP 2's core. Note that CE1 has no direct reachability to the outside of ISP 1; it must always pass through PE1. ISP 1 and ISP 2 are separate Autonomous Systems (ASs).

Figure 10.9 This configuration of three routers provides an example of configuring both an iBGP and an eBGP peering session.

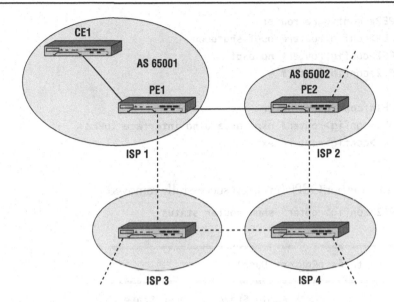

Lab Section 10.1: External BGP Routing

We use External BGP (EBGP), or BGP between routers in different ASs, to provide a tidy example of basic BGP configuration. After establishing EBGP in this section, we'll add additional connectivity in the next section.

Objective In this exercise, you will configure two BGP Autonomous Systems, using eBGP peering. You will configure the BGP routing protocol and required policies to connect the two different Autonomous Systems together and exchange routing information.

Validation You will know you have succeeded if each PE router can ping *every interface* on the other PE router.

Removing OSPF is the first step before configuring BGP, since this exercise uses BGP exclusively between PE1 and PE2. In most cases, removing a routing protocol is a simple two-step process: Shut down the protocol and specify no *xxx* (where *xxx* is a protocol name).

1. Remove OSPF from PE2 only. Remove just the interface to PE2 from PE1's OSPF configuration.

```
*A:PE2# configure router
*A:PE2>config>router# ospf shutdown
*A:PE2>config>router# no ospf
*A:PE2>config>router#

*B:PE1# configure router
*B:PE1>config>router# ospf area 0 no interface toPE2
*B:PE1>config>router# exit
*B:PE1#
```

2. Confirm whether OSPF has been successfully removed.

```
*A:PE2>config>router# show router status


===================================================
Router Status (Router: Base)
===================================================

                        Admin State    Oper State
---------------------------------------------------
Router                  Up             Up
OSPFv2                  Not configured Not configured
RIP                     Not configured Not configured
ISIS                    Not configured Not configured
[... Additional output omitted ...]
BGP                     Not configured Not configured
[... Additional output omitted ...]

Max IPv4 Routes    No Limit
Max IPv6 Routes    No Limit
Total IPv4 Routes  3
Total IPv6 Routes  0
[... Additional output omitted ...]
ECMP Max Routes    1
Triggered Policies No
===================================================
*A:PE2>config>router#
```

2a. Has OSPF been removed from PE2? What other routing protocols are running on PE2?

2b. There is another method of confirming that OSPF is no longer running between PE1 and PE2. What is it?

2c. The output shows three IPv4 routes on PE2. Where do they come from? Explain the results. (*Hint:* Look at the routing table for details.)

3. Assign the AS number to each router as shown in Figure 10.9.

```
*B:PE1>config>router# autonomous-system 65001
*B:PE1>config>router#

*A:CE1>config>router# autonomous-system 65001
*A:CE1>config>router#

*A:PE2>config>router# autonomous-system 65002
*A:PE2>config>router#
```

4. The PE routers are external BGP (eBGP) peers since they have *different* AS numbers. eBGP peers typically use the IP address of the connecting network interface as the neighbor address. On *each* PE router, configure the far end router within a group called eBGP. The far end router should be listed with its IP address and AS number.

```
*B:PE1>config>router# bgp
*B:PE1>config>router>bgp$ group eBGP
*B:PE1>config>router>bgp>group$ neighbor 140.10.0.98
*B:PE1>config>router>bgp>group>neighbor$ peer-as 65002
*B:PE1>config>router>bgp>group>neighbor$ exit
*B:PE1>config>router>bgp>group# exit
*B:PE1>config>router>bgp#
```

5. Once both PE routers are configured, verify that they have successfully established a peer relationship.

```
*B:PE1>config>router>bgp# show router bgp summary
===============================================================
 BGP Router ID : 140.10.0.1   AS : 65001   Local AS : 65001
===============================================================
BGP Admin State        : Up        BGP Oper State    : Up
Total Peer Groups      : 1         Total Peers       : 1
[... Additional output omitted ...]
```

```
=================================================================
BGP Summary
=================================================================
Neighbor
            AS PktRcvd InQ  Up/Down      State|Rcv/Act/Sent
               PktSent OutQ               (Addr Family)
-----------------------------------------------------------------
140.10.0.98
         65002       7    0 00h02m46s 0/0/0 (IPv4)
                     7    0
=================================================================
*B:PE1>config>router>bgp#
```

5a. Have the two PE routers exchanged any route information? How can you verify this?

5b. In the output above, what does the output column Rcv/Act/Sent mean?

6. Check directly with BGP to see the details of routes advertised to the PE neighbor.

```
*B:PE1# show router bgp neighbor 140.10.0.98 advertised-routes
=================================================================
  BGP Router ID : 140.10.0.1   AS : 65001   Local AS : 65001
=================================================================
  Legend -
  Status codes  : u - used, s - suppressed, h - history,
                  d - decayed, * - valid
  Origin codes  : i - IGP, e - EGP, ? - incomplete, > - best


=================================================================
BGP IPv4 Routes
=================================================================
Flag  Network                        LocalPref    MED
      Nexthop                                     VPN Label
      As-Path
-----------------------------------------------------------------
No Matching Entries Found
=================================================================
*B:PE1#
```

7. BGP, like other distance vector protocols, requires an export policy to advertise routes to other BGP peers. Apply an export policy on both PE routers. For convenience, reuse the export policy (e.g., DistributeLB) created in Lab Section 9.1 in Chapter 9. It actually exports all local (i.e., *direct*) interfaces.

```
*B:PE1>config>router>bgp# export DistributeLB
*B:PE1>config>router>bgp#
```

7a. Have the two PE routers exchanged any route information? What three commands can be used to verify this? (You may need to wait a few moments before seeing the final results.)

7b. What is the preference value for BGP routes? How does that compare with OSPF? Which one is *better*, that is, has higher precedence?

7c. At this point in time, how many routes are in the routing table? Explain your answer.

8. Confirm that each PE router can ping every interface on the other PE router. If not, check that you have used the correct addresses and AS numbers in the configurations and have applied the policy correctly on both routers.

Lab Section 10.2: Internal BGP Routing

Shifting from eBGP to iBGP can cause a few extra configuration issues. This lab exercise looks at potential issues and solutions for next-hop values and route preference values.

Objective In this exercise you will add an iBGP peering configuration to the existing eBGP setup. You will configure the BGP routing protocol and required policies to ensure that routing information flows correctly between iBGP and eBGP peers.

Validation You will know you have succeeded if every router can ping *every* interface on *every* other router.

1. Confirm that OSPF is still up and running correctly between PE1 and CE1.

1a. What commands can be used to verify OSPF operation? (*Hint:* There are at least three different alternatives.)

2. PE1 and CE1 are internal BGP (iBGP) peers since they have the same AS number. iBGP peers typically use the system IP address as the neighbor address (which is why an IGP like OSPF is necessary to resolve that address). On both PE1 and CE1, configure the far end router within a group called iBGP. Just like eBGP, the far end router should be listed with an IP address and AS number.

```
*B:PE1>config>router>bgp# group iBGP
*B:PE1>config>router>bgp>group$ neighbor 140.10.0.3
*B:PE1>config>router>bgp>group>neighbor$ peer-as 65001
*B:PE1>config>router>bgp>group>neighbor$ exit
*B:PE1>config>router>bgp>group# exit
*B:PE1>config>router>bgp#
```

3. Once both PE1 and CE1 routers are configured, verify that they have successfully established a peer relationship.

```
*B:PE1>config>router>bgp# show router bgp summary
===============================================================
 BGP Router ID : 140.10.0.1   AS : 65001   Local AS : 65001
===============================================================
BGP Admin State      : Up          BGP Oper State   : Up
Total Peer Groups    : 2           Total Peers      : 2
[... Additional output omitted ...]


===============================================================
BGP Summary
===============================================================
Neighbor
          AS PktRcvd InQ  Up/Down    State|Rcv/Act/Sent
             PktSent OutQ            (Addr Family)
---------------------------------------------------------------
140.10.0.3
       65001       5   0 00h01m41s 0/0/6 (IPv4)
                   7   0
140.10.0.98
       65002     139   0 01h08m17s 3/2/4 (IPv4)
                 140   0
===============================================================
*B:PE1>config>router>bgp#
```

3a. Has PE1 exchanged any routes with CE1? How can you verify this?

3b. In the output above, what do the values in the column Rcv/Act/Sent tell you?

3c. At this point in time, how many routes are in PE1's routing table? Explain your answer.

3d. How does PE1 learn about CE1's interfaces: through OSPF, BGP, or both? What does the routing table say? Explain your answer.

4. Configure the export policy on CE1 so that its interfaces are exported by BGP.

4a. Have the two PE routers exchanged any route information? (You may need to wait a few moments before seeing the final results.)

4b. What is the preference value for BGP routes?

4c. At this point in time, how many routes are in the routing table? Explain your answer.

4d. How does PE1 learn about CE1's interfaces: through OSPF, BGP, or both? What does the routing table say? Explain your answer.

5. Check the routing tables on CE1 and PE2.

5a. Does either router have routes to the other's system and loopback interfaces?

6. Each router advertises its routes specifying a next hop of the local router's network interface. Since PE1 sits between CE1 and PE2, neither of those two routers knows how to reach the far router's network interface. Confirm what route information is being sent to CE1.

```
*B:PE1# show router bgp neighbor 140.10.0.3 advertised-routes
===============================================================
BGP Router ID : 140.10.0.1   AS : 65001   Local AS : 65001
===============================================================
Legend -
Status codes  : u - used, s - suppressed, h - history,
                d - decayed, * - valid
Origin codes  : i - IGP, e - EGP, ? - incomplete, > - best
```

```
============================================================
BGP IPv4 Routes
============================================================
Flag  Network                        LocalPref   MED
      Nexthop                                    VPN Label
      As-Path
------------------------------------------------------------

[... Additional output omitted ...]

?     150.10.0.1/32                  100         None
      140.10.0.98                                -
      65002


?     150.10.0.11/32                 100         None
      140.10.0.98                                -
      65002


------------------------------------------------------------
Routes : 6
============================================================
*B:PE1>config>router>bgp#
*B:PE1>config>router>bgp#
```

6a. What specific IP address does PE2 specify as the next-hop address to reach its interfaces?

6b. Is that address known to CE1? (In Step 1 of the previous exercise, did you remember to remove the toPE2 interface from PE1's OSPF configuration?)

7. A common technique to fix the issue of an unreachable next-hop interface is to have eBGP routers *change* that address to their local address. Configure PE1 to set the next-hop address on all routes advertised/passed along to its iBGP peers.

```
*B:PE1>config>router>bgp# group iBGP next-hop-self
*B:PE1>config>router>bgp#
```

7a. Confirm what route information is now being sent to CE1. (You may need to wait a few moments before seeing the final result.)

7b. What specific interface does PE1 choose for the next-hop address?

7c. Is that address known to CE1?

7d. Why is an IGP still needed among iBGP peers?

8. Confirm whether each router can ping all interfaces on every other router.

   8a. Can every router reach every interface?

   8b. Do the ping results for each router correlate with the routing table information for that router? Explain your answer.

9. BGP routers will only pass along, as a default, learned BGP routes that are the *best* routes. On PE1, confirm which protocol is selected for the routes learned from CE1. (*Hint:* Look at the routing table.)

   9a. Why does the Routing Table Manager (RTM) always choose the one protocol as the source of routes from CE1?

   9b. Does the chosen protocol fit the specifications in the export policy for BGP (i.e., the DistributeLB policy)?

10. Modify the policy on PE1 so that it will include all routes learned within the AS.

In a real-world environment, it may not be required to distribute the CE1 routes into another Autonomous System. It is a design decision and done here for illustrative purposes.

```
*B:PE1>config>router>bgp# exit all
*B:PE1# configure router policy-options
[For layout considerations, the prompt is shorted below.]
>policy-options# begin
>policy-options# policy-statement DistributeLB
>policy-options>policy-statement# entry 20
>policy-options>policy-statement>entry$ from protocol ospf
>policy-options>policy-statement>entry# action accept
>policy-options>policy-statement>entry>action# exit
>policy-options>policy-statement>entry# exit
>policy-options>policy-statement# exit
[...The full prompt is shown again below...]
*B:PE1>config>router>policy-options# commit
*B:PE1>config>router>policy-options# exit
*B:PE1#
```

10a. Note the numbering of the new entry. Does this replace or add to the existing entry?

10b. Does the new entry add an extra condition (an AND function) or an alternative condition (an OR function)?

10c. What is the purpose of the begin and commit keywords?

11. Compare the routing tables on PE1 and PE2. Look carefully at the routes for the CE1 system and loopback interfaces. (You may need to wait a few moments before seeing the final results.)

11a. What is the next-hop address that appears on PE1 and PE2 for routes to CE1? Is it the same?

11b. What kind of BGP peering relationship exists between PE1 and PE2?

11c. Is the next-hop-self attribute required for eBGP peers?

If you have done everything correctly, every router should be able to ping *every* interface on *every* other router.

Chapter 11: Services

The following lab is designed to reinforce your knowledge of the content in this chapter. Please review the instructions carefully and perform the steps in the order in which they are provided.

Note that unlike previous labs, this lab requires a *fourth* piece of equipment that is capable of generating and responding to ping packets as a minimum. You will also need to have the capability of statically configuring its IP address. If your Alcatel-Lucent equipment has copper (i.e., wired) Ethernet ports, a simple desktop or laptop computer is more than sufficient. If not, you will need a fourth Alcatel-Lucent 7750/7450 router with suitable connections.

 These labs are designed to be used in a controlled lab environment. Please **DO NOT** attempt to perform these labs in a production environment.

The exercises for this chapter are split into two sections. The first section creates the supporting infrastructure for services. This infrastructure is not specific to any particular service but can support multiple services in just about any imaginable combination. The second section implements a VPLS service between the PE nodes.

As noted in Lab Section 5.2 in Chapter 5, all lab exercises have been designed to fully illustrate all configuration details but with a minimum number of nodes. While a VPLS across a single pair of routers may seem trivial (see Figure 11.15), please keep in mind that a real network could potentially have *dozens* of routers between PE1 and PE2 and that these additional routers could span a city, a continent, or even the entire globe.

Figure 11.15: The Service Provider Core network provides the infrastructure to connect geographically separate customer equipment in a seamless, invisible fashion.

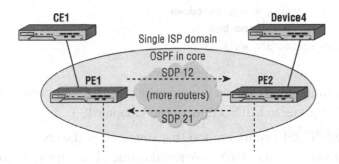

Lab Section 11.1: Services Framework

Figure 11.15 shows the topology for this section. The VPN framework resides within the domain of a single ISP. The edge routers (PE1 and PE2) are the only ones shown explicitly, although there could be many other Provider Core (P) routers. The network cloud is a reminder that the edge routers may have a direct link or may be joined by many intervening routers. An IGP is always a necessity; we'll reuse most of the configuration from Chapter 9. The task in this section is to build SDPs (shown as dotted arrows) between the PE routers.

Objective In this exercise, you will configure OSPF as the core IGP within a single domain, configure LDP, and create a full mesh of SDPs between PE routers. This creates the infrastructure to support the VPLS service in the next section.

Validation You will know you have succeeded if the SDPs between the PE routers are admin and operationally Up after completing all steps, and the two customer-facing (Ethernet) ports are in access mode.

The BGP configuration from the previous chapter's exercises is not needed for this chapter. Although BGP should not interfere with these exercises, you are advised to remove it completely for the sake of simplicity and ease of debugging. The command outputs for these exercises were obtained with BGP removed.

Part 1: IGP Configuration

1. (*Optional*) Completely remove the BGP configuration on *all* routers. (Refer to Lab Section 10.1 in Chapter 10.)

```
*B:PE1# configure router
*B:PE1>config>router# bgp shutdown
*B:PE1>config>router# no bgp
*B:PE1>config>router# exit
*B:PE1#
```

   1a. What command(s) can you use to verify that BGP has been successfully removed? (Refer to Lab Section 10.1 in Chapter 10.)

2. Restore the full OSPF configuration that you saved at the end of Chapter 9. Do this on all routers. (If you don't have saved config files, you will need to complete all the configuration steps from Chapter 9 on all routers.)

```
*B:PE1# exec cf3:\OSPF-Full.cfg
System Configuration
System Security Configuration
Log Configuration
System Security Cpm Hw Filters Configuration
QoS Policy Configuration
Card Configuration
Port Configuration
[... Additional output omitted ...]
Router (Network Side) Configuration
OSPFv2 Configuration
[... Additional output omitted ...]
Executed 225 lines in 0.0 seconds from file cf3:\OSPF-Full.cfg
*B:PE1#
```

3. Unlike in Lab Section 9.1 in Chapter 9, CE1 is now exclusively part of the customer network and is no longer considered as part of the ISP core. Since the role of CE1 has changed for this lab, it no longer participates in the ISP's core routing. On PE1, remove the toCE1 interface from OSPF. (Don't change the OSPF configuration on CE1; it will be modified in a later step.) Verify that OSPF is no longer running between PE1 and CE1.

```
*B:PE1# configure router ospf
*B:PE1>config>router>ospf# area 0
*B:PE1>config>router>ospf>area# no interface toCE1
*B:PE1>config>router>ospf>area# exit all
*B:PE1# show router ospf neighbor

===============================================================
OSPF Neighbors
===============================================================
Interface-Name     Rtr Id       State  Pri  RetxQ  TTL
---------------------------------------------------------------
toPE2              150.10.0.1   Full   1    0      35
---------------------------------------------------------------
No. of Neighbors: 1
===============================================================
*B:PE1#
```

3a. What tells you that OSPF is no longer running between PE1 and CE1?

Part 2: LDP and SDP Configuration

Running an IP/MPLS-based service requires a protocol for exchanging labels between the ISP's routers; we'll use the Label Distribution Protocol (LDP) for ease of deployment. The LDP labels provide the required support to run Service Distribution Point (SDPs).

A VPLS service requires a full mesh of SDPs. The term *full mesh* means every PE router has an SDP to every other PE router participating in the service. In this exercise, since we only have two PE routers, we only need a pair of SDPs in order for PE1 and PE2 to be fully meshed.

1. LDP must be enabled on *all* router interfaces within the Provider Core. Unlike OSPF or BGP, the default state for LDP is disabled. You *must* remember to do no shutdown to enable LDP. Configure LDP on both PE routers.

```
*B:PE1# configure router ldp
*B:PE1>config>router>ldp$ interface-parameters
*B:PE1>config>router>ldp>if-params$ interface toPE2
*B:PE1>config>router>ldp>if-params>if$ exit
*B:PE1>config>router>ldp>if-params# exit
*B:PE1>config>router>ldp# no shutdown
*B:PE1>config>router>ldp#
```

2. Once both routers have LDP configured, verify that LDP is correctly configured on both PE routers and that they have established an LDP session.

```
*B:PE1>config>router>ldp# show router ldp interface
```

```
===============================================================
LDP Interfaces
===============================================================
Interface    Adm Opr  Hello  Hold  KA      KA       Transport
                      Factor Time  Factor  Timeout  Address
---------------------------------------------------------------
toPE2        Up  Up   3      15    3       30       System
---------------------------------------------------------------
No. of Interfaces: 1
===============================================================
```

```
*B:PE1>config>router>ldp#
*B:PE1>config>router>ldp# show router ldp session
```

```
=================================================================
LDP Sessions
=================================================================
Peer LDP Id    Adj Type  State        Msg Sent  Msg Recv  Up Time
-----------------------------------------------------------------
150.10.0.1:0   Link      Established   60        61        0d 00:02:36
-----------------------------------------------------------------
No. of Sessions: 1
=================================================================
```

```
*B:PE1>config>router>ldp# exit
*B:PE1#
```

Every SDP is identified by a numeric label. It's a best practice to design or pick a convention for the numbering scheme, and *stick to it!* We'll use the convention of two digits: the first digit for the near end router and the second digit for the far end router. As an example, an SDP from PE1 to PE2 will be labeled **12**.

3. On PE1, configure an SDP to PE2; on PE2, configure an SDP to PE1. For the first attempt, do not use the parameter `create` when defining the SDP. For the second attempt, don't forget to use the attribute `mpls`! Like LDP, the default state for an SDP is `disabled`. Don't forget the `no shutdown` command.

```
*B:PE1# configure service
*B:PE1>config>service# sdp 12 mpls
MINOR: CLI 'create' is mandatory while creating SDP.
*B:PE1>config>service# sdp 12 mpls create
*B:PE1>config>service>sdp$ far-end 150.10.0.1
*B:PE1>config>service>sdp$ ldp
*B:PE1>config>service>sdp$ no shutdown
*B:PE1>config>service>sdp$
```

4. After both SDPs have been configured, verify that they are both admin and operationally Up. (In some circumstances, you may need to wait a few moments before the SDPs will be Up.) If not, confirm that you have entered all the parameters correctly.

```
*B:PE1>config>service# show service sdp
```

```
===============================================================
Services: Service Destination Points
===============================================================
SdpId  Adm MTU  Opr MTU  IP address   Adm  Opr  Deliver Signal
---------------------------------------------------------------
12     0        9190     150.10.0.1   Up   Up   LDP     TLDP
---------------------------------------------------------------
Number of SDPs : 1
---------------------------------------------------------------
===============================================================
*B:PE1>config>service#
```

5. Removing an SDP is the familiar two-step process: Shut down the SDP and delete it with no sdp. Remove one of the SDPs for practice.

```
*B:PE1>config>service# sdp 12 shutdown
*B:PE1>config>service# no sdp 12
*B:PE1>config>service#
```

6. On each PE router, verify the state of any SDPs (see Step 4).

   6a. Is it possible to get a single SDP in the Up state?

7. Re-create the missing SDP and again verify that they are both admin and operationally Up.

Part 3: Customer-Facing Configuration

This section provides all the steps for configuring the customer-facing Service Access Points (SAPs) on the PE routers. It may not be obvious at first glance why there are so many steps. There is a chain of logic that goes something like this:

A. Customer equipment connects to a VPLS via a SAP.

B. SAPs can only be created on Ethernet ports that are set to access mode.

C. A port with an existing interface *cannot* be changed to access mode.

D. So we first need to remove any interfaces on network ports.

If that doesn't make complete sense, don't worry because the steps below guide the way. Don't be afraid to experiment to see what kind of error messages you get if you miss a step or do it incorrectly.

1. Remove the existing network interface on PE1 that faces CE1. Use the familiar two-step process: Shut down first, then delete.

```
*B:PE1# configure router
*B:PE1>config>router# interface toCE1 shutdown
*B:PE1>config>router# no interface toCE1
*B:PE1>config>router# exit
*B:PE1#
```

   1a. What error message do you get if you try to remove an interface that is *not* shut down?

2. Configure the port facing customer equipment as an access port.

```
*B:PE1# configure port 1/1/1
*B:PE1>config>port# shutdown
*B:PE1>config>port# ethernet mode access
*B:PE1>config>port# no shutdown
*B:PE1>config>port# exit
*B:PE1#
```

2a. There are only two states for a port: One is access mode. What is the name of the other mode? (Use the CLI Help!)

2b. What error message do you get if a port is *not* shut down when you try to change modes?

3. On PE2, configure the corresponding customer-facing port as an access port. This exercise assumes that Device 4 is connected to port 1/1/1. If you are using a different port, you will need to adapt the commands given below. (Also, if you have configured a network interface on that port, you will need to remove it first.)

```
*A:PE2# configure port 1/1/1
*A:PE2>config>port# shutdown
*A:PE2>config>port# ethernet mode access
*A:PE2>config>port# no shutdown
*A:PE2>config>port# exit
*A:PE2#
```

Part 4: Verification

A general first step for troubleshooting services is to check that nothing has been (accidentally) left in a (shut)down state. The next step is to check that nothing was skipped or missed while building the configuration.

1. **IGP Verification**—Confirm that OSPF is running throughout the provider network (i.e., just PE1 and PE2 in this case). Confirm that routes for every interface appear in the routing table. Confirm that all interfaces within the provider network respond to a ping. (Remember that customer-facing ports are now operating as SAPs, not network interfaces.)

2. **LDP Verification**—Confirm that LDP has successfully exchanged all labels that will be necessary for PE1 and PE2 to send data back and forth. Each router needs a

pair of labels—one to reach the far router and one offered to the far router to send data back to the local router.

```
*B:PE1# show router ldp bindings active


===========================================================
Legend: (S) - Static
===========================================================
LDP Prefix Bindings (Active)
===========================================================
Prefix        Op   IngLbl EgrLbl EgrIntf EgrNextHop
-----------------------------------------------------------
140.10.0.1/32 Pop  131071 --     --      --
150.10.0.1/32 Push --     131071 1/1/2   140.10.0.98
-----------------------------------------------------------
No. of Prefix Bindings: 2
===========================================================
*B:PE1#
```

2a. One label is to reach the far router. Is that the Push or the Pop label?

2b. One label is offered to the far router to send data back to the local router. Is that the Push or the Pop label?

3. **SDP Verification**—Confirm that the SDPs are both admin and operationally Up.

4. **Customer-Facing SAP Verification**—Confirm that the customer-facing ports are in access mode. Confirm that the port itself is admin and operationally Up.

```
*B:PE1# show port 1/1/1


===========================================================
Ethernet Interface
===========================================================
Description     : 10/100/Gig Ethernet SFP
Interface       : 1/1/1     Oper Speed     : 1 Gbps
Link-level      : Ethernet  Config Speed   : 1 Gbps
Admin State     : up        Oper Duplex    : full
Oper State      : up        Config Duplex  : full
Physical Link   : Yes       MTU            : 1514
[... 4 lines of output omitted ...]
```

```
Configured Mode    : access    Encap Type      : null
Dot1Q Ethertype    : 0x8100    QinQ Ethertype  : 0x8100
PBB Ethertype      : 0x88e7
[... Additional output omitted ...]
*B:PE1#
```

Lab Section 11.2: VPLS Example

A VPLS is a Layer 2 service that connects multiple sites in a single LAN. It's like creating a virtual switch from a network of Service Routers. In this lab, we will configure the actual VPLS across the PE nodes as shown in Figure 11.16. The PE devices will connect to each other in a full mesh topology using mesh-type SDPs. The CE devices will be configured to use the same subnet (i.e., addresses from a single LAN). The operation of the VPLS will be demonstrated using ping, traceroute, and (optionally) OSPF.

 Note that after the service reference topology has been configured, adding additional services from edge-to-edge does not require any further modification of the supporting infrastructure.

Figure 11.16: Customer equipment connects to the Provider Edge via a SAP. To the customer, the SAP in a VPLS behaves identically to a port on an Ethernet switch.

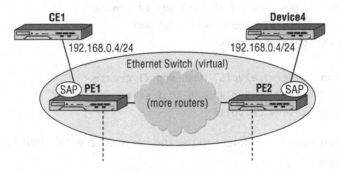

Objective In this exercise, you will configure a VPLS service between PE routers. You will also demonstrate the ability of customer equipment to communicate across this VPLS as if it were a simple Ethernet switch.

Validation You will know you have succeeded if the CE devices can ping each other and if traceroute shows the CE devices as being only a single (virtual!) hop away from each other.

Part 1: Provider Edge VPLS Configuration

1. Create a VPLS service. Every service is identified with a numeric name. The actual value isn't as important as the fact that it should be unique within the ISP's domain. Repeat the configuration on both PE1 and PE2, using an *identical* service number on both routers. Like SDPs, the default state for a service is disabled. Don't forget the no shutdown command!

   ```
   *B:PE1# configure service
   *B:PE1>config>service# vpls 22 customer 1 create
   *B:PE1>config>service>vpls$ no shutdown
   *B:PE1>config>service>vpls$
   ```

   1a. What happens if you forget to use the keyword create when first creating a VPLS?

2. SDPs are used to distribute services across multiple Service Routers. In terms of a VPLS, an SDP is needed to every other router that has an SAP participating in the VPLS. Add the required SDPs to the VPLS configuration on each PE router, specifying that they operate in mesh mode. Be careful with your typing: PE1's SDP to PE2 was identified as *12* when created; PE2's SDP to PE1 was identified as *21*.

   ```
   *B:PE1>config>service>vpls$ mesh-sdp 12 create
   *B:PE1>config>service>vpls>mesh-sdp$ exit
   *B:PE1>config>service>vpls#

   *A:PE2>config>service>vpls$ mesh-sdp 21 create
   *A:PE2>config>service>vpls>mesh-sdp$ exit
   *A:PE2>config>service>vpls#
   ```

   2a. What happens if you forget to use the keyword create when first creating a mesh SDP?

3. Add the SAPs to attach CE devices to the VPLS.

   ```
   *B:PE1>config>service>vpls# sap 1/1/1 create
   *B:PE1>config>service>vpls>sap$ exit
   *B:PE1>config>service>vpls#
   ```

```
*A:PE2>config>service>vpls# sap 1/1/1 create
*A:PE2>config>service>vpls>sap$ exit
*A:PE2>config>service>vpls#
```

3a. What happens if you forget to use the keyword `create` when first creating
a SAP?

4. Confirm that the VPLS is both admin and operationally `Up` on each router. Check
the status summary of the service, as well as the detailed status for all the service
components: SAPs and SDPs.

```
*B:PE1# show service service-using
```

```
===============================================================
Services
===============================================================
ServiceId  Type  Adm  Opr  CustomerId  Last Mgmt Change
---------------------------------------------------------------
22         VPLS  Up   Up   1                       01/01/2000 16:53:17
---------------------------------------------------------------
Matching Services : 1
---------------------------------------------------------------

===============================================================
*B:PE1#
```

```
*B:PE1>config>service>vpls# show service id 22 base
```

```
==============================================================
Service Basic Information
==============================================================
Service Id          : 22              Vpn Id           : 0
Service Type        : VPLS
Customer Id         : 1
Last Status Change: 01/01/2000 16:56:01
Last Mgmt Change   : 01/01/2000 16:53:17
Admin State         : Up              Oper State       : Up
MTU                 : 1514            Def. Mesh VC Id : 22
SAP Count           : 1               SDP Bind Count  : 1
Snd Flush on Fail : Disabled    Host Conn Verify: Disabled
Propagate MacFlush: Disabled
Def. Gateway IP     : None
Def. Gateway MAC    : None
```

```
----------------------------------------------------------
Service Access & Destination Points
----------------------------------------------------------
Identifier               Type  AdmMTU OprMTU Adm  Opr
----------------------------------------------------------
sap:1/1/1                null  1514   1514   Up   Up
sdp:12:22 M(150.10.0.1)  n/a   0      9190   Up   Up
==========================================================
```
*B:PE1>config>service>vpls#

If the service isn't completely Up, start with the troubleshooting steps from Section 11.1: Check that nothing has been (accidentally) left in a (shut)down state. Then check that nothing was skipped or missed while building the configuration.

Note that just like an Ethernet switch, the state of a VPLS service doesn't depend on the CE equipment being properly configured. If the VPLS is down, looking at the customer equipment will *not* help you find or fix the problem.

Part 2: Customer Device Configuration

For this exercise, we will treat CE1 and Device4 as traditional routers. Their interfaces will use addresses from a common subnet, even though they are on opposite sides of a service (which may span a city, a continent, or the globe). The VPLS service will join these two devices in the same way an Ethernet switch would join them.

The minimum requirements for Device4 are that it be capable of sending and responding to pings. We will, however, walk through the full configuration in case Device4 is an Alcatel-Lucent 7750/7450 device.

Determine whether you have the ability to set the IP address of Device4. Set it to **192.168.0.4** if you can. If not, carefully note the address and subnet mask of the interface connected to PE2. You will need to adapt the examples below to give PE1 a compatible IP address and mask so that it is part of the same subnet as PE2.

1. Reconfigure the interface on CE1 that connects to PE1. It should now use an address of 192.168.0.1/24. (We will leave the name of the interface the same, even though a new name like toISP or toVPLS would be more appropriate to this exercise.)

   ```
   *A:CE1# configure router
   *A:CE1>config>router# interface toPE1
   *A:CE1>config>router>if# address 192.168.0.1/24
   *A:CE1>config>router>if# exit
   *A:CE1>config>router# exit
   *A:CE1#
   ```

2. Assuming that Device4 is an Alcatel-Lucent 7750/7450 device, configure the basic router settings and the interface to PE2. If Device4 is some other device and you are able to set the IP address and subnet mask, do so now.

```
*A:NS074662074# configure system name Dev4-CE2
*A:Dev4-CE2# configure card 1 card-type iom-20g-b
*A:Dev4-CE2# configure card 1 mda 1 mda-type m10-1gb-sfp-b
*A:Dev4-CE2# configure port 1/1/1 no shutdown
*A:Dev4-CE2# configure router
*A:Dev4-CE2>config>router# interface system
*A:Dev4-CE2>config>router>if# address 150.10.0.2/32
*A:Dev4-CE2>config>router>if# exit
*A:Dev4-CE2>config>router# interface toVPLS
*A:Dev4-CE2>config>router>if$ address 192.168.0.4/24
*A:Dev4-CE2>config>router>if$ port 1/1/1
*A:Dev4-CE2>config>router>if$ exit
*A:Dev4-CE2>config>router#
```

3. (*Optional*) On Device4, create OSPF area 0. Add the system interface and interface connecting to the PE2.

```
*A:Dev4-CE2>config>router# ospf
*A:Dev4-CE2>config>router>ospf$ area 0
*A:Dev4-CE2>config>router>ospf>area$ interface system
*A:Dev4-CE2>config>router>ospf>area>if$ exit
*A:Dev4-CE2>config>router>ospf>area# interface toVPLS
*A:Dev4-CE2>config>router>ospf>area>if$ exit
*A:Dev4-CE2>config>router>ospf>area# exit
*A:Dev4-CE2>config>router>ospf# exit
*A:Dev4-CE2>config>router#
```

4. Confirm basic connectivity between the CE devices by pinging the interfaces on the 192.168.0.0/24 subnet. If there is no response, verify the previous configuration steps and correct as necessary. Pay particular attention to the configuration of addresses on CE1 and Device4.

```
*A:CE1# ping 192.168.0.4
PING 192.168.0.4 56 data bytes
64 bytes from 192.168.0.4: icmp_seq=1 ttl=64 time<10ms.
64 bytes from 192.168.0.4: icmp_seq=2 ttl=64 time<10ms.
64 bytes from 192.168.0.4: icmp_seq=3 ttl=64 time<10ms.
64 bytes from 192.168.0.4: icmp_seq=4 ttl=64 time<10ms.
```

```
64 bytes from 192.168.0.4: icmp_seq=5 ttl=64 time<10ms.

---- 192.168.0.4 PING Statistics ----
5 packets transmitted, 5 packets received, 0.00% packet loss
round-trip min < 10ms, avg < 10ms, max < 10ms, stddev < 10ms
*A:CE1#
```

Part 3: Verification

CE Network Connectivity

1. On CE1 or Device4, run a traceroute to the 192.168.0.x address on the other device.
   ```
   *A:CE1# traceroute 192.168.0.4
   traceroute to 192.168.0.4, 30 hops max, 40 byte packets
      1  192.168.0.4 (192.168.0.4)    <10 ms  <10 ms  <10 ms
   *A:CE1#
   ```

   1a. How many routers does CE1 see between itself and Device4?

   1b. Does CE1 see the connection to Device4 as routed or switched (at Layer 2)? Explain your answer.

2. On CE1 or Device1, try to ping any of the interfaces on PE1 or PE2.

   2a. Are any PE interfaces reachable?

3. (*Optional*) If Device4 has OSPF configured, check the adjacencies and LSA database on CE1 and Device4. (Refer to Lab Section 9.1 in Chapter 9.)

   3a. How many OSPF adjacencies are there on each CE device?

   3b. Are there any adjacencies with, or LSAs from, the PE routers?

   3c. From CE1, which system interfaces can you ping? PE1? PE2? Device4?

   3d. Explain the results.

   3e. Are the OSPF sessions on the CE devices connected in any way to the OSPF sessions on the PE devices?

4. On one of the PE devices, shut down the SDP to the other PE device. Repeat Steps 1–3 above.
   ```
   *B:PE1# configure service sdp 12 shutdown
   *B:PE1#
   ```

   4a. Explain the results. (*Hint:* Check the status of the VPLS service.)

5. Re-enable the SDP that you shut down in the previous step. You may need to wait a few moments for everything to return to its previous state.

```
*B:PE1# configure service sdp 12 no shutdown
*B:PE1#
```

VPLS Service Connectivity

6. There are now two CE devices connected to the VPLS. Check to see if this has affected the quantity or state of the services present on each PE device.

```
*B:PE1# show service service-using
*B:PE1#
```

6a. How many services are there on each PE device?

6b. What is the status of each service?

7. On each PE device, you can see the MAC database per service using the following command. Compare the exact contents of the two databases.

```
*B:PE1# show service id 22 fdb detail

===============================================================
Forwarding Database, Service 22
===============================================================
ServId  MAC               Source-Id    Type  Last Change
                                       /Age
---------------------------------------------------------------
22      00:1a:f0:5c:6e:1b sdp:12:22    L/0   01/01/2000 18:39:25
22      00:1a:f0:5c:73:c5 sap:1/1/1    L/0   01/01/2000 16:58:14
---------------------------------------------------------------
No. of MAC Entries: 2
===============================================================
*B:PE1#
```

7a. Are the databases identical or different? If different, what is different? Explain the results.

7b. How many local MAC addresses are in the CE1 table?

7c. How many remote MAC addresses are in the CE1 table?

Solutions

Lab Section 2.1 Exercises

3a. Does it matter if a command is typed in uppercase or lowercase?

The CLI is case-sensitive (with one exception listed in Lab Section 2.3). All commands must be typed in lowercase. The only items that would appear in uppercase would be names (e.g., of routers, interfaces, and other settings) that an administrator chooses to write with uppercase characters. These names must be typed consistently, using the exact same uppercase and lowercase as when they were originally created.

3b. If a router is completely uninitialized, what time does it show?

An uninitialized router starts counting from the time 0:00:00, the date 01/01/2000, with the time zone set to UTC. It must be updated by the administrator or a time protocol (e.g., SNTP) to have the correct time.

3c. What is the OS version? Where else does the OS version appear?

The OS version shown in these exercises is 6.1.R5. By default, it also appears between the login and password prompts.

4a. Does the router name *always* appear in the CLI prompt?

Yes, the CLI prompt always contains the router name.

6a. Is the router name still the same as before disconnecting?

Yes, the name remains the same. Simply disconnecting and reconnecting to the router doesn't cause the system name to be forgotten or changed.

7a. Is the router name still the same as before rebooting?

No, the router name has gone back to the chassis serial number.

7b. Why or why not?

The router name is part of the overall system configuration. Nothing was saved before rebooting, so everything was lost. You'll see in the next few exercises how to save configuration information so that it is preserved across reboots.

Lab Section 2.2 Exercises

2a. Upon (re-)booting, what time does a router show?

By default, it reinitializes the time back to 0:00:00, 01/01/2000 UTC.

2b. What are the settings for connecting to the router: Via the serial port? Via the management Ethernet port?

The default settings for the serial port are 115,000-N-8-1 with no flow control. The default management port is fast Ethernet 10/100 Mbps with full auto-negotiation.

2c. In which file are the connection settings stored?

Connection settings are stored in the file bof.cfg. The name for this file never changes.

2d. Which piece of hardware provides the serial number that is used for the default router name?

The default router name is copied from the chassis serial number. See the 18th line of the output for the item `Chassis Serial Number is`.

6a. What are the options for the `reboot` command used in the previous exercise? Which gives more information: using the "?" feature or the `tree detail` command?

There are four options when rebooting: *active*, *standby*, *upgrade*, and *now*. You may choose either *active* or *standby*, but not both at the same time. Likewise, if you chose either of those two, you may not choose the *upgrade* option. Only the `tree detail` command gives the complete list of options available for each command.

8a. How many main categories of events are there?

There are five overall categories: Main, Security, Change, Debug, and LI.

8b. From the above display, how many logs are actually actively recording events? (These are default logs that always exist.)

There are two default logs: 99 and 100. Log 99 captures all events, and log 100 captures "more serious" events.

9a. How are log entries listed: from oldest to newest, or vice versa?

Log entries are listed from newest to oldest. That ensures that the most recent events appear on the very first screen of output.

9b. Each log entry is numbered. Where does that number appear?

The number appears as the very first item of the entry, immediately before the date and time stamp for the event.

9c. Does the number of log entries identified by the log-collector correspond to what is printed out?

The log collector identifies the *total* number of events that have occurred. Not all of them are necessarily still retained in the log. Since log entries are shown starting from the most recent, the number identified in the log collector should correspond to the number of the first displayed entry.

9d. Are there more options we could have used in this command? How can you find out?

There are quite a few additional options to help select and filter out particular entries of interest. Press the [?] key at the end of the command (but do not press [Enter]) to show the options available.

Lab Section 2.3 Exercises

1a. For filenames, does it matter whether they are typed in uppercase or lowercase?

Filenames are the one exception to the rule that the CLI is case-sensitive. Each character, typed in either uppercase or lowercase, will match that character in the filename whether it is uppercase or lowercase.

1b. Can you identify where/how to specify the location for the desired OS version?

The item `primary-image` stores the *directory* name where the router expects to find the OS files.

1c. Can you use any of the CLI Help features to find out what storage devices exist, other than cf3?

Yes. Starting with `file type`, press the [?] key to get the full set of options for the storage devices.

3a. If there are additional chances to find the config, are there also additional chances for finding the OS? If yes, how many?

Yes. There are three (primary, secondary, tertiary) settings (or chances) for finding the config, as well as three for the OS.

4a. What exactly has been saved by the above command: just the BOF's three main items? or all other configuration details?

The `bof save` command only saves the items stored in the BOF. All the other configuration settings (in fact, every setting where the command starts with the word `configure`) get saved in the configuration file identified by `primary-config`.

5a. What exactly has been saved by the above command: just the BOF's three main items? or all other configuration details?

The `admin save` command saves all the other configuration settings (in fact, every setting where the command starts with the word `configure`). You will find that other settings (e.g., ones where the command starts with `debug` or anything other than `configure`) *do not get saved* at all.

5b. The `admin save` command didn't include a filename. What filename did the router use, and how did it choose it?

The router saves configuration details only to the file identified by the `primary-config` parameter in the BOF. It always uses that parameter to get the filename. If you want to change configuration filenames, you must either change the `primary-config` parameter or use one of the file copy commands.

5c. What character has disappeared from the beginning of the prompt, as soon as the configuration was saved? What is the meaning of this character?

The leading asterisk (*) in the prompt disappeared. It is a flag that is visible whenever there are any *unsaved* configuration changes, either for the BOF or the `primary-config`.

6a. Do you have *at least* the files bof.cfg and your main config file?

If you don't have these two files, check and carefully repeat the steps in this section until you succeed.

6b. Is the time stamp on the config files a few minutes earlier than the current time?

If everything is working properly, the time stamp shouldn't be more than a minute or two old.

Lab Section 3.1 Exercises

1a. In total, how many cards are physically present in the chassis? How many SF/CPMs? How many IOMs?

The example output given in the exercise shows exactly two cards present. They can be easily identified since they have a (non-blank) name in the `Equipped Card-type` column. Any card appearing Slot A or B is an SF/CPM card; the example shows only one in Slot A. The example shows one IOM card, of type `iom2-20g`.

1b. Referring to Chapter 2, what kind of labeling is used for the "two (2) card slots [...] dedicated for redundant SF/CPMs"?

The slots reserved for SF/CPM cards are always identified by a letter, either A or B.

1c. Referring to Chapter 2, how many different kinds of SF/CPM cards exist?

There are currently two switch fabric options: 200 Gbps and 400 Gbps (full-duplex) throughput. The terabit version of the Alcatel-Lucent 7750 Service Router uses a 500 Gbps switch fabric, which is a third type. As speeds continue to evolve, expect additional versions of the SF/CPM card.

1d. Referring to Chapter 2, what kind of labeling is used for IOM card(s)?

IOM cards are referred to by the slot that they occupy in the chassis. Generally, there are either five or 10 slots for IOMs, so cards will have numeric labels from 1 to 10.

1e. Is there any relationship between the first character of the prompt and any of the cards?

The first character in the prompt identifies which SF/CPM card is active, either Slot A or Slot B. In these exercises, we use Slot B for one PE router and Slot A for the second PE router. This is intended to make it easier to distinguish which router is used in any given example.

2a. Did the configuration command change the number of *physical* cards or the number of *available* cards?

Configuring an IOM card only changes the Operational State, making a card un-/available. It does not change the number of physical cards, as seen by the absence of any changes in the Equippped Card-type column.

2b. Why did the asterisk (*) reappear in the command prompt? What will make it disappear again?

The asterisk reappeared to indicate an unsaved configuration change. Issuing the admin save command would make it disappear (until the next configuration change).

Lab Section 3.2 Exercises

1a. Can you see any MDAs for IOMs that are *not* configured?

No. Unless an IOM has been configured, it is not possible to get any information about the MDAs that it contains.

1b. In total, how many MDAs are physically plugged into an IOM(s)?

In the example, the IOM only has a single MDA plugged into it. The `Equipped Mda-type` column has exactly one non-blank row. At most two MDAs can fit into an IOM.

1c. Which chassis slot/IOM is the `m10-1gb-sfp-b` MDA plugged into? Within that IOM, is the MDA plugged into the first or second MDA slot?

The MDA is plugged into the IOM in Slot 1. This is determined by the value in the `Slot` column in the command output. The MDA is plugged into the first of the two available MDA slots on the IOM. This is determined by the value in the `Mda` column in the command output.

2a. What is the correspondence between the physical *location* of the MDA and the values specified in the above command?

In the command `configure card 1 mda 1`, the parameter `card 1` identifies the IOM in Slot 1; the parameter `mda 1` identifies the first of the two available MDA slots on the IOM card.

2b. Whether or not there was an asterisk in the prompt *before* issuing the `configure` command, will there be one *after* the command?

Setting the MDA type is considered a configuration change, so the asterisk will reappear in the prompt to remind you to save your changes.

3a. Did the configuration command change the number of *physical* MDAs or the number of *available* MDAs?

Configuring an MDA only changes the `Operational State`, making an MDA un-/available. It does not change the number of physical cards, as seen by the absence of any changes in the `Equippped Mda-type` column.

5a. Whether or not there was an asterisk in the prompt before issuing the configure command, will there be one *after* the command?

Removing an MDA type is considered a configuration change, so the asterisk will reappear in the prompt to remind you to save your changes.

Lab Section 3.3 Exercises

1a. The output above is split into three main sections. The first section is all the output for which (single) piece of hardware?

The first section is all the physical ports for the MDA(s) in IOM 1, as indicated by the section heading, "Ports on Slot 1."

1b. There are a total of 12 ports shown. How does the naming/labeling of the ports correspond with the SF/CPM, IOM, and MDA card numbering/labeling?

Ports on an MDA are named using three numeric values, for example, *1/1/5*. The first value identifies the IOM, the second value identifies the MDA, and the third value identifies the actual port. The (management) ports on an SF/CPM card are named using two values, for example, *A/1*. The first value identifies the SF/CPM card, and the second value is always a *1* since there is only a single Ethernet port on each SF/CPM card.

1c. The MDA is configured as m**10-1gb-sfp**-b, meaning "10 GigE ports using optical SFP connectors." How many ports have the SFP installed?

Only four ports have an SFP installed. These are identified by a non-blank entry in the SFP/XFP/MDIMDX column. In the example, the four ports have a SFP of type GIGE-T.

1d. The last port is listed with a port state of Ghost. Which card is it on? Does the card physically exist? What is the meaning of Ghost?

The Ghost port is listed on the SF/CPM for Slot B. There is no SF/CPM card in that slot, but the system retains a phantom or ghost configuration for it. As a result, the management port on that SF/CPM is designated as Ghost, meaning it doesn't physically exist. You will see similar results if an IOM card fails, or if you configure an IOM that doesn't physically exist, and then MDAs (that also don't physically exist). Try it; there's no chance of physically damaging the equipment!

1e. With default settings, are ports in an Up or Down state? Is this consistent with other hardware (i.e., IOMs and MDAs)?

By default, ports start in the Down state. This is an important point to remember, since IOMs and MDAs automatically go to an Up state as soon as their type is configured.

1f. What is the default MTU for a 10/100 FastE port? For a GigE port?

The command output shows the default MTUs for each type of port: 1514 for 10/100 FastE ports and 9212 for GigE ports.

2a. With the port operationally Up, what new information is available?

There are two new pieces of information, both related to the physical cabling attached to the port. The Link column identifies whether cables are connected *and* attached to equipment at both ends (Yes). The SFP/XFP/MDIMDX column identifies whether the cabling is connected as straight-through (MDI) or cross-over (MDX).

Lab Section 5.1 Exercises

Entity	Number of Host Addresses	IP Network
ISP Network	4094	138.120.16.0/20
Subnetwork assigned to Enterprises A and B	510	138.120.30.0/23
Enterprise A		
Location A.1	30	138.120.30.0/27
Location A.2	30	138.120.30.32/27
	30	138.120.30.64/27
Enterprise B		
Location B.1	30	138.120.30.96/27
	62	138.120.30.128/27
Location B.2	62	138.120.30.192/27
	254	138.120.31.0/24

Lab Section 5.2 Exercises

Divide 140.10.0.0/24 into $8 \times$ /27 address spaces. The following solution is not the only possible solution, but it will be used for all future solutions. Remember that both ends of each inter-router link must be within the same subnet. Note that the gap in the middle between ISP addresses and customer host addresses allows for future expansion of either or both blocks, without creating alternating blocks of ISP/customer addresses.

Divide 150.10.0.0/24 into 8 × /27 address spaces. PE1 and PE2 need to communicate across a common IP subnet! The solution given below is not the only possible solution, but it will be used for all future solutions. Note that the gap in the middle between ISP addresses and customer host addresses allows for future expansion of either or both blocks, without creating alternating blocks of ISP/customer addresses.

ISP Number 1			
Router	**Port**	**Interface Name**	**IP Address**
		Reserved for local loopbacks.	140.10.0.0/27
		Reserved for future use.	140.10.0.32/27
			140.10.0.64/27
		Reserved for inter-router links.	140.10.0.96/27
PE1		System	140.10.0.1/32
		loopbackTest	140.10.0.11/32
		toPE2	140.10.0.97/30
		toCE1	140.10.0.101/30
CE1		System	140.10.0.2/32
		loopbackTest	140.10.0.12/32
		toPE1	140.10.0.102/30
		Aggregate	140.10.0.192/26

ISP Number 2			
Router	**Port**	**Interface Name**	**IP Address**
		Reserved for local loopbacks.	150.10.0.0/27
		Reserved for future use.	150.10.0.32/27
			150.10.0.64/27
		Reserved for inter-router links.	150.10.0.96/27
PE2		System	150.10.0.1/32
		loopbackTest	150.10.0.11/32
		toP1	140.10.0.98/30

Lab Section 5.3 Exercises

1a. Carefully examine the prompt for PE1. Which SF/CPM is currently active?

The first letter of the prompt starts with B, which identifies the SF/CPM in Slot B as active. This was done intentionally in order to make it easier to distinguish PE1 and PE2 in subsequent exercises.

2a. Carefully examine the output for the router's system interface before and after the configuration command. What has changed?

The interface has changed from `Operationally Down` to `Operationally Up` since its configuration was completed with the addition of an IP address.

2b. Knowing that the system interface exists by default, how many additional items need to be configured for it to be operational?

The system interface is a unique interface since it only needs configuration of a single item: its IP address.

4a. Other than the name, how many additional items need to be configured for the loopback to be operational?

A loopback interface requires configuration of two items: its IP address and the parameter `loopback`.

5a. Experiment to see if it is possible to remove an interface that is operationally `Up`.

No, it is not possible to remove an interface that is operationally `Up`. This general rule applies to most entities configured on a router: Shut down first, then remove.

6a. Is there any conflict or problem with reusing the same name for an interface in more than one router? Are interface names local or global?

There is *no* conflict or problem with reusing the same name for an interface in more than one router. Interface names are local to each router.

7a. The command output above shows evidence of another requirement for physical links to be operationally `Up`. What is that extra requirement? (One router's configuration was changed to demonstrate this requirement.)

A port must have a physical cable (connected at both ends) in order to be operationally `Up`. If the cable is disconnected or broken, the port and associated interface immediately go to the operationally `Down` state.

9a. What is the difference between the output from a `show` command versus an `info` command?

An `info` command provides less information since it does *not* show any of the operational status. There are occasions, however, when a more *compact* display is preferable, for example, to do a quick check for missing configuration.

9b. Experiment with creating a physical interface and leaving out either the IP address or the port. Other than the name, how many additional items need to be configured for the interface to be operational?

A network interface requires configuration of two items: its IP address and the physical port. If either of these is missing, the interface will stay in the operationally `Down` state.

9c. Experiment to find out if an interface can be both admin and operationally `Up/Up` on one side and not the other. What are the requirements for an interface to be admin and operationally `Up/Up`?

To be fully `Up/Up`, there are several requirements for an interface: (1) It must be fully configured with both a valid IP address and port; (2) it must be in the `Up` state and not shut down; (3) the associated port must be fully configured; (4) the associated port must not be shut down; and (5) there must be a cable attached to the port that is connected at both ends.

9d. Experiment to see what happens if you try to configure an interface named `loopback Test` without using surrounding quotes.

You will get an error message from the CLI because it interprets the second half of the name as a separate parameter, which should not be there.

10a. Is there a difference between the outputs of the `show router interface` command and the `show router route-table` command? What is the difference?

Yes, there is a difference. The interface command displays only the interfaces and their configured IP address; all interfaces are included, regardless of their operational status. The `route-table` command displays the *subnet* instead of the IP address for each interface; no route will appear for any interface that is either admin or operationally `Down`. You will see in later exercises that the route table displays route information learned from other routers so there are typically *many* more routes than interfaces.

Final Configurations

```
*B:PE1>config>router# info
---------------------------------------------
#--------------------------------------------------
echo "IP Configuration"
#--------------------------------------------------
        interface "loopbackTest"
            address 140.10.0.11/32
            loopback
        exit
        interface "system"
            address 140.10.0.1/32
        exit
        interface "toCE1"
            address 140.10.0.101/30
            port 1/1/1
        exit
        interface "toPE2"
            address 140.10.0.97/30
            port 1/1/2
        exit
---------------------------------------------------

*B:PE1>config>

*A:PE2>config>router# info
---------------------------------------------
#--------------------------------------------------
echo "IP Configuration"
#--------------------------------------------------
        interface "loopbackTest"
            address 150.10.0.11/32
            loopback
        exit
        interface "system"
            address 150.10.0.1/32
        exit
        interface "toPE1"
            address 140.10.0.98/30
            port 1/1/2
        exit
```

(continued)

```
         ------------------------------------------------
*A:PE2>config>router#

*A:CE1>config>router# info
         ------------------------------------------------
#---------------------------------------------------
echo "IP Configuration"
#---------------------------------------------------
         interface "loopbackTest"
             address 140.10.0.12/32
             loopback
         exit
         interface "system"
             address 140.10.0.3/32
         exit
         interface "toPE1"
             address 140.10.0.102/30
             port 1/1/1
         exit
         ------------------------------------------------
*A:CE1>config>router#
```

Lab Section 6.1 Exercises

1a. Can you use a CLI Help function to find out how many log files can be configured?

Yes, the CLI can provide this information. After configure log log-id, type a question mark (**?**). The Help information identifies the valid range of log numbers as from 1 to 100 inclusive.

2a. Use a CLI Help function to find out what other categories of events can be specified as a source of debug information. How many are there in the router ip context?

There are 15 main categories (as of release 6.1 of the OS). The CLI will show these if you type **debug** and then a question mark. There are 10 categories within the router ip context (as of release 6.1 of the OS). The CLI will show these if you type **debug router ip** and then a question mark.

3a. Examine the output on PE1 carefully. Each ICMP packet is numbered in ascending order. Why are there 10 packets showing up on PE1 when CE1 only launched five ping requests?

The debug log on PE1 shows an incoming ICMP *request* as well as the ICMP *response* for each request sent by CE1. Look for the lines

`ICMP ingressing on [interface] toCE1` and `ICMP egressing on [interface] to CE1`.

3b. Can you find where the ingress/egress interface is identified?

See the answer to Question 3a. The interface is identified as the last item on the line.

4a. How many ICMP requests appear on CE1? How many requests are successfully received by PE1? How many replies are sent?

By default, a `ping` command sends a series of five ICMP requests. All five should appear in the command output: `Request timed out.` `icmp_seq=1`, and so on. The debug output on PE1 should show the arrival of every request. No ICMP reply packets should be visible in the debug output.

4b. In which direction (ingress/egress) is all the traffic flowing under these circumstances? Why?

All the ICMP traffic is flowing from CE1 to PE1; all traffic is ingressing on PE1. PE1 does not have any route in its route table to reach CE1's system interface (i.e., IP address 140.10.0.3), so it simply discards the ICMP requests.

5a. Why isn't the ARP table (cache) empty after issuing the `clear router arp all` command? Which MAC/IP addresses remain?

The command clears the ARP table of all entries learned from remote hosts; the MAC/IP address mapping of all local interfaces remains in the table. They aren't cleared because they are local and do not change.

5b. Why is there only a single ARP request/reply pair, instead of a pair for every ping sent by CE1?

The purpose of an ARP table or cache is specifically to avoid the need for an ARP request/reply for every packet. The MAC/IP address mapping is stored in the table for a period of time (e.g., 4 hours) so the information is available and packets can be sent immediately without waiting for an ARP request/reply to complete.

6a. Were ARP messages generated? Why or why not?

Consider the situation of PE1 pinging PE2. As a result of the ARP request/reply messages, both PE1 and PE2 are able to put entries in their ARP table for the other router. Additional ARP messages are generated only if no exchange has occurred between the pair of routers.

6b. How many ARP entries are on each router at this point? Explain.

Each router will have entries for its local interfaces (system, loopback, and network interfaces) plus entries for the adjacent routers. Assuming that CE1, PE1, and PE2 have all had ping activity, then PE1 should have 6 entries (4 + 2), PE2 should have 4 entries (3 + 1), and CE1 should have 4 entries (3 + 1).

7a. Were the pings successful? Why or why not?

The pings would all fail since there is no route that matches the system interface address for either CE1 or PE2.

7b. Were ARP messages generated? Why or why not?

No ARP messages were generated. Without a matching route, the router does not have a designated interface to reach the remote address. Without a designated interface, the router does not have an egress to send an ARP request, so nothing is sent.

7c. When a router is trying to reach a given IP, which comes first—checking the routing table or checking the ARP table?

A router checks its routing table first; the ARP table check is done only after finding an interface to forward the packet.

Lab Section 8.1 Exercises

1a. What is the destination subnet in the above command?

The destination subnet is 150.10.0.1/32, or a single host address.

1b. What is the next-hop address in the above command?

The next-hop address is 140.10.0.98, which is the network interface address at the far end of the link.

1c. Is the new subnet range anywhere within the 140.10.0.0/24 range of ISP 1, or is it completely external?

The new subnet range is completely outside ISP 1. That's the way routing works: The router just needs to know the very next hop along the path; where a packet goes after the first hop is of no interest or concern to the router.

5a. Did PE1 successfully transmit a ping request? How do you know?

The debug log shows that PE1 succeeded in sending a ping request: Debug packet 1 shows the line `ICMP egressing on [interface] toPE2`.

5b. Did PE2 successfully receive a ping request? How do you know?

The debug log on PE2 shows that it, indeed, received a ping request: Debug packet 1 shows the line `ICMP ingressing on [interface] toPE1`.

5c. What are the exact source and destination addresses in the ping packets?

The addresses, as shown in the debug packets on both the sending and receiving routers, are a source address of 140.10.0.1 (PE1 system interface) and a destination address of 150.10.0.1 (PE2 system interface).

5d. Does PE1 have a correct, functioning route to the system address of PE2?

Yes, PE1 has a valid routing table entry to reach PE2's system interface. This can be proven by examining the routing table on PE1, or simply by the fact that an ICMP packet was successfully produced.

5e. Was the `ping` command successful? How do you know?

No. The `ping` command failed. This was shown in the command output on PE1 and also by the absence of any ping response in the debug logs of both PE1 and PE2.

5f. Explain why or why not the ping was successful.

Although PE1 has routing information to reach PE2, at this point in time, PE2 has no routing information to respond back to PE1's system interface.

6a. By default, what source address is used when a ping destination is a *Local* route? By default, what source address is used when a ping destination is a *Remote* route? (This is a good rule to remember!)

When a ping destination is a *Local* route, the router uses a source address of the interface that is used for egress. When a ping destination is *Remote* (i.e., a subnet to which the router has no direct attachment), the router uses its system interface address for the source address.

8a. Did PE1 successfully transmit a ping request? How do you know?

Yes, the `ping` command was successful. The command output shows the number of ICMP requests that were issued (i.e., five in total).

8b. Did PE2 successfully receive a ping request? How do you know?

Yes, PE2 successfully received all ping requests. The debug log shows the incoming ICMP requests.

8c. What are the exact source and destination addresses in the ping packets?

The source and destination are both system addresses: The source address is 140.10.0.1, and the destination address is 150.10.0.1.

8d. Does PE1 have a correct, functioning route to the system address of PE2? Does PE2 have a functioning route to the system interface of PE1?

Yes, a successful `ping` command guarantees that valid routes exist in both directions (outbound and return).

8e. Was the `ping` command successful? How do you know?

When a ping is successful, the command output shows the `round-trip-time` as the last item on each line. The time is usually a few milliseconds (ms), for example, `time=2ms`.

8f. Explain why the ping was successful or not.

The essential prerequisite for successful pinging is a valid route in both directions (outbound and return). These routes existed on PE1 and PE2, so the ping was successful.

9a. Which loopback interfaces are reachable, if any? Explain why or why not?

None of the loopback interfaces are reachable. At this point in time, no routes exist on any of the routers for any of the loopbacks.

10a. How can you confirm that a static route has been successfully removed?

The best way of verifying the static routes is the command `show router static-route`. For this lab, you could also display the routing table with `show router route-table`.

11a. What did you learn: For successful communication, how many routes are required between a source and destination? Do *not* forget this important rule!!!

The essential prerequisite for successful pinging is a valid route in *both* directions (outbound and return).

Lab Section 8.2 Exercises

1a. For the *shortest* path, how many alternatives are there for ISP 3 to reach 140.10.0.0/24?

The fewest number of hops from ISP 3 is one, via the direct link connecting it to ISP 1.

1b. For the *shortest* path, how many alternatives are there for ISP 4 to reach 140.10.0.0/24?

ISP 4 has two choices to reach ISP 1, and both have an equal number of hops. One path goes through ISP 2; the other path goes through ISP 3.

1c. If ISP 3 does not use the shortest path, can traffic still reach 140.10.0.0/24?

ISP 3 can reach 140.10.0.0/24 via a three-hop path that goes through ISP 4, ISP 2, and finally to ISP 1.

4a. Why is a pair of routes to CE1 necessary, instead of just a single route?

CE1 does not have a single *uninterrupted* block of addresses that includes both its system and loopback interfaces. Separate routes are therefore required to reach each of these interfaces.

6a. Can you account for each of the routes in each router's routing table?

The routes are either generated automatically by the router for each configured interface, or they are the static routes defined in previous steps.

8a. How is it possible for CE1 to reach PE2 when there is no route for the 150.10.0.0/24 subnet in CE1's routing table?

This is the purpose of a default route: When there is no other matching route, the default route provides the next hop to a router that (hopefully) has matching routing information.

8b. How is it possible for PE2 to reach CE1 when there is no specific route to CE1 interfaces in PE2's routing table?

PE2 has an aggregate route for the subnet that includes CE1's interfaces. Whether the destination is one or more hops away is not of interest to PE2; it just has the information to reach a router (PE1) that *does* have information to reach the ultimate destination.

10a. Is there any way to improve the handling of these packets? Try out your solution!

There are several options for handling these packets. On PE1, you can install a static route for CE1's aggregate customer IP addresses. This would allow the traceroute to continue one additional hop before failing. A *blackhole* static route could be installed on either CE1 or PE1 to discard traffic for non-existent interfaces. This would silently discard all traffic to non-existent hosts. You could install loopback interfaces for as many of the customer addresses as you wish. This has the advantage of allowing successful testing of the full path.

Final Configurations

```
*B:PE1>config>router# info
#------------------------------------------------
#[... Additional output omitted ...]
#------------------------------------------------------
echo "Static Route Configuration"
#------------------------------------------------------
        static-route 140.10.0.3/32 next-hop 140.10.0.102
        static-route 140.10.0.12/32 next-hop 140.10.0.102
        static-route 150.10.0.0/24 next-hop 140.10.0.98
#------------------------------------------------
*B:PE1>config>

*A:PE2>config>router# info
#------------------------------------------------
# [... Additional output omitted ...]
#--------------------------------------------------------
echo "Static Route Configuration"
#--------------------------------------------------------
        static-route 140.10.0.0/24 next-hop 140.10.0.97
#------------------------------------------------------
*A:PE2>config>router#

*A:CE1>config>router# info
#------------------------------------------------
# [... Additional output omitted ...]
#----------------------------------------------------------
echo "Static Route Configuration"
#----------------------------------------------------------
        static-route 0.0.0.0/0 next-hop 140.10.0.101
#------------------------------------------------------
*A:CE1>config>router#
```

Lab Section 9.1 Exercises

4a. How many routes are in each route table?

PE1 should have 6 routes in total: 4 local routes plus 2 routes from OSPF. PE2 should have 6 routes in total: 3 local routes plus 3 routes from OSPF. CE1 should have 6 routes in total: 3 local routes plus 3 routes from OSPF.

4b. What is the preference and metric value of each OSPF route?

All OSPF routes have a preference value of 10, which is the designated value for "internal" routes. The metric (on the example equipment) can be checked by calculation: 100 × number of hops. The factor of 100 results in the OSPF link cost formula: 100,000,000,000 divided by the link bandwidth. Since all links are 1 Gbps, the result is 100 for all links. On PE1, interfaces on the remote routers are one hop away, so they should have a metric of 100. On CE1 and PE2, interfaces on the adjacent router have a metric of 100; interfaces on the further router have a metric of 200.

5a. How many neighbors do you see on PE1? PE2? CE1?

PE1 has two neighbors: PE1 and CE1. PE2 has only one neighbor: PE1. CE1 has only one neighbor: PE1.

5b. What is the state of the adjacencies? What should they be? Why?

All adjacencies should appear as Full. This is the correct state for fully adjacent neighbors assuming they have completed exchange of their routing information.

6a. What type of LSAs are in the database?

There are two types of LSAs in the database: Router and Network. You will notice that all the system interfaces are Router LSAs, and all links are Network LSAs.

6b. Is the database consistent on all routers? Is the database *identical* on all routers?

The database should be consistent across all routers and, in fact, should be completely identical. This is a characteristic of OSPF: Every router has the exact same set of identical LSAs.

9a. Can the ASBR designation be limited to a particular area?

No, the ASBR designation applies to the OSPF process as a whole.

10a. Can the export policy be assigned only to a particular area?

No, export policies apply to the OSPF process as a whole.

12a. What is the preference value for a route generated from an OSPF interface? What is the preference value for routes distributed via an export policy?

Routes generated from an OSPF interface have a preference value of 10, which is the designated value for "internal" routes. Routes generated via an export policy have a preference value of 150, which is the designated value for "external" routes.

Final Configurations

```
*B:PE1>config>router>ospf# info
#-----------------------------------------------
            asbr
            export "DistributeLB"
            area 0.0.0.0
                interface "system"
                exit
                interface "toPE2"
                exit
                interface "toCE1"
                exit
            exit
-----------------------------------------------
*B:PE1>config>router>ospf#
*B:PE1>config>router>policy-options# info
-----------------------------------------------
            begin
            policy-statement "DistributeLB"
                entry 10
                    from
                        protocol direct
                    exit
                    action accept
                    exit
                exit
            exit
            commit
-----------------------------------------------

*A:PE2>config>router>ospf# info
-----------------------------------------------
            asbr
```

(continued)

```
            export "DistributeLB"
            area 0.0.0.0
                interface "system"
                exit
                interface "toPE1"
                exit
            exit
---------------------------------------------
*A:PE2>config>router>ospf#
*A:PE2>config>router>policy-options# info
---------------------------------------------
            begin
            policy-statement "DistributeLB"
                entry 10
                    from
                        protocol direct
                    exit
                    action accept
                    exit
                exit
            exit
            commit
---------------------------------------------

*A:CE1>config>router>ospf# info
---------------------------------------------
            asbr
            export "DistributeLB"
            area 0.0.0.0
                interface "system"
                exit
                interface "toPE1"
                exit
            exit
---------------------------------------------
*A:CE1>config>router>ospf#
*A:CE1>config>router>policy-options# info
---------------------------------------------
            begin
```

(continued)

```
                policy-statement "DistributeLB"
                    entry 10
                        from
                            protocol direct
                        exit
                        action accept
                        exit
                    exit
                exit
                commit

        ------------------------------------------------
```

Lab Section 10.1 Exercises

2a. Has OSPF been removed from PE2? What other routing protocols are running on PE2?

Yes, the command output confirms that OSPF is no longer running on PE2. The entry for OSPFv2 shows `Not configured` for both the admin and operational states. At this point in time, no other protocols are configured or running.

2b. There is another method of confirming that OSPF is no longer running between PE1 and PE2. What is it?

Confirm there is no OSPF adjacency between PE1 and PE2 by executing the command `show router ospf neighbor` on PE1. There should be no entry for PE2.

2c. The code above shows three IPv4 routes on PE2. Where do they come from? Explain the results.

The routes still on PE2 are all *Local* routes from the interfaces (`system`, `loopback`, `toPE1`).

5a. Have the two PE routers exchanged any route information? How can you verify this?

No, the routers haven't exchanged any routes. The simplest check is to display the routing table (`show router route-table`) and check for any new routes.

5b. In the output above, what does the output column `Rcv/Act/Sent` mean?

The column `State|Rcv/Act/Sent` shows how many routes have been received (`Rcv`), how many are active (`Act`), and how many have been sent. The values for all three are 0, so no routes have been exchanged even though the peer connection has been established.

7a. Have the two PE routers exchanged any route information? What three commands can be used to verify this?

After adding the export policy, the routers will exchange routes. You can verify this by looking at the routing table (`show router route-table`), checking the neighbor states (`show router bgp summary`), or checking the advertised routes on each PE router (`show router bgp neighbor x.x.x.x advertised-routes`).

7b. What is the preference value for BGP routes? How does that compare with OSPF? Which one is *better*, that is, has higher precedence?

By default, BGP routes have a preference value of 170. OSPF routes have a value of either 10 (internal) or 150 (external). Lower preference values are considered better, so OSPF routes will be chosen over BGP routes when equivalent routes exist in both protocols.

7c. At this point in time, how many routes are in the routing table? Explain your answer.

The routing table on PE1 contains 8 routes in total: 4 local routes, 2 OSPF routes from CE1, and 2 BGP routes from PE2. PE2 contains 6 routes in total: 3 local routes plus 3 BGP routes from PE1. PE2 does *not* contain any routes for CE1's interfaces.

Lab Section 10.2 Exercises

1a. What commands can be used to verify OSPF operation?

Three commands for verifying OSPF are (1) `show router status` and look for OSPF being Up; (2) `show router route-table` and look for routes from OSPF; and (3) `show router ospf neighbor` and look for an adjacency with the router of interest.

3a. Has PE1 exchanged any routes with CE1? How can you verify this?

Yes, PE1 has sent routes to CE1. The exchange of routes can be verified with the command `show router bgp neighbor x.x.x.x advertised-routes`.

3b. In the output above, what do the values in the column `Rcv/Act/Sent` tell you?

PE1 has sent 6 routes to CE1, but none have been propagated in the direction from CE1 to PE1. The column titled `State|Rcv/Act/Sent` gives us these statistics.

3c. At this point in time, how many routes are in PE1's routing table? Explain your answer.

PE1 should have 8 routes in total: 4 local routes plus 2 routes from CE1 via OSPF and 2 routes from PE2 via BGP.

3d. How does PE1 learn about CE1's interfaces: through OSPF or BGP, or both? What does the routing table say? Explain your answer.

PE1 only has routes to CE1 from OSPF. The routing table confirms the OSPF information. Parts 3a and 3b of this question confirmed that no routes are received from CE1 via BGP.

4a. Have the two PE routers exchanged any route information?

No, the PE routers have not exchanged any new routes since adding the BGP export policy on CE1.

4b. What is the preference value for BGP routes?

By default, the preference value for BGP routes is 170. By default, the preference value for OSPF routes is either 10 (internal) or 150 (external).

4c. At this point in time, how many routes are in the routing table? Explain your answer.

There are no changes to the number of routes in any of the three routers. No new routes resulted from adding the BGP export policy on CE1.

4d. How does PE1 learn about CE1's interfaces: through OSPF, BGP, or both? What does the routing table say? Explain your answer.

PE1 has routes to CE1 from both the OSPF and BGP RIB. Only the OSPF routes appear in the routing table. As explained in Question 7b from the previous section, the preference value causes OSPF routes to be chosen over BGP routes when equivalent routes exist in both protocols.

5a. Does either router have routes to the other's system and loopback interfaces?

Yes. CE1 and PE2 both have routes to the other router's system interface. The reason for this is that although there is no OSPF adjacency between PE1 and PE2, PE1 still has the DistributeLB export policy applied to the OSPF process. Therefore, the IP address of the link between PE1–PE2 is known by CE1 and the next hop can be resolved. In a typical real-world scenario, however, a more complex policy would be used to make sure the boundary link IP address between two autonomous systems is not propagated into a single autonomous system IGP.

6a. What specific IP address does PE2 specify as the next-hop address to reach its interfaces?

PE2 specifies its local egress interface as the next-hop address: 140.10.0.98 as shown in the command output.

6b. Is that address known to CE1?

Yes. As explained in Question 5a, in this lab case, CE1 does have an IGP route to resolve a next-hop address for PE2's interface of 140.10.0.98. In a real-world network, a more complex policy may be used on PE1 so that CE1 does not know about the PE2 interface of 140.10.0.98.

7a. Confirm what route information is now being sent to CE1.

CE1 is now receiving modified BGP routes from PE1. The next-hop interface value has been changed.

7b. What specific interface does PE1 choose for the next-hop address?

PE1 is now using its system address as the next-hop address for routes sent to iBGP peers.

7c. Is that address known to CE1?

Yes, CE1 has a route to PE1's system interface.

7d. Why is an IGP still needed among iBGP peers?

An IGP is needed to resolve the next-hop address for iBGP peers in order to use routes advertised by those peers.

8a. Can every router reach every interface?

Every router can reach every interface with the exception that PE2 still cannot reach CE1's interfaces.

8b. Do the ping results for each router correlate with the routing table information for that router? Explain your answer.

Yes, the ping results are consistent with the information in the routing tables. PE2 has no route to any of CE1's interfaces.

9a. Why does the Routing Table Manager (RTM) always choose the one protocol as the source of routes from CE1?

The preference values for the routing protocols cause the RTM to always choose OSPF routes over BGP routes when equivalent routes exist in both protocols. As a result, the BGP route information from CE1 is *not* considered the *best* routing information, and thus it is not passed along to PE2.

9b. Does the chosen protocol fit the specifications in the export policy for BGP (i.e., the DistributeLB policy)?

The export policy specifies exporting only local interfaces; it does *not* provide for exporting routes learned from OSPF.

10a. Note the numbering of the new entry. Does this replace or add to the existing entry?

The export policy has been updated with entry 20. Since this is different from the original policy entry 10, it is *added* to the policy criteria.

10b. Does the new entry add an extra condition (an AND function) or an alternative condition (an OR function)?

Each entry creates an OR condition, so routes in the routing table matching *either* entry 10 *or* entry 20 are eligible to be exported.

10c. What is the purpose of the `begin` and `commit` keywords?

The keywords mark the beginning and ending of an editing session. The router does not attempt to use the updated policy until the editing is marked as *finished* with the `commit` keyword. This prevents a half-finished policy from being used, and possibly causing routes to be erroneously distributed to peers.

11a. What is the next-hop address that appears on PE1 and PE2 for routes to CE1? Is it the same?

No, the next-hop address on PE1 is different from the next-hop address that appears on PE2. This is most easily verified by executing the command `show router bgp neighbor x.x.x.x advertised-routes` on PE1 and PE2.

11b. What kind of BGP peering relationship exists between PE1 and PE2?

PE1 and PE2 are eBGP peers since they are members of a different AS.

11c. Is the `next-hop-self` attribute required for eBGP peers?

No, it is not necessary for eBGP peers since the next-hop address is changed by default when crossing an AS boundary.

Final Configurations

```
*B:PE1# configure router
*B:PE1>config>router# info
#------------------------------------------------
#-------------------------------------------------
echo "IP Configuration"
#-------------------------------------------------
        interface "loopbackTest"
            address 140.10.0.11/32
            loopback
        exit
        interface "system"
            address 140.10.0.1/32
        exit
        interface "toCE1"
            address 140.10.0.101/30
            port 1/1/1
        exit
        interface "toPE2"
            address 140.10.0.97/30
            port 1/1/2
        exit
        autonomous-system 65001
#-------------------------------------------------
echo "OSPFv2 Configuration"
#-------------------------------------------------
        ospf
            asbr
            export "DistributeLB"
            area 0.0.0.0
                interface "system"
                exit
                interface "toCE1"
                exit
            exit
        exit
#-------------------------------------------------
echo "Policy Configuration"
#-------------------------------------------------
```

(continued)

```
            policy-options
                begin
                policy-statement "DistributeLB"
                    entry 10
                        from
                            protocol direct
                        exit
                        action accept
                        exit
                    exit
                    entry 20
                        from
                            protocol ospf
                        exit
                        action accept
                        exit
                    exit
                exit
                commit
            exit
    #----------------------------------------------------
    echo "BGP Configuration"
    #----------------------------------------------------
            bgp
                export "DistributeLB"
                group "eBGP"
                    next-hop-self
                    neighbor 140.10.0.98
                        peer-as 65002
                    exit
                exit
                group "iBGP"
                  · next-hop-self
                    neighbor 140.10.0.3
                        peer-as 65001
                    exit
                exit
            exit
    #----------------------------------------------
```

(continued)

```
*B:PE1>config>router#


*A:PE2# configure router
*A:PE2>config>router# info
#-------------------------------------------------
#-------------------------------------------------
echo "IP Configuration"
#-------------------------------------------------
        interface "loopbackTest"
            address 150.10.0.11/32
            loopback
        exit
        interface "system"
            address 150.10.0.1/32
        exit
        interface "toPE1"
            address 140.10.0.98/30
            port 1/1/2
        exit
        autonomous-system 65002
#-------------------------------------------------
echo "Policy Configuration"
#-------------------------------------------------
        policy-options
            begin
            policy-statement "DistributeLB"
                entry 10
                    from
                        protocol direct
                    exit
                    action accept
                    exit
                exit
            exit
            commit
        exit
#-------------------------------------------------
echo "BGP Configuration"
```

(continued)

```
        #----------------------------------------------------------
                bgp
                    export "DistributeLB"
                    group "eBGP"
                        neighbor 140.10.0.97
                            peer-as 65001
                        exit
                    exit
                exit
        #---------------------------------------------------
        *A:PE2>config>router#


        *A:CE1# configure router
        *A:CE1>config>router# info
        #--------------------------------------------------
        #---------------------------------------------------------
        echo "IP Configuration"
        #------------------------------------------------------
                interface "loopbackTest"
                    address 140.10.0.12/32
                    loopback
                exit
                interface "system"
                    address 140.10.0.3/32
                exit
                interface "toPE1"
                    address 140.10.0.102/30
                    port 1/1/1
                exit
                autonomous-system 65001
        #------------------------------------------------------
        echo "OSPFv2 Configuration"
        #------------------------------------------------------
                ospf
                    asbr
                    export "DistributeLB"
                    area 0.0.0.0
                        interface "system"
```

(continued)

```
                              exit
                        interface "toPE1"
                              exit
                  exit
            exit
#-------------------------------------------------------
echo "Policy Configuration"
#-------------------------------------------------------
      policy-options
            begin
            policy-statement "DistributeLB"
                  entry 10
                        from
                              protocol direct
                        exit
                        action accept
                        exit
                  exit
            exit
            commit
      exit
#-------------------------------------------------------
echo "BGP Configuration"
#-------------------------------------------------------
      bgp
            export "DistributeLB"
            group "iBGP"
                  neighbor 140.10.0.1
                        peer-as 65001
                  exit
            exit
      exit
#-------------------------------------------------
*A:CE1>config>router#
```

Lab Section 11.1 Exercises

Part 1: IGP Configuration

1a. What command(s) can you use to verify that BGP has been successfully removed? (Refer to Lab Section 10.1 in Chapter 10.)

The command `show router status` can be used to verify that BGP is no longer running.

3a. What tells you that OSPF is no longer running between PE1 and CE1?

The command output shows only a single OSPF adjacency (with PE2). There is no longer any adjacency with CE1.

Part 2: LDP and SDP Configuration

6a. Is it possible to get a single SDP in the `Up` state?

No, with MPLS SDPs, you will find that SDPs won't go to an `Up` state unless there is a matching SDP that provides a return path.

Part 3: Customer-Facing Configuration

1a. What error message do you get if you try to remove an interface that is *not* shut down?

You get an error message that the `Interface is not 'shutdown'`. It will not be removed.

2a. There are only two states for a port: One is `access` mode. What is the name of the other mode?

The other mode is `network`. You can get this information by typing **configure port 1/1/1 ethernet mode** followed by a question mark. The `network` mode is the default state for Ethernet ports.

2b. What error message do you get if a port is *not* shut down when you try to change modes?

You get an error message saying that the port is `Not 'shutdown' - 1/1/1`. The port mode will not be changed.

Part 4: Verification

2a. One label is to reach the far router. Is that the `Push` or the `Pop` label?

The `Push` label is the one used to reach the far router.

2b. One label is offered to the far router to send data back to the local router. Is that the Push or the Pop label?

The Pop label is the one used to send data back to the local router.

Lab Section 11.2 Exercises

Part 1: Provider Edge VPLS Configuration

1a. What happens if you forget to use the keyword `create` when first creating a VPLS?

By default, if you omit the keyword `create` when first creating a VPLS, you will get an error message and the service will *not* be created.

2a. What happens if you forget to use the keyword `create` when first creating a mesh SDP?

By default, if you omit the keyword `create` when first creating a mesh SDP, you will get an error message and the SDP will *not* be created.

3a. What happens if you forget to use the keyword `create` when first creating a SAP?

By default, if you omit the keyword `create` when first creating a SAP, you will get an error message and the SAP will *not* be created.

Part 3: Verification

1a. How many routers does CE1 see between itself and Device4?

CE1 sees *no* router hops between itself and Device4. This is exactly the same as if the two were connected by an Ethernet switch.

1b. Does CE1 see the connection to Device4 as routed or switched (at Layer 2)? Explain your answer.

CE1 sees a switched connection. If CE1 saw a routed connection, it would expect to see one or more hops between itself and Device4.

2a. Are any PE interfaces reachable?

No PE interfaces are reachable. In fact, *none* of the Provider Core network is visible or reachable from the customer side. This is the essential idea of a VPN: The customer and provider networks appear completely separate.

3a. How many OSPF adjacencies are there on each CE device?

The CE devices only see OSPF adjacencies between themselves.

3b. Are there any adjacencies with, or LSAs from the PE routers?

On the CE devices, there are no adjacencies or LSAs from the PE routers.

3c. From CE1, which system interfaces can you ping? PE1? PE2? Device4?

CE1 can only ping interfaces on Device4. It *cannot* ping the system or any other interface on PE1 or PE2.

3d. Explain the results.

None of the Provider Core network is visible or reachable from the customer side. This is true for both Layer 2 Ethernet frames and Layer 3 IP packets. This is the essential idea of a VPN: The customer and provider networks appear completely separate.

3e. Are the OSPF sessions on the CE devices connected in any way to the OSPF sessions on the PE devices?

There is no exchange of information whatsoever between the customer OSPF session and the provider OSPF sessions. Thus, even for OSPF, the customer and provider networks appear completely separate.

4a. Explain the results.

As soon as one SDP is down, the VPLS service between the PE nodes goes down. The result is the same as if an Ethernet switch were unplugged: All connectivity is lost, the OSPF adjacencies are lost, and all OSPF routes are removed from the routing table.

6a. How many services are there on each PE device?

Each PE device shows only a single VPLS, which is running across both PE devices.

6b. What is the status of each service?

At this point in time, the service appears on both PE routers as Up since it should be fully operational.

7a. Are the databases identical or different? If different, what is different? Explain the results.

The databases should both have the same number of entries. The entries should be for the same MAC addresses. The Source-Id should be opposite on the two routers: What is learned from a SAP on one router should appear as learned from an SDP on the other router.

7b. How many local MAC addresses are in the CE1 table?

There is one local MAC address: 00:1a:f0:5c:73:c5. It is considered local because it was learned from a SAP, shown as `sap 1/1/1` in the output.

7c. How many remote MAC addresses are in the CE1 table?

There is one remote MAC address: 00:1a:f0:5c:6e:1b. It is considered remote because it was learned from an SDP, shown as `sdp 12:22` in the output.

Final Configurations

```
*B:PE1# configure router
*B:PE1>config>router# info
#-------------------------------------------------
#-------------------------------------------------
echo "IP Configuration"
#-------------------------------------------------
        interface "loopbackTest"
            address 140.10.0.11/32
            loopback
        exit
        interface "system"
            address 140.10.0.1/32
        exit
        interface "toPE2"
            address 140.10.0.97/30
            port 1/1/2
        exit
#-------------------------------------------------
echo "OSPFv2 Configuration"
#-------------------------------------------------
        ospf
            asbr
            export "DistributeLB"
            area 0.0.0.0
                interface "system"
                exit
                interface "toPE2"
                exit
            exit
        exit
```

(continued)

```
        #-------------------------------------------------
        echo "LDP Configuration"
        #-------------------------------------------------
                ldp
                        interface-parameters
                                interface "toPE2"
                                exit
                        exit
                        targeted-session
                        exit
                exit
        #-------------------------------------------------
        echo "Policy Configuration"
        #-------------------------------------------------
                policy-options
                        begin
                        policy-statement "DistributeLB"
                                entry 10
                                        from
                                                protocol direct
                                        exit
                                        action accept
                                        exit
                                exit
                        exit
                        commit
                exit
        #-----------------------------------------------
*B:PE1>config>router# exit
*B:PE1 #

*B:PE1# configure service
*B:PE1>config>service# info
        #-----------------------------------------------
                customer 1 create
                        description "Default customer"
                exit
                sdp 12 mpls create
                        far-end 150.10.0.1
```

(continued)

```
                    ldp
                    keep-alive
                        shutdown
                    exit
                    no shutdown
                exit
                vpls 22 customer 1 create
                    stp
                        shutdown
                    exit
                    sap 1/1/1 create
                    exit
                    mesh-sdp 12:22 create
                    exit
                    no shutdown
                exit
#------------------------------------------------
*B:PE1>config>service#


*A:PE2# configure router
^A:PE2>config>router# info
#------------------------------------------------
#---------------------------------------------------
echo "IP Configuration"
#---------------------------------------------------
        interface "loopbackTest"
            address 150.10.0.11/32
            loopback
        exit
        interface "system"
            address 150.10.0.1/32
        exit
        interface "toPE1"
            address 140.10.0.98/30
            port 1/1/2
        exit
#---------------------------------------------------
echo "OSPFv2 Configuration"
```

(continued)

```
        #-------------------------------------------------
                ospf
                    asbr
                    export "DistributeLB"
                    area 0.0.0.0
                        interface "system"
                        exit
                        interface "toPE1"
                        exit
                    exit
                exit
        #-------------------------------------------------
echo "LDP Configuration"
        #-------------------------------------------------
                ldp
                    interface-parameters
                        interface "toPE1"
                        exit
                    exit
                    targeted-session
                    exit
                exit
        #-------------------------------------------------
echo "Policy Configuration"
        #-------------------------------------------------
                policy-options
                    begin
                    policy-statement "DistributeLB"
                        entry 10
                            from
                                protocol direct
                            exit
                            action accept
                            exit
                        exit
                    exit
                    commit
                exit
        #-----------------------------------------------
```

(continued)

```
*A:PE2>config>router# exit

*A:PE2# configure service
*A:PE2>config>service# info
#------------------------------------------------
        customer 1 create
            description "Default customer"
        exit
        sdp 21 mpls create
            far-end 140.10.0.1
            ldp
            keep-alive
                shutdown
            exit
            no shutdown
        exit
        vpls 22 customer 1 create
            stp
                shutdown
            exit
            sap 1/1/1 create
            exit
            mesh-sdp 21:22 create
            exit
            no shutdown
        exit
#------------------------------------------------
*A:PE2>config>service#


*A:CE1# configure router
*A:CE1>config>router# info
#------------------------------------------------
#------------------------------------------------------
echo "IP Configuration"
#------------------------------------------------------
        interface "loopbackTest"
            address 140.10.0.12/32
            loopback
```

(continued)

```
            exit
        interface "system"
            address 140.10.0.3/32
        exit
        interface "toPE1"
            address 192.168.0.1/24
            port 1/1/1
        exit
#-----------------------------------------------------
echo "OSPFv2 Configuration"
#-----------------------------------------------------
        ospf
            area 0.0.0.0
                interface "system"
                exit
                interface "toPE1"
                exit
            exit
        exit
#-----------------------------------------------------
echo "Policy Configuration"
#-----------------------------------------------------
        policy-options
            begin
            policy-statement "DistributeLB"
                entry 10
                    from
                        protocol direct
                    exit
                    action accept
                    exit
                exit
            exit
            commit
        exit
#-----------------------------------------------------
```

(continued)

```
*A:CE1>config>router#


*A:Dev4-CE2# configure router
*A:Dev4-CE2>config>router# info
#------------------------------------------------
#------------------------------------------------
echo "IP Configuration"
#------------------------------------------------
        interface "system"
            address 150.10.0.2/32
        exit
        interface "toVPLS"
            address 192.168.0.4/24
            port 1/1/1
        exit
#------------------------------------------------
echo "OSPFv2 Configuration"
#------------------------------------------------
        ospf
            area 0.0.0.0
                interface "system"
                exit
                interface "toVPLS"
                exit
            exit
        exit
#------------------------------------------------
*A:Dev4-CE2>config>router#
```

Glossary

AAL

ATM Adaptation Layer   The AAL is the layer of the ATM Reference Model that is divided into the Convergence Sublayer and the Segmentation and Reassembly Sublayer. The AAL converts user data traffic to and from ATM cells. On the originating side of the connection, the AAL segments the user data traffic into the size and format of ATM cells. On the terminating side of the connection, the AAL reassembles the user data into its original format. There are four different types of AALs recommended by the ITU-T: AAL-1, AAL-2, AAL-3/4, and AAL-5.

ABR

Area Border Router   A router located on the border of one or more OSPF areas that connects those areas to the backbone network. The ABR is considered to be a member of the OSPF backbone and the attached areas. The router maintains routing tables that describe both the backbone topology and the topology of the other areas.

ACK

Acknowledgment   In general, an ACK is a way for a protocol to confirm that it has received the transmitted data. In TCP, ACK is a bit flag indicating the receipt of a TCP data segment. The ACK is a single bit in the TCP header of a segment that may or may not also contain data. The acknowledgement number (a 32-bit field in the header) indicates the number of the next consecutive byte expected in the data stream.

ACL

Access Control List   A rule or set of rules used to filter data packets ingressing/egressing a router or a switch. Specific characteristics of the data packet such as IP address and TCP port information are used to define the rules.

Adj-RIB-In

Adjacent Routing Information Base Incoming   A table of BGP routes received by a BGP router from its directly connected peers. An import policy, if defined on a BGP router, is applied to filter routes from this table.

Adj-RIB-Out

Adjacent Routing Information Base Outgoing   A table of BGP routes maintained on a BGP router that is to be exported by the router to its directly connected peers. An export policy, if defined on a BGP router, is applied to the local routing information base to generate the BGP routes in the RIB-Out.

ALOHANET

Experimental packet radio network under the direction of Professor Norman Abramson at the University of Hawaii. ALOHANET was connected to the ARPANET in 1972. The original Ethernet specification benefited from the experience of the ALOHA protocol.

ARP

Address Resolution Protocol   Resolves a host/gateway MAC address for a given IP address. A device performs this task by sending a broadcast to the network, requesting (ARP request) the system that is using the specified IP address to respond with its MAC address. If the destination system is powered up and on the network, the system will detect this broadcast (as will all of the other devices on the LAN) and return an ARP response to the original system.

ARPA

Advanced Research Projects Agency   An agency of the U.S. Department of Defense dedicated to the investigation of technology potentially useful to the military. Later renamed to *DARPA* (Defense Advanced Research Projects Agency).

ARPANET

ARPA's Network   Generally considered the first operational packet-switched network. First operational with four nodes in the United States in 1969, it eventually evolved into today's Internet.

AS

Autonomous System   A collection of routers and other Internet devices under a single administrative domain. AS has specific meaning to the BGP protocol.

ATM

Asynchronous Transfer Mode   ATM is the international standard for cell switching. It employs 53-byte cells as a basic unit of transfer. ATM networks can carry traffic for multiple service types (e.g., voice, video, and data).

BDR

Backup Designated Router   A router that is elected in addition to the Designated Router to represent a multi-access (broadcast medium) network in OSPF.

BGP

Border Gateway Protocol   The core Internet routing protocol. BGP is used to propagate routing information between autonomous systems. A BGP update contains network prefixes and the list of AS numbers to be traversed to reach the destination.

BGPv4

Border Gateway Protocol, version 4   The current version of BGP, in use on the Internet since 1994. BGPv4 supported CIDR that addressed the problem of quickly growing routing tables and extended the useful life of IPv4.

BID

Bridge ID   A field in the Spanning Tree Protocol BPDU that is used to elect the root bridge. The BID is comprised of a 2-byte priority field concatenated with a switch MAC address. The switch in the network with the lowest BID is elected as the root bridge.

BOF

Boot Option File   A file that specifies the runtime image, configuration files, and other operational parameters during system initialization of the Alcatel-Lucent 7750 SR.

BOOTP

A member of the IP family of protocols that allows a diskless client machine to learn, among other information, its IP address. BOOTP starts a networked machine by reading boot information from a server. BOOTP is commonly used for desktop workstations and LAN hubs.

BPDU

Bridge Protocol Data Unit   A BPDU is the frame that LAN bridges supporting the 802.1D Spanning Tree Protocol use to communicate with each other.

CBR

Constant Bit Rate   Constant bit rate is an ATM class of service for delay-sensitive applications such as video and voice that must be digitized and represented by a constant bit stream. CBR traffic requires guaranteed levels of service and throughput.

CCITT

Comité Consultatif International Téléphonique et Télégraphique   The CCITT was chartered to promote and ensure the operation of international telecommunications systems. CCITT has been renamed *ITU-T*.

CD

Collision Detect CD is the ability to detect multiple stations trying to access the transmission channel. In Ethernet CSMA/CD, this event is normal. Stations are designed to back off, then try again after a random interval.

CE

Customer Edge CEs are the routers in a customer's network that connect to Provider Edges (PEs).

CF

Compact Flash Specific format of flash widely used in electronic devices as a non-volatile storage medium. On the Alcatel-Lucent 7750 SR routers, the operating system image and configuration files are usually stored on a compact flash card.

CIDR

Classless Inter-Domain Routing An IP addressing scheme that replaces the older addressing system based on Classes A, B, and C. With CIDR, a single IP prefix can be used to designate a block of IP network addresses.

CLI

Command Line Interface A text-based user interface to configure an Alcatel-Lucent 7750 SR node (in contrast to a graphical user interface, or GUI).

CLP

Cell Loss Priority An indicator flag bit on an ATM cell header used to determine whether or not the cell is to be discarded during traffic congestion. If the CLP is 1, the cell is more likely to be discarded.

Cwnd

Congestion Window A parameter used in TCP to control the rate at which the sender transmits data; intended to prevent a TCP connection from causing congestion in the network.

CPM

Central Processor Module The CPM is the control component of the Alcatel-Lucent 7750 SR dedicated for system control, centralized protocol processing, and management.

CS

Carrier Sense   The ability of a device to sense activity on a transmission line. This is a component of the CSMA/CD algorithm used by Ethernet, but also used in other data transmission protocols.

CSMA/CD

Carrier Sense Multiple Access with Collision Detection   CSMA/CD is the method of accessing a LAN specified in IEEE 802.3. A device listens until no signals are detected (carrier sense), then transmits and checks to see if more than one signal is present (collision detection). If a signal is detected, each device backs off and waits briefly before attempting transmission again. CSMA/CD is used in Ethernet LANs.

CTRL

Control   Usually used to indicate a special character code formed by holding the [Ctrl] key on the keyboard.

DA

Destination Address   Indicates the destination device for a network packet. Both Ethernet and IP use DA in the description of their packet headers.

DB

Database   A collection of information in a specifically organized format.

DBD

Database Description   A type of packet exchanged by two OSPF routers as they are forming an adjacency. Usually contains the list of LSAs in their link state database.

DCE

Data Communications Equipment   DCE refers to the gender of an interface on a data device, such as a modem or transceiver. The pinouts are wired so that pin 2 receives data and pin 3 transmits data. In a direct connection between interfaces, one port must be DCE, the other DTE.

DEC

Digital Equipment Corporation   DEC was a computer software and microcomputer manufacturer. Compaq acquired DEC in 1998.

DF

Don't Fragment   A single-bit flag in the IP header that indicates the IP datagram is not to be fragmented. If the datagram is to be forwarded over a network with an MTU smaller than the size of the frame required to transmit the datagram, it is discarded and an ICMP message sent to the sender of the datagram.

DHCP

Dynamic Host Control Protocol   DHCP is a client/server service that is an extension of the BOOTP protocol. DHCP simplifies the configuration of a client workstation since no IP addresses, subnet masks, default gateways, domain names, or DNSs must be programmed. With DHCP, this information is dynamically leased from the DHCP server for a predefined amount of time. Because the information is stored on a server, it centralizes IP address management, reduces the number of IP addresses to be used, and simplifies maintenance. RFC 2131 defines DHCP.

DIX

DEC-Intel-Xerox   The original standard for Ethernet, also commonly known as *Ethernet II*. Compare to Ethernet 802.3, which is very similar but has a slightly different header.

DNS

Domain Name System   DNS is an Internet standard for mapping Internet host or domain names to an IP address.

DoD

Department of Defense   The U.S. Department of Defense.

DR

Designated Router   In OSPF the designated router creates the network LSA that represents the topology of a multi-access network such as Ethernet.

DSAP

Destination Service Access Point   A field in the 802.2 LLC header that indicates a protocol or service address for the data carried in the frame.

DSCP

Differential Services Code Point   A 6-bit value encoded in the ToS field of an IP packet header. It identifies the quality of service handling that the packet should receive.

DTE

Data Terminal Equipment   DTE is a communications interface such as a computer or terminal system. DTE refers to the gender of the interface on a data device, such as a PC. The pinout wiring is such that pin 2 transmits data and pin 3 receives data. In a direct connection between interfaces, one port must be DTE, the other must be DCE.

eBGP

External BGP   A BGP session established between routers in different ASes. eBGP peers communicate among different network domains.

EGP

Exterior Gateway Protocol   A generic term for a routing protocol that is used to exchange routing information between two routers in a network of ASes. BGPv4 is the current EGP of the Internet.

eLER

Egress Label Edge Router   For a specific LSP, the last, or egress MPLS router. The eLER pops the MPLS label and forwards an unlabeled packet outside the MPLS domain.

ESS

Alcatel-Lucent 7450 Ethernet Service Switch   An Ethernet switch that enables the delivery of metro Ethernet services and high-density service-aware Ethernet aggregation over IP/MPLS-based networks. The 7450 ESS is a member of the Alcatel-Lucent 7750 SR product family.

FCS

Frame Check Sequence   An FCS is a Cyclic Redundancy Check used to determine errors in data packet transmissions. In bit-oriented protocols, FCS is typically a 16- or 32-bit field calculated on the entire contents of the frame and usually appended to the end of a frame. The receiving station performs the same calculation and compares the result with the FCS value. A difference indicates an error in transmission, and the frame is usually discarded.

FDB

Forwarding Database   The table in an Ethernet switch or the table maintained for a VPLS instance that contains the list of known MAC addresses and the ports on which they were learned. In the case of the VPLS, the entries contain either the SAP or the SDP on which the address was learned.

FFPC

Flexible Fast Path complex   The chipset on an Alcatel-Lucent 7750 SR IOM that is responsible for packet forwarding.

FIB

Forwarding Information Base   FIB is the set of information that represents the best forwarding information for a destination. A device derives FIB entries from the reachability information held in the RIB, which is subject to administrative routing.

FIN

End of Data   Generally used in data transmission protocols to indicate the end of transmission. In TCP, a single-bit flag (similar to the SYN and ACK bits) that indicates one side has finished its transmission and has closed the connection.

FIN-ACK

The sequence by which one end of a TCP connection indicates that it wishes to close the connection and acknowledges the FIN that has been sent by the other end.

Frame-Relay

A data transmission technique that combines high-speed and low-delay circuit-switching with port sharing and dynamic bandwidth allocation capabilities. Frame-Relay divides transmission bandwidth into numerous Virtual Circuits and supports bursts of data. Frame-Relay does not require significant processing at each node, delegating error correction and flow control to the attached user devices.

FTP

File Transfer Protocol   FTP is the Internet standard client-server protocol for transferring files from one computer to another. FTP generally runs over TCP.

GFC

Generic Flow Control   GFC is a field in the ATM header that provides local flow control. It has local significance only, and the value encoded in the field is not carried end-to-end.

GigE

Gigabit Ethernet   An Ethernet standard that supports a transmission rate of 1,000,000,000,000 bits per second. Both copper and fiber standards are defined.

GUI

Graphical User Interface   A GUI is a computer user interface that incorporates graphics to make software easier to use.

HDLC

High Level Data Link Layer Control   HDLC is an ISO standard for serial data communication. HDLC is composed of a family of bit-oriented protocols providing frames of information with address, control, and Frame Check Sequence fields. It is considered a superset of several other protocols, including PPP.

HEC

Header Error Control   The HEC is an 8-bit Cyclic Redundancy Check that is used to check for errors in the header of each ATM cell.

HLEN

Header Length   A field in the IPv4 header that indicates the length (in units of 4 bytes) of the header, since the IP header length is variable. If there are no options used in the IP header, the value is 5 (20 bytes). The maximum value is 15, limiting the maximum IPv4 header size to 60 bytes.

HTTP

Hypertext Transfer Protocol   A set of rules for exchanging text, graphics, sound, video, and other multimedia files across the Internet. HTTP is the protocol of the World Wide Web.

IANA

Internet Assigned Numbers Authority   The IANA is the body that oversees the assignment of IP addresses, AS numbers, domain names, and other Internet Protocol addresses.

ICMP

Internet Control Message Protocol   ICMP is a protocol that sends and receives the control and error messages used to manage the behavior of the TCP/IP stack. ICMP is defined in RFC 792.

IEEE

Institute of Electrical and Electronics Engineers   A worldwide engineering publishing and standards-making body. It is the organization responsible for defining many of the standards used in the computer, electrical, and electronics industries.

IETF

Internet Engineering Task Force   The IETF is the organization that provides the coordination of standards and specification development for TCP/IP networking.

IGP

Interior Gateway Protocols   Generic term applied to any protocol used to propagate network reach and routing information within an AS. OSPF, IS-IS, and RIP are examples of IGPs.

IHL

IP Header Length   A variation of HLEN—the length of the IP header.

iBGP

Internal BGP   iBGP is a type of BGP used within a single AS. iBGP is a protocol for exchanging routing information between routers within an autonomous network. The routing information can then be used by IP.

iLER

Ingress Label Edge Router   For a specific LSP, the first, or ingress MPLS router. The ingress LER receives an unlabeled packet and pushes an MPLS label onto the packet and forwards it through the MPLS domain.

IOM

Input/Output Module   A module on the Alcatel-Lucent 7750 SR that interconnects two MDAs with the fabric core. The module also performs Layer 3 traffic management.

IP

Internet Protocol   A network layer protocol underlying the Internet, which provides an unreliable, connectionless, packet delivery service to users. IP allows large, geographically diverse networks of computers to communicate with each other quickly and economically over a variety of physical links.

IPSec

Internet Protocol Security   An IETF network layer security standard that is used to encrypt and authenticate IP packet data.

IPv4

Internet Protocol version 4   The version of IP in use since the 1970s. IPv4 addresses are 32 bits. IPv4 headers vary in length and are at least 20 bytes.

IPX

Internet Packet eXchange   IPX is the native LAN communications protocol for Novell NetWare. It is used to move data between server and workstation programs running on different nodes. IPX packets are encapsulated and carried by packets used in Ethernet, and similar frames used in Token Ring networks.

ISDN

Integrated Services Digital Network   An ISDN is a way to move more data over existing phone lines. It can provide speeds of roughly 128 Kbps over regular phone lines. An ISDN provides a wide range of voice and non-voice services, including image and video transmissions, within the same network using a limited set of connection types and multipurpose user–network interface arrangements.

IS-IS

Intermediate System to Intermediate System   An OSI routing protocol, later adapted to TCP/IP networks.

ISO

International Organization for Standardization   ISO is the official international recognized organization that is responsible for establishing voluntary standards, including network technology standards.

ISP

Internet Service Provider   A business or an organization that provides external transit connectivity to access the Internet for consumers or businesses.

IXP

Internet Exchange Point   A physical location that allows several ISPs to interconnect and exchange traffic between their networks. Most IXPs use Ethernet for the interconnection, and the cost of the facility is often split among the ISPs that use it.

L1

Layer 1   The physical layer of the OSI model that includes the required network hardware and physical cabling for the transmission of raw bits and the acknowledgement of requests from the data link layer.

L2

Layer 2   The data link or MAC layer of the OSI model. In networking, it is a communications protocol that contains the physical address of a client or server station that is inspected by a bridge or switch.

L3

Layer 3   The network layer of the OSI model. In networking, it is a communications protocol that contains the logical address of a client or server station that is inspected by a router, which forwards the data through the network.

L4

Layer 4   The transport layer of the OSI model. It is the lowest layer that provides end-to-end connectivity between applications

L7

Layer 7   The application layer of the OSI model. It is the highest layer and defines the protocols used by network applications such as email and file transfer.

LACP

Link Aggregation Control Protocol   A communication protocol defined in IEEE 802.3ad used to communicate link aggregation membership between two nodes. The information relayed through LACP can be used to dynamically include or exclude links from a Link Aggregation Group.

LAG

Link Aggregation Group   According to the IEEE 802.3ad standard, multiple Ethernet ports between two network nodes can be aggregated and used in parallel to form a Link Aggregation Group. LAGs can be configured to increase the bandwidth available between two network devices. All physical links in a given LAG combine to form one logical interface.

LAN

Local Area Network   A system designed to interconnect computing devices over a restricted geographical area (usually a couple of kilometers).

LDAP

Lightweight Directory Access Protocol   LDAP is a networking protocol for querying and modifying directory services that run over TCP/IP.

LDP

Label Distribution Protocol   LDP is a signaling protocol used for MPLS path setup and teardown. LDP is used by LSRs to indicate to other LSRs the labels that should be used to forward traffic. LDP is defined in RFC 3036.

LER

Label Edge Router   An LER is an MPLS node that runs MPLS control protocols and is capable of forwarding packets based on labels. An LER is also capable of forwarding native Layer 3 packets.

LLC

Logical Link Control   LLC is the upper sublayer of the ISO model data link layer and is the protocol layer directly above the MAC layer. LLC provides logical interfaces between two adjacent layers and governs the exchange of data between two endpoints by handling addressing and error detection. LLC governs packet transmission as specified by IEEE 802.2.

Loc-RIB

Local Routing Information Base   A table of BGP routes maintained on a BGP router that represents the routes to be used and installed in the routing table.

LS Protocols

Link State Protocols   A family of routing protocols that exchange link state information and use the Shortest Path First algorithm to calculate the best route to destinations in the network. OSPF and IS-IS are the two most widely used link state routing protocols.

LSA

Link State Advertisement   An LSA describes the local state of an OSPF router, including the state of the router interfaces and adjacencies. Each LSA is flooded throughout the routing domain. The collected LSAs of all routers and networks form the protocol topological database.

LSDB

Link State Database   A link state database, or topological database, contains the collection of link state information received from all routers in an AS. The LSDB is updated on a continuous basis as new link state information is advertised when the network topology changes.

LSP

Label Switched Path   The path from router to router over which a packet travels by label switching within an MPLS network.

LSR

Label Switch Router   An MPLS node capable of forwarding labeled packets based on a label.

MAC

Media Access Control   A media-specific access control protocol within IEEE 802 specifications. The protocol is for medium sharing, packet formatting, addressing, and error detection. Ethernet addresses are often known as MAC *addresses*.

MDA

Media Dependent Adapter   MDAs are hardware modules that are housed in IOMs and in which a physical interface terminates.

MIME

Multiprotocol Mail Extensions   Extensions to the Internet mail standard that support the exchange of binary information such as images and other non-text information. Also widely used to describe content type on the World Wide Web.

MF

More Fragments   A bit flag in the IP header that when set indicates this datagram is one of several fragments of an IP datagram. If the value is zero, the fragment is either the last fragment or the datagram has not been fragmented.

MPLS

Multi Protocol Label Switching   MPLS is a technology in which forwarding decisions are based on fixed-length labels inserted between the data link layer and network layer headers to increase forwarding performance and flexibility in path selection.

MSS

Maximun Segment Size   A parameter specified as an option value in the TCP header during the setup of a connection. Both sides typically specify the MTU of their locally attached network as their MSS and use the smaller of the two as the maximum packet size for the connection.

MTU

Maximum Transmission Unit   MTU is the largest unit of data that can be transmitted over a particular interface type in one packet. The MTU can change from one network hop to the next.

NAT

Network Address Translation   NAT is a method by which IP addresses are mapped from one group to another, and is transparent to end-users. This mechanism allows the connection of a realm with private addresses to an external realm with globally unique registered addresses such as the Internet.

NCP

Network Control Protocol   The original network protocol used on the ARPANET before the development of TCP/IP.

NH

Next Hop   The IP address of the next router that is directly attached in the path to a final destination.

NLRI

Network Layer Reachability Information   The basic information carried in a BGP update. NLRI includes the network prefix and its length.

NMS

Network Mangement System   A system that manages at least part of a network. An NMS is generally a reasonably powerful and well-equipped computer such as an engineering workstation. The NMS communicates with agents to help keep track of network statistics and resources.

NRS

Network Routing Specialist   Alcatel-Lucent NRS I and NRS II are two certifications in the Service Router Certification program. The Alcatel-Lucent NRS I certifies a candidate as having achieved a foundation knowledge in networking technologies, TCP/IP, and routing protocols. Alcatel-Lucent NRS II certifies a candidate as having achieved a solid understanding of IP routing, MPLS, and Layer 2 VPN services, as well as practical experience in configuring these technologies on the Alcatel-Lucent 7750 SR.

NSF

National Science Foundation   A U.S. government agency that funds research in basic science and engineering technologies.

NSFNET

NSF Network   NSFNET was the largest component of the Internet backbone during the early 1990s. The NSFNET was the first major step in moving from the single-backbone structure of ARPANET to the distributed structure of the Internet today.

NTP

Network Timing Protocol   NTP standardizes time among Internet hosts around the world, with a maximum difference of less than 1 second. NTP achieves standardized time by synchronizing the node time to servers that have access to accurate time standards, such as satellite-based GPS or atomic clocks located on the Internet.

OSI

Open Systems Interconnection   The OSI Reference Model is a seven-layer model for network architecture. The model was developed by ISO and CCIT (now ITU-T). Each layer consists of an abstract description of protocols related to particular network functions such as addressing, flow control, error control, and reliable data transfer. From top to bottom, the seven layers are Application, Presentation, Session, Transport, Network, data link, and Physical layers.

OSPF

Open Shortest Path First   Dynamic, link state routing protocol that responds quickly to network topology changes. As a successor to RIP, it uses an algorithm that builds and calculates the shortest path to all known destinations.

OUI

Organizationally Unique Identifier   A 24-bit number that identifies the manufacturer of an Ethernet adapter. The number is purchased from the IEEE, who ensure its global uniqueness. The vendor then adds a unique 24-bit suffix to create a MAC address.

P router

Provider Router   A P router is a core router in a provider network that does not attach to any CE device.

PAT

Port Address Translation   PAT is a form of network address translation that uses a single public IP address to represent all outgoing connections. The connections are differentiated by using a unique source port number for each one—hence the name *port address translation*.

PE

Provider Edge   PEs are the routers in a service provider's network that connect to Customer Edges (CEs).

POP

Points of Presence   A POP is the physical location where an ISP aggregates its subscriber connections and connects them to the Internet.

PPP

Point-to-Point Protocol   A Data Link protocol used to establish a direct connection between two network nodes over telephone line, serial cable, specialized radio links, or fiber optic links.

PT

Payload Type   A 3-bit field in the ATM cell header that indicates special cell types used for operations, administration, and maintenance (OAM).

PWC

Present Working Context   A command in the Alcatel-Lucent 7750 SR CLI that tells the user his or her current context in the CLI.

QoS

Quality of Service   The ability of a network to recognize different service requirements of different application traffic flowing through it and to comply with SLAs negotiated for each application service, while attempting to maximize network resource utilization.

RFC

Requests For Comments   RFC is the name of the result and the process for creating a standard on the Internet. New standards are proposed and published online, as a "Request For Comments." RFC is the prefix for all published IETF documents for Internet environment standards; for example, the official standard for email is RFC 822. RFC documents typically define IP, TCP, and related application layer protocols.

RIB

Routing Information Base   An internal table containing all of the routes known to a router. It includes routes currently being used for IP forwarding as well as all known alternate routes.

RIP

Routing Information Protocol   RIP is a routing protocol based on distance vector algorithms that measure the shortest path between two points on a network in terms of the number of hops between those points. Various forms of RIP distribute routing information in IP, Xerox Network Services (XNS), IPX, and Virtual Integrated Network Service (VINES) networks.

RIR

Regional Internet Registry   A Regional Internet Registry is an organization responsible for the management of Internet IP addresses and similar resources within a specific region. The five RIRs today are ARIN (North/Central America), RIPE (Europe/Middle East), APNIC (Asia/Pacific), LACNIC (Latin America), and AfriNIC (Africa).

RPC

Remote Procedure Call RPC is a procedure call between different applications that run on the same machine or on different machines. There are parameters and returned values as in normal procedure calls. As machines have different operating systems and formats, the parameters and results are converted into a format that can be understood by both partners.

RST

Re*set One-bit flag in the TCP header that indicates the connection is to be re-set.

RSTP

Rapid Spanning Tree Protocol RSTP is specified in IEEE 802.1w. It replaces the Spanning Tree Protocol specified by IEEE 802.1d. RSTP is targeted at switched networks with point-to-point interconnections and allows for much quicker reconfiguration time (~1 s) by allowing a rapid change in port roles. RSTP was incorporated into the STP standard in 2004 as part of IEEE 802.1D-2004.

RSVP

Resource Reservation Protocol A signaling protocol used to reserve resources across a network. RSVP was developed to support IntServ (Integrated Services) but can be used independently. RSVP-TE is an extension to the original protocol that supports traffic engineering and label distribution for an MPLS network.

RTM

Routing Table Manager The RTM is an application that operates in the Alcatel-Lucent 7750 SR CPM to create and maintain a RIB that contains all active static routes in the network. The RTM calculates the best routes from the RIB and stores the information in the FIB.

RTP

Real-Time Protocol RTP provides end-to-end delivery services for real-time traffic, such as VOIP and video, over multicast or unicast network services.

RTT

Round Trip Time Time measured by TCP for an ACK to be received after data has been sent. TCP uses RTT to manage the value of its timers, such as the re-transmit timer.

SA

Source Address   The MAC or IP address of the sender of a packet in the network. Both IP and Ethernet packets contain an SA field.

SAM

5620 Service Aware Manager   Alcatel-Lucent system for integrated network and service management.

SAP

Service Access Point   An SAP identifies the customer interface point for a service on an Alcatel-Lucent 7750 SR.

SDP

Service Distribution Point   An SDP acts as a logical way to direct traffic from one Alcatel-Lucent 7750 SR node to another through a unidirectional service tunnel.

SEQ

Sequence Number   A 32-bit field in the TCP header used to identify the contents of the segment in the overall TCP data stream.

SFD

Start of Frame Delimiter   A sequence of 8 bits that identifies the start of an Ethernet frame. The destination MAC address follows immediately after the SFD. The SFD is preceded by the 56-bit preamble, an alternating sequence of 1010... binary. The SFD is the bit sequence 10101011.

SFP

Small Form Factor Pluggable   A widely used standard format for a compact transceiver used to connect network hardware to an optical or copper cable.

SLA

Service Level Agreement   A contractual agreement between a service provider and customer stipulating the minimum standards of service.

SLIP

Serial Line IP   SLIP is a simple protocol that allows one machine to communicate with another using IP over an asynchronous serial line. It is being superseded by PPP but is still in use.

SMTP

Simple Mail Transfer Protocol   SMTP is the IETF standard for transferring electronic mail messages from one computer to another. It is the main protocol used to send electronic mail on the Internet. SMTP consists of a set of rules for how a program sending mail and a program receiving mail should interact.

SNMP

Simple Network Management Protocol   A standard operation and maintenance protocol defined by IETF. It is used to exchange information between network management system and network devices regarding conditions that warrant administrative attention.

SONET/SDH

Synchronous Optical NETworking/Synchronous Digital Hierarchy   Optical fiber communication standard developed by Telcordia, documented in GR-253-CORE, used in the United States and Canada. SDH is a very similar version of the standard used outside the United States and Canada.

SPF

Shortest Path First   SPF is an algorithm used by ISIS and OSPF to make routing decisions based on the state of network links.

SR

Service Router   The Alcatel-Lucent product family of the 7750 Service Router designed for IP/MPLS/VPN service delivery.

SSAP

Source Service Access Point   A field in the 802.2 LLC header that indicates a protocol, or service address, that is the source of the data carried in the frame.

SSH

Secure Shell   A UNIX-based command interface and protocol for securely getting access to a remote computer. SSH is used in place of Telnet. SSH version 2 (the latest version) is a proposed set of standards from the IETF.

SSL

Secure Sockets Layer   A protocol that provides endpoint authentication and communications privacy over the Internet using cryptography. SSL is layered beneath application protocols such as HTTP, Telnet, and FTP, and is layered above TCP. It can add security to any protocol that uses TCP.

STP

Spanning Tree Protocol   STP is used between bridges to detect and logically remove any redundant paths generated during the bridge database creation process.

SYN

Synchronize   SYN is a message that is sent by TCP during the initiation of a new connection to synchronize the TCP packet sequence numbers on the connecting computers. The SYN is acknowledged by a SYN/ACK from the responding computer.

SYN-ACK, SYN/ACK

A SYN/ACK is a message that is sent by TCP during the initiation of a new connection in response to a synchronization attempt from another computer.

TCP

Transmission Control Protocol   TCP enables two hosts to establish a connection and exchange streams of data. TCP guarantees delivery of data and also guarantees that packets will be delivered in the same order in which they were sent.

TDM

Time Division Multiplexing   TDM is a process of sharing a communication channel among several users by allowing each to use the channel for a given period of time in a defined, repeated sequence. In this method, a transmission facility is multiplexed among several channels by allocating the facility to the channels on the basis of timeslots.

TenGigE

Ten Gigabit Ethernet   An Ethernet standard supporting data transmissions at the rate of 10,000,000,000 bits per second. Both fiber and copper versions of the standard exist.

TFTP

Trivial File Transfer Protocol   A simplified version of FTP that transfers files but does not provide password protection or user-directory capability. It is associated with the TCP/IP family of protocols. TFTP depends on the connectionless datagram delivery service, UDP.

Tier 1 Provider

An ISP whose IP network connects to every other network on the Internet without paying any transit fees.

Tier 2 Provider

A large ISP that pays for at least some of their transit services to connect to all networks of the Internet. The majority of large ISPs are Tier 2 providers.

ToS

Type of Service   Specifically, an IPv4 header field, used to specify the required service priority for the packet. However, generally used to refer to the header field of all Layer 2 frames or Layer 3 packets that specifies the priority of the frame or packet.

TP (TP0, TP4)

Transport Protocol   TP is an ISO communications protocol that operates at Layer 4.

TTL

Time to Live   A field in an IP packet header that indicates how long the packet is valid. The TTL value is decremented at each hop. When the TTL equals zero, the packet is no longer considered valid because it has exceeded its maximum hop count and is discarded.

UDP

User Datagram Protocol   A connectionless transport layer protocol belonging to the Internet Protocol suite. In contrast to TCP, UDP does not guarantee reliability or ordering of the packets.

VBR

Variable Bit Rate   Variable Bit Rate traffic is bursty in nature. In ATM networks VBR virtual connections are configured with two different cell rates: Peak Cell Rate (PCR) and Sustained Cell Rate (SCR).

VC

Virtual Circuit   A Virtual Circuit is a communications link that behaves like a dedicated point-to-point circuit, even though it is not. Data packets are delivered to the user in guaranteed sequential order, as if they were sent over a true point-to-point circuit.

VCI

Virtual Channel Identification   The VCI is part of the address of an ATM Virtual Circuit. The complete address of the VC consists of the VCI and the VPI. VCIs are assigned for one hop only; each switch cross-connects cells from one VC to the next, reassigning VCIs.

VID

VLAN ID   A VID is a 12-bit field in an Ethernet frame that uniquely identifies the VLAN to which the frame belongs.

VLAN

Virtual Local Area Network   A logical group of network devices that appear to be on the same LAN, regardless of their physical location.

VLL

Virtual Leased Line   A Layer 2 point-to-point service also referred to as *Virtual Private Wire Service* (VPWS). A VLL service is a pseudo-wire service used to carry traffic belonging to different network technologies over an IP/MPLS core.

VLSM

Variable Length Subnet Masking   A routing protocol is said to support VLSM if it carries the subnet mask in the routing update. This permits the use of different subnet masks on different components of the network. All modern routing protocols support VLSM (including RIPv2, OSPF, and IS-IS).

VoIP

Voice Over IP   VOIP, also referred to as *IP Telephony*, is a technology for transmitting voice traffic over an IP network.

VPI

Virtual Path Identification   The VPI is an 8-bit field in the ATM cell header that indicates the virtual path over which the cell should be routed. The VPI is assigned on connection setup by the devices at the two ends of a hop. Each switch that the Virtual Path Channel (VPC) traverses cross-connects the VPC from one port and VPI to another port and VPI.

VPLS

Virtual Private LAN Service   VPLS is a class of VPN that allows the connection of multiple sites in a single bridged domain over a provider IP/MPLS network. A VPLS appears to the customer as if they were connected to an Ethernet switch.

VPN

Virtual Private Network   A way to provide dedicated communications between a group of private sites over a common provider network.

VPRN

Virtual Private Routed Network   VPRN is a class of VPN that allows the connection of multiple sites in a routed domain over a provider managed MPLS network. VPRN is an IP protocol solution, and with it the service provider retains routing control.

VPWS

Virtual Private Wire Service   A point-to-point link connecting two CE routers. VPWS, also known as *pseudo-wire*, is a VPN service that provides a Layer 2 point-to-point service (link emulation) that connects two CE routers. The CE router in the customer network is connected to a Provider Edge in the provider network by a physical attachment or a logical circuit.

WAN

Wide Area Network   A network spanning a broad area (crossing metropolitan, regional, or national boundaries), designed to interconnect computing devices.

Index

W

Wiley Publishing, Inc. End-User License Agreement

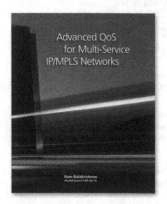